BOOKS BY C. L. SULZBERGER

Marina

Letters and Diaries
of Marina Sulzberger

edited by C. L. Sulzberger

CROWN PUBLISHERS, INC., NEW YORK

Printed in the United States of America
Published simultaneously in Canada by
General Publishing Company Limited

Book Design: Huguette Franco

Library of Congress Cataloging in Publication Data

Sulzberger, Marina.
Marina

Includes index.
1. Sulzberger, Marina. 2. United States — Biography.
3. Sulzberger, Cyrus Leo, 1912 — I. Sulzberger,
Cyrus Leo, 1912 — II. Title.
CT275.S954A4 1978 909.82 [B] 78-7926
ISBN 0-517-53375-8

To Mary and Nicko Henderson
Who were so kind when we most needed it.
With gratitude and love.

Cy

Contents

CONTENTS

Contents

Preface

Marina was so generous that she wanted to give and share everything, her experiences, her glowing happiness. She would chat for hours, curled up in a chair or sitting on the floor. As a result she had an amazingly large circle of friends and also an immense correspondence. She wrote so well that, to my happy surprise, a very large number of her letters were kept — not just by relatives but by friends who adored these continuations of her animated conversation.

There was such a quality of freshness and vivid excitement to her style that, although she was in no sense a famous person whose opinions or judgments would be valued by historians, her letters were simply worth being stored away for the joy of having them to reread for pleasure.

The best of these were to her mother, Dora, generally known as Dodo, but always addressed by Marina as *Mama mou glykia*. They were especially warm, vital, and uninhibited, so loving and so eager to describe each detail in a constantly exciting life that I can only thank my stars Dodo kept them.

But there were many others, sometimes family, sometimes friends, who recognized the unusual value of her observations and therefore treasured them, even deriving sweet amusement (as do I) from her original but effective approach to spelling. Some people, of course, do not make a habit of filing away even things they value highly; but others do, and I thank all those who helped me build this memorial to my wife.

This book is based almost entirely on Marina's letters and snatches of her intermittent diaries. Together these have helped in my attempt to re-create her. I thank those who assisted me by making available what souvenirs they had.

C.L.S.

Marina

I

May 1919 - March 1945

Marina arrived on this earth in Athens on May 1, 1919, the symbolic day of spring, so that lily of the valley (*muguet*) was her flower; freshness, loveliness, and vitality were her character. Every birthday, no matter where she was or how straitened or difficult the circumstances, first her parents, then her widowed young mother, then I, her fortunate husband, sought always to provide her with the staples of springtime. Whatever else, there were asparagus and strawberries, graced by lilies of the valley (except in Greece, where they don't grow and anemones do instead).

The instant Marina appeared, squealing, wrinkled, and rather ugly, her father wrote for her a quatrain, which, being translated, reads:

> All laughed when you were born,
> And you alone cried.
> May you live so that, when death comes,
>   all shall weep,
> And you alone shall laugh.

Marina could not laugh as she died despite all her courage. But her poet father's vision was wholly right in one respect. All those who surrounded her flower-covered bier, on which were scattered fresh rose petals and sweet-smelling herbs and *muguets,* wept.

Hundreds of close friends came to the Greek Orthodox Church in Paris to pay a last tribute (Marina had only intimate friends, perhaps a few acquaintances, no enemies), and some of them were very grand: all sobbing through the glorious Greek Orthodox service with its choral singing, its Byzantine antiphonies, its incense, its wild almost pagan beauty. And then they filed by the mound of flowers that smothered Marina's coffin in order, as Orthodox custom dictates, to say farewell.

Afterward I received a letter from the dear, ugly little Greek seamstress, Madame Titica, who used to come and sew Marina's dresses and who loved to talk and eat with gusto, and with whom Marina used to make a point of chatting and for whom she would personally cook her favorite dishes. "Dear Sir," Madame Titica wrote to me, "you probably didn't see me in the church among all those important people and I was too timid to join in the procession afterward to say goodbye in person to you and your sweet children and I could not send a suitable wreath as a sign of my love for our Madame Marina. Oh, dear sir, my tears were my flowers."

The Athens into which Marina was born was still a small town whose modern construction, surrounding the famous ancient ruins on the Acropolis, dated back only to the nineteenth century. In 1919 the capital had not yet swelled up with hundreds of thousands of refugees from Asia Minor, fleeing the consequences of the disastrous war Greece launched against Turkey in the early 1920s.

Her father's family had originated in Crete but traced its origins back to Byzantium, where an ancestor bore the minor noble title of Protospatharios, first spear-bearer to the emperor. Marina's grandfather had placed a hot coal in the slipper of the last Turkish governor while that dignitary was asleep, and was forced to flee Crete before the island joined independent Greece. Christos Ladas, Marina's father, known as Batsi to his family, was brought up in Smyrna and Trieste (then still the main port of the huge Austro-Hungarian Empire). He rushed back to Athens to volunteer in the Balkan and World wars. There he met — and soon married — a beautiful, lithe young volunteer nurse named Dora Sotiriadis. Dora, for Dorothea, but dubbed Dodo by her two children, came from distinguished ancestry also — a common claim in Greece, as in another small country, Ireland, where every other person boasts descent from a king.

George Sotiriadis, Dodo's father, was a renowned archaeologist and rector of the University of Salonika. The children always knew him as Papou, the Greek version of "Grandpa." He had a long Gothic face and hair like a mass of thistledown during the last four decades of his ninety-one-year life. Marina's grandmother, Maria (pronounced Mar-eye-a) had been born in England and spoke Greek and every other language with an English accent. She came of a famous strain on the little island of Chios, known to history for its mastic, which flavors so many Mediterranean licorice-tasting drinks, and for the terrible massacre perpetrated there by the Turks in the early nineteenth century and immortalized by Delacroix.

Maria's maiden name was Mavrocordato. A legend among some historians is that this name was derived from Othello, *mavro* meaning both "black" and "Moor" in Greek and one of the members of the family, having served as the Venetian governor of Famagusta (an "Othello") centuries ago. Mavrocordatos were among the Greek families sent by the Ottoman sultan to the Turkish imperial province of Rumania because they showed great talent for collecting taxes that the wily Rumanians had hitherto managed to withhold from the Turks themselves.

Christos Ladas was an inveterate dreamer, renowned for his versatility. He could sit at a piano and improvise works which everybody took to be Bach or Mozart or Chopin but which, in fact, originated in his own head and vanished forever once he had played them through with brilliance. He was known for his conversational skill and his ability to charm birds out of trees. Unfortunately, he decided to become a stockbroker, which, by the time Marina was ten years old and the 1929 crash came, was a perilous profession. Having, with happy overconfidence, built a large house with ample land outside Athens in the then completely rural suburb of Amarousion (called Maroussi), he was financially overextended at the time of his premature death in 1933.

Dora made the best of difficult circumstances. Christos' brokerage firm took over the big house and then rented it, to help pay off some of the late partner's debts. The widow moved with her children into a nearby cottage known as the "Spitaki" (little house), which had been built as a dowry for the cook. There Marina and her brother, Alexis, were raised in distinctly straitened circumstances by Dodo and various members of a shifting clan of servants from the island of Ikaria. No matter how badly off the family was, always included among Dodo's helpers — from then until today — was the angelic Ikariote, Eleni, who came to the Ladas household, at the age of fifteen, when Marina was born.

Marina inherited her vitality and enormous charm from her father and her beauty and wisdom from her mother. Alas, she did not inherit the Sotiriadis or Mavrocordato longevity. Both these grandparents died in their nineties, and Dodo, as I write, is alive and vigorous at over eighty. Marina died at fifty-seven.

Her upbringing was exceedingly modest. She went to the village public school at Maroussi, although Dodo managed to scrape together enough to send Alexis to the best private school in the capital, Athens College. Marina was an enthusiastic member of the Girl Guides. Until the end she always treasured her fellow members of the Yellow Crocus patrol, an admirable name for an organization she graced with her springlike gaiety. In Greece, where the crocus blooms twice, the yellow variety comes in spring. The highest point of her young life and her only trip abroad before I arrived on the scene was an excursion with the Girl Guides to the 1936 Paris Exposition when she was just seventeen. The zenith (or nadir?) of that experience was jumping off the fair's parachute tower.

Dodo took the children to the distant island of Ikaria one summer when they were young. She wrote a recollection of this experience: "The cook's village where we were going was on the sea. The ship goes once a week; if the weather is rough it skips a week. The nearest telegraph office is five hours away. There is no doctor, no chemist, no shops. You don't need much in the summer. We had camp beds and blankets. I had quite a store of first aid necessities. In any case we meant to live really simply.

"But no kitchen, no toilet, no water. [Only] a hollow at the back of the house between two rocks, a fire had been laid between two stones, and an earthenware pot on it. Toilet? [I was told] 'Go where you like, nobody will look at you.' To wash? 'The whole sea is in front of you; now it is summer.'

"In our one huge room it was divine. And we didn't need the ship. One week sooner or later makes no difference. And what can a ship bring that one really needs! Everything is made at home by hand. An earthenware pot is the best for cooking on wood that the children gather. Salt you find in little hollows in the rocks. Greens you pick on the mountain. Meat is shot once in a while from the village flocks of semi-wild goats that graze freely on the mountain. It is brought to the village square and divided. Fish you catch; octopus you spear. Beans or lentils or wheat you grow in long plots between the rocks where the earth has been able to collect.

"It is too rocky to carry the grapes or olives to the village down by the sea, so you press them on the spot and leave them there; everybody knows whose they are and when you need some you go and take it. You have a gourd with a hollow reed inserted and you suck the wine out. The men are nearly all sailors. They make their candles, dipping them time after time in boiling fat. The bread is baked at home. The cheese is made out of your goat milk, the honey gathered from wild beehives. You make your strong drink from wild berries. The Italian islands [the Dodecanese were then under Italy] are close and smuggling is a sport. You get sugar, coffee, cigarette paper at cost price; no taxation: and everybody can grow a little tobacco. So you don't need the ship. Time does not count.

"Medicine? There is no chemist but there are so many herbs and all the old women know how to use them from the olden times. If you have pains from rheumatism, let the bees sting you; their poison works. If you are bleeding badly, put spider's web on it; it stops the bleeding. If your eyes get inflamed, women's milk is the best. If you have a bad boil with pus, put some mold on it.

"The doctor is a good man. He lives eight hours away by mule. What can he do? God's will be done! Kalomena, poor thing, has no teeth. She soaks her bread, eats soup. 'What does it matter? We all lose our teeth.'

"The mornings we spend in the sea. No shoes, no clothes, no problems. Even boiled goat tastes good after a morning like that. Sponge divers land to clean their boats, fishing nets drag the bottom of the sea and bring up every kind of fish, shells, seahorses, starfish.

"Sometimes we visit old servants higher up and sit in their little gardens covered with grape vines, eating pomegranates, figs, and grapes, admiring their babies, gossiping. When the old men return from the vineyards or their fishing boats a tray of raki is brought and we sit sipping, hearing the news. After the second or third little glass we hear all about the latest smuggling: how so-and-so had managed to bring a whole load of cigarette paper from under the nose of the patrol boat. Or that Captain So-and-So had got caught and taken off to Samos to be tried.

"I had some vague qualms that this talk was not quite moral for growing children. But which child has not preferred the robbers to the cops or not dreamed of being a pirate or a smuggler? The garden smelled of mint and fig leaves. One of the men would ask for a song and a zither would be brought. It was generally our cook's father, Costandi, who sang. Old songs about the sea and shipwrecks and robbers and a little love: tuneless songs, barely songs, more like a story in a singsong voice. Every now and then you heard the sound of the sea, the echo of the mountains. Then, when one of the children curled up ready to sleep, we would get up and leave, a little dazed: the raki, the slight sadness, the smell of the orange trees.

"Sometimes when there was no moon we would go fishing. That is, we would walk along the shore holding a strip of old tire; it burns beautifully and by its light we could catch crabs or an octopus, sometimes even a sleeping fish, spearing it with an old fork or knife. Sea anemones would lie open like lovely cactus flowers; the slightest touch makes them retract and then they look like a slimy button attached to the rock.

"When going up the mountain we were warned not to rest under any walnut trees. 'I know you will be hot and tired and thirsty and the springs up there have good water but drink it quickly and go on. Nothing is more dangerous than falling asleep under a walnut tree; its shade is bad. You may wake up and find you have lost your mind. That is what the "good people" steal from us. They don't want us to have minds. They live under the earth and come out when the sun is high and everyone is sleeping. The women are quite good-looking, fine women, but they have one defect: their feet are very big and put on the wrong way and when you see their footprints it looks as if they are going forward when they are walking backward. Be careful. But their men are very small and ugly, black and hairy. That is why you must be careful with small children. The "good people" always try to steal baby boys.'

6

"One day we left for the mountain, four miles. We went higher and higher, over rocks, through dry river beds pink with oleander, by large bushes with pink or blue flowers like candles, sweet smelling. If you don't pick one they say you'll lose your love. Heather, white heather, forests of wild oaks, plateaus with wild pear trees. In small hollows, springs with wild mint or lavender, light blue butterflies like moths. We stopped for drinks of water but if we saw walnut trees we didn't even sit.

"We passed small lovely stone cottages with little gardens and big shady fig or mulberry trees. The peasants came out and offered us all they had. They wrapped a few tomatoes or figs in big leaves that are used as hats and as paper since they have none. 'For the road; to cool yourselves,' they said. We went through a dark forest of wild oaks. The muleteer said: 'Hurry, it is a dead spot. Here a father killed his son.'

"After four hours we came to the top. The air was so untouched we dared not breathe it in, in order not to dirty it. Below a steep path led to a ravine with big plane trees, grass with cyclamen and crocuses, blackberries and vineyards on the slope; fig trees, every fig with sap on it; grapes, white, pink, and purple. The children picked buckets of blackberries. We washed them in a stream, put them in the sun with sugar and lemon juice, and after a few hours boiled them without water. No jam was ever like it.

"Costandi told us a story: 'Once when my uncle was in danger, the boat he was on was sinking so all the sailors said their prayers and promised a present to the Virgin if she saved them. They made their vows; each promised what he could. One gave a silver icon, another a ring he had from his father, another a picture of the boat. The captain promised to build a shrine on the rocks they were in danger of sinking on. But one sailor promised nothing.

" ' "Give her something, you bastard; we have all given; we are sinking."

" ' "But I have nothing, only the lice on my body."

" ' "Give her a louse; she doesn't mind. But give her something, we are drowning."

" 'The sailor promised a louse. The boat was saved and, safely on land, they all kept their promises. But the one sailor didn't give the louse, saying: "How can you give the Virgin a louse?"

" 'Months passed. His vineyard sickened. His pig died. His wife fell ill. Everything went wrong. Finally he went to the priest. It was Easter and he took communion, confessed, and told the priest his troubles. The priest racked his brain and asked: "Did you perhaps make a vow you haven't kept?"

"'"Yes, I promised the Virgin a louse that time we were sinking. But how can I give her a louse?"

"'"Give it. A promise is a promise."

"'He went to town the next day, ordered a silver louse, and hung it on the Virgin's icon. His troubles ended. Never, never make a vow that you don't keep.'

"Ikaria is full of scorpions; you get in the habit of looking under every stone before you sit; in your shoes and through your clothes before dressing. The children used to make lassos and catch them. I had also seen some enormous gray lizards like baby crocodiles. I asked Costandi about them and he said they were descendants of Egyptian crocodiles, from the time when Egypt was united to Ikaria — before the Flood!"

Against a background of such delightful purity how was it possible for Marina to grow into anything but a natural girl dusted by love? Love made Marina function: an all-embracing love not only for human beings but for animals and flowers, everything from chasing falling leaves in the autumn to enthusiastically digging out sea urchins on the floor of the blue Aegean.

Endowed with so much zest, Marina's one rule about life was not to waste it. She radiated tenderness, exuberance, charm, and above all love. Although she was not in the least saintly in the medieval sense and not very religious, her faith being heavily tinged with pagan concepts, in olden days she would no doubt have been a saint.

For everybody loved her and her own love was boundless, like the milk in the self-filling pitcher of Philemon and Baucis after it was touched by Hermes and Zeus. She could love one, a hundred, or a thousand people, always adding to the list without diminishing its limitless quantity or tender quality. When she entered a room, it glowed. When she entered a city, all the telephones began ringing. (She could and would talk for hours on that distracting instrument.)

She spoke three languages perfectly and three others imperfectly and had a habit of mixing them together in the same sentence or paragraph, which was, to say the least, confusing to an eavesdropper. Incidentally, she could spell in none of these languages, and employed a system similar to that of T. E. Lawrence, who, in his *Seven Pillars of Wisdom*, spelled each Arabic name differently every time it was mentioned.

Her idea of exactitude was variable. In her letters, in her constantly altering stories of the same event, often illuminated by new and changing flashes of light, she played with truth and improved upon it according to her mood, just as her father had been able to improvise on the piano differently day after day.

Exaggeration was a particular joy to her. Something high was *apo tho os ton urano* (from here to the heavens). Someone without clothes was "naked as a goat." A field in Kashmir contained "billions" of wild tulips. She detested boring objectivity and loved the exuberant torrents of argumentation. Gray was not her color. Even in politics, where she thought of herself as a moderate, it was the "extreme center" and off with the head of anyone to the left or right of her. She was vivid and she was alive. Her eyes could be alternately flashing, soft, loving, understanding, brilliant, and tenderly caressive.

For Marina fiction always triumphed enthusiastically over fact. She proudly rejoiced in the title once awarded her by a great friend Cosa Achillopoulo, *"la reine de l'à peu près"* (queen of the approximate). In 1954 she decided our children should know more about their origins, so she exuberantly tapped out the following at her typewriter. (I have preserved her own completely coherent punctuation and spelling system.)

She chose the Hotel Algonquin in New York, where we were staying on a visit, to sit down on October 20, 1954, and prepare for our Marinette (little Marina) and David her all-too-brief account:

"I have this day decided that I will write down for you everything amusing, awful, interresting, gay, dangerous, important, frivolous or exciting that happens to me, so that when you yourselves are grown up and have children, and when you are sick and tired of reading Mrs. Tigee Winckle, Peter Rabbit, Peter Pan or even delicious Treasure island, to your children, you can have a small change and read to them all about their Greek grand mother who spent half her life doing nothing and the other half doing too much.

"And since Sulzberger history begins with the day I met your father I think I should go back a few years and try and remember all the things that have happened to me since that memorable day when he asked me to marry him, while guns were going off everywhere and the Italian army although defeated, were marching victoriously down towards Athens.

"Some years before I met your father I had become engaged to a very nice tall blond rather dull young man. My mother who is a very wise and wonderful lady was very wise indeed and knowing that young people have a way of getting obstinate if their parents disapprove of something, never said a word against this young man but quietly and feindishly she worked against him by such cracks as, 'The dear boy so wonderfully good looking. You will have a happy life with him if you can stand the dull driary life ahead of him in a small Iowa town.' Or she would say. 'Boiled potatoes are delicious but I wonder how it would be to live on nothing but boiled potatoes.' Well she did it so well that finally the prospect of spending my life in Sioux City Iowa and going to Sunday school meatings and baking pies for the Ladies Home Journal competition, frightened me so that I broke off the engagement.

"Then some years later I met your father who even in those days was a world wind, and my mother sighed and said, 'I know I have always been rather opposed to boiled potatoes but why did you have to switch to a permanent diet of Chutney.' Well she was right. Life with your father has turned out to be pretty well all Chutney what with wars and revolutions and thousands of miles of travel in strange lands, and changing homes and surroundings so often but personally I dont regret it and if I ever had to give advice to any young person in their choice between boiled potatoes and chutney I would take the chutney blind folded.

"But let us get back to the year nineteen forty. I was a nurse in the Greek army and your father was a reporter for the Times and the first time I met him he took me out to lunch alone a thing which I had never done before in my life, and I was very nervous but he was sweet and asked a million questions and made me feel important and interresting and not only that but the same evening he sent me the biggest bunch of blue and yellow iris I had ever seen and you who know what flowers mean to me must realise that from that day on I was finished. You can immagine what days those must have been for me. I was twenty-one and there was a war on and we were winning that war and I was a nurse which of all jobs is the most satisfactory, and on top of all that I was crazy about a young man who had gone as far as to send me flowers and be interrested in intravenous injections and frost bite. Each one of those things in itself was enough to make life exciting, but to have them all together is a rare gift and I was frightfully happy.

"Well this went on for a very short time and then things changed. The little Greek army in spite of all superhuman efforts was defeated when the Germans came to the aid of their less war like Allies and we lost the war and the country was occupied. This is not a war story so I wont tell you the sad and awful things that happened then. I have to keep this story to just the familly otherwise it will be so big your children will be grown up by the time you finish reading it to them. Well before the Italian troups marched into Athens your father asked me to marry him but he did not seem frightfully enthusiastic so I said no I would'nt until the war was over, which he promptly accepted and turned his attention to the menue, ordering *bisque de hommard* which I have not been able to touch since. The next day after a night of tears and deep gloom he left in a funny little boat, and for months after that I had no idea if he had arrived anywhere safely or had gone down like so many others under the bombs of the Germans.

"Those were sad unhappy angry hungry days. The silly thing was that in our tiny garden we had that year planted asparagus and rasberries which are most luxurious expensive things. Well they chose that year to grow rather well, so there we were with nothing else at all to eat except rasberries and asparagus. Not even salt. One day Dodo and I went into town to look for food and after searching for hours and hours came back with nothing at all. Just as we were getting into the buss to go despondently home we saw a pathetic little man selling daisies. My mother and I have a way of seeing things in the same way without words exchanged, and so as I looked at him and then her I knew that this had struck her too as the supreme expression of pathetic optimism. Without a word we got off the buss and spent our last penny (which we had hoped to spend on food) buying up all his daisies. We spent that evening very very hungry, but the house looked as if it wear preparing for a wedding or a birthday.

"Those first months of occupation were dreadful. We were very hungry very very indignant and a bit bewildered and lost. Occupation like every-thing else in life has to be organized and it took us quite some time to realise that it really was true that we had nothing to eat, that we could at any moment be shot as hostages or deported as labourers. Little by little though we learned how to make bread from broom seeds and sugar from carobs and how to eat cat and donkey and how to fight the enemy quietly. But again I say this is not a war story but a family history.

"All this time I had no news of your father and was preparing myself for dismal old maid-hood. One night however there was an air raid and we all woke up very excited at the sound of sirens and bombs. When it was all over it was just a little before one in the morning and we thought that being so late we would be safe to turn on our radio and hear some news from the BBC. Immagine my state of mind when while fiddling with the buttons to find the right station I heard your father's voice saying. This is Cy Sulzberger calling the New York Times from Ankara. In one second I had learned out of the air *si j'ose dire* not only that he was alive and well but that he was next door so to speak. We were all tremendously excited as you can immagine and my mother in a moment of exuberance called to our beloved faithful cook Yiannoula to use up the last drops of coffee in the house and 'make good strong coffee for everybody and whatever isn't left over we wont drink.'

"Well from that day on my one idea was how to get out and join him. But as he had so easily accepted my refusal to marry him I was no longer sure that he wanted to be followed around the world in war time by a wife. So I got a good idea. An American friend of mine from the Embassy, was leaving those days for Persia and I asked him if he would take a letter for me and post it on his way. He very kindly obliged and so I sat down and wrote the most complicated letter of my life. I explained to your father that I was listening to his broadcast and asked him to use a code by which to let me know if he still wanted me to try and join him to marry him. I gave him every way of escape by putting into the code all kinds of possibilities; such as E for Edgar meaning I love you very much but dont think it is a good idea that you should come just now, E for Ernest ment I dont care for you any more. A for Alexander was the key word which would mean I adore you try and come at once.

"After the letter had gone there followed a long period of waiting and hoping and then suddenly one day the longed for message came over the air and it was A for Alexander. But things were not as easy as they sound, because although I knew he wanted me and I was in a mad hurry to get to him I did not know how to go about it. For weeks I tried all kinds of secret ways of escape and somehow they all failed, until one day I decided to take the bull by the horns and just ask the German authorities if they would let me leave the country. I was only a young unimportant girl after all and thought they might not care one way or the other. So I put on my best hat and my last drop of scent and with my heart in my boots started off for the Stadt Commandant's office. I was led into an immense Baroque room and there told my story pretending I wanted to go to Turkey to marry a carpet dealer. Well either the commandant had just been promoted or had just had a new born son or something wonderful had happened to him, or else he was one of those rare things, a nice German. Whatever it was I was lucky because in five minutes he had said certainly I could leave and wished me the best of luck and given me a paper authorising me to leave the country any time I wished.

"But my troubles were not over yet. Although I had the permission to leave, I had no way of locomotion as all travel in and out of the country was restricted to troups in those days and it was practically impossible to find a seat on anything from airoplane to mule. So I waited and waited and finally one day bribed my way onto a German airoplane leaving for Bulgaria. The day before I left I got a strange telephonne call from an unknown man who said it was urgent for him to see me. It was all very thrilling and 'Hollywoodish' and I met this man in a small caffe where he explained to me that he had heard I was going and it was important for me to take out some vital information and give it to the British as soon as I got to Turkey. He handed me a paper on which were all kinds of extremely secret information about the arrival of submarines in the Mediterranean, pipe lines being put down on the side of the Corinth Canal, for oil transportation in case the canal was blown up, airoplane repair factories etc etc. I felt frightfully important and left with the precious paper in my pocket which I was supposed to learn by heart and destroy immediately.

"I returned home and the night was spent in last minute arrangements, advice from my mother on how to face marriage and adult life, and tender fair wells to those members of my family who knew I was leaving, and mutual assurances that everything was going to turn out all right and we would soon be together again and the war won. Under all this tone of optimism we were all desperately sad and anxious but as it turned out we were right to be optimistic and we did all meet again happy and alive even though it took more years than we had expected.

"The next morning at first light I left, and cried all the way to Sofia. With me were two other girls who had received similar permissions to join their *sois disant* turkish fiancees. Actually they were engaged to Greek naval officers in Alexandria. The trip was fast and uneventful and we got to Sofia and the first thing we did was go and eat. We had not had a decent meal for so many months that the sight of food made us dizzy and more than that after we had enjoyed an enormous menue we spent the night being frightfully ill as our tummies had forgotten how to cope with real meat and potatoes and even ice cream. I will not bore you with the details of the rest of the journey which was difficult and tiresome but not dangerous (to our secret dissapointement as we had had visions of ourselves hiding under hay lofts and just barely escaping capture by Bulgarian patrols) but finally we arrived tired dusty and very excited, in Istambul where we thought the beloved whom we had written to from Sofia would be waiting at the station with the orange blossoms, rings and priests all together. But there was no one there to meat us, so hidding our dissapointement we went to a little caffe, to telephonne our Embassy and find out where everybody was.

"Immagine our faces when we learned that the entire Greek fleet had sailed a few days before for Aden and that your father had been sent the day before to Moscow. Shattered and bewildered we went to spend the night with a kind Greek who gave us hospitality until we could get organized somehow. Immagine my amazement and horror when opening my rather pathetic paper suitcase I found in the folds of my one and only Sunday best night gown, the famous paper with all the information on it. Somehow in the exitement of departure I had forgotten all about it and some helpful member of my family had put it into my bag together with the few photographs I had taken with me for sentimental reasons. I had gone through the German Italian Bulgarian and Turkish customs and passport officials and not one of them had spotted it. My knees gave way at the thought of the nice execution squad I would have had to face had any of them been as alert as they were supposed to be.

"The very next day I took this little paper to the British Military Attache and when I told him the story he was angrier than I care to remember and assured me even though he thanked me for my trouble, that if I had any idea about embarking on a spy career I might as well give it up right there and then. The strange thing was that this information was duly sent on to Cairo where my brother who was working as liaison officer with the British air force, was asked to check up on it and find out if the person who had brought it out was trustworthy or not. That is how he first found out that I had come out of Greece.

"For days after our arrival in Istanbul we were followed around by counter espionnage agents of practically every country involved in the war. No one could quite believe that we were as innocent as we looked and all kinds of wonderful intrigue and sinister plots were attributed to us. In the end however they had to admit that there was nothing more to us than love. In the mean time our three men were scattered all over the world and no way of getting in touch with them. There again followed a grim gloomy period of waiting and wondering what would become of us. We were all given hospitality and wonderful care by various friends until we all got war jobs and settled down to wait for our fiancees to get a minute off from the war and come and collect us. I went to Jerusalem to work for a British service. The other two finally got to Egypt but did not get their men until two years later.

"I was luckier. Your father managed to get himself replaced in January of 1942 and finally arrived in Jerusalem to get me. But our troubles were still not over. I had immagined that Jerusalem would be the ideal place for a Jew to marry a Greek Orthodox especially as the Patriarch was a friend of my grand father's and I had had visions of a glorious wedding right in the church of the Holy Sepulcre. But such is the intolerance of religion that it turned out to be impossible. The Orthodox would have nothing to do with a Jew and the Jews nothing to do with me. So we were finally married in Beirut by a sweet intelligent Presbyterean named Doctor Scherer who took it upon himself to explain to God that it really did not matter what we were as long as we were fundamentally good people. If this were a fairy tale I would now say 'so they were married and lived happily ever after' and leave it at that. But THAT, was only the begining.

"J'écoute derrière moi les souvenirs comme le bruissement de la vague sur une plage lointaine.

"The first thing after the begining, was that we started to travel; and travel seems to have been the leit-motif of my married life. I really should have kept a real diary, and I often have had serious talks with myself about this but somehow never got down to it until now, that is why I have to go back so many years for you. When I have caught up with myself I hope to never let it go so long any more. Things seem to change in one's mind as time goes by and the big things become little and the little ones may get overlooked. That first trip with your father was really a most exciting one.

"We went to Turkey and then Egypt and then to Kartoum stoping at such places as Kano which is a strange walled city made entirely of mud in the middle of nothing where the people live by making a die so that everybody's hands are blue. We went to a place called Maidugri where I met my first tame lion walking about the run way. From there to Lagos where I saw my first jungle with pineapples grown wild everywhere and huge frangipani bushes covered with waxy white flowers and strange birds on all the trees. Then to Trinidad and Porto Rico and Finnally my first glimpse of New York and your father's family.

"They were all rather nervous as most Greeks in New York are either florists or grocers or millionaires. The family had also quite properly been brought up with Plato and Pericles in their minds, but they were not quite sure about a Greek bride. I can understand how they might easily have expected a sort of combination of Mrs. Papadopoulos and Electra and how nervous that would make them. However they seemed relieved that I spoke English and was not dressed in flowing robes and that first meeting sealed a

life long friendship which has not been shaken since.

"We stayed in the United States for a few months including a fishing trip to Montana, which prepared me for the fact that the only times that your father is really happy is when he is a thousand miles from anything and anyone, especially out going governments, in comming prime ministers and Security council meatings. Then he went back to the war in North Africa and I was left behind with just one thought in my mind and that how to get back to Europe again. Everyone was frightfully kind but as an Allien the only thing I could do with myself was such driary things as Bundles for Britain, Parcels for Paris or Greek war releif, which was not quite what I wanted. I tried everything in my power to get away which was quite difficult as I was priority Z as far as any officials were concerned but finally by sheer boredom thay allowed me to take a place on a convoy which was leaving for England.

"I left on a freezing cold January morning and took nearly a month to get to England. We left from a pier in New York and the next morning woke up to one of the most beautiful sights I have ever seen. We were near Halifax and from every corner of the horizon, on a clear icy gold day, ships were appearing by the dozen. We were ninety eight all together and all the ships were covered in icicles glittering in the sun shine looking like fairy ships in a ballet rather than grim grey steel determined to get their precious cargoes through the horror of torpidoes and air attack and cold wet death. We all formed up in lines and our ship was in a very good possition right in the middle of the convoy which we attributed at first to solicitude for our black eyes (we were the only ship carrying women) but we found out later that it was not us they were protecting but the eight hundred tons of Nitroglycerine which we were carrying.

"The trip was fantastic. We were not attacked but we ran into one of those storms one sees in the movies. Everything came down and there was more noise than I have ever heard before. Three ships just broke in two and went down. We didn't and after that everything went fine, except that it took so very very long. There was a nice French boy on the boat who kept repeating 'Ze only sing I dream of is to see zis ship from ze outside.' There was also a very beautiful wicked girl on the boat whom all the officers adored so that everyone was jealous of everyone else, until they discovered that she was only beautiful and nothing else and peace returned to the boat.

"The women had been given a severe talking to by the captain who

assured us that there would be no 'women first' attitude if we got hit, as men were so much more precious these days, and he made it very clear that he would stand for no nonsense about our forgetting to carry our life belts around with us and that sort of thing. We humbly complied until we discovered about the T N T and from then on we relaxed and even wore our prettiest night gown to sleep in, so as to appear in heaven properly dressed.

"We finally got to England and I will never forget trying to find your father in Victoria Station in the pitch dark. There had of course been black out in Greece, but the sky in Greece is always so clear and the moon seems to be so much bigger and brighter and stays up so much longer than in any other country, that I had never realised what a real black out could be like.

"I finally found your father standing on top of a huge mass of sand bags. Being short sighted he had given up all thought of seeing me so had decided the only way for us to meet was for him to make himself as conspicuous as possible and hope I would spot him. Which I did. It was a tremendous reunion and that night I lived through my only serious air raid of the war.

"We stayed together in London for a fortnight or so and then he went off again to North Africa while I began the same familiar round of officials trying to persuade them that it was essential for me to get to Egypt. Egypt in those days was the headquaters of the Greek Governement and the nearest place to Greece to which I could go to, as well as work in and my one idea since your father's return to the wars had been to get there and do something useful with myself. Well with great difficulty I managed to get a friend of mine in the Greek Embassy to give me a pretended document saying I was courrier for the Greek governement and had to get to Egypt. With this in my pocket and an official looking enveloppe which only I knew contained nothing more than old news papers, I managed to get a seat on a plane leaving for North Africa. Immagine my embarrassement when I got onto the plane when I found a young man in the next seat to mine, with a huge canvas bag strapped and locked to his wrist and discovered he 'also' was a courrier for the American governement. He took a very dim view of the haphazard way in which I was handling my small enveloppe, and from that moment on he never left me out of his sight. It took all my acting capacity to put on a good show of importance and not keep forgetting my wretched enveloppe in restaurants or my plane seat.

"We arrived in Port Liautey and there for the first time in ages I saw

mimosa and olive trees again and real yellow sun shine. I was so overcome that I burst into tears much to the embarrassement of the jeep driver who was taking us into Casablanca. There Cy had arranged for me to be met by a colonel who very kindly arranged for me to go on to Algiers. Your father was away when I arrived but I spent two very gay days in a fantastic house built by a rich sheik or something for his French lady friend. It was all white satin and lace and the most unsuitable possible surroundings for my two rather druncken newspaper men hosts. But we had a good time and finally your father got back from the front and we left for Cairo which was to become my home for the next year.

"In Cairo your father and I were separated again. He went off to Russia for the second time and I got myself a job with the British intelligence. I was not doing anything very secret or exciting but it sounds better this way than just to say I was a typist and translator. Too many years have gone by for me to be able to give you a really good picture of Cairo during the war. And yet it is all so clear in my mind still. The forced gaiety the dancing and dinning out, the drives to the Pyramids by moon light. All the young men back on leave for a few days and then back to either boredom or death in their respective jobs. No one talked of any thing serious. The men wanted to be amused and entertained and they wanted to dance and drink and forget and that is what we were there for after we left our offices.

"It was wonderful and horrible. Too many things happened to too many people in too short a time. People fell in and out of love all the time, they married and one or the other was killed right away. They fell in love and could not get married because one or the other was so already. Or one fell in love and the other not quite as much. There was enough heart braking matter around to fill fifty books but no one realised it until later. Everyone at that time was too busy not thinking about something. Nothing really mattered except the next few months or weeks or years until death or the end of the war which would once again bring things into their right perspective and 'everything was going to be all right.' It did not turn out that way of course and whereas during the war all one had to worry about was keeping alive and planning for the future, and having as good a time as possible while doing so, after the war, that future we were planning for was right there on top of us and all the planning did not quite turn out the way it should have, for most people.

"The best thing about the future is that it is far away. When it gets close and hits you in the face, it is no longer the future and therefore not quite as easy to cope with. I dont want to sound pessimistic and I have known futures which have behaved very well, but all in all they are better kept in their place. My future in those days I must say, suddenly became very simple and even visible. I was expecting Marinette and felt so frightfully ill that I had to go to bed for nearly nine months so I gave up my job and settled down in a huge bed in the Continental Hotel to await her arrival. It (the baby) was always reffered to in those days as Archymago* the wicked one for making me feel so ill. You will never know how close you both came to being called Archie for the rest of your lives.

"Those were extraordinary days. The entire hotel was more or less taken over by refugees from every European country and they had little to do really except sit around and discuss politics and the future and that was more agreable and more intimate in some one's bed room than in the lobby, so that my room was like Grand Central Station from early morning to very late at night. My greatest problem were the Yougoslaves. As you know that country has always been your father's soft spot and all Yougo-slaves in Egypt new it and came to see him or at second best me. They were bearded Chetniks and bald headed Partisans and I had to find elaborate systems of finding out who was what and sneek one out through the bath room door before allowing another one in in case they were mortal enemies. They were all armed with the same set of photographs of atrocities, which they each claimed the other side had done, and you can immagine what that did to my already squeemish tummy. There were pictures of baskets full of eyes, allegedly put out by both sides, or young men hanging from trees or heads cut off."

---

* Archimago, an evil character in Book I of Spenser's *Faerie Queene*.

Such was the entirety of Marina's merry little autobiography, begun and abandoned amid the Algonquian echoes of Alexander Woollcott, Dorothy Parker, and Bob Sherwood, whose repartee used to ricochet within those staid and tarnishing walls. And to bring the picture wholly into focus, I am sure Marina would not mind a few words appended to her *à peu près.*

In fact I first met her in the apartment of her American uncle and my close friend, Alexander (Shan) Sedgwick, in the spring of 1939. I was then working for Lord Beaverbrook and had been sent to cover the Albanian forces of King Zog, who was supposedly fighting against an Italian seizure of his country. Zog foiled me by achieving one of history's swiftest retreats, and I wound up in Athens. From then on, I always remembered Marina of that moment as a slender girl with dark, iridescent hair and glowing eyes. She moved with secret grace, stood like a marigold, and wafted the scent of lemon-fragrant verbena.

To a jaded man of twenty-six Marina at nineteen seemed but a sweet infant agreeably adorning her uncle's home when she came from her mother's country house to spend the night. Once, when I invited them to lunch, at the last instant Shan and his wife, Roxane, couldn't come and I found myself tête-à-tête with Marina. Months later she confessed that this was the first time she had been allowed to take a meal alone with a man. I offered her a dry Martini, which she seemed to drink with pleasure.

As we grew to know each other, this became a standard preliminary when we dined. Only long afterward, the day of our wedding, did Marina confess she hated all alcohol, above all dry Martinis; she had feared putting me off by seeming a teetotaler.

Without realizing how much she had become of my own self, I was fascinated by the splendid changing kaleidoscopic patterns of her charm. She adored almost everyone she encountered, a joyousness heartily reciprocated by even the stoniest, most sullen of personalities. Each person became in no time for her *Chryssomou* (my golden one), *Glykoulimou* (my sweet little one), *Pedakimou* (my little child), *Poulakimou* (my little bird). I was often that linguistic hybrid, *Sweetoulimou.*

After we were separated by the Axis occupation of Greece in 1941, I suddenly, hollowly, became aware of how much I missed her; more than I ever had missed or would miss anyone so terribly — until her death. I missed her presence, her touch, her smile. I missed her soft long hands, the sound of her voice. I missed the little songs she sang when she was happy: "Swim said the mother duck, swim if you can, and they swam and they swam right over the dam" . . . "Two, two, the lily-white boys, clothèd all in green-o" . . . "Oh I'm in love with the janitor's son and the janitor's son loves me" . . .

I missed the little snacks she used to prepare for me for breakfast and which she called "figwiches," a piece of dried fig wedged between two halves of walnut. I missed her pirouetting little dances, when she felt especially gay, putting on a comic hat and capering drolly about. I ached for her, and even hired two oarsmen to row their boat from Ceşme, Turkey, to Chios, threatening them at gun's point when they tried to turn back midway. From Chios I telegraphed Marina I was coming for her. However, a boatload of Wehrmacht soldiers supervened and I had to turn back once more. Oddly enough, she got my message and packed a little bag; but I never showed up. So there I was in Turkey with my wirehaired fox terrier, Felix, who had been wounded in northern Greece, my typewriter, my gun, my passport, the clothes on my back, and very little else.

One of my first tasks was to devise a new form of transmitting *New York Times* dispatches, which (like those of all other papers and agencies) were taking up to forty-eight hours because of inefficient service and delayed censorship. I hit upon the idea of hiring the Turkish national radio for a half hour each night, after it closed down at midnight. The Turks accepted with alacrity, anxious to earn dollars in their economic isolation.

As a result they had to acknowledge that censorship existed, and my stories were quickly vetted by Selim Sarper (who later became foreign minster) before being put on the air. Then I dictated them, as if speaking into a telephone. And when one dictates, unfamiliar words have to be spelled out: M-Marina, A-Arthur, R-Robert, et cetera. There was much spelling, for I saw to it that as many strange Turkish and Arabic names as possible figured in my pieces. I spelled them with words familiar to Marina — her own name, A-Alexis (her brother), D-Dora, and so forth.

It was in this way (in fact, when she was celebrating her birthday on May 1, 1941, together with her mother, grandmother, and a few friends) that they stayed up late enough to hear, quite by accident, a familiar voice spelling out familiar names over Radio Ankara. Marina and her mother concocted a code and managed to get it out to me. I kept using all the key words urging her to come, insisting I adored her, but at first it was impossible to be sure she heard me or learn what she planned to do.

When Hitler attacked Russia on June 22 and I was assigned to go to Moscow, I left the code with Ray Brock, our Ankara correspondent, and he kept up the special transmission service. My close friends, Geoffrey and Ruth McDermott of the British Embassy, promised to put Marina up and look after her if and when she arrived, and I took off for Russia.

Marina had found occasional couriers among the diplomats leaving Athens as their governments closed up their missions in territory now occupied. One of them brought me a letter she wrote on June 16, 1941: "If you wanted to become a vain conceited man you ought to see my face when I hear you saying M-Marina. The first time I heard it I nearly had a fit. You are the most wonderful man on earth to think of that. (I had hoped you would long ago.) . . .

"You know, I really have the luck of a mouse. Now that it's summer we could have such a wonderful time, swimming and going far away in the country and dinning at the millions of little summer places that have opened, and you would give me lots of guardinias; to Maroussi for week ends, and you would love me very very much because one is so much more susceptible in the summer and everything would be just paradise. Darling you cant think how lonely it is without you. Why does one fall in love with people who go away. It ought never to happen.

"P.S. I hear Turkish women are all horribly ugly and fat and nasty all round????"

Another courier-borne note: "You remember that night in Costi's [restaurant] when you asked me to go away with you? That night I thought the world would stop. But it didn't. I got to thinking and thinking and decided not to come, pretending to myself that it was my mother and my duty to my country and my people. Eyewash. I knew all along that it was because I was scared to death of losing you, not in the way that I would if you left, but in a deeper, more terrible way, if I came with you . . . at a time when you needed your freedom most. . . . I've fixed all my papers and now I'm looking all over Athens for someone with whom I could travel, be he the public hangman if necessary.

"P.S. Love to Felix. Thank God I didn't keep him. He would have starved."

Dodo wrote me on June 27, 1941 (but the letter reached me only much later in Moscow): "From the day Marina got your telegram [from Chios] asking her to be ready to come to you, and unhappily it was too late, she began regretting she didn't come with you. Since then she has been hoping every minute to find a way. . . . Today at last she has a permit for Turkey. . . . I am sure you realize what the decision to let Marina travel at this time costs me, but I would rather see her risk it than see her here so miserable, because I see she really loves you, and I think that you can be happy together and that she really can share your life and its risks."

On August 4, after she had arrived in Ankara and was staying with the McDermotts, Marina wrote me in Moscow (the letter, sent by British Embassy pouch, took a long time getting there): "One Sunday morning which I'll never forget in all my life the Germans walked into Athens and we heard the first German broadcast from our station offering Greece to Hitler as a token of gratitude for his greatness. . . .

Communication in all directions was difficult. Dodo wrote Marina late in the summer (delivered even later): "Really I never knew anyone who had so many people who love one like you." As for Greece: "It is ghastly. I go to Athens once a month. . . . Our spirits are grander than ever and we are getting nearly cheeky."

That October 1941, when Marina had no idea where I was because the Soviet government had evacuated itself, the foreign diplomats, and press to Kuibyshev, but was rather slow about advising the world, Marina wrote to my mother and my Uncle Arthur (then publisher of *The New York Times*).

To Mother she said: "I love Cy so very very much and you being his mother I love you too but saying so on paper means nothing at all. I have had so many disappointments one after the other that I feel I shall be a hundred before Cy gets back. . . . I have loved Cy such a very long time I only hope he loves me as much as I do, and anyway I promise you I will do my best to make him as happy as possible so don't worry as a mother does."

To Uncle Arthur she said: "Cy has told me in his letters that you have been taking a great deal of trouble over my mother and me, and I want to thank you for it very much. It is very hard to write to you, not knowing you and not knowing if this letter will ever reach you, and anyway, whatever I want to say seems so stupid after I see it written down."

By the end of 1941, Marina had gone to stay with her aunt, Roxane Sedgwick (Dora's sister) in Jerusalem, where Shan was assigned as *The New York Times* correspondent with British Ninth and Tenth Army headquarters (a somewhat fictional force designed to take over Iran, Iraq, and Syria). He obtained a job for Marina as a monitor in British radio intelligence on the Greek language network. She soon distinguished herself, according to Shan, by sitting with earphones clamped over her head during an endless speech by Stalin. When her boss asked what it was about, she said, "Stalin says Hitler stinks."

Just before her arrival, Shan wrote Uncle Arthur (who was his supreme boss): "We expect Marina and Felix here shortly. Marina was certainly well looked after by some very good friends of Cy's who are attached to the British Embassy in Ankara, but all the same some sprouting Victorianism in us makes us feel that it is more suitable for a young girl, left stranded financially and hard hit emotionally, being away from her family, to remain with her aunt and uncle. Besides, I frankly feel that Turkey is none too safe a haven for any proven enemies of the Axis. I'm not at liberty to tell you now by letter, but some day you will hear of the exploits of this niece of yours, how she threw her own little monkey wrench into the mighty cogs of the archfiend's war machine and you will be thrilled indeed.

"I may digress now to tell you that Marina is the nicest, the sweetest, least complex girl I have ever known. She is a walking beatitude. I give this as my fixed opinion and make no excuses for prejudice. I have in fact watched her grow up. As a child she seemed incapable of any unkind sentiment. Humanity was her distinction and still is. She sheds goodness and grace. During those dreadful last days in the life of her country she bore up remarkably, allowing no personal consideration to interfere with her duties as a nursing sister."

I flew to the Middle East and we were married on January 22. Shan went ahead to arrange for an official American witness from our legation because the United States consul general in Jerusalem, a routine-minded bureaucrat, had warned him the marriage would be illegal. Indeed, he kept saying this anyway for months afterward. Marina and I wondered if it wouldn't be fun sometime to have a strictly legal wedding with our children bearing her bridal train.

Roxane Sedgwick, Marina, and I drove to Beirut on the morning of the twenty-second. We stopped for lunch in Haifa and were almost late because we became entranced by the restaurant's slot machine. We drove along the lovely seashore through the Crusader town of Acre, past ancient Tyre and Sidon, and found Shan pacing up and down outside the Hotel St. Georges chewing his mustache. He was feverishly distraught. His New England sense of propriety wouldn't even permit us to go to our room together to wash. Finally, after what seemed an age to him, he drove us to Dr. Scherer's pleasant apartment. The minister was waiting with his wife and Bill Porter, a skinny young vice-consul from the American legation, who was our witness and best man. Bill was then just at the start of a career in which he became a highly distinguished ambassador.

Scherer, a tall, bespectacled man with a pleasant, homely face, graven with lines of sympathy and humor, was wearing British uniform covered by his ministerial cassock. He greeted us with affection and invited Marina and myself into his study. There, more nervous than we, he explained that it was highly unusual in his position to marry two people of other and differing religions. The only service he knew was Presbyterian. He hoped we would not mind if he used this for the ceremony. Nevertheless, he intended to preface it with a special apologia, which he read: "Dear God. I know I am departing from custom and, as it were, stepping out of my bailiwick today as I join these two young people in wedlock. But you are undoubtedly aware of all the trouble that exists nowadays on earth. I can only assure you that their two hearts beat as one."

Marina hadn't even time to brush away a tear when the minister rushed us into his sitting room and there married us before a small altar he had erected on a table. Afterward Mrs. Scherer produced a cake. It was not a very splendid wedding but it was the nicest I have ever heard of, and I think it meant more to all concerned — not just the bride and groom, united after so much time and so many adventures. We spent that night in Beirut. A moon was reflected on the old Phoenician bay and waves slapped below.

Next day we moved to the King David Hotel in Jerusalem in order to give our wedding party. Thanks to Shan, there was plenty of booze, and thanks to a stop-off by me in Astrakhan, Russia's caviar capital, there was plenty of caviar for our friends. Unfortunately, because of wartime rationing, we ran out of bread.

Soon thereafter we scurried up to Turkey with Felix, now joyfully reunited with both of us. Then, after saying our farewells, we went to

Cairo, where I arranged for us to fly across Africa and South America to New York. I had resolved to join the U.S. forces since we were now at war (although later I accepted advice from military friends and the *Times* to remain a journalist — a mistake, I have later felt). In Cairo I cut through webs of red tape and obtained priorities for our trip. The journey took six days of flying plus a layover in Lagos. Felix was left behind in Egypt with some pals. He had never truly recovered from his wound and, when bitten by a scorpion in the Western Desert, he died.

Marina reached New York brimful of optimism and excitement. Yet she was worn out (and, although neither of us knew for certain yet, also pregnant). She weighed only 99 pounds, far below the normal even for her graceful thin figure. But her enthusiasm carried her along on its tide and she added legions to the wholesale number of people who already adored her, starting with my mother and stepfather. She put down her own impressions accordingly much later, trying to recapture the memories of those initial weeks:

"The first thing that struck me about New York was how very like itself it looked. Like every photograph or movie one had ever seen. So very unsurprising that I was quite dissappointed for a little while. I suppose that people who see the Acropolis or the Pyramids or the Taj Mahal for the first time must feel this way too, until the light and shadows and all the imponderables come into play and suddenly one KNOWS how wonderful it is and how deliciously surprising. But not even the most cosmopolitan of newcomers to New York dreams of the pit falls and the real surprises this pleasant city has in store for one. Nor how far far more difficult it is to get accustomed to than Kathmandu lets say or Vientiane or Sidi bel Abbes.

"At least in these exotic places the traveller is prepared and like the Queen in Alice quite ready to believe three impossible things before breakfast. But in New York perhaps because at the outset it seems so familiar, the stranger, particularly if he thinks of himself as English speaking, feels quite prepared to venture out into great Avenues and streets and even shops without a moments fear or hesitation. Ah me. Being the wife of a newspaper man I have been to a lot of unexpected places and I have travelled on most things from jets to feet. But I cannot remember ever having been as rattled as on my first day in New York nor as embarrassed as on my first grim trip along Fifth Avenue on a buss.

"This was a long long time ago. Right in the middle of the war. And although I started off by saying that I was not surprised at New York this is only partly true because the meer fact of me being in it was surprise enough in itself. I remembered back to when I was a small child and my parents used to ask me how much I loved them the standard smile provocking answer used to always be — As much as from here to America. America was as far as the furthest limits of my imagination and here I was myself in and part of it. I could not wait to get out and explore. And fall right into the first of my misadventures. Having walked goggle eyed along Fifth Avenue for hours looking at shops that seemed out of another glorious war-less world I finally felt tired and thought quite normaly to take a bus. I felt I could not possibly get lost seeing that New York obligingly runs only up or down (one does not really tackle East and West until a little later) so when a pleasant bus went by and even stopped before me, I climbed aboard with no misgivings whatsoever and sat down but the bus did not move. I thought it must be waiting to fill up or something like they so often do in village stops at home. I looked agreably out of the window and still we did not move. And then I felt a rather sticky silence all around me.

"I did not attribute this to me however until a voice like thunder rose from the huge conductor in the front. 'Hullo Duchess, want room service?' I turned around with that half-smile reserved for public vehicles and elevators and then I noticed that all bus-eyes were upon me and that the silent disaproval was for me. And then the great thick man uncurled from off his tiny seet and stood before me pointing a scowling finger at me and saying. 'I mean you. Did you expect the state to buy you a ticket lady?' I turned a little purple and in a stranger's squeeky voice I mumbled a feable Not at all and started fumbling in my hand bag.

"I had indeed noticed a sort of coffee grinder thing, on entering the buss, and it was full of 'little money' but somehow I had thought, this was the way they kept the change or something. I realised then, I should have payed on coming in and simply mortified at any thought that they might think I did not wish to pay, worst still that I could'nt, I hurridly brought out a big brand new five dollar bill and handed it to the conductor. A groan escaped the man and the assembled buss load and I sensed rather than heard the words Change change. Change what, I whispered, petrified by now and wondering if I had counterfeit money or if this was not the country of dollars after all. And then the man just took me by the hand and before I knew it I had been lifted clear across the buss and firmly pushed into the street again.

"Jellified with shame and embarrasement and still a long long way from home I walked a little my head bent in sorrow. I suddenly saw the reassuring words DRUG STORE in coloured letters. Now I must tell you that in those days when Europe had not yet discovered America as it has done today, to know that a drug store did not really mean a drug store, was a sign of some distinction at least among Greeks. It meant either that one had travelled already or that one had letter writing relations in America or that one had read a lot about it and generally had an encyclopeadic knowledge of the world.

"I belonged to the category that has an American uncle. And very proud and pleased I was to know that one could not only buy everything (even motorcars some said) in a drug store (except drugs said the wits) but one could also eat there. And right at that moment after my recent humiliation I felt that some food and a cup of coffee was everything I needed most. And even perhaps a telephone if I could ever get up enough courage to face yet another inanimate object with possibly a button A to push and change to get from the five dollar bill of my undoing. However the telephone call would come later. Now just food, and time to restore my self respect. Little did I know what was yet to come.

"I walked briskly across the street entered the place and somehow managed to climb up on the highest bartype stool I have ever struggled with. While I was still organising my legs my bag gloves, etc. a beautiful young man came up to me with a little white hat balanced on the tip of his nose neatly and shouted at me 'Whatleitbe?' Excuse me? I said. 'Whatchwant' said he. This I got. 'May I have a sandwidge please,' I said, 'and a cup of coffee.' 'What kind of sandwidge lady?'

"Now in front of me as large as life over the mirror there was a list in great black letters of every conceivable sandwidge combination one could dream up. Later I had plenty of time to study it. But at the moment and in my fragile state I had not even noticed this so I asked most politely (I thought) what kind of sandwidges the nice young man could offer. He looked at me a little strangely and in the voice that I presume he keeps for village idiots he started rattling off things like Baloney (?) cole slaw (?)

salami cheese wurst etc. Cheese I said hurriedly this being the more
recognizable of his offers. What kind of cheese? What kinds do you have?
Another list of ten unknowns of which the word blue for some fanciful
reason stuck in my mind so I said Blue please. And then came the really
flowing question ON WHAT? On what I thought to myself. What else but
bread can a sandwidge come on. But I was not going to get into any more
discussions so I said firmly as I could Bread of course.

"And now the boy put both his elbows on the counter, spiritually patted
my hand and in a gentle half whisper asked What kind of bread? I thought
of the bread made out of broom stick seeds back home but this was no time
for nostalgia or sentimentality so for the third time in this ordeal I asked in
a choked voice What kind of bread do you have? Well in all my life I had
not imagined it possible that there were so many different kinds of breads
in this world. Rie bread whole wheat bread brown bread white bread corn
bread muffins puffins fuffins, the room seemed to echo from side to side
with names of breads. Corn please I shouted thinking that corn was wheat.
The young man looked at me for a full minute shook his head once or twice
and said. 'Its your choice lady not mine,' and with these nerve racking
words he left me, to come back in a few minutes with a colossal corn
muffin, sweet as I discovered to my horror on the first bite dripping with
the smellyest blue cheese (rockfort to me) an agresive pickle on one side a
peace of lettuce on the other and an impressive array of bottles Ketchup
worcester sauce etc.

"So there I was with once again the eyes all around me, pointed straight
at me, like Cheshire cats without the grin and nothing to do but eat. I have
never eaten anything so hateful in my whole life and while I slowly tried to
swallow I studied on the wall across me the endless and delicious possibilities that had been offered had I but learned to read. Hot turkey on Rie
toast, virginia ham on whole wheat with 'delicious crisp oven fresh
potatoes,' the hamberger with a difference the hamberger with a college
education the cheeseberger etc etc etc. I felt alone and small and utterly
forsaken. And not one least bit hungry (ever again). How I paid and how I
got away from there I do not know.

"I met a buss just as I left the place but shied away from it as if it would
bite. Nothing but taxis for me from now on I thought. Just then one came
along and having stopped him I peared very carefully at his side to make

quite sure he too did not have some kind of infernal pre-paying machine. As there was nothing too strange looking I felt reassured hopped in and said with as much of a *femme du monde* voice as I could muster. 'Would you be kind enough to take me to 970 Park Avenue please.' He hesitated just one moment and then turned round and looked at me. Oh not again I thought not something different and difficult again. But all he said was 'Hey lady what kind of sissy talk is that' and started off. I did not answer him I was too tired too dejected and besides feeling slightly sick."

Poor little Marina, just after she was becoming used to these exciting new adventures, it became certain that she was pregnant. Since I intended to return overseas once we had had a rest and honeymoon and since I wanted her to come along quite as much as she wished to (fearing, as she did, isolation in a strange country for the rest of the war), we decided on an abortion. In those days this was a very difficult proposition in the United States. However, a very respected old doctor certified it was necessary because of Marina's weakness, and the job was done. Thin as she was, she recovered rapidly and soon we were off on a long delayed honeymoon in Montana.

Marina audaciously told me she had done a good bit of riding, so I hired the necessary riding horses, packhorses, cook, and guide and we took off for a three-week trip. It required a couple of days to assemble the entourage, so one day I took Marina off to the local golf course for a lesson. She became quickly bored with that endeavor, but walked around with me because there were flowers everywhere, and she gathered a huge bunch as I hacked about.

Marina's brief encounter with golf caused her momentary horror. During my weeks with the Greek army in 1940 and later in Athens, I had acquired a small vocabulary of Greek oaths, which, to her embarrassment, I occasionally used when irked — for example, at bad service in a restaurant. (We would invariably find the offending waiter was a Greek.) Marina begged me to teach her at least one equivalent American phrase. In deep secrecy, swearing her to discretion, I whispered, "Niblick." From then on I would occasionally hear her mutter "Niblick" if she dropped a suitcase on her toes. I had forgotten this when, on my first Montana round of golf, I soon landed in a trap. This was still before irons were known only by their numbers, and I sadly told the caddy, "Give me a niblick." Marina was aghast. She came running out of a field of flowers muttering, "How can you talk that way?"

We took off, four people and six horses. The first day's ride was more than twenty miles. As Marina stumbled from her mount that evening, she confessed that her previous acquaintance with horses had been somewhat less than she had claimed. She blazed, "If I didn't have to ride this damned thing back again I'd divorce you right away."

Those were glorious weeks. We forgot the war, the occupation of Greece, even that her brother, seized on a special mission, was in an Italian military jail. The Germans were at El Alamein and Stalingrad when we disappeared into the Rockies; they were still there when we emerged. We caught all the trout we wanted, including a fourteen-pound Mackinaw I took at the mouth of the Kootenai River. Marina, not impressed, gave it to a forest ranger. We saw hundreds of brown bear, a few grizzlies, and quantities of moose. One day Marina was busy in our tent while I fished nearby. She heard something at the entrance flap and, without looking around, said, "Any luck?" Getting no answer, she turned, saw an embarrassed, summer-hornless moose, and disappeared shrieking under the tent's back wall.

From Montana we went to an uncle's house in the Adirondacks, and by the time we got back to New York, fit, happy, brown as berries, I knew it was time to get to work, and flew to London, having arranged for Marina to follow as soon as possible. She still had a Greek passport, so Washington could not prevent her departure, as it did in the case of American women. In fact, Marina would have kept her Greek citizenship indefinitely had she not eventually become bored by having to wait in one line at each border crossing while the children and I were placed in another, quicker queue.

Marina also had her officer's identification card as a lieutenant-nurse in the Greek forces, and this was to prove invaluable in getting her around a war that was crisscrossed with military barriers. The only trouble was that I could fly to England on an Army Air Force transport while Marina, with lower priority, had to come by convoy.

I left late in 1942, but Marina ran into all kinds of bureaucratic red tape and was delayed for weeks. On January 3, 1943, she wrote me in London: "I miss you even more than I did in Greece and more than I imagined possible to miss any body. You old *maimou mou* [my monkey], maybe it won't be so long now. My feet get so cold at night I don't know what to do without you."

She kept an intermittent diary, simply noting occasional stark facts. "January 13. Wensday. Got to boat 'Leardam' in a launch. One hour out. Lunch on board. Co-travellers all rather dull. . . . January 14. Ships all around us everywhere. Very exciting. . . . January 15. One more day nearer to Cy. A very driary day all the same. Tried on some new kind of lifebelt of rubber. Looked like Frankenstein. . . . January 19. We have been told to sleep with our clothes on. But when challenged the captains admitted that they do not. [The *Leardam* was laden with explosives.] So we don't either. We would be too smelly by the end of the trip. . . . January 20. Terrible storm. We lost our mast. It made a dreadful noise. . . . January 21. A man broke his leg and I am nurse again. Was very depressed as it reminds me of Greece. Also it is our wedding anniversary. Many happy returns. I wonder how long it will be before this bloody war is over and people can have their anniversaries together again."

Fortunately, Marina possessed a toughness that underlay her sweetness, and she managed beautifully on her little Dutch tub in an underprotected convoy at the height of the Atlantic U-boat war. She could ridicule herself with happy equanimity, having ample confidence that she was in no sense thereby diminished; and toward others, no matter how comic they or their situation seemed, she was always compassionate.

As for her courage, it was immense. She bore pain with astonishing indifference, and she was able to endure both physical and psychological hardship of the most disagreeable sort. As a wartime lieutenant-nurse, based in an Athens hospital, her very first job was attending amputations and bearing away stinking buckets of severed hands and feet.

Her diary continued: "January 22. Friday. Terrible storm. Lost a raft and both stairs to the front of the ship. . . . January 25. Saw a mine. Very exciting. The convoy is getting together again more or less. We are 62 degrees north. It seems so funny to be dressing instead of undressing to get to bed. . . . January 28. Some of the people on our ship when last torpedoed met a ship while in their lifeboats. When they were picked up and found out that the ship's destination was far from their original one they said 'no thanks' and got back into the lifeboat. All I can say is that if in the same situation we're offered a lift I hope we take it. . . . January 30. Saturday. I am so sick of this trip I could scream. My little Cy I miss you so. Damn."

On February 5, I met her at last in a blacked-out London railway station, and Marina was delighted with our splendid large riverside room at the Savoy Hotel. This was easily obtained because few people applied for lodging right along the principal marker of the German bombers' nightly path over the British capital. On February 6 she decorated her diary page with a little ink-drawn flower and wrote: "There were flowers for me when I arrived. I had an hour's bath which I needed after twenty-seven days. God it's good to be together again."

We had a delightful time in London. Marina noted in her tiny leather journal: "Wensday. We found a new Greek restaurant. It nearly killed us. Cy said the food had been eaten before. . . . Thursday. Lunch with the King of Jugoslavia and Princess Alexandra at her flat. Very, very nice. Princess Aspasia [Alexandra's mother] talked about Batsi [Christos] and his piano. . . . Friday. Cy gave me the most lovely orchids. We packed his kit in the morning. Gas mask and all. . . . It's awful to have Cy go again. I can't get used to it ever. . . . Saterday. Breakfast without Cy is horrid. In fact life without him is horrid. . . . Wensday. It gets so tiresome to be always so grown up. Half this diary is already full of days without Cy. Damn Hitler."

On February 19, 1943, Marina wrote my mother from London: "We gave a dinner party for Mr. Jan Masaryk [of Czechoslovakia] last week which went off very well. The dinner was very good as we have a charming floor waiter who managed to get us quite a good meal. We had a very good time and we played the game which amused Masaryk very much. You dont know what a nice suite we are living in. Cy is really spoiling me but we figure we will settle down to a budget when we get to Cairo and we might as well have a good time until then. We have a lovely bed room and sitting room looking out on the river and we enjoy it."

Shortly afterward she again wrote Mother: "Last week I spent in the country in a most beautiful house. Georgian and full of treasures. Rodin busts here and there and portraits of all the family by Reynolds and all sorts of beautiful things. The house itself is lovely part Elizabeathan and part

Georgian. It belongs to Lady Fitzgerald whose grandson we knew in Cairo. It was amusing the way we met. We were at a coctail party given by an American colonel for the king of Yugoslavia and there we met Lady Wellesley who is Lady Fitzgeralds daughter. We started talking and in no time found out that we had met her son Dick in the Middle East. Of course we became great freinds and they asked us both to stay but Cy of course did not have time so I went alone after he left. I had a wonderful time and also very interesting from the war point of view to see Lady Wellesley doing all the cooking and washing up herself and lighting the fires in the morning and liking it. She says she likes this kind of life so much better she thinks she will probably go on doing it after the war is over. She is one of the most beautiful women I have ever met and so good and sweet."

Before leaving for North Africa and the juncture of the Americans and Montgomery's Eighth Army coming westward from Egypt, I had managed to get an air priority for Marina through the friendly U.S. major Jules Dubois, acting executive officer for the American chief of staff, G-2 (Intelligence). He sent the following message to Allied Force Headquarters in Algiers and gave Marina a copy to take along, stamped CONFIDENTIAL (EQUALS BRITISH SECRET). This said:

> The Greek Government is sending her to Cairo to perform some confidential work for the Greek Department of Information. Mrs. Sulzberger is a Lieutenant in the Greek Army Nurses Corps. Ambassador Biddle [Tony Biddle, U.S. envoy to the emigré governments in London] has received a letter from the Greek Information Chief here requesting the highest possible priority for Mrs. Sulzberger. Mr. Sulzberger will inform General McClure [Eisenhower's information chief] in person about the confidential mission with which Mrs. Sulzberger is charged. He requests transportation for . . . his wife to Algiers from Lyautey [Port Lyautey, Morocco]. We concur in this.

Marina was forwarded on from Port Lyautey and Casablanca by Captain Charlie Poor and Major Harold Hinton (both distinguished journalists in civilian life), and they were enormously cheered up by this charming task. My friends Kennedy and Deluce looked after her in Algiers, and on April 9, 1943, her diary contained another page headed by a little inked-in flower: "Cy has come back. What luck."

Thanks to the Dubois letter, I managed to get priorities for the two of us on a DC-3 flying to Cairo from Algiers via Tripoli in Libya.

Marina noted: "April 12. Monday. Arrived Tripoli about four. General Strickland was very nice. He drove us into town. Saw enormous concentration camp on the way. . . . April 13. Tuesday. After terrible night at the bedbuggy Grand Hotel, left Tripoli for Cairo. Landed once at Benghazi. Made pipi in destroyed Junkers 52. Great satisfaction."

An even greater satisfaction was the boarding of the same plane by the sheerest good fortune of Uncle Shan Sedgwick, bound homeward to Cairo from Libya, needing a shave, a haircut, and a dry-cleaned uniform. On April 14, Marina jotted in her diary: "Wensday. Cairo. I am a little depressed now that travelling is over. It was a lovely adventure."

At first, and for some months, we had to live in one small, sparsely furnished room of the Continental-Savoy Hotel, even then rather run down and with no air conditioning other than large, limping fans. The hotel was filled with flies, staff officers, and other officers back on leave from distant fronts or special parachute operations in the Balkans. Marina wrote Uncle Arthur of our trip:

"In all these places of course I was the only woman and women being as rare as the dynosaur around there I was treated like a Queen and got very spoiled. I find myself thinking Cairo is rather dull with so many attractive girls around. We met one day [in London] an Egyptian [Coptic] Prince called Lutfallah. He gave us a letter to his brother here who asked us to his palace for Easter lunch and gave us the biggest lamb you ever saw. It came whole at the table in a plater held by two waiters. I told Cy later I thought it looked like a camel but he disagreed and anyway he said even if it was a camel it was damned good. One of the catty stories told about this prince is that when his old brother died some time ago somebody asked him, '*Votre frère est mort centenaire n'est ce pas?*' He answered, '*Ma foi centenaire, millionaire.*' "

Marina noted various experiences in her little tan book: "Sunday.

Dinner with Captain and Colonel Seager. Brothers and one is English, the other American. They hate the Turks which is greatly to their credit. . . . Wensday. We have been married fifteen months. Had dinner alone and celebrated. . . . Friday. Went to the Polish ball and was barmaid from nine to midnight. Know all about mixing drinks now."

Just after her twenty-fourth birthday, May 1, 1943, I took off for a return trip to Moscow. Marina wrote Uncle Arthur to thank him for a check:

"I got a lovely blue chinese bowl with the money, which makes a lot of difference to the room we have in the hotel, makes it look a little less impersonal and cold. . . . Cy left yesterday among loads of soap, tooth paste, silk stockings and typing paper for which we had received pleading requests from all his Moscow friends. He looked like a travelling salesman. It's beginning to be really hot here and I dont at all relish the idea of going to my office. Its just four o'clock and boiling but I suppose duty's duty."

Marina had wasted no time in getting another job in the monitoring services of British Intelligence. But she was suddenly very lonely in Cairo despite the numerous Greeks there, both local and escaped members of her country's forces abroad. She wrote me on May 10 in Moscow:

"I have started work with the British, and its quite nice and interesting particularly now when all the news I monitor is such marvellous news. . . . I'm being very economical and good and this morning resisted a very strong temtation to buy a new dress. I am very unhappy without you my puppy, and although I tell myself that this is nonsense and after all we have been married ages now, and that I knew this was going to happen, and that there is nothing to cry about, but its no use at all, and I miss you more than ever and nothing seems to be any fun any more. I love you so very very much."

Three days later she sent another letter: "My hair looks so nice tonight, it makes me mad to think that you won't be seeing me. What's the use of looking nice, can you tell me? Of course nobody in the world loves anybody as much as I love you. At this point the censor will probably be sick. I had better control myself."

In her diary she confided: "Picnic at pyramids with Robin Fedden and others. What good is a moonlight party without Cy, I ask you? . . . Friday. Bought some grape juice and it reminded me so much of America. Funny how I look back on it with such great fondness. I suppose that I would look back on Timbukto with pleasure if I had been there with Cy."

On May 21 she wrote that, in addition to the British position, she had taken a job with George Seferiades in the Greek information office. George, as "Seferis," was a famous poet who later received the Nobel Prize for literature. Marina said sadly: "Its pretty hard to get up at 7:30 every morning if you work till 2 the night before." Two days later she confessed that she had given away her best nightgown to a friend who was getting married, but added: "I will eat bread and cheeze for a week (or get invited out by American captains) and buy a new and prettier one for you when you get back to like me in."

On May 31 she wrote me again in Moscow: "I go out a great deal as each day I seem to run into more people I know, and there are so many more men than women, I have a lot of *succès*, but don't worry there is no one who is as good as your little toe, and even if there was, I'd rather your little toe anyway." The next day another letter: "I am 24 years old and one month and we have been married a year, four months and ten days, and I love you more than ever and miss you terribly all the time. The world seems to be made up of people missing each other and all because of that bastard, skunk, swine, brute donkey Hitler. . . . I have bought a new dress which is rather nice but whats the use of looking nice if you cant see me. I also made myself a bright red skirt, the kind you like. If only you were here, we could have such fun. We always have such a wonderful time when we are together my darling. Going to bed at night is the loneliest affair. Thank goodness I am usually so tired I fall asleep at once."

Even for those not subjected to its ghastlier horrors, war is a cause of suffering in all kinds of psychological ways, and Marina confessed (Cairo, June 4, 1943):

"I seem to have become terribly social, a regular party girl. Thats what happens when you leave me all alone.

> Cyrus said to Marina I love you.
> Marina said to Cyrus I dont believe you do.
> For if you really loved me, as you say you do
> You would not go to Bolshy land
> And leave me in the Zoo.

Its terrible to be separated, like having your one leg, arm, foot, eye, kidney in Cairo, and one in Moscow.

"I have stuck all your photographs on the walls all around the room so I can look at you all the time. There's the one where you look so angry and disapproving right facing the door, so if ever I am planing anything naughty you look at me, so disaprovingly that I dont do it. Then there is the other one in the frame, which is a bit better you say 'all right this time you may go, I forgive you.' And then there is the poetic one right over my bed in which you love me very much in the melting sort of way."

And in mid-June: "Last night I was coming home late and there were two young officers, one South African and one American, eating sandwidges and the American said 'Please lady sit down and talk.' So of course I did, and we talked for hours and decided that after all there was some good coming out of the war if three strangers can sit around and talk like old friends for hours when they had never set eyes on each other before."

On June 12, 1943, Marina wrote Mother from Cairo: "Last night I got three letters from Cy. These are the first ones I have received since his arrival in Moscow. He seems to be very well and working quote 'like a bird dog' unquote. He is living at the Metropole Hotel. He has a masseuse who comes in every morning and goes over him 'like a steam roller towing a lawn mower' he says it makes him fell good keeps his figure youthful and handsome and besides forces him to wake up in the morning, a thing which as you know only too well he is not too keen on doing. Besides that he has another woman coming in every day to give him Russian lessons. Entirely too many women around him I feel but he assures me that they are old fat and ugly. Ralph Parker who has the room next to his wrote to me too asking me to send him some things for his secretary-girl freind and in his note he adds that anything Cy may have told me about the morality of his life is perfectly true and that he has not yet heard any girlish giggles or the clink of glass against glass emerging from Cy's bedroom.

"All my spare time is spent at the swimming pool here which although rather fashionable and nick-named the snake pit because of all the gossip that goes on and the nasty things which are said about everybody, is rather nice and the only place where one can keep fairly cool and there are lots of pretty flowers and trees around which is a rest for the eyes from the ugliness of this city. There are some wonderful trees here called Flamboyants which are one great mass of bright red flowers. The petals fall on the ground and make a lovely red carpet everywhere. It is really lovely and apparently they last all summer long."

In June I had an awful row with the Soviet press authorities. I resolved to leave Russia, accepting an offer from Captain Eddy Rickenbacker, an American World War I ace on a propaganda mission, to fly from Moscow to Cairo in the bomb bay of his B-24. I wired Marina I would soon come, and she wrote back:

"Oh my dearest how lovely. I have thought of nothing else all day. I have even caught myself making plans as to where we shall go to dinner, and that maybe we shall go to a movie, and that I must get fresh flowers for the room. I must clear up all my things which are spread all over the place, so as to make room for you. What fun, to have all your papers flying around again, and the room so full of things you have to crawl through them. And I shall scold you and make you hang up your cloths. Thank God we have been given two nice rooms and we can breathe again."

"Marina faithfully confided to her diary: "July 26. Sunday. This beastly climate makes one feel a hundred years old. . . . July 27. Monday. Mussolini has been kicked out! Zito! . . . July 29. Thursday. Cy to Turkey. Two years since I left Greece. . . . August 7. Saterday. Aleco Xydis [a Greek propaganda official] wants me to work for him. I'll try both jobs for a week and see. If it kills me I'll stop. . . . August 11. Wensday. So tired I want to die. Two jobs is too much. Work from eight 'til one A.M. August 13. Friday. Sicily is being evacuated! . . . August 18. Wensday. Work. Very brave. Went to dentist and had my tooth out. Wanted Cy so badly to hold my hand. . . . August 23. Monday. Slept a bit and was wakened by [Greek

Prime Minister] Tsouderos who called to tell me that Cy would go down in the history of the Dodecanese on account of the beautiful articles he wrote. . . . September 8. Wensday. Italy has surrendered!!! Yippee!! . . . September 11. Saterday. The British have occupied Samos. Dodomou how you must feel. Maybe we will be together again soon. September 13. Monday. A great tragedy! My truly beautiful ruby watch was stolen. Never again will I have such a heavenly thing. September 30. Alexi has escaped [from the Italian prison in Athens]. Terrific celebration in our rooms till four. I feel as if handcuffs had been taken off my heart. Cy got Eisenhower and the Pope to intervene. The darling." (Actually, gold provided by the British intelligence services and properly distributed in Athens was mainly responsible, just after Italy's collapse.)

She wrote Mother again from Cairo on October 17: "The other day we went to a party with two Kings. The Greek one and the Yuogoslav and I am enough of a snob to have enjoyed it. There were dozens of generals and vice marchals and brigadiers and anything below that was practicaly considered a private. It was a coctail party given by General Wilson who has a lovely house outside Cairo and a beautiful garden and it was quite cool and very pleasant. We talked for quite some time to both Kings and the Greek King remembered my father and talked a lot about him and how he used to play the piano when they were all very young and they would all sit around and talk and sing. I had on my big red hat and looked rather nice says I modestly. It must seem rather strange to you people wearing big red hats in October but its just as hot and summery and unpleasant now as it was in August."

Her diary continued: "October 24. Sunday. Worked. Came back. Found Alexi, How can I write about that. We all had lunch together and tea and dinner and never stopped talking. We talked and sang till 4:30. Alexi seems astonishingly well. . . . October 27. Wensday. It's my darling's birthday. Gave him a book, lighter and cigarette case. We went to an enormous party. Alexi said the food looked like an hallucination. . . . November 18. Thursday. The [our] party was a great success. General [U.S. commander, Middle East] Royce sent an American colonel home in no uncertain way for dining with some Italians who had the impertinence to come and dance at Shepheards. . . . November 22. Monday. Cy so busy I never see him. Rumors that Churchill has arrived in Cairo. Chiang Kai Shek arrived yesterday. Roosevelt and Stalin are said to be here too. How thrilling it all is. The most important conference in the history of the world."

Very shortly thereafter Marina and I motored to Lake Qaroun, a strange, dreamy spot, much tenanted by birds and pleasantly encompassed by solitude. Marina told her diary: "Wensday. What fun to be alone and with nothing to do." A day later: "It's so lovely and lazy. We took picnic lunch and walked back slowly." Finally: "New Year's Eve with Cy. First time it's happened since we got married. We went on the lake all morning. Turkey, plum pudding, bed. Happy New Year."

I had to fly off to Italy right afterward, spending the rest of the winter and early spring of 1944 mostly around the stalemated Cassino position, briefly at Anzio and on the British-Free Polish front extending toward the Adriatic. Marina was again pregnant, unable to work any more, and not up to keeping her little diary. But she sent many letters.

January 11: "I cant write very much as I feel a little as if I were crosssing the Channell all the time but enough to tell you that I miss you horribly. The doctor says I have a heart like a bull and that I am very healthy. I am being very good and did not go to any of the parties. I have been in bed ever since you left. . . . What the hell. Money colds and babies cant be hidden. . . . I cant go on as I am beginning to cross from the Channell into the Atlantic and its getting rough. . . . All my love and the big hug. Dopey" (which had become the favorite pet name, that being the era of Walt Disney's *Snow White*). To this was appended: "Lots of love. Archie."

January 22: "I am still in bed sweetymou and feeling awfully sick. Archie had better turn out to be a wonderful baby otherwise I shall be furious with him for all the trouble he is giving me." ("He" turned out to be Marinette.)

She wrote my mother on March 7: "The other day I saw Prince Peter of Greece who told me he had seen Cy a few days before [in Italy] and that he was dirty and unshaved and dusty and grining all over his face and very busy and happy. I get cables from him and occasional letters. I told him that seing he has a Greek wife and probably half the things from our house are in Italy anyway he was entitled to a bit of looting and that he should try hard and with no compunctions to get at least a Fra Angelico for our dream house and a few Boticcellis for the babies room. (Please censor I am not giving away a secret by saying that my husband is in Italy as he is only a reporter not a soldier and his name and address are given in his by-line on every story of his.)

"I am madly learning how to sew and embroider and have already made young Sulzberger a heavenly set of sheets and pilow-cases in pinc and blue linen all with apliqué flowers on them. I have mobilized all my friends into doing things for me and in teaching me how to do it as well. I have one freind who is wonderful at all that sort of thing and she is being very sweet and helpful. I can still just squeeze into my old cloths but soon I shall have to have others which is an awful bore here as all the dress makers take such ages and all the ready made ones are horrid.

"Cy won 500 dollars off Jock Whitney at poker which he enjoyed a lot and did not have to feel self consious about taking. He said he has only found very few pretty things where he is but is still hoping. I told him I absolutely want at least one Fra Angelico for the living room. He has no idea when he will be coming back but in a way I would rather he stayed on there because if he comes back they may send him off to Russia again and I would hate that."

To me on March 9: "Dearest darling mou. I hear you look like a cross between an arctic explorer, a ragg-picker and a lunatic but that that does not prevent you from being quite cheerful. I am losing my girlish figure little by little and by the time you get back I shall be like a balloon. . . . Dont ruin all the brigadiers at poker and by all means dont lose all your money as Archy who I think is going to be a girl is most extravagant and shows a liking for the good things of life. . . . We are going to have a lot of trouble with her."

I managed to get back to Cairo just before Marinette arrived on earth on September 11, 1944. Marina had cleverly discovered a quite pleasant apartment high up in the Immobilia building, where the censorship and communications were established, so it was most convenient for work, comfortable for our crowded habits, and excellent for Marinette, with a big balcony and two servants. Alas, a fortnight later I had to go back to the war, but Marina wrote often.

September 28: "Marinette really is a most extraordinary child and that is not just my own unhumble opinion. Everybody says so. First of all she has the original million dollar smile. Its a combination of amused tolerant and mishivous smiles all together. . . . I have at last found a nurse. She is a

Greeky [not Egyptian] Greek called Angeliki who kisses me and calls me *Poulaki mou. . . .* If only babies were like camels and one could feed them once a week for good. It seems to me I just fed the little brute and suddenly I realise its five to twelve so off I go again to turn into a dairy."

She wrote Uncle Arthur on October 7: "The funny thing is that she is a complete combination of Cy and me. There are moments when she looks so like Cy that it makes me laugh. She looks exactly like Cy does when she is woken up. Just as grumpy and opens first one eye and then the other and raises her eyebrows in protest just like that old lazybones her father. There are other moments when she looks so like me that it is quite depressing. . . . I heard from Cy that among her other great qualities Marinette has now become an heiress as well and is the proud possessor of a hundred dollars dowary thanks to you, and both she and I thank you very very much. Marinette says that she will spend it all on her first hat but I being older think she aught to save it, which brings it home to me for good that I have now definitely become the older generation and I find it rather depressing."

That autumn Greece was liberated piecemeal, with various irregular and regular military organizations going in from all directions and squeezing the Germans back, singing their lugubrious song:

> "Es geht alles vorüber,
> Es geht alles vorbei;
> Nach jedem Dezember,
> Kommt immer ein Mai."

Marina tried desperately to get back as soon as possible. Major General Ben Giles, American commander in the Middle East and an old golf-and-poker pal of mine, had promised me he would send her and Marinette on his personal plane, but he got into bad trouble by successively flying the American millionairess Doris Duke and then the dog of Elliott Roosevelt, the President's son. He arranged for his chief of staff, General Percy Saddler, to take my family along when he first flew to liberated Athens, but that also got fouled up.

At first Marina accepted these delays philosophically. She wrote: "My sweetouli darling. To say that I miss you and that I have missed you every single day since you left, more than ever before, would be an understatement. I think it is mainly because of Marinette. Every inch she grows and every pound she weighs more and every new little hair or smile or expression I want you so much to see. It loses half its fun by not being shared by you. I think she is so beautiful that it haunts me to think of you missing it all."

Alas, Marina's dream of getting to Athens by Christmas didn't materialize because of Ben Giles's troubles (exposed by an American columnist), and I had to wind up the conflict in Russia, where I was desperately (and unsuccessfully) trying to get permission to join the Soviet forces at the final great battle for Berlin.

Marina wrote me a long, disconsolate letter from Cairo dated "Black Sunday, February 25th, 1945." She said: "The general [Giles] called up this morning and asked me over to lunch and talk about my trip. You can imagine my excitement. . . . The story is that S. [Saddler] has been transferred to Italy and that is why I cant be taken over but I think its really all because of Drew Pearson's story which of course is quite understandable and I've got nothing to grippe about except that I was not told all this time. . . . The general gave me an enormous ham but I dont think that makes up for a lost plane. . . . A million million kisses. Gloomy Gus."

A week later Marina got over her gloom, took the bit in her teeth, and acted. She wrote: "You know in a way you are a very bad influence on me because when you are near me I become feminine and dependent and useless and defeatist. When you are not here and I am on my own I am much tougher. Having cried all Monday I decided that it was time I pulled up my socks and did something and so all yesterday and today I have been running about with the result that I have been put on the diplomatic ship and am leaving soon. Isn't it wonderful."

The word "soon" had been inked in by another hand and subsequent words inked out. At the end of the letter was a note from Ben Giles: "Hello Cy. Sorry had to cut out that definite date. Hope you are getting all the news from the Russkies." Also a postscript from Marina: "If this bloody war is not over soon I shall go crazy. The general did not read the letter so don't be embarrassed about the sweetoulies in it."

At almost the same moment I was writing Marina from Russia, dated:

"The seventh gloomy day in Moscow on which I have heard nothing from or of you," and demanding somewhat peremptorily: "Where are you and what on earth are you doing?" Little did I know that my two darling Marinas were struggling to breathe on an overcrammed little steamer bearing its load of excited temporary refugees back to their own native land. How Marina managed it all, amid her disappointments and the unfulfilled promises of friends, I shall never understand; she even thoughtfully took final moments to write happy recommendations for our two weeping servants, Mufta and Ramadan.

I only learned that the great bridge had been crossed when I received a cable at the grimy Metropole Hotel in Moscow — sent from Athens: "Darling everyone fine Maroussi heavenly uneed anything unworry as happiest just come soon enormous love Marina Sulzberger." (Wartime cable-senders had to sign their last names — even to their husbands.)

II

April 1945 - July 1952

In Greek Orthodox hagiography Saint Marina is customarily depicted holding beside her on a chain a little devil, which, of course, was me. But unfortunately for both of us, she never managed to keep a firm grip on the chain, and even after the war had ended, the exigencies of my job and its geographical scope kept me traveling far afield and often.

From October 1944 until October 1954, as head of *The New York Times* foreign service, I was responsible first for setting up a new global network of correspondents, then for moving them around, and, as it were, seeing to it that they were adequately fed and cared for. In 1954 I started writing a column, "Foreign Affairs," and kept on moving around, figuring my legs were a greater journalistic asset than my brain.

During more than thirty years, I did manage at one or another time to bring Marina along on visits to six of the seven continents. And once the children were old enough to go to boarding school in England, in 1956, their mother was much freer to travel. But at the start, despite interludes, to a saddening degree Marina became almost as much of a peace widow as she had been a war widow.

As the Germans began to fold, Marina — back in the embrace of Greece and family — kept her scanty occasional diaries. She wrote of her twenty-sixth birthday in Maroussi: "May 1. Lovely day but not like last year with Cy." Six days later: "News of unconditional surrender. Strange. I don't feel terribly excited."

For me, V-E day came in Moscow.

As soon as possible I went to Paris, which, although it was grim, desolate, and filled with bitterness, I had decided to make our home base. Because of its beauty, its traditions, and its convenient location, I reckoned Paris was bound to resume its importance as a center of culture and of international conferences. Marina wrote on May 22, 1945:

"Life however pleasant it may be is not really worth while without you and everything becomes sort of dull and second best when you are away. . . . But I still haven't found a proper nurse for Marinette and now that she isn't very well I don't like to leave her. But my darling dont let that make you think that now that we have a baby I'll become an old stick in the mud domestick middle aged thing who thinks twice before joining her husband in Paris because remember I am much more a wife than a mother and however much I adore Marinette I still prefer you to her."

When she did arrive — with Marinette — I had run into an old army friend who obtained for me the unbelievable: a five-room, two-bath suite in the Ritz, which was then a billet for generals only. This was beyond question the most elegant accommodation we ever lived in and, as a military billet, it was free! That delightful factor proved to be just as well. While allowed to have my wife, baby, and a nurse in my suite, I was only entitled to invite one person per week — and for a single meal at that — to the glorious generals' mess. So, apart from that magnificent weekly splurge, Marina and I trudged around Paris's pitiful restaurants, usually confining ourselves to a surprisingly costly meal of celery consommé, braised celery, a piece of bread, sometimes an egg or a morsel of cheese, always an apple.

The rest of my funds went to baby food and keeping our exigent French nurse in those delicacies she insisted Marinette must have (like cold ham, which we often caught her eating herself). Yet even that disagreeable snob was worth having; nannies at that time were scarce as hen's teeth and it freed Marina to go out.

Our life was pleasant until the shocking day when we were informed by the billeting authorities that the Ritz would be turned back to French civilian management. From then on I would have to pay something like two hundred dollars a day for our accommodation. We had been steadily looking around for an apartment but had found none. Paris was crammed with officers of various Allied armies and members of special diplomatic, economic, and administrative missions.

Finally, that winter, I found in London a lovely little Queen Anne house two minutes' walk from Westminster Abbey and Parliament, which we rented furnished, complete with an all-purpose housekeeper named Mrs. Stewart. The only trouble with our new establishment was that it had apparently undergone no repairs since the time of Queen Anne. It was drafty and terribly cold, dependent for heat on two or three fireplaces, and coal was short.

Our landlady, Mrs. Belloc-Lowndes, sister of Hilaire Belloc, was a well-known writer whose novel, *The Lodger*, was a minor classic. She was most friendly and, although over eighty, was massive and fearfully energetic. Always dressed in black, she would drop in frequently, never letting go of an enormous handbag which invariably contained a flask of cognac from which she took nips, explaining that her doctor had so ordered.

She was indestructible and had attended Winston Churchill's wedding as a friend of the groom's mother. When she talked about "the war," it took us some time to realize that she referred to the Franco-Prussian War of 1870, during her girlhood in Paris. The main decoration in our bedroom (hers) was a huge 1914 French mobilization order.

On November 12, Marina wrote Mother from London: "Getting organized in a new house in a country where you need a permit to eat, to live, to walk, to sneeze takes some time and effort and I really have not had time to breath since our arrival. Now at last everything is settled and I can relax again. The house is adorable and you can imagine the relief and fun of having a home of our own after four years of hotel bedrooms. Cy is so happy it is a joy to see him grin as he comes home each night and sits in front of the fire.

"We have a lovely living room very old with panelling and various ancestors hanging on the walls and two fire places. The furniture is all old and very beautiful. There is a bed room for us a study for Cy, bathrooms and a bed room for Marinette and nurse as well as a nursery so its just perfect for us. We have a cook and a maid who comes in half days so for England we are living like kings."

Marina was pregnant when she wrote Mother again on December 22: "I am really dissappointed that I should feel so rotten on the one happy Xmas we were to spend together in our own home but still I'll try and get up Xmas day and hope I am not sick over our best Xmas goose. We were very lucky that way as the office chauffeur managed to find us a lovely bird and its very difficult here these days. Apart from that we have nuts and candy from your sweet parcel and chocolates which Cy brought from Sweden and cheese and butter from Denmark so we are really very lucky. We are being very mean and having no one else in for Xmas day at all as we so rarely have a chance to be alone together but we shall ask all our freinds in Boxing day. Xmas Eve we are going to Canterberry Cathedral to hear the service as we have been asked to spend the day with some very sweet freinds of ours who live twenty minutes from there."

Postwar London was nice, the people were splendid, the taste of victory was exhilarating, but the taste of almost everything else was absent. Food was even scarcer than in Paris. I managed, by hanging it around my neck beneath an enormous Rumanian fur-lined coat, to smuggle back from Denmark a ham, unfortunately uncured and raw. (Imagine having to *smuggle* food into a hungry land!) Marina studied cookbooks in order to prepare it for Christmas, but almost every one, when discussing how to cure a ham, commenced: "Take ten quarts of beer . . ." The Englishman's favorite brew was then even worse than the "near beer" of American prohibition days.

As usual, I had to rush off shortly to what the English call "the Continent," abandoning Marina, Marinette, and "Nur," her first London nanny. Thank God she didn't stay long with us. She was replaced by "Nursey," the heavenly Emily Stanbury, who remained until Marinette and David trundled off to boarding school, and is now again with the family, looking after Marinette's two youngsters.

In January 1946, soon after we had devoured our complicated Danish

ham, Marina managed to get an extra ration book because of "Archy" No. 2, who eventually became David.

She wrote: "I'm doing all the cooking and having lots of fun except I dont sleep very well again since you left. I hate it alone. I miss you more each time you go. All my enormous love Smouli darling."

A few days later she complained, after getting some shots: "That nasty doctor sent me a bill for eighteen pounds. The doctors as they take their fees, say there's no cure for this disease. I really resent having to pay all that money for six injections and for having my pulse taken. . . . I miss you as many atoms of ink as have ever been used to write letters or will ever be used as it would take to dip the world in."

That winter was bitter. Marina told me: "Its so cold that we wear gloves in the house. On Friday it snowed. I wish you had been here. We have never seen snow together. . . . I'm getting more and more depressed."

Sadly, she complained when I had to see Franco in Spain in early February: "It's not anger at you that I feel *you* know that and you know that I know you would not be away from your women if you could help it. Its just anger at this bloody world and this job which for four years has kept us from having a proper home and life like all human beings should. No husband, no home, no country, no hot water. . . . Not a drop of hot water since you left. All night every window every door every board in the place rattles and shakes as if an armoured division were going over it."

A friend smuggled Marina into the United Nations debate on Greece which was conducted at a Security Council meeting in London, and she was most excited: "[Ernest] Bevin [British foreign minister] was terrific. He banged his fists and went purple in the face. He told [Andrei] Vishinski [Soviet delegate to the UN] just what he thought of him and my Mediterranean, anti-KKE [Greek Communist party] blood surged with love for him and my desire to throw an old potato at Vishinski was nearly overpowering." (That was just as the second phase of the Greek Communist revolution was starting.)

It was a nightmare winter for her, but she was incredibly cheerful despite my absences, despite her pregnancy illnesses with David, despite Marinette's habit of waking in the middle of the night and hollering, despite

a sullen nurse and surly housekeeper, and despite the intensely cold, bitter London weather.

In June, Marina, Marinette, and our wonderful new Nursey took off for Athens and a summer with Dodo in Marina's little Maroussi house, the Spitaki. In those days the flight from London to Athens was a two-day affair with fuel stops en route and an overnight halt in Rome.

Yet, like everything else and with all her enthusiasm, Marina enjoyed it. She wrote me from Rome during the overnight halt: "The trip was lovely and smooth except for half an hour before landing and both your Marinas were sick, sharing the same potty between them. . . . Lunch at Marseille was delicious but we lost that. We have a big room at the Albergo Reale for the three of us and Marinette is asleep in a great big bed with all the chairs round her so as not to fall out. She is so pink and sweet I could eat her. Sweetouli I miss you so its unbelievable."

At the tiny Athens airport she found the waiting room crowded with three generations of family and friends. They drove out to Maroussi and "we sat around and had loads of *retsina* [resinated wine] and *mezedakia* [hors d'oeuvres] and everyone talked at once and nurse looked quite lost. We gave her some *retsina* and she liked it."

I had given Marinette one of those sets of Russian wooden dolls that fit inside each other, and Marina wrote shortly afterward: "Its morning and its hot but nice and for once there is no one around which even for me is a pleasure after the seige of the last five days. I'm writing to you in our room and at the same time eating a big peice of black bread and cheese and tomatoe and drinking a lemonade. Marinette is sitting on the floor playing with her Russian ladies who she loves. I don't suppose there will be many left of the small ones after a bit but that is what children's toys are for.

"Last night I went to a taverna party near the sea and it was too heavenly for words. We had *barbounies* [red mullet] and *kalamarakia* [squid] and we sang and it could only have been more perfect if you were there too. . . . I hope you were not worried about the news of a strike. It was the nicest strike you ever saw. Nothing stopped at all. There were lots of policemen everywhere sitting around smoking and chatting with the strikers who were also smoking and chatting and then everyone went home in the evening."

My summer holiday was deferred until autumn because the peace conference that negotiated settlements with Hitler's satellites was meeting in Paris. But at the end of July I flew briefly to Athens for the birth of my son, David, on the twenty-sixth. The evening before his arrival Marina, Dodo, and I dined at a little tavern in the nearby village of Kifissia. We were riding home in a horse-drawn carriage when the labor pains started. Everything had been laid on, including car to Athens, hospital, and doctor. Although both Dodo and Maria assured me it was a boy, I was dubious, knowing they were aware I had set my mind on that particular brand. Since I had to fly back to Paris promptly, I insisted on a full personal inspection and satisfied myself I wasn't being fooled.

I worried about leaving. The day before David's birth I had written: "The maintenance of law and order over large areas of Greece is deteriorating to such an extent that a condition of growing anarchy appears imminent in certain regions. . . . The Communist supporters are strong right in and around Athens." However, the peace conference was top priority. Constantine Tsaldaris, then Greece's prime minister, took me back to Paris with him aboard his personal plane.

On August 5, Marina sent my mother a full account of David's arrival: "Well, its all over and I am a very happy woman. It was all so miraculous you know, because to begin with everything went wrong and then right again. You see Cy accepted to cover this wretched conference when he still believed it would take place in September. Then it was decided to hold it now and he had to be back in Paris which by all probabilities should have been long before David's arrival. He started off to come by car and the car came apart in Trieste. He got to Rome and got a plane ticket but the planes all broke down in Chicago or some other place and he spent five wretched days in Rome bitting his nails. Then he got hives badly and had to stay in bed. He finally got here in a terrible state of nerves, asked about plane passages back and was told that the only one leaving was the very next day. I in mean time went to the baby doctor who said not a hope before a fortnight. We were so depressed we wanted to sit down and cry. Then we suddenly found out that the prime minister would be leaving by plane on Saturday for the conference and having spent a frantic day telephoning and rushing about, we finally got the prime minister who said he'd be only too glad to take Cy on his private plane. This was Thursday. That evening we went out to dinner to celebrate our extra day together and I laughingly said 'Well if only the baby would come tomorrow and were a boy, then everything would be all right after all.' Friday morning I woke up with a tiny pain, but I thought it was wishful thinking or a chill. All that day we sat around played bridge talked and held our thumbs. At about six I got one big pain and as we are in the country and far, Cy thought it best to go down to Athens just in case. . . . But we were still convinced it could not be the baby as it was too good to be true. Then at seven, the ministry rang up to say the plane was leaving Sunday instead of Saturday which delighted us in itself. At 8:30 I got to the hospital and at ten the baby was born. And a boy. Mumy who was outside holding Cy's hand said she never in her life saw such a smile as Cy's when they told him to go in and see his son. He was the happiest man on earth and he could go off to his beastly old conference with a light heart. The baby was the most hidious thing I ever saw, but he has already improved tremendously and now at ten days he is quite sweet. I adore him. He eats like a pig and is angelic. He hardly ever cries and today made pipi in his potty. My nurse is an angel too and its really wonderful. I can relax and know everything will be done properly. Such a difference from little Marinette whom I had all alone and was so petrified all the time that I'd boil her in her bath or stick a pin into her tummy or something frightful. Marinette is such an angel with David. She holds his hand and says 'All better baby brother' when he cries, and helps nurse give him his bath. She is not a bit jealous. She is becoming so big and pretty. I'm dying to show them both off to you. I am quite well although a bit tired and very discouraged as I cannot get into a single of my dresses yet. I have a big roll of fat all round my middle.

"Mummy is in heaven with her two grand-children. She cant get used to the idea of my living here with a baby girl and boy, just as she was, what seems to her only yesterday. As for the great grand mother and all the great aunts, they have all lost their heads. They all come to see Marinette in her bath. It has become the social event of the evening. Nurse luckily is so sweet she lets them all in although it must be quite a nuisance for her. Marinette delighted them all tonight by dismissing them with 'good night ladies.' All together as you can imagine I am a very happy woman and if only Cy were here my cup would be full."

On "David's one month birthday" Marina wrote me: "Sweetouli to your
surprise you will learn that David is really developing into a glamour boy.
He is actually quite good-looking and the longest baby you ever saw. . . . I
adore him. He is so soft and small and warm, and at the same time so
manly and tough-looking."

That autumn of 1946, I managed to shake loose from Paris. Shan
Sedgwick had no transport in Athens, so I undertook to drive a jeep across
the Trieste Free Territory and down through Jugoslavia and Greece. The
trip contained the possibility of hairy moments, so I picked up my old
friend Bob Low of *Time* and slowly we bumped our way to Belgrade.
Jugoslavia's ghastly roads had not improved with war and civil war.

Just before we started off, the Jugoslavs had shot down two American
aircraft loaded with soldiers being flown to Austria. Relations between
Washington and Belgrade were strained and there was loud talk of conflict.
Tito was cold and hostile when I saw him. The local head of British
Intelligence warned me a plot was being laid on to assassinate us some-
where in Macedonia.

The last *četnik* bands of Draža Mihailović (later caught, tried, and
executed) had not yet been hunted down. Part of the area we traversed was
therefore still troubled. But we had no difficulty.

Marina and I had a great reunion in Maroussi. Marinette was already a
little girl, no longer a baby; David was still in the vegetable stage, but
squirming. The Spitaki was charming, with all the nostalgic smells and
softness of the Attic autumn.

My vacation ended when I flew down to Saudi Arabia, where King
Abdul-Aziz Ibn Saud erected a tent city for me outside Mecca, entertained
me at a huge dinner whose other guests were his sons and brothers, and
told me he would never allow a Zionist state to be created in Palestine. I
also saw for the only time in my life a large dhow, or sambouk, loaded with
slaves, seeking custom in a small Saudi port on its way to Oman. The only
way I discovered of getting out without endless waiting was by volunteering
to serve as navigator on one of Ibn Saud's royal flight of DC-3s carrying
pilgrims back to Beirut and Damascus.

Back in Maroussi, we had to arrange our departure for winter in Paris.
We had found a lovely apartment which belonged to a former Greek

military attaché. Because of the size of our expeditionary force — Marina, Nursey, Marinette, David, me, plus baggage — we decided to go by ship to Marseilles.

Our first problem was arranging exit visas. Greece's civil war was bubbling and there had even been gunfire near our house. We had no trouble getting exit permits for Marina, Marinette, Nursey, and myself because we all had entry visas. We had obtained a separate passport for David, who looked like a wrinkled little monkey in his photograph, but when Marina took it to the Maroussi police station to obtain the required stamp, the official in charge examined the document for some time with a puzzled expression. Finally he asked, "Where is the entry?" Marina exploded. "That's the first time I ever met a bureaucrat who thinks the stork carries visas," she said.

That winter of 1946 — 47 was very bad in Paris: not much food, less heat. Our apartment, opposite the Parc Monceau, was huge and splendid and we never before or since had so many rooms or servants. I got a chow puppy, named Pablo, to add to the general confusion. But it was so cold that, although we generally kept only three rooms functioning to save heat, whenever I left a glass of water by our bed at night it was invariably frozen by morning. For twenty-four hours before Christmas we kept a log fire burning in the dining room. Nevertheless, we cautioned all the guests we invited to wear overcoats at table.

March was dreadful. I had to go back to Moscow, where the Big Four foreign ministers were having a crucial meeting. I hated leaving Marina and the children again so soon, particularly as Marina was expecting another baby and we had decided that two were enough. Also Pablo, who had grown fast and become strong, had developed a habit of biting.

I tried to call Marina from Berlin, and just missed her. She wrote me in Moscow on March 5, 1947:

"I am so mad at having missed your call. Apparently I came in just about five minutes after you rang off too which makes it even worse. Well I am getting on fine in the old Fertile Myrtle tradition. A lovely breakfast disappeared this morning as well as lunch. But as a matter of fact that may be my saving. Tomorrow I see a doctor who apparently is excellent and my hope is to convince him that I am in no condition to have a baby and then it can be done quite openly and above board and without complications."

The letter continued with an addition two days later: "I stoped to be sick and then some people came and I couldn't go on and yesterday was an awful day. I went to the dressmaker to try on and on my way out fainted cold dead in the middle of the street. It was horrid. Some people picked me up and I woke up in a shop and after about twenty minutes I managed to get home in a taxi and stayed in bed the rest of the day feeling awful.

"My prospects of getting the thing done here are getting worse and worse. I have been to three doctors apart from the three that you gave me and most of them were quite disagreeable and nasty about things. I thought that fainting and being as green as I am they would take compassion on me but not at all. You have to be dying of TB or heart to be able to do it. I am seeing one more doctor here this afternoon but I haven't got much hope.

"If you knew how I hate going to them. I tell the same story each time (one of them was stone deaf and I had to shout all the horrid details). And they listen coldly and then say No honest man will do a thing like that which makes me feel like a criminal. And yet I think its much more of a crime to have three children you cant take care of properly than two that you can."

On March 19, while I was eating my heart out in Moscow, Marina sent another letter: "Now that it is all over sweety I can tell you that this last month has been one of the most miserable ones of my life. First of all I felt worse than even with Marinette or David. I was sick every ten minutes and I felt dizzy and faint the whole time. I went to all the doctors and it was agony sitting there telling them how awful I felt and how I thought I was justified in not wanting another child and having them look at me coldly and giving me long dissaproving lectures on the duties of a mother.

"One of them even was furious and said he should call the police for my having dared to ask his advice on a crime etc. etc. It was the most soul shattering experience and it gave me such a wicked crime complex in the end I felt as if really it was a wicked sin and yet I kept on telling myself it was better to have two children that I love and could cope with and bring up properly rather than three which would mean so much difficulty in our life and also I did not feel I could bare another such horrible nine months just yet. My body just wouldn't take it.

"Then when I was practically *à bout de force* that angel Mrs. K [my

secretary, Princess Kougoucheff] came to the rescue. One day I was in bed
fealing like hell and she came to see me and we talked about this and that
and then *à propos* of nothing she started telling me about her sister who last
month had had such trouble as she has two children already and was
expecting another one which they could not afford etc etc and that she had
had it taken away. I nearly choked of course and broke down and told her
everything and she was most comforting and sweet and reassuring and
came with me and helped me more than a sister or mother would have
done.

"Well we went to see this person who at first was very reluctant as
apparently if cought you get two years of hard labor not only because this is
a catholic country but because they need population so badly. She said to go
away and come back in a few days and she would think it over and let us
know but of course I should know it would be without aneasthetic. That
was not very apealing a thought but by that time I didn't care what
happened as long as I stopped being sick and dizzy twenty four hours a day.
Finally I decided no pain can be as bad or as continuous as the present hell.

"Since I took the decision I felt better already and much less scared and
even quite interrested to see my own reaction to pain. It was the first time I
would sort of cold bloodedly anticipate physical pain for a few days and I
wondered what it would be like. Having been to a very existentialist play
the night before about some maquis in prison waiting to be tortured and
analysing themselves and their emotions etc I felt even more interrested
and actually not terribly scared.

"The only moment which was nasty was the actual Sunday morning
when I got into a taxi alone and drove off. Going up in that lift and ringing
the bell my mind was not in the least consciously afraid but my stupid
body did all sorts of silly tricks like walking and moving very slowly and
fealling very cold and perspireing under the arms and in my eyebrows. Actually the thing itself was pretty horrid and perhaps a bit worse than having a
baby especially psychologically, but it was over in about half an hour which
is not very much, and the releif lying there all sort of relaxed and weak and
trembly afterwards was so lovely that one forgot everything.

"Its funny how fast the memory of pain disappears. I must say it was
done very well and scientifically and the person who did it was so sweet and
kind and freindly that it made all the difference and helped me to forget all

those horrid cold accusing faces that had scared me so all the past weeks. I stayed there till the evening and then Mrs K came to fetch me and brought me home feeling fine. I kept thinking of you the whole time and knowing how much worse it must have been for you far away and worrying to death."

Well, if that doesn't show the quality of the woman to whom I was married for more than thirty-four years, nothing will! I was so over-whelmed by relief, tenderness, heartbreak, and love when I got this letter that I kept a steady stream of telephone tries for Paris going on and on endlessly. Even during the temporary thaw in East-West relationships accepted by Moscow as host to the Foreign Ministers' Council, the communications system was uncertain. Finally, I reached Marina. Just as I started pouring out my heart, she interrupted breathlessly: "Marinette fell out the window." Then the phone went dead.

It was a full day before I could reestablish contact. Marina explained that Marinette had been all bundled up in her winter woollies, like a ball of feathers, and had been leaning out looking at Pablo in the courtyard below. Fortunately, our apartment was on what we Americans calls the second floor (first floor to Europeans). When she toppled over, she did little more than bounce; not even a bruise. But the twenty-four-hour telephone wait was almost too much.

I heard again from Marina on March 28: "This letter will probably be even more illegible than usual as I have to write with half my hand. The other day like a dope I stuck the end of a tin can into my thumb and its got infected and is enormous and quite painful now. This afternoon I am going to the doctor to have it opened. Is'nt it a bore. I only hope it does'nt developpe into anything worse especially with nursey leaving on Monday. My insides are still a bit wobbly but I suppose that is to be expected. The only thing which worries me is that I feel so nervous and fidgetty and cant sleep at night.

"One night this very sweet new friend called Denise [Boisot] whome I used to know in Cairo and who is here now and very nice and amusing and I went to dinner and the theatre together so as to forget our sorrows because our men are so far away. We had dinner at a place called *la closerie des Lilas* which is the place where Trotski and all his freinds used to go to and also the restaurant which occurs in Of Human Bondage. We lost ourselves two or three times and nearly got stuck with no petrol in Denise's car and it was all lots of fun.

"We saw mourning becomes Electra which was first class. On Tuesday it was the twenty fifth of March* and very patriotically I went to Church and then to the Embassy to pay my respects and then in the evening we all went to a Greek show very patriotic and heroic stuff about our ancestors and flags and Albania etc but we enjoyed it a lot and then we all came back here at midnight and eat soup and sandwidges and started a discussion about Existentialism and James Joyce and surealism and stayed till three in the morning.

"It was just the kind of thing I love. When we came in the porter looked at us and very siriously said. Haven't you forgotten something? We looked blank and he said '*Et Barbe Bleu† qu'avez vous fait de lui donc.*' Then we realized that we were seven women all together and we all had on black astrakan coats. We must have looked very funny going up stairs one after the other.

"The puffin [our nickname for Marinette, dating back to a little song she knew] is funnier and sweeter every day. I had the very bad idea of starting a story for her every night about you and Pablo and all the things you do together and now I am sunk. Every night I have to think of something new that you and Pablo do and it must be exciting and wonderful and my immagination is running pretty well dry. Up to now you have killed Wolves and found great big fish and had duels with Mr. Molotov and all sorts of other things but god knows what I can think of for you to do tonight."

Marina had an astounding capacity to recover from pain or sadness; her spirit was always optimistic. She was soon gaily cavorting about Paris with her friends and children. She wrote my aunt: "We are much happier now that the bad cold is over and spring is doing its best to break through helped along by Parisian women who in spite of the rain and wind have

---

* Greek Independence Day.
† "Bluebeard."

blossomed out in bright colours and flowers and birds on their heads."

I gave Marina two presents to honor her gallantry. The first gift was a dress from Christian Dior, who had just skyrocketed to the top of the fashion world; Marina was proud as an adorable peahen when she strutted about in this. The second gift was a special birthday trip to Greece. As soon as she arrived, she wrote on May 18:

"My dearest darling Smou. It is Sunday and I am up in Maroussi with Dodo and mother [Maria] and Julia [Maria's *older* sister] and Rica [a cousin] and the whole colony and we will play bridge later on and everyone will drink *ouzaki* [a small ouzo] and argue like mad about something or other and it is just like it always was and I am terribly happy. The thing about Maroussi and Greece which I love so is that they always live up to my expectations. Repetition is never worse than the last time.

"You were so sweet and good and kind to let me come I shall never forget it. It is rather fun now and then to be without a household without servants to cope with no meals to order no accounts to finish no nothing although I do miss you all like the devil. Yesterday I saw a balloon in the street and my first instinct was to go and buy it and then I had a horrid feeling in my tummy to think that you were all so far away and I could not buy you any balloons or order your meals. . . . I must go down now and entertain the family with stories about the children. They simply lap them up. They are so sweet all of them and I adore them and I adore you for being so angelic and letting me come to see them. You are the nicest husband there ever was. I shall try and be the nicest wife."

She was. Even her grandmother, dear Maria, wrote me while she was there: "Dear Cy. Very much obliged to you for the loan of Marina for these few days. We appreciated it very much." For that self-contained old lady who disliked the very thought of expressing any emotion, this was a huge concession to sentimentality.

A few days after Marina had returned to Paris, Maria wrote her: "Dear dearest mou. I read that nothing happens to people from overwork but a lot to people who don't work at all. I hope Cy won't disprove that. If you can't make him moderate it, tell Uncle Arthur to stop him. What's the good of doing too much for a short time instead of less for longer? The present condition of the world isn't temporary; it has come to stay for years. And even Cy won't make it any better by wearing himself to tatters. I'm glad you're back with him."

Later, she told Marina in another letter: "Tell Cy from me that nothing worldly matters much and most things don't matter at all so what on earth is the good of him wearing himself out sweating for a lot of quarrelsome politicians or diplomats when he could have such nice times and just as profitable ones (I don't mean in dollars) writing, thinking, creating, at home instead of watching to see whether Molotov is looking particularly disagreeable or, worse still, too pleased. Detachment and serenity are worthwhile acquisitions."

That summer we all went back to the United States for inspection by my mother and stepfather, who had not yet seen the children and who had rented a house in the mountains of North Carolina. It was blissful. Marina, as always, had completely won the hearts of my family (so did the children and Nursey), and she adored the forested countryside.

Finally, after visiting uncles and aunts and a theatergoing stay in New York (a city I detested but Marina loved), we returned to Paris in the leisurely fashion of that agreeable era, aboard the Cunard steamer *Mauretania*.

I have a foible, which I suppose is a form of minor criminality, of swiping soap from hotels; Marina had the same weakness for acquiring free stationery. So I was not surprised when the next letter I received from her, on returning to Europe and departing on another journey, was neatly stamped: "Cunard White Star — RMS Mauretania." I had to go off in the middle of an increasingly cruel winter to arrange emergency communications for various correspondents of *The New York Times* — emergency evacuation of their families, emergency deposits of dollars and gold coins — just in case general strikes then threatening should (1) cut off regular telegraph and telephone links by which news is reported and (2) develop into a politically revolutionary strike that might require sending wives and children to safe havens.

Discouraged, overtired, and somewhat ill, I had called Marina. She wrote:

"I get so sad when you talk to me and sound so utterly exhausted and weary and unhappy. Sweety nothing in the world is worth the effort in your voice last night. Dearest, this is a strange thing to say to you in a letter but really, don't think that it means anything to me to live in Paris and have servants and pretty hats. I like it but I'd be just as happy any place else.

"As for the children, their adult life will probably be so much worse that its just as well they dont get used to too much. Anyway they are too young to be affected yet, one way or the other. By this prologue I mean really why dont you leave the whole business and lets go away somewhere and rest and become happy and normal again. You know I cant remember any more when was the last time that you said to me I feel wonderful. . . .

"I really felt so strongly about it since you talked to me last night and your voice was half dead that I had to write and tell you once more that I dont care how or where we live as long as you are well and happier. . . .

"I'm in bed, warm cosy and reading John Donne's Devotions. I've unpacked all your books which are divine. I am not going to read one detective story or bad novell this year. . . . Marinette comes in every morning asking for you. Lets hope this will be your last trip for ages and ages."

During the summer of 1948, Maria found a modest villa at Villerville on the Normandy coast. When I was in France I would hurtle down on Sundays (and sometimes for entire weekends).

Marina wrote me (in Palestine, which had exploded into Arab-Israeli war): "The house looked sweet and right away we got to work and made beds changed furniture around put out photographs and flower vases and the place looked lived in. Then we went round the village making friends with the boutcher the baker and the farmer's wife and we got a woman to bring milk cream and butter once a week and the baker will make us white bread and another man brought us coal and wood so everything is fixed.

"The joy of the children was a real thrill to watch. The first morning we spent in the garden painting the garden chairs red and green. Can you immagine the children each with a paint brush and allowed to do as they please. I may say we were all covered in paint from head to foot but they loved it. In the afternoon we went to the beach and there new delights. Shells sand water everything their little hearts could wich for. We all had tremendous appetites and eat like pigs and went to bed at nine and woke up at six because of the birds who were making a terrible noise outside our windows."

She invited Fuego, the Boisots' Alsatian, as a houseguest and friend for Pablo. This did not turn out too well initially.

"The first encounter with Pablo was awful because Pablo turned nasty and vicious and bit poor Fuego to bits but now he is used to him already and they are good friends and have a lot of fun together. I look really like the Pied Pipper when I go to the village with four children [ours and Boisots'] and two dogs. The policeman was horrid at first and said dogs were not allowed without a leach etc but then we smilled and cigarettes crossed hands and we payed a hundred and fifty francs to the *music municipale* which is rehearsing for the 14 Juillet and now he does not say anything any more. . . .

"Yesterday Marinette said We never see our father but he is very nice. David does not go to sleep until nursey or I give him a kiss for father. If we forget and some times we pretend to on purpose he yells, Kiss for father *s'il vous plait.*"

During the 1948 – 49 winter Marina decided to attend the Sorbonne and had full intention of taking some sort of degree. But the rules then prevailing for that institution stipulated knowledge of a classical language, preferably Latin or ancient Greek. Speaking modern Greek, of course, and having studied its classical predecessor for four years in high school, she naturally opted for that choice. However, to her astonishment and fury, she discovered it was taught according to the Erasmian pronunciation, which is totally different from that employed in Greece itself and approximately as if one had to learn English with a Japanese accent. In the end she grew so impatient that, although for a considerable period she attended Sorbonne lectures, she abandoned her Flemish-infected Greek instruction with outrage.

She told Mother on November 29: "Paris looks Xmasy already. There is a thick grey fog and frost on the ground everywhere. Quite a change from

Lisbon where it was hot enough to bath a week ago. We had an amusing time there wining and dining with several ex kings pretenders etc. We went to lunch with Umberto* who is very sweet but really just like any other young rather handsome Italian aristocrat. One meets them by the dozen here. One other day we went out with Don Juan* who seemed to have much more caracter and is very amusing and gay. His wife is adorable and has lovely sad eyes although not pretty. Its absurd really because she looks so much like Louis XIV. They have a little girl who is blind so I suppose that even if all their other troubles did not exist she still has good reason to look sad. But she is really nice and friendly and pathetic. We also saw Carol and Mrs. Lupescu,* and they looked very moth eaten poor dears. Her sister is married to Dr. Voronof and the four of them always had their meals next to us in the hotel. They were all very odd looking I must say. Mrs Voronof has masses of bright red phony hair just like the old fashioned advertisements in hairdressers windows. Cy also had a long talk with Salazar so from the point of view of celebrities we did rather well if one can still call poor nostalgic ex kings celebrities. One got the impression rather that they thought us both celebrated and lucky. They are so bored in their provincial little lives that anyone coming from Paris looks to them like all that is enviable. Poor things. What a world."

Right after Christmas, on January 7, 1949, she again wrote Mother from Paris about an unexpected journey: "First of all thank you for all the lovely presents. The children were so thrilled with theirs that it was a joy to look at them. They were extreamly spoilled this year as we gave them all kinds of things and on top of it all yours arrived and they were in heaven. When they walked into the room with the tree David was absolutely speechless and Marinette took one look at her pram and doll and her eyes became enormous and she said: 'That is just exactly what I wished for in all the world and now I dont want anything else.' In our present day world of sorrows and discontent it warms one's heart to hear a phrase like that coming straight from the heart. Then when she got your presents *en plus* she said to me. You know I had even not asked for those from Father Xmas

---

* Umberto, ex-King of Italy; Don Juan, pretender to the Spanish throne; ex-King Carol of Rumania and his famous consort.

65

because one must not ask too much, but he knew and told grand mama about it. How kind he is. We had a very quiet family dinner and the only guests were my two cousins who are adorable and Turner Catledge who has been staying with us.

"It was lovely and such fun to see the children so happy, and then on top of it all I got the one Xmas present in the world which I wanted. Cy went to have lunch with Mr. [Averell] Harriman on Friday and just at the very end of lunch he said to Cy, You know I am going to Greece for a week why dont you and your wife come along. Can you imagine. I nearly died. And what a way to travel. No expenses no passports no customs no waiting around the airodromes. Just straight from the taxi to the plane and in eight hours we were home. I had not spent the holidays at home for eight years. I must say that week was the most full in emotions I have ever had. You can understand the delight of seing them all again. I kissed my way from one end of Athens to the other.

"But at the same time it was heartbreaking because of course I was so awfully conscious of the minutes flying flying inexorably and I could not possibly see them all and also you know how terrible it is to find old old friends, all looking older more tired a bit more shabby a bit more white a bit more discouraged. All of them pretending that things were fine and being gay and happy to see me and all the time underneath knowing them all crushed by poverty struggles, discouragement. A problem that can be solved in some way, for which there is hope and promise of deliverence, can be borne however tough it may be, but when there seems to be no solution no hope and the struggles and fights go on and on and on, then it kills one. And they are all so brave and cheerful and try their best but it is such a half hearted best. It broke my heart. But seing my mother and grandmother was so lovely and they were so sweet and so pleased to see me it made me feel all warm and soft and young again. The joy of being told to put one's coat on so as not to catch cold.

"But I feel so terribly guilty at my own cosy comfortable easy life. They need every scrap of help anyone can give them. Do you know there are about a hundred thousand refugee orphans in Athens with nowhere to go no one to look after them. Its too too dreadful. But dont let me depress you too with all this. The whole world needs help and where can one start."

In January 1949, I was in America. Marina wrote: "I was at the Sorbonne all morning and it was lovely. Spent the evening at home with the chicks and a hot bath and Mr. Bertrand Russell." In her classes she had met an unhappy Czech refugee. "You know I was rather sad because the other day I had a boy and a girl from the Sorbonne to tea so as to study together and I said how ugly I thought this house was and the girl who poor darling (I found out after) is a Check jewess whose parents were both shot before her eyes etc got very cross and said it was all very well for me to say this place was ugly but to her it was a palace etc etc. It made me sad because I only said it was ugly it did not mean that I was not happy with it or not conscious of my bloody good fortune etc etc I only said it was ugly from an easthetic point of view but when one is unhappy one's values get all confused and every word means the same thing and there are only to big categories in the world the haves and the have nots. You see what I mean by unhappiness not always making better people. Anyway on Saturday I went to school looking like something out of the gutter to prove to her I was not a *sale* capitalist. And also will take her to lunch in a bistro tomorrow."

The Sorbonne was a confusing experience for Marina. She wrote me: "Yesterday I went to hear a man giving his thesses. You know its when you are already a teacher in some school and want to pass from that to being a proffessor in University. I must say it was most interresting and terrifying. Five of the God the fathers sitting behind a formidable looking desk and the miserable looking young proffessor giving his thessis.

"His subject was Flemish painting in the 16th century. You should have heard them take him apart. After saying My dear friend we felicitate you on your excellent work which etc etc etc but. You have added nothing new to what has been said before, you use the word plebien too often and what do you mean by it. What is humanisme in your mind.

"There was nothing left of the poor young man (not so young at that) but a pool of tears and humiliation. After they had eaten him up even his toes, they said. '*La Faculté se retire pour discuter votre cas*' and we all sat breathless and in three minutes they were back and he had passed with mention *très honorable* which is the highest you can go. Ouf. But what cads."

In her next letter: "Imagine, at the theatre I met Elisabeth de Miribel and said hulloa and wont you come to lunch one day and she said 'I dont think I can see you this is one of my last days and I am going into the Carmelites on Tuesday.' I remained absolutely dumb. What can you say good luck or best wishes or what. Poor girl. I must say its a tough decision to have taken. Never to talk again. It gave me quite a shock but apparently its not out of sorrow or despair or anything. She just feels the call and is very very happy."*

Saturday, March 26: "Damn. Poor little Marinette has mumps. She woke up this morning with a face like a red ballon. . . . Adieu Sorbonne Spinoza Descartes etc. but *ti na kanome* [what are we to do anyway]. What a bore but this is only the beginning. We have measles hooping cough etc to face. . . . Marinette asks about you all the time. This morning she said. 'I expect he will have an argument with Tito.' "

David was packed off to England with Nursey, to get away from the mumps — but it turned out to be whooping cough also! He greatly admired the policemen's hats.

Marina wrote: "Marinette is not suffering but she is still coughing and in bed. It is a shame because the weather is the kind that makes one feel drunk. Absolutely gold and blue and all the flowers are out in the parc."

A friend invited Marina and Marinette to fly with him in his company plane because "at four thousand mettres it is supposed to do miracles for hooping cough. We shall see but even if it does not cure us it was fun and lovely to look down on Paris with this glorious weather and all the blossoming trees. The woods are like a dream with primroses and violets all over the place. David has hooping cough too. Nursey called yesterday and said so. He is coming back as planned when the mumps quaranteen is over and they can finish their hoops together. I think I have hooping cough too but also with no fever."

Nevertheless, she went to a dinner with the David Bruces, Averell Harriman, and Geoff Parsons, then editor of the *New York Herald Tribune*'s Paris edition. Marina recounted in her letter: "Parsons said We cant get our men into Portugal since Cy went there because Cy wrote things he [Salazar, the Lisbon dictator] told him off the record and I said. Now Geoff

---

* She was one of the first Gaullists, granddaughter of a French president, de Gaulle's secretary in London, then envoy in Canada. After a few years as a nun she left her convent and rose high in France's career diplomatic service.

dont be catty you know perfectly well that Cy has never brocken his word in his life and you should be ashamed of talking like that and he sort of blushed and said 'well I dont mean he broke his word but Salazar did not like what he wrote.' "

In April 1949, Marina wrote Mother from Lausanne: "One night we had dinner with King Leopold [of Belgium] and his wife the Princesse de Réthy who is the most beautiful girl I've seen in years. And in a nice strong healthy way. You feel she looks the same on waking up as she would at a court ball. Very nice too. He is good looking but rather stupid and most reactionary. The Belgians may be right in not wanting him back."

That June the family returned to Maroussi. Marina exulted: "To have a place that never lets you down. I would have ten eyes to look ten noses to smell, the smells of childhood, the earth, ten mouths to chew pine needles with ten sleaves to send a head of wheat wriggling up. It had just rained an hour before we arrived and everything looked scrubbed and clean a bit self conscious like a child who has been told to stay tidy until the grown ups have seen it.

"The little house was beaming and smiling and spotless and your flowers everywhere. The *Regierungsrat* bed* is all fixed and I slept all afternoon to wake up with a large spoon of *vyssino* [cherry] jam. The children as happy as can be and so is nursey. The maid is wonderful and so clean and punctual its unbelievable. . . .

"Its raining again now. It has been cool all day and bright and unbelievably beautiful. How is it that no other place in the world smells like this. The jasmine comes right into the house. The children made necklaces of it. They had water melon for lunch David's first in his life. What fun to be so young that there are so many many 'first time in my life' to come for them. They picked apricots off mother's [Maria's] tree and were in extacies. Mother who normally does not care a hoot about who gets her apricots, apparently has been guarding these with a gun from her window for the last three weeks for fear anyone would take them before the children arrived."

July 14: "We are having an even more wonderful time than I expected. I

---

* The *Regierungsrat* was an enormous Nazi official who inhabited the Spitaki during the occupation and broke the bed with his massive weight.

have laughed more and in a nicer gayer simpler way here in ten days than a whole year in Paris. In spite of pennylessness troubles, wars, problems unending these people have more laughter in them than all the French gathered together at a fancy dress ball. And they are all so generous and so good and so kind. . . . Really the more I grow the more divine I think this country is. And so moving with all the soldiers in the streets [the civil war was in high gear] even they looking as gay as possible and singing and sort of *ti na kanome* atmosphere."

July 22: "First of all let me say that time has not made things look any less divine and if anything I love this place and everything about it a million times more if possible. Everything about it is either laughter or tears and both are of the good kind. . . . Last Sunday when we went out with the wounded soldiers that Rox and Shan take for pic-nics every week it was the most wonderful and moving thing in the world.

"All these boys without legs or arms or eyes all full of song and gay because they were going out into the open after so long and we danced until my legs dropped off and we sang every song we knew and at one point one of the boys a nice fellow with his arm in an enormous cast came and sat next to me and he was rather quiet so I asked him what was the mater and he said. 'You know I want to apologize to you because I know its such bad maners not to be gay and contribute to the *glendi* [party] and I am very sorry to be a bit depressed but you know my arm is hurting quite a bit and also I just heard that my sister and her two children have been killed so you must forgive me.' What can you say or ever ever do for people like that.

"Yesterday I took a taxi from Maroussi and kept him waiting for hours and then when I asked him what I owed him he said. 'Bah I've not known you for twenty years for to make you pay for a little trip like this.' Its so wonderful and everybody is so kind and good and even the bad ones are delicious."

July 29: "I went to Mykonos last week and it was heaven. It was so beautiful I had forgotten what clear sea could be like. I felt like drinking it all. We swam all day and walked about and eat the most enormous amound of odd things like octapus for breakfast *loukoumia* [Turkish delight] for drinks etc. We stayed at a friend's house which was lovely and saved us some money besides. We were dreadful *pique-assiettes* and managed to get invited here and there for tea and breakfast. And even so we spent all our money and had to borrow some to eat on the way back but all that made it even funnier and very gay. We went to Tinos on the way back and lit a candle and said a prayer."

We spent the late summer together, part of the time with the children and part of the time on an island holiday. I have no letters from that period; because I had Marina herself, happy, warm, suntanned, swimming like a mermaid, diving for sea urchins. When we got back to Paris, I had to dart around northern and southern Europe on journalistic chores, coming back for Christmas, then taking off for the Balkans, the Middle East, and a backbreaking trip around the whole world in those lumbering propeller aircraft of the era. Marina took the occasion of my absence to go off on a motoring holiday with the Boisots and a girl named Gilberte Léauté. I received a letter in Belgrade:

"We drove to Germany via Rheims where we saw the cathedral which is perfectly lovely. Nancy where there is a lovely *place* all Louis XV, and then Strasbourg where we spent the night. Its a delicious place not French at all and not quite German either but a queer mixture. We had dinner in a darling little tavern where they had the most divine music box enormous with all kinds of people dancing on it and bowing and drummers and trumpets and a little train a blind man with a dog and everything. It playes eight tunes. We thought we were dog tired when we arrived but started playing bridge right there at the dinner table with cards that Gilberte had brought along, and stayed up till one o'clock. We walked back in the snow and had a lot of fun because we had in the mean time forgotten the name of our hotel and could not find it.

"The next day we drove to Colmar to see the famous Grünewald Triptych and as we got there at twelve and the museum was closed till two what do you think we did to waste time. We played bridge. Its such fun travelling that way with no definite program no special plans or hours. The Grünewalt is extraordinary. Very beautiful but very germanic. You know a Christ who has been dead for days and is all green and horrid.

"From Colmar we crossed the frontier and that was funny too. We got out and the Customs people said. *Alors l'anglaise. c'est vous.* I said I am sorry I am Greek. But your car is English you live in England. No I live in Paris. Ah but your husband is English. No he is American. Ah but he is in England. No he is in Yougoslavia. They were so confused that they gave up trying. Then the others went on to Austria and I drove to Geneva where I spent Friday, Saturday and Sunday with Alexi.

"I got a letter from Walter* in which he wonders why I have not long ago been elected president of the reformed spelling league because when he looks at my spelling of words my version seems to him always so much more logical than the popularly or unpopularly accepted versions."

Poor Marina was having bad luck with her adorable letters to me, which often arrived late, after many forwardings, or sometimes not at all, as I moved gradually eastward on my circumnavigation.

On March 18, 1950, she wrote: "With the first letter on this paper I adress a prayer to Hermes (isn't he the God of post offices) that this the seventh effort of mine since you left does at least reach its destination. Its really too disheartening especially for a letter hater like you who has made a reall point of writing twice a week to have my lovely litterary efforts disappear in the gloomy darkness of some Arab post office."

Marina wrote that in spring, when the blossoms were bursting, they all drove to Chantilly and "we went to visit the chateau which had only been reopened recently and you cant imagine the treasures it contains. The chateau itself is quite hidious inside all very nineteenth century with gold and stuff but the pictures, Smouli, are something amazing. All the Fouquet miniatures for the 'Très riches heures d'Etienne Chevalier.' The book of hours of the Duc de Berri and enough Clouets and fifteenth century portraits and drawings to make you lose your mind.

"Then after we left the chateau we went for a walk in the forrest and imagine how crazy we went when we found fealds and feailds and feilds of dafodils. We picket and picket until we could hold no more. The children were speechless with delight. At one point Marinette said isn't it so unhappy that father is so far away. We drove back in extatic silence at about seven

---

* Goetz, art critic and dealer, old friend.

thirty the car full of flowers to the brim and Pablo in blissful sleep at our feet after a day which for him too must have been as happy as for the humans. He chased birds eat dead leaves dug holes and had the time of his life."

On April 2, 1950, her letter said: "I admit that for the last six or seven days I have not written but the truth is that it was such glorious weather that it went to my head a bit and I was out of doors all day with the children either picking flowers or just roaming the streets or just sitting at the window looking. You know what it can be like here and how tipsy making it is. Now it has started to rain again so everything is back under control. I only bought one hat and that at a small cheep hatter so under the circomstances I think it was pretty strong minded of me.

"Marinette is on holiday from today. Her report from school was pretty bad but just a bit better than last time. They are both full of spirits and delicious. She said the other day. Do you think you could get yourself another husband for awhile. Surprised I said why. She said Well the second husband might not mind if you cut my hair and then when you had cut it you could take father back and you could explain that you had to cut my hair off because your husband said so and you must obey a husband. Like that everybody would be happy. What wonderful logic." (I adored Marinette's pigtails.)

On May 2, the day after May Day, her birthday, she wrote to thank me for presents, saying: "For one thing after a week of rain and cold it suddenly became lovely and yesterday was so lovely and warm and gold that even the communists could not find much wrong with life and paraded up and down grinning and smiling at everybody and all their aggressiveness evaporated in the warm sunshine. We had the traditional strawberries and asparagus and in the afternoon I took the children to Sasha Bruce's birthday party. It was lovely I must say all those little children in their best starched muslins running about on the grass they looked like fairies. They had the time of their lives and looked less like fairies at the end of the party."

Referring to pieces I had written about the Indian subcontinent's North-West Frontier region, she wrote: "I must say if you want to settle for ever in Swat you could not have done a better job of preparing me for it. I am ready to eat ghee and wear jasmine around my neck for the rest of our lives. I also loved the story of the nomads and the children to whom I read bits of it also want to travel now on camels backs in baskets with baby goats and sheep and camels."

In late May my trip was winding up, and I flew in stages from Japan to Alaska and finally to New York. Marina wrote: "Somehow writing to New York I feel you will get it easier and its worth writing even just to say good night. When I wrote to Afghanistan and I knew the letter had to go through so much to get to you I felt that it really had to be a good one full of news and tit bits well expressed but for New York I feel all the letter has to do is to take a plane and once there wait on a nice desk for you so it really doesn't have to expect too much of me."

I got back to Paris in June and later that same month, after a tremendous reunion, the entire family including Nursey embarked on the *Ile de France* to spend a long holiday in the United States. We had rented a cottage near my Aunt Louise's in the Adirondacks, and eagerly looked forward to the pleasure of doing nothing but enjoy, enjoy. Traveling on the same ship were General Al Gruenther and his wife, with whom Marina and I played bridge every afternoon or evening (most tolerant on his part, as he was one of the finest players in the world). One day he was called to the phone. He came back, said nothing, finished the hand, and then, shuffling the cards, remarked deadpan: "Cy, you'd better put your soldier suit on. North Korea has invaded South Korea."

Nevertheless, I was exhausted and also overcome by the prospect of being with all my family beside a forest-bordered lake, then filled with fish, and that's where we spent an idyllic summer. When that pleasant interlude finally floated to an end, the children had to return to school, so I took them back to Paris with Nursey while Marina remained in New York with my mother in order to complete the formalities of taking out American citizenship. This had all been most graciously arranged by Jimmy James, my managing editor, who sent a man to the naturalization courtroom to help out if necessary. According to Jimmy, the latter reported:

"The judge asked her if she fully understood that by becoming a United States citizen this meant abandoning the citizenship of her native land, Greece. She said she did. The judge then asked if, in the case of a war between the United States, her country of adoption, and her native land, she would acknowledge prior loyalty to the United States. She blazed with indignation. 'What,' she said, 'is this great big nation planning to attack little Greece?' The judge threw up his hands, swore her in, and turned as fast as he could to the next application."

For us 1951 was an exceptional year because I spent more time with the family than I had ever before managed. By then we had moved into the first apartment to contain at least a few sticks of furniture belonging to us. We were well established on the Left Bank of the Seine along the Boulevard St. Germain in a duplex flat plus a new pair of servants, Grat and Justine, worthy, loving, loyal, and eccentric French Basques.

General Eisenhower came to Paris as commander of the NATO forces, and we played endless golf and bridge together. Since I reckoned him a likely U.S. president, I thought it good journalism as well as pleasant husbandry to use his presence as an excuse to minimize my absences.

That Easter, Marina wrote my mother: "Its funny how for all one's life one knows that spring will come how it always comes and how it always takes us by surprise, and enchants us. To sit at my window and see those deadest of dead looking bits of stick suddenly come to life and get covered with little green buds and leaves is something that I will never get used to and which makes me always take hope when things look blackest. If a thing which looks as dead and ugly and useless as the tree outside my window, can again and again start breathing and become the thing of beauty that it is today then why not Europe why not the Russians why not the whole world."

The only trouble with having spent most of that year with Marina — as I look back nowadays — was that I paid with fewer of her lovely letters. During the summer she rented a house at Guéthary, on the French Basque coast just north of Spain, which we shared with Greek friends. I went down for a delicious holiday, alternating between beach picnics and golf.

Marina summed up the whole year neatly in a letter to Avi von Ripper [wife of Baron Rudolf von Ripper, both close friends] on August 21, 1951: "Since the end of June I have been to America, I have bought a house in Bucks County [which we quickly and sadly sold at a loss when we discovered its state of disrepair and that its highly commended "trout stream" was a muddy trickle], I have been to banks, borrowed money, rented the new house, arranged mortgages, rented the land to a farmer, taken the airoplane back to Paris, was offered a house here in Bidart [near Guéthary], took it sight unseen as it was very very cheap and sounded nice, packed the children and nursey off, flown to London with Cy where we stayed ten days the one more hectic than the other with such divertissements as Reuters' hundredth anniversary dinner with two thousand people including [Prime Minister] Attlee and the Archbishop of Cantaburry, cocktail parties for the world press, innumerable Greeks, and even a terrific ball where I dragged Cy *malgré lui*, and had lots of fun as it was the prettiest thing I have ever been to with candle lit gardens fountains, lobsters champagne, a whole Spanish village build in the garden for the occasion, flammenko singers, a regency ball room and a merry-go round, covered with daisies and Cocteauesque statues all over the place. Plus such attractive guests as Laurence Olivier and Vivien Leigh and hundreds of beautiful women and even handsome men which was quite a welcome change from Paris which has everything in the world except men that one would even look at twice.

"Well at last all that quieted down a bit and I finally took off for the Basque coast in the car with a friend of mine and we got here about a week ago. Now I have gone to the other extream and see no one, do nothing but sit in the sun swimm eat and go for walks. Its peaceful quiet and delicious. Only nursey is on her holiday and I am looking after the children so life is not quite as restful as it could be. By eight o'clock when they are finally in bed and a delicious silence descends about the house, sometimes I wonder why one ever wants a family.

"Last week I went to a bull fight for the first time in my life but I was not taken by it. Perhaps it was that it was a very third rate fight, but what bothered me most was not the blood or the horror of the picadores, it was the public. There was one very young torero who had been badly wounded about ten months ago, and this was his first reappearance in the ring. He was obviously scared and pale as death before he even started, and he did not give a very good show admitedly. And the public went mad. Insults and booing and yelles of 'go home, coward, imbecile, we have payed good money and he never gets near the toro, boo hiss get out.' I hated it. To be risking your life and have people insult you on top of it seemed to me unbearable. And another thing. The bull did not look at all dangerous (he is, very) so that it made the whole thing look sort of much ado about nothing, and one could not help thinking of Ferdinand wanting to go off and eat grass and smell flowers, instead of beeing slashed to bits by picadors and matadores and banderillos and what not."

We shared the Guéthary house with Georges and Mary Averoff and their daughter Marilia plus her nanny, a great friend of Nursey. Georges, a Greek diplomat stationed in Paris, and Mary had been friends of Marina's since her childhood. Marina wrote after my return to Paris:

"There is no news and my artistic talents if any seem to be asleep. I cant allow myself any of my special kind of exagerations and extravaganzas (as Vogue would say) when writing to people who see through me. Strangers might think it 'kute' you would only think 'what is the matter with her.' Its really a big price that one pays for living with the person one loves. All mystery taken away. No weeknesses allowed. Still its better I suppose than not living with him at all.

"Mary and I decided this morning that the world would get on so much better if there were segregation. All men on the right bank [of the Seine] let us say and all women on the left with the children the servant problems the socks to darn etc. The men to be seen after six in the evening for conversation love making or just sitting together reading listening to music, etc. But the mornings definitely spent separately. The men to provide a monthly check and not ask questions. Their mid-day meal provided for by expert women lent for the occasion by the left bank and taking it in turns to look after the needs of the right bank."

On October 15, Marina wrote my mother: "Yesterday we had a lovely day with General Gruenther at their new house in Versailles. He gave a birthday party for General Ike and we were invited which was most flatering as we were the only people there who were not big shots or very close friends. There were only about twelve people and we really had a lovely time. The general was divine sitting in the middle of the room opening his presents and saying funny things about each one. Then we had a wonderful very American dinner with turkey cramberry sauce ice cream etc and then danced and played cards. I was so thrilled for Cy because as you know newspaper men are not the men that important people go after as usual and the fact that in so short a time Cy has become not only an acquaintance but a friend they want around at their smallest most intimate parties, really does speak well for his charm. But please dont tell anybody about this, please please because he made me promise not to tell anyone as he does not want people to think we brag about it."

Two months later Marina repeated the caution: "Mother darling I have a favour to ask of you. Please dont talk too much about Cy's freindship with general Eisenhower because you know how he hates being talked about. [My cousin] Ellen was saying in front of me how you were saying that we saw so much of the Eisenhowers and he was furious with me for even having written to you that we know them because he is so afraid that the general might think we boast about it. You know how Cy is. And the general is such an ostentatious figure that even if one sees him once or twice one is considered a best friend and already most of the other journalists are mad with jealousy because of our friendship with him as also with Averill Harriman and people like that so the less one talks about it the better. Please forgive me for writting this but it is so terribly important to him that is why I mention it. Cy does not even like me to say if we have been there to dinner, but I know that it amuses you to know that is why I write these things to you but please just dont talk about it to anybody. If I know you wont then I can go on writing without getting into trouble with Cy. The Harrimans are leaving the day after tomorrow and it will be a great loss to us because they independently of everything else are really good friends and fun to be with and we shall miss them very much."

On January 21, 1952, we celebrated our tenth wedding anniversary in Paris, and then I had to rush down to Madrid the next day to see Franco. Marina wrote me:

"I want to thank you for having been so sweet on Monday and given me such a lovely present and such a delicious lunch to top off ten years which in spite of their ups and downs have been good years and which I would not exchange for any other ones."

In February, Marina took the children off on a short skiing holiday in Val d'Isère. She wrote: "This is a lovely place although we are all three in one tiny room and sleeping in one bed with a child is a bit tough. However we ski a lot, the sun is glorious the food delicious and everyone very nice. I

improve every day and today came down an enormous slope. The children
are not enthusiastic skiers yet."

In June 1952 we went to London for Queen Elizabeth's coronation.
Marina described this to Mother:

"I do want to say that the really wonderful thing about the coronation
apart from the splendour and colour and deep symbolism of it all was the
man in the Street. Immagine hundreds of thousand of people standing in
the cold and rain for forty eight hours, without ever a complaint without
one push one shove one grumpy face. And immagine them all here not 'to
see the show' but actually and truly to pray and pay hommage to their little
Queen. I have never in my whole life seen anything so moving as the sight of
an entire city silent and praying under the icy rain. You could hear a pin
drop in the streets of London through the entire service which was being
broadcast from one end of England to the other.

"Every person in that vast crowd of frozen people was participating in
his own quiet way in this their most important religious service, and not
one word of that exquisite solemn liturgie was lost upon them. You felt
really that every symbol every rite every word carried its true meaning with
it, and that both the people and the Queen were pledging themselves to
keep their oath of service and duty mutually to the best of their ability. I
wept the whole way through it was so wonderful. As for the parade it was
straight out of Cindarella but you will see all that in the movie if you have
not seen it already. It is marvellous and not one thing has been left out of it.

"As for the city itself I cant tell you how gay and bright and heavenly it
was and everybody from the hotel porters to the Prime minister going out
of their way to be friendly and affectionate and kind. We were wined and
dined and everybody falling over themselves to be of use. Too wonderful
especially after the perpetual sour faces and bad manners of the French.

"After the coronation we went down to Oxford where they were having
an open air traditional ox roast. The ox had been sent to Oxford from
Denmarck as a token of esteem. It would have been wonderful except for
the rain and bitter cold. But what was funny was that our friends whom we
were staying with had the entire Yougoslav delegation to the coronation
staying with them. Typical of our life to go from a coronation to a
communist house party. I think that the commies had been impressed in

spite of themselves because when we asked what hopes they thought 'The Revolution' had in England they had to admit that the crowds they had seen in the streets did not seem particularly keen for a change of regime.

"We had a lovely time in Oxford and then I went and spent the day with Lord and Lady Harcourt who live quite near here in the most divine Elisabethan house you ever saw absolutely filled with wonderful paintings and things like a two hundred peace Sèvres dinner set made specially for the Spanish Embassador in London in celebration of George the third's recovery from his first attack of madness. When he left he gave the set to the then Lady Harcourt who our friends suspect was more than 'just a friend to the Spanish Embassador.' In the afternoon we went to the garden party at Blenheim Palace which is quite near them and that was really quite thrilling. The Palace itself is a fantastic place and the grounds and gardens are beautiful beyond description. And in that setting to meet Princess Margaret Mr. Churchill and hundreds of colourful members of the commonwealth in Turbans or feathers or top hats was really quite delicious. I was even presented to the Queen of Tonga who was the star of the parade having done the whole thing in an open coach and nearly drowned."

The big news that summer was Eisenhower's formal decision to run for the Republican nomination. When the two party conventions came, in July, I attended and had great fun because of my friendship with Ike, which allowed me to spend crucial moments with him.

Marina had to stay in Paris throughout much of July because of the long French school year, and she was delighted when there was an exhibition of essays pinned to the wall of David's class in the École Communale [public school] the children attended. The topic was "What My Mother Does." Marina had been much moved to read about the labors of the scrubwomen, grocers, factory workers, concierges, and other parents of David's classmates. This interest was suddenly replaced by deep embarrassment when she read her son's carefully printed-out contribution: "*Par fois Maman tappe à la machine des lettres.* David." (Sometimes Mama types out letters.)

She wrote me in the United States: "*A propos* of education the children had their first encounter with anti-semitism a few days ago. Some children were saying that *les juifs sont de sales gens* [Jews are dirty people]. Marinette told me that she told them that was not true and if so why did they like

III

July 1952 - October 1954

Late that summer of 1952, I finally flew to Greece, and we decided to take the children with us to Andros, a lovely island with remote beaches where on moonlit nights we could see the shadows of large gray mullet reflected on the sandy bottom just offshore and where flights of quail and turtledove rested on their great southward trek to Africa. I borrowed a gun from the postman of our little village and lugged it, at first rather weakly, favoring my cicatrized belly, over the stone walls that separated herds and orchards. Afterward we dispatched Nursey and the youngsters back to Maroussi while Marina and I joined friends on a fishing caique, sailing by the Sporades and finally spending a delicious weekend on the mainland at St. John of the Ivy, opposite Euboea.

Our plan that year was to install the children back in school, sending them with wise and faithful Nursey to English friends for Christmas, and then to take a long swing through Africa together. Until then Marina's only extensive trips had been during the war or on summer holidays in Greece or North America, occasionally punctuated by visits to nearby lands like Spain, Switzerland, Italy, or Germany. But I had at last persuaded *The New York Times* that, since I spent more time traveling than any employee they had ever had, it was but fair that once a year the paper should pay my wife's expenses on an extensive journey with me. We chose Africa as the scene of our first joint exploration. This at last marked Marina's transmogrification from the sad status of what I have called a "peace widow."

For a moment our great project seemed threatened. I had to make a preliminary voyage to India and Pakistan, where one of our correspondents was in trouble, and the idea had been that Marina and I should meet in Cairo, a halfway house between Pakistan and France. But Marinette came down with scarlet fever when I was in New Delhi. Marina, once she discovered the illness had struck in its mildest form, simply suggested that "if you can drag on this part of your trip a bit longer the better it will be for me." She then busied herself in late November getting the children their respective Christmas presents (an electric train for David), which they would receive just before leaving for London "so as not to have to pay fortunes in customs in England and I am giving nursey just small stocking things to take for them there."

We had a joyous meeting in Cairo, where Marina had not set foot since her wartime departure for Greece. We only spent forty-eight hours there, I having completed my Egyptian journalistic labors. Nasser had ousted the king before her arrival. She was happy to move on. On December 17, 1952, she wrote to Dodo from Addis Ababa:

"My capacity for astonishment is being worn to a frazel. My eyes pop out of my head about fifty times a day. The one thing that is certain is that the unexpected simply does not exist. Anything can happen. We arrived here five days ago and were first of all astonished at the sheer beauty of the place. Also at the endlessness of this continent. It really made me feel how tiny and also how desperately lovable Europe is. After hundreds and hundreds of miles of malevolent angry brown and black sand and rock hills in the Sudan, the plane suddenly comes over a sort of blue paradise with streams and rivers and sudden patches of the most brilliant yellow I have ever seen. I say blue because the whole country is planted with nothing but Eukaliptus trees which look dark blue from a distance and also give a strange strong smell to everything.

"Being three thousand mettres high (one feels frightfully fluffy and light headed the first few weeks here) the atmosphere is so clear that you can distinguish even the leaves on a tree many miles away. It is the most brilliant and harsh light I have ever seen. In the rainy seasons it is all a poison green but now it is all bright bright yellow with the blue trees and far away in the distance grey blue hills. I say hills but they are more than three thousand mettres high but being so high on the plateau one's self they don't look big.

"The town is like a rather scruffy Nea Ionia [an Athens shantytown]. African huts mostly tumbling down and with the original pretty thatched roofs replaced by horrible corrugated iron. Here and there you see enormous half finished modern buildings the kind of what I call totalitarian architecture, remnants of the Italian occupation. Everyone here agrees that it is a damned shame the Italians ever left. Before them there was no light no roads no water no nothing, and now that they have gone the country is rapidly reverting to type. Everything is falling to peaces.

"The Emperor, whom Cy is seeing tomorrow in a borrowed cut away and after several rehearsals of bowing and scraping and leaving backwards without bumping into things, is complete master of everything and has even the right of life and death over his subjects. He refers to himself as Emperor of Ethiopia King of Kings the concquering lion of the tribe of Judah. He claims direct descendance from the Queen of Sheba and King Solomon with whom she spent a gay night once, the result of which was the emperor Menelik great great great ... grandfather of this one. He is absolute monarque but actually his powers dont stretch very far because this country is composed of utterly impassable territories with gorges going down five and six thousand feet separating the plateau from the rest of the country completely and there are forty or fifty different tribes all hating each other like poison.

"Who ever says that race prejudice is a European invention is crazy. No Amhari (that is the sort of superior tribe around here) even dares show his noze in Tigre or Danakil terrotory. They have extreamely sharp knives and dont hesitate to use them. Here in Addis Ababa you see a lot of the tribes mixed up but none of them dare go very far inland. They are hated much more than any European. Some of them especially the Somalis wear everything from black homburgs to brilliant coloured turbans on their heads.

"But god what a frustrating country. Bureaucracy in the hands of a primitive people is like a new toy and boy do they play with it; It took me litteraly the entire morning to buy some stamps and send off Cy's telegrams. As for our passeports we still have not got them back. They did not like the stamp on my small pox vaccination (never heard of the Institut Pasteur) so I had to have a new one all over again and it is only by sheer screaming and banging on tables that they decided to relent and let me go before the forteen days theoretically necessary to check on the reaction.

"Cy's American impatience was strained to the breaking point. Everybody here of course is used to it and never expect anything done at all. Most foreigners just live from day to day and spend all their spare time shooting and fishing in the country which is great fun. They all ride too as there seem to be hundreds of wild ponies about the place. We have not seen any exciting animals yet except for some lovely coloured birds.

"Most of the shops belong to Greeks which makes it very easy for me. There are more than ten thousand foreigners around of whom the Italians are still the most numerous and prosperous. If Mousolini had not been such a dumb cluck as to enter the war, they would still own this place and a jolly good thing it would be too for everybody concerned. It is a crime to see so many thousand miles of potentially fertile prosperous land going to waste. The more we travel the more Imperialist I feel.

"I will probably end up like an old English colonel. We met a dream one this morning when I went in despair about my passport who was straight out of Gunga Dinn. He said to us 'You must be patiant my dears. This is not England you know. What. What.' As if we were likely to forget it for a second. A place where people are christians and yet believe in genies and spirits and wont let you take a photograph for fear it might imprison their spirit in the little box. Where they are past masters at poisoning, eat raw meat and banana roots after they have allowed them to rot in earth for a few weeks (tastes like camembert they say) and where they hate each other so much that it makes our own little European likes and dislikes look like squables in a YMCA."

We went on to Kenya, Zanzibar, Tanganyika, and what was then Southern Rhodesia. In 1952 all were still British colonies. Marina covered these adventures in one long letter to Dodo from Salisbury, last stop on this first lap, dated December 28, 1952:

"Mama mou glykia. This place is exactly like a woolly west town in America that one sees in films of pioneers gold diggers etc. One has the impression of walking around in a film *décor* and that any moment a man will slip round the corner (the sherif) and stick a gun into the back of a cow boy gangster. Not that the place looks wild at all but so new and obviously unhousebrocken yet. But I must say of all that we have seen of Africa up to now this seems by far the nicest. . . . It is not tropical and one sees all kinds of European trees masses of grass and English looking flowers, ranges of lovely blue mountains in the horizon etc. It is covered with lakes and rivers not to mention small things like gold diamond and lead mines I think and the climate seems ideal.

"We only arrived here about twenty minutes ago so I dont know much about the place except that we are in a nice hotel Cy is having a bath and I am taking advantage of his bath to write to you which I have been unable to do since Ethiopia because we were moving around so fast. From Addis Ababa we flew to Nairobi which is about four hours away (hundreds of miles really but that does not seem to bother anybody around here). Nairobi is a bit bigger than here, but also madly new and pioneerish looking. Very small really the center of town but spreading out over miles of residential district with large 'villas' gardens grass enormous trees and really very pretty and madly suburban looking. And so frightfully English, in spite of the inumerable different specimens of humanity one sees all over the place, from black, shiny Masais, to pale dissatisfied sinister looking Indians and blond Englishmen. Hundreds of Greeks of course.

"We met an old friend, an Englishman from Cairo who has married a Greek girl (*décidément* we are a wonderful race) and he took us around everywhere as did the American consul and his wife who also asked us to Xmas eve dinner and Xmas lunch and a large garden party before with 'Le tout Kenya' so we really did see things. We did not see any lions but sixteen giraffes all at once several ostriches, a monkey and millions of dear gazelles etc. Kenya is not tropical either and looks European but of course with most exquisite Jakarandas Flamboyants and bougainvillias of all colours from white (which is rare) to pink orange mauve and scarlet. You see trees of every colour pink yellow blue and it really is lovely but the kind of landscape I immagine that one gets pretty tired of soon. No change at all. What amazed me is to find so many hundred of thousands of Indians in Africa. They are descendants of Indian traders or labourers originally imported by the British or immigrants. Every small clerical post, every shop laundry tailleur, plumber governement minor officials etc are

Indians and disliked heartily by both Europeans and Africans.

"The women are so covered in strong spicy scents that in the plane to Zanzibar which was full of them I felt quite sick. The Africans around Nairobi are mostly Kikuyus and nobody knows which of them are Mau Mau and which are not which makes it very hard to trust them with ones home and babies but what else can they do. Some of the servants, called boys everywhere, have been with families ten or fifteen years. That poor family called Micheljohn, which was murdered, was murdered by their own boys which they had had fifteen years and looked after and done everything for. It is impossible to get a clear idea of what is going on anyway as each person you ask has a different opinion. Some say its the end, some that its nothing some that you should shoot them all and be done with them but everyone more or less agrees that the government has made a mess of things.

"People go out to dinner with their guns in their pockets and on Xmas night there were ten more murders. For the present, most of the murders have been of Africans as a terrorist method of making them join the Mau Mau. All that and then one day in the paper we saw an advertissement saying 'Where but in Kenya can a man whose grand father was a canibal watch a really good game of Polo.'

"Zanzibar is a real film island. One expects pirates and slave traders and beautiful ladies in white lace to come out of every corner. The houses are very tall dassling white with innumerabel tiny windows quite high up all with bars on them and even *jalousies* here and there. All the doors are very heavey dark sculpted wood with brass nails and loks beautifully polished. Over every high white wall you see hibiscus by the hundreds and jasmin red white and pink all on the same branch. The whole island is one mass of colour. Coconut trees mangoes which are a perfectly beautiful tree a bit like a large oak from far.

"Flamboyants as I have never seen and millions of other flowers everywhere. Little black children run around picking mangoes and coconuts in pretty baskets and through the trees you catch a glimpse of bright blue see everywhere. It is not a very big island, its main cultivation is cloves. It is a big tree a bit like a lemon tree and the cloves are the unopen buds of the flowers, which are picked and dried. The whole island has a faint smell of cloves. Here too the population is mixed African Arab and Indian. At this time of the year when the monsoons blow they are expecting the big dhows to arrive from Arabia bringing merchandise. Is'nt it most romantic? To think of those boats which have not changed in shape since the Ptolemis, sailing the same route to the same place in more or less the same conditions. The only thing that has changed is that they dont have slaves any more which used to be the great trade of Zanzibar. We did not see the sultan unfortunately because he was away for Christmas. We stayed two days which was enough really because it was very hot and especially so damp that even standing still we dripped.

"From there we went to Dar Es Salaam which is the main port of Tanganyika. There we stayed only one night and were given a tremendous party by the American consul. The other guests were straight out of novels too. A Greek rope king who had gone there a bare footed boy forty years ago to end up a millionaire philanthropist with his fat cosy wife who talked about *Ah to Parisaki mas ti omorgo pounai* [Oh, our own little Paris, how pretty it is] but presumably a heart of gold. An English colonial official exactly as you would expect him, in mess jacket and rather snotty and aristocratic but with a frousy wife. An English power company man and wife all enthusiastic about this great growing country and its future (enthusiasm not shared by the colonial official), a fast drinking American couple, the consul and his wife who obviously hate each other like mad but who called each other my darling and my dear all night, and us rather dazed and extreamely scruffy having had to go to dinner un-ironed as the maids at the hotel were already off when we arrived. We left this morning and flew here as I say arriving a short time ago.

"I must say this about Africa. I would not come here to live from choice of course but if I had to I could be quite happy. Its beautiful, new, unexplored, young exciting and one could make a very happy life for oneself. You would go mad gardening here. This friend of mine in Nairobi who is new here too and did not know how fast things grew, planted some lettuce and he says that 'It was all I could do to grab two for dinner, before they shot up into hulking great trees.' Even things like heather and geraniums grow to tree hight. You could have a garden such as you have never even dreamed of. And one can ride and swimm and fish and see wild animals and for children it must be wonderful to grow up in so much space. You cant immagine what a feeling of enormousness one gets. Thousands of miles of utterly unused uninhabited land. We were told that over a thousand people a month are arriving in Rhodesia to settle. Mainly from

England. This town is growing like a mushroom."

On New Year's Day, and again from Salisbury, Marina wrote Dodo: "Mama mou glykia. *Me to kalo* [good luck for] the New Year and all all my best wishes. May Alexi be well well and for ever and may it bring us several unexpected reunions. What better wishes can I make. I am dashing this off to you before we take off for Pretoria at six tomorrow morning. Why does'nt one plane leave at a christian hour. Today we spent a heavenly day. We drove out to a native reserve and met Big Cheif Chinamora who I am afraid looked much more like a nice black *klossa* [hen] than an African warrior but who was frightfully sweet and most friendly. He told us all about his five wives called Jessica Eulalia Gertrude, Chiko and something else, two catholics one church of England one nothing and one presbyterean (how the church looks upon polygamy and conversion as a working combination we did not find out but gather that native Christianity is a sort of *sui generis* brand, where polygami and occasional whitchcraft spirit worship etc are accepted).

"We asked him how many children he had from these wives for whom he told us proudly that he had paid twenty five pounds plus several heads of cattle each, and he could not remember off hand so he got out a sort of little account book and said, 'Ah here it is.' Under each wive's name he had written down the names of the children and date of birth. Most methodical. He had seventeen sons and eighteen daughters. The smallest a few weeks old. The little ones I must say are adorable. He himself was rather dissapointingly dressed in grey flanales and a tweed jacket. He put on his red council robe for us and his crown made of otter fur, but even then looked more like a father Christmas than a warrior.

"After that we pic niced under an enormous mango tree in the grass, with millions of flowers around, flame lilies, little bright orange flowers, pink, mauve, blue, sheer heaven, and with a divine view on a green valley and great enormous granite rocks scatered all over as if by the hand of a great giant. Near by we saw on rocks Bushman paintings of stags, girafes, etc. No one knows how ancient they are but they look prehistoric and are quite lovely in deep reds browns and black. This is really the nicest day we have had since we have been in Africa. One must be in the country. The towns are dreadful and the English in their colonies too awful for words. Common, overbearing and of course now with New Year drunk as owls.

We fall over them every where in the hotel. *Kalynikta* [good night] darling Dodo mou and a million kisses."

A week later she sent another letter from Johannesburg. She said:

"Well, here we are at the other end of the world and I cant help fealing that we should be walking on our heads. Not that most people are'nt, figuratively speaking, in this strange continent. We spent six charming days in Pretoria. Not charming because of Pretoria which is a driary little place but because as always we found all kinds of friends and in particular one very sweet American couple and the wife sort of adopted me put her house her garden her swimming pool and her children at my disposal and so I had all kinds of fun rather than sitting in a hotel bedroom which is what I am always afraid is going to be my fate and never is. In Pretoria we did not rather I should say I did not, see much in the sense of improving my mind, but I went to lots of parties and met innumerable extreamely driary people exactly like the people one meets at most Embassy parties only worse but then I came back to the house with this friend Hellen Guillion and she gossiped about them all and was very amusing and witty. As in all these African towns, the center itself is dreadful driary 'hick towns.'

"But everybody lives in the suburbs and they are quite charming especially the gardens which are heavenly everywhere. One day I was taken out to 'see' Pretoria by a gentleman in the 'Native affairs office' but you know they are so proud of everything, their history their progress etc (the less history one has the more one talks about it it seems to me), that instead of showing me native villages and things they took me around to 'model' locations (locations are where natives live) and pointed out to me the showers the kitchens, the plumbing and even the dentists equipement. And I who had hoped to see a Hottentot or a Zulu.

"However I went into the appropriate raptures over the dentists tools and heard for the thousand's time all about the great Treekk (it is'nt really written like that but it ought to be). Everything in Africans seems to have double letters, Dingaans treachery, the second Boer war, several other Treks and all about the fathers of the nation who are all called Pretorius or Julius or Cornelius. You know I am distressed at how often it is the good high minded bible reading god fearing people of this world that do the greatest harm. Nothing is more dangerous it seems to me than a litteral interpretation of the bible. Here the natives are considered 'hewers of wood and carriers of water' as it says in the bible and nothing more. I could understand it for political reasons expediency self protection etc but when it is considered the word of the lord to kick them around and everyone feels nice and cosy about it then No. However let me not get heated up about the racial problem because it would take twelve pages and say nothing. Here it is the *leit motif* of every conversation but of course nothing leads anywhere.

"I did have fun one afternoon when I was taken to a farm where natives come or rather came from Central Africa and they settle on the farm, live there build their mudd huts called Rondavaals and in exchange work the land for the farmer. These natives are the happiest kind as they have not become contaminated by life in the big cities and are very happy working eating sleeping and having thousands of babies. I must say their houses were spotless and sort of pure in their extraordinary simplicity. One round room with a pointed thatched roof where they all live until the boys and girls get too big and then they build an outer circle to the original house and the boys sleep on one side the girls on the other.

"When they get married the whole tribe gets together and builds the couple a new house. It only takes about a fortnight. Inside the house was one large iron cooking pot, the family blankets all neatly folded, a few straw mats, and one home made long thin guitar. That is all their life besides work and love making. Rather nice. The women all wear stiff beed neclaces and bracelets on arms and legs up to their knees. They are put on when you are born and when they get too tight as you grow bigger they are cut off and new ones stuck on. It looks quite pretty but most uncomfortable. Besides the beads they were a minute little skirt only on front, and nothing else. The men have gone European and wear Zoot Suits and big hats.

"We left Pretoria yesterday and drove here [Johannesburg]. It is only thirty five miles away, stopping on the way to see the famous monument (guess in honour of whom? the Voortreckers of course) which is the ugliest thing I have seen anywhere.

"I must sound very cynical and *blazé* but it is'nt that. I am all for the tear in the eye at the stories of pionners and things, and undoubtedly these people were marvellous and brave and everything but when history results in hatred all over the place it makes me cross. Of course that is true all over the world except that here you feel it more because it is so concentrated and they all live on top of each other. If the Greeks hate the Bulgars it becomes sort of theoretical and condition reflexy in the end, or the French the British etc. But here the British hate the Dutch the Dutch loath the British and together they hate despise and kick around both the Indians and the Africans who in turn hate them and each other. *Pou na vris logariasmo.* [Where's a solution?] It is really very very sad.

"Mama mou glykia from here we go to Bechuanaland which promises at last to be more true to my idea of darkest Africa. Plumes and paint and war cries. I will write a gay description from there. If it is true, I would not be surprised to find the Zulus wearing tweeds and flannels and playing golf. All all my love and a big big kiss.

"P.S. The favourite food of the natives on that farm I went to see is Vlitta [a kind of Greek dandelion]."

On January 17, 1953, to my mother from Cape Town: "I keep wanting to put down June or August as the date. I am sitting with nothing on in our bedroom and the sun is streaming in through half closed shutters while out in the streats crowds of girls and boys in shorts or open dresses holding towls and bathing suits are off to the beach. There are little black boys selling fantastic flowers in the streets and the fruit stalls are heavy with pine aples mangoes bread fruit, peaches and bright yellow and red plums. Hardly a January landscape. We got here last night from Johannesburg on a fabulous train. As comfortable and spacious as the best American trains air cooled and with delicious food. It took us more than thirty hours. It seems incredible to my European mind to take so long and still be in the same country. It is nearly a thousand miles and most of it over the flatest brownest land I have ever seen. And I keep thinking of a little line in a poem *Le ciel est pardessus le toit si bleu si calme.* Never have I seen so much sky. I feel like one of those Victorian dolls which are kept under a glass dome.

"Here the sky seems to be all around one so blue so calm. Much too calm to cover a country where hatred of everybody seems to be the leit motif of everyday life. Everybody hates and despises the natives and to make it even more incomprehensible they do so with great smugness in the name of our Lord. Remember in the Bible Ham the son of Noah laughed at his father when he was lying drunk under a tree. And Noah was very cross and said to his son Your descendants will be black people and they will be hewers of wood and carriers of water. So there you are all pat and easily explanable to a conscience which might now and then aske question (which it does'nt). And if that were the only problem it would be easy but when you get the Africaners hating the British, the British hating the Indians, the Indians hating everybody in sight and so on then you really get an idea of what this country is up against. That and an earth outwardly green and cool and mellow as a parson's garden, and inside boilling over with gold and diamonds and uranium, breeding greed desires ambitions frustrations and all the lower forms of human passions. To think what a nice quiet peaceful people they would have been if they had not discovered all these treasures. The Midas touch is really learking over this place."

After Cape Town, which she adored (especially the cloud-fall tumbling from the rock around which the city is built), we flew up to the (Belgian) Congo, also the French Congo, and finally on to Accra, capital of what was then the Gold Coast and under qualified British rule. From there she continued her African travelogue in a letter to Dodo dated February 5, 1953:

"This has been by far the most interresting bit of the trip and the most 'African' as far as landscape goes. We got to Accra on the Gold Coast a week ago and were very kindly taken to stay in a government house as the hotel is too dreadful for words. As you probably dont know, the Gold Coast is to all intents and purposes independant. It has its own governement with its own black ministers and only the minister of defence and finance are Englishmen. It is a strange and difficult experiement and often disheartening but on the whole working well and it is the first place in Africa where you get a fealing of real unself-conscious racial equality.

"Last night we went to dinner at an American's house and the other guests were all natives. One journalist, one lawyer one girl brought up in England and the daughter of a judge, and one girl the daughter of a fisherman who had by sheer diligence and hard work got a scholarship gone to England and was now running a successful business on her own. As caracteristic a group as one might wish and we got into a discussion which was enchanting in its sheer familiarity. Exactly the same words and arguments as you might hear in Montmartre Greenwich village or the Plaka [the 'Greenwich Village' of Athens]. We went from race prejudice to politics to religion and back again. The interresting thing to me was that most of them claimed that they had been brought up and educated as good christians but had all given it up after their stay in London.

"You see both in religion as in education they, being primitive and natives, accept every word they hear with the same fierce belief as they did the tales of Avenging gods fetiches who answered praeyers, etc. And not being familiar yet with abstract thought, or 'expediency' (lucky things) as soon as they are disappointed their disbelief is as violent as their original acceptance. When they saw their own missionaries, who to them had taken the place of tribal gods, going to the beach on Sundays instead of church or when they asked a christian god for good crops and did not get it, their anger and disappointment was ten times what our own would be. The same with their politicians. Their admiration of education knows no bounds; it is tied up in their minds with good jobs progress less mortality and being able to stand up to the white man.

"As such, education and by that I mean letters, which is the thing that has replaced their own principles of education based on respect for their elders their tradition their gods, honour for the clan or tribe etc, civic and ethical education rather than the book learning which the missionaries are giving them, where was I? Oh yes education I say is the most desirable thing on earth and those among them who possess it are small gods. As a result there again they are in for violent dissapointements. Their senator who is an educated man and in whom they have unlimited faith, promises them that next year they will have more water. They will do anything for him but if on the exact date the water has not come, they may well kill him.

"It is all such a mixture of two civilisations two ways of life and thought that the problems to be faced are interminable. For instance up in Togoland, where we went yesterday, an old old chief is lying dying of cancer. He is a good man and a good chief but a theoretical christian. The authorities however have sent up two hundred policemen to be on the spot when he dies so as to prevent his family and friends from killing the customary two hundred people who are supposed to accompany the dying chief to his last dwelling place. In another part of the land only a short time ago the fishermen were having bad luck so they killed five young girls and fed them to the fishes and the next day they cought fish which confirms their belief more than ever. Still this is the only place where even an effort is being made and as such a real paradise compared with South Africa.

"The Gold coast itself is not too pretty but we have seen a wonderful castle built by the Danes in the sixteenth century for their slave trading. It is right on the sea and quite quite lovely. Their are lots of them all over the country. From here we went for two days to the Ivory Coast which is French and there I got my first glimpse of real tropical forrest. I was thrilled. Thick black forrest where the sun hardly ever penetrates. Fantastic trees sixty and seventy mettres high with things dripping from them. Extraordinary fruit and flowers everywhere and birds of course. We saw no snakes but they are there. I also went to a cocoa plantation and picked a cocoa been for the children. Funny how one eats chocolate for all one's life and never bothers to think what it comes from. I also saw coffee plantations tea, vanilla, and the cola part of coco cola which is a green sort of fruit and has bright red nuts in it which are the cola beens. They are aphrodisiac mildly and as such greatly in demand by the poor natives who have a dozen wives each.

"From the forrest we went to the lagoon country which is perfectly lovely and exactly as one expects. Miles and miles of water calm and grey and very peaceful and the naked black men rowing in those narrow narrow canoes like a *fassolaki* [string bean] really. It is most beautiful and hot as hell and full of malaria bilhartsia tse tse flies and crocodyles. But we did not see the crocodyles. The people are naked in the villages and wear most lovely brightly coloured sort of roman togas in the town. They are extraordinarily elegant and carry on their heads anything from a bath tub a tray covered with china, a load of wood, a *cazani* [large pot] full of hot soup or a live goat. They can carry up to twenty pounds weight on their heads as well as the babies on their backs.

"Everyone as usual have been very kind to us and as soon as I finish this I am going to be taken swimming by a nice lady and serf riding which must be terrific. The coast is perfectly lovely but even so no sea can stand up to the small toe of the Mediterranean. The Indian Ocean is grey green and the Atlantic grey brown. . . .

"It has been an absolutely fascinating trip but I am glad to get home and stay there for a bit. I find that six weeks away from the children is about as much as I care for."

Later that spring Marina arranged with Avis Bohlen that our two families should take a house together in Mallorca that summer. Chip Bohlen had been named U.S. ambassador to Moscow in April and, having already had much Soviet experience, knew how advisable it was to get away when possible — especially for the children.

Early in July she wrote me from our shared villa: "Formentor is quite quite lovely and so like Greece that it is disconcerting. I feel as if I were suddenly face to face with someone who looked just like you in every way and yet was a complete stranger. As soon as we arrived before even looking at the house we went for a swimm and then had supper of eggs and potatoes fried in olive oil and then went straight to bed about ten o'clock.

"The children immediately went exploring. We have a ruined house in the forrest two steps away from us which is rapidely becoming a smugler's den, a ruined forteress a prince's palace etc. David has built himself a house with wood and palm leaves and is happy as a clam. We went down to the sea quite early and stayed all morning swimming and rowing a rented boat. I must say this is the most restful wonderful day I have had in a long time. I feel a million miles away from everything and everybody. Too much so in a way because as I say it looks so familiar that when I saw a yacht in the water my first thought was 'I wonder who is on it' meaning any possibilities of rich Greek friends."

July 8: "Dear Piro. I cant tell you how I wish you were here. There is something about the air which makes one sleep like ten proverbial dogs. Everyone around complain that they cant keep their eyes open in spite of ten solid hours every night. I myself am dropping this minute with that delicious sleepiness which comes from a whole day spent at the sea. The children unused to having me at their disposal are really taking advantage of it and at every moment of the day I am rushing after this one in the water or climbing a tree for that one or helping with the building of a house with logs or reading Ivanhoe not to mention the agony of slipping wet bathing suits off and running after endless shoes hats shirts lilos, books and slippers left about on beach and garden. My Spanish is improving and I now know the words eggplants *colokithakia* [zucchini] shoes ironing board and Saterday."

Just before the Bohlen family departed in September and I flew to Mallorca for a final weekend, Marina wrote. She said the mother of Vane Ivanović (an old Jugoslav friend of ours who now lives in London with his lovely wife) "asks us on her boat all the time and to dinner and dancing and all kinds of things and she has the Prince de Monaco [father of Rainier] staying with her on the boat and they all stand at stiff attention in front of him and call him Monseigneur and curtsey even in wet bathing suits which puts Avis and me into histerics. Yesterday they took us all to a bull fight and it was pretty awful as two of the three men were goared to bits and we were nearly sick so as to recover we all had innumerable drinks. I had a rhum drink of some sort and felt very fluffy. Then we all went to a night club and watched fandangoes and really got about a thousand cc of Spain at one dose. Avis drove back from Palma in fifty five minutes with what one might call a certain abandon of style which made us feel very young and reckless. Today we feel less so."

The year 1954 was excellent for us. I took Marina on a long motor trip from the top of Italy to the bottom, stopping off in all kinds of towns and cities in order to talk with representatives of right and left, church and labor, to try and ascertain if (as our ambassador, Clare Luce, was predicting) the country was on the immediate verge of becoming Communist. I concluded that it wasn't and Marina was emotionally as well as politically glad because she was irked by a dinner the ambassador gave for us at the end of our tour when, after the meal, she joined the gentlemen for brandy, coffee, and serious conversation, leaving the ladies with Henry Luce, her husband and the publisher of *Time*, who did his best to keep abreast of feminine gossip. Yet, as our old friend Gastone Guidotti of the Italian foreign ministry told us just before we left: "Mrs. Luce is the most important ambassador you ever had here because she is a member of your Politburo. If there is anything we really want done we persuade her — she circumvents the State Department and telephones the White House. *Time* and *Life* are more valuable to us than experience." Marina took great delight in repeating this wise cynicism around Paris.

She summed up her impressions to my mother on February 27 from Perugia: "I have seen so much beauty in the last five days which I would like to share with you, but it is always such a rush such a battle between even the need for sleep and the desire to see just one more church one more Giotto. This is the first time I have been in Florence for more than one day and I wore out a pair of shoes litteraly running from church to church for fear of wasting a single moment.

"My mind by now is one great turmoil of Ghirlandajo Fra Angelico, crusifications anunciations pietas and nativities. I think of the Medicis in the same way as my grand mother about the family friends 'oh yes dear so and so who married that rather common woman but with lots of money, or poor old so and so too sad that he had to be killed by those nasty Pazzis.' I have not thought or seen or heard anything but Medici for four days. Yesterday thank god one of Cy's appointments did not show up so for the first time poor lamb ever since we started he was able to come with me and look at something other than his typewriter. In the afternoon we went to have tea with [Bernard] Berenson and it was a delight. Such a house, mother dear. Big, tall dark yellow of that particular Florentine colour unique in the world covered with thick creepers and standing in a most heavenly walled garden with terraces paved in green pebbles like in the Greek islands and full of delicious smells and religious looking Cala lilies.

"The inside of the house needless to tell you covered from inch to inch with lovely pictures statuettes precious books and all that in great comfort with big cosy arm chairs and a delicious tea with hot buttered buns and Berenson himself in spite of his eighty seven years bright and dapper pink cheeked and full of vitality with a red carnation in his button hole dropping 'bons mots' right and left. It was really delightful.

"Then today we had a really unique day. As Cy had to see a priest in Assisi we were obliged to take the Perugia road to Rome rather than the shorter one via Sienna which we already know so we had the opportunity of driving through Arezzo and getting a glimpse of the Piero della Francesca frescoes which are utterly beautiful and from there on to Assisi which is the most lovely thing I have ever seen. The whole town built of pinkish yellow stone is sort of clinging to the very steep side of a hill and looks like those pictures of Thibetan monasteries. The church of San Francesco is quite quite lovely. It is Romanesque very big but beautifully proportioned and also build of pink and yelloish stone which in the early afternoon looked completely transparent. There are two churches one underneith romanesque very low cealinged and rather dark and cript-like and covered with fresques by Giotto Cimabue and Lorenzetti.

"While we were there the choir of young brown clad novices was singing their prayers and it was utterly lovely. Then one goes up a little stair case and comes out onto a hung pink terrase with arcades looking out onto a view exactly like the backgrounds of so many of the pictures we have been looking at. Pointed hills, cyprus and olive trees and a small green river winding its way into the sky. On the other side a wonderful cloistered courtyard with other little monks playing in it. And from there into the gayest Gothic church I have ever seen. Very simple very tall walls entirely covered with Giotto and Cimabues and a green and blue cealing with stars. Lovely stained glass windows also. We were so enchanted we could have stayed for ever."

That proved to be a fateful spring. Hammerheaded French generals conceived of a strategic insanity by establishing a major base in the valley of Dienbienphu, hoping to attract an attack from the Communist guerrillas France was fighting and to end what had already become a drawn-out Indochina war. They attracted the guerrillas all right but, under the brilliant leadership of General Giap, the Vietnamese mustered an impressive array of mortars amid the surrounding hills, blasted the French, overran their perimeter, and administered a terrible defeat which pushed France out of Southeast Asia and sucked the United States in. The resulting international confusion forced me to delay my departure on a journey we had arranged weeks before, as I first saw Secretary of State Foster Dulles and other American leaders in Paris and then, almost immediately, again in Geneva, where they met with the French, Russians, Chinese, and various Vietnam factions in an effort to patch up a settlement. The patchwork didn't endure long.

In May, we drove to Venice to start a long trip with my cousin Marian and her amiable husband, Orvil Dryfoos, then vice-president and soon to become publisher of *The New York Times*. We motored via Trieste and Belgrade through northern Greece to Athens and then flew on to Turkey and Cyprus, being royally entertained all the way. Eventually the U.S. Air Force flew us down to Izmir on a special plane, and we were greeted by a batch of conducting officers with a sightseeing schedule for Ephesus and other places. The schedule included a memorable phrase Marina never forgot: "14:30 arrive Parking area near the Home of the Virgin Mary. Walk to the Shrine with a Coffee Stop enroute."

Before I became a columnist toward the end of 1954, I was entitled to the regular *Times* foreign correspondent's home leave of three months every three years. It was the last occasion we enjoyed the privilege. Marina had been such a good sport on our Montana horseback trip in 1942 that I asked if she'd agree to an even more arduous enterprise that summer, a canoe trip through northern Canada just south of Hudson Bay. She wrote to Avi von Ripper on June 11, bridging the gap between springtime in the eastern Mediterranean and summertime on the edge of the Arctic.

"My darling Cuega [Cau Cueg, the name of the von Ripper house at Pollensa], I do envy you Mallorca and more than ever will I miss you and my mediterranean home spiritual while chasing down a frozen river in a canoe, as is our latest summer plan. We are leaveing the children with my in laws and going off in a canoe somewhere in darkest Canada. We will sleep in sleeping bags, wake up, whisk the icecles off our brow and fish, fish, eat fish, talk fish, and obviously miss the biggest of all fishes who will somehow get away thus ruining an otherwise perfect summer. Ah me.

"However for the moment I am taken up with getting my Paris spirit back after six weeks in the homes of everyone from Pericles to Raymond of Toulouse. We have been wondering over Crusader country. Cyprus was a surprise and delight to me. Immagine a golden island where time really has stood still (to coin a phrase) and where the immagination can really have a good old orgy. Old Gothic abbeys covered with rosemary and jasmine and the stone pale yellow instead of the typical gray. Cypress trees in the cloisters as well as palms and lemon trees. Everything smelling so sweet and that shimmering atmosphere which comes with great delightful heat and makes the cicadas so happy.

"And leaving the Abbeys or the castles Othello's house, or Richard's hunting lodge, one is not suddenly brought back to reality by a petrol pump or a post office building. The hole island is in keeping and the fishermens houses blend in quite happily with Crusader's castles Hellenistic tombs Roman temples or Greek stadiums. The people speek a Byzantine sound-ing Greek and the whole thing is one joy after another not the least of which is conspiring under bushes for the overthrow of British rule. You know the Authorities have taken that phrase from Othello 'Welcome to Cyprus sirs' and use it everywhere in airports etc. The Cypriots who know their Shakespear have added under it the 'aside' from the same act 'Goats and Monkeys sirs.'

"I became more nationalistic than ever in three short days there. My brother came for three days and we had a wonderful time spear fishing swimming or discussing the middle ages. That was really the best part of the trip otherwise Italy was fun except that it never stopped raining. Geneva was hell made even more so by the fact that a German ran into our car and smashed its behind so it had to go to a garage for five days. Yougoslavia was interresting. The difference in the last three years is tremendous. Good roads, more things in the shops more food hot water in the hotel and no pale frightened faces. We saw the merchand of Venice in Belgrade and although '*Hvala Lepo Gospodin Shylock*' does not sound quite like the original, the acting and the costumes and the revolving stage were really first class.

"Athens was heaven of course but too short for a town where I love simply everybody. In Turkey the St Sophia mosaics were the high lights of the trip. Too too wonderful. Ankara was driary and Smyrna dusty. Ephessus was lovely not so much for the quality of the ruins but the fact that they are abandonned and overrun with marvellous wild flowers Iris and snap dragon and sweet smelling grass and one sees one Greek colum with wild roses climbing up it and a bit further down a little wild white peony. Half Hubert Robert and half Dali. Really wonderful.

"We got back to Paris two days ago and already it is beginning to close in on us. We found a mass of those sinister little white enveloppes addressed to M. et Madame, which bring evil news of receptions coctail parties luncheons and teas. As I have to shut up the house get the winter things hidden the children's summer cloths done arrange for next year's school etc etc and nursey has gone off on a holiday, I dont suppose I will have much time for being bright and gay however. We leave from Cannes on the sixth of July and will return, late in September, if we have not been eaten up by a bass man-eating trout muskalonge (?) or other sweet water fiends that is. I will write often from my exile. Have a wonderful summer think of me when eating figs grappes and gaspatchio."

Once we had arrived in the United States and were preparing for our boreal adventures, Marina wrote Susan Mary Patten: "After a day of infinite struggles with packing some things for Canada some for the Addirondaks in different bags to be checked at Grand Central and others yet to be mailed ahead to Cape Cod for the end of August we got off hot and messy and greatly relieved to get away from that huge Frankenstein of a town, which seems to me steadily stealthily but surely to be acquiering a life of its own with but one aim and that to destroy man.

"We go to the Addirondaks tonight for about ten days and then the children go off to Cape Cod with the in laws and Cy and I go off to the wilds complete with sleeping bags ruck sac and determination. Last night there was a party here and every guest gave us a different peace of advice. Terribly cold so take warm clothes. Terribly hot so beware of sun stroke. Be sure to take a lot of medicine against snakes poison ivy mosquitoes red Indians etc. Dont forget to take lots of morphine just in case. . . . All most discouraging to me but not to Cy who just cant stop grinning and can hardly wait to get at his fishing tackle. If by any chance we dont ever get back you can have all my books and the blue vases in the bed room. My cloths are not worth leaving to any one."

Before going to Canada we stayed at Knollwood, my Aunt Louise's place near Saranac Lake, New York, for a few days. Marina wrote to Avi von Ripper on July 25:

"I am so full of a 'real American' lunch of fried chicken, corn on the cob potatoe pan cakes and deep dish apple pie that I will probably fall asleep in the middle of this letter but it will have been a good try anyway. If this place were only about twenty degrees warmer it would be paradise on earth. It is wild and beautiful and green and the lake changes colour every five minutes. But it is freezing cold and my mediterranean blood rises in revolt at the thought of being subject to such treatment. As a matter of fact were it not for the aqua skiing I dont think I would ever wet even my small toe. That and the fear of making a *bruta figura* before my American family makes me plunge every day into water which is nothing but the melted ice off all the wretched mountains which surround us.

"I console myself with the thought that it must be frightfully good for *cellullite rejuvenation refermissement des muscles* etc. The skiing and ridding is what will keep us I hope from looking like Fatty Arbuckle when we get back. I cant tell you what huge quantities of food we consume in spite of the latest anti calory crase that is shaking America only slightly less than the cancer problem. No one smokes any more and people comme up and shake their heads at you if they see you with so much as a match in your posession and take that crypto-pitying look that one usually reserves for the semi dead.

"As for the callory problem it is solved by calloriless coca cola called Cali Coli calorilless sugar tobbacoless cigarettes unfattening butter etc. Cy is eagerly waiting for the day when they will put out non alcoholic whiskey and unfattening unintoxicating martinis and then he will turn in his American passport and become a Bulgarian.

"We have been here a fortnight today and I must say that for the moment I dont like it. I have a new thing to add to my blazon of the present century dedicated to the common man. Up to now it was just a Coco Cola bottle Proper on field of azure with a Reader's Digest rampant in guile and argent. Now I will add a Motel Couchant. The entire country is slowly and inexaurably being covered by them. In the shape of Suiss Chalets, Victorian Villas, or the more uninhibited type of resort architecture. They cover every inch of formerly lovely land-scape and advertise self service Do it yourself precooked eggs, premade beds etc. as if they were the greatest blessings on earth. Ah me, how I love the old 'never do a thing yourself if it can be done by anyone else' civilisations. This passion for independance leaves me quite cold and I admit franckly that if anyone tries to iron my shorts for me or do my bed, I will not pull myself up to my full hight and declare hautily that I can do it just as well as anyone.

"We were not long enough in New York for me to get into any [Senator Joseph R.] McCarthy arguments, or see what people think these days but hope to get an idea when we get back in September. For the moment the accent is all on body building. It has been raining steadily since we arrived and I must say that my enthusiasme about the Canada trip such as it was is dwinddling rapidly, under the steady patter of bigger and better rain drops. I have visions of my crawling dripping wet into an even wetter sleeping bag all the while fighting off man eating moskitoes. Well well. I keep remembering last summer and saying to myself that Cy really deserves his turn, but oh what would I not give to be wiggling my toes right now in your pool while arguing about Piero della Francesca and even the 'Liberation' of the modern artist till four in the morning. Here we go to bed at ten. However the children and Cy are having a wonderful time and Cy has not got a frown left. He never growls and is bright and chatty even before breakfast. As for the children they dont know where to start. The skiing delights them and the horse back ridding they adore. I went with them too and the first time my behind suffered quite considerably but now I am hardened.

"We get up at a decent hour every morning have a huge breakfast and then go off on the lake either with a canoe or a guide boat or the motor boat. Cy fishes all day or plays golf. I swimm (reluctantly) and ski for hours which I must say is heaven. I read and even get on with my *gros point* carpet which will be a dream if it ever gets finished. Some time in the evenings we play bridge. All very middle aged and *comme il faut*. This pleasant life comes to an end next week when Cy and I go off to Canada and the children to Cape Cod with my mother in law. Then at the end of the month we join them there stay a week or so and come back to New York. I wont be able to write from Canada but will send juicy madly exaggerated descriptions of our adventures when we get back."

And to Dodo: "We went ridding in the afternoon and I made a *bruta figura* by being thrown from my horse head first onto a rock. Luckily I was not hurt but felt quite dizzy and tonight as I got into the bath I knew that every bit of me exsisted. We got back from the ridding and then we all including eight children went to a pic nic in the speed boat. It started to rain just as we got there but we had rain coats and after half an hour it cleard and we eat wonderful lamp chops and pan cakes with mapel cirop which is the *spécialité de la maison* on all pic nics. We had a really good time and David seemed marvellously happy. He even got a camera from one of the neighbours [for his birthday] and is taking photographs constantly with more success than me, I hope. I am most discouraged. I took some wonderful pictures the other day of both the children aqua planning and diving or surrounded by baby white goats and none have come out. But I am still trying. The children are frightfully well and I do think having the time of their lives. I am so interrested to see the differences between them. For instance Marinette is ready for anything once. She will dive off the highest places, swimm to the middle of the lake, tip a canoe jump on a horse without the slightest hesitation. But once she has tasted the thrill she is not quite so sure the second time that it is really as much fun as all that and becomes much more nervous the third time. David is quite the opposite. He is most reluctant to try anything *en principe* but once he had done it and found out that he is still alive, nothing will stop him.

"I must say this is a dream place to bring up children because there is so much for them to do and that with the touch of *filotimo* [pride] brought out by the presence of seven or eight other children, makes them do all kinds of things which of course in Paris they would neither dream of doing or be able to do. David is wonderful with any kind of boat now and they both swimm quite well. Marinette has at last mastered the head first dive and is thrilled. They both eat like horses and although David is not fatter he is taller even in the one week we have been here and his chest has filled out.

All together this is a most succesful expedition.

"Yes we will live in Paris still at least for another year and I hope probably more. I must say the more I see of this country the less I like the thought of living in it (*entre nous*). Everything here seems to happen at once to everybody even things like trying to get thin, or wanting to wear pink. Even cancer. No one smokes any more since that article in *Life* about smoking giving people cancer of the lungs. Ah but its too difficult to really describe what it is about America which does not suit me. Things like people constantly talking about other people as being malajusted or insecure or undevelopped. Words one never hears in Europe."

Our biggest adventure of 1954 was a canoe trip through the sullen lakes and forests of northern Ontario.

Alas, it was quite impossible to sit down in a wind-and-rain-swept tent and compose a letter to anyone at all, above all in the absence of a typewriter, which by then was Marina's chosen instrument of creation, and in the full knowledge that the nearest human being during most of our trip was ninety miles away and the nearest post office probably about a hundred and fifty miles. That combination is enough to discourage the most enthusiastic correspondent.

On August 2 she wrote to *Mama mou glykia*: "We are on the train going o Kapuskasing from where to take the canoes. My this is a big place. It is taking us 24 hours to get to the start of our trip. All our fellow passengers are immigrants as this train goes all the way to Vancouver. It is the first time I have ever seen refugees so near to their goal and it gave me a strange Cavafy feeling of "what will become of us without the barbarians?"* I thought of all the aches and heartrendering separations, all the violent struggles to reach the ultimate decision of leaving homes, brothers, pasts, to refuse the easy way out of letting oneself be crushed. But up to this moment there was still action, uncertainty, fuss travel, to keep their minds off other things. Now, tomorrow, they will be finished with half-truths and they will all be face to face with their new reality. How very frightening.

"My heart bled for them. There is something terribly pathetic anyway I have always found in people carrying heavy suit-cases, and when I saw

---

* Constantine Cavafy (1868-1933), a Greek poet who lived in Alexandria.

them struggling downstairs with those agonisingly cheap bags, so heavy to the arms, so desperately light in terms of the accumulated posessions of a life time, I wanted much to cry. I wish I were more susceptible to the exsitement of adventures, new life etc. and less so to the sorrow of a passed left behind. It probably comes from my own passed being so full and so incredibly happy that no future can possibly hope to stand up to it.

"As far as the immediate future goes, as always when I am well into it, I enjoy it more than the prospect of it. As long as it does not rain all the time, I will actually enjoy it I think. This may be my last letter for three weeks. Dont worry. I do hope I catch one big fish at least."

The very next day, from the surprisingly comfortable Kapuskasing Inn on the borderland of endless forests, rivers filled with logjams, and the edge of the arctic tundra, Marina dashed off another brief ink-scribbled note to Dodo:

"Well we are off tomorrow at five in the morning. We have two canoes and two wonderful guides. One half French and half Cree Indian. The other half Irish and half Cree.

"This is a most astonishing place. It is a town entirely build around and because of the huge paper mill across the river. We were received like royalty by the manager and taken to the hotel which is first class. The unexpected joy of a suite, hot bath and turkey for dinner plus the stopping of the rain restaured our morale, somewhat shaken by 24 hours in a dirty train.

"The trip is less wild than Cy hoped, but still sounds good. We sail down rivers into lakes and out again and what I am looking forward to most is shooting rapids. I dont like still sweet water, but have a passion for rushing streams. Apparently half our trip is what they call 'fast water.' We fish for trout and pike. We will see moose and dear and bears. This is great trapping country and we may meet lumberjacks and trappers who spend all their lives in the wild forrests and come to this place once a year to sell their skins. Rather exciting. I am really quite thrilled now that we are actually off."

On the whole, it was up to her expectations. She was saddened by the fact that there is no true "land" extending beneath the infinite stretches of conifers whose commercial value lies in their potential as paper pulp, the only ground being a mixture of long, greedy roots and swamp, interrupted by bushes, stretching from lake and river along the northern flats. On the other hand, we canoed across and through white-water rapids, portaged long distances through virgin forest carrying heavy packs and canoes, staked out camps at least ninety miles from the nearest human being, and although it was out of season for hunting, I was allowed to bring a .22 rifle with me to "protect" us from bears. This occasionally supplemented our fish-plus-canned-food diet with ducks picked off swimming and a not quite full-grown moose nibbling subsurface weeds at the entrance to a stream. Marina was surprisingly delighted when I shot him six times through the throat and, after he fell, Vincent (the guide) cut off one haunch and threw the rest into the bushes "for the bears." Our haunch, which tasted like young veal, thanks to Charlie the cook, fed the four of us for a week.

When we finally emerged from what was genuine wilderness, Marina was both pleased to get out and proud to have been there. We cleaned up and headed southward to the U.S.A. and Cape Cod, where the children and Nursey were staying with my mother and stepfather.

August 29, from Cape Cod: 'Mama mou glykia. Some times when the weather was fine it was really beautiful and rather thrilling to be a thousand miles from everywhere. At times we paddled into little lakes which were so still that everything was reflected perfectly in the water giving one a strange sensation of being in a completely Platonic world of essence and existance as our philosopher friends might say. It was rather striking to see how things in conjunction with their own exact reflexion seemed to be themselves, and acquire a new meaning. Perfectly ordinary logs of wood seen both in reality and in shadow acquired the shapes of dragons, witches, castles snakes and strange monsters. Made me wonder if our own exsistence, our thoughts, even our acts, if always coinciding with a second version of themselves, would turn into strange monsters too. Double goodness turning into wickedness double evil into good etc.

"You can imagine that I had plenty of time for considerations of this sort while paddling endlessly down river. But the thing which fascinated me most about the trip was when we entered the vast empire of the Spruce Falls Paper Company. Immagine that it owns seventy thousand square miles of bush. That's bigger than Albania. Only the trees actually belong to them and the rest to the government but there is mighty little else let me tell you. Seventy thousand miles of timber land uninhabited except by here and there a trapper who sets his lines and waits. The company has what it calls camps in certain places where the lumberjacks live, that is to say eat and sleep and from there take off for work cutting down trees which they then float down the river to Kapuskasing where these mighty glorious trees are turned into Kleenex W.C. paper and newspaper pages.

"It was strange to see people living the complete and perfect elementary life. Men from as far off as the Ukrane or Tschekoslovakia or unfortunate shivering Italians or great strong Swedes and little wiry Finns some of them hardly speaking English and not caring anyway and you can immagine that the art of conversation is limited in such a community. A company of strong tough silent rootless reckless men drifting in and out of these camps (they are not regularly employed and they are all such wanderers that they never stay in one place much anyway). Working seven eight hours a day payed colossal sums some make up to thirty dollars a day, sleeping eating fabulous ammounts and when they have enough money wondering off to some city to spend it all on one colossal binge of hooch and women secure in the knowledge that their arms are strong and that when their money is gone there is always more to be made in a country so vast and so young.

"I found it strangely disturbing some times to be with people so different from myself. Our guides for instance whose life is made up only of essentials did not know the difference between warm food or tepid. To them food is food to keep you alive and a detail like liking ones coffee warm or the fish fried all the way through seemed fussy and queer. But one thing they all had in common. A deep deep love for the bush. In a town they feel cramped and that goes for the occasional women we met too. Formans' wives for instance whose one sorrow is that their children eventually grown old enough to go to school and then they have to move to the big city (the size of Halandri [a Greek village]). They all love the river and the fish and the hunting and particularly the winter.

"I who was shivering even in August was slightly taken aback by everybody's assertion that the winter is the real thing. That then they get the most work done have more fun etc. But now I understand it. To begin with it must be quite a sight that huge expanse of white and second their transportation problems are eliminated and everything freezes over and they can drive their cars for hundreds of miles over frozen river, and do ten times more work standing on solid frozen earth rather than waddling through the sodden black earth of the summer.

"Some of the portages we had to go over were quite awful. A portage is when the canoes cant go over a waterfall and we had to get out and carry our stuff plus the canoes for a mile or so over deep forrest so thick that we had to cut our way through and so wet that we were up to our knees in mud. I got my inevitable giggling fits at the sight of Cy falling six times in a row in the mud or getting inextricably cought up in branches or bushes and cursing heartily. But luckily not too loud so I avoided any real congugal scenes. But having seen that I understood why they all prefer the winter with everything clean and tidy. And if one has the right kind of cloths I suppose one isnt TOO cold. Must stop but will continue tomorrow. . . .

"The last place we went to was called Opazatika lake which means Lake of Poplar islands in Indian. It was the prittiest of all the places and the whether was comparatively good so we enjoyed that last part more than the rest and would have stayed on another three days especially as Cy had not yet cought the forty pound pike he was looking for but only a twenty pound one but then three nights before our scheduled departure I got a hook right into the bone of my second finger and although Cy tried to cut it out with a razor, looking ten times more miserable than I did in the process, the hook was too deep to get at so the next morning we started for the town in order to get to a hospital. And that was quite astonishingly quick considering that we were in the middle of nowhere at the time we started paddling for home and by sheer luck just as we were taking off we saw a lonely trapper who appeared from nowhere in a little outboard motor canoe, so he offered Cy and me a lift to the first camp, while the guides struggled with the canoes and came later.

"At the camp they arranged for a boat to take us to the next camp, from where they gave us a ride in a little home made train of the company, and then another boat, and one way or another we got back to Kapuskasing less than twentyfour hours after I got hooked. We were lucky it had not happened while we were on the river with long portages separating us from civilisation. We found a charming doctor who x rayed my hand and cut out the hook. That night it hurt a lot but considering everything it was an easy way out.

"Mama mou I had left the letter on the porch of our house yesterday, unable to finish it after all and such a storm came up this night and is still raging, that it soaked everything including the typewriter which I cant use. That's why this letter is such a dreadful mess. Also reading it over I find I have not written half the things I wanted to say or managed to convey the atmosphere of vastness, remoteness and strange contentement that surges from that place. It is the habit to consider simple pure life as good and virtuous. I am not one who agrees completely to that. I dont see why to eat sleep work love and die without such trimmings as Proust, Bach's Toccata or Fugue, Dior, *sole meunière*, Chanel No 5 Shakespear and hot baths is morally *better!* But there is no doubt that there is something, something about the elementary, which satisfies and keeps one sort of happy."

To her brother, Alexis, she wrote on our return to New York: "How you managed to live all these years in this infernal city without a nervous break down, seems a miracle to me. For the second class citizen who does not know the complicated tricks of existence here life 'sure is' complicated. We have been back from our various Fenimore Cooper expeditions about a week and I am already a wreck. Today for instance I came down from our room in the hotel and in a breezy European manner asked the porter to post several letters for me. He did not even answer, looked at me as if I were the village idiot and pointed with his head to a corner in which there stood an infernal looking machine, the kind of inanimate object whose sole function is to destroy man, its inventor. Needless to say I did not have the right change, and when I got it did not know which hole to push it into and I pulled the wrong lever and pushed the wrong button and cought my finger in a beastly looking wire and alltogether it took me twenty minutes to perform that simple operation and so much weariness and anger that I would have given up letter writting for ever, were you not my only and devoted brother.

"And that incident was just one of many. I went to buy dressing gowns for the children and first of all no one knew what a dressing gown was. After a lot of research in semantics we discovered they were 'wrappers' and I was told to try the Liliput Bazaar. Express to seventh floor. It turned out however that my children after three months of Borden's full cream pasteurized homogenized sterilised mezmerized sanforized milk, had nothing Liliputian about them so we had to descend to the 'Teen agers departement.'

"Teen agers were too big so we started on a desperate round from Toddlers to Little Sportsmen to 'In betweens' to 'Big littles and little Bigs' and after a nerve-racking morning in which we were considered old fashoned stick in the muds because we wanted just plane navy blue wool and not Kelly green Orlon or Apple blossom Acettate or never-never red Nylon with orange girrafes on the pockets, we gave up and decided to wait until Paris. This happens daily wheather I am looking for underwar tin openers or sheets. Which does not mean that I dont spent millions anyway carried away by such absurdities as 'Suspants, the lift that never lets you down,' the cream that gives you school girl complexion all over, and the only pyrex dish fit for kings.

"Last week we went on our last bit of holiday before Cy starts earning the daily bread again. We took the children up to Knollwood and camped out in the woods.

"We drove back after four days there and stopped on our way in Fort Ticonderoga which is really rather lovely and gave the children a good and graffic dose of American History which fitted in rather nicely with their previous knowledge as some of the guns belonged to the Duc du Maine or Montcalm whom they know from good old Septième [Paris school] days. We slept in motels which in spite of my prejudiced hatred for them as the symbol of twentieth century mediocrity together with Coca Cola and the Readers Digest, turned out to be most comfortable gay and practical. Now we are back in 'lil ole New York' and frantically shopping and packing as the children leave with nursey on Wednesday to go back to school while I remain here to hold Cy's hand while he starts work again.

"We will probably stay a month and much as I hated the thought of letting the children go home alone now that it cant be helped I am rather glad to see New York 'in season' for once. We usually arrive in July whisk off to the country and then leave again in September before any play is open or any self respecting conductor will be seen even loiterring anywhere within a mile of Carnegie Hall. So I am rather looking forward to a few good concerts Opera plays and especially a few dinners and things so as to drop some provocative remarks about Senator you know who [McCarthy], the recognition of Communist China or Mendès France and see what happens. For the moment none of the gruesome stories about one's best friends grovelling in the path of the Bastard seem true but I cant really tell having consorted with nothing but Canadian lumber jacks, Cape Cod fishermen and the dressing gown ladies, up to now.

"We are going to Washington soon and I am going to see Mamie

[Eisenhower] which I must admit rather pleases me. I have never set foot in the White house and the chances of our having another president friend are rather slim I would say. It looks as if we might have a Governor friend however as dear Averell [Harriman] is trying like mad for it and got the nomination the other day as you probably know. How I envy you your [Greek] trip and the whole summer. Each drop of rain that fell upon my Mediterranean head, each icicle I whisked from my brow, each frog, blood sucker or worm I saw swimming in the so called clear waters of the North, each beastly fish I cought, each portage I stumbled through each bigger and better pine spruce or birch that I sat under, made me more and more nostalgic for salty water, yellow sun, dry earth, no green, *barbounis* [red mullet] and all the unique delights of our part of the world. *Papoutsi apo ton topo so kai as einai* [Better shoes from your native land even if only the shoe lace is left]."

Nineteen fifty-four was the year that marvelous woman, Anne O'Hare McCormick, died and I inherited her column in *The New York Times*. I knew well I had neither the wisdom nor stylistic grace of Anne and that I had to devise a new approach to the task. Therefore, I resolved that I would constantly travel all over the world, making up with energy for what I lacked in intellectuality or literary craft.

Marina wrote her mother on September 26: "I have to admit to you that the children are unrecognisable. They hardly lift their heads from their commics or the television set and I may say that murder rape arsen and violent death hold no secret for them any longer. They have also become completely familiar with acid indigestion, under arm odor, costipation bad breath, and undesirable hair. They can tell you what number to call for that extra large, inexpensive, satisfying tube of tooth paste, Wash-day joy, hair remover and the soap that gives you that wonderful miracle school girl complexion all over. They can tell you how 'not to offend' or get rid of dandruft.

"As for their language they have now added to their French, Greek intonation and Devonshire Aas, such expressions as You can say that again bud. Atta boy, You are damned tootin, Hot digerdy, and all kinds of superlatives like Super, smasher, knocker and Cool. Apparently the old expression Oh he is hot stuff is out now. You have to be 'Cool.' Man but is that song cool! Hot diggerdy. Ah *Thé mou. Ti girevi i alepou sto pa zari* [My God, what is the fox doing in the market?]. How did I ever get tanggled up in all this can you tell me. Well they will be back in Paris in a week or so and then they will probably pick up some nice French Argo to add to all this and things will be just 'Super.'

"Last night Marinette had the treat of her life. It was a belated birthday present from me. We took her to the Opera to see a Midsummer night's dream. She had on a bran new dress of white embroidered organdi and red shoes and bows in her pig tails and looks sweet. It was the Old Vic which has just arrived in New York and did a combination of the Play with the Mendhelson music and the Saddler's Wells ballet. Actually I found it too much of a good thing between Shakespear and Mendhelson and the dancing and the *décor* which no 'Wood near Athens' ever dreamed of looking like, but for Marinette it was a perfect way to start off with one's Shakespear. The costumes of the fairies were divine and Titania was any girls dream with her red gold hair and white tule dress covered with gold stars and all together I think she adored it. Anyway even if it had been humpty dumpty, the idea of being up at midnight would have been a treat."

Marina confided in another letter to *Mama mou glykia*: "In all the other letters I had given you detailled accounts of my strugles with the New York jungle, compared to which Canada was a peaceful paradise. I had described in colourful exageration, the beastly buss drivers the irrate shop ladies the excentric taxi drivers the grave difficulty of such simple operations as posting a letter, calling long distance or the use of the English language. But *tant pis*. Let all that go by and I will start fresh from 970 Park [my mother's home] where we economized since the children left us a week ago.

"You see, as I had explained in detail in several other letters, Cy has to stay on a bit here because of his new job as columnist and he wanted me so desperately to stay with him that in spite of my deep objections to leaving the children again I felt that this time for once he really needed me more than they did so I stayed behind and now we are staying with my mother in law and it is all a frantic rush of hard work for Cy and for me a hopeless attempt to see everyone. There are all the people mother in law wants to show me to, there are all my American friends ex from Paris or Rome or Zanzibar. There are Americans from just plane America and of course least but certainly neither last nor few my own beloved Greeks (a heaven of extrovertness in this frustrated world) including dozens who in Greece itself would perhaps not be 'mous' as Cy calls them but whom exile and a mutual longing for the *patrida* [fatherland] suddenly turns into blood brothers.

"Those are mainly pleasure but there are also newspaper men politicians 'Socialites' as Haarper's Bazzar would say, etc etc etc who all telephone ten times a day and want us for week ends begining luncheon breakfast dinner or tea for one reason or another. Cy whose yearning for the desert land of fish is growing with every invitation, is in a state but there is nothing to be done about it especially on Monday when we leave for Washington, which is a smaller town and where we will really be snowed under. We will be staying with an old friend called Polly Wisner and she telephonned yesterday to warn us that every single meal is already taken up and that senators Republicans Democrats and coleagues from other papers have all been at her telephone for the last week. This all souns very pompous and as if I wanted to make out that we were madly popular but it is not as immodest as it sounds.

"Cy's new job has a lot to do with our being so *Recherché.* Also the fact that we are new faces in a town where everybody has seen and disliked everybody else for the past thirty years. However I suppose it is good for Cy's job to see all these people, so what can we do. Aliki [Russell] with whom I spent the afternoon yesterday was terribly sweet and tried her best to lend me all her New Dior cloths hats etc so that I would make a tremendous impression and uphold the prestige of the *patrida.* Just this minute I received letters from the children and nursey from the boat as well as a cable saying they had arrived well and Sebastian [our tekel puppy] had nearly died of excitement at the station. They are already at school but of course I dont know news of that yet.

"Nursey the angel is perfectly capable of coping with arrivals departures etc and each time I think of all she does for us I thank the good God who sent her to us. She left here with eleven cases of things in the hold and got them out of customs and everything. It was mostly china and linen that my mother in law gave us as well as towles sheets things like that which I bought as even with customs they are cheaper here than in Paris. We will be well fixed for quite a while from the domestic end I hope. She will also see the children well established in the new school and all that sort of thing and anyway we will be back in Paris in another three weeks or so I hope. Cy has not started yet and is awfully anxious to make the first articles especially good. That is why he wanted me around I suppose. Its so much easier to have some one to be grumpy at when under a strain.

"The United Nations are in session which adds to the number of acquaintances from all over the world. We went to a party last night which turned into a fierce Cyprus debate. Aliki was there too and she and I had to hold the floor for hours against all kinds of outrageous statements but on the whole it was a good natured rather teasing affair. It is funny that both John Russell and Sir Pierson Dixson in charge of Cyprus affairs here, more or less, should have Greek wives. Makes their troubles double I should think."

IV

October 1954-January 1956

I was nervous as a kitten when I began my thrice-weekly column in the autumn of 1954, and was consequently most grateful when Marina agreed to stay by my side. I decided to start my new venture — which allowed me to express personal opinions, whether or not they agreed with the editorial policies of *The New York Times* — by calling upon my old friendship with Eisenhower. Although the President was skittish of the press and had not yet received a single newspaperman, he made an exception in my case, and I took Marina along to the White House so she could see Mamie while I talked world affairs with Ike.

Our visit to the White House started with a long chat with the First Lady in the private apartments. Mamie was in her study, sitting beside a TV, writing letters while three hillbillies blared away. She embraced Marina and then took her sightseeing, pointing out that she and Ike shared a double bed, showing her a model of their Gettysburg farm, and then displaying a mass of signed portraits to the presidential couple, including one from Emperor Haile Selassie and his empress inscribed to "President Aisenhower." Marina recalled the rest of their meeting in a memo for me:

"Mrs. Ike took me around some more rooms and then as I offered to leave her in peace, she said: 'Oh, do have a cigarette.' We had three. We talked about the difficulties of entertaining people who sometimes spoke no English. Also about their finances which are going to the dogs, as their huge salary is taxed 90 percent. She said it costs them about $25,000 [annually] for Ike to be President. She is obliged to buy dozens of evening dresses and hundreds of hats.

"She says that it is quite tiresome being a First Lady, as she never gets a chance to go for a walk by herself or browse around in little shops. One day in Denver she walked into a five-and-ten in an act of revolt and had a lovely time. She was just about to buy a brassiere when she remembered the secret policeman behind her and was too embarrassed to have her measurements taken, so had to give up the whole idea. She told me that all the food and flowers and upkeep for the two of them and any unofficial friends they entertain, is paid for by them.

"Also any repairs to the top of the house — this I am not quite sure I did not misunderstand. She said that nothing had been done to the White House until she came because Mrs. Truman was 'too busy doing nothing' and Mrs. Roosevelt was 'too busy running around the country.' She repeated that Ike hated being President but had 'only done it because he felt it was his duty.' "

We returned to Europe in November. Marina was overjoyed to remain in the Boulevard St. Germain apartment, spending as much time as possible with Sebastian, our dog, and the children, who went to the little public school around the corner. Soon I had to pack up and go to England, Germany, and Austria. With much happiness Marina accompanied me to Vienna, about which she had heard so much and which she had never seen. After that I flew off on another globe-girdling tour via the Middle East, Far East, and United States, which brought me home only in April, shortly before her birthday.

Marina wrote in French to her friend Kitty Solomos in Athens on January 26, 1955: "Vienna I found a bit disappointing at first glance. After Paris, you know, whose harmony is so perfect, all other cities seem a bit village-like. But this being said, Vienna is filled with charm despite the baroque statues everywhere with the inevitable naked ladies falling over on top of delphiniums or baskets of roses with a Neptune, wearing a beard and carrying a fierce trident, doing no one knows what on top of them. One ends up by even liking the entire mixture. The churches are very lovely and the Esterhazy Kinsky and Windischgraetz palaces are ravishing. But despite their well-known charm, I found the people a bit ridiculous. *Küss die Hand. Grüss Gott. Gemütlich.* Naturally we went to the Opera and I admit it's marvelous. Splendid voices and a perfect orchestra."

I was in Beirut when I got Marina's first letter (January 30), confessing: "I rode home very gloomily thinking of you and hating the idea of your long trips and your fealing so awful and the fatigue ahead of you. I console myself with the thought that once you get to all those strange places you may find things to fascinate and amuse and interrest you and you will forget how tired you are.

"Friday I went to a completely Greek concert directed and composed by our Mr. Petrides who thinks himself a sort of Bach Beethoven and Alban Berg roled into one when he is in fact quite good but pretentious. We all applauded with due patriotic fervour but it was a bit tough. Two hours of mediocre music was a strain on even the Greekiest of Greeks. . . . All my most enormous love and admonitions to be careful and to try and not get too tired and do please look at the wings and things of planes before you get into them."

A few days later she wrote: "Last night I went to the Ismays [Lord Ismay, NATO's first secretary-general] a small party with the Reinhardts [U.S. diplomat, later ambassador to Italy] and Spiedel [General Hans Speidel, Field Marshal Rommel's chief of staff] and de Staercke [Belgian ambassador to NATO]. It was fascinating as I sat on a sofa between Spiedel and Ismay and they discussed Dunkerque each one from his own point of view. Spiedel couldn't have been friendlier and sent his most fervent regards to you and good wishes for your trip. He is taking me to hear Fidelio in March as the Stuttgart Opera is coming.

"It was strange to be sitting on the sofa listening and then we got to talking about the occupation and I told about the *Regierungsrat* [the administrator billeted in the Spitaki] and Dodo drinking champagne with the German officer to Alexi's health and then de Staercke told about his escape from the Gestapo and it was all so cosy and utterly unembarrassed which is a tribute to Spiedel. The Ismays also send all their love to you and Pug was sweet and made jokes about me being in circulation as a bacherlor for two months, with a gleame in his eye."

On February 16 she wrote: "Yesterday I had dinner at the Pattens with Cecil Beaton and the Cabrolles and Lilia [Ralli] and Nancy Mitford and some other people, the kind of party you would not have liked at all but I enjoyed a lot. The talk was all about the Royal Wedding in Estoril from where both Cecil and Lilia had only just returned and they are both frightfully good raconteurs so we were really regaled with various delicious tit bits of European royal gossip."

That month Marina gave a fancy-dress party for the children and their new friends at the American School, to which they had transferred. She wrote: "It was fun and our own two looked divine. David was a very handsome sheik with a beard and wicked eye brows and Marinette who had been to the hairdresser looked too delicious in her Victorian hairdo and Great Aunt Semira's dress. As David told you in his letter Susan Mary sent her a posie of pink and white flowers all done in silver paper and addressed to her. That is the kind of sweet thought Susan Mary has which makes her doubly lovable. We had two hundred sandwiches five huge birthday kind cakes five kiloes of petit fours and at the end of the evening there was not a crumb left."

By that time I was in Bangkok for a conference of the SEATO alliance and came down with a ghastly attack of gout. Marina wrote me on March 1:

"My dearest sweet Peter the Gouty. I cant tell you how sorry I am for you and that I am not there with you to comfort and console you. You must be having a wretched time. Is it as bad [an attack] as in the Gold Coast? As far as your stories went no one could ever tell that you were not in the best of spirits. Even Mr. Shakespear himself however could not have made anything seem terribly exciting it seems to me. Was it as dull and irritable as it sounds through the papers? Poor you. Conferences are bad enough but to have such a dull one and gout besides seems piling Pelion onto wherever it is. . . . I have never been colder than yesterday at the funeral of Mr. Claudel [Paul Claudel, one of France's great writers]. Notre Dame was like a tomb already. There were lots of speeches and lots of violets and lots of people and I did not even get to shake the hand of Mrs. so it was all useless."

Three days later she was again regaling me with her Parisian adventures:

"Last night I went to Pamela's* for dinner and boy was I glad you were not with me. It was nothing but marquises and horsey lords and the conversation consisted entirely about who was sleeping with whom in St. Moritz or Klosters or Davos. Lord and Lady X were there, you know the lady who was shot by her crazy buttler last year and caused quite a scandal. Her husband nearly caused another one last night when we went dancing in a night club after dinner. Apparently he was making eyes at a very pretty girl at the next table and then he moved up a few chairs and put his elbow on their table. The girl's escort pushed him off and they both lept up and very nearly came to blows which was all madly embarrassing. Then he refused to participate in the bill on the pretext that he had been offended by a client of the management. Nice fellow. But as usual the food was excellent and the women lovely looking and all dressed by Dior. You would have hated it. I rather enjoyed it in an amused detached way, not being what they called o.c.d. [our class dear]."

Her next letter wound up: "Good by for the moment my sweet Pirandello, and do write and please be careful what airoplane you get into. I saw that one fell on its way to Formosa the other day and my heart stopped. I will only feel comfortable and relaxed again when you are safely tucked up in the big bed asking for a *tizane*, slightly grumpy but not too much, and just made a score of three hundred and eighty nine at scrabble as opposed to my hundred and four. I will even read Barchester Towers to you (but not cheerfully)."

That March, Marina went over to England and stayed at Oxford with our chums, Pussy and Bill (now Sir William) Deakin, then warden of St. Antony's College, the university's newest and most experimental institution. She had a grand time and also visited several boys' preparatory schools for David. We had decided to send him to England in 1956 because Marinette was pleading to go to boarding school with her best friend, Isabelle de Waldner, and we had acceded. Marina wrote:

---

* Born Pamela Digby, first married to Randolph Churchill, mother of young Winston Churchill, M.P. Later wife of Leland Hayward, then Averell Harriman.

"Oxford seemed more unreal to me this time than the others. Even Isaiah [Sir Isaiah Berlin] whom I like so much seems to be trying a bit too hard to say the unexpected in a clever way. We had dinner one night with [Sir] Maurice Bowra [warden of Wadham College] and the conversation consisted entirely about people and gossip and stuff like Maurice saying 'So and so is ghastly, he really is too disgustingly high minded, of course he is neurotic which helps a bit but nothing can make up for his loving his mother so' or Pussy told a story about some wolves who had attacked a pack of dogs and the general cry was 'Oh, we do hope it was the dogs that were eaten up, it would be too maudlin if the dogs won.'

"Bill went out of his way to drive me to the school called Beachborough which is about sixteen miles from Oxford. It seemed enchanting: a lovely old house, beautiful grounds young pleasant looking masters a friendly matron and seventy little boys in grey flannels all looking most relaxed and happy and playing in a huge room entirely taken up by an electric train. I was astonished and delighted to see even a teddy bear here and there in the boys beds which did away with my last reservations and Dickensian thoughts on English upbringing."

She got back to Paris in time to get a letter from me about a visit to Kyoto and a geisha house to which Japanese friends had taken me and about which I wrote a column. With merry disapproval, she commented:

"It is my turn to call you Smouko as you seem to have gone all Japanese. I must say even before your letter I suspected something was up from the lyricisme of your Wednesday article. Your letter confirmed everything. Well I am at least happy that your moral is up and you feel better. I like to get cheerful letters from you even though I sometimes suspect that the cheerfulness is not entirely due to the landscape. Five years of lessons in learning how to please [at geisha schools] must certainly do something to those ladies which cannot be easy to resist. However if I am going to make a scene I will do it from near and enjoy it. . . .

"One bit of amusing news is that Rowley Winn has inherited the most beautiful house in England, the only one on which Adam and Chippendale worked together [Nostell Priory] as well as a colossal fortune. He has ten of the most beautiful Poussins ever found which were in the attic unknown to anybody, as well as Giottos and god knows what else and one of two or three existing first folios of Shakespere which he sits and looks through by the fire on mild evenings. He is happy as can be. What fun for him."

Right after Easter, Marina wrote me in Honolulu as I was starting homeward:

"Spring seems to have reached us after all and all the leaves have suddenly come out, taking everyone as always by surprise. Beautiful warm evenings which make one feel delightful but restless. . . .

"Yesterday (Easter) was a dream day. We went to St. Firmin [Lady Diana Cooper's manor near Chantilly] and all the children picnicked on the grass which was studded with daffodils and primroses and they looked for eggs and rolled on the grass and fell in the little stream and loved it. Diana could not have been nicer. Kissed me on both cheeks asked after you and said your articles were excellent. Randolph [Churchill] and his [second] wife were there and he too was in a pleasant mood. He said when someone had asked his father recently when he would really retire he sighed and said 'Pretty soon, pretty soon, I can no longer bear those hungry eyes.' [Meaning Eden's, of course.] How very wicked.

"Randolph also told a sweet story about the time his father had threatened to retire from eighteen successive cabinets because of his fight with Lloyd George over the dreadnoughts. Asquith* apparently had done everything to get them to agree and every time they had left practically spitting at each other and finnaly he said 'I will give you both a last chance. Meet on Monday morning and have a last argument.'

"Churchill arrived at the meeting and Lloyd George handed him a letter grinning. It was from his wife Dame Margaret who lived somewhere quietly in Wales and said. 'Dear David. I read somewhere in the papers that you are haveing some kind of disagreement with Mr. Churchill over dreadnoughts. I know nothing about dreadnoughts except that obviously it is essential to have enough and it seems to me it is better to have a few too many than a few too few.' That is how Lloyd George was finally persuaded to agree to Churchill's demands. Isn't it a sweet story."

---

* David Lloyd George, the British prime minister, opposed the head of the Admiralty, Winston Churchill, on naval construction. Lord Asquith was first British prime minister of World War I, prior to Lloyd George.

Marina took an automobile tour through the Loire Valley to allow the children and Sebastian to visit the famous chateaux. Then, just in time for her birthday, I arrived back in Paris. She wrote my mother:

"I drove down to Cherbourg to get him, through a Normandy so covered with flowers that it was all I could do to keep my eyes on the road and not go flying into a feild and stay there picking. The weather has turned so hot that one feels like July and there is a mad scramble for trunks and getting out last year's summer things to try and squeeze into them in a hurry. Cy seems very well and although tired, much more relaxed and chipper than he usually is after such a long trip. Yesterday to celebrate my birthday we started off full of joy and optimism for our usual *muguets* place and immagine that it took us an hour and a half to go ten kilometres. The entire road was one solid unbrocken line of motor cars as far as the eye could see. We finished by turning off at the first free left turn and picnicking by the side of a dusty road."

Just before going to Greece for the 1955 summer holidays, Marina started the complicated process of moving from our apartment, which had become too noisy and also too expensive, to a charming old house on the Avenue de Ségur. When the fundamentals of the move had been completed, she flew off with the children and Nursey. From the Spitaki she wrote on July 16:

"I must say that all the English here seem to make the same mistake of bringing the Cyprus problem up constantly at parties when everyone else is thinking of other things. [Cyprus was then struggling for its independence from British colonial status, led by the EOKA guerrilla organization and Archbishop Makarios.] It is quite irksome and I could not resist saying to one the other day: 'One can do anything with bayonets except sit on them.' I was told a rather funny story. Apparently Sir Charles [Peake, British ambassador to Athens] when he was in London found at Sotheby's the inkwell which was given to Byron by the Greek people and bought it and the Greek general staff learned about it and asked him if he would sell it back to them so that they could give it to the King as a birthday present. He said yes, so the King was given by his generals a bronze ink stand representing Britain leaning gently over a Greek wounded soldier and ministering to him. 'A singularly inapropriate gift at the present moment what what . . .' as Sir Charles commented."

On July 29 she wrote: "I have no idea where you are or anything but presume it must be work and travel as the Swiss ladies are hardly dangerous; however one never knows." [I had been in Liechtenstein and Switzerland.]

We did not yet own a house in Spetsais, an island where both Dodo and Marina had spent two generations of summer vacations, but we had rented one for August and September. Marina wrote:

"We are off on Wednesday complete with deck chairs tied together with a string, a primus stove and the orphanned cat in a basket. Dodo is staying [in Maroussi] so as to be there for Maria's name day on the fifteenth and then she will come. She acts a bit as if she were going out into the great wide allien world by coming to Spetsais and only constant reassurances that the house is as far from the Poseidoneion [main hotel] and the Social circle of the Tapia [central plaza] and that she can put a hood over her head and see no one if she wants, quiet her fears. She and you ought to get on splendidly, you anthrophobes. Even I must admit I have been so very anthrophil in the last weeks that I might welcome the quiet of a darkened silent room after lunch."

Her last letter before my arrival in Greece recounted: "I had a splendid day yesterday on the Fuller boat [Hod Fuller, a great friend, an American retired Marine general married to a Greek]. Taki [Horn, a Greek actor] and Freddy [Fredric March, an American actor] spent half their time doing take offs on Hamlet or immitations of each other and it was really wonderfully funny and gay. The sea was drinkable and so warm and green that it makes one a bit crazy. I was terribly humiliated however once again in my [spear] fishing. I managed to miss even a sitting octopus and a sole which is big and wide and motionless. Quite hopeless. But the day was heavenly. . . . I forgot to say in my last letter how thrilled I am at the possibility of the Russian trip."

In September, after our holiday, when we got back to Paris and moved into our new house on the Avenue de Ségur, we were invited to Moscow by Chip and Avis Bohlen. Marina wrote my mother:

"My brain is so full of curtain rods, towel racks, smoking chimneys, leaking toilets and such sordid things that I am not fit for human company any more. Little by little however out of the chaos, a tiny light is appearing and at least the children's and nursey's rooms are quite nice and I can go off to Russia knowing that they are all right. You ask for a description of the house. Well here goes.

"Front door (which does not open or shut properly) up five steps (with carpet that kept slipping off and threatened brocken legs constantly). Hall of the oddest shape and black and white tiles and a large staircase with hidious twentieth century stained glass window at the top. On the right a small library where Cy will work when it is fixed. For the moment all our books are on the floor in it. You know the kind of exasperating things that happen. I ordered shelves for the books, waited six weeks and they finally arrived two days ago so awful with such small distances between them that no books would fit so they have had to be taken away again and another six weeks of waiting probably.

"On the opposite side a huge and pretty living room. Red damask on the walls, red moth eaten carpet, three large round windows. Our own furniture fitted rather nicely but we still needed a desk or a commode or something for it. If one has one valuable bit then even the rather shabby other stuff stands out better. Off the living room a dining room not bad. The furniture there is all the Countess's [our landlady] plus a huge revolting portrait of the dowager with one of her sons in black velvet and lace collar, you see the type.

"Then you go up-stairs and half way up there is a tiny door in the wall so small that one squeezes in side ways and down three narrow steps, into a bath room where the gas heater recently exploded with an atomic noise. Off it is the tiniest guest room you ever saw with a hole in the floor. That is where our beloved Chip Bohlen is being given hospitality. I had to have that all repainted and buy a bed and curtains and carpets and everything. Even light bulbs.

"Then a bit further up stairs is the bed room floor. David has a room which we had redone in white wall paper with tiny green Empire wreaths all over it. He has a dark green carpet, cream curtains with a green trimming, a brass bed with Aunt Iphegenes white bed cover, and a very pretty table with green leather and brass in-lays and a chair which I bought for fifty dollars at the flea market.

"Marinette's room has pink wall paper with a white design sort of like tiny Xmas trees. She has a wooden bed, white heavy silk curtains and bed cover, deep red carpet. Then nursey's room is peach and white stripe wall paper, cream curtains and persian looking carpet in pale green with animals and flowers.

"I must say the flea marquet is great fun and that is the part I enjoy most but one has to go every other day and look and look until one falls on to something nice and cheap.

"And on top of all that Russia. It could not have come at a worse moment this long awaited visa. For one thing my mind is so distracted I have not even had time to be excited yet. For another I am torn between my desire to follow Cy if he gets to Central Asia and take this unique opportunity of seeing places like Bokhara and Tashkent and Samarkand and on the other I do so hate to leave the children over Christmas. Chip on his way back from Geneva is staying with us and as sweet and bright as ever. He goes off to Berlin tonight and we join him on Wednesday and take off in his plane from there."

We had a minor disaster in Berlin. Our flight landed in a snowstorm at Tempelhof airdrome, where Bohlen's U.S. Air Force plane was awaiting us. We had brought along a consignment of extra-special old French cognac, Armagnac, and framboise, all highly esteemed by Chip, but some slick German porters, shifting baggage from one aircraft to the other, managed to make off with this amid swirling snow. Our only house present, apart from such Christmas gifts as perfume for Avis, was therefore a huge parcel of endives, a salad vegetable especially craved by Chip in green-less wintry Moscow.

Marina's first letter, quite properly, was to her beloved Dodo.

"Mama mou glykia," she wrote on November 28, 1955: "The terrible thing about being in Russia is that whatever you think about it is both right and wrong and anyway one is so nervous about being either overprejudiced or not enough that one's own thoughts are mixed up from the very start.

One does not travel in other countries peering into people's faces, watching their cloths and shoes, or trying to discover the hidden significance of a smile, a frown or a turned up collar. Here one does.

"Also one feels a sense of responsability. I can't go back and not KNOW whats going on in Russia. One is not expected to know about the Chambre des Députés, after all or the intricacies of French politics after a fortnight in Paris. No one cares if you know about senator so and so on your return from Washington, but from Moscow everybody expects you to know but at the same time expects you to confirm their original ideas anyway. If you like it well you were influenced, if you dont like it, well you did not see enough. So I am not even trying to form an opinion.

"I shall go around and try and see as much as possible and leave it at that. The start of our trip was fascinating. East Berlin where I spent the whole of Friday was like a sort of preview of what was to come. The first grim buildings the first slogans the first banners and words such as Cammaraderie International and Republique writen up five feet high on all the walls. Also the first snow.

"I was very lucky to be smuggled in to a press conference about the Dresden pictures which have been in Moscow up to now and were just returned to East Germany with great fanfare as if they were a gift from Russia. The pictures are marvellous and I went around with the correspondent from the daily worker and another from a Polish paper and it was all sort of other worldy and as I said before the words Deutches Republik Freundlich etc. used at every turn. What struck me most about East berlin and again here is a tremendous pathetiqueness. The huge new buildings all look like badly built summer resorts of the twenties. The shops full of lights and *Art nouveau* decorations, show three rayon stockings of bad quality.

"One gets a fealing that all this violence and upheaval has taken place in order to give people something they already had and the grim determination with which they tell you and themselves that this is the best of good worlds is really the most pathetic of all.

"We took off from Berlin in a snow storm and visibility zero but luckily it cleared up soon and we came into Moscow by brilliant wheather and it was I must say terribly exciting and in some ways exactly as I expected. The people in boots and fur hats and long coats, the wide boulevards the huge buildings. I have seen nothing yet as yesterday was Sunday and we did not go out except to go to the Bolshoi Theatre in the afternoon to see Swann Lake which is the first thing any tourrist simply has to do. I must say I have never seen such dancing in my life. The costumes rather gawdy and bad taste and again that sad fealing of old fashioness. Not old enough to be picturesque just terribly demodee. But the orchestra and the dancing absolute perfection.

"The audiance was fascinating too. It consisted entirely of Kyra Perse-phonies, Metaxias, a few Yiannoulas [Greek peasants] only not quite as well dressed, their male counterparts and hundreds of delicious children in yellow pig tales and white aprons sort of like some Northern parody of Alice in Wonderland. How they grow up to be so ugly I cant think. Because the first impression is that one is surrounded by ugly dowdy people. The men's cloths are terrible and the women at best had on sort of brown dresses with a touch of satin at the V necks and cuffs. Lots of gloomy brique too and not one woman with lip stick on. Hair mostly in a tight bun at the neck. Lots of uniforms too but one cant quite tell if they are bell boys post men or colonels or just that they had the uniform left over from the war and go on wearing it without the insignia.

"All together a sense of driariness, which of course one need not attribute to the regime. I believe that cold climates do that to places. I had the same fealing in Vienna. Red noses and turned up collars always make me feel desperate. I have been reading gallantly all I could about Russian history and getting nowhere. Everyone seems to be called Ivan or Vladimir and everyone killed someone else to get to be grand prince and the places they become grand princes of are also called Vladimir. Tomorrow I am being taken to the Kremlin which I must say looks terrific. Moscow as a city is much prettier than I expected in spite of the huge new Soviet buildings which as I say are half pathetically self consciously avant guarde, of the twenties."

On December 3 she wrote the children: "This country is a bit like Alice in wonderland, 'In this country said the Queen you must run very fast in order to stay in the same place.' However I think that the chances are that we will be allowed to stay on so my angels I do hope you will have if not a perfect Christmas at least a gay one and lots of presents. Think of us who will probably be in a train going to Baku or Khiva or Akmolinsk. Minsk and Pinsk and Akmolinsk. Someone has already made a song with those names

I believe. It will be terribly terribly cold and there are no proper beds and no W Cs at all. Dear me. But they are all fascinating cities and it will be greatly exciting when we get back to talk about these strange parts of the world.

"For the moment I must say we have had a glorious time. We live at the Embassy and I play with Charlie and Celestine [the younger Bohlens] to try and cheer myself up for not having my own chiks around.

"Well we live in this house which is enormous and quite pretty and very warm thank goodness. Outside it is bitterly cold. Everybody has high boots and fur hats and we wanted to buy some fur hats for all the family but immagine that even the worst immitation ones cost thirty or forty dollars.

"Far [what the children called me] always has loads of work and I go sight seing. I have seen so many churches and pictures that I dont know which is which any more. I also look at the shops and restaurants and things which are so pathetic they break your heart. The people are so badly dressed that it makes one want to cry. Not so much poor or cold or anything like that. Just terribly badly made.

"This afternoon we are going to see Lenin and Stalin's tomb and I am a bit squeemish at the idea of seeing two dead gentlemen. I have not gone to the Kremlin as one has to go on a conducted tour and there has not been one yet. It looks dreamy from the outside. A huge palace and lots of little churches with brilliant gold domes glittering under the snow. The snow makes everything look prettier even though it feels awful when it trickles down over the top of one's boots. There is one church called St. Basil which is exactly like Hansel and Gretel's ginger bread house. It is all curly queues and domes and long thin towers and it is red and gold and blue and yellow and really each dome looks like an apple and then an ice cream cone and then a tangerine and a pine apple. It would be a glorious thing to pop into a Christmas stocking."

She sent two successive letters to Susan Mary Patten. The first, dated December 7, said: "One is suddenly plunged into a sort of never never land where everything is both true and false, good and bad, where every preconceived idea is both confirmed and denied, and to try and convey to anyone else the welter of impressions is hopeless. We have been here exactly a week today and it feels as if we had never been anywhere else. All other worlds are shut out and I forget that I have children and a home elsewhere.

"For one thing the endless planes, all white, all flat make one feel that there is nothing but Russia all around one and that there is no use trying to get out. It has a strange horrid fascination however, like looking under the bed for a burglar and secretly hoping he is there. Moscow itself is much prettier than I expected, and right there is a phrase typical of what I said about things being both true and untrue. If you see Moscow from a certain quarter glistening in the sun light all covered in snow with the golden domes of the Kremlin it is quite lovely. If you see it from another street and covered in mudd instead of snow, and you dont come back to delicious warm cosy Spasso House [the U.S. Ambassador's residence] after a freezing walk, but to the indescribable gloom of the National hotel then, you think it is the end of the world.

"If you want to think it is wonderful and the expression of all that is wonderful in a brave new world you look at the faces going by and you see in them the fire and determination of a brave generation. If you are prepared to dislike it, you have even grater scope for your immagination. The tired pale faces the bent heads, the silence, and the indescribable lack of taste. To me that is the most heart breaking side of Russia; the side I least expected too. You simply cant laugh or feel I told you so-ish about that. The horrible blue velvets the unbelievably pathetic efforts at dressing for the Opera the shop windows the *Art nouveau* lighting the nineteen ten summer resort architecture, the cement houses which started off white and in no time at all turned a deep horrible death bed grey, the cookery book showing in garish colours a plate with one brilliant red saussage six canned peas and a peace of spinache drawn from the immagination. I have to keep back tears of sentimentality at every step. And I dont think that all of that can be ascribed to the regime. It is an undeniable disadvantage in life to be born a Russian. People who can think of nothing but how to keep warm for six months of the year inevitably developp a secretive gloomy personality. The turned up collars, the slouchy walk the bent heads, are not only due to politics but mainly to the effort of trying not to break your neck on the ice. On the other hand to my Mediterranean eye, snow and fur hats and big boots always give an impression of festivity and prosperity. Not even a millionaire in Greece has fur boots and high fur hats. The children all look delicious like baby father Xmases skating and sleighing all over the little squares.

"Needless to tell you that our point of view can hardly be called that of the struggling proleteriat. We have caviar at every meal go to the ballet every night and hob nob with Ambassadors even at breakfast. I have done a lot of sightseing and am more muddled up than ever. I keep forgetting how late everything is here. You see a church or an Icon which you swear is eleventh century and it turns out to be eighteenth. Baroque squiggles have been added on to nearly everything, so it is hopeless to try and be learned about things. But as sheer esthetic pleasure it is wonderful. The dark blue domes the gold and red, the greens the flowers and garlands on everything. And of course the gleaming white snow as a back ground for everything. St. Basil is like nothing one has ever seen before. It has Persian turbans and forget-me-nots on it. It has one red and white dome one green and yellow two green and red, and one gold and flowers all over it. It has not one symmetrical inch or any real architectural raison d'etre except sheer exuberance. And quite lovely.

"The picture galleries are marvellous. The Icons are lovely and the Impressionists heaven. And millions of wonderful nineteenth century anecdotic horrors. The Unexpected return of the warrioer, The death of Uncle Igor, The marriage of the pretty virgin to the wicked rich merchant. Etc etc The Napoleonic campain is rampant, with as much blood as any good Russian could wish for. Also wonderful historic ones. Ivan the terrible liquidating the Poles. Ivan the great liquidating the Tartars, Ivan money bags liquidating I dont know whom.

"We also went in the Metro which is really something. Each station ladies and gentlemen as you see is different. You have the Soviet rennaissance with great bronse figures and hands holding flambeau for lamps, you have Soviet Roccoco. Soviet Louis seize Ritz. Soviet Cosy corner etc. Too splendid. You go down two hundred feet in a giant escalator. The smell is indescribable. It is the national smell of Russia and a combination of damp fur humanity cheep cent, lifeboy soap and boiled cabbage.

"We are running very fast to Intourrist and getting tickets and everything and are just holding our thumbs on trip plans. Which means that we wont be back for Christmas, thanks to you really. I feel so terribly guilty about leaving all the work to you and Kitty [Giles, who were looking after the children and Nursey] and do hope you wont be swamped. If by any chance it is difficult to have the children dont hesitate to put them off. I am so torn between wanting to get back and hating the thought of Cy alone in Akmolinsk for Christmas. I must say the trip sounds fabulous but my enthusiasm is dwindling slightly at the thought of 25 below zero in places with only out-door W Cs and not even a candle to keep warm at.

"Today we went to Zagorsk which is a wonderful place with a monastery three churches a bishop's palace all pink and white, and it was so cold that the tears from our eyes froze as they fell. It really hurt. We tried to take pictures and our hands would simply not respond. But it was wonderfully sunny and beautiful the gold and blue domes behind the black delicate branches of the trees and the white snow and blue sky were simply terrific.

"Of course there are things not quite so lovely. The appartements are so so sad it kills one. The hotels are the end of the world. And human relations non existant. We had long talks with two Russians and we never knew when one said for instance that he thought the food in America was 'not very original' if he was being polite or if he had actually adored American food and was afraid to say so or if he had loathed every mouth full and was being kind."

Two days later she told Susan Mary: "After two weeks of prevaricating we have at last been given a month's more [visa] extention. But we still dont know when we leave for Central Asia. You really cant immagine what it is like. Every day something changes. First they say we can go to Alma Ata then they say we cant. Once they say we can fly from Tashkent to Tiflis then they say there is no plane on that route so we must fly back to Moscow and thence to Tiflis. Some days they say we can go to Khiva and some days that Khiva does not exist. Anyway we have given up worrying and the fact of knowing at least that we can stay is in itself the most tremendous news."

To Dodo she confided: "I see now why reading about this place means nothing. All books or articles or photographs remain somehow two-dimensional. Not that one really understands anything when one is here, but things somehow fall into their rightful place and one of the rightful places is an acceptance that one cannot understand about this place.

"To begin with, it is too big, too flat. too white. too cold for anyone to grasp it all at once. And second more than anywhere else in the world, one's impressions depend so much on how and in what mood they find you. And if you have to work for your living and especially as a journalist, you might as well go mad at the start.

"Like Humpty Dumpty says to Alice. Words mean what I want them to mean no more no less. It depends on who is the master. Or like the King says to the messanger. There's nothing like hay when you feel faint. I should have thought said Alice that cold water would be better. I did not say it would be better, says the king, I said there is nothing like it.

"We have done a great deal of sight seeing and I must say there are some beautiful things. We went to the Kremlin yesterday. As it is dark at half past three everything is flood lit and the huge Square with the five churches all glistening and shining in the white snow around is really like a fairy tale. We were taken into the Palaces which is only on special request and saw the fifteenth century rooms and then the sixteenth century ones and one really feels as if one has walked straight into the *décor* of Boris Goudounoff. Not beautiful but grand and Oriental and wicked. One can easily imagine Ivan the terrible killing his own son, mothers blinding their children. The nineteenth century part is so ugly, so really lower middle class, such bad taste that one realises that all ugliness around this place now, can not be entirely ascribbed to the regime. Actually that is the sort of heart breaking side of this place. The patent leather flowers in women's hats, the tragically gay *Art Nouveau* lamps all over the place, the monstrous bright blue plush everywhere; the huge restaurant rooms enough for a thousand people, with six tables occupied. The people themselves I dont think for a moment feel tragic, but they look so very pathetic. One is sort of lead to believe that everything will be huge and organized and made of cement. So that the innumerable pale pink, yellow and pistache coloured buildings, with stucco guarlands and colonaded facades, with half the paint coming off, look sort of like frivolous old maids cought up in a *Kraft durch Freude* parade.

"My greatest surprise was a collective farm. I dont know why but in my mind a collective farm was a separate unit to beguin with. Something with a wall around it, and large low cement buildings and even the cabbages growing in straight rows like Nazi soldiers, and the chikens all organized in cement chiken coops, producing eggs at a certain hour.

"Well immagine a village, like any other Northern village except that the houses are all woodden and croocked in fifty different ways as they sink here and there into the snow. They look utterly riddiculous like a child's drawing. They are painted blue or green or stripped and as the farmers have nothing to do all winter, they spend three or four months carving window frames or eves or pediments, and the houses look exactly like something out of Hanzel and Gretle. The fact that five famillies may live in them, that they get their water at a pump many miles away and dont have even a semblance to a W C seems in itself surprising, un Soviet like. But so much gayer than I expected, at least in looks.

"And there again you have the phenomenon of things being both good and bad at the same time, depending on your mood and where you lay the emphassis. A man came to dinner last night who is an engineer from General motors and he has come to visit factories and things and he made a very wise remark. We asked if he had been impressed by what he saw and he said. Yes very. But it is the same emotion as I would feel if I were listening to a child of twelve playing the violin like a genius — for a child of twelve."

"We have been very lucky to see Ulanova dance twice. She is the best ballerina in the world of the last twenty years and is forty eight now but even so I have never seen anything like it. She wiggles her little toe and it is pure delight. We saw Romeo and Julliet which is Prokovieff music and quite lovely. and also Gisele. She is such a wonderful actress as well as a dancer."

On December 13: "Mama mou glykia. I am amazed at the number of people who come up and talk to one in the street. Dozens of people ask you the time, but that's often an excuse to start a conversation. It breaks my heart not to be able to answer. One old woman came up to me and talked for ages about how horrible everything was and how she had been trying to get out (she was a Volga German she said) for two years and was not allowed and how if you are a foreigner it is so awful because they wont take you into hospitals if you are ill or find you a place to live or anything. I dont know how true this is but it was strange walking down a street with an old woman complaining bitterly to me in German about life here in general. What one gathers however as most certainly true, is that if one does not 'belong' to something here one can really not exist. You have to be a worker or an artist or a something to tag after your name to be able to get a permit for housing for instance.

"We met a man the other day who was saying that he was asked to a party by a Russian girl at her 'house' and it turned out that the house was one fifth of a small room shared with an old woman another young girl a man and an eight year old child. When one of them wants to give a party (which they often do being very gay and party loving) the others all very good naturedly take it in turns to leave for a day. God knows where they wait for the party to finish.

"The lack of living space is having a terrible effect on the young and there is a tremendous wave of juvenile delinquency. The same man who went to the party promised to take me to one of the law courts when we get back from Asia. He has been following them for six months and he says the most sad thing is parent's pleading in defense of their children. You see the young have nowhere to go and a lot of money which they cant spend on anything. Their parents both work all day so they cant keep an eye on them or give them any sort of family life, and the youth clubs and things which they have everywhere are really too driary so they all dissappear in the streets or to restaurants from 11 in the morning and drink too much and when they drink they go crazy. There is a whole group of what they call Stiliagi who are the rich sons of succesful party members and they are the sort of bright young things, the 'vile bodies' of the new era. They hate anything home made, will give their eyes for a foreign neck tie or grammophone record, they gather at each others homes (some of them have as many as three cars and two appartements) they speack English or latin amongst themselves and wont be seen dead with anyone who does not belong to the *parea* [gang]. They are snobs and rebels.

"Extraordinary how human nature seeps through everything sooner or later and really *plus ça change plus c'est la même chose*. There is a lot of worry about this and a lot of talk about education and surveillance of the young but the more you put their two feet in one shoe the more they rebel, and the governement in spite of all its talk is really quite baffled as to what to do. A night club opened some months ago under the terms of the new 'relaxed policy' and in a few days there was such chaos so much jitterbuging so much class distinction between the stiliagi who wore foreign cloths and danced better and sneered at the others and all the young people waited in lines for hours to get in and thought of nothing else, that they had to close it up again. There is a reall starvation for entertainement of any sort. The French films which came two months ago were the most tremendous succes and even the taxi drivers spoke of nothing but 'not missing' the new film."

On December 28 and 29, Marina wrote to Dodo: "I better start at the begining. We got our tickets to go off at three one morning. Not a nice hour. We sat up talking with the Bohlens till then (Cy is on a water wagon which makes sitting up and talking a bit more strenuous for him) but then a car came for us and we took the longest coldest drive out to the airport with a driver whose method of taking a corner was just to jamm on his breakes and skidd around the middle of the avenue sideways like they do in circuses phiou!! Immagine then our sorrow when we got to the airport to be told vaguely that the plane had been postponed for several hours (they did not quite know how many). This is standard procedure in Soviet transport but we did not know it at the time. By the end of the trip if ever we left at the prescribed time and on the prescribed vehicle we were so surprised we could hardly speak.

"Well we drove all the way back and sat huddled in our room for a few hours and then took off again only to find that they still did not quite know when we would leave. We finally took off at ten thirty. The plane was small but quite comfortable but the crew looked most un-scientific in big boots and sort of cosy mufflers and the hostess looked more like a *candilanaftra* [beadle] than a hostess, with a huge sick-coloured shawl over her head and red hands. We flew for hours over the flatest whitest land you ever saw and our first stop was at a place called Uralsk. Flat and white also and as desolate as a tomb. A tremendous wind was blowing and hardly had we made foot step marcks in the snow than they were covered up again and you saw nothing but a huge white sea, and things that looked like waves only white. We had some hot soup of cabbage there and recovered a bit and then took off again for another place called Aktiubinsk.

"From there another three hours and we were practically over Tashkent when the pilot said there was fog so we could not land and we flue another three hours back to a place called Djusali. It was about four in the morning by then and we had been in the plane about seventeen hours. We got out and to our surprise we were offered beds in a really warm room. We had hardly curled up in them however when there was a bang on the door and we were told that the pilot had decided to face the fog anyway. Well what can you say especially when you dont know any Russian to say it in. To cut a long and most tedious journey short we got to Tashkent twenty seven hours after, instead of eleven that it should take. Well we went to our hotel which is really something unique. This tiny place with a really huge hotel, smothered in that very particular smell which is half cheap scent (called Stalin's breath by some of the more irreverent foreigners), half boiled cabbage, a lot of damp furs and age old dust. It leaves one quite breathless. We were taken to our room which was as big as a stadium, had a grand piano in it, several tables innumerable sofas a rubber plant, and everything covered either in thick hidious carpets or crocheted doilies. Not much to wash in and a turkish style W C really rather awful.

"Tashkent is really terribly dissapointing as one's first glimpse of the real East. It is the capital of Uzbekistan and the Soviets have made it into a rather large unutterably driary town. Grey and ugly and terribly dipressing. The only interresting thing is the poeple's faces. Uzbeks Kazaks Khirgiz, slanting eyes, round eyes, I felt that I had stepped into the pages of Batsi's [her father] German Encyclopedia which we used to look at as children, on the chapter about peoples. Do you remember it Dodo? They wear the most extraordinary hats. Huge fur things or tiny embroidered scul caps, and they have marvelous Omar Kayamish beards. But there the Omar Kayamishness stops. No flask of wine, the bread nothing to talk about and wilderness remains wilderness enow.

"However we had a huge breakfast of some rather awful soop floating in sheep's fat and brushed up as we had an appointement to see the Mufti who is the religious head of the Moslems of the Soviet Union. He is ninety six and his eyes must have seen plenty in those years. We went to the Mosque and waited outside for the service to finish and that was rather picturesque. There the men wore long Kaftans and turbans and looked as I had expected them to look. Then the Mufti's son came out to greet us, in long yellow caftan and lovely white turban and beautiful beard and he took us off to his house which was a bit like a persian house with collonade and inside courtyard but instead of roses and jasmin and a veilled princesse we saw laundry hanging across the pale blue courtyard and some women in the unutterably driary cloths of this regime.

"But we were taken into a room where there was a rather wonderful table layed out for us. Fruit plates with pears and pommegranates, and crystalised fruits and almonds. Quite a sight especially as we have not seen fruit since we arrived. We sat down and to our dismay a huge meal was produced (we had just had one remember). As we knew that it is considered very nie-culturni not to eat in a Moslem house we struggled through huge bowls of soup, and a pilaf with everything imaginable in it, while a three fold conversation took place, from Cy in English to the interpreter in Russian to another interpreter who put it into Tourkie or Uzbek for the Mufti's son. Not very interresting and you felt that every answer was well thought out so as not to give anything away. But even so one got the impression that these boys have done a pretty good job of crushing Mohamedanism around Central Asia.

"After the meal we were taken in to see the old Mufti who is very Impressive and we had a tremendous exchange of courtesies. Our honor to be here Our honor to have you here, our double honor to be received etc etc bowing and touching our hearts and heads. All rather marvellous. Then we went on a tour of the city but it is hard to go around with the interpreter because they keep showing one the new playground and the new party headquaters and the new maternity homes rather than the old city. We went at last to the marquet which was rather colourful. People in colosal fur hats really looking as if they had stepped out of Tamerlane's horde. Some veilled women some little children in pretty gaily stripped caftans.

"But the things they sold broke one's heart. Instead of the silks and spices of the orient, one miserable machine made pull over in mauve and yellow. Or one pair of second hand shoes one bycicle chain, a few dried raisins. We bought two little hats for the children but with the dollar at four rubbles everything costs an absolute fortune so we could not get much.

"Mama mou I have just been asked to go skating in the park of Culture and Rest so I must leave this and go on tomorrow. I think I will post this as it is, because the pouch leaves in the morning. Otherwise it will wait till Monday. You will get the second installement next week. Remember we are in Tashkent and about to leave for Bokhara the next day."

"December 29th. Installement 2. Mama mou glykia. I hope you have already received the first part of this letter which I posted a few days ago. I had stopped in Tashkent. Well from there we took a plane to Bokhara which is only three hours away. That is really the end of the world. Much as I tried to tell myself that we were near to the frontiers of China. Much as I repeated to myself that here on the right was the Kyzyl-Kum desert, that on one side was India on the other Afghanistan, that this was really the heart of the world, the silk route from China, the place from where the best carpets in the world came from, it still remained a flat grey muddy desperate place. It used to be the Capital of the Emirs of Bokhara and there still stands an incongruous Victorian summer palace in the outskirts of town all curley queues and turrets and about as out of place as a Quacker spinster at a flammenco party.

"The Emir has always been an exceptionally wicked man and in that sense I must admit that anything that happens to the Uzbeks or the Tadjiks since his removal cannot help but be for the better. He used to have people decapitated at the slightest whim or thrown into the Vermin pit which is a huge hole filled with sheep lice and scorpions and things and leave them there to be slowly eaten to death. He even threw two English men in to it at the end of the ninteenth century. He had three hundred wives but in spite of that he had to have a new thirteen year old girl every other night.

"The town looks like any of the worst Moslem towns in the middle East, flat houses built of uncooked brique and sort of really mudd coloured. The only thing worth seeing is the Medresseh or school for mullahs which has a rather lovely tiled courtyard and the tower of death which is an enormous brique tower from which the Emir threw people off as punishement. It also served as a light house for the caravans of camels coming from China. I suppose I should be more thrilled at even having been in Bokhara but really it was too driary for words. I immagine that it looks better in the summer. Being essentially Asiatic it needs the blazing sun, the deep black shadows, the birds flying overhead and camels on the horizon.

"As it was we saw only wet mudd and it was much too cold for birds or camels, or people for that matter. Luckily something as usual went wrong with our transportation and we were told that we should either take the train that same night to Samarkand or wait three days for the plane. So we took the train which was in itself quite an experience. Again I repeat the only really rather exciting thing is the people and sharing a compartement with someone who looked as if he had walked right out of Genghis Khan's tent was rather terrific.

"We arrived in Samarkand the next morning rather tired as a Russian train rattles and jerks not only back and front but sideways and up and down. There we got a history profesor to take us around and that I must admit was more gratifying. We saw Tamarlane's tomb in a wonderful moske with a turquoise blue dome. The tomb is made out of one single enormous peace of green black jade.

"The prettiest thing of all was a thing called the Shah y Zindah mausoleum. A huge place with little narrow walled streets and on each side little Mausoleums for Tamarlane's family. Ulug Beg his grandson who was wise and peace loving and a great philosopher and astronomer. Some of his favourite wifes, his nanny his teacher and the tomb of a nephew of Mohamed who is said to have saved the city by cutting off his own head and walking with it in his hands towards the enemy thereby driving them away in terror (And no wonder). He is called the Living Saint and will rise again one of these days to make the Uzbeks kings of the earth. I must say I do hope he doesnt do it quite just yet as I would hate to see the Uzbeks in charge of anything.

"One thing I felt so strongly on this trip. The Russians really look like blood brothers compared to the real Asiatics and I would not be surprised if before my life is over the West is not allied to Russia in order to face the on coming Asiatic hordes. We also saw the Moske of Bibi Hanum Tamarlane's favourite wife which is rather lovely. They all used to be completely covered in pale blue and dark blue green and white tiles and little finely carved colonettes. The only tiles now remaining are the Dome of Tamarlane's tomb and in the Shah y Zindah.

"Samarcand is quite driary too and again you see amongst the pleasant one storey houses in pink and blue and green which look quite a bit like Greek island ones, great huge ugly play grounds, an enormous rather pretty but quite unecessary theatre and all kinds of party headquaters, new maternity wards etc. The old and new civilisations do not blend well together architecturally speaking, or sartorially. The few people one sees dressed in their own costume look really exciting. As soon as they wear the driary old Soviet box suit they look like grocers.

"It really is too bad that they gave us our viza in the winter (at least as far as Central Asia goes) because the thing which is so lovely in the summer is the flowers and the view of the fantastic mountains. Immagine mountains like huge walls coming out of the desert straight up, and the valleys around simply covered with scarlet tulips or those pink and white stripped ones, and small brown iris and huge dark blue gentians. I have only been told about them and my heart warms and my fingers itch.

"As far as the rest of Russia goes though the winter is really much better. I cant tell you how wonderful Leningrad is on the frozen river and covered with snow. But Leningrad comes later. We spent one more day in Samarcand and then took a train back to Tashkend. Most of that day was spent waiting. One thing no one can understand unless one has been here, is the amazing inefficiency and the deep sincere lying that goes on. You ask about your tickets and they say first Oh yes you have them. When you go to pick them up, first they stare blanckly. Then they say oh it is impossible as there are no planes from here. Then they say the weather is bad that is why the planes are not flying, forgetting that a minute ago they said there were no planes. Naturally Westerners are inclined to see in all this some sinister meaning but if there is one it is absolutely impossible to decipher it. When the Bohlens wanted to see the Vermin pit they were told it was impossible because the bridge over the river was under repair. The fact that there was no river anywhere in sight did not seem to bother them. It is the crasiest place in all the world really.

"Interviewing people for work is enough to drive a newspaper man out of his mind. You ask about city problems let us say. Oh we have none. How about the murders we read about in the papers. Oh those are not anything really. They are quite exceptional that is why they get into the papers of course. The best argument yet was about a word which one man insisted ment one thing and another that it did not exsist. When a dictionary was produced and the word was in fact not in it, the first one shrugged and said — But my dear fellow what is the use of putting into a dictionary a word which everybody knows. Dictionaries are only for difficult words.

"One simply cant win. Well anyway having spent half the day on the bench outside the hotel we finally did get away and this time on a marvellous plush train all green velvet and wonderfully luxurious and old fashioned. We had hardly settled in when a wonderful lady looking like a huge gipsy came to visit us with a ripe melon under her fat arm as a gift. She told us through the interpreter that she was the vice president of Tadjikistan off to Moscow and the meating of the supreme Soviet. She was rather a wonderful creature and a perfect example that wherever communism goes Eastwards in spite of its messiness it introduces a better standard of living. She said that in her childhood she would have had to go veiled or be rapped by the Emir or slave around a stove for some exacting husband. Now here she was. 'I dress as I like' she said proudly showing off a dress down to the ground in black crepe de chine covered in orange yellow green and scarlet flowers with a V neck around which was a little yellow frill. 'I can go to Moscow and sit in the Supreme Soviet with our great leaders, and I have a simply glorious gay time visiting Red corners, playgrounds, parcks of culture and rest.' It was all too marvellous. Ah me. We finally gently but firmly indicated that we were rather sleepy and putting the mellon in a safe place we curled up and went to sleep.

"If we ever get back to sleeping in beds that dont move or shake or bounce I think we will lie awake all night. Another day in Tashkent not very exciting except that I bought a lovely pair of high soft boots for David and an embroidered hat for Marinette. Things are so expensive it leaves one breathless. Our guide bought a pound of raisins for a New Year's cake and it cost twenty roubbles that is to say five dollars.

"We took the Bohlens and Charlie Thayer [Avis's brother] to a restaurant before the Asian trip and for five people it cost a hundred and twenty dollars. That was where I saw I think the most heartbreaking gesture of all. The waiter serving the water from an old caraffe went around to Cy first as the host, put a drop of water in his glass waited for him to taste it and then went on serving the others. Oh dear. Did I write this to you already? So many little things strike one that I cant remember what I have written and what not. Like the ice cream women. Do you know what you find at every street corner in Moscow with the icy wind blowing your heart out and twenty below zero? Little old women selling ice cream connes and doing the briskest trade you ever saw.

"We got back to Moscow Christmas Eve exhausted and so dirty it was hard to believe. We each sat in the bath for an hour and then had a charming evening with all the Embassy staff and the British coming in and sitting under a huge tree and singing carols. There is no protestant church here and no catholic either and last year the priest was thrown out on some excuse so they hold services in the Embassy. I must say all of them sitting on the floor in the large domed drawing room of the Embassy with the lights only from the Christmas tree candles, and singing Onward Christian soldiers, they looked very much like some modern version of the Christians in the catacombs. Rather moving in an absurd way. Next morning we all had stockings under the tree. How Avis did it I cant immagine. She had both of us and Charlie and another young girl guest all unexpected and yet she found presents for all of us and we had a very sweet Christmas. We telephoned to the children in Chantilly who seemed quite happy but I felt rather weepy without them. I cant write any more because I am sure the letter wont fit in an enveloppe. All about Leningrad in the next letter."

That letter was sent from Moscow on January 2, 1956. It started off: "We are all recovering from a very heavy New Year's Eve and Day and everybody is more or less asleep or slouching on chairs in a very Chekovian fashion. So I decided to pull myself a bit together and write to you. Our new Year's eve was very Russian. First we went to a ballet and then we had a table at the Metropole Hotel where 'le tout Moscow' celebrates. Immagine that it cost forty dollars a person for the dinner without drinks. It was a rather extraordinary sight. Everybody had on their best best and you have never in your life seen anything so appalling. The efforts of the people in the street towards embellishement of their driary cloths are heartbreaking. This was not even that, as there is really no excuse for such bad taste except that they must like it.

"For one thing I simply cannot believe that a gentle God gave the ladies of Moscow such figures. It must be over eating or something. They are ALL short and completely square and you really cant tell which is front and which is back except that the mountainous projections are higher in front than in back. Dresses of crushed velvet mostly or "Atlazi" in the most sick making blues yellows or magentas you have ever seen. White shoes with ankle straps and hair permananted until they look like astrakan furs. However they all looked extreamely happy and within an hour everybody was extreamely tipsy and several people were leaping into the fountain in the middle of the dance flour.

"About four in the morning the nineteen twenty four tango was replaced by folk dancing and mazurkas and polkas which were very gay and lots of people came and danced with us from other tables and we did a lot of fraternising and cementing of Russo American friendship. It was all very gay very ugly very very awful in a fascinating sort of way. When finally we decided to go home there was no transport of any kind. Typical of a place like Moscow which prides itself so much on its Stakanovite efficiency that there were no cabs no busses no metro no nothing. So we walked home through the snow in our Sunday best silk pumps but it was rather fun. Everybody else was doing the same and there was a lot of learching and slipping induced not only by the icy roads but by liquor as well and a lot of hearty greeting from everybody. We walked for more than half an hour and when we got home were quite frosen and our shoes were ruined but we had fun and some of the fumes from russian cigarettes and the worst champagne you ever tasted had dicipated. Having got home at Five we slept most of the day yesterday and then could not go to sleep at night so stayed up again till all hours playing chess and talking, that is why the household has barely assembled itself today.

"But I have not yet told you about Leningrad. The reason we went, apart from wanting to see it, was that Porgy and Bess have come to Russia under the 'better understanding among peoples, through culture and art' theory and the Bohlens were going to the opening night and we went with them. We went off on a train so perfect for Anna Karenina that you expected Vronskie to come out of every compartement. Wonderfully confortable and old fashioned and does about thirty kilometres an hour. The station too was quite unreal and looked like the setting for a film called 'last train to Berlin,' or 'the train will whistle three times,' or something. You excpected to hear 'muffled footsteps running in the snow' all the time and lots of 'Who goes there' and the beautiful blond disguised as a peasant in a mink coat to sneak out onto the platform and shake her head twice in the direction of the hero.

"We got to Leningrad the next morning and it is really a glorious town. A real town, with a plan to it and really heavenly buildings. Most confusing as one feels one recognises a style and somehow it is not quite that. Italians French English and Germans have all worked on it, and somehow managed to produce something that is essentially Russian. I immagine that seen away from Russia all these buildings might appear second rate, but in this setting they are just right. The Roccoco is even more exuberant than in Vienna, the Neo Classic Greekier than ever, the Baroque heavier, but the whole thing because of the flatness of the country, because of the back ground of snowy white, of frozen river and crystalised trees, and especially because of the bright colours of the buildings, becomes a perfectly enchanting thing. Immagine a [Place de la] Concorde in butter yellow, pale pink, pistache green and turquoise. And all the details, the pediments the plaster guarlands the tops of colums, dusted with sparkling white snow so that you dont know quite what is architecture and what nature.

"The winter palace is green with white decorations and all statues and urns and colums and quite delicious. The river is most exciting frozen solid. And things like the Bronze horseman, the Alexander Column, the Admiralty tower are all so thrilling because they remind one either of a poem about them or a play or an opera or something. But the most fabulous thing of all is the Scythian gold in the Hermitage. A real Ali baba cave. We were lucky as they dont show it to everybody. We had special permission, being with the Bohlens. We stood with the guide in front of a huge iron door, left our hand bags which one is not allowed to take in with one, and he knocked three times on the door where upon leaving behind us the eternal smell of cheap scent and cabage and wet fur, leaving the ugly faces, the ill cut suits and half dead faces of the outside world, we stepped into six of the most fabulous rooms I have ever seen.

"The Scyths were, they say, the original inhabitants of the Crimea and the Ukraine and the Greeks had colonies on the Black sea border and came to know and trade with them. Herodotus has long descriptions of them and a story that they were *Androfages* [cannibals] and that one could not really travel in their country because of the masses of tiny white plumes which floated about in the air. Well *androfages* or not they did not eat the Greeks who established a brisque trade with them taking from them wheat and honey and furs, and selling to them luxury goods, such as pottery and silks and especially the Greeks used the gold from the Scythian mines to make jewelery for the Scyths and that is what you see in the museum.

"The Scyths buried their chiefs with everything they had used in life including wives friends servants etc with the result that even after the tombs had been robbed several times, when in the late nineteenth century the tombs were really excavated they found the most fabulous things you have ever seen in your life. I cant possibly describe them to you but there are neclaces and ear rings and crowns of such beauty that they leave one breathless. And swords and ceremonial cups and shields from the work shops of Phidias. One pair of earings, with twelve horses carved on top perfectly exquisite and you can imagine their size. Each horse absolutely perfect and not bigger than a pin head. Incredible.

"After the Scythian gold we went into more rooms with all the later things of the Tzars. Fabergé and gifts from Sultans or Queen Elisabeth and enough jewelled snuff boxes watches, souvenirs to make one drool. A souvenir of the discovery of America on the Santa Maria made out of one emerald. Just fabulous. We came out of there so dizzy that we could hardly look at the pictures of the Hermitage which is too bad as they have the most wonderful collection of Rembrandts in the world as well as everything else.

"That night we went to see Porgy and Bess nervous as cats that our 'Western culture' would not be well received, but we need not have worried. These people are so starved for any sort of outside world manifestation that they would adore Little red ridding hood done by a kindergarden. And I must say that the all negro cast was colourful enough to please anybody. The first night they arrived at the hotel they took over the orchestra and played boogie woogie and jitterbugged and the whole town went wild. The next day the restaurantt was closed and we dont know if it was just chance or wheather the authorities thought there was too much decadance bandied around. But you should have seen the cast. Dressed in the most amazing tweeds and tartan stockings and huge fur hats and smiling and beaming at everybody. It was quite a sight to see ninety negroes floating down the Nevski Prospect with the snow as a back ground and the people following them around by the hundreds."

She sent a final letter to Dodo from Moscow: "We leave tomorrow by train for Kiev and after a day there we go to Prague and Paris and I must say I cant wait to hug the children again. . . .

"We drove out to one of the Cheremetiev palaces called Astankino which is really delicious. All yellow with white columns and the most enchanting interior you ever saw. Count Cheremetiev married one of his serfs and built a little private theatre for her in this place where they spent their time acting and having a wonderful time. The palace has the prettiest chandeliers I have ever seen and the most heavenly colours on the walls. Green and turquoise, or red and pink most unexpected and marvellous. In the last room they have a display of hand cuffs and the chains with which the slaves were beaten or tied up in the snow. Once the Empress Elisabeth was bored in the winter so she decided that it would be fun to make some statues. They picked some of the prittiest slave girls took all their cloths off stood them in various positions in the park and then poured water over them and let them freeze into live statues. And she was one of the nicest by far.

"Today [January 6] is Christmas here so we are going to church tonight. It will be fascinating to see what kind of people still go to church. And tomorrow we go to the Kremlin in the morning where there is a huge Christmas tree about twenty metters high in the great St. George hall where all official receptions are given by the governement. It is really in honour of Charlie and Celestine Bohlen that we were invited. Every year there is a party for all the school children in Moscow and grandfather Frost comes and gives them oranges and presents and things."

We entrained for Kiev and then, after a fairly short stay, went on to Prague and eventually Paris. From that delicious capital she wrote her *Mama mou glykia* on January 18:

"Oh the sweetness of the Western world. Oh the beauty of Paris, the joy of seing warm brown earth again let alone the orgy of parental love we have indulged in, in the last few days.

"We got back Saturday after a whole week of rumbling along in a Soviet train. The second thing I did after the kissing and hugging, was of course to go to have my hair cut and washed and my nails made to look capitalistic again and while at the hairdresser I heard two girls talking. *Dis-donc Colette, tu trouve que tangerine serait une jolie couleur pour mes cheuveux? C'est plus nouveau que noisette n'est pas?* It may leed to destruction and revolution this kind of talk, but oh what joy it was to my ears after seven weeks of *Narodni Delegatsia Respubliki* and the great struggle for peace and the common man.

"Russia may or may not be the country of the common man but it most certainly is that of the common woman. I can't tell you what a joy it is to see females with waistes and ankles again. . . .

"And at some point some Soviet factory must have made a mistake and produced seven thousand kilometres of prune coloured crushed velvet, because that is all you ever see. The women, the curtains the seats in the opera, the bed covers in hotels everything, everywhere. So that even Prague seemed beautiful in comparison and little had I ever expected to look upon the Cheks as blood brothers, but I can assure you that driary though they are they still look good after Kiev.

"We took nearly two days to get to Kiev after we left Moscow and then it was a pretty desolate place. In summer it may be better with the Dnieper flowing by and one or two lovely churches and oh joy a few hills here and there which after the flatness of Moscovy seem like the Parnassus, but in winter it is muddy and nasty. We spent a day and a half there and visited the churches and some catacombs filled with the bodies of eleventh century monks who had burried themselves deliberately for self flagelation I suppose and walled themselves in these caves until they died of starvation and other things I immagine.

"The caves must have some kind of alcaloid earth as the bodies did not melt and it was considered a great miracle. You go down led by a monk with a cape who looks as if he had walked straight out of Maxim Gorki's *Bas Fonds* and all over the place you see the coffins with here and there a hand or withered foot stiking out. Very gruesom and thrilling and awful. We also visited a collective farm which looks like any other kind of farm only bigger and flatter and certainly colder. But the peasant farmers were very friendly and the little houses sweet painted many colours and a bit like the houses of the three little pigs. What was lovely was the drive there through thick beautiful pure little Red Ridding Hood forrest with huge straight fur trees and all sparckling white. . . .

"Mama mou glykia good night now. All my most enormous love and a million Western kisses. Long live capitalism, privileges, class distinction, erudition and art for art's sake. Bits of fluff of the world Unite. You have nothing but your Jacques Faths and your nylons to lose."

Her final summation went to my uncle on January 24:

"Sweet Uncle Arthur. I cant begin to describe our trip as it would take an abler pen than mine, and sixteen pages to do it in. The men en masse all look like commarade Khrushchev. I do think that is pushing loyalty a bit too far, even for a communist country.

"I must say that Paris seems more beautiful to me now than it ever did before and I am ashamed to tell you that frivolity, decadence, and mushrooms smothered in cream and white wine, may lead us to ultimate destruction but in the mean time they feel mighty sweet, and desirable to me after nothing but 'social realisme' and the 'Struggle for peace' for seven weeks."

V

April 1956 - September 1957

Paris was a big change from Soviet dreariness. On April 4, 1956, in a letter to her old friend Eleni Panayatopoulo, Marina wrote: "I went to a big ball for the Queen of England and felt like a traitor [because of Cyprus]. But she is charming I had to admit. And the ball was beautiful. All the women had tiaras on and the most spectacular dresses and such jewels as I had never seen. And everybody had bran new gloves on with the little thread still hanging down as no one in France ever wears long white gloves and all the ladies had just bought them that afternoon. Rather funny."

After a trip to London to buy clothes for the children, who were going to English boarding schools that September, Marina wrote Uncle Arthur (June 10): "I was amazed at the exuberance of London society were'nt you? I must say the commonly accepted ideas about people are nonsense. How did the legend ever arise that the British are strong silent reserved people. I found that they make Paris look like the Y M C A. I have never in my life seen sex life so rampant as in London. And how they all talk about it. At any coctail party at any dinner, I found people pouring out their love life to me at the drop of a salted almond. Theirs and everybody else's. On and on until I felt that I had come from some quiet provincial town where nothing ever happens.

"It was rather fun, and I got back to Paris fealing that this was indeed a quiet place especially as spirits are rather low what with Algeria [the war there] the cost of living and the steady rain which has been pestering us for the last six days. It did not rain one drop for months and now just as all the open air festivities which are such an integral part of Paris life, are starting, it is cold and wet as a soup. The races were ruined, all the garden parties all the charity balls, and even dry cleaners are complaining that they are ruined because nobody is having their summer cloths freshened up for the holidays."

I had to go to the United States that summer for the political conventions. Marina decided to take the children and Nursey to Mallorca for a holiday before depositing them at boarding school and coming on to join me. She wrote me from Puerto Pollensa, at the beginning of July:

"My dearest sweetest Prune. It really broke my heart to watch you standing all alone behind that barrier last night. Somehow when you go and we stay, it does not seem as sad. But I do so hate the thought of you in that house all alone. It is going to be a long and hard summer for you, but somehow we must manage so that this never happens again."

With her usual infinite curiosity, Marina drove off to Palma with Avi von Ripper our old friend who lived in Mallorca to see a bullfight. On July 26 she wrote:

"I must say it was terrific. Out of six bulls the four were fought perfectly from begining to end. All three matadors got both ears and the tail. It was spectacular to a degree and there is something fabulous about that proud throwing back of the head, that shout of Hee Hee Toro that chest offered to death in front of a thousand people. Also it was the first time I have ever seen a nice public. You know how I loath it when they whistle and shout and boo. Well this time the first boy Littri fought his first bull very badly and he was hissed and booed and I was under the seat with my tummy in a tight knot weeping for him. The *Bruta figura par excellence* and in the most heart-breaking way of all.

"Well then the second boy came out Antoniete and he did all the Cape stuff absolutely beautifully but messed up his kill terribly. He was so mad at himself that after it was over he put his head on his arm and wept. Then the third one Chicuelo a tiny little man in pale green and silver came out and was marvelous. Such complete control of both his own body and the bull. His kill was perfect straight high and right in between those deadly horns. The public went wild and he got both ears and the tail.

"Well this got the *filotimo* [pride] of the other two and in the second part of the fight they vied with each other as to who would be braver. They offered their backs to the bulls they met them on their knees they did Veronicas and whatever the other passes are called one after the other so much so that even the public was yelling Ahi Ole Chico Basta basta. It was incredible. Chicuelo killed his second bull first try. The other two in the second try but they had been so wonderful before that the people forgave them and hats bags flowers cigars and handkerchiefs came flying into the ring. It was quite a sight.

"I must say we did cause a sensation arriving at the bull fight. The car is fire engine red and low and smooth and Avi was wearing an orange dress a pink and orange cloack and a silver tinsel hat like something off a Xmas tree and the usual ration of huge jewels. We flew to a standstill with a screach of brakes and every head turned in our direction and there was whisteling and exclamations of *Que guapa ahi Madre que guapa.* Rather fun."

I had traveled to America by ship and had written Marina that our liner approached only a couple of hours after the sinking of the Italian ship *Andrea Doria*, which was bearing our close friends "Cian" and Jane Cianfarra and their two daughters. By one of those weird accidents, Cian and one of his daughters were killed — the only casualties of the entire disaster, I believe. Marina, who had already learned of the awful affair, wrote me on August 1:

"I can hardly think of anything but the Cianfarra tragedy. I read it in the Times which arrived quite late and my first reaction was pity that Jane was not killed too. It simply does not bare thinking of. What will she do? Have you seen her. Is she badly hurt? I will try and write but what ever can one say? It is too too ghastly. God help us. It might easily have been the ship you were on. I keep thinking one should never separate and yet here was this sweet family all together and three of them are gone. [One daughter was saved later.]

"We are still at the Rippers and today was a glorious day. Bright and gold. There is a kind of *fiesta* in the village so all the servants are out and we did the cooking for some guests at lunch and it was all very peaceful and nice.

"Yesterday evening we went on board the Creole [the huge yacht of Stavros Niarchos] for dinner. She had arrived the night before. Stavro was very friendly and I must say she is a glorious boat. I did not see the Cézannes but Aliki and John Russell were on the boat and I went to Aliki's cabin which is like the Ritz. Both send enormous love. John had fallen off his horse on his head, playing polo and had had concussion rather badly and Teheran is no place to be ill so he had been given a bit of extra leave and they had joined Stavro in Portugal. There was Mrs. Luce on the boat too but she had a soar throat and had supper in her cabin. A few English Dukes and marqueses finished the party. Ripper got drunk which was embarrassing for me as I had brought them and Stavro was rude to Avi telling her she was too tall to make love to which was embarrassing to me also so on the whole except for the pleasure of seeing Aliki, it was not a very successful evening. Except snobishly speaking we are supposed to have scored one over the rest of the group. Really!! I am gladder and gladder that we don't live here."

On August 5 she wrote: "You sound cheery except of course for the Cianfarra news. How incredible the saving of little Linda sounds. I will certainly write to Jane. It seems easier somehow now that I know that she has at least one child alive. When I read that both the children and Cian were dead there simply did not seem anything possible to write.

"But more cheery things from me too. Yesterday great excitement as the Woodwards gave a South sea island ball. I got myself a little grass skirt in the village and Ripper went as a beachcomber comme Gauguin and Avi marvellous as a nun with a slit in her skirt and pink sequin pants underneath. The party was spectacular. The whole garden was lit with torches and little lamps and there was a sort of tea house affair of raffia and bambou and the tables were spread with water melons and bananas and sea shells and we had Hawaian (sort of) food served from huge shells and there was an orchestra and I had a delicious time.

"I danced all night and you know how I love dancing. There were lots of most attractive people and all the guests had made an effort to dress up and it was not the awful fancy stuff where people spend fortunes on elaborate costumes but everybody had found some old thing to wrap around themselves and lots of flowers and there were gardinias everywhere. The harder drinking folks objected to the fact that there was only a sort of sweet rhum drink with gardinias floating in it (anathema to any drinker I should think) but naturally as it was so icky I loved it and actually had two boals full. We stayed till four."

In early August 1956, I received a cable in New York advising me from Peking that the Chinese government had issued me a visa which I could pick up in Hong Kong. I had been steadily applying for the permit in every Communist capital I visited. Naturally I was delighted, and wrote as much to Marina, who replied on August 13, still from Mallorca: "Your China letter arrived today. Really what next. But how exciting. I envy you and hope you manage it."

She and the children had by then moved to Vane and June Ivanović's at Formentor and loved it. "I have been out speerfishing twice. We go at 5.30 A.M. It is fascinating. Most women either get sea sick or cold or scared so I am considered the cat's whiskers and am being taken down with bottles next."

August 19: "Sweetest Pir: I took to the bottle this morning. That is I went down with the aqua lung and absolutely loved it. It has all been so perfect. The fishing, the [water] skiing, the real swimming and sporting life, and also the social side which as you know I rather enjoy.

"If you go to China and don't get your holiday, cant you take it in the winter and we can go somewhere and really rest. Christmas perhaps with the children who have a whole month."

When she got back to Paris at the end of the month, Marina received my letter explaining that after all I hadn't gone to China. Uncle Arthur had given Foster Dulles his word that none of our people would go there without the Secretary's personal authorization.

So, sadly, in the end I turned around and went back to Europe. The affront to the Chinese was such, as Peking viewed it, that I was not given another visa for seventeen years. Chou En-lai personally implied to me in 1973 that this refusal had been the reason.

I nursed my Chinese sorrows in northern Canada, where I spent a brief fishing and hunting holiday in solitude. Marina wrote me:

"Sweetest Cyrus L. Boon. I do hope you are having a glorious time in the company of fish and moose and wilderness. I dont know when you will get this but it will be waiting for you as well as the others when you come back to the world of posts. . . . I am terribly excited about the Indian trip." The children had both gone off to English boarding schools. When she went to deposit them, she observed: "I remember them in pink shorts and suddenly see them in grey flannels and cant get over it. London is seathing with mothers and school children in greys and different coloured caps. The station was one mass of mothers and boys and over night bags and strained porters."

Right after that Marina joined me in New York. On October 9 she wrote Kitty Solomos (in French): "I must say New York in October is superb. Sunshine and red, gold and yellow leaves on the trees. And stores that make you dream. You have to go down Fifth Avenue with your eyes blindfolded so as not to end up in a debtor's prison. One loses one's head."

On October 13 she told Nursey: "The country is unbelievably beautiful. Clear crisp golden weather and a Greeky Greek sky. Next week we go off in the car to visit lots of small towns and see what people think."

Twelve days later she added, as the world began to crumble (first Poland on the eve of revolution, soon to be followed by the 1956 Hungarian uprising and the Anglo-French-Israeli Suez invasion): "Cy well but madly busy. Is'nt the news fabulous. Cy has been writing brilliant stuff about Poland.

"We went to a huge political party night before last with every democrat in New York and it was fascinating but a bit depressing as they all looked like thugs to me. Mr. [Adlai] Stevenson my candidate is not too good. He looks awful on T.V. Far appeared on television too yesterday morning at eight. Who can look good on anything at eight.

"PS Guess what I have just done. Had tea with the President and Mrs. Ike. As I was with a friend in the bar [of the Hotel St. Regis] they paged me on the phone and it was the Commodore Hotel saying that Mrs. Ike wanted to see me and could I come some time. I dashed into a cab and passing through a dozen secret policemen I was taken to their room where we chatted for nearly an hour. I must say it was nice of her to think of it when she must have a billion other people to see. I felt a bit of a traitor being a democrat myself but I must admit that Ike is irresistible."

We took an automobile trip through Pennsylvania, West Virginia, Kentucky, Tennessee, Georgia, South Carolina, North Carolina, Virginia, Maryland, and so on, which coincided with a tragic series of events in the distant outer world: the windup of the Polish rising, with Gomulka moving in; the bloody, double-crossing Soviet invasion of insurgent Hungary; and the Suez disaster. To listen to this sadness on the dashboard radio of a car taking a pair of explorers through the hinterland of the United States was incongruous.

Marina was amazed at what she saw. First we traversed the Amish country of the Pennsylvania "Dutch." Marina was startled by their bleak mode of dress and overwhelmed by their copious cuisine. She could never master their name properly and for the rest of her life called them the "Shimmies."

She was delighted with Kentucky. In Paris, seat of Bourbon County, I had my forty-fourth birthday in a grimy little hotel. Marina gave me a precious set of silver goblets designed to serve well-frosted mint juleps, something she had saved for secretly and purchased in New York. I wanted to put them to use at dinner that night, the only fete I would ever celebrate in the heart of the bourbon area. However, it was a Sunday. The hotel manager explained there was a blue law and no alcohol was allowed. At last he murmured furtively, "If you go to such-and-such restaurant and tell them it was my suggestion, I'm sure they'll fill your coffee mug and let you drink a couple of slugs. But don't take those silver things along." Marina didn't know whether to be delighted or ashamed: it was a Greek restaurant.

On November 5 she wrote Kitty Solomos (in French): "We have just finished an extraordinary trip throughout the American South. It was as new for me and as different as even Russia. An immense country and so flat for the most part that one felt as if one were on a part of the earth that was falling away and the road seemed so endless that I felt sooner or later we would find ourselves in empty space. A little like Christopher Columbus must have felt on his ocean. Serious people, profoundly religious, who consider even dancing a sin. No alcohol, no cigarettes, and church twice a day. Everywhere along the way placards a little like those which say Drink Coca Cola saying Christ Is Coming, are you ready to receive Him. Jesus is looking at you. God is on His way; prepare your house for Him. Very strange and nutty in a rather moving way. One must admit that Christ has chosen his moment badly if he really intends to come now. My God, what a world. Friends against friends. Allies enraged. Deaths everywhere and the least possible illusions on the morality of the Western world. I have never been so depressed from the viewpoint of humanity."

When we got back to Paris, she wrote Nursey who had returned to live in England (December 9): "House like a tomb. No children, no you. I called them on the phone and they both sounded like Selwyn Lloyd [London's foreign minister] to me. How British can one get in so short a time. Kitty who was in the house and a great blessing in those first empty hours of return was listening in and making faces and groaning 'Get them out of there fast. Let them remain extrovert Mediterraneans and not shy reserved Englishmen!' I think that a few days in their own home will unjell them again but I must admit it gave me quite a shock to be told How do you do mother."

The very next day she confided to my mother: "The shops seem sort of shoddy after New York and prices sky high. People gloomy and acrimonious blaming everybody and anybody except themselves. Fierce indignation about America having let Hungary down and Suez hardly mentioned." She added in a note to Alexis: "Here I am an old woman in a wet season and as cross and overtired and overworked as can be. Our great vulgar car is standing at the door a sarcastic imobile symbol of man's stupidity. Most people the government included are preoccupied with finding black marquet gas coal mazout [fuel oil], hoarding soap and salt or changing their money into something else. The blame for everything is put entirely on everybody and anybody else."

In this blue mood, Marina prepared a Christmas dinner for no less than twenty people and arranged for the four of us to go off skiing in Les Contamines, then a small, remote, modest village, now a snappy resort near France's border with Switzerland. Amidst these arrangements, she wrote my mother:

"I heard such a sad tale today. It made me shudder to think that I complain because there are too many people whom I love and am loved by, too many invitations, too many calls etc.

"Well I had lunch with the Polish ambassador who asked to see me. His wife just died. She had been a very sweet rather colourless little thing but very nice so once or twice I had gone to see her for tea and then when she was ill I took her some flowers once and visited her in the hospital once. As you see the minimum possible of human courtesy and niceness if one can call it that. Well apparently she died two months ago and she died with my name on her lips saying I was her only friend here the only person who had been gratuitously nice to her. My god it makes one die this kind of thing. To think how often out of laziness or selfishness one does not do even such small favours. Really the unfairness of life leaves one breathless even if one is on the sunny side of it one's self. Think what sheltered lives we all live and how we know nothing about the unloved uncared for unspoilled people of the world. Ah me."

When the children returned to school, I took Marina off on her long dreamed of trip to India, which she fancied filled with fairyland rajahs and ranees, colourful silks, and great troves of glittering diamonds, emeralds, and rubies. To make it even better, we had a brief stop in Athens.

She wrote Susan Mary Patten from Karachi on February 1, 1957:

"Our departure from Paris went off better than usual and those Bourboulis [imps] whose only work is to disrupt conjugal harmony, were quiet. Cy's shirts for once were not at the laundry his only pair of blue socks had not disappeared his cuff links were in their box and the zipper on his suit case was not out of order. All surprising and agreeable and we left full of hopes for the future. Our week in Athens as always was perfect. How is it that that place never never lets me down. The same large group of old friends to meet us and see us off, the same wordless understanding with my mother and grandmother the same smells the same tastes.

"Even the sun which had been doing queer things of late, came out for me and for a week it was like spring with almond blossoms everywhere. I went up to the top of Hymetus with an old friend and there too everything was just right. I found anemones and crocuses (the very first ones of the year I think) and just as the sun was going down and everything was pink and dark dark mauve a shepard started playing the flute, and a few goats came tumbling down the hill their bells filling the air with the only sound possible in a moment like that. Just right just right everything is always just right for me there. But what a hopeless rush. I never went to bed at all and even had breakfast with friends or relatives and still did not see half the people I should have. We left Athens Wednesday afternoon and after a very long flight got to Karachi yesterday noon and today I have been in bed all day with a bad cold. A rare luxury to be able to stay in bed.

"We are staying at the Prime Minister's guest house which is very pleasant I must say. Cy is out seeing and talking to people and I am watching a party going on downstairs in the garden under a huge marquee with lots of marvellous white clad servants with great turbans. A military band is playing 'They tell me that falling in love is wonderful' and makes it sound like the battle hymn of the Republic. It is most Kipling-esque the whole thing except that the guests instead of being rather glamorous Bengal lancers or Brigadier generals are State department officials just off the plane and their searsuccer suits *look* as if they had been slept in which indeed they have."

On February 5 she wrote *Mama mou glykia* from the Governor's House in Lahore, a huge viceregal palace where we were staying: "I feel like Lady Mountbatten at least. We arrived here last evening after a pleasant three hour flight from Karachi and were met at the airport by the biggest car and most elegant chauffeur with a turban a foot high and sparckling white and were whiscked off to government house as the governor's guests. The palace is a dream. Half Arabian nights half comfortable English country house. Our room has pointed arched doors and little pointed windows high up in the cealing and one feels like Sheherezade. There was dark pink peach blossom in every vase as well as a huge fire in the fireplace and a table ladden with fruit and drink of every sort from whiskey to papaya juice. Three servants in red and gold standing motionless at the door. That is a bit disconserting especially as I have a habit of going around with no clothes on and they come in and out on silent feet and never knock so you never know where they are.

"The palace is in a large garden and lawn and at one end there is a huge clump of trees decorated at night with little lights and on top of the highest tree a half moon in tiny lights. The real moon was only a bit higher in the sky and it was very gay to have two moons all to one's self. In the evening there was a huge dinner party and everyone there was so exactly like themselves that it was hard to believe I was not making it all up.

"The Governor small clever fat and with penetrating black eyes. The British Minister for Commonwealth Nations, straight out of P G Woodhouse. Lots of fat colonel Blimps and their frumpy wives in evening dresses from 1919 and long earings and pointed satin shoes like gondolas.

And some simply lovely looking Pakistani ladies, in yellow or gold saris. And young Pakistani officers in red trousers and black coats looking as if they had stepped out of the 'Bengal Lancers.'

"You would adore the house. Very big but cosy. Huge white columns in front and a semi circular front porch. The inside is huge cool and white with the pointed Asiatic Arch everywhere and mahogany doors and stair cases and wonderful polished brass doorhandles. The cealings at least ten metres high. And bright yellow sun streaming in from everywhere.

"Interrupted to go sight seeing. What a town. Ploncked right in the middle of what to me seems wilderness and desert a green Mogul town full of huge mango trees and big red sand stone buildings which I am sure are responsible for the Victorian craze for red houses. We went to the biggest Mosk in the world whose name I cant pronounce which can hold over a hundred thousand people and is pink stone and white marble. Then to the fortress which is like stepping right into the Arabian nights. Pools with water lilies formal Mongol gardens huge trees, cypruses cut into various shapes and buildings covered with mosaics or fresques or inlaid with semi precious stones. Too wonderful for words and an amazing sense of space and biggness but with the right proportions.

"From there we went to the Shalimar gardens which the name alone makes one feel dreamy. Unfortunately it is too early for flowers but the trees and bushes and pools and high walls around them and the fountains are enough. Then to a place called Jahan Khan's tomb cool and quiet and all marble inlaid with precious stones (most of them have been stolen through the ages but there are a few left still). The tomb is all decorated with cyclamens and anemones made out of amethists tourmaline cornelian and other stones and coloured marbles. This is early seventeenth century and much more delicate and simple than the later things. Later on the Sikhs start using glass and mirrors for inlays and it becomes gaudy and vulgar although rather fun.

"Exhausted and dusty, although it is not hot yet (I wore both my sweaters but no coat) we dashed back just in time for lunch with the minister of finance. They are really attractive people the Pathans. Wonderful looking tall dark blue eyed with gentle voices and not the nasty sing song Oxford accent of the Indians. Both the minister and his wife absolutely charming although they nearly killed us with too much food. You think you have finished after soup and roast chicken and then to your horror a new dish appears rice curry, meat vegetables and all of it spiced so it takes half your head off. However we managed that and now we have just come back to meet another official who is taking us to the Bazaar. Cy has collapsed and I think will skip the bazaar especially as we found a message that the governor hopes to have tea with us, a Maharajah wants us for drinks and some other minister for dinner at seven thirty.

"Thank god we dont have any appointments in Peshawar. If this goes on we will be dead before we ever reach Afghanistan. They are the most hospitable people in the world. In Karachi I was given a glorious peace of gold cloth by a Minister whom I sat next to at lunch once. Well mama mou our friend has arrived so I am off to the Bazaar with strickt injunctions from Cy not to go crazy and spend all our money on the first thing I see. So good by for the moment. More travel-talk soon. I hope I dont sound too much like the National Geographic."

She added in a note to the children: "It is a very old house and our room has pointed arcades and tiny arched windows high up in the cealing like the windows in a fairy tale. We expect a pigeon or a Princess to pear through at any moment. We have a huge fireplace which burns all night and in the morning the sun comes pouring in like gold. We look upon an enormous lawn and gardens full of flowers and trees and birds and at night the trees are guarlanded with little coloured lights and at the top of the tallest tree a half moon in little lights also. Last night the governor gave a large dinner party at which we met the Wali of Swat's son and most beautiful wife. She is eighteen and has a child of two already. She was wearing a lovely sari and yellow trousers.

"I forgot to tell you that in Karachi most people move about in rickshaws instead of Taxis which are like tiny carriages painted all the colours of the rainbow and decorated with flowers birds etc. They used to be drawn by horses but now they use bycicles. Also all the heavy things are drawn in wagons by camels or donkeys. The donkeys look so tiny and sweet next to the camels who are enormous."

Marina wrote my mother on February 13 from Kabul, after we had first visited Peshawar and the principality of Swat: "We have just taken the most amaizing trip by car from Peshawar in Pakistan over the Khyber pass into Afghanistan. A friend of Cy's in the Embassy here most kindly drove down to fetch us and brought us back. The distance in miles is only about a hundred and eighty but in hours it can take anything from eight hours to three days. There is practically no road in parts after you cross the frontier. The Khyber pass itself is more dramatic by association than by looks. Not very high and the mountains around mostly of this untidy brownish sandstone. But on each side these strange mudd villages with high walls around them and turrets, looking for all the world like medieval feudal domains, only made of mudd. The landscape is such that you wonder what kind of human beings can live in such surroundings.

"The tribes live on their cattle but what the cattle live on one cant immagine. The nessecities of these people are really down to the lowest possible minimum. A mudd roof and four walls to keep out as far as possible the snow or the scorching sun and some bread and water and a few skins to sleep on. No furniture. When they are rich in the spring after selling their skins and reaping their little wheat or luxury of luxuries a little rice, they come to the cities and buy guns, and jewels for their wives and sit in the 'story tellers bazaar' and have a wonderful time.

"Beyond the Khyber pass you get into really lunar landscape. We drove for two hours over sandy desert. A completely round valley ringed on all sides by fabulous mountains (the Hindu Kush in the far back ground) with nothing nothing in it but stones. After the valley you come to Jelalabad which is the first bigish town in Afghanistan with a Bazaar and orange groves. Rather pleasant and after so much dust and mudd your eyes feast on a little patch of green here and there.

"Needless to tell you that practically as soon as we left the Khyber pass the other car which was travelling with us (another man from the Embassy) burned out its choke and by miracle the Pathan chauffeur managed to tie bits and peaces together and we started off again but at thirty miles maximum speed. We had to drive behind him in case he broke down again and the dust we swallowed is indescribable. Well then we started getting into the mountains and there the road is just an illusion. It follows the river all along and the landscape here is tremendous. But in parts of it the army was blasting and we had to wait for ages for them to clear a passage for us to go through. On one side sheer rock dangling by nothing. On the other a sheer drop into the river. I must tell you I kept my eyes shut quite a bit of the time.

"Well we finally got through that. The soldiers looked like something out of an anthropological dictionary. Mongols with slit eyes Persians out of

Omar Kayam, and faces straight from the old testament. But the uniform is modeled on the Chinese army and it gave one the creeps slightly. Well then we came to the most terrific gorge I have ever been through. A narrow winding path cut right into the mountain with a thousand feet of precipice on one side and a thousand of rock above. And the sound and furry of the river dashing itself against the rocks. Simply beautiful and frightening and utterly dramatic in the pale light of a moon that had just appeared behind the clouds. We drove for several miles up and up and up and immagine our amazement when at the top of the mountain six thousand feet high we came out in a perfect flat plateau again ringed by a new set of hills and completely covered in snow. A river flowing in the middle and a few caravanserais ghost-like in the moon light. Here and there some camels and around a fire a ring of bearded turbaned bedwins. Too wonderful for words."

She told the children about Swat: "We went to Swat for two days before Afghanistan and I must say it is a lovely place, especially after the rest of Pakistan which is so frightfully flat and camel coloured. We drove over the Malakand pass which is where Mr. Churchill fought the Pathans sixty odd years ago. The pass is not very high but even an ant hill feels high here. It is brown mountain not grey or blue like in Greece. Rather wild and unkind looking. And after some time you pass into the valley of Swat which seems all the more beautiful as it is so unexpected. A pure small round valley with rivers everywhere green and blue, and with the mountains coming right down into the very town, covered with snow like powdered sugar. Green fields of corn and rice, sugar cane everywhere and even now in February some narcissus and oleanders. Later in about three weeks it is one mass of peach blossom anemonies and every immaginable other flower. Here and there on the hills we saw ruins of Bhudist Temples and tombs but they are not very exciting.

"The most exciting are the people. They all look as if they had walked right out of the old testament. They all look like Christ or St. John. They walk so quietly and so beautifully behind their donkeys or camels or water buffalo. As for the women they all look like Rebecca at the well. Or like a ballet. One hardly ever sees one alone. They go about six or seven in a row with their large coloured trousers and veils flowing in the wind carrying the largest possible jugs on their heads and every movement looks as if it had been taught to them by Madam Krilova [Marinette's ballet teacher]. They are the most beautiful people I have ever seen anywhere with large soft black eyes and perfect lips and noses.

"But oh my darlings what dirt. It seems strange in such glorious surroundings with little green streams and blue hills and flowers and gold sun, that people should care so little. For it is not dirt such as not washing (which certain members of my family sometimes indulge in too) it is dirt such as you cant imagine. It is little children playing boat in the gutter with *balou* [excrement] floating all over the place or a dead donkey lying beside them. It is the village women going to infinite trouble to scrubb and wash the family cloths in the sewer, and then when they are sparklingly awful, hang them to dry on a patch of deep grey glucky mudd. It is washing their faces in the same water that they previously tinkled in. It really breaks your heart.

"We saw mountains of lovely looking fruit. Oranges and gouavas and papayas and Far would not let me eat any of it. No wonder when you think what it has been watered in. However we stayed at a most enchanting hotel all porches and columns and with very good food, so much curry that I don't think my mouth will ever stop burning again. Also buffalo butter and ghee which is boiled buffalo fat not too bad. We went for a lovely walk in the Bazaar and bought some honey and new Swat hats for Far and David. Then we drove to the hills and the snow. The Wali has a summer palace up in the hills which looks as if it had been designed by Steinberg for the New Yorker. You know the one I mean all squigles and things. There was snow everywhere but glorious sun shine too. All over the hills were tiny mudd houses where the peasants live. We saw the Wali who was very nice and gave me a gold embroidered hand bag. One thing is sure they are the most generous people I have ever seen. They consider it a deep insult if you refuse anything. and they would give you the shirt off their backs.

"Far has a very tough time refusing things to eat like a whole chicken fried in ghee and covered in red pepper which is all he needs for his gout. But there must be something about this food. One eats and eats and eats and one can still eat more. I am hungry all the time. The Wali to my great dissapointment wore grey flannel trousers and a tweed jacket. He did have a fur hat but that is not much. We slept with every blancket we could get hold of in the hotel and a great fire in the fireplace and we still were so cold that we made a gentlemen's agreement with Far that we did not have to wash anything except face and hands. I must say I am rather looking forward to India and warmth again."

Once in Kabul, we stayed with Armin and Alice Meyer, counsellor of our Embassy and warm, true friends. Marina had never been in Afghanistan, and the mere experience excited her although she didn't feel well, having caught a bad cold in Peshawar and more or less moved from cold bedroom to cold bedroom. She wrote a mass letter with copies to all close relations on February 15 (1957):

"My sweetest darling relatives. I am sick. I wrote you a glorious long letter in triplicate and had put the carbon paper in up side down so I have to start all over again. I don't mind except that there is always so little time. Not that there is so much to do here in Kabul. The town is as big as Maroussi let us say with one storey houses all behind tall white washed walls. Even the palace is really quite small. The roads are mudd except for a few paved by the Russians last year. The mudd which is just at its best now that the snow is starting to melt, is the most splendid you have ever seen. The gouey grey clinging type.

"There is a bazaar but not very exciting. The little fruit shops are sweet and full of pomegranates and birds (in cages) which is very pretty. But what makes one forget the dreariness of the town is the place where it is built. On a high flat plateau with a ring of perfect mountains all around it which come right down into the town. They are even now covered with snow and sparckle in the sun shine. Little streams trickle down them and they tell me that in a month they will be covered with wild tulips. The sky seems so close at night that you feel you can put up your hand and pick a few stars. As for the moon light it is clearer even than in Greece. But oh how cold when the sun goes down.

"Actually we are staying with these American friends of Cy's and we were most pleasantly surprised at the house which is nicely heated by large stoves in the walls like in Russia. When you are indoors you might as well be in Athens or Lyon or Prague. Which is surprising as from the outside you expect anything from sleeping on the floor on animal skins, to gold beds with silk rugs on them. The ladies here are never allowed out unless they are covered from top to toe in what they call a girga which is a sort of tent which hangs from their little scull caps. Immagine my astonishement yesterday when in the street three little hooded figures where walking in front of us and suddenly they stoped to get into a little horse carriage (the taxis of Kabul) and I saw under their girga three little pairs of blue jeans and moccasins. In their houses apparently they can wear what they like. But they never go out to a party never leave their houses and never see anyone except the family.

"The men in the streets look rather different than in Pakistan. They are Uzbeks or Tagiks like we saw last year in Samarcand and they look more like Genghis Khan's people. Actually Ghengis Khan came through here seven hundred years ago and still today when things dont work they are blamed on him. He really went to work and destroyed everything. But so did nearly everybody else. Alexander came here and Mohamed and the British for years and now the Russians are trying their best.

"The drive from Peshawar to here was the most exciting thing we have seen as yet. We went over the Khyber pass which is more exciting as an idea than in actual beauty. But one thinks of the Punjab riffles and the King's own Khyber dragoons and all the Kipling stories and it all becomes very moving. In one of the Afgan wars nearly five thousand British troops left Kabul for Peshawar after an agreement with the tribesmen to let them pass, but they did not keep their word and only one single man came back alive. I kept thinking of that as we inched our way up that fabulous gorge and was rather glad that times have changed and the Pathans are no longer so blood thirsty.

"On both sides of the road after the Khyber you see these extraordinary mudd villages of the various tribes. They look exactly like those built by David in the sand at Guéthary. Or like medieval feudal fortresses with high walls and turrets and look outs and crenelated walls. But made of grey mudd. The country all around is the most bare and ugly I have ever seen. Mostly brown sand stone and sort of untidy lose earth. Not one single solitary tree or even a blade of grass. And no sign of water anywhere. How those people live I cant immagine.

"They are wonderful fierce looking people with riffles and cartrege belts and glorious beards and turbans. The women here are not veiled but wear red baggy pants and black shawls and seem to be able to carry anything from a water melon to a wiggley baby on their heads. Well then we crossed the frontier into Afganistan and it really looks like another world right away. First the army is modeled on the Chinese and they give one quite the creeps. Tough and yellow with Mongol faces. Herodotus says when he first saw them that they have eyes like birds noses like cats and mouths like dogs and beards like wolves. We saw a lot of the army as they were building bits of the road.

"I forgot to tell you that in the distance the highest peaks were those of the Hindu Kush (the Indian killer as those mountains are called) because so many people travelling in caravans over them, never got to their destination. When Alexander's soldiers got to it they called it the Caucasus where Promytheus was supposed to have been tied until he was saved by Hercules. They called it that partly to flatter Alexander showing him that he had gone as far as Hercules and partly because they thought and rightly that this was the end of the world. So did I for a while as the car slipped and skidded up that narrow path."

On February 19, after we had reached New Delhi and were again received as state guests, Marina wrote Dodo:

"I am sitting on a collumned terrace of Hyderabad house, with a garden at my feet full of such roses and blossoms of every sort (and somehow even panzies and sweet William seem more exotic here) that I think I am dreaming, especially after the grim toffee coloured regions we have just left. The weather is like a soft shawl around my shoulders and the sun is going down, making everything pink and even more sweet smelling.

"Hyderabad house belonged to the Nizam of Hyderabad (naturally) until he was disposessed by the government. I felt sorry for a moment but was told not to worry about him. He was given about ten million dollars a year *apozimiosi* [compensation]. We arrived here yesterday after an epic trip out of Kabul. You see kabul airport looks a bit like the strip of land between mother's house and ours let us say, so that as soon as the snow starts to melt or a cloud appears it is impossible for planes to come or go. We were planning to leave kabul Sunday and get here in time for today which was imperative as we were lunching with Mr. Nehru and could not possibly miss it especially as he is leaving again tomorrow on an election campaigne. Well Saturday dawned grey and muddy so our host came to us and suggested we take a lift on the air attache's plane to Peshawar. Once out of Afganistan there are ways more or less of getting places. It is Afganistan where you can get stuck for three weeks.

"So we bundolled our little belongings said fairwell and off we went together with two other young men who wanted lifts. We got to Peshawar flying over the most amazing mountains I have ever seen. Really god was not at his best when he made that poor country. You feel that he just dumped things any old how. Sand and rock and left overs. We got to Peshawar in good time and then started flying round and round the airfield for over an hour. We could not understand it until the co-pilot came and told us that the Air attache's ears were stuffed and he did not want to go down. Dear me. Well there are some compensations to being an air attache in Kabul I expect and coming down or not as you wish must be one of them. However even the best of planes cant stay up for ever, ears or no ears so eventually we kangaroo landed, thanked him rather sourely and off he went.

"From here on we were on our own. We thought of taxi, train, even camel, so imagine our pleasure when far off on the field we saw a little tiny pale blue plane which belonged to an American construction company. We begged for a lift and were granted one by the pilot, a glorious Texan in coloured shirt and ten gallon hat who looked totally out of place amongst the turbans and camels of the landscape and completely sweet. The plane was as big as a tiny taxi and we squeezed in, Cy sitting on the floor and off we went. It was like a toy ride except again for the fabulous unkind mountains below us. A tiny pale blue airoplane flying over prehistoric lands does not give one a sense of over confidence and I felt that nature would claim its own. But not at all. It was a most pleasant trip and we landed in a place called Gujrat (I think) in the midst of a field with water buffaloe and *mangano-pigada* [old-fashioned wells]. All totally absurd. From the so called airfield we got another lift by truck to the town and there to our joy and astonishment got a bran new pale green taxi complete with embroidered curtains and flower vase which for fifty ruppees took us to Lahore where we arrived exhausted but triumphant late in the evening.

"The young man from the Embassy who was off on his first leave in ages behaved as if Lahore were Paris New York and Venice roled into one. We had a very gay dinner at Mr. Faletti's hotel and then all four shared a room as the hotel was full for the annual horse show. The next day our luck held out and we got seats on an Indian air line to Delhi. Here too the pilot circled the field for hours. It could not be *his* ears again. No he was practising landing our hostess told us blandly. Really!! However we made it and now here we are installed in super luxury in the poor old nizam's palace.

"Delhi is like paradise after Kabul! Huge trees and flowers and glorious weather. Just a few weeks and the real heat starts. One great disappointment all our mail has got lost somewhere and no news of the children. I could cry. I spent the morning sight seing and shopping with some Indian ladies whom I knew in Paris and who are kindness itself.

"Then lunch with Mr. Nehru in a garden such as one dreams of. Birds and flowers everywhere and even a baby panda which is without a doupt the most angelic creature on earth. Mr. Nehru at his best. I must say he can be irresistible when he wants. I could never be a journalist. I always believe the last person I have been talking to. In Pakistan all seemed so clear and simple and the Indians all just a bunch of cads who had snatched Kashmir away illegally. Here it is the Pakistanis who are the wicked agressors and when you listen to them you wonder how you could have ever thought otherwise. I do that is to say.

"Of course in such a garden one could have told me anything and I would have agreed for the sake of the peach blossoms and the roses and the fountains and the Jakarandas. As for the Panda I simply never wanted to leave him. A triangle for a face and eyes way down on his nose and he eats dates with his front feet and, well its no use trying to describe him. He is just an angel.

"Today Cy has a beastly cold and the only thing we did was go to lunch with a millionaire in another of these fantastic houses and gardens. This one actually is the one Gandhi was murdered in. When you see the flowers and grass and coloured birds everywhere you cant immagine violence associated with such a place. Apparently our host was a great friend of Gandhi's so that when he came to Delhi he always stayed with him. He was holding a prayer meating in this glorious garden when this fanatic Hindu who felt Gandhi was preaching too much raprochement with the Moslems, came in and shot him three times. The more we hear about Gandhi the more like Socrates he sounds.

"I am so glad of these few days rest in Delhi. No planes or any form of transport for a minute or two. I have unpacked fully for the first time since we left Paris and I must say I seem to fall in quite easily with this Nizam type of existance. You have never seen so many servants. The only dreadful heritage from the British is the early morning tea business but we seem to have at last conveid the idea that we dont want tea at seven. Meals are so fabulous in this country, we have to constantly remind ourselves that there are always five courses at least."

Marina wrote the children on March 1 from Delhi: "Well now the most exciting part of the trip has started. Our visit to Jaipur and Agra was marvellous. We went first to Jaipur and the road there (about a hundred and thirty miles from Delhi) is rather exciting especially as the Rajputs (the people who live in Jaipur) are the most colourful I have ever seen. The men wear enormous turbans, yellow orange or magenta pink and the women huge skirts like gipsies and veils on their heads and silver bracelets on arms and legs. How they can work with all those veils in the way I cant immagine but you see them everywhere in the fields looking like princesses.

"The country is very flat except near Jaipur where it gets hilly and there are castles on every hill top. Jaipur itself is in a valley with a river and quite fertile. There is wonderful tiger hunting here but much as we looked we did not see a single tiger. But I did go to the zoo and saw a mother tiger with several babies too sweet for words. The zoo was so funny because outside the bars were dozens of monkeys holding their babies by the hand and looking in at the other animals. It is the first time I have been in a zoo where the monkeys are outside looking in. The most prized posession of the zoo is an English pig. I suppose that is natural in a country where tigers and monkeys and peacocks and parrots run wild. In one place the monkeys who are sweet pale grey ones and with nice behinds not hideous untidy pink ones like usual, come and eat bananas and things out of your hand. The tiny ones are adorable.

"Well first we did a lot of sight seing in Jaipur where it was Sunday and all the people were out voting (it is election time here) and they all looked like peacocks in the most sparckling coloured clothes I have ever seen. Gold and silver embroideries and reds and greens and yellows everywhere. Then we went for drinks with the Maharajah who is an athletic nice looking young man with not much to do now that India is a republic so he plays Polo shoots tigers and has three wives. The wife we met was like something out of a fairy tale in pale green muslin and long black hair and eyes like a doe.

"Then the next morning we went to the old Capital of Jaipur which was built in the 18th century by some Rajput prince and it is the most wonderful haunting place I have ever seen. You drive up through the valley onto a steep hill with a lake on one side and a palace and garden built right in the middle of the lake. The Moghul princes had a passion for gardens and from this one they went duck shooting. We left the car there and climbed on a glorious elephant and off we went (feeling rather high up and wobbly) through the great gates of the city wall and up and up a cobbled road to the very top of the hill where the biggest palace is. We were followed all the way by two little musicians in rags who played, one, on a strange thin little guitar and the other with two little cymbals which looked like the tops of a sugar basin. One simply could not immagine that such sweet soft music could come from such weard looking instruments. I tried to whistle the tune but I have forgotten it already.

"The palace itself is wonderful. All terraces, and inside, courtyards, and gardens and collumned porches from where the ladies used to fish in artificial pools in their gardens. Everywhere the same flower inlay works, and the same mirror work on the walls (like grand ma's desert plates which amused you so much when you were little do you remember them?) You light one match in these rooms and it is reflected several thousand times and the whole cealing looks like the sky in August with a million twinkling stars. Those people really knew how to live. The view from up there is fabulous. You look down into the narrow green valley with the hills steep as walls on both sides and the actual old walls like a fish fin across the back of the hills.

"The whole valley is covered with old temples, strange looking tall lumpy things unlike anything I have ever seen before. Hindu and Jain temples. The Jains are the people who must never kill anything and who have such a hard time with ants and microbes. Here and there huge palm trees sway in the wind and the lake which from near is so gluky, from up there looks emerald green. I have never seen a more hauntingly beautiful sight and with that moaning music in our ears and the elephant like a huge historical anachronism, I felt I had walked right into a dream. From Amber as this place is called, we went to another place called Fatipur Sikri which is an abandoned pink Mohgul city. Some Rajah built this most enormous thing all pink sand stone and then discovered there was no water so just left it and moved back to Agra where the Taj Mahal was built. One gets a fealing of how many millions of people live in this country when you see the ease with which they built great cities and then just left them.

"Agra is a pleasant town and a nice hotel full of flowers. We went to the Taj Mahal and I must say it is every bit as lovely as they say. Sparckling white marble and lovely proportions but impossible to describe really or to see what it is like from the pictures, as it is not so much the thing itself only, which is lovely, but the way it changes colour with the sun on it, the way it is reflected in the pool just in front of it, the way the shadows of the dark tall cyprus trees fall, the birds that fly everywhere, the flowers, the tremendous sky and clouds above, and behind it the great slow silver river. There are crocodiles in the river but again we did not see them. The smell of the flowers is too lovely for words. We went in the soft mauve evening and really one feels one can just sit there and look for ever. I am so glad we managed to go. It is the prettiest thing we have seen yet on this trip.

"Last night we went to dinner in the old city of Delhi and then later strolled around the little streets. There you get quite a different picture of this country. Mudd a foot high and people sleeping right in it covered with a few rags. Babies rented out to beggars. Pock market faces everywhere. Rotten fruit and filth floating in the gutter which runs by the side of the street and is the center of life. W.C. garbage pale washing water drinking water etc. Sacred cows and all kinds of other scrawny animals live side by side with the people and the dung is most precious as fuel. They dry it in the sun and use it for cooking and heating. Millions die every year. But they seem most cheerful and dont look as if they cared. It seemed impossible that we should get into the car and drive for a few minutes to find ourselves back in the splendours of Hyderabad house only a mile or so away from so much filth and misery."

On March 7, Marina wrote Dodo from Kathmandu, the capital of Nepal: "How I wish I had eyes to look for you also and ears to hear for you also. Only noses I am rather glad I have just one for myself, and even that I could have given up for a few days. The smell of rancid ghee and dead sacrificial animals is quite something. But I anticipate. Let me start at the begining. They say that Kathmandu in the ancient days was a lovely lake and in it grew two lotus flowers, one pink and one white. They fought with each other constantly as to which one was the prittiest until the gods tired of this bickering, slashed a thin passage in the mountains and let the water out destroying the flowers and thus creating the valley of Kathmandu, something so beautiful, so like Shangri La that one can hardly believe it is a real place.

"It is through this narrow opening of the gods that the plane comes into this country whose only form of transport is the plane and the human foot. Never can you immagine a more hair raising flight. Our wing tips grazing large trees and great mountain peacks towering above the plane. The slightest air pocket and one is skattered upon the face of the hill. Holding our breath in terror and amazement we looked down onto a hidden valley, surrounded by green hills (the foot hills of the Himalayas) so tightly terraced that they themselves look like Boudhist temples. Tiny cultivated squares some green some brilliant yellow, mustard plant, and some all white (radish flowers). Even from the plane we could see the flowering rodhodendrons and in the distance five hundred miles of snowy mountain range and *Everest*. Eleven of the sixteen highest peaks in the world surround this little valley.

"We landed to our surprise and releif on an air field which only barely meets the minimum prescribed size and at each end falls sharply away into two great ravines. Like landing on an air craft carrier. There we were met by some charming Americans of the mission to Nepal and driven off to where surprise after surprise awaited us. First the Hotel. A huge neo classic stucco building of several hundred rooms and as fitting to the landscape of hills and pagodas as a hamberger heaven would be on the Acropolis. And on its terrace what do you think. Several dozen American tourrists complete with Kleenex revelon nylon and blue hair. If I had seen elephants and cobras I would have been less surprised and certainly less disappointed.

"Here I thought I was a close second to Marco Polo and the Caronia tour was there before us. It is all the more incredible when you think that up to the revolution in 1950 hardly any foreigners had ever been allowed in the country and that the only way to get to it had been by train to the Indian boarder and then on foot for several days over the mountains. Every single thing in the country including the few royal motor cars, a steam roler, the largest crystel chandeliers for the Rana palaces, and grand piano and glass and gold grandfather clock have been brought in on human backs. You see people even women carrying such loads on their backs, held in place by a band around their forheads, that I could not even lift one inch off the ground. They spend their whole lives walking across the hills into

Kathmandu bringing in wood or fruit or whatever they have for a few ruppees.

"The country which is all utterly lovely is devided into strips sort of. First what they call the terai which is marchy malarial fertile valley and jungle, near the Indian frontier. There they have tigers and elephants and every kind of wild animal and there it was my dream to go but it takes so very long on foot. There live the peasants who are more like Indians and who are separated from the valley of Kathmandu the capital by wave after wave of hills so that most of them never get to the big city in their lives. They are the poorest people you can immagine and by far the happiest gayest sweetest smiling people in the world. They are half Hindu half Boudhist with a smattering of Tantric which is pagan and weard and full of phalic symbolisme. In the middle of the country is the valley where mostly Gurkas live who make wonderful soldiers. Also the King and up to 1950 the famous Rana family whose ancestor established their hereditary Prime ministership by cutting off the heads of fifty or more nobles who stood in his way. The Ranas reigned supreme for ages until they were thrown out in 1950 and now everybody is trying to democratise the place and make them prosperous and modern and I am afraid those wonderful smiles may change for the harrassed brows and stomach ulcers of the jeffersonian Democrats.

"We only had five days in Nepal and I spent the whole time rushing from temple to temple either in an old jeep or some of those glorious taxis so big and draughty that they bare the same relationship to a cadillac or a Jaguar that an elephant bares to a race horse. There are two ancient cities which are really phantastic. They look somehow like medieval European cities with tall brick houses with overhanging carved woodden eaves and also heavily carved bay windows. The streets are narrow and dark and everything from child birth to what must inevitably preceed it, to eating, washing quarelling arguing and of course buying and selling, takes place right in them.

"The dirt is fabulous. It is something I cant quite understand. For instance you see the temples and the offerings of flowers garlands and the prescribed holy cakes, bowls of rice, fruit etc, as well as intestines of sorts and you also see a dog eating them up, a baby too, a man doing pipi and a little girl dancing all together. It is fearcly smelly and messy and nasty. The people though have lovely faces and you can immediately tell the people from the Terai who are more Indian looking from the Gurkas who are more mongul and then of course the Thibetans who live in the frosty regions of the Himalayas with the yaks, and come down for pilgrimiges or commerce. The men and women both have long pigtals interwoven with flowers ribbons amulets and rancid butter, both have beardless faces, and the only way you can tell which is which is that the men are usually taller.

"They smell so high you can hardly breath when near them. And they are so friendly and curious you cant help but be near them. They come up to you smilling and peer into your face and ask for money but in a most unservile way, and they are always fascinated by our stockings and the seam which they think is a tattoo. Constantly you feel a little hand strocking your leg to see if it will come off. One day I went with a lady to a Bhudist Temple which was crowded with Thibetan pilgrims, as this is a holy year of some sort and en mass they were really fascinating. Such amazing faces. Really the Pinko-grey races are much less pretty.

"On our way home we met a funeral. Never in my wildest dreams had I thought to see the burning of a human body. The body was in a sort of altar thing made of wood and cloth and we stopped to see because we thought it was the burning of an effigy of some sort. When we realized it was the actual dead lady we nearly passed out but stayed, out of amazement rather and horrid curiosity. This is most unusual because normally the dead or rather dying are taken down to the sacred river where they are put with there feet in the water to facilitate the passage of the soul into heaven via the sacred river. This poses quite a problem for doctors (European) who have to say when the time has come. If they say wait a little longer then for sure the patient dies that night and this is dreadfully bad luck both for the dead and the living. But many many people might have been saved had they not spent their last days with their feet in muddy cold water. Some go down as far as a week ahead.

"After they die they are burned on what they call ghats, sort of stone piers and their ashes strewn to the sacred river. Our unfortunate corpse was probably too poor or had died in the house or something because it was burned right there in the middle of the village green. The ceremony involved the building of the fire and a lot of walking around it three times and mumbling and chanting and throwing sacrificial offerings such as rice corn cakes flowers shells herbs etc., onto the fire. Also water strangely enough. Dozens of beggers were given rice and fruit. We did not stay to what promised to be a rather gruesome end, as the fire was really not adequate at all. The wood is so expensive that poor people can only afford token ammounts. They then throw the half burned body into the river. This same river is used for washing drinking laundry etc. Also in a most undivine way, it runs dry-ish for more than part of the year till the monsoons. I spare you the details.

"The temples themselves are quite amazing. Bhuda was born in Nepal and so was the Pagoda and from here spread to China Thibet etc. The Temples are four or five tiered, of red brick with profuse carvings everywhere in brilliantly coloured wood. The domes and steeples are usually gold leaf and crawling with dragons tigers snakes and all kinds of fantastic animals. The base of the eaves are where the pornographic releifs are; and they really are something. The reason given is that Lightening is a virgin goddess and when she sees these scenes she gets shocked and goes from the Temple leaving it unharmed. Personally this sounds like a most feable excuse to me. You simply cant immagine what goes on.

"All the temples are very much alike and not really beautiful in themselves but utterly fascinating of course. There is a Bhoudist one right on top of a hill which you climb a thousand steps to get to and the view from there takes your breath away. From there it looks really like the enchanted hidden valley of dreams. Monkeys live by the hundreds in this Temple and come and eat from your hand. The peasant houses are also brick dark red at the bottom and white at the top with thatched roofs. The valley is covered with flowers including rodhodendrons camelias and gardinias and both men and women wear flowers in their hair all the time. The thing though that strikes one most in this country where everything is striking is the sweet happiness of the people. I have never seen such gentle gay smiles, I have never felt such a natural immediate affection emanating from everybody. You are given a jeep driver let us say, and you cant speak a word to each other but at once he makes you feel that you are his charge and somehow you feel that he would watch you and protect you with his life if nessecary. No wonder the British officers adored their Gurka troops. They are really the nicest people I have ever met and I hope to god the airoplane, the Caronia tourrists transport and democracy dont make them less nice.

"I must say the Americans we met there were an exceptional group of people too. One nicer than the other and they looked after us like long lost relatives. All together this was by far the most marvelous part of the trip. Some day I would like to go back, before Neon lights and Cinema-scope ruin the place, and go to the Terai and see some real jungle and tigers. The Prime Minister had just taken a group of friends to the jungle for a tiger hunt and they had all got at least one. They came back breathless with excitement including the owner of our hotel who is a white Russian ex-ballet dancer, ex-trapese artist ex-night club owner in Bombay and god knows how many other exes. A fascinating caracter quite in keeping with the whole adventurous fealing that Nepal still gives one.

"P.S. We left Nepal yesterday morning and after the horrid flight which seemed even more frightening now that we knew what was ahead, we arrived without mishap in Benares which is really ghastly. The total opposite to gay crystaline beautiful Nepal. We went in a boat on the Ganges this morning and I hope never to see such a sight again in my life. Dead bodies about to be burned, seething ugly sick humanity nacked bathing its horrid bodies in a horrid river.

"Lepers beggars and filth everywhere. And the indians again after the nepalies, seem rather awful. Full of complexes and chips on their shoulders and they never give you a straight answer to the simplest question and all together most irritating. Except for Ceylon which I am looking forward to mainly because of the sea and the flowers, I must say 'je regrette l'Europe aux Anciens parapets.' Never has Christianity appeared so sweet and pure and clean and unclutered to me before."

Out next stop was Colombo, Ceylon, and Marina wrote *Mama mou glykia* on the day of our arrival, March 14:

"We arrived here at three in the morning last night as the plane was late. Even this dream island does'nt get to me somehow. And more and more I feel European and Christian. Only the flowering trees and the birds are better on this continent. And I am so tired of infiriority complexes that I would like to spend a week with a hideously proud agressive Englishman just for a change. And to hear a few thoughts expressed in an original manner.

"I suppose people do express themselves differently when talking in a language they are tought and not born to. But I must say I am bored to tears by expressions of National pride and achievement. Of such thoughts as 'the imparting of knowledge in our way of life is thought to be elevating to the spirit.' Oh dear maybe it is the heat that makes me so intolerant today. It is stifling and so damp that I have little trickles down the back of my legs and my hands slip on the key board although I am writing with nothing on and all fans going. I have not seen anything of Ceylon yet.

"Cy is off seing the Prime Minister Mr. Bandaranaike and Mr. Kotelawala so I have the typewriter to myself for an hour or so. The island looks dreamy. Palm trees and yellow sand and such flowers and fruit everywhere. Frangipani and a dozen different kinds of jasmin including a dark red one. On Saturday we take two days off and go inland to an ancient city and also to see rubber tea and coconut plantations. Real picture jungle at last. Probably this is the last letter I will write to you. We go to Bahrein from where I may have time to scribble something but if we do go to Saudi Arabia it will be a tremendous rush to get back in time for the children. The trip back will be ghastly. We stop at so many places like a blooming tram. Baghdad and Basra and Istanbul and Geneva Milan Rome and god knows where."

We had quite a good time in both Ceylon and Bahrain. In the former we visited Kandy, rubber plantations, forests of plane trees, frangipani, manioc, cashew, and jackfruit, and we watched amiable elephants having their backs scrubbed by their keepers in muddy rivers. We saw a six-hundred-year-old sacred Bo tree, its branches filled with ravens, and suddenly came up to hillsides covered with tea plantations. We spent a night at Nuwara Eliya, more than six thousand feet high and so cool that we actually wore sweaters in the evening.

In Jufair, Bahrain, we stayed with Sir Bernard Burrows, then British "political resident" for the entire Persian Gulf. Marina was delighted when Ines, his wife, invited two or three of the leading sheikhas (wives of sheikhs), and they had a long conversation in which neither side understood a single word spoken by the other but spanned the gap with smiles and nods.

Back in Paris, Marina learned that Pussy Deakin's father had died; he was a charming Rumanian journalist who had suffered for years in prison. She wrote her:

"It seems so awful not to be able to find one word of comfort, one word that one has not used already in other people's cases, for other people's sorrows. How sadly human beings are tied to words and second hand expressions when it seems unessecary and yet imperative to tell someone one loves how much one shares their sorrow or their joy. My Pussy you must know how much I weep for you and how much I would give to help. And yet here I am unable even to write. I cannot bring myself to say the things that come to mind about courage and that at least his suffering is over. It is true and perhaps in time you too will come to see it as a liberation for him. But not now, not yet. There is no comfort for such sorrow. All I have to give is sympathy and love and at moments like these even love is helpless."

By that time Marina had had enough of travel for a bit and felt happy that she no longer had to "curl up like a question mark" in an airplane seat.

She wrote my mother from Paris on April 26:

"We had a simply wonderful Easter. Nursey arrived all aflutter and the children's delight at and with her was quite touching. Then this sweet couple the Carters who are always so good to us asked us *en masse* to spend Easter week end with them in Senlis and the weather turned suddenly to glorious summer so that for three and a half days we lolled in the sun shine picked *muguet* (thought of you) went to large children's pic nics rode bycicles with no hands eat like horses played bridge in the evening and golf in the day time for Cy and were all together blissful. Sunday we went to church and then to an Easter egg hunt at Lady Diana's who has the most exquisite house in the grounds of the Chateau at Chantilly. She has a garden à l'*Anglaise* with a slopping lawn dotted all over with primeroses violets and tulips and ending in a little stream at the bottom. She had seventeen children all rushing around amongst the flowers looking for Easter eggs and the *coup d'oeuil* was like that story of Oscar Wilde's called 'The Selfish Giant.'

"She also had a grown up house party made up entirely of brilliant Oxford professors or writers or intellectuals of one kind or another and somehow everybody got on frightfully well and you saw things like Professor Maurice Bowra of Oxford riding a bycicle with a tiny girl pearched behind him or Peter Quennell (History Today) rolling in the grass with three small boys on his back. All this in between fearce argument on the nature of Christ or monophysism. It was enchanting. Cy got a lot of exercise and a lot of bridge and the fresh air made him sleep well so he was full of smiles and pleasure. We got back Monday night in monstrous traffic jams but too cheerful to care and now we have our friends the Deakins staying with us for three days. I have sent them all packing this morning which gives me a chance to sit down for a second and dash this off to you before they return and need entertaining. Also the children are spending the day with Rothschilds in Chamant so I can breath for a brief second."

After Nursey had returned to her little Devon cottage, Marina wrote her from Paris (May 17): "Lady Burrows is coming from Bahrein to stay so is Mr. Dedijer [Vlado Dedijer, Jugoslav communist] the father of Milica remember? He at least speacks English. Then the Rippers on the 24th. And as if that was not all last night Far came home to announce that Mr. Adlai Stevenson was coming to breakfast this morning. We asked the Pattens too and you can immagine the confusion of Grat, our eccentric butler. He served the orange juice after the coffee the grape fruit with the bacon forgot the bread gave us spoons instead of forks and infuriated Far by giving him alone the largest cup and all the jellies. Ah me. This at nine this morning. They have just gone and I am expecting some more people for lunch so in between am dashing this off to you."

She elaborated on the Stevenson breakfast to Avis Bohlen on May 25: "We hit rock top the other day socially speaking when we started our entertaining At Breakfast. Mr. Stevenson was here only for a day or so and as all his meals were taken he himself suggested breakfast. Panic in the household. The best coffe pot not big enough the best cups one too few etc. In spite of all instructions Grat kept the grape fruit for last (as desert I suppose) forgot the orange juice entirely and brought the eggs ten minutes after we had all finished the bacon. We had asked Bill and Susan Mary and Cy's young secretary whose father is a big democrat in Kanzas City so it was quite a party. A friend called at nine and Grat pompously said '*Madame ne peut pas venir au telephone elle est à table avec du monde.*' The caller said '*C'est pas possible ils sont la depuis hier soir.*' '*Pas du tout Madame. Nous recevons à toute heure dans cette maison*' said Grat. But it was great fun and I was charmed all over again and am more of a Democrat than ever."

The next day she wrote Alexis, her brother: "We have the Rippers (six feet two and seven respectively) Vlado Dedijer (seven foot) and Ines all coming at the same time. Can you immagine Ines and Vlado sharing a bathroom. Its going to be quite a week especially as Vlado will want to hit the town and eat his way to ulcers as he is facing jail when he gets home [to Jugoslavia]. I must say he pushes courage a bit too far. Hardly let out of prison he gets a job as history professor gets an invitation to lecture in Scandinavia France England etc. and as soon as he has his captive audience shoots his trap off about the deplorable state of affairs back home. It is enough to irk even a Jeffersonian democrat. Anyway we will do our best to feed him up before he goes back to bread and beans.

"Last week we saw Laurence Olivier in Titus Andronicus. Super acting but the play is a gay little thing with twenty three corpses even before the curtain goes up. Vivien Leigh has her hands and tongue cut out after being raped people go mad are burried alive, burned to bits heads cut off and ends with a splendid banquet seen at which the Queen of the Goths eats her children who have been made into a stew by Titus. *Thee mou* [My God]."

I went to Oxford at the end of June to stay with the Deakins and attend a seminar at St. Antony's College, of which Bill was warden. Marina and the children meanwhile took off for the summer holiday in Greece. She wrote from Maroussi on July 3:

"Well here we are installed in the Spitaki and nothing nothing has changed at all. Even the children are conscious of some eternal quality about its ever sameness. Marinette in the *pagoniera* [icebox, our name for a tiny room] found the bed turned sideways and begged to put it back to its old position at once. 'Nothing must be different.' "

Three days later Marina continued: "Last night I went to a marvellous concert. Maria Callas. The theatre [below the Acropolis] was packed all the way up to the olive tree and I must say a delightfully pretty well dressed audience headed by Mr. Karamanlis in his white suit looking wonderfully scrubbed behind the ears and like the dream prime minister of Zenda or Ruritania. His wife too. Then the moon of course was glorious as always and the theatre superb and a smell of jasmine everywhere.

"Well Callas walked on to the stage in a Dior dress looking like a princesse and her meer presence filled the theatre. A ripple went through the audiance. She looked radiant and somehow beautiful with those strange Minoan eyes which reach her ears on the side of her face. Heavy black hair and a sparckling complexion. And what an actress. And you know it is not easy in a recital with a rather mediocre orchestra. Anyway she sang like an angel. The amazing thing is that her voice is not really that good. The lower notes are pure honey but the high ones squeek a bit. It is all sheer mastery of her art and a talent for putting herself across such as I have never seen. After a moment's hush there was such a burst of applause you could hear them at the Syntagma [Athen's main square]. Really such fun to watch a triumph. The little bitch really is wonderful."

On August 15 she wrote to Susan Mary Patten from Spetsais, where we had rented a house together with our English friends Frank and Kitty Giles:

"So much love and beauty and welcome, make one a bit selfish and although I have wanted to write to you for days, always some smile some invitation, some offer either from friend or wave or fish or moonray, make me forget my less immediate wish for the urgent satisfaction of the present. What a blessed country where at every corner the delicious cry of 'Marinaki Mou' rings in my ears. Friendly family friendly rocks friendly trees and herbs. Only the fish have left us and in vain do we don mask and flippers and breathers and go down as in search of Mobby Dick only to come back with a defenceless sea urchin.

"We hardly ever go in 'to town' but fish and pic nic on our own and each day more blessed than the next. Cy in a mood so mellow and gay that he is a pleasure to behold. One thing about this country. As one has to react to it (*noblesse oblige*) in the right way and as its beauty and importance sensually is such one is more or less bullied by the moon and the sea and the mountains and the smell of thyme and jasmine into a permanant state of exhaltation.

"All our visitors burning with love and desire and the slightest impediment becomes an Agamemnon problem. To love to want to weep perchance to live, they all vibrate like twenty year olds and it is too delightful all the more so in a way because deep down you know that it is a game and that it is only their way of responding to their atavistic responsibility as relatives of Olympus and Sounion and Salamis. One cant love weekly or cry gently at the foot of the Acropolis so we let ourselves go. This delightfully exaggerated situation I may say is joy to me as a listener and an observer and as aplied to love or any kind of sentimental emotion.

"But when it is also given to red-tape ministries, aplications for money demands for work etc it becomes soul destroying and frustrating. All my friends are poorer than ever, all in trouble of some sort or another and all unable to see any hope of amelioration. What a strange mixture of pleasure and trouble this place is."

On August 20, Marina wrote Nursey about a family visit to our friends George and Mary Averoff at Skylogianni, their place on Euboea:

"The house is charming and very Victorian and old fashioned and at the same time a Maroussi like atmosphere. Lots of sweet peasant maids called Elenis and Jiannoulas and Tassoulas. Huge dishes of food set in the middle of the table and everyone passing to everyone else. Fourteen at table even for breakfast.

"On the fifteenth of August [Mary Averoff's name day] we had a great feast in the garden with roast lambs on the spit and *kokoretsi* [tripe sausage] and *loukoumades* [Turkish delight] and David drank so much retsina that he had to sleep it off and had his first hang over. In the morning we went to several churches in the village and it was really nice and moving. The property is lovely. All that I like best in Greece. Such sea that you want to drink it and be one with it. Under water landscapes like fairy casttles. Then the wide yellow fields with olive trees and figs and the smell of hot pine needels. Then a river (actually with some water in it) and plane trees all the way down and heards of baby sheep searching for shade. Huge walnut trees and black berries and then row after row after row of hills pale yellow turning into dark blue mountains in the distance. And Everywhere that most delicious of God's after thoughts the cyprus tree just to give the right proportions to everything."

Marina wrote my mother from Spetsais on September 12:

"Terraces with arches for each position of the sun. The sea all around us and this glorious whiteness of the lime white-wash which seems to catch even the tiniest ray of light and magnify it a thousand times. The whole island sparckles and shines and everything is white and blue. No wonder the Greek flag is those colours. It could not possibly be anything else.

"Our days (each one the same and each one unique) consist of breakfast *en famille* around eight. Fresh figs off the tree dripping with dew, eggs and god knows what else. We all have appetites like horses including Cy who complains that we feed him too well and he has to spend the rest of the day climbing hills to take the extra weight off again. We sit at the breakfast table for hours conversation ranging from fishing to ancient greece from mythologie to the state of our finances or from food to religion. Then there is a vague potterring about *sois-disant* house keeping but in fact we have Eleni with us who is without a doupt the dream come true. Forty four plump pretty curly haired and has been with us since she was eleven. There is nothing she cant or wont do. She can iron and wash a shirt in two seconds she can produce a meal for twenty without batting an eye she can sew she can sing and she can do the entire house and even have time for us all to sit on her lap and be told for the millionth time about the day we fell into the water as children or the day we did this or that or the other.

"Then comes the great exodus. To see us leave you would think we were at least first cousins of Cousteau. Under-water guns, flippers, masques, spears, we really look like men from Mars. All that and we occasionally bring back one small defenceless red mulet or a sole which presents a large flat imobile surface. Our singular lack of skill or success has done nothing to damp our enthusiasm and every morning three generations of us dissapear under water only to surface occasionally with a tale of woe about the biggest one which got away. Some times we take pic nic lunches and light fires and cook susages and an occasional octapus. Other times we come home to large meals and an immense afternoon sleep and reading and relaxing. Later we go for long walks the variety of which is unending on this lovely lovely island. Then dinner and bed at nine and all of us as sleepy as if it were dawn. The children have a huge band of friends all children of the children I use to play with. It is so amusing to see the full circle. Marinette has a whole group of boys aged forteen or fifteen (so glamour-ous) trotting around with her and is turning into a real teen ager complete with blue jeans and pony tail and fresh talk. They really are rather divine children and this year they are old enough to go off on their own and they are having a glorious time I think."

VI

October 1957 - December 1958

That autumn of 1957 Uncle Arthur asked if Marina and I would care to join him and Aunt Iphigene on a Far Eastern trip, starting in Japan, where we would meet. Marina was excited all over again, although she had not yet simmered down entirely from her Indian experiences. As for myself, Uncle Arthur was not only publisher of the *Times* and therefore my boss, but I was also particularly fond of and close to him, so much so that sometimes I called him "Uncle" and sometimes plain "Arthur." My own father, his older brother, had died when I was thirteen, so I regarded him as half a surrogate parent and half a brother.

The prospect was therefore pleasing, even though it meant more work for me than my normal tours, as I would have to participate in a certain amount of additional socializing as well as earning my daily bread. Marina was delighted, already conjuring up visions of Shinto ceremonials, Zen rock gardens, and fragile geisha houses. We took off from Copenhagen and flew over the North Pole with only one brief stop in Anchorage, Alaska. As soon as we reached Tokyo (October 3) Marina wrote Dodo:

"After thirty two hours in the air I feel as dopey as can be. Ears buzzing knees wobbly and oh so sleepy. But what a trip. We left pretty, conventional, predictable Copenhagen to launch into an amazing astral world of Northern lights and space. The airport, dark shiny and mysterious was like a vision of the future. Great shivering elegant masses of steal trembling and shuddering to go. Planes everywhere and that wierd quality the human voice takes on through a microphone. And little people like us with pathetic over-night bags scurrying into the night like sleep walkers cought up in some fantasy of their own making.

"Luckily we had berths so we could stretch out and sleep rather well the first night. We had all that night and all the next day in the plane and got to Alaska (did not even see the Pole as there were clouds) in the evening, only there it was morning and the sun was just about to rise behind strange sharply pointed mountains and everything was mauve. The land was flat and round and I really felt that if I walked a few miles the earth would start curving downwards under my feet. What a country. What courage to go off and pioneer that frozen land. By air it looked half Dante half Davy Crocket seen by Arthur Rackham. Grey and marshy with black and yellow patches and mudd mudd mudd. And around these huge spicky mountains like a lunar landscape.

"The foot of man has never touched this land as it is soggy and cold and malevolent. And full of great grizzly bears and, further down seals by the millions and god knows what else. Then the great ocean and everywhere islands like Spetsais or Poros only frozen frozen frozen. We flew right over a volcano which puffed out great flames at us. It looked like a toy. Then we were given lunch only for us it was dinner and we were really ready for bed again only the day was just starting.

"We managed to sleep some more however and got here about an hour ago full of dramamine and really groggy. Luckily it is evening here so we don't have a whole day to cope with. Only dinner with a Minister of something. I have not seen the Uncle Arthurs yet as we just are unpacking and getting ourselves together. Cy has already popped off to see the American Ambassador an old friend of ours with a pleasant wife. Nephew of general MacArthur. Poor Cy this trip is going to be hard for him as the rest of us dont have to earn our living. We were handed a program a mile long with receptions dinners teas and god knows what all. He is struggling already to get a few hours off to do some work.

"I cant tell you a thing about Tokyo yet except what I saw through a haze of dramamine on our way from the airport which was not much. The

Japanese look less Japanese somehow than I expected. As if they were pretending somehow. The hotel is the wierdest looking thing. It was designed by Frank Lloyd Wright in nineteen twenty for Mexico and looks like some Aztec monument. Everything is so low that even I keep bumping into things."

She wrote to my mother on October 10 from Kyoto: "Tokyo is an ugly town and tell Grand Pa [my stepfather, an architect] I think Mr. Frank Lloyd Wright should have been strangled at birth. The Imperial hotel is about as ugly as one could immagine and the rooms so hot and breathless now I hate to think what they are like in the summer. And the closet arrangement such that you open one door and two others fly open and you are trapped for ever.

"But the Temples . . . We went to a place called Nikko which is the most beautiful Thing I have ever seen. And now Kyoto which is a dream. Oh such wall painting and such cealings. Birds and flowers and tigers all multicoloured on gold backgrounds. I who dont really like Oriental art find myself perfectly entranced by it all. And the gardens, and the little red lacquer bridges: and the midget pines and the pointed tall hills all around. I have never been in a country which looks so like engravings of itself. And Fujiyama, snow-covered in the sky.

"Last night we went to a most enchanting geisha party. The little girls with faces painted chalk white and huge hairdoes and so exactly like dolls that it was a surprise to hear them sing and giggle and dance. They sat by us and fed us and filled our glasses and danced for us and tought us silly games and it was enchanting. We rushed around madly sight seing and I must say I am dead tonight, Uncle Arthur bearing up quite well and in a very good mood. Although he does have to skip some of the more strenuous sights. Aunt Iph sweet. A Mrs. George Woods is with them who is charming and gay. She and I have a Japanese room in the hotel and sleep on the flour and have our own private garden. This is Kyoto where Cy did not come as he had so much work. We go to Nara tomorrow and then to Miki Moto's pearl island the next day and back to Tokio from there."

On October 11, back in Tokyo, she wrote an adorable letter to Dodo: "I got your first letter to follow me in my travels. It reached me here in Tokio where we returned tonight after a week travelling around the country. How can you even think that all I say about loving you, is in any way exagirated let alone a pretence. One can pretend to lots of people and all too often in life one has to. But not to one's mama and not gratuitously, when there is no reason on earth for it. So please stop wondering and accept it once and for all as the gospel. I herewith hasten to add that I adore you and miss you and that if only I could share some of the pleasures of this trip with you and the children, it would be really bliss.

"I wrote to you a few days ago about Kyoto and its beauty. From there we went to another ancient capital called Nara. Full of gardens and temples and wisteria. Then we went on to a pearl island. I must say it was fun. For one thing the drive to it took us through simply exquisite country. These hills are so enchanting. There is no doupt in my mind that hilly countries are the best. These hills are everywhere and dark dark green.

"You know how it amuses me to recognise trees all over the world. Well here I only recognise less than half. Pines and cidars and great forrests of bambou. (I had some *au gratin* the other day and they were delicious sort of half artichoke half celery and not quite either) and of course *mouries* [blackberries] and figs. The hills are all terraced and all over there are these lovely tiny fields of rice bright yellow at this time of year and in them peasants working. The rice is so high and they so small that all you see moving about are masses of pointed straw hats. Too sweet. More scare crows per inch than anywhere else in the world. Gay exuberant scare crows. But no crows.

"We only saw a few storks about but they too looked as if they had flown right out of a screen. There are rivers everywhere and little streams and torrents. It is really utterly enchanting country. Then we saw the Pacific. For me the first glimpse. And in it litteraly hundreds of little islands no bigger than a whisp and all covered with trees right down to the water and so near each other that you feel you can jump.

"We went by little boat to the place where they cultivate the pearls. We saw the girls dive for them (just like diving for sea urchins, with a mask and an *apohi* [hand net]. They bring the oysters out and then they are half opened and a tiny bit of sea weed is inserted into their flesh, as well as a small bead. Then they are shut again and put back onto great trays which are then hung into the sea from great rafts. There they stay for four years, looked after like a *pépinière* [nursery]. They give them the right kind of planktum, they keep away the smernes [a fish] who are their great enemy, they make sure the water is not too cold for them etc. In these four years the sea weed produces an infection which makes them form the pearly covering for the little bead. It was fascinating to watch. Then we were each told to chose an oyster from a great basket and it was opened for us and we all got two and some three pearls. We looked longingly at the great sacks of pearls all over the place but one is all we got. But it was fun anyway and such a pretty island.

"Mr. Mikimoto who invented the whole idea about forty years ago only died last year. He was a macaroni manufacturer. We flew back to Tokio this afternoon and Cy has gone off to a bachelor dinner with the Prime Minister Mr. Kishi. Few men entertain at their own houses here. Even the Prime Minister has taken Uncle Arthur and Cy off to his geishas place. Every man *qui se respecte* has a mistresse. I must say they are quite delicious looking and I dont blame them, but a bit of a bore for the wives who sit at home."

Six days later, from Taiwan (Formosa) to *Mama mou glykia:* "In a minute we are off to lunch with the Rankins, Pauline and Karl. Do you remember them. They were *en poste* in Athens for years. Am sure mother and Rox do. He is ambassador here now and they still adore Greece and greeted me like a daughter. We got here two days ago and have been doing nothing but eat since our arrival. I feel like a zepeline but it is well worth it. I have never tasted anything so wonderful. Not like Japan.

"We had two fourteen course meals in one day. They included shark's fin soup not very good and birds nest desert also not good. Like sweet slimey *fide* [vermicelli] in white of egg. But the rest simply out of this world. Roast Peking duck is all crust and straight from heaven. Roast suckling pig powdered with sugar and pickled garlic. Fabulous. A sweet made of lotus seeds. Delicious and so romantic. I have learned to use chop sticks quite well.

"This is a beautiful sad island. All green and lovely volcanic hills full of exotic plants and earthquakes. Hybiscus of every size and colour especially a dark yellow which is a dream. Camelias azeleas forty different kinds of bambou and fifty kinds of fern from a tiny leaf to great big tree. And everywhere this divine ginger flower which smells like all the jasmine tuberoses and foulia of the world put together. The island is I think as big as Greece. I am not sure but anyway it has 10 million people living on it. A few aborigines who are Malay and strange wild folk. A few million local people who have been succesively occupied by the Portuguese the Dutch the Chinese and most hateful of all the Japanese. The rest are refugees and governement in exile people and they all live with one dream to reconquer the mainland. It is a bit as if Spetsais were the Free Greek governement and lived in hopes of reconquering the rest of Greece.

"The optimisme and energy and courage are totally disarming and sad. They really are the nicest people. The men are most beautiful (surprise) but the women less so than the Japanese. But here one does not feel so much that great wall of spiritual difference as in Japan. Of course the ones we met are all most Westernised and educated in Foreign countries and speak excellent English which helps. They have such lovely manners that the way we talk sounds like truck drivers. We had tea with the Generalissimo and Madame Chiang yesterday who were quite delightful. We dine there again tonight. I was rather thrilled. I remember ages ago coming back from Paris with the guides *katastroma* [sleeping on the deck] and playing the game I am thinking of someone begining with C. It was the general. At that time in full glory. Ah me what a world. No more time for banal philosophical considerations. Cy has gone to Quemoy for the day, one hour's flight from here. Do you remember all the fuss about Quemoy and Matsu the off-shore islands, last year. Or was it the year before that? How history flies by us these days."

When we got to Hong Kong, she wrote Dodo (October 24):

"This is really a place of adventure and colour. For one thing it is absolutely beautiful. Very much like Greece in formation but not in colour. All this part of the world being more or less volcanic is much more brown than we are. There is no blue in the mountains. Nonetheless it is simply lovely. Hong Kong is an island and Kowloon is part of the mainland of China. The collony all together is about twenty two miles long. It is queer to think that only twenty two miles away is Communist China; a world which in Paris seems so remote that it is practically mythical.

"Hong Kong, the island has this in common with Greece, that it is very hilly and you have the sea at one moment on your right at one on your left and often on three sides. The town is built on lots of Lykabetuses [Athens' small mountain] and I must say one is rather hopeful that the person driving has not had an extra gin. As they are apt to do in British Colonies. Apart from its physical beauty this place is seathing with spies refugees black marqueteers opium smuglers and strange adventurers of every nationality. One has a fealing that everybody is what he says he is and something else. Being a free port you can immagine the trading and the ammount of money that changes hands.

"And all given an extra touch of adventure by the fealing that it is all happening on borrowed time. Actually the whole colony is only rented from China and has another forty years to go before it becomes Chinese again. But forty years is a life time these days and in a place where you are supposed to be able to double your investement in four years, forty is a wild dream. The people here, as Cy says in his column, are like the peasants who plant their vines on the side of Vesuvius because the soil is so rich that it is worth the gamble.

"And of course like all cheap places it is madly expensive to be here because one wants everything. We have been frightfully touristy and gone into every corner shop and the local shoe lane and I must say it is enough to make you cry not to be able to buy and transport everything. Porcelaine out of this world. Not only antiques but the ordinary modern chinese stuff is absolutely delightful and that special yellow which I so like. A soup bowl cost about six drachmes. And the linen and the materials and the precious stones. Not to mention things like cameras radios etc. which are tax free and duty free.

"One feels one simply cant afford not to buy them. I got some silk one pale blue and one white with black bambous. I also got a clasp for my pearls in rubies. I have to hold on to myself not to spend every penny I own. But it is fun even just to look. The Chinese writing is so pretty that all the streets with the names of the shops on flowing ribbons, look like streets decorated for a celebration. The shop signs are all red or blue or green and it is marvellous. As for the little Chinese girls with their tight dresses and skirt slit up to the thighs they are too sweet for words. I bought a Chinese dress but my behind is a bit too big and too low for it. I shall have to wear it sitting down. We leave in an hour or so for Manila and Cy has gone to have breakfast with a man so I have grabbed his typewriter."

In Manila we saw our old chums the Bohlens. Chip had been withdrawn from Moscow by Foster Dulles, a secretary of state who disliked him because of his independence, brilliance, and refusal to be cowed; also for his sharp sense of humor, Dulles being the butt of several of his jokes which were funny enough to be repeated throughout the intellectually incestuous atmosphere of Washington. So Chip was exiled as ambassador to the

Philippines. We then flew to Singapore via Saigon, where Arthur and I watched glumly for five hours while they went through our plane and all its baggage because of a bomb rumor, and Marina and Aunt Iph chatted innocently over the teacups in the airport, where they had been told a cylinder in an engine was being changed. Singapore was lovely, but Marina had no time to write. Finally from Bangkok, whence we had flown for a day to northwestern Cambodia, she sent a long letter to Dodo on October 30:

"I have been to Ur and Babylon and Nineveh. I have seen the greatest wonder in the world, not so much in beauty as amasement. We spent the day in Angkor yesterday and each moment I kept reliving the adventure of the French naturalist who eighty years ago and quite by chance came upon this strange fabulous stone city under the jungle. Imagine mama mou a Boudhist Brahman Versaille lost in a wilderness of trees and lianas and orchids. Scattered among colosal trees, like in a dream, stand walls and gates and highways, temples and palaces and shrines, sanctuaries to strange seven armed Vishnus and eight headed Cobras. Great grey stone stairways leading to nothing and balustrades of Bhudas playing at tug of war with great winged devils.

"Enormous pineapple like structures climbing ever higher into the sky and as you look great faces appear in the stone, which you had not noticed before. The face of Shiva the destroyer or Vishnu the sustainer or Brahma the creator. A face thirty or forty feet big and facing four sides of the towers, to dominate the world around it, which in this case is jungle. Jungle at last as I have dreamed of, with great festoons of leaves both climbing up and hanging down from trees so huge that one cant see the top. Trees with such a variety of parasite leaves and fruit and flowers that it is impossible to tell which are his own. And water everywhere.

"Imagine that this astounding kingdom built they think in the ninth century on labour such as one cannot believe possible and of such splendour that makes Louis Quatorze a pauper depended mostly for its income on the sale of Kingfisher's wings. Green and blue wings to adorn the heads of Chinese emperors and War lords. So they had pools and lakes and *pièces d'eau* simply everywhere to attract these precious birds. And now these long discarded ponds are full of water flowers thick and peasoup green and creepy. Except for the lotus which at last at last I saw in bloom. All these years I have been reading about them and seing them in carvings and as symbols but always where we went it was not the season. But yesterday for the first time I saw a pool so full of white and pink and deep rose flowers standing straight up from their huge round scoloped leaves that even the thought of crocodiles would not have kept me from wading in to pick some. Aunt Iphegene however did.

"All over there were birds and jungle sounds. Here is a constant battle between archeologist and vegetation. They cut and prune and fight and always the great roots come up and push and tug and bring great massive stones down as if they were pebbles. But can you imagine Mr. Mouhot in 1860 I think wandering the creepy jungle and suddenly seing the first wall and pushing his way with difficulty through curtains of leaves which seem as much alive as the moskitoes leaches snakes and other horrors of the forrest to find himself in the first great courtyard of Angkor Wat. This is the biggest structure and the one which is in best condition. It is at once temple and palace. Temple to Vishnu and palace to the king who was considered divine and as such personifier of the deity.

"You walk up a tremendous road flanked on each side by statues of elephants and snakes and lions as well as the lotus pools I told you about and come to the first courtyard. Great massive blocks of grey stone turned yellow or green by moisture and the jungle, and covered all over with bas reliefs of dancing girls and battle scenes and faces. The faces are also stained in white or green by damp and it gives them even stranger expressions than they already have. At times they even have weeds and orchid leaves growing from eyebrows and lips.

"A strange stillness is everywhere and is at once a glimpse into the past, a death of some tremendous lively gay pagan civilisation, and also like peeping into some sinister future when our descendants if any might wonder around the Empire state building or the Hotel Matignon ruined and overgrown with giant roses or honeysuckle. In this first cortyard there are chapels and corridoers and huge pointed cealings with millions of bats flapping around and a strange smell of damp and death. Boudhas peer out of every niche and on every side other sunken yards which might have been pools to catch the coolness of the evening. 'Black Shade, sweet nurse shroud me and please me.'

"The heat is so tremendous outside that it is like going into another world of shadows and cool darkness as you leave the courtyards to climb up hundreds of the steepest shallowest most slippery steps I have ever climbed, to the top of the second court. And from there still more steps and the traditional five towers and the great pinaple cones climbing to the sky which is pale blue and full of lovely clouds. From the top you gaze down onto the cascade of stone steps you have just climbed and into a wilderness of green so thick that one has to sit for a while and dream of all the birds and tigers and creepy things that must live there as well as of the flowers one might have picked. I found some tiny pink orchids but that was all except the lotus.

"Unfortunately our aged relatives (*entre nous soit dit*) are not in their first youth so that we galloped along often not even getting out of the car in places where I could have spent a week. I got awfully cross at one moment but luckily that other self asserted herself and I allowed but for them I would not be here at all. Of all our trip this has been the best. I have not written to you for ages I know but as the stays get shorter it becomes increasingly difficult to find a moment to sit down and be alone. As it is I pleaded a tummy ache to skip lunch and write to you today and in a moment they will all be back and we shall visit the Palace of the old Kings of Siam.

"Great coloured Temples covered with gold bells that tinkle in the wind. Goodness how romantic and divine this all is. Less so the every day life of today. Freedom brings with it its own tragedies and all over the Far East freedom seems to be confused with red tape. Even Malaya which has been independant only since the 30th of August already has customs people at the frontier with Singapore (her sister) and officious officials throwing their weight about and asking for your age sex and name of grand mother at birth in seven *exemplaires*, before they sell you a stamp. Another evil of independance (besides the busyness suit which has so unfortunately re-placed sarong, tagalog sari etc.) is the radio, which blares at one from every corner and all conversations have to be yelled to the accompaniment of Bangkok blues or Mambo.

"Its funny psychologically that if you go to a strange place and live in a hut with the natives etc you are terribly glad when anything goes right at all. But if you go to the same place and are put in an air conditioned hotel with plastic shower curtain spitoons modern atrocity furniture and bell boys, then when the telephone does not work the shower comes down unexpect-edly on your head you ask for a dress to be ironed and get some one else's shoes back instead, then you begin to feel and act and even occasionally think like a South African version of Senator Faubus. Most disturbing. We stay here till Saturday and then go to Rangoon and there we separate. The Uncle Arthurs are going to India and we to Indonesia."

My idea was to stay in the general Pacific region, going home via Indonesia, Australia, and New Zealand, while Uncle Arthur and Aunt Iph would continue westward from Burma across India to Europe. Louie Woods had already left our party in Hong Kong. However, the entire plan was disrupted by unforeseen disaster. We had flown to Rangoon, and there we intended to split up, my uncle and aunt heading westward.

A day after we were installed in the old-fashioned Strand Hotel at Rangoon, a pleasant city with smiling people whose principal hobby nevertheless seemed to be murdering each other, the two elders and Marina and I were to meet in the lobby at 9:00 A.M. for a morning of sightseeing. When we descended a bit early, we found Aunt Iph already waiting. "I wish you'd go upstairs and take a look at Arthur," she said to me. "I can't help feeling there's something wrong with him."

When I reached his room, he was still wearing pajamas, dressing gown, and slippers. He kept rather nervously moving from one chair to another in their suite. He talked ceaselessly but with what seemed to me a slight slur. "I don't know what's come over me," he said, "but I just don't feel right. You three go off and I think I'll rest a bit."

The previous evening U.S. Ambassador McConaughey had given a dinner in our honor, and, just before we left the table, I saw Arthur take his handkerchief and dab several times at his eye. He was sitting right across from me on the other side of Mrs. McConaughey. As we filed into the sitting room, he whispered, "I have the most awful sudden pain in my eye." We left early, and when we parted company he said, "I feel much better now." Yet he looked exceedingly drawn and tired. I remember saying to Marina when we were undressing, "I'm afraid he's had a stroke."

When I saw Arthur that morning, I was sure I had been right. I made him lie down on the bed, saying, "You've just been doing too much." (After all, he was sixty-six and, although extremely vigorous, had been greatly overtiring himself with excessive travel, excessive sightseeing, excessive tedious receptions, lunches, and dinners, and was feeling generally fatigued.) I called up McConaughey from the next room, murmured that I feared something was seriously wrong with my uncle, and asked if he could get the best possible doctor to his room as soon as possible.

When I put down the phone, Arthur had again wandered shakily into the room and started fiddling idly with ashtrays and books, and seemed restless and disturbed. I tried unsuccessfully to calm him, then descended to the lobby, where I told Aunt Iphigene and Marina that he seemed a bit off but assured them that it was nothing to worry about; they should take the sightseeing car while I stayed with him. Then I returned. Fortunately, a few minutes later a nurse from the American Embassy arrived. She was a pleasant, decisive woman, and she firmly put Arthur to bed, where he remained until a quiet, calm Indian doctor, who practiced in Burma, showed up, quickly diagnosed the case, and summoned an ambulance, and off we went to the doctor's clinic, a tranquil place by a lake just outside of Rangoon, where a murder had been committed the preceding night. Shortly afterward Aunt Iph and Marina followed.

It was indeed a stroke. For about three days it was nip and tuck whether Arthur, who got speedily worse, would survive. After the first few hours in his hot little bedroom (there was no air conditioning then), he sent Aunt Iph away to find him a cold drink and whispered into my ear as best he could, "I hope I don't make it. Don't tell anyone." From here on I will let Marina recount the story, compiled from excerpts of the many letters she suddenly had unexpected time to write.

To Dodo on November 9: "I have not written for ages. Uncle Arthur had a stroke five days ago here in Burma so you can immagine the distress and anxiety and re-organisation. Luckily it was a very light one and already we know he is out of danger, but we still dont know how long he must stay in bed. I must say both he and Aunt Iphigene were marvellous. Gay even making jokes, and wonderfully calm and self posessed. Its no joke to be semi paralysed in Rangoon as you can immagine. Luckily the nursing home is quite pleasant, on a lake and gets some kind of breeze and also we managed to borrow and install an air conditioner so now he is more comfortable. It is incredibly hot and sticky here.

"There is not much I can tell you about Burma because all we have seen are the hotel (shades of the empire with Bloomsbury furniture and pudding and mutton for lunch when it is not Chinese food) and the Hospital. They tell us that there are glorious things to see further away. Great rivers and the jungle once again no further than my arm and yet out of reach. And hills and strange wild tribes with nice names like Chins and Chans and Karims and Nagas. There are also seven different civil wars going on and raiders called Dacoites and insergents and it all sounds most glamourous and fascinating but here we are doing cross word puzzles in the hotel or hospital room when we get too tired of reading about boudhism and ruins we cannot visit.

"I sound browned off but actually I am not. If this had to happen thank god it happened while we were still with them and could be of some help. The very next day they were supposed to leave us and go to South India (Madras or Bangalore would hardly be anybody's favourite spot to have a stroke in) and we were going to Jakarta. It would have been perhaps better in Singapore but this is not too bad. People have been most kind and we are always glad to get an invitation to dinner so as to get away from the grim hotel dining room and the mutton. Two days ago was full moon, always a holiday in Asia and this particular one the light festival and we went up at night to the Shwe Dagon pagoda which is a fantastic place in the middle of the town. Like most things in South East Asia one is told that it is several thousand years old but as earthquakes, rain, people and time all are destroyers around here, everything is rebuilt repainted re-decorated every twenty years or so, so one can hardly tell what is what.

"This one however is most extraordinary with a huge sort of pyramid in the middle all gold and all round it inumerable red and gold shrines thickly populated with Boudhas and all the various offerings to the gods. Four huge entrances lead up to the high terrace where the shrines are and all four are lined with tiny shops on each side selling every conceivable thing. Lotus flowers and incense and temple bells and sacred ombrellas made of coloured guilt paper and garlands of paper flowers and robes for the monks in that glorious orange and safron and yellow cotton and there are barbers to shave off the monk heads, and astrologers and bowls of rice for offerings and everywhere people in their gay dresses. They wear a kind of long sarong in bright coloured cotton and the women all have flowers in their hair and the men funny pink or yellow turbans.

"The night we went up there were millions of little flickering lights and it was just like a *panigiri* [village fair] with people asleep on the ground and others chanting or chatting or eating. On this night all the best weavers in town come and weave all night a great cloth of yellow and orange which is later cut up to make robes for the priests and given away. Most of the young people chose their favourite weaver and bet on her and there is great cheering and shouting encouragement to the rhythme of a great drum. I must say it was delightful. The priests all look like bald ancient romans and not at all religious looking. It is a strange faith which frowns upon the destruction of a moskitoe or a worm but thinks nothing of human life. Great gang wars go on amongst the various monasteries and often monks from one district atack monks from another and cut off their heads.

"If all goes well we shall probably leave here in ten days and fly as directly as possible to New York so as to tire Uncle Arthur as little as we can. It cuts our stay in America very short and I shall probably fly directly to London to pick up the children from there. Cy has to be back in Paris too by the 15th for the NATO conference. He has been wonderful. Like so many men he is difficult to live with when little things go wrong and in a real crisis he is splendid. But very tired and I cant wait to get him out of here as well as Uncle Arthur."

Finally we were able to get Arthur off to the American Hospital in Manila, where he could rest on the way to the United States and where we had the Bohlens to raise our spirits.

Marina's next installment of this sad event (from which Arthur never recovered, although he lingered on eleven miserable years) was again to Dodo, on November 24 from San Francisco:

"Fourth and last lap of a rather anxious trip. A whole week on the way since we left Rangoon last Sunday night. It really does something to one these long long laps. Especially when the time changes constantly and today is tomorrow or yesterday. We left Manila in great pomp. The President sent his car for Uncle A and the Bohlens theirs and several other people plus the ambulance and the doctors so we were quite a motorcade. We were allowed to drive all the way to the plane and Uncle A was lifted in by a kind of crane they use for luggage.

"Typhoon Lola was blowing to the north of us and typhoon Kate to the

East but thank god we steered clear of both and landed safely what seemed a year later in Honolulu. Two whole nights and a day on a plane. Thank god we had bunks and sleeping pills. I must say I found it hard to believe I was in Hawai. You know somehow for us it is different. All Americans go their for thier holidays there. But to us in *Psorokostaina* [poor coastal Greece] it means travel posters and fancy dress parties and Robinson Crusoe you know.

"We stayed in the ugliest hotel I have ever seen mustard coloured and magenta pink and full to bursting with vacationing Americans who with all due respect are about the end. They wore more orchids and octapuses and things on their beach clothes than in nature herself who is pretty lush anyway. Man and wife, models, mother and daughter. Long pants short pants every horror in the book. But even they could not spoil the real beauty of the sky and the hills and the fabulous flowers. Such hybiscus mama mou. Every shape and colour and size. And orchids everywhere and palms right down into the water. I went surf riding which is the most exciting thing on earth."

Back in Paris for Christmas, Marina wrote Nursey on December 21:

"Last minute Xmas shopping. We got a pretty tree and the children decorated it all afternoon while I still unpacked (in between answering the phone and receiving visitors). You know the usual flurry of return but this time after three months and minus you, and Far in such a state of nerves that you cant say boo to him. He deserves them though poor darling. He was dreamy all through the trip and this is reaction. We neither of us sleep at all at night. No wonder after so much flying.

"The children arrived fresh as daisies and so full of beans. I cant believe there was a time when David was squashed by Marinette and rather tongue tied. Now none of us can get a word in edge-wise. He had a glorious time on a farm in Oxford while the school was shut down from flu. My two days in London hectic. We will call you at noon Xmas and wish you everything in the world.

"We got onto that plane as usual looking like refugees. At the last moment I bought a huge porcelaine swan (impossible to pack) and some lovely false flowers (also unpackable) and I had with me two hats from

Siam and the Philippines as big as bath tubs. However with much pushing and giggling we made it and Ike's visit to Paris must have made them all pro American again as we went through customs like a letter in the mail. So now we are here and in another day or so I hope to have some kind of organisation."

At least the year 1957 ended on a happy note. Marina wrote my mother from Lech am Arlberg in the Austrian Tyrol on January 6, 1958:

"Christmas went off fine. Then at the last moment André de Staercke the Belgian ambassador to NATO asked us all to spend the New Year and four days with him in his divine house on Lake Maggiore. General [Lauris] Norstad [NATO commander] a co-guest would take us all in his plane. So after a frantic changing all our tickets around so as to come here from Italy, we all started off for the air-port. Imagine our dismay when the pilot said the whole of Northern Italy was under heavy fog and no question of landing. Then the general said it was too gloomy to go back and have dreary lunch each on our own so lets just go up and eat and fly to Milan and back as there was one chance in a thousand that it might clear.

"What it is to have your own plane. We had a delicious lunch and what made it even more unbearable was that only a few mettres up it was crystal clear. We flue over the very house bathed in golden sunlight and the lake blue and shimmering, with tears we turned towards Paris when suddenly a signal came over that there was a tiny clearing over Turin. We zoomed down and landed and even as our wheels touched the ground the fog closed in again and by the time we got out of the plane we could not see our hands in front of us. It was as if a fairy hand had lifted the curtain for a second just for our benefit.

"The drive from Turin is only a hundred miles but it took us nearly five hours because all was black. Still we made it in time for supper and the next three days were dream like. The children bowled with Cy and the general and listened goggled-eyed to tales of war and diplomacy, while sipping Mouton Rothschild for the first time in their lives and eating caviar and foie gras. We went for walks and rowing on the lake and had a lovely time. Then the others went back to Paris and we made our way here by taxi train buss etc. Rather long but pretty. The hotel here is sweet and David and Andrea [our nephew] whizz about most bravely. Marinette and I more cautious.

Cy reading, sleeping and walking as the skiing is rather dull. No snow at all except on the nursery slopes. Cy goes back tonight and we stay another week."

On January 11 she wrote to Jane Joyce, whose husband, Bob, was U.S. consul general in Genoa and who were among our closest friends:

"We trudge along at ski school and groan and moan but today was a great day as we did a slalom without sticks and all feel like champions. Ah me what a nicer sport this would be if the snow were warm and if things did not hurt so much. Bushes stones the ski boots themselves prickly under-wear everything seems to be against one. I must admit I much preffer sports for which one has to undress rather than dress up to the ears. There is a chair lift here which is a night mare of dangling feet in mid air and agony to get off of as well. Costa [Achillopoulo] my beloved friend is a great comfort to us all encouraging patiant and totally uncritical. We play games in the evening or go for sleigh rides which I must say is glorious. I cant claim that it reminds me of my childhood in the Greek islands but somehow I suppose everyone reacts the same way to dark trees moonlight on diamond whiteness shades of wolves and Anna Karenina. Songs too and yoddling and tyrolean dancing. All very gemütlich. We eat knoedle and knopfen and krapfen and things floating in tepid broth but our appetite after a day on the slopes is undiscouragable."

She continued that account in a letter to Avis Bohlen on January 23 after returning to Paris: "There was only one lady in the hotel who was rather well dressed in silk skirts and *après-ski* and things and she was there with 'a gentleman friend.' How things have changed. Whereas only a few years ago our mothers might have sniffed and pulled their skirts aside at her passage, we all felt that she was the most *fréquantable* person there. She had made it, so to speak. She was romantic and glamorous as opposed to all of us rather dreary married couples. Well Cy stayed only four days and then had to return to the daily bread but we stayed nearly too weeks and it was heaven and we came back with all the greeness of Asian flue gone and full of pep if also full of bruises. My behind was like a Mediterranean sunset.

"Then we had another week here. Marinette had a red haired gigley school chum to stay and we 'did' Paris. I did not want her to go back to her parents and tell them we were not couth, so off we went conscientiously to the Louvre Versaille St. Chapelle and the Commedie Francaise. Rather fun really but of course I did not have a moment left to myself, and yesterday all these pleasures came to an end and dismally we took the plane back to London."

She also wrote Alexis about the Lech holiday on January 30: "Robert Graves [the English poet] was there with innumerable children from four to forty and the children got most chummy and skied and danced together all the time. Robert Graves looks exactly like you would think. Huge and rather flabby and bushy hair eyebrows and little hairs coming out of his ears. Beige baggy corduroys and a Yougoslave hat. Unshaven slightly dirty and really dear. Adores his own theories which I must say are well expressed but founded more on arbitrary 'I knows' than actual fact.

"We got into long arguments about the Greek myths and Christ but got no where as he won't be argued with. You know how easy it is *après coup* to explain things by freudian causes and effects. Appealing but not necessarily so. We played 'the game' [charades] every evening. We went for sleigh rides in the moon light in forrests which looked like the original of little red ridding hood's place. So romantic."

On March 5 she wrote Kakia Livanos, a Greek friend, about a visit she and Susan Mary Patten had paid to our old Middle East chum, Rowland Winn, who had inherited the house and estate of Nostell Priory and the title of Lord St. Oswald:

"I have just returned from ten delightful days in England. I went to take the children out for half term and oh the pleasure of seing their little faces again. I really miss them horribly and to have them to myself again even for a day was glorious. I took them out two week ends and spent the interveaning week in London and in Yorkshire visiting a friend who has just inherited the most fabulous house. It was built by Adam with the help of Chippendale who was the local carpenter and his friend Angelica Kauffmann and her Italian husband Zucchi the famous stucoist. The four of them worked on the house for several years and it is the only house I know for which the furniture as well as the walls windows terraces etc. were designed by the same architect. I simply cant describe to you the beauty of the fire places cealings painted doors mirrors, stair cases etc. Not to mention Rembrandts Holbeins etc., etc.

"I slept in a green lacquer chinese Chippendale room of such beauty that

I stayed awake half the night not wanting to fall asleep and miss a single flower or bird of the wall paper a single sprig of embroidery on the canopy a single motif of the cealing mantle peace window frame etc. And all this in the heart of the black country surrounded by infinitely dismal mines and flat grim country. The boy to whom all this now belongs is a red moustachioed guardsman called Rowland Winn whom we knew in Cairo.

"In London as always everyone so kind and hospitable. I was saddened to find the English more anti American than ever. I don't mind them being Anti American but I do mind it when they are so for the wrong reasons. The thing that makes me maddest is when they still harp on Suez claiming that it was all Americas fault that they stopped. Either you have guts enough to start something on your own and then finish it on your own or you dont. You cant claim later when you have gooffed that you did so because America shook a finger at you. I even heard one man say that America had done more harm to Europe since the end of the war than Russia.

"I must say the only thing all the so called Allies have in common seems to be a deep dislike of each other, as well as a huge exhasperation at their respective governments. As for France it is really messy and so expensive that Dubonnet and leeks seem like champagne and asparagus. However the weather is glorious and the trees are blossoming and all the women are trying desperately to achieve the 'baby doll' look without actually spending a thousand dollars on each new dress. Actually the baby doll look is too dreamy for words and makes all other cloths look like what the cave women wore."

That was an agitated spring. I had to see Tito in Belgrade, Nasser in Cairo, and also fly to Syria, Lebanon, Holland, and Germany. But as the warm weather started, it became increasingly clear that the biggest story of all was France and the best place for a journalist to be was Paris. The Algerian crisis unfolded with all its explosive doom and General de Gaulle took over power to destroy what was left of the feeble Fourth Republic.

On May 13, 1958, the day a military revolt against the French government was launched by French officers in Algeria, Marina wrote Avis Bohlen:

"Well the only consolation for not having you around Europe is that everything is so bloody in a way it is good to be tucked away somewhere and try and forget all about it. We have just heard that there are riots both in Beyrut and in Algeria and the American consulates set on fire, the flags torn down etc. Several people killed and here in Paris all the salad baskets [Black Marias] are out as they expect riots here too. Its all too grim and beastly. Mr. Pflimlin [prime minister] is already accused of having 'sold' Algeria before he has even taken office. What follies what utter madness rules the world. . . .

"I interrupted this letter two days ago and have not had a chance to finish it until now. The situation suddenly became so terrible that we were all hanging on the radio wondering if we would not be in full civil war any minute. Its all ghastly and in a strange way exciting like living in a play. The town is so full of policemen that one cant move. Meetings of the chamber constantly, everybody expecting the parachutists to land at any moment and take over the capital. Lots of wild talk and also lots of apathy. No one seems to take things seriously. Its the wolf wolf story over again and who knows when the wolf will suddenly appear. Cy tense and working all night. The general's statement yesterday plunged everybody into even greater uncertainty and chaos."

Exactly a week later she told my mother: "It has been impossible to concentrate on anything at all these last days. How can I possibly describe to you the extraordinary atmosphere in this extraordinary country in this extraordinary situation. A governement which does not govern, an army which revolts while swearing allegiance to the republic. A little people said by everyone to have had enough yet who strolle amongst the machine guns and armoured cars on their usual post prandial walk as if all this were happening in Timbuktoo. De Gaulle announcing that he does not want to be a dictator but wants 'special powers,' that he is for the governement but that the army did well to act as it did in flagrant rebelion against this same gouvernement.

"One feels like in a dream where everything is possible and nothing. Paris looks like an occupied city. Not an inch where there are not clusters of gendarmes in grim looking helmets machine guns on their backs, gas masks at their hips, and totally uncoinciding smiles on their pleasant faces. From far it looks like the eve of Balaclava. From near like preparation for the 14 Juillet parade. Only one thing is certain. No one, not even Cy knows what is going on or what will happen or what should happen or even what they wish would happen. Rumours as you can immagine are eagerly and carefuly collected and exchanged stingily like we use to exchange marbles when young. One big one for two small ones. One totally mad for three semi official. One minute the 'paras' are about to land at Le Bourget. The next Algiers in toto has seceeded and joined with Nasser and [mutinous General] Salan to lead the war against France. Then again nothing will happen at all and 'you foreigners' are mad to get excited about a little thing like an army insurrection which is not an insurrection when the gouverne- ment itself intrusts the insurgents with the public safety. Madness Mad- ness.

"Of course in this kind of atmosphere how to sit down and write? Or do anything at all. Any excuse is good enough for not doing unpleasant things like balancing one's check book or calling the plumbers or darning one's socks. And frivolous things like fittings or getting summer clothes ready seem much too unpatriotic on the verge of a disaster which insists upon not coming. Result that I spend half my time on the telephone exchanging delicious grousome bits of misinformation, and the other half sitting about with women friends quarreling arguing and expressing violent opinions on things we know nothing about and do not understand. No one does, that is at least a consolation. I wonder if all revolutions are like this in the flesh. Not a bang but a wimper as Cy says in his column."

She wrote Marinette the same day, at her English school: "You cant immagine what Paris has been like this week. Thirty seven thousand helmeted machine gunned policemen all over town. The Cours de la Reine and the Invalides like a picture from the Crimean war. Bivouacs guns and huge dark blue and grey salad baskets. The telephone never stoping and everyone exchanging the wildest rumours. General de Gaule is coming, the Parachutists have landed the communists are attacking. Far calling and saying Dont leave the house and whatever you do dont use the car as they are after Americans. The radio going all day long and everyone expecting shooting and blood shed at any moment. House wives rushing to get a little stock of sugar and flour for the 'barricades.'

"All this under a brilliant blue sky and the chestnut trees more beautiful than ever and tourists strolling down the streets with cameras and *Le tout Paris* going to the races. It is the maddest town you ever saw and in all this nothing at all happens. One feels partly relieved and partly let down. All the excitement and worry and it all fizzles out. There was a general strike called for yesterday and everything stopped for an hour and then like lambs everyone went back to work.

"You have the strange phenomenon of thousands of governement police protecting general de Gaule when he comes to give a press conference against the governement and supporting the rebel army. No one French really considers the generals as rebels. They are good Republicans who just dont happen to agree with the governement and therefore disobey. You have mister Soustelle under arrest escaping under the nose of his guards in the boot of his car and getting to Algiers before anyone knew. If it were not so tragic it would be really musical comedie. There is a state of emergency and one needs vizas to leave the country and there is censorship again like during the war. Everyone expects the worst and says 'It is surely for tomorrow.' And tomorrow comes and nothing happens. Ah me."

On May 26 she added to Marinette: "Tremendous excitement again since last night as Corsica has revolted. No one knows a thing and everyone expects anything at any moment. But come what may I shall be with you next week. Last night we stayed quietly at home with the telephone ringing every few minutes with new reports that Marseille was in open rebelion or Toulouse or Perpignan none of it true as far as we can find out but everything is so confused that it might be true."

The summer of 1958 we took a holiday in Colorado with the children in a couple of log cabins loaned to us by our old friends Jimmy and Nancy Smith [he was former U.S. AID administrator]. The cabins were well above Aspen, en route to Independence Pass, so we lived at an altitude of about nine thousand feet. I went to America early, to see Eisenhower and two relatively little known political figures named Jack Kennedy and Dick Nixon. Marina spent a fortnight in Greece with her family before coming back to pick up the children and bring them to the States. She wrote:

"I had a glorious three days in Pylos where it was utterly beautiful. We swam and fished and visited a Venitian castle and we went to the excavations of King Nestor's Palace. Imagine they have found the bath. Do you remember a lovely pasage in the Oddysey when Telemachus goes to Nestor's to ask if they know anything of his father. He meets the King on the beaches and he is at once asked to dine and wine and come to the Palace for a rest. After the King's daughter has given him a bath (in the one we saw presumably) he comes out all refreshed and only then etiquette permits the

King to ask of him Who are you? What is your name? Are you perhaps a bandit or a pirate, or perhaps a friend? What lovely lovely manners. Greece looked more beautiful than ever. The oleanders were as big as Dahlias and morning glories and *ligaries* [a bush] at every step. And it all smelled so heavenly and the roads are all repaired and we eat fresh fish and so much garlic I could not even stand it myself. I got back Tuesday night and then yesterday and today went to Pikermi and watered the lemon trees."

On July 16, just before leaving Athens, she sent me a letter in the United States saying: "I have had a dreamy time. Last weekend I went to Epidaurus with Taki [Horn] and spent the week end with the entire theatre. Not only was the performance of the two Oedepuses, Tyrrant and Colonno perfectly wonderful but it was such fun being with all the troup and sitting around afterwards for hours listening to anecdotes and theatre stories and laughing till we ached. I had never seen Colono before and it is a marvellous play. And as always nature took such an active part in everything. At one moment when Oedipus old and dying curses his children for their wickedness and announces his comming death, the sun set which until then had been mild and mauve suddenly turned scarlet and fierce and flamming. And the mountains seem to come nearer and a wind came up and blue the chitons of the chorus so that they looked alive and angry too. There were forteen thousand spectators most of them peasants and shephards and old women with head scarves. It is very moving."

By August 12, when we were well established in the Rocky Mountains and Marina had recovered from her first day or two of altitude dizziness, she wrote Susan Mary from our cabin:

"All this could hardly be further from my natural habitat. Great mountains hovering above our heads, even though we ourselves are already nine thousand feet up. A rather small gloomy lake at our doorstep. Marshy fields full of flowers I do not recognise, smells I do not know; great clouds overhanging and when they are pushed away by the wind the sun comes out hotter and nearer than even in the Greek islands. Further away a lovely lovely river full of round slippery stones shining in the sun light and rushing waters so cold that only the misguided belief that it is good for my figure induces me to go in every other day. This pleasure is somewhat marred by the ever presence of snakes of all sizes. But we wade in the river with blue jeans and shoes and I dont catch any fish but enjoy the motion of casting and the deep silence and the solitude.

"Our log cabin is so far from the rough idea that Nancy had given us that it feels like the Ritz. We have two little houses one for us and one for the children. We have nice 'rustic' beds covered in cotton bed spreads exactly like what one would expect in a woolie west movie (the sweet pionners house just before the Indians scalp everybody). We have (oh blissful surprise) a gas stove hot water and a shower and detergents for the washing up. And a wooden WC with a seat which does help a great deal in view of the snakes. We have a jeep and every now and then drive into Aspen to get groceries at the Super marquet and books at the lending library. Aspen I have not taken to. It has a self conscious 'old wordliness' about it and innumerable ye quaint old gift shoppees. The 'summer people' all wear clothes as closely resembeling Hopalong Cassidy as possible and if not that long shorts and souvenir hats.

"Everybody is frightfully nice and good natured and says 'by now' and 'folks' and everybody has a drawl. Besides that there are the 'artists.' I even saw a lady in black tights and a false red beard the other day in the drug store and I rack my brain to see what opera she could come out of and cant think. Strangely one hears the sound of Bethoven or Scarlatti being rehearsed every morning from inside a red brique building which must have been the Hotel de Ville in the old silver mining days. We have not gone to any concerts yet nor seen anyone but the Smiths arrive today and they will probably urge us into a slightly less solitary existence.

"For the moment our life consists entirely of fishing walking wading in the river and for me housekeeping. Oddly enough I enjoy it. Perhaps the fealing that ninety per cent of the women of the world do this all the year round except on holiday makes me feel that it is right and proper that I whose life is one long holiday should be doing this now. Perhaps it is to see that I can after all do it. Perhaps too there is something pleasantly unproblematic in simply having one's day's work cut out for one. Breakfast washing up beds sweeping laundrey lunch washing up dinner washing up etc. etc. It is sort of soothing and so far removed from summit meetings, the Middle East, Grat's excentricities, the Empire line, who to have dinner with whom etc. etc. that for while it lasts I really rather love it. If only I did not dislike mountains and the rather soft gloom of lakes I would be very happy. The children seem very happy and as for Cy he is in heaven. We wake up frightfully early and go to bed at nine really sleepy. Every evening after washing up I read a chapter of the Iliad to the children and we are now practically on family terms with Atreus Thyestes Priam etc."

When we had returned to Paris and had put the children back in school, Marina told Avis Bohlen (September 27, 1958):

"We rode a lot and went to bed at nine every night and never saw another human being and Cy looked fifteen and woke up smiling and we did not even know about the off shore islands [the Quemoy and Matsu crisis] until we hit New York weeks later.

"And we all got on frightfully well with each other and each one thought the other three were wonderful. And Cy and David went off alone together unrushed and unhurried and Cy tought David to tie a fligh and to cast and to aim at a beaver and the names of fish and trees and they got to know each other the way men should. And Marinette and I cooked and cleaned and felt wonderfully like pioneer wives. The country around is beautiful and we went for a pack trip up to what seemed like inhuman hights and I was petrified going over the narrowest steepest pass thirteen thousand feet high on loose stone and I thought my last hour had come and the horse slid and slipped his way down into a gorge which seemed like the valley of death to me. Great crenelated red rocks rising high high into the sky like sort of ruins of super human temples.

"It is not country made to the measure of man at all and hardly my home spirituel so I was really quite surprised at how much I enjoyed the summer. Mostly it was the utter peace and quiet and our being alone together just the four of us and time on our hands. And such a rest from our fellow men who on the whole I love as you know but we had had a bit too much of them what with Parisians and Burmans, New Yorkers and the 600 Philippinos of that monstrous cocktail party [the Bohlens had given for us]. And the *évènements* in May when Cy worked till dawn every night and going back and forth to London to see the children. Anyway by the end of June we were like old rung out dish cloths. Then Cy went to New York for work and as the children were still in school I nipped off to my own native land and had three weeks of sheer joy, surrounded by a hundred loving friends; speaking Greek ALL the time, going to the theatre in Epidaurus which was a dream and sitting in or under the sea for as long as I possibly could.

"We left Aspen ten days ago and spent a few frantic days in New York or more precisely in Macey's basement and in a frantic search for clothes for Marinette who is at that hideous stage when girl's cloths dont fit her and woman's are too big and the only things which did were too expensive so all was frustration and hurry and by the end of a few days there we felt we needed another holiday. Then I flew the children back to school, put them on their respective sad little trains and last night got back to a house full of still unpacked bags summer cloths to put away curtains to hang carpets to dust and the usual up-heaval of late September. Not to mention the inevitable cloths problem. Everything one owns is naturally not Empire and one looks provincial and dreary with one's waiste where God ment it to be and one counts and recounts one's bank balance and it remains the same and mighty small whatever way one looks at it. So one plans and one gets a glassy look in the eye and does not listen to other people's problems until somehow it all falls into place some time in November and one no longer cares.

"The telephone has not stopped all day. I must say much as I enjoyed the solitude of Colorado it is fun to get back and find one has been missed and people gather around and still love one. Amongst my other chores is to somehow get a dead beaver* whom we brought over from Aspen tanned and made into a rug for David. His first silvan catch. You should have seen us arrive in the hotel in New York complete with frying pan sleeping bags and beaver skin over our arms. I do think I am a wonderful wife and mother. The things I do."

Marina wrote my mother on November 30: "Tuesday we are giving a large dinner party. I have one prince (Paul of Yougoslavia) one movie director, one actress, one author, two Ambassadors and one ship-owner. Nobody knows anybody and god knows how it will go but I felt that all these people always meet the same people wherever they go and this would be a change for all of them I hope it wont be a change for the worst."

---

* Jimmy Smith had permission from the State Conservation authorities to kill beavers that were destroying his dam and irrigation system.

That Christmas was especially memorable for the four of us. Poor little Sebastian had died of distemper, leaving a hole in our hearts. Therefore I secretly arranged to purchase in England a three-month-old beagle puppy. He was smuggled into our house on Avenue de Ségur with great craft by our cousins, Monica and David Curtis, who arrived from London to spend the holiday with us. Benjamin, as he was named, on the theory that a dog his shape required quite a long, low name, was hidden away in the cellar by Justine and Grat. Grat adored animals and immediately became the slave of Benjamin, my present to Marina. When we assembled before the tree Christmas morning to exchange presents, the door suddenly opened and in raced Benjamin bearing a large card attached to a ribbon around his neck:

> Benjamin Beagle is my name.
> I'm beautiful but dumb.
> I hope you'll love me all the same:
> Merry Christmas, Mum.

Marina indeed loved Benjamin with a passion, above all when she discovered that he adored the water surrounding Greece even more than she. Beagles are not normally water dogs, but he loved swimming so much that he had to be chained on a boat to prevent him from jumping off. He liked diving from rocks, swimming back, and plunging in all over again. Even during his final summer at the age of fourteen, he could still swim. At the end of 1972 he fell very ill with the ailments of age. Finally, in pain and with mistrustful sadness, he had to be put down by the vet. Marina, who was just as brave as she was loving, held him tenderly in her soft arms, wordlessly weeping while the doctor gave him his final injection.

VII

January 1959 - October 1961

In 1959, Marina traveled a lot, including visits to five of the earth's seven continents: Europe, North America, Africa, Asia, and Australia. The year started off pleasantly, with another holiday in Lech, which Marina described to Kitty Solomos on January 19 (in French):

"I must admit the ski trip was delicious despite my strong prejudice against mountains snow cold whiteness etc. The children adored dancing in the afternoons, the largest cream cakes in the world, and evening sleigh trips through mysterious black forests with blue-eyed ski teachers who had voices like nightingales singing into the night to the sound of their guitars. Because our appetites coincided with the number of kilometers we skiied and the number of times we fell, we ate as if starved. . . .

"This letter has been interrupted for several days by a disaster. When I went to the bank for money I didn't have a sou left. How come? They showed me ten days worth of checks made out to cash and with my own signature. But when I saw the endorsement on the back it was that of a Spanish refugee who was the lover of the little maid we had helping Grat and Justine. I went to the police and within an hour they found both of them, too stupid even to get out of Paris but spending money wildly on dinners, American cigarettes etc. Aglaia (the maid) took all responsibility and begged to get him released. Oh my God . . . love!"

On February 14 she congratulated Monica Curtis, who had just produced a baby girl in London: "Has she got huge eyes and does she look like Greta Garbo and Bardot combined? And does she already speack Greek and Latin?" Immediately afterward we flew off to North Africa, and she wrote Susan Mary, from Rabat, Morocco, on February 16:

"Let us face it I DO NOT like the Arab world. Its no use starting off with Much as I like etc. I just dont. The Moorish arch leaves me cold. The palm tree swaying in the desert wind I find Hollywoodish. Even the biblical faces and the donkeys and the beards I have had enough of. What I would take if pressed and that in a non Arab country would be a moorish garden. Great walls enclosing deeply shadowed garden tiled and fountained and ripling with water and with shadows and with smells of all kinds Jasmine and mint and lemon blossom. And in each great silent wall a tiny carved door leading to another garden and another one with pea cocks, one just lemon trees and orange, one with only flowers in pots. That I would like. But the rest . . . No wilder shores of love for me.

"I have been struggling with a story of Morocco and I cant even disentangle the Berbers from the Arabs or the Dynasties of the first few centuries let alone when you get into Lyautey times. The only thing that stands out as far as I have got is that these brave folk have contributed nothing but killing to civilisation as long as they have existed. Oh dear I dont know why this should surprise me except that I was so ignorant of things Maroccan. I still am but frankly now I dont care. I am dying to drop the wretched history and return to my juicy detective story and finish the last flower in my tappistery.

"From here we go to Marakesh which everyone says is lovely. *Nous verrons.* I promise you not to come back with inlaid brass coffee pots or camel blankets not even chunks of silver jewelry. I only wish you were here for one thing. The wild flowers I must grudgingly admit are a dream. Iris as tall as I am, and calla lilies and a million strange wildly coloured things. Beautiful."

We flew on to Algiers, which was then in the midst of a sputtering and doomed war against Algerian rebel patriots fighting savagely for independence. Marina wrote my mother on February 27:

"Cy has gone off to spend the night with a farmer so as to get an idea of what life outside Algiers is like. We did not want to impose on an unknown farmer's hospitality unduly so I could'nt go. Too bad as I really have seen nothing except the town of Algiers and here one does not understand anything.

"Strange how every-dayish every day life can be even in the midst of drama. The faces one sees on trams or in caffes and barber shops bare no trace of tears. Yesterday and tomorrow covered with blood and hate and grief and terror, today going about their business as if nothing ever happened. Only now and then in the sunny mimosa scented day is one reminded of all this, as one's bag and pockets are searched at the door of any caffe or shop, for bombs. So also by the young parachutists *"les hommes peints"* as they call them who in their green and brown and mustard coloured suits patrol the crowded sidewalks clutching a machine gun under their arms like some nefarious ombrella or walking stick. What a tragic situation. All that is good and determined and brave in man mingled with so much that is ugly and mean and grasping under the glorified excuse of patriotisme so that one cannot distinguish the one from the other and as much harm is done by galantry as by selfishness.

"And what a bore it is to see everybody's point of view. How much easier to be fanatical and prejudiced and black and white (no pun ment). Here whatever one's sympathies may be or one's sense of justice or history one simply cannot blame anybody. The tough selfish little Frenchman as well as the one who gave up his whole life to make this place what it is big and rich and sparckling white, cannot be blamed for wanting at all cost to hang on to what he has achieved at such a price and with so much hard work and sacrifice for a hundred and twenty nine years now. When you see Arab towns and compare them with this you realise what they have made of desert land.

"On the other hand who can blame the Moslems for wanting their own country for themselves especially when you think of a hundred and twenty nine years of little humiliations of being treated like mudd and hardly

allowed to live at all. God knows if only France had done thirty years ago
what she is rushing to do now in terms of social reforms maybe all this
would not have happened. On the other hand maybe nationalisme is just an
inevitable historical reality and nothing could have prevented it. Whatever
it is I have very distinctly the fealing that our breads are numbered as they
say in Greek. Quite soon I think the French and the British and the
Europeans in general will vanish like the Dacians or the Illyrians or the
Carthageneans and we shall just be glorious names in history books. Unless
of course we blow ourselves up before that.

"But this is the kind of theoretical gloom which in no way really means
anything and our private spirits are perfectly high and pleasant. except that
we are both suffering from over-feeding. That is the real trouble with
travelling after middle age. One cant in a hotel or as someone's guest have a
cup of tea dry toast or salad and the result is that our livers are protesting
violently. We cant wait to get home and lead a quiet life. From here we go
to Tunis tomorrow."

In early April we went to London to pick up David for his Easter holiday
and pack Marinette off to Malta to spend her vacation with a schoolmate,
the daughter of the British admiral there. Marina described this to my
mother on April 3:

"Well Marinette's departure was epic. First a race to the shops bags
shoes toilet water sponge bags two new dresses bathing suit. You might
have thought she was off to get a husband the way I carried on. But her eyes
were sparckling and her feet dancing and what can be nicer than a happy
happy child. Her plane left at the ghastly hour of four in the morning as that
is a much cheaper plane than the day one. I think it was a queer economy
because to pass the time we took her to a play and then to dinner at the Ivy
and spent as much as the better plane seat would have cost. However we
felt virtuous and more and more so as the hours dragged and it was still
early. Finally we got her off and staggered back to our rooms and bed about
ten to five.

"The next day Cy's resistence being most low I got him to his taylor
believe it or not and at last he has a new dinner jacket and a gabardine suit
to replace the one he looks like Fagin in. Then the day after David arrived
three inches taller and looking like an orphanage child, trousers to ankle

and sleeves to elbow in the best suit bought for him only last September. And off we went at once to Winchester [where he was scheduled to go in January 1960] to see the school and the house-master. All three of us were most agreeably surprised. We found the house so much cosier and more human than we expected. And the housemaster simply charming. Warm and kind and wise. Then he took us all over the college which is one of the most beautiful places in England. If David manages to get in it would be wonderful. It is such a privilege to be accepted at all. However the exams are stinkers. The headmaster gave us some sample papers of last year's entry exams and as far as Algebra and Latin go it might as well be Chinese for both Cy and me.

"Then we came back and went straight to Chantilly to our friend Lady Diana's for a quiet but pretty and flower picking Easter. Tonight I take David off to the South of France for a few days to our friends the Deakins who have a house near Toulon."

In June, Marina accompanied me to my twenty-fifth reunion at Harvard. Of this she wrote our English friend Michael Edwards:

"For five days now we have been in the constant company of two thousand people. From nine in the morning till three in the morning we have been moving around in a huge amorphous group eating drinking talking and smiling benignely on our husband's friends and memories. But let me start at the begining. I left London last week and got on to the tiny narrow short economy size plane with some trepidations and had a beastly trip. In the seat next to me was the fattest lady you ever saw with six little bags and basquets and nets including one with dried dead fish. . . . She was an Armenian going to see her son in California and spoke not a word of anything but Armenian naturally and alas six words of Greek. She was petrified and kept nudging me all night for reassurance and also shifting her various bags around so that the only thing of me that went to sleep at all was my foot and leg causing great pain.

"I arrived stiff as a poker and rather worn and weary to be skouped up by Cy and put on a train for Boston without even the time to wash my face. Innumerable cups of coffee in the train helped somewhat but not enough to help me face the hideous concert that night in Boston's symphony hall. Hours and hours of 'Toreador,' Invitation to the Waltz, and the 'Nutcracker Suite' played by a military band. This sitting at a table with a hundred other Alumni (why do I hate that word so) and eating fruit cup and cold chicken. However little by little we sorted ourselves out and to my great surprise the whole thing turned out quite pleasant and touching. There is something irresistible about an academic background about a university town filled with young men on the threshold of things (what a cliché) and about men who have not seen each other for twenty five years, meeting again and remembering. The conversation of course was mostly about exams just squeezed through about so and so and this and that all twenty five years old and all the more fresh and bright because most of them had not even met since their graduation.

"The usual smattering of heart break too. Some older looking than they should some sick some faillures some very very poor. But I must say I was impressed by the general gaiety and dignity of the thing. I did not see one single man drunk or foolish in spite of the rivers of alcohol poured into us. Most of them had their children with them and there too I was impressed by their looks their charm their manners and the cosy way in which the generations mixed. We had two dances and a huge reception and pic nic with what looked like seven thousand lobsters and swimming in the ocean which was nice and then of course the last day was the graduation ceremony which never fails to bring a tear to my eye. A thousand young men 'welcomed to the fellowship of educated men' a thousand parents glowing with pleasure and pride. A Latin Oration hymn singing and all the oldest and corniest and dearest causes for emotion. But oh my were we tired when we got on to the train last night.

"Soon I shall have to face the outside world. This made even harder by the fact that we live on the 23rd flour of the Savoy and I need dramamine each time I come or go. What a monstrous civilisation this one is. I feel more alien to it each time I come and madly disloyal but there it is. The press button. A world totally defeats me and you may be sure it will take me half an hour to master the stamp machine when I get down to posting this letter."

Marina wrote my mother on July 3, after we had returned to Paris:

"I was suddenly out of a clear blue sky (litterally) abducted to the Italian lakes by the Norstads and our friend the Belgian ambassador to NATO who has a dream house right on lake Maggiore. Cy was in Oxford and I was sitting quietly minding my own affairs when Isabelle Norstad rang up to say Laury had to make a speach in Rome so they were flying down for a few hours and then spending the week end with this Belgian and would I like to join them. If so would I be ready in an hour to take off. How can one resist such an invitation? Of course I went.

"What a way to travel. Soldiers *au garde à vous* half the way there, no passports no formallities except a lot of vice-generals trying to make things as easy and smooth as possible. A huge plane with beds in it and a shower. We got to Rome in a twinkling and while Laury [Norstad] poor fellow was addressing God knows what European community, André [de Staercke], the Norstad daughter aged eighteen, another young girl and I went sight seing as fast as our legs would carry us. Under my friend's guidance even the things I knew best became new and exciting. We also had a bit of luck. We went to St. Peter's and as the next day was the name day of the Saint they were preparing the church for its great ceremony and everything was lit up and the double choir of the Sisteen Chapel was rehearsing. It was fabulous those volumes of song filling the prodigeous spaces of that pagan church and we alone in it like some great princes of the Rennaissance. We could hardly bare to go.

"Then we flew to Milan and by car to my friend's house where we spent Friday Saturday and most of Sunday eating sleeping and swimming in the lake which is on his doorstep visiting churches fishing for trout in a 'torrent' and altogether having a most enchanting time. The Norstads are sweet people and so beautiful and the Romantic décor of Magnolia trees and dark Italian lake was just the right setting for them. One felt tubercular and tragically in love merely by being there. Ghost of Stendhal and Chateaubriand. However we came back no more in love than usual and far from tubercular after a combined Italo-Belgian cuisine. At four in the afternoon we were still sleeping and swimming in the lake. At five we took off and at eight we were in our little homes back in Paris. Pure magic carpet stuff. Cy got back the next morning looking very well and having enjoyed both his philosophico-scientific week and his children. He says they both look well and cheerful."

On July 18 she confessed to my mother: "I really am spoiled. Sometimes I feel quite ashamed of all the delicious things that happen to me. Hardly had I got back from Italy than my friend Pam Churchill took me down to Cannes with her for four days. She has a house there for the summer and she had two other friends staying and I must say it was an orgy of aquatic joys. You know me at the sea, it makes me twenty years young just to think of it. And here I was in the brilliant sun and salt air and a garden just like a Greek one full of cyprus trees and hibiscus and a marvellous view and grilled lobsters and all around us her various millionaire friends at our service. It is such fun to enjoy other people's money. All the pleasures and none of the responsibility. There were yachts and speed boats and sail boats and cris crafts and everything that floats at our disposal. I was never out of the water I think for four days.

"Even when Pam took me to a large rather chick dinner I had to go with my hair dripping down my shoulders. I skied and sailed and slept and talked and had a dreamy time. Cy did not feel like coming. He is frightfully busy and then this sort of thing is not really his cup of tea. He would always so much rather be alone than with his fellow man. We constantly argue about that. However I got back two days ago and we have spent these two days quietly at home playing scrabble and talking and working and it has been fun."

To her girl-hood Greek friend Catherine Negroponte on July 23: "We go off on Saturday to Athens for a week and then Spetsais for six or seven. I cant tell you how I look forward to it. After the hurely burley of winter it will be sheer bliss to do nothing. My only worry is that since Stavro [Niarchos] established his hunting lodge on Spetsopoula the bloody place has become shick [chic] and more and more I hear of people who have taken houses there. It will be like Capri and everyone in Pucci blouses and tights pants and sipping martinis. Well not I. An old bathing suit and bare feet and not talking to anyone. I feel like an empty sack."

As always we had a delicious summer holiday in Greece with Dodo and, for a time, her mother, Maria, to inspect the great-grandchildren. We rushed back to get the children to school, close up the house, and take off for Singapore, Indonesia, New Zealand, Australia, Fiji, Hawaii, New York, Washington, and Paris. While Marina waited in Christchurch, on New Zealand's South Island, I flew down to the Antarctic.

We were moving so fast that Marina had no chance to carry on her usual extraordinary correspondence about our day-to-day adventures on the trip until she was stranded in Christchurch, because a rigid rule forbade the presence — even for an instant — of any woman in the small American colony farthest south. So her somewhat scrambled recollections begin with a letter she wrote my mother on October 21 from her forced New Zealand bachelorhood:

"I wrote to you at length from Djakarta but as I said then I felt as if I were putting a message in a bottle and throwing it into the ocean; which makes it hard for me to write again without knowing what you have had and what not I shall either repeat myself or leave lots unsaid. Better that and we can catch up on all you dont know when we see you in a very short time now. At any rate I know I did not write about the famous lunch given by the American Ambassador for us to meet the President of Indonesia.

"It was a wierd thing but at least in their country place up in the hills which is really I suppose the way they keep sane. Going up into those cool blue hills with runing waters and great dark thick pine trees one might be in Switzerland or the Addirondacks except for the added attrac ion of palm and banana and glorious deep scented frangipani trees. After the dank damp sweet gluewy heat of Djakarta it is sheer heaven to breath air again and not a thing which feels like liquid blotting paper. The Embassy house is charming and has a lovely swimming pool and heavenly flowers. Gardenias grow like weeds. Well it was a huge lunch mostly Americans and about six Indonesian couples. Then Mr. Sukarno himself arrived looking just exactly as one expected. There seems to be one model for these neo-independent-democratico-dictators. Same self-designed uniform padded shoulders funny black velvet hat wide wide brown trousers and a breezy nod and wave. Mrs. however is really beautiful. She is his second wife and had a very bad reputation before he married her and so most Indonesian ladies avoid meeting her.

"But I dont blame him for wanting her. She was lovely and sweet smiling. Indonesian ladies are much more talkative and cultivated and gay than most Asiatic women. The agonies of shy silence I have been through with Indians and Pakistanis and Saudi Arabs. But in Djakarta they were charming and most interresting and interrested. President Sukarnos greatest weakness is women and his next favourite dancing and singing so imagine the whole dignified assembly being shoved off their feet immediately after lunch and made to hop up and down to the tune of a few fiddles a drum and two saucepans borrowed for the occasion from the Ambassadors kitchen. The national dance is a sort of simplified and extremely monotonous cha cha cha and there we all were sweating like sponges and smiling bravely leaping and bouncing on terrace and lawn and getting down on our bended knees and squeeking up again and all together looking too absurd for words.

"Ah me this awful race for popularity with the underprivileged nations. If we dont dance maybe the Russians will and then they will like them more than us and so they may go communist so by all means DANCE. Who said *Tout comprendre c'est tout pardonner?* He did not know what he was talking about. Every single thing in Indonesia like in all ex colonial places is comprehensible. The infiriority complexes the suspicion the dislike of Europeans the incompetence (they were kept deliberatly back for three hundred years) their wish to throw their weight around in their turn etc etc etc. But understanding does not make one *tout pardonner*. Not when your car has brocken down for the eighteenth time in the middle of nowhere in heat worthy of hell. Not when it takes three hours to make one telephone call. Not when you are finger printed eight times for an exit visa etc etc etc. You go out of your mind with irritation and frustration and its no help to repeat to yourself that it could not possibly be otherwise.

"The trouble with independence here is that it came a hundred years too late when everyone else is more or less giving it up in favour of interdependence and when help from others is no longer considered humiliating but only useful. Fierce pride and incompetence, freedom and ignorence, make bad companions. This is the richest country in the world and half its population goes hungry. However people like children have to grow up their own way and make their own mistakes and in the mean time we as well as the Russians play the seducing game and are beaten at it. A pity childishness is only endearing in one's own children.

"We left Indonesia for Sidney a few days ago and what a long trip that is. It is hard to remember how huge everything is here. From Perth to Sidney is twice as far as from Paris to Athens. We stayed in Sidney only long enough to see the Koala bears in the Zoo and they alone were worth the trip surpassing in adorableness any thing imaginable. Round balls of fluffy furry angelicness.

"But we had to take a plane immediately for Christchurch, New Zealand, as the navy had moved up its trip to the Ice as they call it here, and we left the next morning. Christchurch is a funny rather charming typically English town with pseudo Gothic cathedral town hall little gardens a river called the Avon weeping willows and mutton and sago pudding at every meal. We spent yesterday getting Cy's equipment which is marvellous.

Even with a hundred below zero and winds faster than a hundred and eighty miles an hour he can be cosy in THAT costume. And he left at eight this morning very excited. Alas I have just had a call to say blizzards are blowing so they cant land and he will be back this evening ready for another try tomorrow. One does not fool with Antarctica.

"In the meantime I who thought that for the first time in my forty years of life, would find myself totally alone in a place without a single friend and rather looked forward to the peace and rest of it have been greatly mistaken. For one thing there is little news in Christchurch so I had two interviews with the local papers which both mentioned I was Greek and alone here. Ever since this morning the phone has not stopped. Greeks everywhere, Greek wives who met their New Zealand husbands during the war. They want me for lunch for tea for supper. They want to adopt me to look after me to nurse me. It is too sweet.

"One sweet girl came to see me just now. Her husband was wounded in Crete and her parents hid and looked after him at their own danger for eighteen months. He finally got away and only after five years managed to get a letter to them asking for their news. He had been told they were all dead. His letter took months to come to Crete and their own back to him even longer. The girl was forteen at the time but he had fallen in love with her then and remained faithful all through that time and as soon as he found out they were alive came over and married her and they have three children now and a garden and are very happy. Another one is taking me to her farm on Sunday. Then a lady from the radio station came and interviewed me. Then another asked me to the movies. So its all I can do to sit down and write to you. But very heart warming. I suppose I shall be here about a fortnight. *Faute de mieux* I am just steeped in books about the Antarctic but rather hampered in my reading by ignorence of such things as latitudes longitudes magnetic poles statute miles etc. I think I should go back to school instead of meeting Greeks."

After I got back to Christchurch, we left promptly for Wellington, the capital on New Zealand's North Island, from where Marina wrote Jane Joyce:

"Most of the Greco-New Zealand couples were war ones of course. One girl was a seamstress chez Madame Tassoula the dressmaker of the *quartier* in Salonica. Mme Tassoula (later deported and tortured by the Germans) hid three boys in her house where this girl met and looked after them. Not a word of English from her not a word of Greek from the men. 'But his eyes were kind' she said and we were young.

"He was cought by the Germans but after the end of the war went back to New Zealand bought a wild farm and wrote to her from there to come and find him. She packed her little bag and without a word of any known language started off steerage to cross the world and find him. Now they have a sort of biblically beautiful farm and a thousand sheep and four children called Socrates Xanthipi Anthoula and prosaically Tom (for some English grand father). Even the animals have Greek names and a large rock on the farm is called Acropolis. I spent one of the sweetest days of my life with them. I met at least six couples like that and they were all so nice to me and took me for pic nics and drives and walks so I really had a wonderful time and saw a good deal. It is rather a wonderful country with sea and mountain everywhere in most human proportions and distances so that one could ski and swimm on the same day and even the poorest worker plays golf fishes trout and rides.

"They have one glorious sounding sport. They climb high on the side of a mountain on the solid rocky part and then at the top crawl onto a side which is covered with loose stones rubble pebbles etc where the mountain has been shredded by wind and snow and ice, and there they stand up straight and wiggle a bit and the whole thing starts moving gently downwards like a huge natural escalator. It is a bit dangerous and if you wiggle too much you can be covered up by a land slide but they all seem to know how to do it and enjoy it. It sounds heaven. They also have little planes that land on mountain peaks with skis where they deposit the skiers who can then ski down for the whole day.

"Much as I like following the spring around the earth it does make one rather un-chick. I am wearing an old skirt and sweater the same one for the past fortnight not having expected spring in the antipodes to be as cold as this and having come only with cloths for the tropics. In Java it was so hot that one got stuck in the tarr on all streets which had it, which was not many. When not stuck to tarr one was stuck to the car seat one's own self or the sheets and moskitoe nets. Talk of underprivileged people. What a ghastly climate. I suppose it is the price one pays for living in a place where every leaf every blade of grass is worth its weight in gold like a super Hédiard [a Paris luxury food shop] *en état nature*. Coffee tea rice tapioka tobacco quinine rubber teak every conceivable thing not to mention mangoes papayas bananas and all the Robinson Crusoe things. And yet half the population is hungry. Ah me. Funny how one cant get over one's childhood ideas of geography. South sea islands and the East Indies are even now filled with dreams of blue sea and birds and flowers for me. The sea around Djakarta is brown and gluky and full of sharks and beastly things and the sea birds are in cages and very few. And in the jungle the huts have nylon curtains. I know there must be places where this is not so but they are for the explorer or rich tourrist on saffari and not for hard working news paper men who hunt prime-ministers and not birds of paradise. But who am I to groan and protest when I am supposed to be so lucky to be here at all.

"To tell you the truth I have had travelling, and would not mind never moving again if I had my way. We still have Australia ahead of us which for some reason bores me even at the thought of its size. I hope and pray that we may stop on the way back in Fiji or Tahiti or Tonga. At least that bloody well ought to be South Pacific-ish. If not I shall stick to botanical gardens and zoos from now on."

She described the next lap briefly to my mother in early November:

"Wellington is a larger prettier port town but without the little town charm of Christchurch. Middle class old world England stuck at the up side down end of the world. Cricket and crocket every Saturday afternoon church on Sundays and the Salvation army singing under our windows. Only the drinking laws are crazy. They are only allowed to drink from four to six with the result that at six ten I walked out yesterday to get some cough drops for Cy and at every street corner I met a group of ten to twelve men all bleary eyed and tottering. It looked like the setting for a woollie West story. Weard. This is written on the run more or less as we leave Wellington in ten minutes for Auckland and thence to Melbourn."

Afterward *Vogue* asked Marina to write an article about New Zealand, and I quote a part of it in normal magazine spelling:

"This, alas, is a letter about how I did not get to the South Pole. I was left behind in Christchurch, the taking-off base for Antarctica, waving goodbye sadly to Cy, who looked like the well-dressed explorer: fur hat, four different pairs of gloves, quilted pants, quilted everything, and the softest, warmest, most elegant underwear I have ever seen. Considering that the temperature drops to a hundred and thirty below on that frozen continent, and that the winds blow at a hundred miles an hour, I am glad to think that those poor sailors can keep warm, if nothing else. I asked Cy, as a joke, if they had iceboxes down there, and he said yes, not to keep the beer cold but to keep it from freezing solid."

Nineteen sixty started with a big event. David, to our surprise, had passed the entrance exams for Winchester, Britain's toughest "public" school, and went off in January to start. Before that, however, Marina took the two children and Billy Patten off again for a ski holiday in Lech. When they returned and both of us had accompanied David to his new school, Marina wrote my mother from Paris to congratulate her on her seventieth birthday:

"I am only sorry that I have not had the privilege and pleasure of being your daughter in law and friend for the whole seventy years. It would have been fun for us to have grown up together. But perhaps Cy would have been a problem then."

On March 11 she wrote Avis Bohlen, after the news that Khrushchev was coming to Paris in the spring:

"The entire nation is in a frenzy over Mr. K. The Louvre flapping around dusting old paintings and things suitable for his tastes. The curator of Versaille in a state trying to find places to hide his thousand secret policemen inside *cache-pots* behind tapestries under chandeliers etc. and checking every flour board cealing etc for hidden bombs. The Quai [d'Orsay] convulsed because they have only just been told that he is bringing SIX grandchildren with him and where to put them and what little diplomats to mobilize for the *jardin des plantes*. All inhabitants of Balcan or Iron curtain origine whisked off on an enforced and prepayed holiday to Corsica much to their delight and the indignation of the Corsican Hoteliers who would much rather have rich English tourrists on their beaches than pennyless potential political assassins. Mrs. K is going to visit the Galleries

Lafayette a whole day much to their horror as all other buyers have to be kept out. Four thousand police for the Ile de France alone. But I do hope they take her to Dior and the Ritz and Hermes too and if we cant beat them at their own game maybe we can seduce them a *grand coup de decadence* and capitalism. Immagine if he 'chose freedom' too and refused to go home. Not that he has been much at home lately. How he runs that country as abscentee landlord I cannot immagine."

Marina wrote my mother just before the children came home for their Easter holiday that Bill Patten had died (March 26, 1960). She said:

"For days of course we did nothing but be with Susan Mary his wife. I went with her to England just for one day to get their little son [Billy] back you know the one who was at school with David before he moved to Winchester and it was a simply ghastly trip. He was so pleased and surprised to see us and his little face lit up with joy and to have to tell him the reason we were there for was too heart-breaking.

"Then Cy had to do a lot of arranging for her and funeral and flowers and telegrams and we were really such close friends and she was a bit lost so all that took a great deal of time. Hence my long silence. I even had to give up going to England to bring the children back from school which was sad as Mrs. [Polly] Wisner gave a tremendous party for them in the evening with orchestra and buffet and over fifty guests and I would have adored to see them at their first semi grown up party but what could I do. It was the very day of the funeral and we had to be here. Any way even without us they seem to have had a glorious time and danced till one in the morning and then they came back on their own followed by a bevy of young Americans one nicer than the other and all mad about Marinette who preened and pranced like a peacock with so much male attention I am rather afraid at the expence of her studies.

"The first part of the holiday went very fast. Then we took off in the car with a friend of mine and her daughter and her dog and our dog and drove down to a tiny village near Toulon which was a dream. There we were joined by Susan Mary and her children and it was so good for her to get away to a quiet place with no people and some peace to cry in. She is wonderfully brave and Bostonianly self controled but deep down she is miserable all the time poor pet. Anyway we took charge of the children there so she could rest or stay alone in her room if she wished and that helped too. . . .

"We had a glorious time drove all the way to Aigues Morte in the Camargue which is this Medieval city from where the Crusaders took off. We went to Arles and St. Giles of the glorious Romanesque church and constantly to Avignon and to Aix for ice cream and Toulon to look at the ships and we pic niced in field after field of wild narcissus and we picked lilac and tulips and sniffed our way around the mountain side for the wonderfully nostalgic smells of thyme and rosemarie and all those Greeky Greek herbs that made us feel so much at home. Really Provence is a divine place I would not mind living there for ever. Cy came down to join us for three days and was sweet and gay and relaxed. Our old freinds the Deakins from Oxford live there so it was quite a reunion. We had a whole lamb roasted on the spit on Easter day and red eggs and spring onions so it was as Greek and as Orthodox as possible away from Greece."

Aunt Nina, her father's sister, died in Athens, and Marina wrote her cousin Monica on May 3:

"You know I used to think that words are no good in moments like this but in the past weeks I have seen my friend Susan Mary whose husband died after a long and terrible illness, and I have seen her comforted and warmed by the hundreds of letters she received and so I wonder if perhaps words do help in a way. Not help of course in making one's grief one's infinite pain any less awful but only a tiny consolation in the thought that others share it with you.

"And if after all, after life is what one leaves behind one in other hearts then one does like to hear how great the love and admiration and warmth was that one had for Aunt Nina. To you I know what she meant, to you and to Peter, but to us too she was so much more than an Aunt. Theia Nina does not just mean Aunt Nina. It means a whole set of emotions and ideas and feelings. It means coming in to dress for an evening and opening that famous cupboard door in search of untold treasures. The last drop of scent borrowed unscrupulously. Beads handkerchiefs a hundred last minute touches to one's appearance and happiness. It means a cotton and needle to repair disasters to a peticoat a hem a sleeve.

"It means long talks deep into the night about everything under the sun.

It means security. Aunt Nina will fix this Aunt Nina will know, Aunt Nina will help. It means laughter at the most unexpected moments and a twinckle in the eye. But far beyond all this and perhaps understood only much later in our lives she means courage and hope and tenacity such as I have never come across in anyone in my whole life except perhaps in you. Optimisme and hope in the face of every blow that unkind fate could deal to one human being. And in spite of all her troubles all her own worries and physical pains always compassionate always ready for others, always always time to hear one's troubles to think and help. Awful and unthinkable as death is there must be some satisfaction some tiny consolation at the thought of the job of life well done to the very end. To go quietly without a single remorse a single regret as far as others go, a single gesture of courage and goodness left undone, must be a help."

The famous Four Power summit conference, featuring Eisenhower, Khrushchev, de Gaulle, and Macmillan onstage and Gary Powers' unfortunate U-2 spy plane offstage, was held that spring in Paris to the accompaniment of Mr. K.'s rants and roars.

Marina wrote Jane Joyce: "Did I say I was not looking forward to the summit. Well world catastrophy *bruta figuras* insults and threats of war apart, I have never enjoyed anything more. We never went to bed at all and had the wildest week in years. Chip and the [Llewellyn] Thompsons [U.S. diplomat] some nights ending up at the LIDO (yes) and then at several places for 'just one more drink' and Chip at his wildest best and thriving as he usually does on action and crisis. Then several other Alsop evenings* with Stuart acting the part of 'Elsworth' returning to Paris for the first time since the war and taking a sentimental journey up to Montmartre. I really have never laughed so much in my life.

"Then there was another act of the stingy brother not wanting to share the bill with Joe. He was absolute heaven and I love him. Joe too was wonderful and strangely he the profet of doom when doom was more or less upon us optimistic as never before and glorying in the company of what Diana Cooper calls his camp followers. All those beautiful women he

---

* Joseph and Stewart Alsop, brothers and eminent American journalists.

always has up his sleeve. Now they have gone but every chief of mission in Europe is here so a series of garden cocktail and other parties all rather nice if you dont have to give them yourself and only stay half an hour to see old friends."

I flew off to America for the political conventions that nominated Kennedy and Nixon, the first time both presidential candidates were younger than I. Marina wrote me from Paris on July 3:

"After those agonising moments at your departure it took me nearly an hour to get to the hairdresser. Eventually all fancied up in a great coiffure I got home and dressed and then Peter [Payne, her cousin] took me to Versailles to dinner with the Alexanders. Oh dear. Thank god you were not there I kept thinking. You know that I am a snob basically but my god I felt more and more like a *tricoteuse* as the evening went by. For one thing the dullness, for another the food consisted of cold ham and one old jellied egg and some lettuce. Then I sat near a Prince Hohenlohe of sorts to whom for want of something to talk about I said 'We went to see the Ben Jonson play last night' and he answered 'Oh is he playing in Paris these days.' Honest to goodness. Then the talk came round to the awful state of affairs in the world in general whereupon there was agreement that things could not possibly ever become any worse. In a world where Princes travel without valets and have no lands and live in small houses just like anybody else how could things be worse. I was sickish.

"But nothing to what came later on in the evening. We all trotted off to Versailles and I must say one thing, the arrival was a dream. One drove in through the great gates and all along there were troops dressed in Louis XV uniforms and carrying torches and horsemen of the regiment of Louis XIV and drummers playing a fanfare or whatever and it was too beautiful for words. But then the ball was in the Orangerie and one had to wait for hours to park the car or advance at all and eventually we got into the Orangerie which is half tunnel half corridor and not at all made for a ball. Luckily because we came in with Alexander and the Queen of Italy and all that we were bowed and scrapped into a relatively comfortable table and there somehow sat in spite of the thousands of people pushing and peering and photographers all over our laps and it was too awful and there we sat with a cha cha band blasting our ears off under the shuddering statue of the poor old *roi soleil* until about one when a hundred and forteen debutantes came crawling in to curtsey and smile and crawl out again.

"Then the awful thing happened. The Queen got up to leave and we all stood up and I turned back to try and get Peter who had been pushed to another table and he came forward to look for me and Maria Pia* said to him dont worry she is going home with Alexander and so Peter went off and left me alone in this ghastly thing with no car. Peter got to Alexanders and did not find me and came dashing back twenty five kilometres to look for me and I was looking for him and half the night was spent this way."

1960 was a bad year. First Bill Patten died; then Aunt Nina; and then, on July 12, quite unexpectedly, Ripper. Marina wrote me the next day:

"Is'nt it awful about Rip. I cant even begin to realise it. Between him and Bill we have really lost two good friends this year. I talked to Avi just now who sounded completely *abattue*. Luckily Gwen and Rudi [her sister and brother-in-law] were with her and I shall stay with her for a bit as she probably needs company. He was buried in Mallorca at once as that is the law in Spain. Much as they quarreled and fought and bickerred I think she will realise now how indispensable he was to her life. Poor poor things. God help us and grant us many many years together.

"I am going to the Talleyrands tonight to spend 14 Juillet there quietly. I would just as soon have spent it here alone but for one thing they get a bit hurt if one never goes and for another I can take Beagle and give him a bit of fresh air."

From the Talleyrands', at St. Brice, she wrote morosely to Avis Bohlen on July 14: "This is going to be very brief because I am off to Mallorca tomorrow to breath a bit of salt and wind before plumping into the greenness of the Far West. Also our poor friend Ripper died two days ago so although I was going to Mallorca anyway this makes it all the more imperative that I get there soon to hold poor Avi's hand awhile. What an awful year it has been. Between Bill Patten and Rip, Cy has lost his two oldest friends in Europe."

From Puerto Pollensa, where she was staying with Avi, Marina wrote

---

* Daughter of Umberto of Italy, wife of Prince Alexander of Jugoslavia.

me on July 19: "Never have three days seemed longer to me or sadder or more oppresive. I came here because Avi is in such an awful state poor little thing and the nights seem endless to her. Rudi and Gwen had to go back so she was quite alone when I arrived. And in such a state. Remorse bitter regret looking back all the time all the things she did or did not do which caused him pain and suffering, all this comes out in one long sad ballad to which I can say nothing except add my own tears and perhaps a kiss and a hand held tight so we sit in the scented air of that garden where every leaf is his, every branch every stone and which with the total indifference of nature to the fates of her men seems more beautiful and luscious than ever this year.

"She found him in the garden you know. He must have felt the need for air and gone out for a breath. She woke up later on and finding the bed beside her empty rushed out to look for him and found him in the garden. She was alone in the house and the doctor did not come for hours and then neglected to send for a priest with the result that poor Rip although a catholic was buried without a priest in the protestant patch where all the infidels go and naturally rumor is rampant and they are all saying in the village that it was suicide or something strange and they are even saying that the Guardia Civil opened the grave and found only bags of stones and that he is not dead but only hiding.

"Avi does not know this thank god but she knows about the suicide rumor. The whole thing is so appaling and of course I understand now that they were denounced as *contrabandistas* which means that this has not got to be proved. Secret denounciations dont have to be proved and it means that if the lawyer does not manage somehow to get a more lenient sentence she looses all her jewels all the other things and both cars. She is without a car now and you dont know what a sence of claustrophobia one gets tucked away in this place whose very beauty is heavy and strange. His presence is everywhere in every bit of furniture in every picture even in the food and drink. Oh dear how awful it is. And unlike with Susan Mary with whom it was easy at least to be sincere when one said she had done everything a human being could do to make his life happy and better with Avi it sounds false and hypocritical to say that she was not the cause of a great deal of suffering so everything is worse. Oh dear what misery.

"She sleeps hardly at all all night but at least sleeps late in the day time whereas I wake up at eight and roam around the house till two or three starving on top of it all because I am not used yet to Spanish hours and trying to think of something to say or do which might help. I find nothing. Your letters to her have just arrived and the obituaries and I must say in all the drama we could not help laughing at you saying so admiringly that he had fought on the loyalist side. Thats ALL she needs just now to fix her up proper with the authorities. I just dont know what she will do with her future. She does not want to give up this house which is her only home and which is ALL him and yet she does not know if she can afford to keep it and also knows that she cant spend the rest of her life here alone.

"All my love and a huge kiss. Dopey

" P.S. Dont lets ever die except together."

Finally we all got to Aspen, Marina from Mallorca, having gathered up the children in Paris, I from Chicago and San Francisco. On August 9, Marina wrote my mother from the tiny porch of our log hut:

"Our little cabins looked just the same only we have a real ice box this time so we dont have to put the milk in with snoopy the snake and that makes a nice difference. Yesterday we went into the village to do all our shoping and Cy went to the seminar [of the Aspen Institute] which turns out to be fascinating. A judge, a head of M I T, Chip Bohlen, several proffesors, some business man and all brilliant and extreamely well informed. Yesterday they discussed human rights and today it is de Tocqueville Jefferson and Horace Mann. I sent the children in to listen as it will be so good for them.

"Later after the discussion was over the Bohlens came back with us here and we spent a pleasant day fishing and walking and I gave them a delicious stake and corn dinner and we sat by the fire after dinner talking about Greek philosophy and things and the children were all ears as Chip is such a wonderful talker. Tomorrow we shall go in too as they are discussing the Greeks and then there is a concert in the afternoon and a dinner for all the participants in the evening.

"As soon as we set foot in this place Cy is a new man and is sleeping again and all smiles and cheery. They have all gone to the seminar now that is why I am able to sit down and write letters and relax. The beds are made the food on the stove the washing hanging up on trees and all is peaceful and pleasant. The weather is crystal blue and the lake full of jumping fish. A pity I hate trout so."

On August 29, after the Bohlens had left, she wrote Avis: "Cy refuses to put his nose out of the place so we have seen no one. Except tomorrow we go to the Smiths who are our hosts after all. But one momentous thing (alas) did happen. David and Cy actually GOT that beaver SHHHHHHH . . . Yes indeed and skinned him and cleaned him and we have been curing the wretched skin for days with vinegar and salt and its been quite a to do. And then the next day Cy sent us all off and cooked all by himself the whole day and I think it was the Beaver à la Lexington with a bit of Sulzberger thrown in that he did for us and I have to admit grudgingly that it was very good. There was so much onion and woocester sauce and ketchup and cinamon and god knows what else that the beaver was incidental and therefore quite good. Cy proud as punch."

We returned to New York in time for a UN meeting made famous by Khrushchev banging his shoe. Marina wrote Susan Mary Patten that September:

"New York is nuttier than a fruit cake and funny and all the camp followers are turning up and its just like Paris. There are policemen under every hamberger and every three blocks the traffic stops utterly as there is some crowd of different origin gaulking or yelling or applauding their respectively hated chiefs of state. We have Kadar [the Hungarian Communist boss] next door but he seems less turbulant and overshadowed by enemy number one Fidel [Castro]. The stories that go around about him range from plucking live chickens in the lobby of the Commodore hotel to spending all his time in negro brothels none of which are quite true nor quite faulse. He looks like the worst type of self conscious beatnik. His bush shirt is dirtier than our children's when they come back from school his beard worse and his posture at the UN is half lolling half dosing half scratching and his face only lights up when Mr. K even sneezes.

"Great excitement yesterday when the President [Eisenhower] arrived and everyone quite pleased with his speech which I found average. Then today I was still asleep when darling Chip called to say he could get me in to hear Kruschev (much as I have read his nasty name I still cant spell it) and so I lept out of bed and went as Mrs. Andy Burding but I must say that unless one goes to the delegates lounge which is delicious as one sees a thousand old friends and hears a lot of gossip, just to go up to the third floor of the visitors I would just as soon see it on television from my own bedroom. Nkrumah talked for two hours and he might have been K's half brother and then K himself spoke from eleven thirty to a quarter to two raving and ranting part of the time but most of it indulging in the Russian passion for statistics. You know under the Tszars the Uzbeks produced ten tons of this and now as free Soviet citizens they produce ninety three million point eleven etc. One could have screamed. He raved for Castro and against the secretary general* who sits impassive as if he were made of plasticine and in general the whole thing was rather boring."

She wrote to David (back at Winchester) on October 8: "I am so sorry it is cold but very flattered at what you say about my cooking. Maybe I can get a job as school cook and then I can keep back all the best bits for you. I feel very selfish when you are cold and uncomfortable and badly fed because we here are warm as toast and sunny and alas overfed. We have been going out constantly and poor Far and his passion for slimming is having a very hard time.

"Yesterday he had such a lunatic day poor chappy. Not only anormous ammounts of work but after a long long lunch with the heads of the FLN [Algerian National Liberation Front] (who incidentally took him to the best French restaurant in town) he got back and was just starting off on his work when the receptionist on his floor called to say 'There is a most enormous black gentleman and a most tiny white one outside asking for you.' Far let them in and it was indeed the largest black man he had ever seen and a tiny white one who introduced themselves as *'Mon excellence le ministre des affaires étrangères du Katanga,'* and the little white chap was his body guard secretary chef de protocol etc. Poor Far they sat down for the whole afternoon and he could not get rid of *mon excellence* and he could not imagine what excellence wanted of him.

"When he asked him how it happened that he wanted to see him Mon Excellence said he had been told to come by *un de vos très grands amis.* But as Far cannot recal a single *ami* in Katanga he was more bewildered than ever

---

* Dag Hammarskjöld.

and *excellence* said the name of the friend was a state secret. So you can imagine how fatigued poor papa can be after lunatic days like these. But we did go to see a terrific mad outrageous wicked play by Brendan Behan called 'The Hostage' which was wonderful although pretty *osée*. We also went to a huge party full of movie actors and musicians and television people but that is the kind of thing I enjoy more than he does. We go to Washington tomorrow for a week. Mr. K at least is leaving soon. That will cool things off a bit."

In Washington we stayed with Chip and Avis, and Marina wrote Susan Mary on October 20 (1960):

"We watched the third debate on TV with the Bohlens and the Grahams* and all disagreed on everything till two in the morning. You know I am beginning *malgré moi* nearly to be very much for Kennedy. Possibly because Nixon is so unspeakable but also Kennedy sounds very convincing and sincere when he talks. I see Marietta† a good deal too. I think half my popularity in this country is based on the fact that I am your friend and dont think I dont feel smug and self satisfied about this. And so possessive.

"Marietta looks more beautiful than ever and working like the devil I must say it will be a huge relief when the elections are over and we know one way or the other. Funny that I should feel strongly about this. I think somehow or other I always end up by fealing strongly about most things. Even madly pro the Pittsburgh Pirates who won incidentally in a most exciting game.

"But the debates on the whole are frightening. Give one really a fealing of organisation men sales talk etc. Nothing seems quite real quite genuine because everyone knows everything all the time. How much make up they have on even at what degree of heat Nixon sweats and the argument about it before the show because he sweats easier than Kennedy who gets cold too easily. Ah me. Not one thing left unsaid.

"You know I remember once walking in a garden in Kenya and my host

---

* Publishers of *Washington Post,* Phil and Kay Graham.
† Marietta Tree, who became a Kennedy envoy to UN.

showed me a kind of high green forrest and kicked it viciously saying these are the lettuce seeds I brought from England. Everything grows so fast here that I have trees instead of salads. Well our present civilisation gives me a bit that fealing. The ground here is so fertile there is so much reseptivity imagination power riches possibilities that even the tiniest idea the soberest thought the wisest new perception, once planted aquires such proportions as to smother even its own unsuspecting creator and turn from something good and wise and sober into a kind of Frankenstein of itself. Television mass media education standards of living everything somehow seems to get too big too quick and totally out of hand. Never have I had so strong a feeling of living in a world which is the victim of its own self. And no way out."

The same day she told Michael Edwards: "Our life has been frantic as you can imagine. Ours and everyone elses although the more lunatic aspect of the city has quieted down a bit since the shoe shaking spitting biting departure of Mr. K. Now our only problem is to remember that Niger and Nigeria are NOT the same place and for god's sake where is Ouagadougou. All our diplomat friends tremble that this will be their next post as well it might. Although for the moment they only send one embassador for every four of the new countries. What with the UN the world series (that is base ball in case you dont know it) and the elections life is one long disagreement with everyone. We argue about everything and to my Balcan spirit this is most agreable."

She wrote David on October 30: "Now of course no one thinks or talks of anything but elections. I am becoming more and more pro Kennedy and fight with anyone who is'nt and its all most exciting. The campaign is getting nastier by the minute and everyone calls everyone else names but they tell me this is usual and when its all over they dont remember the insults. We are going to the Times on election night and to the Harriman's after which will be fun and I hope we will walk around Times square too and see the crowds. Apart from missing you I must say I have enjoyed this as it has been most interresting to see the campaign get under way."

As soon as we were back in Paris, Marina wrote David on November 17:

"It seems somehow longer than ever since you left on that fancy plane perhaps because so many things have happened and we have seen so many

239

people and got a new President and all this makes the time feel much much greater. I must say though now that I am once again sitting at my funny brocken down old desk with *Il Turco in Italia* on the gramophone Beagle in one corner Far next door whistling periodically and the room around in its usual chaotic condition, I feel as if I have never been away really and it is good to be home."

The year ended in much Christmas confusion. Marina summed it up to Avis Bohlen on December 30:

"I hardly survived Xmas. Having just returned from such a long absence and then a trip to London for the children, it had all come in a rush. The children arrived blossoming thank goodness but each with a friend so that in a house of four bedrooms we were eight people. Beds we managed but it was closet space which was the problem and the rush hour at bath and WC every morning was quite something. Well now the two ladies have gone and one child so we were a bit less *congestionnée* for Xmas. But . . . we had to give a ghastly egg nogg party on Xmas morning for the whole of the Times which is a kind of tradition now which we cant get out of, only this year the paper has twice as many people here because of the international edition.

"We were up at seven opening presents and what not and then rushing around with Cy as a kind of Clausewitz in charge of operation egg nogg which ment that he stood in the middle of the kitchen giving orders while we all ran around like mad for rhum milk beaters spices punch boals etc and all the time tasting the ghastly concoction and *tappant* at eleven the first guests arrived all of whom were strangers to me. I kept introducing Mr. Greenbaum as Mr. Guinsberg and Mr. Jacobs as Mr. Isaacs until even the children thought me anti semitic which indeed I was practically being at that moment. Especially as I had just started a monumental cold and could hardly see.

"There was a grim moment when the lunch guests (twenty including several babies) arrived before the egg noggers showed any sign of leaving or ever wishing so to do, probably due to the gallons of rhum Cy had been using with such abandon. Luckily Cy's devoted secretaries did a fairly diplomatic job of suggestion and in the end we got the *avant dinners* off and sat down to our turkey and plum pudding which were ruined by then but not ruined enough to keep our guests from staying till seven o'clock that evening. By then I was not only blind but deaf and dumb as well so I took to my bed and have been there ever since and I must say that except for a few aches and pains this has been better than a Carribean cruise.

"I lie in bed spoilled by Marinette who coddles me and brings me hot drinks every hour, I read love stories (Torrents of spring which I had not read in years and how divine it is) listening to music putting the last stiches (at last) to Cy's rug and neglecting everything in a most delicious and self indulgent manner. I even pretend I am too ill to talk on the telephone so this has been a real and I must admit much needed rest. I was so tired particularly of my own self and my own voice I could have wept. But today I felt there was no more excuse so I have got up and struggled to my desk which is naturally one mountain of papers. How is it that even if one sends a thousand Xmas cards they never quite coincide with the ones one gets? Ah me."

As had by then become a tradition, we took off early in 1961 for the skiing slopes of Lech, where I stayed practically no time, leaving Marina a gay *"Gruppenführer,"* as she put it, for a host of children revolving around our own two and Billy Patten. When she returned to Paris, she wrote Catherine Negroponte on February 15:

"Now is the time where all women go about fishy eyed and abscent minded and where else is their mind but at Dior and Balenciaga. Even the least frivolous the most serious of people at this season seem to get a primitive bird like urge to change plummage and every thing in the cupboards looks dowdy dreary and unwearable. I have been to several collections and Dior is a dream. Ah me for a gold mine, I said as a joke to Lilia Ralli who was sitting next to me. I suppose this dress costs a million and she said No I am afraid it cost one million four hundred thousand. Ah well. *Tant qu'à faire* why not a billion?"

On March 30, after several weeks in Greece, mostly spent searching for a house to buy in Spetsais, Marina wrote my mother:

"I think I have found the dream place. Three terraces and three gardens on different levels and it is in the right place and near the sea and a glorious view and this one at least is within our means. We went over it several times and it needs a lot of fixing but all possible and Cy saw it and liked it and had I not had to come back because of the children I might have been able to pay and sign next week. As it is mummy has a power of attorney and will do so as soon as all the legal papers have been put together. I cant tell you how happy we all are about it and needless to say we talk of nothing else since our return and we are down to curtain colours and kitchen tyles even before the house is legally ours. It is a lovely passe time. Apart from house hunting my month in Greece was a dream. As always all old friends and everyone so gay and warm and full of tales.

"But the glorious part of it was the island. You know as it is a long time since I was in Greece in the spring it was like seing an old friend for the first time. Everything looked different. The place I knew all burned and parched and brown and ageless, suddenly looked young and fragile under a pale blue sky covered with little green grass and tiny daisies and everywhere but everywhere the glorious combination of severe dark cyprus tree and frivolous pink almond blossom as if a swarm of butterflies had landed on every branch. And the scent of thyme and orange blossom and stock, for me the for ever Easter smells of my childhood.

"And we sat with the fishermen and the sailors and the gardeners and sipped wine and talked of other summers other lives, while their wives and sisters kept discretely in the back ground as befits good women. It is only the summer folk, the Athenian women who are exsempt from this rule. And of course they have known my mother and me for sixty and forty years now which is many years. I cant tell you how good it was and we went to church each night and thanked the Virgin Mary and asked Saint Nicolas to help us find the house (which he did) and told him we would give him a new lamp for his help (which we will) and all this, seemed perfectly right and real there even to me who am hardly a deep believer.

"Cy came and went and came again and then we joined up by chance at the Rome airport and travelled the rest of the way back together and since yesterday it has been the opposite of exodus a kind of mass return of the family. Beagle out of his mind with joy at having us all back again."

In April, Susan Mary married Bill Patten's best friend, Joe Alsop, and Marina wrote Mother:

"How glorious and how considerate and dear of you to send me again such a yummy birthday present. As usual it came just at the right time. I

242

must say my mother picked a good season to have me. Xmas for my winter clothes and May for my spring fluff. Needless to tell you I have already picked just what I want and believe it or not for only a very little more than you gave me. I went to dear Mme Gilberte at Lanvin and asked if she had something I could squeeze into for the evening so that I would not look like an orphan at all these receptions given for Susan Mary and Joe Alsop. So she thought for a while and then came up with a simply beautiful dress which was on sale. It is red organza over white and the bottom all embroidered in silver and a big bow at the waist. And I just got into it as if it were made for me.

"I am keeping it for the biggest of the parties which is on Monday night at the Philippe de Rothschilds for eighty people. We went to one party at the Norstad's last night which was pleasant enough as we were all old friends but everyone was so desperately gloomy over our total shame of Cuba* that it was not a very gay party. We all tried to talk about other things but it sounded forced and rather grim. What a terrible thing for us to make such a ghastly mistake especially after we had already had the same over Suez and Hungary and especially with a young president whom everyone thought of as the great new hope and there we are doing exactly the same mistakes over again. Enough to cut one's throat over.

"Tonight we are having eighteen for dinner all of them ambassadors and things and I am wracking my brain to think where I must sit whom. The average age of our guests seventy including Walter Lippmann and Helen just back from Russia. I dont expect this will be a gay affair either but at least it may be interresting if only the men dont insist on sitting out over coffee and saying all the interresting things behind our back. We have to go out every night for the next few days and you can imagine how much Cy likes this. However the days are entirely concentrated on the children and I must say they are nicer than ever. David came back utterly thrilled from his trip with Cy to Germany and as sweet and nice and gay as could be.

"I went constantly to Chantilly to help poor Lady Diana close up the house as she is leaving for England for good and it was sad to know that this is our last glimpse of that glorious house and forrest. But as she is leaving she told us to pick every single flower in sight so you can imagine that we

---

* The Bay of Pigs.

did not have to be told twice. We were drunk with picking. The house looked like a dream and we even had a small vase in the W.C. It was too wonderful."

Marina moved masses of clothes and household goods to Spetsais by ship from Marseilles via Piraeus. She and Benjamin Beagle then flew to Athens, whence she wrote me on July 7:

"Beyond all hope I had a most delightful journey. When I left you at the foot of the stairs, I found myself in an absolute ocean of humanity. Thank god we had left early enough. There must have been a thousand people waiting for their passports to be stamped, and me in that crush afraid that someone would step on Beagle and he would bite them. And droping my heavy clumsy parcels and wearing my coat, so that I was swimming in heat. Well eventually I squeeked through to the other side just as they were saying Olympic flight etc *embarquement immédiat porte 40*.

"We always seem to leave from *porte quarante* which is the most distant one, be it for Athens or Singapore. By a miracle however I found one of the little trolleys and Beagle was still a free dog. I asked the hostesses if there was a way of walking him onto the plane but they said no. So I sat as near as possible to the entrance and was joined there by a sweet American family of five and the littlest boy of course stroked Beagle's head (out of the carrier bag) and we got to talking and they had just read your column about dogs in the paper, and then the man said his name was Mr. Stulpvogel or something and had worked for the Times for ten years in Advertising. Then they promised to carry a few of my ghastly parcels and then the hostess said *Les familles avec enfants les premières* and grinned at me and said *vous aussi avec un enfant*, so the Stulpvogels and I made a commando rush and got the first seats in the plane where there is so much leg room and even managed by just being ourselves (women children dogs bags etc) to scare all other pasangers off so that we had the only empty seat between me and Miss S aged nine. Then there was an argument between her and her seven year old brother as to who could hold his lead and who could stroke his ears and who could give him a bit of their *medaillon de veau*, so everything was lovely.

"Two hours and thirty minutes which is nothing. And then even in Athens there was not the usual chaos (inside at least) and the gun the cartridges; beagle bags etc all came through easily and politely. The porter told me there had been one thousand seven hundred arrivals that day in Athens. Humanity is really becoming too peripatetic for its own good. At first I saw no one, and my heart sank a little at the thought that at last I had in fact been taken at my word, but then huge smiles. Fany *and* Kitty were there. Dear sweet loyal friends. Kitty had a little party for me with Nata and Paspatis, and Nico Baltazi and it was all very gay and dear."

I came to Spetsais in late August for my month's holiday — the first in our new house — but the vacation was interrupted by a summons from Moscow to see Khrushchev. I collected a visa at the Soviet Embassy and then flew to Paris to pick up my Soviet files and some slightly warmer clothes. Even in September there is a difference in temperature between Greece and Russia.

Marina wrote Avis Bohlen on September 1, just after I had left:

"I should have written to you ages ago and often started on a letter but either I was interrupted by the workmen who wanted to move my desk in order to fill in a hole or some great crash in the next room announcing some new disaster. They say that if you don't build a house and marry off a daughter you dont know what trouble is. Well I am learning. But in spite of everything I must admit that clumsily or not miracles have been accomplished. Imagine that the first workmen moved into the house on the 5th of July and by the 20th we were living in it. Sort of Potemkin village living but nonetheless we had water electricity a real W.C. and oh marvel a bath room which is the show place of the island. I brought mad extravagant gay wall paper from Paris and somehow it is up and my pride and joy. And we even have water.

"When I was a child one relied only on god's rain but with progress we can now buy water from a wierd kind of floating rubber whale toed by a *kaike* which brings it to the port and from there with great fuss and shouts and confusion it is pipped up to the houses. So we feel rich in water and it is strange how like a starved child who grows visibly at the first mouth full of cod liver oil, the plants here are (bad English that). I have a jasmine and a rose which looked like dead twigs and since the Hydronaut, I have watered them twice and they alredy look like a jungle. So marvelously satisfying. God I do hope that you will all come to us one summer.

"The children are in heaven. The island population is eighty per cent under twenty. The village square in the evening is like a small civil war. Children of every size and shape swarming everywhere. They fish and swim and sail and bycicle and walk and ride donkeys and flirt. David is like a moth buzzing around the various glowing lights of bikinied Lolitas. Such a change from austerely masculine Winchester. Marinette too has a bevy of beaus around her and the only complaint one hears all over the island, is from parents who claim they never see their children. Cy poor lamb arrived full of woe. Gout in both ankles an infected hand an abscess in his tooth, and disconsolate. And hardly had the blessed atmosphere of this place started to sooth and mellow him, than he was called to Moscow. I could cry. Just as the shooting season opened and his foot was good enough to walk on. What lives our men lead.

"We had one fascinating day last week when we went across to the next island to see my friend Melina Mercouri of Never on Sunday fame making a movie with Tony Perkins We spent the day watching them film and I must say whatever millions they may make whatever fame and glory they acquire is well deserved. The agony of sitting under the blazing projectors for hours on end with a crowd of people around you the make up chap over your nose the director at your elbow all kinds of wires light contraptions and everything and then to have to relax be natural and play your part seems quite impossible to me. Melina spent the entire morning to say quite literrally 'Who?' But we enjoyed every moment and found Mr. Perkins (Tony to us) irresistible.

"So you see that life in spite of my groans and moans is not only household problems and workmen. As a matter of fact the one drawback this year is that there is too much social life and yachts coming in to port all the time and even two households entirely of British Lords and Ladies for the snobs of the island. Angel girl enough chatter. I arrive with Marinette in New York on the 15th take her to Radcliffe on the 18th spend a few more days in New York and then I hope to come to Washington and see you all again. Cant wait."

She got one letter off to me in Moscow: "What a life. Not even a fortnight's rest after such a year and so many hurty feet arms legs teeth. I cant decide weather to be pleased for you or furious at fate and you know who [Khrushchev], who decided to see you now. I do hope at least that having bitched up your shooting and fishing and fig eating he gives you some fabulous tale. That he has decided to give up all and become a trapist monk. Or that he is divorcing Nina P to marry Maryleen Monroe and settle in California and will give East Germany to the French just to show his good will. Or something.

"Marinette was in such a state when she arrived and we had gone. They found a boat in distress and had to go and give him help and tow him in. She galopped off to telephone you on Sunday night [in Paris] but you had not arrived yet. And Monday there was such a furious *meltemi* [storm] that all the Express* people got as far as the Tsilivinia (just after Hydra) and had to come back so the post office was a night mare of people trying to cancel buisiness appointements children telling their parents they would not arrive others trying to arrange for taxis to pick them up in Costa [on the mainland] etc so it was impossible for us to get through to you. Which does not mean that I did not spend half the day at the post any way.

"First the wood gentleman called from Pyreas which means they have to come and find me and I have to galumph down in the heat and then wait for ever. He wanted to ask me if I wanted the *skouretta* [shutters] dark or Swedish which was Chinese to me so I had to go and get the carpenter and call back. This was only the begining. Then I called the *plakakia* [tiles] man who said that the *plakakia* I ordered and payed for do not exist any more so he is sending me some others more or less the same colour. One cant very well quarrel effectively over a bad telephone and if I send them back and wait till I go to Athens and chose new ones it will be a month before they can deliver etc etc."

When I got back to Paris after a very long talk with Khrushchev, there was already a note from Marina, who had flown on ahead in order to take Marinette to Radcliffe, where she entered as a freshman. And on September 19 she wrote David, still at Winchester:

"I am a most dejected mama. I have just come back from leaving Marinette and feel as if I had lost an arm or a leg. Its not so much the physical separation which we have had before after all, but the feeling that she was entering another world, that now that she was grown up sort of the generations were more apart instead of less so. I suppose they join up again

---

* A hydrofoil to Septsais.

later but all the two days in Cambridge I felt like 'poor dear old mummy fussing and fretting' instead of the mum whom one swimms and skis and laughs and picks things with. Oh well. It had to be but I am very despondent and the fact that it is raining and grey and hot does not help. I got back last night dead tired and today New York feels in deep gloom and mourning for poor Mr. Dag [Hammarskjöld, just killed]. I dont know how the UN will open tomorrow. What a ghastly thing to happen. Poor poor man. Oh me the world seems in a mess does'nt it. At least papa is arriving next week."

Marina moved in as a guest with Pam and Leland Hayward, the theatrical producer, and then, when I arrived, was kind enough to agree to go up to the Adirondacks with me for a few days, although it was already October and cold, because she knew I was worn out, having sacrificed my holiday to Khrushchev. She wrote Marinette: "Ah me I hope you marry a non fisherman." But before that self-indulgence I had to go down to Washington to convey a private message to Kennedy from Khrushchev and to try and ascertain what the Soviet leader was really seeking to convey.

On October 6, Marina wrote David: "We went to one dance which was fun for me and awful for Far. Then I met the President at a lunch in honor of the new publication of the diaries and papers of the Adams family. He looks divine and what a smile. Far saw him too for hours and had a good talk. Now we go off to Saranac lake for ten days to rest and fish as Far is really dead beat."

In another letter, to Marinette at Radcliffe, she added: "It was quite funny because Far went to see the President later that afternoon and he said to him 'I met your wife today. What connection is she with the Adams family?' Total bewilderment of Far until the thing was cleared up. The poor president naturally could not think how I got into that party unless I were an Adams. So now they all tease me and call me Abigail and say I am the Greek branch of the Adams family."

Just before taking off on a Latin American swing, Marina wrote twice to David. The first, from the Adirondacks on October 14, said:

"Think of us in Knollwood. We were lucky to have one week of perfect weather. So much so that even I did enjoy being out in a boat on the lake.

Every time I go out with Far he catches nothing and when I stay away he catches six. On the whole he only had one skunked day. I row a lot and walk and read and we play scrabble in the evening and sleep. But I was getting much too fat so decided to give up eating and to my surprise find the process extremely disagreable. I find I wake up in the night thinking of toasted cheese sandwidges and strawberries with cream. Ah me I do find middle age unpleasant.

"Yesterday the weather changed and the temperature must have dropped god knows how much in a few hours. One evening it was so hot that Far got a sun burn and the next morning there was snow on the ground. I hate winter. Luckily I was going back to New York tomorrow anyway and if it continues like this Far will come back with me as there is no point in staying up here all alone if he cant fish. But it has done him a lot of good anyway even ten days."

From New York (October 26), she continued: "I hate the very thought of this trip. Two days here one there just hotel bed rooms and the insides of airoplanes. I could cry. But poor old Far could not face the trip alone either so what choice did I have. I am so tired of moving I could die. Even in the month here we have moved 11 times. From hotel to hotel from Washington to Saranac to Boston back to another hotel etc. I feel like an exile and a refugee. I miss you all so including Beagle. Far works and works. He is giving this lecture at Harvard tonight which will be interresting and amusing to see what young American students think of foreign affairs."

VIII

November 1961 - December 1963

Latin America was never Marina's favorite tourist area. But she was a darling, loyal wife and in late 1961 she flew off with me to Mexico. On November 3 she wrote Marinette, now having the time of her life in the first Radcliffe class that was to be graduated as "Harvard men":

"Well here we go again. The trip was so bumpy I thought we had had it but we played two handed bridge all the way over and I lost all my money to Far and that kept my mind off death and my gloom at the very thought of this trip. We arrived in the afternoon and the altitude is such (nearly eight thousand feet) that I felt too fluffy and tired to move. Far had to go to a man's dinner at once so I had supper with our correspondent's wife here and another lady and they were both sweet and kind but I felt oh god yet two more people in my life whom I shall never see again and as we sat talking of children and clothes and Toltec ruins *J'ae été prise d'une immense fatigue*.

"In my foolishness and ignorence I had imagined Mexico City as small and tree grown with gardenias everywhere and huge hats over tiny people selling papayas in the street and dancing the hat dance. *Pas du tout*. It is the 10th biggest city in the world and modern and hell. But lovely weather.

Clear and cool today. I should'nt write about it even as I have seen nothing yet except the hotel room and Mrs. Kennedy's (not the president but Paul Kennedy, the Times correspondent) tiny flat. Tomorrow we will do some sight seing but I am ashamed to say that Aztecs Toltecs Mayas etc leave me quite cold. I dont like funny little grimacing statues.

"I am too Greek for that perhaps. And I hate pyramids. However maybe I will like them more later. As for pronouncing things like *Quetzalcoatl* or *Ah Xupan Xiu* and *Nezelxualcoatl* its quite out of the question. I dont know which is a place and which a person. It may come though."

Four days later she wrote Marinette again: "Well the first place is over. I must say I liked it a bit better as the days went by although I still feel like an old dish cloth because of the altitude. I want to lie in bed all day and not move. We did have one pleasant day when we drove to a place called Cuernavaca and the landscape around was lovely and at last a little like what we expected. You know mountains and cactus and donkeys. Not a single sombrero though. We had lunch at a dream place in a garden full of flowers of every size and shape and colour and smell and with dozens of parrots and peacocks everywhere. One parrot came and perched on our shoulders and laughed and chatted and took my hand bag and teased me. Far says he is the closest to a beagle in the bird kingdome he has ever seen and wanted to take the old boy back with him. Can you imagine Grat's face."

From Panama she sent a letter to David on November 12: "I must say the three days in Guatemala in spite of its charm and tropical jungliness which I rather adore, were pretty dreary. To our surprise and slight dismay when we arrived at the airport we were met by a very nice but totally strange gentleman from the embassy and out of the kindness of his heart he said 'You are going to stay with me while here. Mrs. B and I will be so glad to receive you.' Well you know it is rather hard staying with people one has never seen before. Mrs. B turned out to be a perfectly lovely sweet young thing but so shy she could hardly open her mouth.

"One night we went to a huge dinner at the president's palace and both before and after dinner most of the guests took us aside and showed us with glee the bullet holes in the wall where the previous president had been assasinated. Hardly any central American president dies in bed. We were also told that to say South America when in Central America i.e. Guatemala El Salvador Costa Rica Honduras Panama and Nicaragua is most insulting. I suppose like saying Balcans in Greece. I am learning geography at any rate. I would never have known that Belize was the capital of British Honduras not to be confused with just plane old Honduras mind you. Belize incidentally has just been wiped out more or less by hurricane Hattie the beast.

"Everyone everywhere everytime, talks of nothing but politics and everyone hates everyone else, and everything from the coffee crops to the Russians is the Americans' fault. Oh me. We did have one lovely day in a place called Antigua which is the second capital of the Conquistadors the first one having been destroyed by earthquakes. It is a lovely little colonial town with baroque ruined cathedrals and pink and blue and yellow one storey houses and flowers to make one's eyes water. I must say that the more we see of South America, pardon Latin America, the greater my admiration for the conquistadors. To think of a handful of Spaniards arriving god knows how in this totally strange land fighting not only fierce Incas Mayas Aztecs (and they had a nasty habit of cutting your heart out with stone knives) but mosquitos the jungle the heat dysentry scorpions etc etc and not only lasting out but finally conquering a land as big as ten times Europe. And then to come back to Spain and be kicked in the teeth by Ferdinand Isabella Charles and innumerable beastly Philips.

"The strange thing is that all the people here hate them as the Greeks might hate the Turks let us say and yet they ALL descend from them except the pure Indians and they are despised poor things. Screwy. We also drove through nice thick jungly bits and lava beds to a coffee plantation which was fun. But otherwise as I say rather dreary. Then we flew to Panama and arrived only a half hour ago. It is hot and clammy but nice and we have a lovely view of the Pacific and hundreds of little black sail boats in the distance a little like Hong Kong. I cant tell you anything about Panama yet as all I have seen is the hotel and a glimpse of a gambling casino. I hope Far will let me go in one night and if I win pots I shall bring you back lapis lazuli cuff links. I have already got you a pleated shirt in Mexico but the ones here look nicer so maybe I shall get some more. I keep thinking of all the things I would like to carry home to Spetsais like old Spanish carved doors and mill-stones from the Indians and yellow Hybiscus and gardenia bushes."

She told Marinette about Guatemala on November 12: "The palace was very pretty as nearly all the colonial houses in Guatemala. They all have enterior patios. All the houses practically are one storey high because of earthquakes and look most humble from the outside and then you go into these exquisite patios with such flowers and fountains and birds as to make your heart's delight. One day the minister of health took us to Antigua which is the first capital of Guatemala in the sixteenth century. Very pretty baroque ruined cathedral etc. Did you ever read *Le Carosse du Saint Sacrement* by Merimée I think. Very much like that. Then he took us on to his *finca* which means farm on which one plants coffee, *hacienda* being one with sugar cane I gather. We drove through real jungly tropical stuff and ravines which had been made only a few years passed, by lava. Black and strange. He described the noise and the smell and the heat when this molten river comes down and it sounded apocaliptic. But however pretty it may be I was glad to leave."

Marina's industrious correspondence was frequently behind itself in geographical terms. Thus she wrote to David from Lima, Peru, on November 16: "Did I write to you about the [Panama] canal. I am so befuddled with flights that I cant remember if I wrote or thought I wrote. Anyway we went on a lovely trip in the governor's launch and were lucky as we just got to the locks in time to see a huge Japanese ship being lifted fifty feet in the locks by great billows of churning bubling water, in only a few minutes. Except for the locks which look man made and are tremendous, the rest of the canal fifty miles long looks so much like a lovely tropical river that one simply cant believe that men actually cut this out of rock and mountain and jungle and brought the water up about three hundred feet above sea level. It is a very exciting thought. But to look at it looks like being in the 'African Queen' jungle all over and they say crocodiles.

"But human nature depresses me on the other hand. The Panamanians by this very canal that feeds and lives them have been made into resentful angry yet parasitical folk. Without the canal the place would be still nothing but a malarial mangrove swamp. And they know this but at the same time resent the Americans who live in better houses buy things cheaper live more agreably and no doupt at the begining were rather beastly and discriminatory. We gather that Miss Margot Fonteyn and husband [a Panamanian politician] really made asses of themselves that time when they thought to make a caffee society palace rebelion and overthrow the governement.

"After we sailed about the canal the next day I went to the other two cities San Cristobal and Colon both named after Columbus which are at the Atlantic side of the canal. These are nice little towns full of arcades and a nineteenth century atmosphere and thousands of little shops with every possible thing from Zanzibar to Paris. Chinese Japanese Indians Syrians all smoking at the door of their little Ali Baba caverns. It was fun. We drove for two hours through thick jungle and they say that at night you can see all kinds of animals including great boas who slide across the road. They have boas in Panama city itself at times when the rains are very strong.

"I know now what they mean by rainy season. When it comes down which it does without a moment's notice it really is like the bath tubs of heaven all emptying at once. On the way we stopped to look at the cobbled trail which still goes through the jungle all the way from the Pacific to the Atlantic which was the trail taken by Henri Morgan the pirate and his men when a handful of them sacked the city of Panama and pinched all the Spanish gold. They must have been the toughest men alive both the English and the Spaniards. To think of walking through all that gluck and in heavy armour at that. They tell me that if you just dig a bit here or there on the side of the trail you can still find hundreds of sixteenth century hand blown bottles scattered about. The local coco cola bottles I expect of all those hard drinking pirates. I was dying to dig needless to say and had visions of a row of pirate bottles in the downstairs bath in Spetses but alas as usual no time and deep mudd and the thought of all those boas rather damped my enthusiasm I have to admit.

"Then we flew to Lima yesterday and I spent most of today sleeping as that damned plane is supposed to leave at three, left at five and just as one dozes off they wake you up to give you awful grapefruit juice and nasty eggs. So not a wink all night. Lima is pleasant. Lots of baroque churches and large squares with statues and houses with closed woodden balconies all around. But unfortunately we had hoped to go to Cuzco and Machu Picchu the Inca strong holds in the Andes forteen thousand feet up but it takes at least four days and we cant do it. I am heart brocken. And even the jungle here is too far to see. Only the coast line is near which is desert as far as the eye can see. Its strange how from Europe one tends to think of all of Latin America as much the same and yet here we are a few hours flight away and every place is so different. Spiritually they are much the same though. And to me not very atreactive. All they do is revolt assassinate their president and start all over again the same thing while all the while grumbling that it is the US fault. Oh dear."

Marina was not by instinct a revolutionary and she wrote my mother from Peru on November 21: "Why sweat on the earth when you can sell souvenirs to Americans and at the same time carry on and feel put upon. All this is most human but also irritating. And I must say one gets a little tired of the kind of black mail that goes on in every place it seems to me. Be nice to me and help me and pay my debts else I shall go Fidelista. As if I kept saying to Cy be nice to me or else I shall get measles or be run over by a car. Lima I have enjoyed more than the other places thanks to a very old friend Pat Davies you know whose husband is one of the Foreign service victims of McCarthy and now living here runing a furniture factory. They have tremendous courage. No joke to be pennyless and out of a job and forty five with six children and to start life all over again in a foreign land. Well they did it and seem happy and with not even a trace of bitterness which is marvellous.

"There is this tiny strip of desert beach all along the length of the country where there is no rain and which is cold and austere and then quite suddenly out of the desert rise these fantastic lunar hills brown and black and malevolent and after them row upon row upon row of the Andes dividing the country into two length-wise. These are something to see apparently. They go up to twenty seven thousand feet a little less than the Himalayas and some have high jungle on them and most of the Indians and the Llamas live there and its poor as hell and then on the other side is the thick unlivable-in jungle and Brazil. Two hundred miles from Lima (New York Boston, so to speak) is high jungle where white man's foot has never been. This is a rather exciting idea dont you think?"

Marina didn't get a chance to write anyone from Chile, because, as soon as I was able to rush through my work, I whisked her down to the deep south for a trout-fishing weekend. She eventually reported to Marinette from Buenos Aires, on November 28:

"We stayed in Santiago two days. Far was going out of his mind with a program of lunch dinner breakfast tea, when we chucked the whole thing and went off to the South to fish for two days. He has been dreaming of this for years as you know, as the trout was said to be a kilometre long. It wasnt, but it was good enough and even I cought one or two. But for once even I enjoyed it because for one thing we were on the most beautiful river on earth just exactly what one dreams a river to be like.

"First of all the water was like melted emeralds. Then it was really fast water. And those boatmen handle the little boats as if they were fish themselves. I cant tell you how marvellous it was to come swishing down that river and sort of poise at the very edge of a whirlpool motionless for a second or two and then go diving on. How they do it I cant imagine but we went swirling from one side of the river to the other upstream as well as down with just a flip of the paddle and really felt like a fish. The water was as clear as Spetses only bright green and every mile or so the little banks changed.

"Here it was beach with pebbles and little yellow iris, further down it was slopping green valleys with just imagine field after field of lupins and foxgloves and delphiniums all over the place. Really pickables, things five foot high like in an English garden. And little yellow orchidy things and believe it or not TREES of fushias. Then later the banks went high like granite canyons with huge tropical leaves hanging down and sort of douanier Rouseau-ish. I really think it is the most beautiful place I ever saw. This was the first day. The second was less pretty. But better fishing.

"Another river but volcanic and black and rather creepy. The volcano in the distance is fabulous. A blue and shiny white triangle right in the sky, all snow and shimmering in the sun. We stayed at an incredibly shick hotel quite a surprise down there at the reall foot of the world (Tierra del Fuego is but a little away) and Far was really happy to get away for forty eight hours from presidents and ministers and economists and all the people who come and say Some of my best friends are American that is why I can tell you that if the USA does not do this that and the other they will lose us and we will all go communist and then you will see. I am so fed up with this I am on the verge of becoming an isolationist Barry Goldwater type. Go communist and see if I care.

"Far as usual is much more balanced in his judgement and not as irritated as I. But really I feel this continent is as bacward in some ways as the Congo with much less excuse. We then took a bumpy train back for twelve hours got to Santiago at one in the morning woke up at seven took off for the airport where the plane was hours late and arrived pooped in Buenos Ayres where we were greeted by grumpy people, heat, had to carry all our own luggage which made Far cross with my Mexican basquet which gets heavier with each country, so all together our first view of Argentina is slightly jaundiced. The town is quite pretty but there is no sight to see except shopping and this is a nightmare.

"Oh well. Only ten days or so to go. If I last that long. Otherwise you will have to look after Xmas and my funeral both. No more my precious as we must meet some senators down-stairs for a drink. The place is crawling with senators for the Alliance for progress or whatever its called."

While still in this somewhat negative mood, Marina confided to Michael Edwards on November 28: "I have to make a sweeping statement here and to hell with objectivity and fairness. I hate the whole continent. Everything except the flowers and the rivers and the jungle which has an endless fascination for me. I dislike with a passion the Aztecs and the Toltecs and the Mayas and the Incas and primitive art bores me to death.

"They are all fierce nationalists and not one patriot among them (sweeping statement again never mind). Not one politician who does'nt bank in Switseland not one land owner ready to give an acre away. Not one minister who does not take a cut from everything from the customs to the brothels. And another strange thing. In Mexico you dont see a statue or a picture or even a mention of Cortez. The Spaniard is the great black enemy. And yet not one single person admits to so much as one drop of Indian blood. Its as if the British hated William the conqueror and yet spat on the very thought of one drop of Saxon blood. Crazy mixed up people.

"Guatemala is pleasant and jungly. Peru sombre and one gets an idea of the fabulous enormity of the Andes. Really like a great fierce petrified ocean. Wave after wave of malevolent peaks as high as the Himalayas nearly. But at the foothills at least not nice solid blue rock. Just crumply brown and grey sand stone. But in Lima oh what gardens. I have never in my life seen such flowers. And roses out of a fairy tale. Chile is nice. But crazy. A ribbon of a country stretching like a macaroni all the way to Tierra del Fuego with black dead dead coppery desert in the North so bleeck that you think god must have made a mistake, then delicious country in the middle all tidy green fields and a mixture of cherries and figs and tropical vegetation and English looking herbacious borders and cows French Iles de France forrests German valleys etc.

"The people are that way too and I do find it delicious to have a national hero called Bernardo O'Higgins. The Chileans are the most hospitable people and nicest on earth. Their secret weapon is the coctail party and had we not stolen two days to go fishing in the South we would be dead of cyrosis by now.

"Buenos Aires is a pretty town but the people seem à *première* view rather horrid. Imagine that we were standing under an awning in front of a shop today waiting for a taxi in a torrential rain, with several other stranded pedestrians and the owner came out with a look of glee on his face and roled the awning up, shut his door and sat watching us get soaked. I have never met such pure nastiness in any land. I have little to do as there is no sight seing and the country around is flat as a morning after, so I go window shopping which I must tell you here is a nightmare. Not the hand woven bits and peaces of Guatemala or pottery birds and baskets of Mexico or Peruvian silver nic nacks that an ordinary mortal might aquire in a moment of abandon. Souvenirs here consist of emeralds minks crocodyle luggage leather coats of infinite beauty and little odds and ends of that sort. What makes it worse is that all these goodies go here for a tenth of what they would anywhere else."

On December 11, Marina wrote the children from Rio de Janeiro: "Here I am in Copacabana which sounds like all the nightclubs in the world and in fact means something of the Virgin Mary.

"On Monday we take off in a German plane and fifteen hours later we are in Paris, France, via Dakar. But I must tell you this is the most beautiful city I have ever been in. It has everything. Imagine living on Fifth Avenue and having Agia Paraskevi [a lovely bay in Spetsai] at your feet, and a huge mountain at your back and the jungle all around. Great smooth rocks coming down right into the back yard of everything and great trees and flowers and ocelots wondering about a few miles from the heart of the town. And what sea.

"I sit at our window for hours looking at waves like in Wellfleet [Massachusetts]. And the beaches stretch for fifty miles in every direction and they are not nasty city beaches with water melon rind and papers everywhere. Clean and white and tiny boys selling the most beautiful kites made like hawks and eagles. Every one but everyone adores and plays and talks and thinks foot ball. They are nice nice people. Alas having just got fairly comfortable in Spanish now suddenly we cant even understand yes or no. What a language. Nothing sounds like it looks. The last sylable is dropped completely. SSs are SH oos are uus. Its a nightmare. Far has been very busy so we have not done much but he has promised to take me to see one decently danced samba and if possible to a macumba which is not a dance as you might think but a voodoo ceremony. I cant wait. Today we drove for lunch into a tropical forrest and then up to the famous Christ at the top of a hill from where you see the whole city and the ocean on three sides and as far as the eye can see white beaches. It really is incredible.

"The plane takes fifteen hours so I plan to buy an arm full of orchids and put them in the plane ice box and if they last as long as they say they do they may be there to greet you as you come off your plane.

"The beaches along this whole province are thirty and forty miles long. I droole also at the thought of unexplored interior and the amazon and head shrinkers and Indians who fish with blow arrows. And at the same time cities like Chicago. No Brasilia alas. It looks astonishing in pictures. But the weather is too bad for planes and by car it takes three days and by train four. It was one of those extravaganzas the country is paying for *en masse* and we are told no good to anyone and no one wants to live there. But all the architecture is sort of like the Brussels world fair. Upside down triangles churches like water lilies chapels like number eights etc. Would have liked a glimpse. No more."

The trip home was less swift and easy than anticipated. We lost a wheel on takeoff, and the Lufthansa captain announced on the loudspeaker that it would be easier to land at Dakar when the plane, having crossed the Atlantic, would be much lighter after using up its fuel. He managed to come down beautifully on two of the three normal points — amid wild applause from his passengers. We then had to spend a steaming night and morning sprawled out in deckchairs at the uncomfortable airport while little frogs leapt all over and around us. Finally a new wheel was flown in from Frankfurt, fitted aboard, and off we went to Paris.

It was a relief to be home for Christmas with both children and a hugely wiggling Benjamin Beagle, to say nothing of Grat and Justine. On January 4, 1962, Marina wrote Michael Edwards:

"Thank god Xmas only comes every now and then. What a struggle. And I am planing to form a new committee for the salvation of over-developped nations. Everyone frets about the poor under-developped folks and no one even sheds one tear over those poor overdevelopped people who have so many cars that no one can move any more. Whose standard of living is so sadly high that they have to queue for hours outside Fauchon to get their poor little *foie gras*, and who can hardly think of the scent scarf toy or jewel departements anywhere as they look like small civil wars from frantic customers. However we managed to overcome these difficult problems and had a cosy Xmas with twenty for lunch including the Chambers* and mad bridge. The children are too divine and I have four of them in the house which was glorious and made me feel young and gay too."

When Marinette was back in Cambridge, Marina wrote her from Paris on January 19:

"One night we went to see Melina's new play, its *Prova Generale* [Dress Rehearsal] and sat in her dressing room while she put on a red wigg then a black one and looked entrancing and while the room kept filling with the oddest people. Greek tailors, *metteurs en scène* Tony Perkins who greeted David like a brother, the *maquilleuse* with paint brush and pot etc. It was most amusing. The play is not good at all but Melina is good.

"We went to a very beatnik *vernissage* on the Faubourg Saint Honoré where everybody had black stockings on and high heals and white lip stick and high hairdoes and needed a good bath and smoked out of long cigarette holders and generally looked *avant guarde* and super foolish and no one looked at the pictures at all but at each other and then they put records on a pick up and everyone started to twist to David's huge delight."

Marina sent a lovely letter thanking Uncle Arther and Aunt Iph for a Christmas check:

"Your glorious present makes up for all the wear and tare of being married to a Sulzberger for twenty years. My head was so heavy [with a bad cold] and everything streaming so that I could do nothing coherent at all. Except one thing. Lie back and think how I was going to spend your present. And it kept me awake all night, the dream I mean.

"And I went from a small sail boat to a speed boat to a whole set of Chippendale, changed my mind again, and thought perhaps a set of Staffordshire for at least sixty guests. On and on and I must say it was a

---

* Ambrose and Virginia Chambers, Americans who lived in Paris and were dear friends.

delightful way to spend a cold. I simply cant wait now to be less germ infested so as to go straight to the flea market and behave like a millionaire. You were angels to think of us and I only hope that some day you will come to see for yourselves what we have done with the present and sit on our terrace and sip ouzo and look at the sea and the sky.

"Have you seen in the papers the awful scandal that has befallen our gracious church? My mother writes that it was awful as the opposition went to town on it and had a glorious time. They are brutes. Nothing is sacred for them although perhaps it was unwise of the Holy Synod to ellect a notorious homosexuel to the highest clerical position. Ah me.

"But you know what those wretches in the opposition will do. I must tell you the funniest of all. Months ago Cy had written a fairly unimportant story about some of the CIA activities in a country which out of discretion he had called Banania. It was about a candidate in certain elections being payed to keep quiet after he had been defeated. This as I say months ago and one of that whole series of South American articles. Well a few weeks ago our telephone rang and it was Athens on the phone. I of course thought it would be for me but no it was Cy they wanted. It was a journalist and friend of Cy's wanting to know 'How Cy had found out about Mr. M and the CIA' and wanting Cy's permission to quote him. Immagine! That they decided out of a clear blue sky that Banania must obviously mean Greece (if at least it had been Olivia or Tabacia or Garlica) and that here in the very words of a well known and consciencous American journalist was proof that the Greek elections had been croocked."

She wrote Marinette on February 3 as the French government was facing a serious rebellion by an officers' group in Algeria called the OAS:

"Last night we had a dinner here for sixteen. One of the stuffy ones but it ended up rather pleasant and the less stuffy guests stayed till two. I gave them bisque of crab which everyone had to eat with their fingers which lessened the formality of the party at the start and then somehow people got involved in talks about Orthodoxy or sex or Russian Icons as opposed to Greek ones which was a nice change from Algerie. Everyone keeps saying this is going to be the crucial week and then it becomes the crucial hour and the crucial month and nothing crucials at all.

"But they are stopping cars and people more and more and asking for identity cards and searching cars etc. There was a huge plastic [bomb] rue de Verneuil the other night. Far had a two hour interview with you know who last week [General de Gaulle] and was delighted with it although he does not wish this talked about as it is always confidential. But it is nice that he can see him any time when hardly any one else does.

"I just got a letter from George Paspati saying the Hybiscus which I had brought from Peru and gave him to take back to Greece when he went through here, have cought and have six or seven leaves each so we will have white and yellow and pink hybiscus in the *patrida* [fatherland] after all. We must call it the Marina. I would adore to have a flower called after us."

Again, on February 14: "David seems mighty homesick too but this has done nothing to his spirits. Today I got a huge enveloppe with *Plastique* written all over it (ha ha) from him with a letter written on parchement two feet high in Gothic letters saying he is studying pornography. I quote 'when I say good pornography I mean good litterature not good sex. At the moment I am reading Sartre who is good both ways.' Then he quotes long passages in Latin. It is the funniest letter in the world but I cant forward it to you as it would cost a thousand francs to mail.

"Papa is in Algiers but getting back tomorrow to my great relief. I hated his going. But he went first to the Sahara with a governement group and I gather they had a wonderful and fascinating time. I dont know if you ever have time to read his articles but the last ones have been marvelous. As usual nature in some strange quirk of its sense of humour participates not at all in human dramas and Paris has been too beautiful and golden although cold.

"I wanted very much to go to the République two days ago to see the parade in honour of the eight killed last week but then I thought it would be too silly to get my head opened at this moment so did'nt and felt like a sissy. It always distresses me when life goes on so gay and pretty in one *quartier* when another is tormented, or that history in the making is felt so little by those not actually participating in it. Except for reading the papers about horrors one might as well be living in another city. Tomorrow morning I go off to Orly to collect papa and I am so glad he is out of that rat trap."

On March 15, Marina wrote Nursey: "Papa came back [from Algeria] shattered. He has seen as you know quite a bit in his life but I have never seen him as sad as on his return. The sheer lust for killing. He saw women jumping up and down and yelling with glee as men poured gasoline over a car filled with wounded men and set fire to it. Its not even politics any more. Its bestiality.

"Here in Paris we live the strangest things. We read about this and that in the papers but as if it were not you so to speak. As if they all happened in another town. One hardly ever *sees* them happen and our life changes not one scrap. Anti aircraft guns on the Elysée Palace and the Arc de Triomphe armed policemen everywhere, we are stopped constantly for identification but that is all. I am constantly amazed at the invisibility of history in the making. The nearer you are to it the less you seem actually to see it. The plans for next week OAS are known as Operation Apocalypse. God help us when the cease-fire is signed at last."

Just before taking David to Greece for his Easter holiday, Marina sent a letter to my mother:

"Last night we went to a ghastly party for the Windsors but at least we played bridge and Cy won forteen dollars off the Duchess. The only consolation because otherwise it was deadly. And tonight we have another dinner at the Italian Embassy for all the people Cy went to the Sahara with last month. It may be fun but he is so tired he does not enjoy anything much."

On the day of departure, Marina dashed off a slightly regretful word to Marinette:

"I am so sad to be spending our first Easter away from you and Far. Oh dear again my kangaroo complex. I wish I had you all in a little pouch beside me for ever.

"Mother [her grandmother, Maria, then ninety-four] has been quite ill. Her leg suddenly swelled up and they all thought she had flebitis and took her off to hospital where she kept scolding the doctor for trying to keep her alive and saying but dont you understand that I am burning with curiosity and impatience to see what death is like. Please stop all this nonsense. The doctor did not know what to do and mumbled I cant poison her after all just to please her. Well anyway after a few days of being an insufferable patient the swelling went and she is home as right as rain and complaining bitterly on all these 'faulse alarms.' She really is a fabulous caracter. I am so glad she did not die before we see her once again."

David and Marina drove slowly across Italy to Greece with Bob and Jane Joyce. From Athens, Marina wrote me:

"David was swept away from nine this morning by a bevy of young admiresses to a pic nic at Kantza where the Camba wine comes from and I dont know when I shall ever see him again. Good for him to get away with his contemporaries after being stuck for five days in a car with three old things. I must say he was marvelous. Gay and eager and talkative and at the same time neither precocious nor over-talkative. I myself was astounded at his erudition. As far as I ever see he only reads Mad. So where does he get all his knowledge. A mystery.

"We got off the boat in less than half an hour which was wonderful and then drove straight to Olympia where our optimisme was justified but only just. We got a lovely suite with bath only because the people who had it had had a *panne* and called to cancel six minutes before we arrived. They had been turning people away half the afternoon. We had a wonderful bath and supper and sleep and woke up the next morning to what do you think. Catacylsmes of rain. I bribed Bob and Jane never to tell anyone, and we ran through the ruins but then had a lovely two hours in the museum which is both wonderful and not wet. Then we took off for Athens and on the way had everything. Thunder lightning hail and SNOW. We lunched at Vityna in a hovel very bad *keftedes* [Greek meatballs] and cold macaroni but both Bob and Jane were sweet and nice about it all and most receptive. So we finaly got to Athens at seven rather exhausted but most happy."

When they reached Spetsais, and our new house, Marina told my mother: "The house was a dream. What we had left an old rubble heap full of dust and plaster and bits of briques and wood is suddenly a glowing garden. All the lemon trees in blossom and such smells as surely even paradise does not enjoy. Stock and roses and pale red flax and we had tiny new potatoes from the garden and peas and beans and of course fresh onions and even string garlic which made us all happy and a menace to our fellow men. The house still needs some cealings and flours painted and much more furniture than I had thought.

"We went for walks all over the island which was all dressed up as for a ball. Gentle sweet pale grass everywhere and wild orchids and gladiola and asparagus which we picked and eat every evening. We went riding and for lovely pic nics and even swamm once but that was a mistake. It was breath takingly cold in the water but wonderful out. David was a dream. I simply cant understand how a boy who to my knowledge never reads a book can have learned so much by osmossis or whatever it is. All through Italy as well as Greece he seemed to know everything whether Rennaissance history or the Normans of Sicily or baroque churches or ancient Greece or Roman history and all this rather shyly and quietly never showing off intimate and cosy and relaxed and yet never fresh or precocious. I could eat him."

She wrote Marinette: "Never never has Greece been so beautiful. As for Spetses all the gods had come down to arrange things just for us. Mummy put her hand over my eyes as we arrived and led me to the edge of the terrace and then said Now look. Gone the plaster and the rubble and the bits of stone and wood and in its place waist high stock white and pink and peach and lillies and lilac and all the lemon trees in bloom with such a smell as surely even paradise cant know."

On May 8 she told Uncle Arthur and Aunt Iph: "You know it is so many years since I was in Greece in spring and it was like meeting an old friend whom one is used to seing in old blue jeans and work on their hands, suddenly all dolled up for a gala at the Opera. It was like Ireland. Green green everywhere and oh the lemon trees and the lilacs and tiny red anemonies everywhere. And in the back always the severe dark straightness of the cypress trees, just to add dignity to so much frivolity and colour."

She wrote Avis Bohlen on June 29 before returning to Spetsais from Paris for the summer vacation: "Marinette and I leave tomorrow by train with a dozen bags basquet brown paper parcels Beagle AND a bycicle built for two which David aquired in a benighted moment and wishes to use for transporting various lady friends from one end of the island to the other. But it shows what a decadent and spoilled century we live in when you hear people Ouing and Ahing and commiserating with me as if I were off to the salt mines because I have to face three nights on a train. And all this with *wagon lits* and first class after all. I do admit I am too old to face it sitting up. But we will have books and tappistery and thank god Marinette still seems to have a hundred things a minute to tell me so actually I am rather looking forward to three completely quiet days except that I am so eager to get home and start fixing the house."

That summer I received an adorable letter which bore all the signs of Marina's typing and spelling but which, dated July 8 from Spetsais, was signed: "Respectfully and lovingly, your dog, Beagle." The text follows:

"My beloved papa.

"I am writing to you for mama and Marinette who are both so busy with the house that they have hardly stroked my ears ten times since we arrived. They are pushing furniture around sweeping floors (hate me because my feet they say are terrible on newly polished wood but what can a dog do) opening linen closets etc etc and ten times a day admiring the new frigidaire which they seem to think is a beauty. It has been so hot since we arrived that I dont even think of sleeping on the pink [sheets] but get well *under* any bed I can find.

"But let me tell you about our trip. After you left us we settled quite comfortably in our little compartment and mummy and Marinette seemed to think it was a bit tight but I was fine. I dont know what people make such fusses about. As long as I have someone to sleep on I dont care about anything. The next day we had all kinds of adventures. First of all THERE WAS NO WAGON RESTAURANT. Think of that. We could not even have a drink of water until Belgrade. Well for lunch we got some biscuits and a bar of chocolate (I had two and the women one each) and then in the evening we were about to go to bed with nothing when a kind little gentleman from the next compartement a Greek from Canada came very shyly and begged us to share his humble meal and we very politely said we did not want to deprive him but I was nudging mama not to be too damned polite so in the end she accepted and we had bread and ham and cheese which was delicious.

"We had one other or rather two other *awful* moments. One was in a place called Milan where Marinette had taken me out for you know what. It had been quite difficult up to then because you know what a dog is he cant just do and run. I needed a few sniffs and things and we never seemed to have any time and besides I was a bit sheepish with the whole train leaning out of the window and giving advice and encouragement. So any way in this place the man had told Marinette we had a whole half hour so there I was pulling towards a special place and thinking of a lovely big success when suddenly shouts and yells and agony the train was leaving with mama green at the window and Marinette and me racing like lunatics and thinking what we would do with no money and passeports in a strange land. It was agony but luckily the train was just being shunted to another track. But *quelle émotion*. That was our first suspence.

"Then came the worse one at the Yougoslave frontier when a nasty looking man with a red star in his hat asked mama where her visa was and she said they had none and he said they should take down all the luggage and get off the train. Luckily mama was so stunned that she did nothing and then a little man came up and said shush have you got four dollars. We did'nt and they would not take francs or travellers checks but thank god a nice little American gentleman from the next compartement lent us some and somehow the other little man persuaded the nasty man to stamp a visa in the passeports right there in the train and we were saved. But there was a lady in the compartement with three little girls who told us that she had been thrown off the train on Friday and with twenty suitcases had to spend the night in the street. They would not even let her sit in the station out of the rain and she had to go back to Trieste and spend two days there getting a visa and buy new tickets all over again and she had joined our train at last on Tuesday. She was fit to be tied. Mama looked greener and greener as this tale of horror unfolded, at the thought of what we had just escaped. I also heard her say that the travel agencies ought to be shot. It would have been so easy to get a visa and take a luncheon basket had we but been told. However as it was we had all the emotions and suspense without any actual drama so all was for the best in the best of worlds.

"We crossed the Greek frontier with great ease and a nice customs man never opened a thing and gave us water melon as we seemed so hot and sticky and by this time everyone on the train was great friends and lots of children were pulling my tail which I rather like (*entre nous*) and I was getting all the left overs from the lucky people who did have pic nics and enjoying myself. Then on Wednesday we did get a restaurant and we had macaroni and meat and it tasted wonderful. Well we arrived on Thursday and mama and Marinette dashed and changed dresses to look nice for the lady they call Dodo and at ten in the morning we arrived and there was a lady called Kitty there too and Uncle Shan with his car so there was a lot of

human kissing and hugging and chatter and then Mama and her mama
went to get the tandem out of customs and I went with Uncle Shan and
Marinette to a nice house with a terrace and lots of new smells. Then
mama came and the telephone started to ring and all kinds of people came
in and after that I saw neither Marinette nor mama for two days. They were
buying frigidaires they said and all kinds of other things for the house and
they also went out to dinner with Uncle Shan who gave them a party with
Costa and Paddy [Leigh Fermor] and a man called Junky (ha ha) Flyshman
[Fleischman] who has a yacht and they went on and danced by the sea and
Marinette looked so happy when she came in and kept on saying this is the
life for me. Mama looked pretty cheerful too.

"Then on Saturday first light it seemed to me we all started carrying
endless suit cases (I was given a basket but thought it beneith my dignity
and also *entre nous* did not quite understand what they wanted of me. They
also put a horrid leather thing round my nose in order to get on to the
Neraida* my old friend the boat of last year but I got rid of that pretty
quick). Uncle Shan was with us too as he had only come from Hydra to be
nice to us. What a nice human. The trip was all right. People tripped over
me and said *PoPo to skilaki* [tut tut, little dog] which I gather is not good but
mama explained that I was nice. And then the lovely moment came when
we got off the boat and I took off my coat and neck tie and went right into
the sea and rolled in the dust and did EVERYTHING I like barcked at
everyone ran after everything and like that we got to the house which is
even nicer than I remembered.

"But the women (by this time they were four with Dodo and Eleni my
old friend who cooks so well) set to work right away and have not stopped
since and that is why mama said now Beagle make yourself useful do go and
write papa and tell him everything because I really must get the house
straight soon. I think she misses you quite a lot and I hear your name
cropping up in conversation all the time. So do come soon. I wish to walk
with you up the mountain and you know what the women are to me for
that. They did take me for a swimm today I must admit but a quick one as
the man for the frigidaire was arriving to see if it worked properly. It does. I
do believe that cat is on the roof again and we cant allow that. Mummy just

---

* Benjamin had absconded on the Spetsais— Athens boat *Neraida* one summer.

says to please give you all all her love and a huge kiss and a hug and so does Marinette and Dodo and I add a lick and please forgive my spelling. Its not as bad as mama's but not perfect either."

I had written a book (*The Resistentialists*) in which an old Jugoslav partisan friend, Vlado Dedijer, figured very favorably. Nevertheless, to my astonishment, he was furious and actually threatened my son David in retribution. Marina wrote me on July 22:

"As for David I would not really worry. But how horrible. How horrible that unhappiness and disillusion and sickness can bring a man to such a pass. And how sad for you and all of us that it ruins so many years of hard work and thought. Less so for me because I always disliked Vlado but for you who were so fond of him it is awful and I feel deeply for you.

"I hope you got my telegram. Of course I think you should publish your book. As far as your friendship and conscience has gone you have done everything. And one simply cant go on being bullied by a nut much as one might wish to sympathise because of the causes of this lunacy. You know that I have never liked the man nor do I basically believe that it is the tragedy that caused the madness. [His son had committed suicide.] No one ever knows and I should not be so categorical, but people do so often bring about their own fate and Vlado has caused so much pain and suffering around him for so long that it was bound to come back some day to him. However we cant really discuss the metaphysics of his personality by letter. I only want to say that of course you should go ahead and publish and I dont even think he will sue when it comes down to brass tacks. As for the threats to David he does not even know what David looks like its been so long since he has seen him. The very fact that he even thinks in these terms shows that he is basically a son of a bitch. So let us publish and get the damned thing over. I am so tired of having you made unhappy by a bunch of tragic jerks."

Late in August, just after I had started a Spetsais holiday, my mother died suddenly and I flew off to New York. Marina wrote me there:

"We all miss you so much that I am writing to you even though in my heart of hearts I hope that it will never get to you because you will be on your way back. I have not gone swimming this morning because I cant bare to think of myself in the sea and you in a sad sad synagogue somewhere doing and being and thinking all the things you dislike most. Oh dear how I wish I were there with you so at least we could talk afterwards. All all our thoughts are with you. So my darling sweet Pee. Keep your courage up and come back to us soon so that we may console you and sooth you and rest you and look after you. The first hunters have arrived today The wind is bird wind and even he is waiting for you. All my love and a most enormous hug. Dopey."

That summer of 1962 was not a good one: my mother's death, the trouble with an old friend, a bad attack of gout. Then my Uncle Dave, to whom I was devoted, died in September. I felt too tired to fly back again for his funeral. The only good news was that the Bohlens were coming to Paris, where Chip was about to become U.S. ambassador. Marina wrote Avis:

"What joy to know at last from your own lips that it IS true and that we are once again to live in the same town. Your letter was so sweet and I promise not to move without your permission nor will I ever wish to do so. You have left so many friends behind and everyone will be so thrilled to have you back that except for a few revolutions and things I cant see what can go wrong. Even Mr. Balmain will be at your feet begging to dress you. What a joy to think that in about a month we will be curled up on a sofa talking our heads off. I ment to write the moment I got your letter and believe it or not in this glorious lotus eating island I never got one single moment to go near my desk.

"Cy arrived a week earlier than expected and I was so worried that he would be furious to find the house overflowing with people You know what a solitary fellow he is. But he took it very well and was full of gaiety and in a marvellous mood and then his third day here we got a telegram that his mother had died in the night and he went off to the funeral and spent a ghastly week in New York and got back here only to go to bed with the worst attack of gout in years. It is too wretched. Last year he only had six days before Mr. K got him trotting off to Moscow and now all this. In his own house and the only pleasant quiet weeks he has the whole year. Oh dear this Anglo Saxon up bringing where men cant cry and show their sorrows. In his own introvert way he was devoted to his mother and it has been a great blow. And then this morning a second telegram that his Uncle David died too. One has that awful fealing that the older generation is going fast. And however grown up and even old one may be one's self having an older generation behind one is like a kind of solid wall or like a warm arm round one's shoulders. One for whom one is always the child always excusable who might say to you put on your coat dont catch cold dont forget to say thank you or wipe your feet. When there is no one left to say this one is really on one's own."

As September drew to an end, Marina wrote with nostalgia to Marinette:

"What a change from the hustle and bustle of August. And the island seems to be following the house. Gone are the Lolitas and the tiny shorts and the transistors to be replaced by solid looking hunters and sailors home on leave. The Tapia looks like a Greek island again and not like Portofino. The sky is pale pale and the sun too and there are cyclamen everywhere and the second flowering of the thyme which is mauve too so all seems gray and mauve middle aged colours instead of gold and blue of youth. I found a new gardenia and a *fouli* and if paradise does not smell exactly like this then it wont be paradise. The painters are everywhere and the pale blue floor downstairs looks very nice. Sadly I put away more things every day. How I hate endings. End of summer end of youth end of a good book even."

We got back to Paris in October, a very grim and tense October as it turned out to be, for it featured the Cuban confrontation, a showdown between Kennedy and Khrushchev that almost exploded the first nuclear holocaust. Unfortunately, Marina was in such a hurry making preparations to unpack from the summer, pack for a scheduled trip to the United States, say hellos and goodbyes, that she wrote few letters, and, to my infinite regret, this particular period included a considerable span for which Dodo, her most faithful reader and correspondent, has mislaid her file.

On October 24, Tom Finletter, U.S. ambassador to NATO, gave a farewell dinner party for his German colleague, von Walther, and Marina and I were the only non-NATO people there. This was already the height of the crisis period and no one spoke of anything else. There was much gloom, and the general belief was that either we must invade and take Cuba in order to seize the Soviet missiles or trade the latter's withdrawal off against a similar withdrawal of American missiles from Turkey (which, when history is written, will be seen as the true basis of the settlement). And on October 25, the day after the Bohlens' arrival, we dined *à quatre* with Chip and Avis, even before our new ambassador had presented his letters of credence to President de Gaulle. The first thing Chip told me, after an enthusiastic and alcoholic round of greetings, was that he had just received a cable from President Kennedy complaining about my column on the crisis and asking Bohlen to set me straight.

On October 26 we flew direct to Boston, where Marinette, diminutive and pretty, was awaiting us, and celebrated my birthday the next day with a cozy family party. Isaiah Berlin, the brilliant English scholar and writer, came for coffee in the morning after having just been in Washington and seen Kennedy. Marina and I were much struck (and I noted this in my diary that evening) because Isaiah "wonders if deep in the President's mind he may not have a presentiment that he may not live a long time because of his known but unmentioned illness and that he must make his mark on history quickly."

Early in November we flew to Washington and on November 8 dined at the White House. Marina's only record of this I can find comes in a letter to Kitty Solomos (in French).

"I must tell you that despite my protestations that I didn't want to budge again, I enjoyed myself like a mad-woman above all in Washington. First we spent three exquisite days with Marinette in Cambridge. She was so pretty so nice so sweet so gay that my heart beat faster whenever I looked at her. Afterward there was a sinister week in New York spent above all on condolence visits with the family. I admit the Egyptians were right to bury everyone together with their dead master. I had tears in my eyes all the time.

"After New York ten fascinating days in Washington amidst the full Cuban crisis, dining each evening with people deeply mixed up in it and who were called to the phone ten times during the meal and would return with the mysterious air of 'knowing something.' Fascinating and what a pleasure for once to be on the winning side.

"One night we dined at the White House. A very small group, only ten. I was as excited and nervous as a debutante. Not only the idea of the

President, the man who in the end held our destinies in his hand. After all, that feeling I already knew from the time of the Eisenhowers. But the personality of the man. He is without doubt for me the sexiest and most irresistible man on earth.

"I was on his left and I would have given my right hand to seduce him. Alas. He loves or makes love or talks politics. Nothing between. Unhappily I didn't fall into either the first or the second category. But just to listen to him talk is irresistible. She [Jacqueline Kennedy] is extraordinary also. She has a tiny little voice, idiotic and affected, long eyelashes which she uses constantly, big, wide eyes like a naive little girl so that one waits for her to speak worldly platitudes. But in fact when she opens her mouth it is to say really intelligent things, thoughtful, intellectual and generally interesting and one sits there open-mouthed and as completely entranced by her as by him. The entire evening I thought *Ti gerevi i alepou sto bazari* [What is a fox doing in the market?]. And listening to the secrets of negotiations on Cuba, the letters exchanged between the President and Khrushchev, about the missiles and the preparations for total war, etc. It was so unreal that I myself should be there.

"We also went to one ball where I got into an argument about de Gaulle with a cabinet member and to another where I flirted with the minister of national defense. All this as exquisite as you can possibly imagine. Cy in a good humour, thank God, but very very tired. As a result we gave up his idea of a Latin American trip and came back to Paris by boat where we arrived yesterday evening [November 29]."

In January 1963, Marina wrote Marinette that we were cold and were strictly rationed on fuel, and that Benjamin Beagle objected to getting his feet frozen when taken for a walk. *The New York Times* was on strike (putting me on half pay) and I was grouchy. She added, however: "Far had a two page letter from him [de Gaulle] saying how much he liked his book and this together with a note from his publishers saying they think the new book superb has done a lot to restore his strike-stricken morale." As a mother she had to add: "Every time I go by the closed door of your room I get the glooms."

On February 18 she continued: "A new assassination plot *pour mon Général* discovered just in time and round the corner from us too. One phoney countess in the plot with a face that looks as if it could have

Marina as a lieutenant-nurse in the Greek army (1940).

Marina with her uncle Shan Sedgwick (1941).

Marina and the two friends with whom she left occupied Greece in midsummer 1941. From the left, Dolly Constantinidis, Marina, and Nadia Papadopoulos.

Marina at her favorite sport — flower-picking (1941).

Marina and Felix (Greece, 1941).

Marina meets her first chipmunk (Montana, 1942).

Marina outside our Montana home (1942).

Marina just after our marriage (1942).   Myself just after our marriage (1942).

Four generations: Marina, Marinette, Maria, and Dodo (1945).

FEBRUARY 6
Saturday

First day in London. How good to be on land again and with Cy. We have a lovely suite at the Savoy. There were flowers for me when I arrived. I had an hours bath which I needed after 23 days. Cy is even sweeter than before. God its good to be together again.

JULY 5
Monday

Hairdresser, lunch with Lilia Ralli, very pleasant talked for ages. Lucette came after lunch and then Elly. We talked. Lucette is depressed. Went to work. Took Elly to buy a ring too. In middle of work I telephone from Cy that he has arrived. great reunion. I had oranges in bed. Talked, & left

Two happy pages from Marina's diary marked with flowers at the top (1943).

Marina in a Dior dress posing for *Vogue*.

Marina at our first Paris apartment (1948).

Dodo by the fireplace in Maroussi (1947).

Marina in the backwoods — Lake Opazatika (1954).

Marina in northern Canada (1954).

Marina and the children skiing at Val d'Isère (1952).

Marina and myself in Uganda (1964).

Marina with U.S. Ambassador David Bruce shortly before her death in 1976.

launched a thousand plots. Seven plots in three years. Even worse than Louis Philippe."

Dodo, who loathed travel, finally agreed to pay us an Easter visit, and on April 12 Marina proudly boasted to Marinette:

"Yesterday we went for a pic nic at Senlis and it was more beautiful than the day. Dodo had not really believed me when I wrote for years that there were seas of daffodils. Mrs. Hayward and young Winston [Churchill, her son] were here. He is leaving for America to go and get the honorary citizenship for his grand father. Rather nice. He was so funny telling how he was put in jail in Morrocco for telling the customs people that his name was Winston Churchill. *Vous vous foutez de notre geule* they said and in he went. I have filled the house with flowers for Dodo."

She counseled our daughter, who was in love: "I wish I could think of consoling solid principled things to tell you and that the ONE thing you should do is this or that. Old fashioned parents who could seriously believe that Trust in God and do his bidding and all will be well, must have been such a comfort to lost children gropping in the dark for some deeper knowledge. Alas neither my generation nor yours is given that kind of crutch to hold onto any more and one has to struggle on alone. The only thing I say to myself is that on the whole and *plus ou moins*, etc. life in itself is the meaning of everything. A nice day a kind man a smiley *vendeuse*, finding a parking space a Beagle wiggle to take only a few and tiny things, are good in themselves and dont have to have an inner or deeper meaning. In a way I think because we are so attractive to each other as a family we become a triffle more difficult *vis à vis* the outside world. One learns *siga siga* [little by little] not to mind and only to be doubly pleased when one finds the kindred spirit."

I had to fly off to Ottawa for a NATO meeting, and Marina wrote me on May 23: "I am so glad you will see our Founelle [Marinette]. How silly that we should all four be in different corners of the globe."

Orvil Dryfoos, husband of my cousin Marian and publisher of *The New York Times*, died suddenly of a heart attack just before I left Canada for New York. Marina wrote Michael Edwards on May 29: "I have had a deluge of letters from Cy telling me how heavenly he thinks I am. My morale sky high. No one knows yet what will happen to the paper now that poor Orvil is dead, but it will certainly not be Cy. He would die too."

By the time I got back to Paris, Marina had left for Greece with Marinette, who (neither for the first nor last time) believed herself hopelessly in love and was engaged to a young man who fell by the wayside before a year had passed. On July 9, Marina wrote me from Spetsais:

"All the whitwash has to be redone most of the paint has come off in globs and there is a hoard nay a legion of cocoroaches everywhere and those other horid animals that turn into balls when you touch them. However Lissaio the angel man [master builder of Spetsais] has been alerted and already a small boy has arrived with a huge bucket and even huger broom to start white washing. Marinette is well and sweet but seems in a stupor of love and sits silent in the moonlight for hours. Beagel is in heaven. So are we all in fact and just hope the time goes fast until you come to heaven too."

And I had another of Benjamin Beagle's delightful letters:

"Dear Father
"Please forgive me for not writing to you before but you know what it is like when one is suddenly let lose in a place like this after a whole cold wet winter in the city. The strange thing is that I can still find the same old smells, and you must admit that they are quite different from car tires and those admitedly delicious [Avenue de] Ségur smells but of course nothing can compare with the ones here. But its not only the smells and the *pipi* and the old friends and enemies growling at Mangoufi the Kalliga dog who I simply cant stand. Its the swimming that is the best. For some silly reason mummy and Marinette wont let me jump in right away but tie me up with all kinds of silly things (they invariably forget my leach which any self respecting dog may grumble at but can accept) like belts or bits of rope and as much as I yell and shout and argue which seems to make all the humans in the boat a bit restless they still wont let me swimm all the way to Agia Paraskevi [a distant bay]. They say if I have understood Human correctly, that some huge fish that eat dogs and humans have been seen off the cost

most often this summer so everyone is even more difficult than last year about leting me jump off in mid stream so to speak ha ha. But even so I manage to get enough swimming and all is glorious.

"My special arm chair in your's and mummy's room is most comfortable and I sleep in it every night and even occasional naps in the day time because it is so cool this year that I have not needed to creep under your bed once. Mummy went to Athens for two days last week and came back with all kinds of goodies for our house dog biscuits for me and a Mr and Mrs Colonna in toe (or is it tow). They seem very nice and he is so useful because he is so tall they make him curl and uncurl the jasmine and the other creepers when necessary without even a small ladder.

"Mrs. Joyce your friend has a tiny dog and some gossips in the village say that he is my son but I assure you that this is a grosse calumny. He does not even look like me really I am a million times better looking. However he is a nice kid and sometimes I take him for walks and even frolick with him in the house except one day we nearly brought the table with a lamp on it down on the floor and mummy said I was not behaving like a responsible grown up dog and she was quite cross which is unlike her as you know she has a kind of weakness for me.

"As for Marinette all she does is write letters to that new chap. But I have to admit she is looking most pretty. This week end I have hardly seen mummy as Mr. and Mrs. Colonna are here and she is very busy being nice to them. She came back from Athens with a new table for our room and some garden tables all very pretty. I must leave you now as she is yapping for the typewriter to write to you herself. Yours very beaglily. Beagle."

Marina added in a separate letter to me signed "Mumble," one of her many pet names: "Beagle at any rate has found his soul-country. He swam for two hours yesterday non stop and non stop bark. He is the most lovable pest on earth."

Marinette was worrying about her new soul mate and then two letters from him arrived together and Marina wrote me:

"Once again her eyes look as if they had been polished with gold dust." And on August 3 she said: "Life trickles through one's fingers in this lotus eating land. If I paint a chair in the morning or have something to do in the garden or have to go to the Tapia to get amonia or insect repellent, by the time that it is done it is swimm time and then lunch time and then sleep time and then people drop in or one *has* to take a walk to dispel the food and sleep and then it is time to eat again and talk a bit and then at night it is too beautiful to be in doors or concentrate on anything except the smells and the moonlight, so how can one do anything at all."

On September 11 she wrote Marietta Tree:

"My grown-up guests were infinitely less trouble. They were heaven in fact and ranged from Maurice Druon who because of his latest book on the Greek myths was given a huge hand by the whole island and a surprise party with everyone dressed as ancient Greeks, to the last ones to come the darling Bohlens and in between several Greeks, French, Italians, and even two Egyptians all of them adorable appreciative gay and fun. The most surprising and satisfactory was Kay [Graham, whose husband had just killed himself]. We wrote of course as soon as we heard about poor Phil and cabled and asked her to come but never thought she would be able to. But to our delight she appeared and stayed a week and was marvellous. Such amazing courage and *retenue*.

"I suppose that after so many years of anguish death may seem less hard to bear. Anyway here it was good for her as everything was so far removed from anything in her passed that she could just relax and swimm and walk and I think she liked it. Having Chip and Avis here at the same time who are old friends must have helped too and Bob and Jane [Joyce] of course. So odd to think of so much of Washington finding its way to this bear-foot island. While the Bohlens were here we went shooting at Spetsopoula once or twice and even to a lunch party for Princess Margaret and 'Tony'* and you should have seen us scrounging around for our least faded shorts and trying to get Chip out of bed-room slippers into something more decent. But the visit turned out much nicer and cosier than we expected and great fun in fact. His Lordship spent all morning teaching me how to ski on one ski which he eventually managed both to his pride and mine and I at least found him irresistible.

"P.S. The best *mot* of the season. David asked a young English girl if she had seen Mycenae and she said No who the hell is he. Later when the story

---

* Lord Snowdon, her husband.

was repeated to another boy he asked Well who IS he. The same boy when asked if he had been to Karajan answered No where is it. In that though I dont blame him what with Kranidi across the bay Menidi round the corner etc why not the ruined temple of Karajan."

When Marina got back to Paris, she wrote Marinette (October 6):

"I cant tell you how awful I feel. My girdle pulls my stockings tickle my sweater scratches I am scared of motor cars, dont know how to answer the telephone and am generally deeply *dépaysée*. It was raining when I arrived last night and has been raining all day today. I unpacked gloomily and put away shorts and sandals and desperately tried to get my feet into shoes. Luckily the old crocodyle ones are flabby enough because three years old. I feel both nacked and hateful of clothes and at the same time passionately desirous of some glorious Chanel suit just to flit into and not think about.

"Far and Beagle and Françoise [Payne] were waiting for me at the airport which was nice and for once I arrived not ladden with paper parcels and baskets but only carrying twenty tuberoses which I blew myself to on the way to the airport. The whole house smells which is better than that horrid smell of *moquette* which greeted me last night. Oh dear how much nicer summer is to winter, Greece to France, and being together to being torn apart like us. Far is off to Cairo next week. That jerk Nasser did not answer soon enough else he could have gone from Athens and saved himself this trip."

Nine days later, after Marinette had endured one of those emotional slides that come in any nineteen-year-old girl's life, Marina wrote her:

"So my precious think all these things over, *et ne m'en veux pas* for preaching. Who will if I dont? And thank you for turning to us in your saddeness. This you must always do even if we preach afterwards because after all parent-child love is the only one that fears nothing. One may get cross furious impatiant amused, irritated etc etc but the love itself is there, like the blood in one's vains like the heart or the nose on one's face and no amount of *éppreuve* will ever change or harm it."

While I toured the Middle East, Marina indulged herself in that aspect of Paris life which bored me. She wrote Marinette:

"Last night Mr Bernier and Olivier (Peggy is in Copenhagen photograph-ing the Rosenborg museums) took me to a thing called the *domaine musical*. It is five concerts a year at the Odéon under the patronage of some intellectual ladies and directed by Pierre Boulez and I went because for one thing I like being with George and Olivier and also one cant hate something one knows so little about. Well now I know a scrap more and hate it all a scrap more. I thanked my lucky stars neither you nor David were near me because we might have had such a ghastly *fou rire*. There was a lady singer with the funniest accent who kept singing *La capitalu de l'eternelu de la hambru*. I thought I would die. And even the one better peace sounded so much like the back ground music for a Boris Karloff movie. You know wind blowing doors slamming things creeping. All right but not what they all breathlessly call ART.

"But the audience was heaven. Up stairs hundreds of young thin pale beatnics and down stairs old thin pale beatnics with beards and cashmere shawls and long long feet, *parsemmée* with *le tout Paris* in their second best mink in order to look intellectual too. I loved it and then Mr Bernier took me to a party in a grim rich appartement in Passy of a sort of lady Maecenas of music, with the worst examples of the worst abstract painters of our time, all over the walls and a lot pink *petits fours* and warm champagne and again hundreds of bearded philosophers painters and all the orchestra. It was such fun."

On November 9, she continued:

"Part of my whirl was Nureev the other night. I thought of you so much and our crazy Marathon movie and would have given anything to change places so you could have gone in my place. Swan lake very badly done by the Royal ballet ugly costumes and also to do a bit of name dropping the eighteen swans look quite measly compared to the seventy two of the Bolshoi. However all the boredom is justified by the six minutes when he dances in the third act. People like that come once in a generation and I promise you the whole theatre held its breath while he sailed through the air like a wind blown leaf. And Dame Margot Fonteyn was spectacular too. I was asked to a little party for her tonight and my host said come and have a drink with Margot Arias which I thought the hight of humble snobism. Too funny.

"But the great event in our life was dear sweet Gina Bachauer* playing at Pleyel last night. I gave a cocktail party before hand just to make sure people would go and Peter and I sent out hundreds of invitations because you know how huge Pleyel is, to fill. And I asked all the musical people I could think of and on the whole it went off very well and today the critiques are very good."

On returning from the Middle East, I still had to go to North Africa and Marina was to accompany me but was worried about David, who had had a hand operation and was facing his College Board Exams, which we hoped would lead to Harvard. She wrote him on November 18: "I hated the thought of leaving Far all alone again for weeks and weeks and I hated the thought of not being with you for once that you have your three days. And I spent sleepless nights, until today when Far with a big smile said he thought it could be arranged for me to do what he calls 'one of my combined operations' and leave him in Casablanca or somewhere and fly to London on the night of the 6th.

"I cant tell you how happy I am about all this. We leave here either on Sunday or Monday for Algiers and then Morocco and Far will probably go on to Spain and maybe Portugal but anyway will be back well before the 17th when Marinette gets here. I have started counting the days. It is so wonderful to think of us all under the same roof again after three months."

And then everything was changed — for everyone, everywhere — by the tragic murder of President Kennedy on November 22, 1963. Three days later Marina wrote to Marinette:

"It was so strange to get your letter this morning written on Friday before you knew anything about the President. A little like Louis XVI's diary of the 14 Juillet when he wrote '*Aujourd'hui rien*.' We have all been so stunned we have been going round like zombies since then. We were just about to take the Deakins, who were staying with us, to a play when Denise [Boisot] called. She had just heard it on television.

"Far and Mr. Deakin went to the Times office and Pussy and I to

---

* Greek, despite her name, renowned pianist, Marina's childhood teacher.

Denise's and really it is so amazing to sit in your arm chair and watch the most world shaking event flashed to you half an hour later across an ocean as if you were there. It leaves one dazed. The first tears came when I heard for the first time the passed tense applied to the man who a minute before we had watched smiling and waving to the crowd. He WAS etc. etc. It just cant bare thinking of.

"You dont know how grief struck France is. For a people who are not too pro American or too sentimental it is wonderful to see everyone from the post man to De Gaulle with grave ashen faces as if they had lost a personal friend. And all this when he was a public figure only three years.

"David called to say England was even more shocked and stunned. The Head master and all housemasters and boys sent special messages to him and the other American boy and I think he has been profoundly surprised and pleased by all this. Its good as youths are so apt to make sweeping judgements and it is good for him to realise that appearances of indifference are not always true. He sounded profoundly moved and sad. Thank God we are going over next week for his exams.

"You can imagine that our plans for going to Geneva were cancelled. Thank god. It would have been so awful for poor Far if we had been on our way there and lost in some small Savoyard village knowing nothing nothing of all this and Far had a column about international communications or something. As it was he could rush to the office and write another one. So we are not going anywhere the Algerian trip having been postponed anyway till after Xmas. I am just as glad as it would have been so short if we had to fit David in too.

"The road yesterday was one mass of cars and policemen as half the heads of state and Royalty of Europe went by on their way to Washington for the funeral. Here there is a service at Notre Dame at five in order to coincide with the American one and I am going with Mrs. Chambers and Mme de Rose. Oh dear how awful it all is.

"I can imagine what it must have been like for you there. Did you by any chance see last night's television when Mr Ruby killed Oswald. Really how uncredible. To kill a man before all those detectives and give up your own life in the electric chair for it, out of straight sheer anger and indignation is rather crazily wonderful I must say. Unless of course there are secret things behind it all that we shall never know. I hope not. I am rather sorry for Mr Ruby. Is'nt it strange to hear everyone denying Oswald like the pest.

The communist party, the pro and anti Castrists even his wife. Ah me. Good by for the moment my precious darling girl."

For us as a family, at least, the period that had included all these deaths — my mother, my uncle, my newspaper's publisher, and my country's president — ended on a warm personal note. Marina wrote Marinette just before she came home for Christmas:

"David is NOT going back to Winchester. This I consider fabulous. After endless discussions and not knowing what to do for these nine months that he has ahead of him we went and asked the advice of the cultural attaché here who suggested the American college in Paris. We did not even know there was one. But there is and they will take him in the middle of the year as a favour and they can get his college board results earlier than April and for the first time in seven years I shall have a child at home again and I can hardly stand the pleasure. Half the night I did not sleep making up menues to fatten him up. And in a week I shall have you both to hug.

"The other night we dined with a gentleman from the U.S. Embassy in London who was telling us about their side of the Kennedy tragedy and he told us funny little unimagined sides to great events. Practically none of the great who went to the funeral had their passports in order. The Duke of Edinburgh's was at the Sudanese Embassy getting a visa and as it was Saturday nothing would induce the Suddanese to open up their Embassy and get it. Somebody else had lost theirs and yet another's had expired so in the end our freind said they were giving travel permits practically on visiting cards. Now that all the sad things have been said, one can turn to the less so."

Marina put a touchingly dear little letter on the chair where I kept my clothes, just before New Year's Eve:

"Here I am sitting at my desk surrounded by what seems like seven thousand unrequitted Xmas cards and thanking people like Isabelle and Hope and Count Motrico when I suddenly thought 'Why is one only polite to people one does not care that much about and leave the really important ones out because they don't expect any formal thanks.' So I decided it was high time to write you a bread and butter letter or rather a cake and jam letter. You have given me bread and butter for twenty years now and on top of it so much cake and so much jam that it is hard to say thank you for it. Perhaps that is why one only thanks for a bottle of sherry but not for a life time of niceness. One really ought to invent a few new words. However even with the old ones what I want to say is very simple. Thank you very very very much for a lovely Xmas and all all my best wishes for the New Year.

"May it bring with it, personally speaking and leaving out such obvious things as peace and all that, no gout no siatica a pleasant trip or two, our Marinette happy, our Polar* near us and well and into Harvard, a few ENORMOUS trout in Aspen, a good renting of the Spetses house, some work on THE book, some beating of Chip at golf, a few more talks with you know who [de Gaulle] and only very very few grouchy days. May it bring a lot more things too but even if we get only Polar and Marinette all right out of all these wishes it will be plenty. *Ne quitez pas* and all all my love and thanks. Dopey."

---

* Polar and Puffin are nicknames for our children, David and Marinette.

IX

January 1964 - December 1965

The year 1964, which began with David at home for the first time in ages, started in a traditional liver-busting French way. Marina wrote Jane Joyce on January 9:

"Chip and Avis got back safe and sound and of course the first thing that happened was that we went to supper there on their second night 'a quiet supper à quatre' and needless to add the cards and chips and brandy bottle came out and even more needless to add, both the men having begged us to be sharp with them and not let them play too late, we were all up till three and today the men are humble and the women cross. The aweful trouble with being a woman is that you cant really hit a man when he is down, and you certainly cant hit him when he is up for the simple reason that he is bigger than you and wont let you, so what can a poor woman do.

"Oh well. Christmas is over thank god and we are slowly struggling up and back from a stupor of caviar *foie gras* truffles venison and plum pudding. All this was served to us over New Year's eve, on our *tournée* of the Seine et Oise. New Year's eve at Alain and Mary's [Rothschild] with Alphands and other assorted Rothschilds, and New Year's day at Cecile's. Too bad one cant take a plastic bag with one and take the food away for rainier days. It would be lovely to have a truffle now and then, and caviar now and now, but all of that stuff together just kills one."

Twenty days later she sent Jane a postscript: "I am sadly reduced to just waiting and planing no further ahead than . . . Uganda. Please do me one favour. If by any chance I am eaten by a Bahutu or a Baluba or raped by Field Marshal Okele, do try and hush it up and tell people I met a more romantic end. Nothing can be more unkind than the inescapable trite joke attached to one's sad end. Think of everyone even one's best friend bursting into chuckles every time one's name is mentioned. Marina. Ah yes is'nt she the one etc. In a week or so we are off to Spain Algeria Morocco Egypt where to his great surprise Cy has been invited to go to Abu Simbel and Sinai *tous frais payés*. Then possibly Ethiopia and Kenya Uganda and Zanzibar."

Shortly before our departure Marinette called from Cambridge in tears and confessed she had decided to break off her engagement — which was more than all right with her parents as we had never been raving mad about the project. Marina wrote her on February 8:

"I must tell you my precious that personally we all here in the family think you are right. Right to say that you are too different in everything, in caracter in approach to life, in mentality. The moment he came to Spetses I saw it. And I am only too delighted that you saw it too before it was too late. He is young and he will get over you let us hope and there is no one in the whole world who has not had an unhappy love affair in their lives. Its part of what makes life. I will not add to the distress you must already be feeling by saying what a chump we all think you are. But I do want to say that having made two big mistakes in your life, you must now do something which wont be easy. You must both pull yourself together and not allow yourself this over enthusiasm which results in distress all around.

"So dont fall into deep discouragement, and self dislike and things like that. I know you will go through *un très mauvais quart d'heure*, but let it be a *quart d'heure*. Dont let it colour your whole life and caracter. I am sorry my precious that you have to go through this very bad bit of your life, alone. I would give my right arm to be with you and talk things over or just sit silent but sort of around as a comfortable shoulder to cry on. But in the end everybody solves their problems alone. This is a platitude by now. But platitudes have a way of being true. And whatever your black thoughts may be, tell yourself that this is not as bad, as if you had realised all this after you were married and had a child and were really *engagée* towards two humans instead of *semi engagée* to one."

To cheer her up, she told of a dinner party we had given which included General Lemnitzer, the NATO commander, and the Philippe de Rothschilds.

"Mrs. Lemnitzer asked Pauline de Rothschild, 'Did you make your own dress deary.' She was wearing a heavily embroidered Balenciaga special. Pauline's face was too funny. She answered. 'Alas no. I am not clever enough for that.' "

A few days later we left for Africa via Rome, whence Marina wrote Marinette:

"Rome is more beautiful than I remembered. I must bring you some day. And so lovely to see the sky again and yellow light and flowers. We had dinner at the Embassy the first night a deadly stuffy affair for visiting admirals and we were squeezed in at the last moment, but everyone left early and we were able to sit and talk to the Reinhardts [U.S. ambassador] at the end quite cosily. The next day I walked the streets and looked at churches and the Campidollio.

"Last night we dinned at some friends in the Piazza Navona which is a dream. It is the old chariot racing ground and has kept its exact shape over centuries although there is not one roman stone left. Very Ben Hur-ish in shape indeed, but with all these beautiful deep orange houses around it with flat facades and so many windows and on one side a tremendous Baroque church and in the middle three Bernini fountains. Everywhere you look there is something to please the eye. I have kept my eyes resolutely closed when it comes to shops however so as not to be tempted and keep my very very few dollars for the bazzar in Cairo."

On March 2 she told Marinette: "It is funny writing to you from your native city. We walked by the Immobilia building as a pilgrimage this afternoon and Groppi the pastry shop which you were too young to visit, and it all looks a little brocken down and seedy. The town has moved away and the snappy part is now where all the big hotels are cropping up like weeds. They are really suffering from Hiltonisation in this country. Even the Minister's* wife told me that the local joke is 'Dont whatever you do leave your flat empty for the weekend, because the minister will confiscate it and make it into a hotel.' If ever there is a depression and people start staying at home again the poor minister will have to shoot himself. However for the moment I think there are more Dutch Germans and English here than in their native lands and the minister is all powerful.

"He had us met at the airport and we whizzed through formalities in a minute. The fact that they later lost our passeports for five days is but a very typical Egyptian detail. However we cant complain as we have really been given the treatement. Our trip to Aswan and Abu Simbel *à l'oeil* was tremendous. We flew to Aswan and there too were met by a tiny gentleman in a huge Mercedes and first he took us to see the first of the temples that has already been moved from the water's edge. It is called Kalabja and was built by Augustus when he was placating the conquered by seeming to adopt their gods. Then it became a hyding place for Copts who were persecuted by the Romans.

"It is quite lovely but the most beautiful thing is the view. We climbed to the top of the temple and looked out towards miles and miles of a strangely beautiful nothingness. It is all as far as the eye can see granite and sand desert. Brown and grey and beige and the only bit of colour is the Nile which here is really bright bright blue. He looks so quiet and calm that it is very hard to imagine that in a year or so he will be turned by the damn partly into such a towering force as to make the biggest hydroelectric plant in the world, and after that into a lake five hundred kilometres big which will cover all that we were looking at, desert and rock and hill, village and valley and that the temple we were standing on so far away would then be in the middle of a tiny island surrounded by waters.

"I hope some day we can come back and see this strange landscape's new face. After the temple we were taken to see the present hydro-electric plant which is always terribly boring and which for some reason every propaganda minister will always show one. Then the Hotel which is lovely. There is a beastly new Hilton right beside it shutting out the view from one

---

* Deputy Prime Minister Hatem.

side but luckily we were in the old Cataract hotel still full of Indiano-Victoriana; red velvet and white polished balustrades and mosquitoe nets which we alas neglected to use and I now look like the cholera kid of all times. We had drinks on the terrace and watched two boats come sailing in with the loads of Marks and Spencer tourrists. But you cannot imagine how lovely they looked with their colosal mast at least thirty feet tall and curved and the sail really looks like a wing on a huge sea gull. And the moon was full and the Nile here is quite narrow and private looking and full of rocky lunar looking islands. No wonder the Agha Khan wished to be burried right there. It is most beautiful.

"The moment we finished dinner we were taken by yet another little gentleman to the damn. I promise you it is one of the most incredible sights of my life. At first I was rather dissapointed and thought it looked like any other *chantier*, just miles and miles of mud and workmen. They work twenty four hours a day in shifts and they have twenty thousand workmen. At night they work by huge flood-lights and it gives it a strange even more unreal atmosphere. We drove round the works for a while and then suddenly came to the edge of some works and looked down. Down two hundred mettres. Here was the future hydro-electric plant. They had dug down and out through the granite and in the gigantic hole thousands of men were working.

"The strange light and the noise was fantastic. Noise from cranes the size of the Empire State building. Noise from Russian trucks whose wheels were as tall as I. Noise from machines making cement from sand, and sand from granite and every concievable gurgling noise. Things sucking out water, others sucking out sand or spuing sand and water. And all these men looking as if they had walked straight out of the bible with their robes and their turbans and their beards. Much much closer to the bible than to a Russian construction firm. And all the while the Nile flowing by, still and silent as if tottaly unconcerned with what all these people were going to do to him. It really was the strangest sight and most awsome that I have ever seen. I am sure the building of the Pyramids must have looked something like that.

"We got home quite late and were woken up the next morning at four to catch the Express [hydrofoil] which would take us to Abu Simbel. Alas our ministerial friend had got things mixed up and instead of the honor seats up stairs with windows, which he had boasted of we were the last to be seated and given the nasty last row seat. No window and what with the vibration (we were siting on the engine) the noise, the heat and the smell of gas after five hours I was ready to die. But when we did finally get to the Temple I admited it was worth while. You hardly know it when you arrive, so sudden is the appearance of the temple, right out of the rock and practically in the water. You suddenly look up and there are four gigantic statues carved right in the rock.

"The whole temple is carved in the rock. Inside there are six rooms, three where the priests kept their paraphernalia and one *pro-naos* [porch] one middle one for the King and the last one for the High priest alone. Here there are four sitting statues again of Amon, of Horus of one other god and of course Ramses. He was not a humble man. Twice a year on the day when Ramses won the great battle against the Hittites, and the day of his birth day the sun upon rising comes through the three doors and illuminates only the face of the King and then moves to the other three faces. It must be quite an exciting thing to see and how they calculated all this several hundred feet into the heart of the rock god alone knows. The walls are of course covered end to end with reliefs grafitis and symbols of all kinds. Great battles, coronations and everywhere everywhere Ramses himself.

"There is a second temple next door which he had built for his wife Nefertari and here Far says he found the three most beautiful women of his life. It is a relief of Nefertari with two attendant goddesses. I must say they are lovely. Very tall and very very thin with *bouffant* hair and long slim arms. Huge eyes and wide wide mouths. Very *nouvelle vague* somehow. Well we had just done the rounds of both temples when we heard the well known pa-pou pa-pou of the Express and off we had to go again.

"This time it took even longer and the sun was hitting us just at the back of the head. On our way we found the other express. They have two. It had brocken down so we tried to help them and then we broke down. You know what it is like to brake down between Athens and Spetses. Bad enough. In the middle of the Nile and with Arab mechanics bending over the gas tank every man of them with a lit cigarette in his mouth, it is much much worse. However, I dont know why but we suddenly took off again and got to the hotel just in hair raising time to catch the train back to Cairo. I was so tired by then I would have slept on a pile of pebbles but in fact the Hungarian built train was most comfortable. We got back this morning to find alas and alack that our trip to Mount Sinai is off. We shall never know why as every reason given has been a different one. The revolution after all, optimistic as it may be, can not change the national character overnight, and twelve years is overnight."

The next letter Marinette received was from Nairobi, dated March 11, but it included an account of Ethiopia. Marina wrote:

"Sunday our hosts [Ambassador and Mrs. Ed Korry] took us to a pic nic near a tremendous gorge which was simply beautiful. You look down into miles of ravine down into a river bed which eventually joins the Blue Nile. We saw a whole family of baboons, so I am sure mama baboon was saying come come quick and see the funny humans. We moved and talked and stared at each other so in exactly the same way. Then we went to a lovely lovely farm run by an old English couple, he eighty four and she eighty two who have been there for fifty years, through wars and masacres and changes they go on planting strawberries and plums and peaches, sweet william and love in the mist. There is something rather glorious and indestructibel about the 'Good' english pioneers. They gave us tea in the garden with plate after plate of scones cake fruit quince jelly etc vanishing into four little Korry tummies and reapearing full.

"We picked flowers and looked at the sun set which in Ethiopia is the most beautiful in the world. As the whole landscape is blue and mauve anyway from the young Eukalyptus and the sun set turns everything pink and deep gold and it is breath taking. How I could cry that we could not travel a little. There is Gondar with its Arabian fortresses so Crusader like that one thinks one is dreaming. And Lalibela where King Lalibela cut eleven great Orthodox churches right out of the rock. But not like Abu Simbel where they are cut into the rock. This is like a colossal square of rock separated from the rest of its mother rock, then scooped out and carved in the shape of a cross which they then decorate with bas reliefs and paintings. The pictures of it look quite unique and I could cry all over again and the thought of poor far having to sit for hours and listening to gugh about Somalia instead of travelling. Really humans make me a bit tired. This place called Ogaden in Ethiopia which now the Somalis Kenyans and Ethiopians are 'ready to die for the fatherland' is such a horrid peace of desert bleak and bare and a hundred and thirty in the shade (of which there is none) that in the old days an Ethiopian would either resign or shoot himself if he had to go there for anything. And now it has become the garden of Eden that they are all slaughtering each other about.

"So then we arrived here [Nairobi] yesterday morning after an hour and a half flight. The jets do make a difference. Even I can take an hour and a half. Eleven years ago when we were here last it took four. Nairobi is delicious. Half English half Indian, half twentieth century half Trader Horn. You go to a Drive-in movie in the national park and the Giraffes get in the way of the camera. Do you remember Mr and Mrs Dunford whom we had taken to Malmaison four years ago. Well Cleo (Mrs) has taken charge of me so I hope to see a few animals and so glad to see a bit of the country. Last time it was all Mau Mau so we never were allowed to leave the city.

"It is the most perfect temperature in the world. Cotton dress and sweater type. And so so blue and gold. If I find sarris I shall get you one. My shopping up to now limited. Far has no time to write to you himself poor fellow (its hard enough to remember that Zambia is ex Northern Rhodesia and keep the names of Mr Gadinga Odinga Mrs Bitti Titti Mr Mbah Kaounda Karune etc, clear in his mind. I do hope we meet Field Marshall Okello but I think he has made a bit of a *bruta figura* and no one wants him."

On March 16, from Dar-es-Salaam:

"When I wrote I had not yet visited the [Kenya] animal reserve. I cant tell you what fun it was. A giraffe with eyes exactly like Audrey Hepburn and eye lashes bigger than even your faulse ones. Gazelles of all kinds of course and wildey beasts and Zebras looking so dressed up and dear. But of course the lions are the great tourrist attraction. They are the hardest to find anyway. You cant imagine how odd it is to get to a patch of bush with yellow grass no higher than ten inches and you look and look and see absolutely nothing and then slowly there is a kind of ripple and you see a most beagle-like hand stretching and a yawn and suddenly under your very nose and out of seeming nothingness arise one two three ten lions.

"How they make themselves so flat and invisible I will never understand. I went twice, once with an old Greek friend whom I found here who had been in the [Girl Guides] yellow crocus patrol with me (you can count how many years I have known her) and once with Far. And we were lucky we saw the lions both times. The first time they had just killed a poor wilde beast and it was extraordinary to watch them carry it to their brothers. They all sat around and munched and licked and they really looked so friendly and cosy and soft, one simply cant imagine that it would be dangerous to get out of the car and stroke them. One is hardly allowed the window down so I suppose it is. We also saw hyppos and a crocodyle.

"The stay was quite pleasant although Poor Far had a most frustrating time. Three times he had an appointement with a minister at nine in the morning and three times he waited for hours and either he never turned up or said it was a mistake. The continent on the whole is perpetually near chaos as was inevitable and it makes it very hard to work. Inevitably one applies Western frames of refference which dont really exist and we persist in thinking it frightfully rude to give an appointement and not be there, to call a meeting and not show up, to have a reception given in your honor and never appear, and yet probably in Kikuyu customs or Bantu or Hutu this may be accepted behaviour. But it still makes it hard to exist in a twentieth century society. It is too bad they became independent in the moment of automation and cybernetics, or tel-star and sputnic, because now they can never never hope to catch up with anything.

"Their worse problem I think is the 'what are we to become without the barbarians' complex. You know once the barbarians left everything was going to be all right; there would be jobs and money and milk and honey for everyone. And of course there is'nt and they cant blame the colonialists any more so they blame their own leaders and so it goes. Field Marshall Okello is the tragico-funniest thing now. Having in a fit of *excès de zèle* killed 12 thousand people and considered himself the elect of god in the Zanzibar revolution, he is now told that it is easier to overthrow old governements, than to run new ones, and please please would he go away. No one wants him and he flits between Zanzibar Tanganyika and Kenya and everyone is polite but firm and he is pushed off elsewhere. He gave a press conference the other day in which rather sadly he said 'If god does not need my services any more I shall go back and be a house-painter.' We arrived in Tanganyika last evening and had dinner with the Embassador and Mrs and then came to our hotel which is the ugliest little thing you ever saw. We have *soi disant* air conditioning but it does'nt condition much. It is like a Turkish bath.

"Dar es Salam itself is not much of a town. It consists of about six blocks and it is mostly shops. They sell lovely shells in the streets and nice baskets, both good for Spetses. But I have not succombed yet as I might find my own in Zanzibar where I hope we will go on Thursday. The N Y Times is not very *grata* as one of the four men who had been thrown in jail during the coup was ours, so we are not sure we will be allowed in. Or what is more important out. But we will know tomorrow. So I shall try and collect my own shells. Buying them is somehow a tiny bit cheating.

"From here we shall go back to Nairobi on Sunday and then to Rwanda and Burundi and then after that if Far can write himself three columns ahead of time we are going off on a few days holiday to fish. He has been dreaming of Nile perch (which is not a perch) ever since he was a small boy so this is his last chance. This will be in Uganda. We went off and bought ourselves khaki trousers and shirts in a safari shop and although I dont look like Ava Gardener or Capucine, to my surprise I dont look as awful as I had expected so my moral is up. If on top of that I too catch a fish or shoot an Impala there will be no end to my dinning out. I met a lady the other day who shot a crocodyle by mistake. So one never knows. I am sticking to both the chair and the typewriter so I will leave you and go and have a shower. The sea here is truthfully hotter than a hot bath in Paris. Disgusting."

The next letter to Marinette was sent on March 29 from Kampala, Uganda. Marina said:

"We have been having a fascinating time since I last wrote from Tanganyika but travelling so fast that I had no time to write in the last week. We flew to Burundi whose capital you may not know goes by the fancy name of Usumbura but which they are about to change to Bujumbura just to mix people up even more. It is a simply lovely place although one cant call it a town really. A sort of suburb with no center, lots of pretty houses build by the Belgians, lovely gardens as everything grows *à vue d'oeil*, glorious views from everywhere as it is all hills and at the foot of the town a lake which is beautiful.

"But oh dear God must surely have made this continent on Monday and Tuesday, as he seems to have just learned about world-making. He certainly knew how to make mountains lakes rivers trees flowers but he had no sense of proportion yet nor any idea of detail. It rains all the time for three months and not at all for nine. The loveliest lakes overflow and drown people and anyway you cant swimm in them as they have crocodyles. The prittiest streams have bilhartsia worms which are a deadly illness, or malaria or god knows what else. The sweetest fruit are poison the loveliest flowers die at once when picked.

"It really takes true christian patiance and all the virtues, for people who work here and try to get something accross. Add to that justified but nonetheless tedious chips on shoulders infiriorito-superiority complexes, and you get a picture of the real difficulties when trying to treat them as serious democrats with an equal vote in the U N. And of course add to that the gigantic courtship payed them by the Russians and more so by the Chinese and you can see why people age fast when *en poste* on this continent.

"From Burundi where we were lucky to stay with Mr. [John] Bennett the British Embassador and old friend of Far's (I dont know where else we could have stayed as there is no hotel) we drove to Rwanda the next door neighbour, and now since independence, ennemy, over the most beautiful if bad road in the world. Hill after hill after hill with trees and coffee and flowers. Neither the Burundi nor the Rwandans have villages which is strange. They live as far from each other as they can which is not very far as the countries are tiny and over populated. Rwanda is even more beautiful but Kigali its Capital is really nothing but a few houses. But we were so glad to travel at least a part of this long trip by car and not the eternal plane from which you see nothing."

Marina began to write an article for *Vogue* (in the form of a letter to Deppy Messinesi, an editor. She never finished or sent it. After her death Marinette found it in Marina's desk. This manuscript recounted:

"We have just returned to Kampala after a tiny safari (the very word seems like name dropping even to my own ears). You should see me. With clothes hair eyes finger-nails all covered with red dust, I am just exactly what Vogue would deplore the most. The African sun beating down on us, in our tiny boat on the waters of lake Albert (name dropping again) is so fierce, that my face is like a peace of scratchy burned toast. But it was all wonderful. We had been travelling around East Africa for months and we desperately needed a few days off, to try and forget for a moment all about politics and politicians, international, national, or race relations, tribal feuds, economic needs, *liberté égalité fraternité*, and the dismal lack thereof, in this fair world of ours.

"More than ever in Africa, I was glad that it is poor Cy who has to do the writing on these trips, and not me. I could no more understand and then explain to others the troubles of independence than fly. All I could feel was that they are endless and heart-breaking. So while Cy struggled with statistics and ever contradictory information, I just walked and looked and listened and talked. Luckily French and English are spocken by all. Or practically all.

"One day at a particularly difficult ladies lunch having exhausted most subjects of small talk I asked the lady across the table, when did the jacarandas bloom, and she answered gravely 'Yes I have four. One of seven one of five one of two and a baby.' Serves me right for leaving the beaten track. Silence fell heavily upon us, until the ladies at each side of me, one an English missionary and the other a gigantic African lady minister of womanhood or something, both turned to me simultaneously and one said 'You can't think how hard it is to keep jello fresh in this country,' and the other asked 'how many tribe you country.' Two civilisations, two worlds meeting verbaly head-on over my soup plate.

"We could not go on a serious safari with tents and bearers as I had visualised it because these take a minimum of three weeks and alas we had neither the days nor the dollars. But for one week, the safari companies can take you to one or another of their established camps and very nice cottages with beds and baths and really if anything too comfortable and one can shoot small game, that is any kind of antelope, cob, congoni wilderbeast, wild pigs, any number of birds and even a zebra. But who would want to shoot a zebra? They are so beautiful and so frightfully elegant and upper-class, in their black and white ensemble. So are the guinea-hens in grey with white polka dots, the personification of middle-aged chic. The 'Mrs Exeters' of the jungle. But so infuriating. Cy discovered to his deep humiliation that they can walk faster than he can run.

"One day mortified beyond words at having failed to make them fly, he was running after one in a field while I was watching from the land-rover with our white hunter. Suddenly I saw one of the African boys (we had two with us) run right in front of Cy's loaded gun. I turned to protest to the white hunter at the danger of this but he said 'No no dear lady he is just trying to stop your husband from running right into those elephants there.' And sure enough not twenty yards from Cy stood a family of elephants, looking exactly like a small grey hill. Neither of us had noticed them. Later we saw dozens and dozens of them and of all the animals around us these were the hardest to believe. The country side is so pleasant and familiar like any wide open prairie land in Europe or America that one keeps forgetting where one is periodically. So that the sudden sight of fifty elephants is constantly an amazement, like seeing a tractor in a Georgian living room, or native dancers at a super-market. Except for the monkeys, the elephants are the animals who gave me the deepest fealing of family life. Father is always very serious looking; the tiny ones they are a dream, and all look as if they were dressed up in granpa's cast-offs. Everything is too big for them and flaps about in great grey folds around their chubby legs and throats. . . .

"Then we went fishing on lake Albert, but I came to the conclusion that there is no fisherman's god. Cy had been dreaming of catching a Nile perch since he was a boy. We sat in a small boat for a whole day and he who would have given his right arm for the privilege, never even got a strike and I who really rather dislike fish cought several huge ones in no time at all. How unfair can fishing get. The lake is too big to be loved. But parts of the shores we floated by were marvellous. Great rising walls of sheer rock, overgrown with strange unfamiliar Douanier Rousseau like plants and leaves with water falls with monkeys everywhere, and here and there a patch of pink, not flowers but flamingoes. No flowers anywhere oddly enough. I looked everywhere for the profusion of exotic blooms but there was no profusion and the one time when I mistook a scarlet leaf for a flower, and started off to pick it, our white hunter said 'I would'nt venture into the underbrush if I were you, Not in those shoes. Not with all those gaboon vipers around.' Apparently the Gaboon vipers are pink and blue and exquisite and kill you dead faster than a bullet. He did not have to tell me twice. Green is bad enough but pink and blue.

"The most unexpected thing of all however, for me was when we were sitting in our little boat and suddenly there would be a swirl and a churning of water and there right under our nozes would slowly rise something looking exactly like the old leather sofa in the library, only with absurdly delicate pink ears and small malevolent pink eyes. Hypos. By the dozens. We were told that they can overturn a boat in no time. I so hated the thought of floating around in that creepy brownish water, even though we were assured they were no crocodyles there. We did see some crocodyles later at Murchison falls. They are fabulous. The falls I mean not the crocodyles.

"It does not look like water at all, this great giant of gurgling roaring pounding whiteness. We walked down the steepest cliff to the pool below and I must say I have never seen a sight closer to a surrealist hell. The water is frightfully high all over Africa this year, so there was but a tiny strip of beach left, and most of it was covered with polished white bones, and an infinite number of dead things including a hypopotamus. The heat and the smell and the noise were unbearable and even here to my sorrow I cought a fish and Cy did'nt. Its justification for a man to leave his wife."

We were in Morocco, cruising about another piece of Africa where I had to keep previously arranged appointments, when we got the news that David had been accepted by Harvard, to our great joy. Marina wrote Marinette from Rabat on April 22:

"We have just returned from a trip to Fez which is quite lovely. The city walled and crenelated and full of tiny streets and dark alleys and everything looks and feels just as mysterious as one could wish. The bazar full of fruit and material and copper and slippers and dirty dirty people and all great fun. The hotel we stayed in (I sent you a post card but it will probably arrive after the letter) was by far the prettiest we have ever been in. An old palace turned into a hotel when the old prince died, it is all on different levels with courtyard after courtyard in multi coloured tiles and with fountains everywhere and such flowers as one dreams about. Our room all very moorish and fancy was right in the garden and with a lemon tree at the door. What with the moon light and the scent of the orange blossom violas calas etc it was almost too romantic."

From Morocco we flew to Algeria. She wrote Marinette on our return to Paris:

"Black Africa is bad enough but god preserve me from the half-black, half communist, half-thinking Frenchified arab. Never have we been subjected to such a plethora of *idées reçues*, of undigested ideas old fashioned slogans and deep rooted muddleheadedness. Also tragic and pathetic and nice which makes it all the worse. We saw Frankie Wisner [a young American diplomat and friend] who was sweet and most kind and helpful and who is admired and respected by both the Algerians and his own Embassy people. It was deadly boring though most of the time as I sat in the hotel garden reading detective stories. We went to one nationalised farm one that father had known under its French owner five years ago with a machine gun on the roof and barbed wire over the roses. The barbed wire and the roses are still there but it belongs to the workmen now and they say that they are not really better off under the present State but their children go to school and they are their own masters and have their own dignity. True indeed and touching. I picked so many flowers that even I had my fill. Not as fabulous as the road from Rabat to Fez which holds the record but good enough. I brought them all the way back to Paris with me to Far's horror and they look lovely in the living room right now."

On May 5, Marina philosophically concluded from Paris to Louie (Mrs. George) Woods:

"On our way back we went to Morocco and Algeria too and that was pretty depressing. Worse I would say. You know the tragic thing is that in the end war is so much easier to wage than peace, and a gun lighter to bare than a hoe or an axe or a typewriter. All these young men who for seven years were willing to give their lives for their freedom, are not in the least bit ready now to give their time, their hands their work and their slight anti-climax fealing, for their country, and the result is slogans big words rhetoric, a lot of sitting about in caffees arguing, and utter chaos. Poor poor things. Poor poor humanity; trying so hard and doing so badly. Oh well maybe the trying is the thing in the end."

Exactly three weeks later she added to Louie: "If I was eloquent on Africa, you should hear me now on the over-developped countries. If someone does'nt do something about them soon, I dont know what will happen. Today I left my house at dawn to go personally and get the plumber to come and fix our toilets which risk to flood the house next door. After much waiting I was told he would 'try' and come middle of June. I thanked gratefully and went to pick up my coat from the cleaners promised for the week before. It was not ready but they did tell me that the price for cleaning had gone up since last week from four to eight dollars for a coat. I came out to find a parking ticket on my screen.

"Got home to find that seventeen people who have been kindness itself to both of us in such disparate places as Peru Zanzibar Omsk and Rio, were all in town at the same time and wished to see us. I went out to lunch drove eighteen times around the block without finding a place to leave the car, came home left it took the subway and arrived dishevelled hot weepy and with an ulcer forty minutes late. My hostess was tearing out HER hair because living in a modern building, something has gone wrong with the lift but it is built in such a way that to fix it they will probably have to tare down the house. Oh well.

"Not to mention Peruvians killing themselves at foot ball games, Mods and Rockers tearing up their home towns, gangsters kidnapping Mme Dassault under Miss Callas's nose at the Opera etc etc etc. However, if one does survive it IS so beautiful and if one has to die one might as well die in the Place Concorde as in Dar es Salam. I still remain a staunch European. If only we could come back just a tiny bit to our old human scales. A taxi driver said *bon jour* to me the other day and I practically kissed him."

In June 1964 we went to the United States. From the political conventions which nominated Johnson and Barry Goldwater we rushed on to Aspen, Colorado, with its log cabins, trout, and utter tranquillity. Marina wrote Avis Bohlen on August 12:

"I am not telling about the Conventions because you probably saw Susan Mary and she must have told you all. All I can say is that it was hell and depressing beyond words. On the way up here we saw a silly nasty article asking for Chip's recall imprisonment cashiering if not castration, because he is supposed to have said: 'If Goldwater is nominated duck the missiles boys.' Alas there seem to be more lunatics in this country than I had thought. The Goldwaterettes in yellow felt skirts high boots and cow boy hats were too sickmaking.

"Cy sticks to his fishing and solitude like a leach and nothing will stop him not even a serious attack of gout. It really is too miserable on a holiday. Like a small boy who would always get measles at Xmas. And he loves all this so. The children are arriving next week. Thank god. Their jobs at the World's Fair were fun and they have both made a little money (although much less than they thought what with taxes and having to pay for their transport and lunch) but they looked pale and exhausted. So I am glad to give them a fortnight of fresh air and stakes and lots of sleep before they plunge one in her last and one in his first year of college."

On August 21 she wrote Nursey: "The children got here Saturday rather green and skinny but now they sleep twelve hours a night at least and David and Marinette's newest friend a boy called Dicky Mackintosh eat so much that I cant believe my eyes when another dozen eggs and whole packet of bacon vanish under my nose. Needless to say I love to see this. Marinette domesticated and Americanised far far beyond me has taken over as well as the shopping because she says I am too extravagant and dont know the difference between margarine and butter. Today however we made two cakes and both were miserable faillures.

"Far and I were here twenty days before the children. He blissful fishing all day and refusing to see a soul or go anywhere, and I quite happy too because there are lots of old friends in town whom I went down quite often to visit when pa was safe away fishing, would have up here for pic nics and then I went to the concerts and even to a little bridge now and then so we were both happy.

"Yesterday we had such a storm I thought the cabins would burn down struck by lightening. The light was so strong it was like day and the noise like a bombing. And it poured sheets and sheets all night. Thank god we were not in tents. But today all is clear and beautiful again except for snow on the high peaks which even for here is rare in August. But because of so much rain, this year the spring flowers are still out now and you cant think of the number of times I think of you when I get back with arms full of delphiniums and some strange mountain lilies called Mariposa and deep blue gentians and some other tall pale blue things like canteberry bells but not quite and even the hair bells grow as fat as daisies. Its too lovely."

After visiting the children at Cambridge in late September, we returned to Paris. Marina wrote philosophically to Marinette on October 7:

"By the very nature of things senior year at college is bound to be a rather sad one. Plus the fact, all emotional things apart, that it really is the tail end of the fairy tale, the never never land in which one really has no other problem save that of a good hour-exam or getting asked to a foot ball game or a dance, and how to squeeze an extra ribbon out of one's pocket money. A few months more and then one is out into the huge outside world thinking in terms of real life and real problems jobs, what to do with one's life how to understand one's fellow humans (a practically insurmountable problem) how to get on with them even without understanding them, how to hurt and get hurt as little as possible, how to earn a living etc etc etc. I wont go on depressing you even more than you already are my darling baby. I wish you were still six and I could read you a story and see your eyelids close."

She wrote David on October 26: "The Opera was wonderful except I hated the Wieland Wagner *décor.* As for the Chagal cealing it is lovely but more like something for a travel agency than the Opera. His brilliant reds and blues make the curtains look shabby as hell and the shabby pinks and reds of the seats and curtains make his reds look vulgar and out of place. A great mistake I think. One letter from Far from Mexico while waiting for his plane to Cuba. His article yesterday was about Tshombe which makes me think that he is sitting biting his nails waiting for the bearded one to see him in Havana. I hope all goes well for him.'

In San Francisco for the Republican Convention that summer, Marina had encountered a cab driver who judged from her accent she was French and begged a favor. She told the children on November 6:

"I did have one small triumph this week. Do you remember the story I told you about the taxi driver in San Francisco whose grand daughter I had to find. Well I found her. I first went to 86 Avenue Foch the address he had given me and asked for the Mr. Xavier de Vilmorin and he did not live there any more having left years ago. So I called Louise de V. and asked her help and of course this was just her cup of tea. Two days later she called me and indeed this gentleman turns out to be a second cousin of hers and as Louise modestly said *'Toute grande famille aristocratique a sa mauvaise branche.'* This one is from the *mauvaise branche* and was indeed a magician in a music hall and then a circus because he was in love with a circus girl. Then he married this American girl (my taxi driver's daughter) and was truly beastly to her.

"From here on *les choses se gattent.* She did not kill herself while with her Vilmorin husband, but ran away with another man and was killed in a motor car accident which may or may not have been deliberate. This the poor father obviously did not know. Anyway when she died the other man sent back the child to its rightful father who hardly knowing the child did not want it one bit having in the mean time re-married the daughter of the famous Malgache queen Ranavalona who is a perfectly beautiful ivory coloured lady. So the child is taken by the aristocratic old grand mother who sends her to a convent and tells her she is an *enfant trouvée* but that they adopted her and she will be the heiress.

"So I am in the worst possible spot. Wanting to play the little fairy I now dont know what to say to anybody. Maybe its better for the child not to suddenly discover a Californian taxi driver grand father. Maybe its better for the taxi driver not to know his daughter ran away with another man. Oh dear. So the only thing I wrote to the old gentleman is the address of the grandmother so he can get in touch with her and sort things out. Just goes to show that sometimes by interfering with fate one can make matters worse. But is'nt it a strange tale."

On January 4, 1965, Marina wrote Kitty Solomos (in French) that if Christmas came only once a year* she would stand less risk of going to jail for debt. We had been twenty-two for dinner and, "having spent a fortune on all kinds of useless things, I tried to economize on the tree and it ended up square. We spent New Year's at Chamant at the Rothschilds with a mountain of foie gras. Now I need a face lift."

We went to Rome for a week and then took a short rest at Cademario, in Italian Switzerland, from where she sent a letter to the children on January 18:

"The trouble with sight seing in Rome is the more you see the more there is to see. I had one wonderful day with a first class professor in the Vatican museums. We saw the Raphael rooms better than I have ever seen them and the Sistine [Chapel] of course and luckily there were not too many people and then the professor got special permission to show me the Chapel of Pope Paul the fifth I think but I have a hard time keeping my Popes straight. Both the walls covered by huge frescoes by Michael Angelo when he was eighty or so. Fabulous. And angry St. Peter on the cross

---

* Western and Greek Orthodox Christmas are on different days.

spitting fire with indignation. Then another day Elie de Talleyrand took me to see several little churches Byzantine mostly. Or rather Byzantine stuck on to pagan temples and baroque over that. Just the opposite of Paris where all is so one century, here everything is pell mell with such a sense of continuity no wonder the Italians dont believe in anything and do believe in everything at the same time.

"But one thing they all seem to believe right now unanimously is that this is the end. Each one we talked to for different reasons, some afraid for their fortunes others for their positions others because they have neither. The believers hate the church because it let them down over communism, the unbelievers hate the church because it has let them down through the centuries. And so it goes on. One friend talked about the new Axis Jesus — Karl Marx.

"But in spite of everything, Rome still beautiful and the people delightful hospitable cynical and gay. I dragged poor Far to a huge dinner for fifty princes Dukes old Marquessas etc at Countesse Volpe's and I did not think such palaces functioned any more. The palace as big as the Louvre nearly and door men in black and red capes and flaming *torchères* at the entrance. Pictures tappisteries, hanging terraces statues. Everything. Everyone there dull but contrary to Paris where if you go to a dinner where you know no one, you may drop dead before they will pass you the salt, here everyone without exception came to us greeted us asked us to meals, to call them next time etc. There was no next time as we left the next morning for Milan where we spent only one rainy night and then came on to here which is a rest house just above Lugano. We have rooms with the most beautiful view down into a deep valley and the lake at the bottom and high mountains all around us with snow.

"Today it snowed even on our terraces and yet the sun is so warm we take sun baths with no clothes on. Then we take bubble baths and sauna and we have massage and no lunch and up to today we did nothing but sleep and rest but tomorrow we will start walking and even bowling. Far was so tired he could not have gone on one more day. So this is wonderful for him and not so bad for me either. I looked like hell when we arrived. I still do but it may change."

Four days later she wrote the children: "Far looks like a new human being already. He is so good about his diet and eats nothing all day. I on the contrary get so bored that I eat everything in sight which is not much. We go tomorrow and I must say I will be quite happy even though this has done us both so much good. I went to the Sauna also and then believe it or not actually roled in the snow stark naked AND enjoyed it. I must be crazy."

Back in Paris, on February 22, she wrote some philosophical counsel to Marinette: *'Si belle que vous soyez Madame, vous n'êtes pas aussi belle que votre vie.'* I remember Dodo repeating to me time after time when I was young and what a good lesson it was. There is no man in the world who wont forget the most heavenly of women for his job for fishing for talking *avec les copains* for indulging in his favourite sport or work or hobby. The great difference between men and women is that men love solidly faithfully and intermitently while women love all the time to the exclusion of all else, or not at all. This causes troubles, but there is nothing to be done about it. There it is.

"I am so sorry my baby that you think *la plaisanterie* is over, another eventually takes its place. Even down to the end when bridge and gardening or playing with the grand children replaces sex and other biological delights. Its only the passage from one type of *plaisanterie* to another that causes one moments of panic and sadness. I am talking of course of avarage all-human things, not the really great catastrophies that some times crash down on people's heads. I am talking of measles and flue not cancer, or war. And much as it does'nt help *sur le moment* it is good to remember when one has flue that cancer is worse. But I dont have to tell you that, because it is thank god deep in your caracter, to see the good side of things I mean. As for independence it is one of the trickiest things in female lives. To be handdled with kid gloves. Either one is too independant and then considered unfeminine and tough, or one is too much dependant. Nothing but time and experience can teach one how to hyde one's too great independance, or to pretend a non existant dependance, if that."

In March she wrote jointly to both children: "Our Gala for Zorba [*the Greek*] went off very nicely and we made quite a bit of money for the Greek students. I had a coctail party here before. I say I because poor papa was in the bottom of his bed with a high fever and fealing sick as a beagle from his various shots for going off to Saigon. Having had the flue before, the various bugs must have found him week and tired and disgustingly went to work on him and he has been miserable for a week. But I could not put all the guests off at the last moment so they all came and I had *keftedes* [meatballs] and *bourekakia* [cheese pasties] and *taramossalata* [fish-roe mousse] and that kind of thing and to my surprise when we all left at about twenty to nine there was'nt a crumb left. The film was lovely as you said Marinette but I dont happen to like Kazantzaki.

"However it was a very elegant *soirée*. Prince Michael came from Greece for it with his new little wife who was sweet and very well dressed and self possessed. Princesse Olga* looked lovely. I took Maurice Druon with me to take Far's place. Then after the movie we all went to Maxim's and to my astonishement I found myself sitting IN Anthony Quinn's lap. I sweated blood to get a word out of him at first and all he said was yes or no and then he said 'I hate women of the world' so I assured him that I longed to be a woman of the world but had never really managed it and on this he cheered up greatly and we had a very good time.

"Then my poor benighted country's gouvernement having decided to decorate Mr. Quinn chose no better place to do it in but Maxim's. Maxim's eyes have seen many a thing in their day I am sure but never a decorating ceremony. It was too embarrassing and endearing and under-developped for words. When Mr. Quinn came back to the table blushing purple his decoration across his chest it still had its celophane wrappings on it. And to top all suddenly onto those few inches of space between the tables at Maxim's, lept a dozen Kretans seven feet tall complete with boots moustaches pistols bouzoukia etc and tried desperately to create a tottally uncreatable folklorish atmosphere in that so so nineteen hundred *décor* we were in. It fell flat as a wall to wall and I could have died with sadness. Three people away from me was Mme Calas looking simply beautiful and Mr. Onassis and a lot of *tout Paris* caracters who did not know Krete from Kanzas. Mr. Onassis talked to me for quite a while asking me how my nice son was and saying he read every word Far wrote. I thought him quite bewitching quite naturally.

"Poor little Far is off to Saigon tomorrow and at the meer sight of the suitcase Beagle has been either sitting in it or roling on his back feet in the air doing his utmost to make himself attractive so as to be taken too. I try to tell him I am not going but he does'nt really believe me. He came with us to Chamant for the week end and had a wonderful time. So he wrote a splendid bread and butter letter to Ma Dame excusing himself that his human is'nt as good as it should be etc. She was so pleased that he is now

---

* Greek princess, wife of Prince Paul of Jugoslavia.

permanently invited for any week end he wants. Far will be gone about four weeks I think. I hate to see him go fealing so badly but perhaps when he gets into the open jungle air he will feel better. Far says that ninety per cent I will be able to come to the U.S. for your graduation Marinette. He has to come anyway to give a speach at the War College."

That spring I flew to Vietnam, Thailand, Ceylon, and India while Marina stayed in Paris. My tour was rapid and many of her letters got lost. It was always inspiriting to receive her vigorous and often biased comments, such as that of March 28:

"All the Greeks tell me the situation at home is catastrophic. All [George] Papandreou does is make impossible laws one day and unmake them the next. Such as forbiding emigration and then three days later allowing it again. Such as stoping payments on the installement plan and putting them back again when all trade stops. Ah me. Poor old Greece."

When I returned, she wrote Marinette on April 8:

"Far's trip came to an end sooner than he thought and there he was. I went to pick him up at Orly at seven in the morning and the plane was two hours late so I had ten coffees and endless *croissants* which undid all the good *Silhouette* has been doing. Far was dead tired and pale but luckily we managed to get off right away to Normandy where he fished for three days and cought a lot and most satisfactorily big trout, so all the fatigue was soothed out of him in one go and now he is fine again.

"On his way back Far had bought two large boxes of caviar cheap at the airport in Teheran so last night we had Mrs. Hayward who is here for two days, to dinner and Mr. de Staerck and Prince Paul and Princesse Olga and we had the caviar and the trout and made an extraordinary *bella figura*. It was most cosy and agreable and Mrs. Hayward really is the youngest and prettiest grand mother in the world."

We flew over to the United States in May, but, not long after I addressed the National War College, I had to return to Paris, leaving Marina to have fun in New York, Washington, and Cambridge with all our friends and the two children and also to attend Marinette's graduation from Radcliffe. David had an interesting summer job; Marinette hadn't yet decided on her future after graduating; Alexi got married to his third wife on June 17 and Marina was optimistic that this one would stick. "How lovely it is that we are such a wonderful loving united family," she boasted happily, adding quite untruthfully: "And you the best of us because you have all our qualities and none of our faults." A fine way to describe a morose and solitary misanthrope!

Marina wrote me before leaving Washington, where she stayed with Susan Mary and Joe Alsop, about a dance she attended where many high officials were present. Her comment: "Somehow I kept thinking how sad half-wars must be for those who are in it: More so really than whole wars: when everyone is in the same boat there is a kind of *camaraderie* of suffering whereas to the mothers wives children of those poor marines [who had recently landed in Vietnam] it must be bitter to see their vice president or secretary of defense doing the frug." To this she added in a subsequent letter: "Joe is in a black pessimistic mood. He says Washington is beginning to feel like the Bounty before the mutiny with a tremendous fealing of restless crosseness everywhere."

1965 was a Greek holiday summer. Marina wrote Virginia Chambers on September 5:

"They say God maddens those he wishes to destroy and I am afraid that the whole of Greece has gone out of its mind. It would seem that there is not an honorable man left in all of Greek political life. And if there are a few the 'people' seem to want him least of all. The strangest phenomenon is taking place. All of peasant working lower middle class and a great many rich and upper seem to have developped a passion for Mr. Papandreou who has managed in less than two years to ruin everything he has touched. I am not talking of politics or ideologies now. Simply the technique of governing. The previous regime had left the coffers full and a well runing country. Now there is not a penny in the treasury, and even simple things like the post office the telephone buss services dont work any more. And as for the last six weeks of the crisis its like a nightmare. With every imaginable and ridiculous and shaming thing possible happening. Oh it makes me weep. I do believe we are a deeply self-destructive people."

I joined Marina, Marinette, and Dodo in Spetsais for September. David, occupied with his summer job, did not come. Then Marinette had to float out into the uncertain, frightening post-university world of real life, driving as far as Paris with her mother and the Joyces. They returned via Jugoslavia and I, by plane, via Bulgaria. Marina wrote David on October 18:

"We went to Ochrid where we saw the gloomy lake and some lovely churches and frescoes and to several other churches and monasteries on the way all through Macedonia which is really beautiful. Tremendous mountains, deep grey glorious rock a thousand feet high on one side and deep rushing waters on the other. Apple orchards and green valleys and the most handsome people I have ever seen all smiling and kind and not at all scowling proletarians. Beagle was a huge success. *Koutch* [dog] is the Yougoslav word for him and everywhere people stopped and stroked and spoke to this forgotten symbol of better days. He is now the most cultured dog in Europe having been to museums and monasteries cathedrals and palaces and beautiful Venetian baroque villas. I must say we saw lovely things. The Dalmatian coast is a dream. In a place called Kotor we drove for ages almost in the sea with the whole coast row upon row of these abandonned Venetian Adam houses. By Adam I mean where he got his inspiration for his classical revival. They are all in honey white stone with terraces and great staircases, balustrades and hanging balconies, and all of them roofless and deserted and for sale for less than five hundred dollars. Only the surroundings, beautiful as they are, have something depressing closed in and airless about them. Too bad as I would love a sixteenth century Venetian villa.

"One night we went to a restaurant there and before we knew what was happening a great partisan of a cat had flown at Beagle who needless to say yelled and jumped into Marinette's arms making a terrible *bruta figura* of us all, while the cat attacked me and in an instant rivers of blood were coming down my leg. Commotion. Waiters etc advice from everyone and then a large bottle of Slivovica was poured over my leg for disinfectant and we left in a huff to dine elsewhere. One other time we got stuck in a pile of rubble and had to be hawled out by a group of gay young men who happened to be passing, one of whom kissed Marinette on the lips to her utter amazement. Ts Ts what dissolute behaviour for a puritanical friend of the people. But those were our only adventures. Split was lovely too and we visited Diocletian's palace all one morning.

"Then Venice which was the best and I loved to see Marinette with eyes as big as saucers in wonder and excitement. We did all the right things, gondola and *capuccinos* at Florian's in the Piazza San Marco and the Doge's palace and we also saw a fabulous Guardi exhibition. From Venice we only stopped at Verona and Bergamo. And home at last yesterday where we found Far had returned unexpectedly before us as Tito was ill so he cancelled that bit of his trip and came home with gout and a stiff neck poor dear. And worse news of all Justine is sick and wants to leave and I think I will shoot myself. This house without Grat ... and *three* Beagles [Benjamin's children]. Young Beagle is adorable I must say but I dont know how we can possibly keep him. What other servants will ever look after three dogs while we travel? Oh dear the holiday really is over."

On November 20, 1965, Maria wrote her adored granddaughter, Marina, a two-page letter carefully scrawled in pen and ink:

"Perhaps this is a goodbye letter as we are not regular correspondents. Anyhow I was thinking of you quite a lot lately, especially of that rare combination in your make-up, brilliance and goodness. The characteristic of brilliance is not generally a flow of goodness. Happily for you, you have got it, as it is the thing which lasts longest into old age and that which gives most comfortable and non-egoistic satisfaction to those who are blessed by it. I shall be ninety-four tomorrow and wonder how long I am going to last. I am having a very happy ending and have had a happy life, thanks to husband and children, and I hope you will too and expect it with your character and your surroundings."

Just over six months later she died quietly in Maroussi.

X

December 1965 - December 1967

Marinette left right after Christmas for a job at the National Gallery in Washington; David returned to Harvard. We followed them in February 1966 on the first lap of a long Pacific swing. In Washington, where Marinette already had an apartment with two other girls, Marina became so passionate in expressing her hawkish Vietnam views that she confessed in a letter to Michael Edwards:

"I never thought the day would come when I would find democracy perhaps not such a good idea. I do of course but its only trouble is that it is such an essentially aristocratic conception for first class minds and for small countries and human problems that when it becomes a massive thing like the American one and with super human or perhaps all too human problems to solve and a lot of middle class minds, discontents, politicians searching for self advancement etc get mixed up in it, it can be terribly dangerous. Perhaps never so dangerous as any alternative so what to do?"

She wrote Virginia Chambers: "We went to dinner one night with Mrs. Longworth* and then to a dance given by the Alsops for the departing

---

* Alice Roosevelt Longworth.

[Mac] Bundys which was very gay I must say, with the *clou de la soirée* Ethel
Kennedy dressed in an extraordinary Op art dress to the hips almost and
décolletée to the navel in black and white oil cloth. It looked awful but one
had to admire her courage and her gaiety. Then we had one bad day when
Cy had to have a tooth pulled immediately because of a sudden abscess. It
is so odd the different aproaches to life. Last year poor fellow he had one
out in Spetses with a probe which looked like a carpenter's tool and a drill
operated by foot like an old sewing machine. This time he had the dentist a
surgeon an aneasthetist and two nurses and almost did'nt need the
aneasthetist, at the thought of what it would cost. In fact it was only twenty
five dollars and he says the nicest group of people he has ever seen. But only
just awake and groggy he had to dash off and see the President* who rarely
has real lunch never offered Cy any and kept him for hours including a visit
to the barber shop together."

At the end of the month we flew to Hawaii and then Tahiti. From the
latter (in Papeete) Marina wrote David on March 11:

"What do you suppose happened to me in Hawaii. I swam and played
with a dolphin. In the hotel there was a great sort of assortement of pools
and lakes with rare fish and turtles and in the biggest were three dolphins
playing around and showing off and leaping in the air. Utterly delightful.
The day we arrived we watched them being fed and it was lovely. Then the
next day I saw a gentleman go swimming in the pool with them although it
said forbidden, and so I decided to try it too. At first I went in rather shyly
and just stood in water up to the hips and in no time at all the biggest of the
dolphins came up to me and sort of pushed me with his nose exactly like
Beagle and I stroked his head and his tummy and his chin and to my
surprise he was not at all slippery not even like a moray and felt most cool
and clean like linoleum. He was shiny dark grey and paler underneith and
with a lovely smile. So after we had conversed like that for a few minutes he
turned on his tummy again and then I cought his fin (which incidentaly
when he is in the water could give one heart attack *à l'improviste* because it

---

* Lyndon Johnson.

looks just like a shark) and then he took off and I with him like we do with Beagle's tail.

"For just a few seconds I imagine, but which felt like a year we were away together and realy very fast and then he went down and I too but not for long because I was not quite quite sure in my mind if he liked this as much as I did and if he didn't the *tête à tête* underwater might 'end in a cry.' So up I came and I think it is a whole new *étape* in my life. Now I will say that was before I swam with the dolphin.

"Hawaii seemed nicer to me this time perhaps because of the dolphin perhaps because Far seemed so well. The hotel was lovely and most luxurious and the full moon was wonderful. It really is unfair that one has to be either a working man or a worn middle aged tourist to get to these lovely places. I wrote to Marinette that in my ideal state no one under thirty will be allowed to work. Up to twenty they study and learn and from twenty to thirty they are kept for pleasure and travel and mind improvement and invention and what ever, by the state and at forty they have to go to work. Incidentally I was thinking of our discussion in the car when you said we helped Ho chi min come to power. But the French did so much more and the whole picture of independence was so complicated and confused it is only too easy to sit back now fourteen years later and say who did what. It means nothing.

"But away from politics to Tahiti. I must say it is most most beautiful. But the sad thing is that after the Greek water I am afraid I am snob for any other waters on earth. First thing I did was to get goggles and in a way I wish I had'nt. The water is thick and I can hardly see one inch in front of me and what I do see is so creepy and unkind and full of menace that even when a leaf touches my toe I leap three feet in the air. I did see some glorious orange fish and some yellow ones with fringes and a lot of zebra ones and tiny brilliant blue ones but the coral reef itself seems wicked. Also the beaches both sand and pebble and even the rock is sort of volcanic and coal black which is not in the least bit inviting. Psychologically so I suppose, because it is clean but it looks so angry and wild.

"Yesterday we drove about the island which is about eighty five miles around and has only forty thousand inhabitants which in this part of the world where one counts in millions everywhere hundreds of millions, seems almost uninhabited. We went to the place called Venus point where

Captain Cook first observed Tahiti from and where the Bounty movie was made. Palm trees bananas bread fruit mango trees and such flowers I have never seen in my life. No birds and all the beautiful girls must have left on the Bounty because we see one in ten who is at all presentable. But they do look exactly like Gaugins. We went to the little Gaugin museum about thirty miles from here and it is charming full of his things and copies of his pictures and life history and an amusing chart of the first pictures he sold for a hundred and forty francs and the last one which went for a 100 million to Goulandris.

"The ginger flower grows wild everywhere and the scent and the moon make it really the most romantic place in the world to look at if not to live in. The city is awful. Papeete is almost not a town, sort of untidy and a small harbour and one shabby caffée and one really sordid nightclub where one imagines 007 coming in for a moment but in fact it is cheep and ugly. But our hotel is dreamy. We have individual bamboo huts and they are very hot and sticky but pretty and the sea is at our door. Last night there was a Tahitian dance and it is exactly but exactly like what you do. Only in grass skirts and crowns of flowers it looks better than in black tie. I must stop now because to my sorrow I must have my hair done. We are invited out to dinner by *'Le gouverneur général de la Polynésie Francaise'* which is a dreamy title I think and I cant go with sea weed in my hair. Oh another horrid thing the sea urchins are albino white greyish."

We flew to New Zealand, and Marina wrote to David: "We were expected to stay at Government house. 'Their Excellencies' [Sir Bernard Fergusson and wife, now Lord and Lady Ballantrae] were old friends of Far's from war days and not excellencies then but cosy friends so you can imagine our surprise when we found in our rooms a little printed card telling us how to behave. You will address Sir Bernard as Your Excellency you will curtsey to them the first time you meet in the day and the last at night (at least a small blessing that we did'nt have to bob up and down ALL day) they leave the room before their guests and you address them when addressed. Just like royalty. It was very funny really except that curtseying is so pretty I think one should always do so. We dressed for dinner even when the four of us and Far who said proudly in his *clochard* manner that he did not have a dinner jacket was politely but firmly squeezed into the young aid's costume in which I may say he looked very handsome.

"Auckland is pretty being on two oceans, and full of gardens and hills but oh dear how deadly. The welfare State may be comfortable but it sure is'nt stimulating. They all sound like the sheep they raise. However two and a half days was most bearable and pleasant although being a constant guest is a bit of a strain especially to Far who has work to do as well. So this morning we flew off again and arrived in Sydney after a most agreeable flight of only two and a half hours which in this part of the world where even farms are hundreds of miles from their next door neighbours, seems like nothing. And the moment we arrived we were infuriated by having to be vaccinated all over again because some ape like character did'nt like the looks of our French stamp. Nothing is more bone headed or disagreeable than a colonial Englishman and in no time at all they make one feel like a second class citizen and I felt like punching them. However, after a pleasant lunch and a strole we feel much better and kindlier disposed towards Australians as a whole.

"Oh I forgot to tell you the most exciting bit. In Auckland at government house we met two of the Astronautes who came to pay their respects to the Governor. Borman the forteen day fellow and Shirra and their sweet wives. I did not think it would be so moving, but I cant tell you how I felt at actually shaking hands and talking with these two quiet humble intelligent young men who have seen and done things no one in the whole world has even imagined. They could'nt have been more attractive. The young son of the house aged 8 and away at school had written to his mother to tell her a few intelligent questions to ask the astronautes as he was afraid his mother would not know what to ask and so Mr Borman very sweetly when he was shown the little boy's letter sat down and answered each of his questions in writing so the boy will have a really precious document eventually."

After returning to Sydney from Canberra, Marina wrote David: "Canberra has changed quite a bit since we were last there, but still does'nt look quite like a capital city yet. But we had a pleasant time. Or rather I did because poor Far was glued to his typewriter and had to see Prime ministers defense ministers etc.

"The governor general Lord Casey turned out to be an old acquaintance from Cairo days and they asked us to lunch and it was very nice. They are seventy five and seventy two and he still flies his own plane and they look sixty and bright as berries. Strange and nice how these middle Eastern friendships endure. We met again after twenty years as old friends. The

British High commissioner also was an old Cairo friend and this was lucky for me as his wife took me in charge and I saw what there is to see which is not much admitedly but better than sitting in a hotel room. I was taken to a scientific research place for animals where for instance they study the flights of sea gulls to see what they can do about them on landing strips where they are a great hazard particularly in Sidney which is so near the sea.

"We also saw thousands of kangaroos who are really most absurd animals a bit donkey a bit hare and a lot nothing like anything. We took a train back so as to see the landscape a bit but it is very flat and uninterresting except for the sky which is enormous and like a bowl all over one and with most lovely clouds. They have had a dreadful drought poor things a million sheep have died. Think of having a million sheep. But on the whole this is I must admit a very dull place for a short visit. If one lived here and had a nice house and went to the desert and the great barrier reef and did serf riding and spear fishing and all that it could be agreeable I am sure but for a few days it is pretty deadly."

In a joint letter to Susan Mary Alsop and Marietta Tree she wrote from Sydney: "I was surprised to find people here almost as devided on the issue [Vietnam] as they are in the U.S. And here it really is their life's blood in danger. Indonesia is the big news here though for the moment, although no one seems to know from day to day what goes on. The airport is closed one day open the next. Sukarno is under heavy guard one day and gaily drinking champagne at a coctail party last night. We still dont have visas but Cy thinks he at least will get in from Bangkok. I got a letter from my mother today saying she worried about us with visions of our being surrounded either by stray bullets or sharks or microbes. Too sweet but we have had none of these exotic dangers as yet. We are still in full flesh pots."

From Singapore she wrote Marinette on March 29:

"Well I must tell you I am rather glad to be out of Anglo-Saxon Pacific into the real thing. Our flight here was endless. Nine hours made longer by a small child in the next seat who kept spitting and drooling on Far while mama looked on in love and admiration. We stopped in Darwin for a moment where it was 94 in the shade. We arrived here in the evening and at once were plunged into the rather glorious atmosphere of the real East.

Lights and signs in Chinese and lanterns and *karotsakia* [pushcarts] with every conceivable thing for sale and Chinese ladies in trousers and the tiniest waists and the malays in sarongs of batic over their white trousers and frangipani everywhere. Our hotel is a dream too.

"Today I was taken around by a nice old gentleman to the botanical gardens where monkeys are like squirrels in central park and orchids like geraniums and it was lovely especially as we finaly got to a hill from which there was THE most lovely view of the ocean with dozens of green feathery islands and junks and sampans as well as large freighters in the distance and there, not further than one's hand it seemed was Indonesia. I was lucky that it was a brilliant clear day because this is the rainy season and the other two days it was drizzling all the time and I would'nt have seen anything. But today it really seemed as though I could swimm to Indonesia. This lovely green and deep blue view was all the more delightful, because this is the one thing my Greek mind finds difficult to get used to. Everything is so flat that although this is my third trip to the pacific this is one of the first times I have looked down into it. It looked just like an eighteenth century drawing done by one of Cook's or Bougainville's men as it were."

Marina stayed with our friends Tony and Felicity Rumbold* in Bangkok while I flew to Indonesia, where a military government had seized real power (although pretending to keep Sukarno as president under house arrest) following a Communist coup attempt in which some 300,000 of its sympathizers had been slaughtered. Another "shadow play" in Java, where shadow plays were invented. When I returned, we flew off to Phnom Penh, the Cambodian capital. Marina was captivated by the bowing white elephants maintained at the royal palace. From there we took another plane to South Vietnam. On April 13 she wrote David:

"I will never again think of the thirteenth as unlucky. The fact that we are here and all in one peace is proof of this. First of all we took off in a DC3 with a Cambodian pilot which was not too reassuring, as our brief encounter with his compatriots in our five days in Phnom Penh had convinced us that they are as a nation far from quizz kids as Far would say. Well in this case their very disorganisation and incomprehension helped in

---

* British ambassador Sir Anthony Rumbold.

our being here because they either ignored or forgot or never read or understood the urgent signals from Saigon saying the airport was closed to all traffic so we merrily took off.

"It was a lovely day (and there again our luck was in because only a few hours later, but we were on the ground by then, a storm such as I have rarely seen blew up). Well a little before we had to fasten our seat belts suddenly we heard a tremendous grgrgr and there almost ON us was the biggest U.S. army plane I have ever seen. He flew around us once or twice and then went off but this was not as scary as I would have expected (or if we had been the enemy I suppose). And then we made a most perfect landing which made me slightly ashamed of my white-supremacy attitude towards the pilot.

"As we landed we saw a great deal of smoke and then a great tongue of flame shoot up from a corner of the field. Also there seemed to be very few people anywhere and a kind of strange quiet unusual in airports where people are usually falling over each other. One little man wheeled the ladder to us but there seemed to be no officials around and no one for luggage. But we ascribed this to Asian sloppiness which we are just beginning to get used to. In the airport we saw some American officers and men, some smiling some waiting with that quiet look of people in airports, some heartbreakingly asleep on thin thin sofas. But no one seemed unduly grave or anxious. For a while we waited and nothing happened and no one took our passeports and then we sort of asked around and discovered that no one expected us because the airport was closed to EVERYTHING and everyone.

"A few hours before there had been a Viet Cong mortar attack and a fuel depot was burning, several planes had been destroyed and alas alas seven young Americans only that instant arrived in Saigon had been killed and many many wounded. I cant even bare to think of these boys killed before they even set foot in the accursed place.

"But what I will never get used to is the strange quiet way things have of LOOKING so peaceful and normal. When I describe this to you dont you get visions of horror and excitement and hurry and noise. Nothing. Had we gone on to Hong Kong on the same plane we might not even have known. And this I cannot understand or stand. It seems unatural to me that the world doesn't stop each time. But not only does it not but eventually after hours of trying to get connected we got through to Franky [Wisner] and he came and got us in his car and brought us here to Mr. [Ambassador Bill] Porter's house which is air conditioned and spaccious and pretty and we have a lovely confortable room and we lunched at the famous Caravelle hotel and met a few other journalists and the more I listened to them talk about the demonstration the Buddhists the governement the students etc the more I feel like a blind-folded bat in a black tunnel on a dark mid-night.

"Everybody here seems to know what they dont want and are ready to jeopardise the war, the country, their own lives for this, but if asked what they do want they dont know except for vague generalities which mean nothing. It is bad of me to talk like this ten hours after I set foot in this agonised agonising place, but I ask and ask and no one answers me.

"Phnom Penh is a pretty little town but hotter than two hells and we had very bad luck as it was not only Easter but also the Queen's birthday and Cambodian New Year so everybody black brown yellow or pinko-grey was out of town so poor Far was skunked work-wise. Still I doubt if the fate of the world or his career will suffer too much because he did not see Monseigneur Sihanouc. I was taken for a boat ride on the mighty Mekong. The water in Spetses is better.

"We were so happy to find your nice letter waiting for us. Not only for its news of you, but also as a deeply needed link with another and perhaps saner world. Mr. Sukarno in his more fierce moments reffers to us [Westerners] as NECOLIMS. Neo-coloniast-imperialists or as OLDEFOPS old established forces. And by golly as far as I am concerned he is absolutely right. Your most devoted and loving Necolim mother."

On April 20 she sent a long letter from Saigon to Denise Boisot:

"How can I describe this most evil of cities to you, which is so full of contradictions for the eye as well as the spirit. Imagine mountains of uncolected garbage, and petals floating gently in the breese. Imagine rats everywhere and the daintiest most beautiful women I have ever seen. In the floating pale coloured robes on their bicicles, the ribbons of their picture hats trailing behind them as well as the skirts of their long robes, they look for all the world like some exquisite dragonflies flying over a mangrove swamp. Imagine black marketeers at every corner, and blue eyed slender

319

innocent young American soldiers, pimps and prostitutes from thirteen years old up and bald Buddhist nuns and reverant fathers who may be Viet Cong and Viet cong who may be American agents. Imagine the sound of humming birds and the ever present thud of artillery fire in the distance.

"Helicopters as numerous as sparrows and taxis as rare as an objective man. Imagine an unbeleivable mass of American technicians, diplomats, military, agricultural advisers, psycological warfare experts, Aid people, economists, volunteers, and to make one telephone call takes all one's energy patiance and Christian virtue. And then the people we are trying to save. Everybody hates everybody else much more than the enemy. Everybody is more interrested in gaining personal power than wining the war. In most countries alas you have political parties, but here on top of it you have religions and regionalism and tribes and a people who have never really been a nation and whose only interrest is power money and doing the other fellow in.

"And in an ironic tragic way innocent Americans with every gesture make it worse. A soldier gives a small boy a tip and he will make it even more difficult to get the boy off the streets and into school. He makes over a thousand piastres a day shining shoes, running errants pimping etc and will at once spend it on girls or drugs even at the age of twelve. America spends a million dollars a day here and this causes inflation. America brings her own food in so as not to add to the burden of the country and this finds its way to the black market and causes even greater problems.

"The city people hate and dispise the peasants and the peasants hate and despise the Montagnards. The Annamites hate the Cochin Chinese, each tribe hates the other. They dont all hate the Americans yet but they will if we dont win the war and they make it almost impossible for us to do so. And if we do win it they will hate us too. They really are the most horrible people I have ever met and yet everybody we have seen here, rightly or wrongly, is prepared to stay for ever and leave their bones if need be, to save a people who dont care about being saved. And if you talk to two people about any given problem you get four answers.

"Here we sit in scented gardens at night with frangipani flowers falling gracefully into our soup, talking gravely about all this, and except for the artillery noise in the distance, I sometimes think I am making it all up. There was one huge demonstration since we arrived but as the Buddhists had just won a certain victory, at least on paper, from the government it was not violent, but quiet and grave and looked more like a parade.

"But I am deeply frustrated. Our host the Ambassador wont let me circulate out of the city and in spite of offers by everyone including young Frank to take me to a village or a hamlet or the jungle, I have to sit here and *poiroter*. As I am a guest I can naturally not growl or argue and I am so afraid I might have a 'dont you know there is a war on' thrown at me that all I can do is bow my head in vexed silence. Cy is off with General Westmoreland at this very moment the lucky thing. So I console myself by walking around the city. But there too I am frustrated.

"I went to the Chinese market this morning and it was lovely. The Chinese are so clean and tidy unlike the Viets who are filthy. And I saw mountains of mangoes and other lovely fruit, baskets full of *fouli* which they make garlands of like in Cairo, tuberoses and lilies for one *cent* a flower; beads, bolts of lovely coloured cloth, unrecognisable vegetables dried fish and above all oh dear dear, so much Chinese blue and white porcelaine that I could die. A dozen bowls cost twenty five cents. A huge *cache pot* or lamps cost a dollar. Big and small plates three and five cents each. And how to carry them? I bought a dozen for Marinette and hope to camouflage them in my underwear before Cy has a heart attack. But I cant camouflage a pot or a lamp. And oh how lovely they would look on the terrace.

"A sadder occupation is going to hospitals and orphanages. Luckily I have sun glasses to hyde the tears I cannot stop. I think of you so much when I see these children. Either dead parents or indifferent ones or lost or children of soldiers both French and American. So starved that at eighteen months they look like baby monkeys. And I played with one small boy yesterday who had been adopted six years ago at the age of three months and since then his parents had had children of their own so a week ago they decided they did not need him any more and left him at the door of the orphanage with twenty piasters in his little pocket and a rice cake in his hand. I almost took him with me. But he is a catholic and they wont give him to anyone but catholics. For god's sake. And he is one in thirty thousand at least.

"You know I can see so well even after a week how this place gets one and one cant leave. The thought of being in the flesh pots of Hong Kong in a week seems almost unbearably immoral to me. But Cy says I am too old to be romantic. But not too old to be heart broken."

From Hong Kong Marina sent letters to David and Marinette on April 28. The first said:

"Well we are out of Indo-china physically, but I am still there spiritually. It feels somehow like leaving a sinking ship (although god willing it is'nt sinking) to go from Saigon to Hong Kong. There EVERYBODY needs help and rightly or wrongly are doing what they think they should. Here there are two kinds of people more or less. Those intent on spending money, and those interested solely in making it. Its a good combination, but the other feels better.

"Not too much more to go. Five days here, a few in Tokyo, a few in Alaska and then back to you two. If Far does'nt get a day off there to go fishing I shall cry. He has not lifted his head from his typewriter since that one half day off in Tahiti. And everyone seemed to want to tell him their troubles in Viet Nam so he had to struggle to find time to write. He really is a marvel. But oh so tired."

To Marinette she confessed: "Out of Viet nam, I feel as if I had left an orphanage for a night club, and somehow ashamed and guilty. I cant understand how that place got me so strongly in such a short time. Perhaps it is because it was a short time and all I saw was the good side of people, the nuns and the ladies working desperately for the leppers, and sergents trying to adopt little sick and ugly babies, and I did not see or care about jealousies and nerves and the million discomforts of life which in the long run I know are almost harder to take than the big ones. NEVER finding a taxi, getting wet every day, never fealing cool and neet, never relaxing and never thinking talking or discussing anything but the war and politics.

"And I must say I came to the conclusion in spite of my deep desire to stay there and help that the Vietnamese are the least savable people in the world. But shsh dont tell that I even presume to have an opinion after just two weeks. This is *entre nous* and not necessarily right. You know we keep thinking poor things they been fighting for twenty years, but this is not so, they have been fighting for two thousand I suspect. There has never been a time in their history when they were not fighting each other if no one else. So much so that they have never written a book never built a temple not a nice one, never even stayed too long in one religion before they felt they had to split and worship something else and fight some other sect."

On May 2, the day after her birthday, she wrote David:

"Luckily it was a nice day and we took the hydrophoil to Macao. I was a bit dissapointed as I had expected a little sixteenth century Portuguese fishing town and it was not at all that. Rather a large town with not much caracter and we struggled up to a few Buddhist temples and one catholic church (built in 1936) and then a mediocre lunch. But after lunch we were taken to the casino and that was great fun. We both lost all we had started off to lose until the very last moment and it was only a few chips left and Far put them all on a number and I begged to take just one off and I took it and put it on seventeen and it came out so we made back exactly what we had started out with which ment we had about an hour's great fun and suspence on nothing.

"The only thing which was absolutely beautiful were the junks in sail. They really look like great brown water birds going backwards. Hundreds of them which is nice because in Hong Kong they are almost disapearing and replaced by motors. The sails I mean. Also it was rather strange looking straight through a tiny strip of no man's land into communist China and seing the path that the refugees usually take."

A week later she wrote him from Japan: "We just got back this morning from Hiroshima. You know it is incredible the survivability of man. Luckily it was before you were born, but I remember long conversations about how nothing would ever live or breath or ever grow again where an atom bomb had exploded and here was Hiroshima twenty years later flourishing ugly prosperous and twice as developped as if they never had had it. It has even served the new Hiroshimites well, as tourists flock there and international money has gone in by the ton.

"I dont mean this, in this way at all, but that is how one is amazed by its present appearance. And the museum which is full of gruesome pictures is'nt really moving or frightening I dont know why. Possibly because nothing nothing can ever approach the horror of those days in August, and so one is at once relieved and surprised by such a gay city. We went to a

great rodhodendron garden, you must admit its the last thing one thinks of
in connection with Hiroshima and as it was Sunday EVERYONE in town was
there on pic nics and you have never seen so many people in your life, all in
gay kimonos and the greatest quantity of small children I have ever seen
and in almost every corner groups of Koreans (the hated minority here) in
the most enchanting gay gauzy costumes and all absolutely pickled oddly
enough and doing a kind of poor man's *bouzouki* [a Greek tune] with one
drum and a fiddle and dancing about a bit like trained bears, but so gay and
funny. And all over the place a strange mixture of Japanese yéyé with
electric guitars and very pointed shoes and long hair, playing *N'avoue jamais*,
or old and old fashioned ladies (possibly retired geishas of reduced
circumstances) with things I imagine as dulcimers, primly playing japanese
squeaky love songs. And every inch of hill covered with the most beautiful
azaleas and rodhodendrons and maples and pines and bamboo so exactly
like they look on engravings or painting or lacquer boxes that one thinks *tin
tin* for all those artists all they are is a bunch of photographers.

"That is true of all the country in fact. Never have I been to a place
which looks so absolutely like one thinks it should. Even the waves I am
sure must curl inwards and have dark blue and silver spray like on the
screens. We went to a lovely island from Hiroshima by ferry called
Miyajima, where they have a bright red temple built on stilts so it looks at
high tyde as if it came right out of the ocean, which is indeed what it does. It
is a sacred island so no one is allowed to die there or be born there or even
to fish or hunt so the only thing they do is trade with the result that except
for the temple all one sees is thousands of little honky tonk shops full of
plastic toys and temple bells and candy but here somehow they dont look
vulgar, just gay."

We flew to Anchorage, where I had to make a speech, and then,
although it was late May and snowing heavily, we hired a tiny float plane
and a bush pilot flew us off to a lake in the wilderness where there was a
canoe, a boat, a tent, some rations, and a bed. Poor Marina: it was bitter
cold and she promptly put a kettle to boil on the woodstove, climbed into
bed with her nose streaming and her two sweaters huddled about her
shivering shoulders, and loyally made the best of a bad time while I fished.
All night she wondered woefully what would happen to us if the bush pilot

never showed up or couldn't find us in the snow. The fishing was lousy. I suppose the trout were too cold to do anything but huddle at the bottom; that's certainly what Marina did. One of the great moments of her life was whirring off through bumpy storms to Anchorage. Next day we flew to New York. Shortly thereafter we were back in Paris and, amid mad whirls of a beagle tail, Marina made ready for another Spetsais summer.

On August 1, when Marina got to Spetsais, she wrote me:

"The moment Beagle got into the village he was like a calling card. People saw him and came rushing around saying 'Kyria Marina' must be somewhere around too. The first swimm with the Joyces he barked non stop ALL morning and was drownable. Melina [Mercouri] has rented a house next to us. She has turned left wing in the silliest manner so we had a rather tense Viet Nam evening but not a quarrel and she is full of charm and an old friend anyway. Then on Saturday [a group of friends] turned up on a yacht and they brought me back to Athens and we had an absolutely lovely time. We sailed under the biggest moon I have ever seen and we sang songs from our youth. I must say it is fantastic luck to have so many old friends whom one finds again and again intact after a life time."

As usual, I joined the family at the start of September. Marina wrote Avis Bohlen on September 9 that Vivien Leigh, the actress, had been staying with her.

"Melina Mercouri had the house next door to us working on a musical version of Never on Sunday and then to top it all Greta Garbo arrived on a boat with Cécile [de Rothschild] so we really had a star spangled summer. Before that we had had a week with twenty five Nobel prize winners here on a seminar thing, so the film world as well as bio-chemistry have no secrets from us any longer. It was all very lunatic but great fun."

She added to this saga on September 30 in a letter to Michael Edwards: "One night we had Garbo here and Melina who really spent herself on seducing her for patriotic as well as proffessional reasons and she danced and sang and was heavenly and then we all accompanied her down to the pier still singing and Garbo with sobs begging us to sing 'Her' song just once more. So we all sat on the steps of a taverna and sang and sang until at one moment (this being two in the morning) the poor owl-like pyjamaed sleepy tavern-keeper flung open the window to give us hell, but before he could say a word Melina was shaking him by the hand and saying 'Good morning how do you do may I present myself I am Melina Mercouri and this is my friend Greta Garbo.' What could the poor chap do but murmer a dazzled 'and I am Mr Stroumbos' and join us in the song. It really was glorious."

Marinette became engaged to a splendid young Englishman, Adrian Berry, and was back in Paris preparing for marriage. Marina wrote David on November 11:

"One should be allowed forty eight hours a day when preparing a daughter for marriage. *Préfecture de police*, consulates medical exams dressmakers etc etc.

"Two nights ago Maurice Druon invited Marinette and me to the American ballet of Merce Cunningham and it was the most *avant garde* thing and the music when there was some, which was not all the time, was made up of turbo jets taking off, pneumatic drills on a binge, motor cycles starting, cars not starting, brakes grinding, tramways screetching, and occasionally as a soothing interlude such melodious things as fire engine syrens or telephone bells. The noise was so deafening that it prevented one from really seing the dancing which was in fact quite good."

She added, to Fred Warner: "It seems to take longer to get marriage papers than a Russian visa. I must say I get more thankful by the day that we only have one daughter to marry off. I dont know where THEY will spend their honeymoon but one thing is certain: Cy and I will spend it in prison for debt. We got back in the middle of October from Greece and ever since then it seems to me I have done nothing but spend money. You cant think how difficult it is to choose a decent mother of the bride costume. I threaten beige lace and my friends protest politely that I am too young and then I suggest a mini-dress and that wont do, and I am sure Pam will look spectacular so something drastic will have to be done. Pauline offers to lend me one of her splendid mink hats so I can do a bit of one-upmanship there."

Marinette formally adopted her mother's faith because there were good, interchangeable relations between Greek Orthodoxy and the Archbishop of Canterbury's flock. On November 24, Marina wrote her cousin, Monica Curtis, of Marinette's christening:

"Saturday we had to go to the church in the morning for the christening and it was both nice and moving and also rather funny. The poor bishop you know is supposed to bless the infant's new baby-wear which is provided by the god mother and in this case Mary Averoff had given Marinette a lovely pale blue set of panties and *soutien gorge* which was neither white for purity as it is supposed, nor in the least bit innocent. So in order not to embarrass the poor bishop we had to leave it all in the Gallery Lafayette box.

"It was freezing cold in the chapel so luckily the kind bishop decided it was not necessary for Marinette to be dipped entirely in the *colymbithra* [baptismal font] (not to mention the fact that she would have been ten times too big to fit into it) so she just had water sprinckled over her and oil on her forhead her wrists her chin and her feet. Then we had a glass of sweet wine and a blessing and there she is, welcomed into the faith of her mama.

"But humans seem to be much more demanding than god in this case because you cannot imagine the endless *va et vien* between the British consul (a bitchy old maid) the *Mairie* the Ministry of Foreign Affairs and the *préfecture de police*. Less disagreeable but equally exhausting is the trying on of wedding dress, veil, shoes, bags, glove. Cy in good health and delightful mood in spite of our constant nipping into his bank account."

Just after Christmas, Marina wrote Susan Mary Alsop (December 29):

"My entire family is here or about to be here and I do a kind of *navette* [shuttle] between Ségur [our house] and Orly [airport]. My mama as usual a darling but she looks a little like a lamb being taken to the slaughter house when I take her to Madame Grolet for her dress for the wedding. It is grey with a few *paillettes* at the throat and wrists and she wears it as if it would bite her. She has been most resigned about the dress but put her foot down over hat and shoes but as we will all be standing in church no one can see our feet much.

"Our dresses have arrived at last and as usual having ordered mine now I have dreadful second thoughts because it is bright green and I am afraid I will look like a salad, especially if it is a cold wet day. But Marinette's wedding dress is pretty and when they tried the veil on her the last *essayage* I had tears in my eyes she looked so sweet and so unreal to me."

The wedding went off perfectly in an incense-filled Greek church where the Archbishop Metropolitan Meletios officiated, and was followed by a haze of champagne. David was the first of the family to fly off afterward. He had to work hard on his thesis. Just to make things worse for him, he and a friend, Hector Vasconcelos, were beaten up by some anti-Harvard Cambridge ruffians, exciting Marina's limitless indignation. She wrote him on January 21:

"Now I worry about those unspeakable townies and I am organising a possie to come and beat them up in June. What absolute brutes. My poor sweet. Your poor eyes. And poor Hector. A brocken jaw is ghastly. Do give him my deepest sympathies. I could kill that policeman for not arriving a few minutes earlier. Here all is well but sad. Your room is empty. Dodo left too and Rox and Shan and Paris feels empty and cold.

"We went out to dinner at Versailles at M. [Gerald] Van der Kemp* and *le tout Paris* was there including Mr Eliot Ness of the Untouchables who is much better looking in real life and Mrs. Untouchable who is a dizzy blond in a lepard dress, but rather sweet. The women were all beautiful and most elegant but on the way home Far was groaning that all the men's brains put together would not come to more than a ping pong ball and no heavier. He does'nt like caffé society that's for sure. But the food was delicious and the house inside the Palace on the left as you drive in, is perfectly lovely.

"On Monday I took Shan to the airport and if you think you looked funny leaving you should have seen him. One very splendid gentlemanly suit case and one super smart leather brief case and after that progressively down hill. One *tagari* [Greek peasant bag], one nylon transparent shopping bag, one silver fish net bag, one paper parcel and one red cardboard box big enough for a donkey containing six small champagne glasses without even

---

* Curator of Versailles.

one bit of paper between them. Each of the other bags had one shoe, two cheeses, one shirt etc. We finally got him into some kind of organisation and Grat tied his three ombrellas and two canes onto his hand luggage so I hope he got home all right. Rox and Dodo were a bit better but not much."

On February 8 she wrote Christine Claudel* (in French):

"We had a dinner for eighteen including the Alphands,† four ambassadors, Prince Paul, Princess Olga, the Van der Kemps, etc. and wanting to do the best possible I ordered everything from the best caterer: a very elegant dinner. Imagine my state when at twenty minutes to ten not a soul from the caterer had shown up. No dinner, and the telephone at the caterer's didn't answer and there wasn't even an open store to run out and buy eggs.

"I am certain this produced three ulcers in me and ten kilometers of new wrinkles. Finally they arrived at a quarter to ten when I was ready for suicide or murder. Everyone was very sweet, I must say, Florence Van der Kemp suggesting she go down and make some spagheti, Prince Paul saying we aren't hungry in any case. But sometimes a catastrophe like that makes a dinner party because everybody was laughing."

On April 21 there was a *coup d'état* in Greece and a conspiracy of colonels set up what became an increasingly tough dictatorship. I flew to Athens and met all the leaders, most of whom struck me as mediocre except for the real boss, Papadopoulos, who was intelligent — and very nasty. Marina wrote Susan Mary Alsop:

"The very fact that I am rather relieved than otherwise depresses me. I would have been struck by thunder, what am I saying, ten five years ago, had I been anything but scandalised by a military takeover and a dictatorship in any land, let alone my own.

"And yet if one has to *se rendre à l'évidence* and admit the fact that we are an under-developed and under-Papandreoued nation, what other solution

---

* Wife of a French diplomat.
† Hervé Alphand, former French ambassador to Washington, and his wife.

was there? Except of course that this is not a real solution unless by some miracle these colonels turn out to be crosses between Einstein and our Lord Jesus, which is not likely. Ah me I feel depressed and out of touch with my generation and less and less 'with it.' When I read the other day about the gang in London which tore the poor Greek embassy apart even down to the matresses and water taps, who it turns out did not even know what they were protesting about, it was just for arts sake, and who when they were put in jail screamed and yelled and had a question asked in Parlement about the ethics of having their contraceptive pills taken away from them for that night, I really want to shoot myself I feel so old fashioned and scandalised.

"And the odd thing you know is that the screaming and protesting and poetico-litterary indignation comes from friends not foe. The Communist countries have not said peep. Its the British and the French with that phoney aproach of *Ah la Grèce qui est la mère de la démocratie*. They forget that we also are the mother of oligarchy and tyrany and the grandma of all political disunity *à travers les ages*. And how about Mr. [John Kenneth] Galbraith protesting about Andreas Papandreou and his execution when he is not even in prison and no one talks about shooting him yet."

We were again in New York when Israel's Six-Day War began. Marina wrote Marinette, who was in Spetsais with Adrian:

"We are in the same room at the Carlyle and of course as of Monday glued to the T V watching the security council and the news and holding our breath. Odd how basic human beings are *quand même*. You should see the doves and the Vietnics becoming hawks for the middle east in one second. And as I wrote to Dodo I cant help smiling in view of so many centuries of anti-semitism at the ammount of people I hear saying 'We're for Israel. We have licked them hollow etc.' And the public image changing from Shylock to Blue eyed warrior and breath taking courage. They are too too marvellous. Needless to say I wanted to take off for there at once."

David had just finished Harvard, and we attended his graduation proudly as he had gone through in three years — with honors. We went down to Washington, and Marina wrote Michael Edwards on June 17:

"Dinner with Mr. [Dean] Acheson on his really lovely farm in Maryland. So bright and amusing and interresting but too too bitter and destructive. Once in power one should remain there otherwise the short taste and then loss of it seems to make people cinycal and sour. Mr. Archibald MacLeish was at my side through dinner and I loved him. Talked of poetry and D. H. Lawrence and suffereing. Today lunch with lots of women friends and then tea with the President. I AM name dropping."

On June 23 she wrote Marinette from Washington:

"Far alas had to go back to New York not only because of Mr. Kosygin but also to see the head of the Bulgarian communist party. But I stayed on with David, who has to be here a few more days to settle his fate. As of yesterday he has been taken into AID [for Vietnam] which I am a bit sad about but also relieved that the suspence and indecision are over. He will train for ten months right here and that at least ought to be great. He is looking around for someone to share a house with and also awaits last minute instruction.

"He had hoped that the training would start in September but now thinks it will be August. So as soon as he knows for sure I want to pack him off to you [in Spetsais] on the first plane so he can eat and sleep and swimm and think of nothing for four weeks at least. Far would like him in Aspen but I say he has to have this last fling sort of. The graduation was nice but not as intimate as yours. The big day four thousand six hundred people got degrees honorary et al, so the parents were sitting almost in Boston common. But then the degrees were given after lunch at Eliot House by master Finley* who is a genius. He had a most extraordinary little speech for every boy very special and very different and with those hops and gestures and squeeks that you know so well it was really a performance not to be forgotten. . . .

"Yesterday or rather day before Far went off at six to see the President and David and I bought sandwidges and waited to have them with him in the garden. Ten o'clock eleven no Far. I asked David if I should start worrying and he said the President would probably give him better sandwidges than our horrid tunna on rye. Well at one A.M. Far came bouncing in having been to dinner on the Honey Fitz [the presidential yacht] with all the ministers and things and had a good talk both before and

---

* Professor John Finley, an old and brilliant friend.

after and says the president was in high spirits because of the grand child probably born that morning. Far was driven back here in the presidential car and the President said to him 'If you have nothing better to do could you come to lunch tomorrow also.' "

To Marinette on July 6 from New York: "Israeli jokes are rampant here. One is a man saying to his friend where are you going this summer and the other answeres To Israel to see the Pyramids. Another about L B J sending a black patch to Westmoreland. Another in the New Yorker of a meeting of the Defense secretary and all you can see is McNamara's head and ten faces with black patches. And so on and so forth.

"We have just returned from a superb five days in Fisher's island with the [Jock] Whitneys. David too. It really was marvellous. We had two cars to pick us up one for us one for the luggage. The private plane is all polished wood and chintz and soft cushions. The house is a dream of bright colours and pretty things and white wicker beds and arm chairs and flowers in baskets at every corner and such comfort and it is all covered with pale pink fat old fashioned roses.

"But one cant have everything in life that was apparent. Their sea is beige. Shallow and sea weedy and to add insult to injury it is melted ice. David and I did go to the other side, not the sound, which at least had big waves but that too was so cold it felt hot, so we only stayed in for a few waves. Then it rained cats and dogs but no one minded because everyone there, Haywards, Mrs. Selznick us and the Whitneys are bridge fiends and we played in the morning twice, which really gives one a super sense of holiday. And believe it or not we were too shy to say the stakes were far too high for us, so we played at a cent a point with our hearts in our boots and won every rubber and came away with tons of lovely money some of which I gave to David and some went to the hair dresser this morning. Gosh this is an expensive city.

"Mrs. Whitney gave me two delicious dresses and the softest pull over in the world. What hospitality. And a huge bunch of roses to take back to the hotel. Did I tell you we have moved to the Blackstone because for the same price as one room in the Carlyle we have three here and Polar is with us and not eternaly farmed out *chez quelqu'un* so it is lovely."

Toward the end of July, Marina and I went to the Smiths' log cabin near Aspen, my idea of paradise, and Marina addressed a letter to all the family in Spetsais: "Aspen is more beautiful than ever because they have had so much rain and the wild flowers are something fabulous and the air is like iced honey and crystal. I have not yet gone all the way in to the river but only up to the behind and that is pretty cold too. I miss you so terribly in things like that.

"At night we have a new friend. I think he is a marmot but I am not sure. He is cat size and several shades of brown and he is the cheekiest animal I have ever seen. I gave him a sandwidge and he eat it from my hand chatting all the time and I dont think it was thank you that he was saying. Rather god damn these things that come and live in my house and spoil my peace and quiet. I wish they would go back to Paris, France. He makes such a noise at night upseting saucepans and tin cans that I am afraid we will have to take steps, but he is rather irresistible."

Marina kept a diary on and off for years. That summer in Aspen can best be described by the following excerpts:

July 28, Aspen, Colorado: "Martin Marmot so familiar. He now comes and goes as if we were his guests. Ate a sponge, soap as well as his sandwidge."

August 8, Aspen: "We found a basketful of mushrooms. Floated down river on a rubber tyre. Marvelous fun. Rain all night."

August 14, Aspen: "Went fishing all day. I caught a 17-inch trout. Cy even happier than I. Cooked him *aux amandes*."

August 29, Aspen: "Went fishing all day at a most beautiful place between Basalt and Carbondale. Cy caught more than 50 fish."

September 5, New York: "Feels awful being back. Air is like cotton wool."

On September 11, Marina wrote Marinette from New York: "We are off to Washington for about a week and then back here for two days and then Venezuela. Every night Far springs a new country on me. Yesterday it was Angola and South Africa."

From Caracas, she wrote David on September 24:

"The town seems to sprawl without shape or form or *'Centre ville'* with huge appartement buildings rising into the sky like fingers sort of semi-detached and next to them empty lots and then a slum next to a bank and then pretty but totaly uninhibited villas going from Spanish to moorish to nothing. We were met at the plane by a gentleman from Protocol with the lovely name of Ploutarcho Garcias and another one from our embassy and whisked through customs which I love and taken to a very charming hotel with our own little garden in front with morning glories and a swimming pool. So we are very comfortable but a little bored.

"And everything in this vast continent is so huge that one cant even leave the city without taking a plane. The sea is an hour away but all the beaches have been messed up by a huge earth quake they had in July. So my great hopes of a visit to the jungle and aborigines is once again frustrated. Anyway the last group of foreigners to go into the jungle never came out was never heard of again and the only visible trace of them is a tribe of Indians with blue eyes and this was in the sixteenth century so perhaps its just as well. But I am sad just the same. Perhaps Bolivia will prove more fruitful. The Ambassador there has asked us to stay and as he is as avid a fisherman as Far we might get a tiny try.

"Today my friend Ploutarcho came to take me sightseeing and took me up a thousand metre mountain in a *téléférique* and by the time we got to the top my hands were clammy with anguish. You know me in Lech. This was sheer agony but the only consolation was the thick green jungle under us which somehow looked soft just in case. Anyway Ploutarcho and I made it to the top and it was almost worth it because the mountain falls sharply off on the other side as well in a great green sweep all the way to the sea. But I had barely time to say Ahhh when a huge white cloud came and covered us and after that it was like being in a milk bottle. There is a forteen floor hotel up there and we were IN it before I saw there was anything there.

"But as far as sight seing that is all except Bolivar's house. There seems to be a Bolivar house almost everywhere in this part of the world. This one has a lovely garden and I visited it this morning alone and was just about to steal a gardenia when a gardener popped up from nowhere so I asked him for it instead and he gave me a whole bunch of *foulia* too and jasmine so our room smells like Maroussi."

From her diary I extracted the following additional comments:

September 24, Caracas: "Dinner at Timoteo's. Only Venezuelan food in town. After we eat it I know why."

September 25, Caracas: "Tea with Mrs. Leoni [wife of the president] while Cy was seeing him. First time a president in Venezuela has an official residence. Bran new but an old hacienda style. Absolutely lovely and a dream garden. Pet monkey. She is charming, young. I talked Spanish for two and a half hours. God knows what I said. President Leoni seems nice. I have given up even trying to understand who is left, far left, China, Moscow, etc. Only no one is rightwing."

September 27, Lima, Peru: "Arrived at 2:30. Met by Pedro Beltrans [old friends, former prime minister] and embassy man. How I enjoy all these privileges. Makes life so easy. We stayed at Pedro's lovely old house. At dinner he said Peru is in a financial mess. Who isn't?

On October 2, Marina sent a long letter to Marinette from La Paz, Bolivia, saying:

"La Cordillera Real de los Andes in name alone is pleasing, and when you fly over it it is sheer magic. The most god and man forsaken part of the world and one can see why. There is no blue in it anywhere except lake Titicaca which is dazzling. But the sheer enormousness of grey brown yellow and black rock high high high into the sky takes one's breath away (literaly as well as metaphorically). The airport is the only one in the world which is as long as it is high because at this altitude planes need much more space to brake in. It is thirteen thousand something feet, but to my great surprise I did not drop dead as I had expected judging from my fatigue in Aspen which is only nine thousand. I did have a terrible head ache the first day but since I feel fine except if I forget and run upstairs but then everyone is prepared for that with visitors and as soon as you move everyone shouts Dont Run.

"The first view of La Paz which is in a bowl surrounded by these fabulous snow covered mountains is like a Daguerrotype of Shangri-la. I mean it is all brown and black and dusty like an old photograph but the landscape is sheer magic. It is really very ugly as a town with almost no vestiges of colonial architecture except for a moth eaten cathedral and one house, but somehow it has enormous charm and one feels at home and loving right away. For one thing it is so nice to be at last in a place where the people dont wear their national costome only on National holidays and where things are really as primitive as one had hoped (except for the

Embassy [where we stayed with Ambassador Doug Henderson], which is lovely and comfortable and has central heating. An African wardrobe does not allow for much warm clothing.) So one has the best of both worlds. The Indian women wear these enormous skirts ten or twelve one over the other in most psycedelic colours and shawls and the delightfully absurd bowler hats at a jaunty angle and long pigtails and carry their babies on their backs and look wonderful.

"We went to the Indian market today and every little shop had dozens of kinds of herbs and dried flowers and incense and beatle nuts and a lot of unrecognisable things and everywhere huge baskets full of Llama fetuses (believe it or not) which is the most horrible sight you ever saw. They are dried in the sun and really look straight out of MacBeth and they are used to put a hex on your enemies and all I can say from the quantities we saw is that they must all have a lot of enemies around. It is incredibly elementary. Sharp thorns to card wool with, brushes for their hair made of broom twigs, stones for spinning wool etc. And everywhere the softest furs of llama and alpaca and vicuna and SHshsh I bought the most beautiful chinchila bed cover for Far for Xmas and it is so soft I have hidden it in the back part of my suitcase and god willing I will get it through sixteen countries and safe to Paris somehow. It cost fifty dollars. I also got a lovely Spanish colonial picture of Saint Gertrude with flowers and a gold face.

"Yesterday we spent a perfect day. Our hosts who are angelic (and have six nice children) took us to the Zogo valley. We travelled less than three hours, climbed over lunar landscape to about seventeen thousand feet through the most dramatic mountains with snow and above us even higher peaks like crusaders castles straight into the sky, and saw packs of Llamas and Alpacas and here and there a deserted Spanish church from 1530 or so and then suddenly started down on the narrowest most frightening road down to five thousand feet into real true jungle at last. Great water falls everywhere and then a river full of trout and Far and the ambassador went fishing but alas cought nothing, and all around thick rain forrest with such flowers that I was almost drunk with pleasure. Arum lillies and those round bushy bright blue things which cost a fortune in flower shops (could it be anchusa) and huge bushes of fuschia and *le comble* I found five orchids, some feathery pale mauve and white and one amazing yellow and red one. I was beside myself.

"We picnicked by the stream (Aspen sized) and paddled although it was icy and the Ambassador who is a great orchid collector climbed a huge tropical man eating type of tree and picked several different plants. It really was just the kind of day I always dream about and never get because no other country has all this so near. In three hours from the high Altiplano to the tropics is really a luxury.

"One other day I was taken to some pre-Inca ruins by a marvellous old German lady archaeologist who has been excavating here for fifty years. She is eighty two and looks so like Maria that I had to hug her. But alas I am such a snob about ruins. Mud bricks look like mud bricks to me even if they are a thousand years old and I had a hard time matching her enthusiasm when she pointed out a squiggle on a sand stone and asked me to admire.

"The great event of course here is the trial of Régis Debray the French journalist who was cought by the governement in the valleys with the guerrilas and also the almost irrefutable proof that Che Guevara is here. Poor fellow. He is such a romantic figure and so brave and mysterious, but bringing violence to other people's countries for its own sake never did anybody any good and the big mis-calculation was to think that all it would take to arouse the poor down trodden Indians and miners here would be a bit of propaganda. Instead of which they found a really apathetic people who anyway consider them both foreigners and white-men and therefore to be avoided. So they are starving and boiling and having a very nasty time for nothing and they have had a great many deserters who spill every bean they can. There are lots of Cuban refugees here. Also half the people have been in exile for ten fifteen years and others just made millions and left like the Patiños the Hochschilds etc. It is not a very admirable nation lets face it which is sad because the country is really splendid."

We then flew on to Uruguay, and Marina noted in her diary:
October 9, Montevideo: "Marshall law! Odd how one never feels anything of a crisis unless one is a minister, or killed. It is raining like hell. Dull day."

From Brazil in a letter to Marinette on October 15:

"We are living in super splendor in the British Embassy with Sir John and Lady Russell, which is only a little bigger than the Royal Palace in Athens and the same style of architecture and I get lost every time I leave our gracious air-conditioned rooms, but as I spend ALL the time with Aliki catching up on ten years of gossip it does'nt matter. Friday we went to Brasilia and I have rarely hated a place so much in my life. It made me angry and tired with distaste. I know I am a square and conservative and like small places with gardens, and that is not possible in the world of tomorrow but even so there seems to me no excuse for those rows on rows of superblocks all like large peaces of toast rising into the sky.

"The landscape is enormous horizonless colourless and the only nice thing is the sky and yet Mr. Niemeyer [the urban planner] has not built one balcony one terrace one garden from which you can see this sky. No pavements no roads you can strole on, nothing but nothing to humanise the place. He has even turned the buildings with their backs to the street because he feels people should be isolated, so that the main street is one long row of back yards except they are not yards just walls and service entrances. Also as there is no transportation the city has sprung a whole series of ghetoes. All banks and bankers in one *quartier* all schools and churches in another, all diplomats in yet another. The one hospital next to the one cemetery (practical but charmless) etc etc. I really got the creeps especially when a lady gave me her address and it was Super block 113 building 1685 Flat 140039 road J6 Brasilia. How 1984 can one get?"

She added to Nursey three days later: "It is incredible to be in a city [Rio] with beaches EVERYWHERE. It is exactly as if one could undress in the middle of the Concorde and go swimming in the Rue Royale. All the men take a sandwidge from their banks offices papers etc and cross the street to do their exercises on the beach and take a swimm. How they can concentrate on work I cant think."

On October 24, from Accra, Ghana, Marina continued her account to Marinette:

"We left Rio on Wednesday night and after a cramped sleepless night, got to Dakar at five in the morning, and went to a small sticky ugly hotel, only to be whisked off to do some sight seing (thank god there is nothing much to see in Dakar which looks just like any other provincial french town with a lot of charm) but no Notre Dame no Acropolis no Taj Mahal which is good because even those we could not have seen through half closed pink eyes. And in the evening we had to go to a huge dinner in honor of some visiting generals and their wives and it was one of those ghastly affairs where no one knows anyone else, and I heard myself so many times saying 'No I am not with the Embassy my husband is . . . yes to seven more countries . . . no only this morning . . . on Saturday etc,' that I was almost tempted now and then to change it and say 'No I am a snake charmer on my way to Hollywood or something.'

"And as if this were not enough we had another dinner of the same type the next day this time in OUR honor. The Senegalese are most beautiful tall tall and so thin they wave in the wind and the women wear great togas of tulle or mousseline with gold threads in them over their mamy-dresses and head dresses over a foot high and move like soft animals. I saw a dreamy one dressed like for a gala at the opera with a baby on her back and a basket bigger than her on her head, gently squat in the middle of the main street and with one hand pop out a bosom to feed the baby and with the other make a *cornet* of pea-nuts for a customer.

"One morning I went to an island in the bay which was a Portuguese slave station which was very 'picturesque' but so hot that by the time we reached the top to see where the battle between Free French, English and Vichy had taken place in the war, we were ready to faint and melt away. We swam but only for coolth. The water was grey and thick.

"Then the plane to here left at four in the morning, so once again we missed a whole night's sleep and arrived in Accra to find that there is a ballet troup here of American negros and they were giving a gala that night so there was dinner first here at the Embassy then the ballet and then a dance for them back here in the garden. I thought we would drop dead. Our hosts are blacks too [Ambassador and Mrs. Franklin Williams]. Very very nice.

"Sunday there was a day long pic nick at a beach thirty miles from here and I must say it was all I had hoped for. Endless stretch of sand and palm trees and huge waves but no under-tow so I could swimm for miles not like in Rio where three feet is as much as one can do. I walked alone too and found really wonderful shells some deep orange ones and lots of cowries. And Today we go off to the capital of the Ashanti country and to some villages which will be fun. Poor Far cant come as he has to see the President who only gets back from London today. He is a hero your poor Father. I get all the fun and he does all the work."

Of her trip to Kumasi, the Ashanti capital, she wrote Marietta Tree on October 27:

"I went with the Embassador a few days ago into the bush in Ashanti country where he had to dedicate a leprosorium and also a couple of schools in different villages and except for the car, and in one village a loudspeacker, we could easily have been in Mungo Park's days. Right in the heart of the forrest we first payed hommage to the chief in full regalia, gold crown gold sandals dozens of gold bracelets and neclaces, surrounded by clan heads each with a different staff of office, also gold, in their great hand woven togas in brilliant yellows and blues and greens looking like shiny black Romans; standing under great scarlet and gold ombrellas and drums talking all the while. When we had bowed and shaken a hundred sticky hands, we went back to our seats under a palm leaf shading, and then the royal group came and saluted us with great dignity and slow drums and pipes.

"It really was extraordinary. Then we all danced and they sang for us and we danced some more, wet to the skin with the heat, and then the Ambassador was given a toga too and sandals and two hundred eggs and two live turkeys. They were a bit of a problem in the car but luckily we could give them to the nuns at the next stop at the leper colony so all was well. In one village they had had a death and there the drums were quite different and the whole village was in their mourning clothes which are hand printed cloths in strange designs each with a symbolic meaning. I was really very lucky because I could only see a thing like this with the Ambassador."

We were moving too fast for her to write with her usual regularity. I quote from her diary:

October 27, Accra: "Cy's birthday! Not very wonderful for him. He worked all day. Saw General Ankrah (the boss). Gave him a Sant Iago from Bolivia. Beagle gave him a fertility goddess."

October 29, Lagos, Nigeria: "A glorious day although cloudy and not even warm. But we went to a beach on the ocean with Mr. Olsen [the U.S. chargé d'affaires] and the Friendly's [*New York Times* correspondent and wife] and took serf boards and had a wonderful morning. Excellent pic-nick and rest. Cy's third day off since we started."

October 30, Lagos: "Odd to be in a country in full civil war and not to feel it at all."

November 2, Kinshasa, Congo [later Zaire]: "Two new columns of mercenaries said to be advancing in Kivu. Told not to leave embassy alone. Rumors rampant but not even the ambassador knows anything certain."

November 3, Kinshasa: "Bob Mc Bride [our host and friend, the U.S. ambassador] is really charming and Mobutu [the president] and Bamboko [the foreign minister] seem to depend on him entirely. They call up every hour. We left at 2:30 A.M. for Johannesburg."

November 5, Johannesburg: "Johannesburg on Sunday is like a tomb. No movies, no radio, no humans. Just church. Small walk in park."

November 8, Luanda, Angola: "Luanda is lovely on a thin strip by the sea. As soon as one leaves this it is hideous sad brush land, with horrid Arthur Rackham baobab trees, tiny cactuses, huts, corrugated iron roofs, dust and dreariness."

November 13, Salisbury: "Cy saw Sir Humphrey Gibbs (the governor general who is in house arrest) but not Ian Smith. Smith preaches only to the converted. How sad for such a lovely country."

To Susan Mary Alsop, Marina summarized her impressions in a letter from Salisbury on November 11:

"One thing that struck us both in Ghana and Nigeria though was the enormous difference between West and East Africans. The British here had never really been colonisers in the sense of settling down and taking over the place. They had always been traders and administrators and sometimes enemies but never owners. With the result that one feels no chip on the shoulder here, no complexes; great dignity realism and humour and great conscience of the troubles ahead and the almost impossibility of staying in the race when one has had the misfortune of coming of age in a world already old.

"In Ghana at least being smaller they have a semblance of homogeneity. In Nigeria and a million times worse in the Congo, there is enough human and land discrepancy to make six nations. In Nigeria hundreds of different tribes and 800 languages not counting a kind of moslem military lingua franca called Hausa. We could make little of what was going on as one cant believe a tenth of what one hears. A few days before our arrival a plane had bombed Lagos but the damage had only been to the museum garden with the result alas that the famous Benin bronzes had been packed away in cases (by the American wives) only to see them to their horror stored for safety where do you suppose? Under the only bridge in Lagos, the only strategic target of the slightest interrest, and there the cases of treasures lay. Ah me.

"The plane had been brought down and six white bodies had been found in it but no one *really* knows if they were mercenaries or just people from Biafra trying to get to Sao Tomé a Portuguese island not far off. One is supposed to have been a reporter from *Match* and another a splendid Baron von something very romantic who is a well known gun runner from Madrid. But who can tell. The week before two photographs of white soldiers had been published in all the Lagos papers as definite proof of mercenary presence in Biafra but on closer inspection one turned out to be a world war one soldier and the other an unabashed photo of John Wayne in confederate uniform. Ah me again. One is constantly torn between affection and despair.

"No affection in the Congo though. *Everybody* there seems vile. The whole thing was all the more unreal because the trees are all in full flower at this season. Flame trees like scarlet banners and jacarandas the colour of a windy morning, and yellows and pinks just like the city was decked out for May day parade. Sitting in our Embassy garden (we stayed with Bob MacBride, a kind of gentle modest pro-consul with Mobutu and everyone calling him on the phone every hour and a fealing he was everybody's last hope) with the mighty Congo river at our feet, flowers everywhere, a swimming pool and a bloody Mary in one hand a cigarette in the other, listening to tales of death and horror, we felt like visitors from the moon. In town however I did feel uncomfortable. I never did in Saigon or anywhere else in so-called danger spots. But here there is such a fealing of total illogic that even in the market place buying a basket one felt that any minute they might turn on you and tear you to peaces for some unknown tribal reason.

"In the old days if a member of one tribe hurt a member of another, even inadvertently it was either war to the finish or a member of the offending tribe was sent over to the other as payment, this usually a young boy or virgin to be sacrificed by fire and thus wash out the offence. Even today if someone is hurt by a car lets say the problem is not between the victim and the driver but between whole clans. So you can imagine what feelings are when white mercenaries come, kill, and go.

"In Katanga apparently not only the government troups but the Katangese gendarmes also spend most of their time killing anyone who happens in front of them. The Belgians never trained any officers so the troups now have no one to order them or guide them and it is total chaos. One of the French mercenaries apparently arrived here some time ago rather badly wounded in the head and leg, and the French consul went to call on him and ask if he needed anything or anyone advised back home of his whereabouts but he said No he had noone except his mother who had long ago given up caring. Asked if he needed money he said no he had more than he could ever spend but what he wanted was some other war to go to, as soon as he could leave this hospital.

"Johannesburg is deadly. Enormous changes since we were here last but still deadly and one cant help feeling it is apropriate that the Afrikans word for whites is Blanks. When one sees the 'Whites only' signs even on the benches in the park one wants to cry with shame. We also went to Luanda in Angola for a few days which is a charming Mediterranean town and a relaxed atmosphere although in a pinch I am sure the Portuguese can be as horrid as anyone."

Still in Johannesburg, she confided to Marinette on November 21: "You know I have such a long list of thank yous to god each night and things to be grateful for but now I have to add another one and that is that I dont have to live in Pretoria. God what a dull dreary place. The suburbs are pleasant with nice Dutch houses and wonderful gardens and those magic jacarandas everywhere but flowers is not all.

"There is not a bloody thing to do and on a week end everything is closed even book shops and I had just finished my Boer war book (incidentaly after forty years of having been pro-Boer like everyone else I think I am now pro-British even in that and also as Far keeps saying what fantastic luck that Peter Stuyvesant was beaten by them else we Americans might have been Boers too). And so I had nothing to read but the Gideon Bible. And I promise you a Sunday in Pretoria with the old testament is enough to turn one into a card carrying hippy. Far had a lot of people to see, the most liberal of whom make Barry Goldwater look like a communist, so I was in the dreary hotel room all the time and to add insult to injury it rained non stop for five days.

"We also went to Botswana which was a great disappointement. Endless ugly flat bush and the only nice thing were the thousand of birds everywhere guinea hen and partridge and dove. But poor Far, it was like me walking through a garden and not being able to pick. He came to see Mr. Seretse Khama but '*ça ne vaut pas le détour.*' It takes four hours normally but our hired car broke down and it took us seven by which time I was getting more prejudiced by the minute.

"Then we also made the mistake of wanting to see Mafeking a town which after all caused so much pain and joy to so many English mothers and wives and the hero-place of my spiritual master Lord Baden Powell, founder of the Scouts, (Yellow Crocus patrol) and so we drove another five hours to the place. I had at best expected crenelated walls a small fort guns etc and at least a monument or little museum and there is NOTHING. The deadliest little market town with groceries and a few Indian shops where the Afrikaner farmers come for their weekly shopping.

"P.S. The two most popular songs in Malawi these days are 'Groundnut Flower' and 'Brush Away the Flies from Your Baby's Eyes.' "

Marina stopped off in Athens for one week to see Dodo and her friends. The year wound up in Paris. She noted in her diary:

December 13, Paris: "Came home to find King Constantine had attempted counter revolution. No one knows details but Salonika radio in government hands. Sounds bad."

December 14: "King seems to have fled to Rome. What a fiasco. Only a few hours to defeat. Left with all his family, luggage *and* a dog. Cant have been very optimistic *au départ*. What agony. What tragedy."

December 16: "No news. King is giving his own terms. After Nasser [the Six-Day War] this is the next best thing. You fail — and then you give your own terms."

December 21: "Pick up Marinette. Divine as always. Her meer presence warms the house.

"P.S. Adrian arrived this evening."

December 23: "Polar arrived. Skinny but well. I cooked excellent dinner for 18."

XI

January 1968 - December 1969

On January 22, 1968, Marina wrote Marietta Tree, who had invited us down to Barbados:

"The trouble is that Cy has to travel so much for work that when he does not *have* to I dont think I can get him to go further than the Etoile. We have just been asked to go to Mouton by the Rothschilds to glimpse their new [wine] museum, but Cy cant possibly leave Paris at this moment and I am heartbroken. The trouble is that 'at the moment' may mean anything from a week to for ever."

Next day she wrote David:

"Far saw the general [de Gaulle] yesterday and to his horror the Elysée itself put out a little notice saying so. He has been so discreet about his meetings always and has not even told me about them, almost dropped dead when he saw it in the *Agence France Presse* in big letters. I think they have a new public relations chap who boobooed. He also saw M. Pompidou this afternoon so he wont have much trouble thinking up collums for the next few days. But he is working on his book and that means he cant sleep at night. Luckily Beagle keeps him warm and soft.

"We are going through a festival of Bohlen good by dinners. Tomorrow at the Quai d'Orsay, then several Rothschilds and the Billottes. I think they will see more of us this week than all of last year."

She added subsequently: "Our dinner at the Quai last night was superb. It always amuses me how people take on the physiche of their surroundings and there we all were in 1968 looking as second empire as can be. I sat between Mr. Alphand who could have been Thiers as it were and a man whose daughter is married to *l'oncle* Bicco who hangs on our dining room wall. Odd no? Anyway it was not too yéyé as you can imagine me being almost the youngest there but it was a lovely *coup d'oeuil* and both Mr. Couve and Chip managed almost affectionate sentimental fairwell speaches even though they had to skate over some thinish ice on the *'liens traditionels de nos deux grands pays.'* Excellent dinner including *foie gras* and I always wonder how they manage to serve it hot to sixty people as god knows how far the kitchens are in that huge ministry."

From her diary:

February 3, Saturday: "Lunch Avis. Cy took Chip and Cecil Lyon [U.S. minister and close friend] to Lucas [my favorite restaurant], and the owner. Mr. Alex gave them a special cake with flags and *Merci* written on it. They drank two magnums of champagne and 1913 marc and god knows what else. Cy will miss Chip beyond words."

We flew to London to await the arrival of Marinette's baby, our first grandchild, staying at the Bruces' vast Embassy residence in Regent's Park. Marina noted of Jessica's birth:

February 11, London: "Baby girl born at 2.30. Girl has long black hair. Looks like everybody. Marinette tired but well."

She added to David: "She had a horrid time poor baby and finally the baby was coming with her head in the wrong direction (Far mumbles *'ça ne m'étonne pas*, none of the women in the family have any sense of direction')."

On April 24, Marina wrote Avis Bohlen: "You have probably already heard that Louise de Vilmorin is sharing a house if not a bed with André

Malraux. As the avarrage age of these starry-eyed lovers, is well over sixty, there is hope in the world yet. Maybe if our generation turned into flower people too, it would solve all our problems except for gold. You left Paris probably just in time to avoid prison for dept. Even since you left things have doubled it seems to me and of course the rent-freeing is going to throw more people out into the street, than one can imagine. I believe that one would make pots of money by renting a moving van and a few able-bodied men to take all the disposessed from their elegant ex rent-controlled houses, to the hovels they are reduced to."

That May the famous strikes and riots began in France, almost over-throwing de Gaulle.

At the head of the page in her diary for May 6, Marina had written, "Troubles started," with a heavy line underneath. The entry read: "Student war in left bank. Several hurt."

Two days later she wrote David, who had been in Vietnam since February:

"The news about the five journalists and the German diplomat [who were killed] was all that is needed, to turn a mother's heart to stone. Every moment of the day I think about you and when I do forget for a second, then I remember with double vigour and stand distressed.

"We too have had our little Tet offensive these days. Monday and Tuesday there have really been street battles of extraordinary violence. Last night I was almost cought in it and half glad half regretful that I missed it by six minutes. I had taken Mrs. Chambers to a movie and drove her home as to top everything we had a taxi strike, and was coming home at around mid-night via the quaie when at the first bridge before St. Michel we were stopped by a huge police barrage.

"Behind the Sorbonne where there were CRS [security police] by the thousands looking like Homeric hoplites with their helmet and shields against briques and bits of the pavement which are the student arms as well as the No Parking signs up-rooted everywhere, and used as battering rams.

"Suddenly great shouts and the first tear bomb but I could not see anything only a lot of red cross cars and the shouts and the tears. I managed to unscramble and got home via Montparnasse, turned on the radio and heard that there was serious fighting Rue Vaugirard and the crowds were pouring into Montparnasse. It was exciting and tragic and out of sixty students arrested only four turned out to be students at all. Two policemen are still in a coma.

"The awful thing is that no one yet knows exactly what they are asking for. Everyone says it is a minority of five thousand out of sixty but the fifty five dont seem to lift a finger to stop all this. 'Like many of the upper class, they like the sound of broken glass' I think is what it comes down to although they do have a lot of legitimate gripes. Mainly that when they graduate they dont find jobs."

Marina's diary continued:

May 15, Paris: "Strike of papers and taxis. Things worse all the time. Students took Odéon."

May 16: "On one o'clock news, hospitals call all doctors to be on emergency standing. Workers took over Renault and six other factories in France. Is it the revolution?"

May 17: "News stranger all the time. Twenty eight factories taken by workers. De Gaulle still *insouciant* in Roumania [on a state visit]. Red, black flags everywhere."

That day Marina wrote David in Saigon: "The situation here is completely out of hand. And only two weeks before exams so that the students have really cought '*leurs pieds dans leurs barbes*.' After Pompidou came back from his little propaganda frolick in Persia he made two splendid speaches and gave in on everything to the students, but I dont think they want to get what they want. At the begining everybody but everybody was for them partly because they have so much on their side and partly because one cant be *pour les flics* [police], but now the whole thing is so confused with romantic anarchy with lyrical illusions and underneath really sinister elements of total destruction [specifically because of the Vietnam conference at this moment] that they are rapidly losing most sympathies. Last night when it was thought things were quieting down they suddenly occupied the *théatre de l'Odéon sous prétexte* that they did not want the bourgeois theatre to function, and took the decision to attack the Majestic which is Vietnam conference headquarters and plant the black flag on its roof. It is all so crazy and sad.

"Traffic is at a standstill constantly and the telephone works once in every eight times one tries. And there seems to be a deep contradiction everywhere. They scream against exams and for the democratisation of the university and above all because of the *manque de débouche* after graduation particularly for the *faculté des lettres*. Well either there are no exams and then everybody can get a diploma and then of course there wont be jobs for everybody, or there will be a natural selection at the start and then jobs for the graduates, or then a graduate will no longer consider himself something special and worthy of the state's special attention but education will be a personal thing for one's own improvement and joy.

"However I think one of the big troubles with humanity is that it surpassed itself when it invented logic *and* justice, and as neither are natural or apparent anywhere else except in the human mind which is infinitely superior in the blue print of its thought than in the application of it, and so we are in constant *tiraillement* and contradiction with ourselves and surprised by the lack of logic in the world when we should really be surprised (agreably so) if it did exist.

"Talking of illogic I went to a lunatic dinner last night chez Bordeaux-Groult and there were several stuffy nice elegant intelligent *tout Paris* and Quai d'Orsay guests and also Dali who arrived with Léonor Fini with a hair-do like a huge black poodle and arab flowing robes but above all with a creature in white trousers and transparent silk blouse and long yellow hair, smoking a long cigarette holder and carrying a gold headed cane, who was even to my inexperienced eye, manifestly not of the female sex. Our eyes popped out of our heads and conversation stopped dead *jusqu'à ce que nous ayons retrouvé nos esprits* and then we all talked at once.

"Apparently the person in question is famous, was in the navy, changed sex and is now known under the name of Amanda and according to Léonor Fini who was only too glad to confide details to Jacques de Beaumarchais her table companion, the details of the operation made his hair curl; and also she told him that the lady is now the most expensive lady in town. Who knows maybe the puritan anarchists have something after all.

"I told Dali about our picture and he acted as if he had found a long lost child and is coming to see the picture after thirty four years. He remembered it quite well but thought it was one of about two hundred which vanished during the war. He was sad because he has just published a book on lost or little known works of his and would have loved to have this one in the book too. His agent *homme de confiance* or what have you a tough little Englishman who Kitty says looks as if he may well have done 'a stretch' somewhere, but bright as a button and amusing, told me he knows three museums which would give us sixty five thousand dollars for it any time, but I do hope we never have to sell it.

"Dali looked just like himself moustache cane and all, but I could not really concentrate on anything but the green faced beautiful creature he had brought. The voice deep but possibly female, what was a dead give away was the feet and the standing posture. Rather creepy the whole thing, but they left early, and you can imagine that the rest of the evening was spent in lude speculations on all aspects of the problem, which in itself was funny as I have never talked of anything but serious detached subjects with either the Beaumarchais or the Gillets. It really was fun and funny.

"The North Vietnamese were deeply insulted when they saw the original conference room because it did not seem elegant enough to them so they had to change to the dreary ball room which at least has a lot of gold and red velvet and now they are happy. They also did not accept the governement cars at their disposal but bought seven of their own. So there. Ah me. Equality equality what foolishness is committed in its name. The capitalist Americans were quite happy to go on foot."

Her diary continues:

May 20, Paris: "Got my last drop of gas and wont use the car any more except in emergency. Went to market. No sugar or oil. No salt."

May 26: "We drove to Mouchy with Averell [Harriman, head of the U.S. delegation to the peace talks] and Mr. [Cyrus] Vance [his No. 2]. Their car of course. Pleasant but no one can really concentrate on anything."

May 27: "Huge meeting. Yells of Down de Gaulle, Down Communist Party, Long Live Anarchy."

May 28: "Warm, lovely day. No one knows if we are heading for civil war or not. Paris looks *en fête* with so many people on foot. One understands the French revolution better now. Life goes on gay until possibly the last moment."

May 29: "De Gaulle suddenly cancelled cabinet meeting, left for Colombey. He vanished from 12 to 6:30 and reappeared by helicopter. Where was he for six hours?"

May 30: "De Gaulle's speech at 4:30. I wont leave. No referendum. But elections. Army said to be at all Paris gates. Went to the manifestation at Concorde. Six hundred thousand people. Fascinating. Most peaceful gay parade."

May 31: "No sign of resistance from workers or students. Thank God, but what cowards. Deflated balloons like hot air."

June 1: "Everyone feels relieved, happy and sort of let down. As if we had been through a kind of nightmarish holiday and now we are back in dreary everyday life and another period of that difficult old man."

On June 12, Marina wrote David:

"It is an enormous tribute to the organisation of France as a country that it can live for six weeks with almost general strike and not feel it more than we did. I mean superficially because of course the poor people who could not go to their jobs obviously felt and what is more will feel the pinch when banks open again and there is no money in them. People like masseuses and piano teachers or any one who lived from their day's work of course are *catastrophés*. Little *entreprises* too, the barbers the dry cleaners little restaurants tailors, all the small luxury shops etc are closing down. But as always in moments of exciting crisies one does not think of them.

"At first it was most exciting and Denise and I were in the streets all day, almost wishing to be cought up in a *baggare*. At first too everybody was for the students and for the workers and against the CRS of course. But as week after week went by and the romantic rather nostalgic very 1848 atmosphere became more and more absurd, sympathy turned to exhasperation and even to deep hatred.

"I went often to the Sorbonne and also sat in the Odéon listening to the young rebels and the over-all fealing in the end was boredom and *une immense fatigue*. Slogans like *à quoi ça sert de bouffer quatre fois par jour si on s'enmerde* or *baiser avant de vous faire baiser*, are hardly inspiring revolutionary principles and when they have to write *à bas l'Impérialism* when there is not an inch of imperium left to the Western world, seemed to me such a lack of imagination and sort of stealing from our generation. It would have been more understandable if they wrote *à bas le marriage* or *à bas la famille* or something newer even. But *l'impérialism les assassins, les oppresseurs* seemed to me rock bottom of nonsequitors. Also at the same time, *à bas la société de consomation* and *vive la hausse du niveau de vie* . . . Which is which?

"However the poor children poetic and foolish as they are, had a point *au départ*, and were really frustrated when the workers walked in and stole their revolution from them, not in the name of nebulous destruction of the establishment and society etc but with most specific and pragmatic *revendications*. And then they got what they wanted and more, and in their turn had their strike stolen from them by the anarchists, the *Chinois* as they are called. Then to top all, people got really frightened, you know cars burned houses pillaged, chaos and confusion everywhere (only good thing no parking tickets for anybody) and once again issues confused and half a million people manifesting from the Concorde to the Etoile yelling for the General and for *légalité* and *la République* and *le drapeau tri-color vaux mieux que le rouge ou le noir* and *la Marseillaise plus que l'International*. And there we were, workers *femmes du monde*, students business men any old thing shouting patriotic things and *vive de Gaulle* even the most un-gaullists of all.

"The shouts were *Mitterrand au poteau, Sauvageau* [the student leader] *au boulot. Waldeck au Crochet les cocos passerons pas, Saleaud saleaud saleaud, Mitterrand repondit l'echo* to the tune of a nursery rhyme. Also at one lovely moment outside the Travellers where there was a big American flag, *L'Amerique avec nous*, and *au Viet Nam s'il le faut*. All very moving and exciting and then one got home and realised that having the general back stronger than ever is not a solution either. *Du reste on n'a pas tarder de le voir*, because for three days after the de Gaulle speach and the freeing of gasoline (simultaneaous and probably not fortuitous, and everyone tootling off for their *Pentcôte* holiday) everyone heaved a sigh of relief and hoped it was all a nasty caprice of history, but then it all started again and the last two days have been nasty.

"All last night we could hear the dull burst of the tear gas bombs (I never knew they made so much noise), and the warm Parisian night was like a battlefield. One cant imagine how fast a barricade goes up. In no time at all trees pavement stones even cars are pushed into place and there is the barricade six feet high, to which the students then set fire, god knows why? Everyone talks of police brutality naturally but on the whole I think they have been saints. I watched a group one night for hours being really hurt by flower pots thrown off balconies, not a brave way of fighting anyway, and called SS and even peed on by students and not flinching.

"But of course there must be some brutes among them and god knows they had enough provocation to do even more. Especially as the whole things was not *sérieux* in its final analysis because wanting to destroy society, liberate inhibitions, crush the establishment etc *c'est trop facile*: and then what. But I must admit that I did envy Mr. Cohn Bendit [student leader] his moment of bravoura. The only man in Europe having fun. The whole thing of the dyed hair, the squeezing through frontiers the arrival at the Sorbonne and giving a press conference under the very nose of a paralysed governement must have been too delightful. All the Nanterre students have given up their summer holydays in order to work and debate and even physically build back what was destroyed. They are all frightfully ernest and rather pathetic. Grapin their director was a deep convinced communist which makes it all so much sadder and more confusing.

"The fact remains that the communist party *qui fait figure de grand bourgeois* really saved the situation, for various reasons and not least of them that they hate anarchy even more than the squares, and also not for the world would they wish to be in power at this moment when so many nasty unpopular measures must be taken. I must tell you that already in a few days bread has gone up and milk which is psychologically as well as pragmatically a very bad thing. The day that gas came back to Paris there was such an *embouteillage* that Eda [my secretary] took five hours (litteraly) to go from the office to her house in Passy and Uncle Peter* six from his office to home. It was really nightmarish and shows how easy it is to destroy an over-developped city.

"What was fantastic all things considered is that with so much power of blackmail in their hands the workers never turned off either the gas or water or electricity which would have paralysed everything of course. I think that the French are too over sophisticated and civilised to stay more than ten years under one ruler, that they like and need change and *la baggare*, but at the same time for those very same reasons of sophistication and civilisation, cant make real bloody revolutions, because they respect life and property and their own comforts too much. Ever since man began we are told that you cant make an omelette without breaking eggs; but

---

* Peter Payne.

perhaps now we are learning that we can. At least not human eggs. Economically *reste à voir* how terrible the consequences will be.

"We have had both Mr. Vance and Averell to meals but they dont say much for the moment. What can they say? Mr. Vance is very nice but not as exciting as I had planed for him to be. Averell on the other hand nicer than ever. We played gay pleasant bridge with him and Mrs. Chambers last Sunday and then were going to again when he had to fly off to Bobby Kennedy's funeral. What about that. I feel like a swimmer in a stormy sea who as soon as he lifts his head from one great wave, is struck all over again by another. The tension even subconscious must have been so great these passed weeks that everyone we know is paralysed with sheer physical fatigue.

"Now Far's manuscript has arrived and we have more than a thousand pages to correct and I have not lifted my head from it for two days. It is fascinating. I have to go back to it in a minute, but had to take a little time off to write to you my darling after almost six weeks of enforced silence. All this month not only could I not leave France but even if I had been able to I would not have wished to for the world unless it were a matter of life and death elsewhere. Funny these odd loyalties one developps *malgré soi*. Lots of people left, I must tell you, left in a hurry and with suit cases full of money and are now sneaking back sheepish and also a bit worried that they came back too soon because *on n'est pas encore sortie de la bergerie* by a long shot. However this time I do have to go to England so I leave on Sunday and will stay until after the christening on the 29th. When I go to Greece god knows as with all these *événements* the house is still half painted, and everything up in the air.

"What killed me above all was to see the *revendications* of the Yougoslav communist students who also occupied their university. What they were asking for was the abolition of social classes the downfall of the bourgeoisie, great economic differences between workers and the establishment and greater participation in government for students and workers. *On pense rêver.* All this (exactly what the French are asking for too) not a generation after their country was one river of blood in the name of equality. Ah me. Humans really all *adorent ce qu'ils ont brulé, brulent ce qu'ils ont adoré,* and I have come to think that the most brilliant thing ever done politically was Napoleon crowning himself Emperor exactly ten years to the day after a mad crowd decapitated its King."

In June, Jessica was christened at Oving, country home of Adrian's parents, with Susan Mary [now Alsop] acting as her godmother.

Marina wrote Avis Bohlen:

"The Odéon became known as the *'Prison sans Barrault'* [Jean-Louis] who incidentally behaved like abject cowards and Madeleine Renault is supposed to have said 'Why us, we are not a bourgeois theatre why not try the *Folies Bergères.'* The only moment that I felt a little frightened was the famous Wednesday when you know who [de Gaulle] vanished for six hours. Rumour of course was rampant but the most persistant one, was all too naturally that he had gone to the army and that he would call on article 16 and then by all that is logical, we might easily have had civil war. So imagine our *stupeur* the next day, I lunched with Ethel De Croisset and we went to see M —— who was white as a sheet and said 'go at once, this is the one place you must not get cought in; if they come, they will come here first etc.' Then she said, 'well at least the children are in the country, and as for us, well we have had our good lives.' Ethel and I were stunned. We decided to go home to my place to listen to the general's speach which was at four.

"But by the time we had walked to the Invalides we saw that there were crowds of young and they all had transistors so we stopped and listened to it in the street and then he was so different from the little old man he had been the previous week, so strong and sure of himself that we were sure then that the tanks were at the gates. But we decided to go to the Concorde anyway. There amongst thousands of people we bumbed into Marie-Alice de Beaumarchais, and together watched and it became little by little, and in the most orderly fashion, the most corny old fashioned nostalgically patriotic thing, I have ever seen since the war. Great tricolors everywhere, the Marseillaise at full blast, and from every street, every corner thousands upon thousands of people. Old young poor rich, poured into the Concorde shouting *Vive la France vive le tricolor plus beau que le drapeau noir, plus belle que l'International est la Marseillaise.* In spite of mixed emotions one had a tear in the eye. And then at six the whole teaming massive body of humanity, started to walk to the Etoile hand in hand, singing and shouting slogans. *Mitterrand Charlatan, Waldeck au Crochet, vidanger la Sorbonne, liberté de travail* etc etc. And the great mini-revolution was over. Who will ever understand the French."

At last Marina went to Spetsais. She wrote in her diary:

August 25, Spetses: "Mayia gave wonderful party at Zogaria. We went with horses and arrived just as the sun set. Everything scarlet and gold. Have seen the same for forty years and never get used to the beauty."

On September 19 she wrote Avis Bohlen: "The baby is a dream. She is not at all pretty although she does have huge black eyes, but she is the gaiest baby I have ever seen. Laughs and gurgles and kicks all day, and Cy is almost as delighted with her as with Beagle which is saying a lot. The rest of us gaga, but we the three mothers keep arguing, Mummy saying HER daughter is the best, and I claiming mine as the most enchanting and Marinette sneering and saying neither is as good as hers. Adrian is completely Greekyfied and everyone loves him.

"But the best thing of the summer was David's arrival which none of us had dared to hope for. He managed three whole weeks and arrived on the 10th. I went to Athens to meet him and his plane got in on the dot of three in the morning. He was the first off the plane, and then I lost him and half an hour went by and then more and in the end a little man came and called me in to the customs and imagine, somewhere en route his health certificate had got lost and they said sorry he has to spend six days in the contageous desease hospital. We almost died.

"As all this was taking place another plane came in from London bringing one of his oldest friends, to stay with us, and so he and David and a guitar and I sat in the customs until eight when the pest-car came to take him away, playing the guitar with all the customs men sitting around us singing too and plane after plane going through almost unnoticed. Well then the next morning I got to work and pulled every string imaginable. It was so obvious that he could not be in Viet Nam without his inoculations that I did not feel I was asking for anything too unreasonable, and the Embassy I must say did its utmost, particularly general Eaton, and in the end I got him out after forty eight hours instead of the six days, and arrived triumphant to collect him only to find him playing backgammon with the crew of a Chinese ship, and five black Portuguese from Cap Verde or somewhere.

"*Quelle émotion* however. We were like limp rags when we got to Spetses finaly. But he is in wonderful form and seems to be enjoying every minute of his holiday. I was worried that all the young would have left as universities have just opened, but somehow young seem to grow out of the bushes in this place and three nights in a row he had about twenty five to dinner. Then two girl friends appeared and took him and his friend off for three days to the Mani and they just got back brown and dusty but delighted. Cy arrived in late August and miracle of miracles has not had any gout at all. I still face the same insoluble problem of his love of solitude and this islands continuous togetherness, but I think there is simply nothing to be done about that. Either we go to Aspen and stay alone like weeds, or come here and live with people."

On October 2 we were back in Paris, preparing for a trip to Eastern Europe. Marina wrote David:

"Far looks forward to this trip I think. The Balkans are much more his home spirituel than anything else and he is far more fascinated by a Bulgarian village than a Korean one.

"The last few days in Greece were lovely. I kept wishing it would rain and storm to make it less hard to go, but not at all. *'Nai'* [Yes] day [elections] was more brilliant than all the others and in spite of so called Marshall law and coercion the town had a lunatic festive fealing about it. I sat all day at Kolonaki [Square] and the whole of Athens went by, stopped had a coffee said keep my place I will be right back I just want to dash off and vote *ohi* [no] and come back. But the poor boobs [the colonels] had it all so badly organised that it took some people ten hours to vote. As for the railway stations, Pyreus etc it was total catastrophy. No one could leave their jobs much before Saturday so that the whole of Greece almost was trying to get somewhere from somewhere else, and naturally there were not enough boats trains or anything.

"However none of this disturbed our lords and masters too much and I was wondering myself, theoretically speeking if one had a totally honest governement which might sincerely get 100 per cent of the vote, what could it do to make it look less. *Ce n'était pas le cas* as you can imagine, and in a lot of the provinces the voters were only given the *nai* paper and also were not given a curtain to go behind to vote. But I suspect that even with none of this they would have had an enormous majority because of this extraordinary apathy that has descended upon us. As long as there is quiet and a minimum of money no one wishes for anything else and as long as it is someone else's brother husband father who is in jail or without a job etc, oh well you can't have everything. You will be glad to know that all our friends almost, voted no."

From Belgrade she wrote to David on October 19:

"Some day we must go to Venice together. We had two and a half lovely days there and it was the first time in ages that Far had taken any time off for sight seing and sitting at caffés sipping capuccinos or Harry's bar for bloody Marys, and it was wonderful to see him relax and enjoy it all. He needed the rest after two hectic days in Paris trying to get his columns done as well as the wretched speech for Nato, and then another five in Rome equally rushed.

"The coctail party for us at Nato was horrible. We stood for hours convulsively shaking hands and smiling at people we would never see again and sipping fizzy lemonade and this was followed by a dinner at which I sat next to a sweet but dim air vice marshal who kept repeating 'Greece ah yes lovely, did a lot of her in my youth, the Acropolis you know and Homer and all those chaps, lovely lovely.' Rome was dreamy too, pale yellow sun light and soft warm weather like a little shawl around one's shoulders.

"In Venice we took a gondola naturally but Far drew the line at "Venice by night" when the gondolier sings to American ladies with blue hair. Then we took the train to Belgrade which is unrecognisable since I was here last fourteen years ago. It is a real city now with huge new buildings and all dolled up and no more peasants bringing their pigs to market and only a few selling roast chesnuts at street corners. But on the other hand long haired youths and duffle coats and minis everywhere and even a hippy corner, quite near the university and a tremendous air of intelligent excitement.

"One is almost led to believe that it is worth losing everything but everything, because then the appearance of Italian shoes in the shop windows or foreign cigarettes or pull overs, becomes a great social achievement. These are the best looking people I think in Europe. I turn round ten times in every block to stare at some dazzling girl or young man. The play on at the moment at the theatre is Genet's *Le balcon*. Of course everyone is desperate about Czechoslovakia but there is nobody here who is not determined to fight if it comes to a show down here too. They really are a wonderful crazy manly people.

"This is a tough trip on Far as every word represents an endless struggle. As for me, after I had seen the Kalemegdan which is the old forteresse (Roman Turkish Austrian etc) and the war museum there is really nothing at all to do but sit in the room and read. I managed all the Roman and Byzantine bits of 'The Balkans in our time' and rather relished the succesive invassions Huns, Avars, Iliryans, Dacians, Slavs, Magyars, Pechenegs, Polovtsi, Gegs, Tosks, Slovacks, Slovenes etc etc etc. But when I got to the part when Roumanian Transylvania becomes Hungary and then Roumanian again etc I got so confused I gave up. Thank god Greece at least has only one people one tongue one religion. They say about here that it is six republics with five nationalities four languages three religions two alphabets and one political party. What a miracle that is."

From Marina's diary:

October 26, Varna, Bulgaria: "Varna, the playground of the East. How tragic. Colossal hotels all new, all falling apart already. Our room so ghastly we begged to be moved, so we got the royal 'appartamenti' which was awful too. No plugs in bathtub, all the enamel gone from everywhere. Sad. Sad."

October 28, Bucharest: "Bucharest immediately looks western, latin, civilized, almost gay. And does not smell like Moscow, Belgrade or Sofia. Athenée Palace super de-luxe. We have *three* rooms, bathtub spotless and with plugs and hot water. Everyone speaks *something* and everyone kind and smiling. Dinner at the [Ambassador] Davises who are absolute pets. Met Bishy Catargi* whom I had hoped to find."

On November 1, Marina told David that in Bucharest "People have been angelic to us and Papa's hopes were all gratified as he had an interview with

---

* A Rumanian prince whom Marina knew when he was a boy and used to come to Greece. He and his mother were old friends of mine. She "adjusted" and became close to Ana Pauker, a Communist boss.

Mr. Ceausesco which lasted a long time and apparently it was shown on television last night and also made the head lines this morning. This is all very very surprising and pleasing and we have been asked for drinks at some aquaintances house and also for dinner, which is an enormous change. Also the best is that having had all his appointments and work so quickly Far has been working like a slave for the last three days with the result that we can take the week off and drive to Moldavia to see the monasteries which are unlike anything in the whole world. We are spending the night in one of them called Moldavitsa and everyone tells us the nuns are angelic and cook one the best meals."

She added thirteen days later: "We did drive to Moldavia to visit those fabulous monasteries of the 15th century. They are the only ones I have ever seen anything like it. Neither Gothic nor Byzantine, they have enormous low wooden roofs like gigantic funny straw hats, and they are painted over every inch of them both inside and out, with the most beautiful frescoes imaginable. And the colours, as fresh as the day they were painted. Paintings of angels and devils and the old testament and Adam and Eve and Greek Philosophers all mixed up, in the most brilliant blues and red and gold. Dazzling in the sun shine. In one they gave us hospitality for the night and it was biblical. The nuns wore lovely black velvet pill box hats and the veil over it so that they looked more like *châtelaines* than nuns and we were taken to our vaulted rooms by little winding stone staircases and slept in very high wooden beds, with those nasty Germanic sort of eiderdowns with sheets blanckets etc all buttoned into one, which fall off at the first deep breath, but luckily we had a huge tiled stove which took up an entire corner of the room.

"They gave us a marvellous supper of hot corn bread and cheese and fresh cream and pickles and raw onions. Then we went to church which in spite of Lenin and Marx was full of peasants in beautiful embroidered leather jackets and the women in wide fluffy flowery skirts. The most un-like our own Orwellian conceptions of collective farming and People's republics, that you can imagine.

"Then we went on to Budapest which is still very beautiful at least the center of the city by the Danube with this hill and the castle and the cathedral at the top. But as soon as you get to back streets all the bullet holes are still in the walls everywhere. It must be bad enough to have the

Russians breathing down your neck when you love and admire them like the Bulgars do but here it really must be hell. November 7th is the National day from the October Revolution, and the poor things had to celebrate it and have parades and things, which must really kill them. That night we were given tickets to a gala performance of a new ballet by Katchatourian called Spartacus and written specially to commemorate the revolution. It is the first time it has been given and hopefully the last. The music was sub-Cavaleria Rusticana and the dancing a pathetic cross between Romeo and Juliet and their idea of West Side Story. Hell. And everyone so pathetically dowdy and sad.

"Although at least in Budapest they do see foreigners and accept invitations although they never ask back but rather out of poverty than politics. I wish you had been with me as the antique shops are sort of state-controled pawn shops, and the campiest thing you have ever seen and simply over-flowing with Victorian pictures, landscapes and portraits and interiors for really very little money. You with your good eye I am sure could have picked up a few treasures. The china and silver were beautiful but most of it one cant bring out. I did buy some Herend porcelaine, which I will give you when you get married. It is very pretty with one rose and a green line. Far nearly fainted when the three large paper parcels arrived, but we came back by train and luckily the civilised French dont wake you up in the middle of the night for a few pennies worth of *contre bande*. In Roumania Bulgaria etc we were got up every time two or three times and both in and under our beds searched. We have seen some superb pictures on this trip. Lovely Icons in Bulgaria, beautiful German and Italian in Bucharest and three Grecos of great beauty and even in a tiny town called Esztergom outside Budapest, the most exquisite religious paintings of the 15th and 16th century. Sort of tucked away in a dusty old building.

"We were very impressed by the Americans in all these countries. Almost without exception the whole Embassy staff spoke the language fluently and Hungarian is really a tough language to even pronounce. Then we had a day and a half in Vienna and really if anyone again rants against the consumer society I shall personally punch them in the nose. There is nothing up-lifting or moraly inspiring about queing half an hour for card-board-like toilet paper. The difference when one reaches Vienna and the capitalist world again is like light from darkness. Just straight planning and efficiency, leaving aside all ideals or morality. Sacher's is a dreamy hotel and it was lovely to have lots of hot water again and smiling waiters and even as far as it goes to understand the language around me. I dragged Far to Rosencavalier.

"We took the train [back to Paris] yesterday afternoon and arrived a few hours ago to find our Beagle and our Grat and our own beds again and it is sheer delight. Poor Far has to go off almost immediately as our Czech visas came through while we were travelling and also the Russian ones. But I think I have had it and he does not mind my not going (he will just work hard and fast and be back in at most three weeks).

"Tomorrow we are going to Mr. Harriman's seventy-seventh birthday party. The first one we ever went to was when he was sixty, and there was so much brass there we did not know where to look. Eisenhower and Acheson and Bradley. Admiral Kirk and General Gruenther were the lowest ranking men there except for us. How long ago and how yesterday-ish it all feels."

As Marina had written, I went off alone to Moscow, Warsaw, Prague, and East Berlin. It was just as well she didn't come. The whole area was gloomy and tense. Czechoslovakia had recently been occupied by its allies to put an end to Dubček's "socialism with a human face."

Marina wrote me in Moscow on November 23:

"My little prune, but I miss you, and in an odd way even our various red and silver, or prune coloured hotel bed rooms. Dreary as they are, they somehow become little nests from the outside world which is so big and where there is so much choice, and looking back on it all, the rather dull hours in strange lands surrounded by strangers odd languages unknown currencies and landscapes, become sort of precious."

She wrote two letters to David in Vietnam. The first, on December 12, after a trip to England to see Marinette, said:

"I spent one week at Stanton Harcourt and all of Saturday I stood shivering and wet in a cabbage field while the sporty British took shots at some equally sodden pheasants who could hardly fly. Eight guns and about a hundred and eight beaters, all going chuck chuck chuck chuck urging the poor birds out of their warm grass to be shot at. However I was given a brace which I took to Monica [Curtis] who was delighted as she had guests and her economics dont run to pheasant. Stanton Harcourt was mainly a joy because Mrs. Guest* was there too, and I love her, and also the house is lovely and the first thing one sees in the hall on arrival is one Bellini and two Velasquez.

"PS I have been reading a book on the thirty years' war and the description of the peace negotiations for the Treaty of Westphalia are so funny and so exactly like here and now [on Vietnam] that I clipped the bit out and sent it to Averell. Right down to the shape of the table, and all. The protocol was such that the French Harriman, the Duke de Longueville, and the Duke of Pomerande who headed the Spanish delegation, never met one single time in all the four years the negotiations lasted, for fear the one would enter a room one inch ahead of the other. Then the Catholics and Protestants also quarrelled and the allied Sweeds and French and the members of the delegation between them and, *pour comble,* after four years when the terms of the Treaty were finally accepted, they were sent in code and 'the horsemen of the apocalypse still continued to spread death and destruction over Europe' while for three weeks they searched for the key to uncode the message. *On pense rêver.*"

On December 27 she sent him a sad letter: "One should be with one's children at Xmas, war or no war, grown up or not. But luckily as I said in other letters Mrs. Chambers had asked us to go to her house, so it was not so gloomy in the house except for Beagle and Grat who were sad not to have a fuss and flurry around them. I decorated a tiny Xmas tree and cried a little remembering the inevitable quarrel over, garlands or no garlands, lights or no lights etc. Where have all the lost years gone and who cleft the devil's foot?

"Far says he was more pleased with his presents this year than ever before. I gave him a beautiful Icon from Roumania painted on glass of St. Christopher and St. George on horses. Marinette gave him bright red

---

* Our friend Lily Polk Guest.

woollie pyjamas and he loved them rather to my surprise and between us so many books we will have to have some more shelves or move out."

She ended the year in her diary:

December 31, Paris: "For me it was a nice year but for Cy miserable because of office politics. For France bad. For the world bad too."

On January 19, 1969, she wrote Avis Bohlen: "After our lunch with little Avis Cy had to catch a plane to Dublin as he is going over there to see a few priests and theologians and 'cover' the new wars of religion. I really do think the world is going madder by the minute. And it is the 'human rights' chaps, that are beating up the others. How the words tolerence, freedom justice etc ever even got into our human vocabulary one wonders. I am going to join him in London tomorrow. It will be Jessica's first birthday soon, so we are just going over to give her a hug. I must say she is a darling. Like a small round ball of love, and so soft and warm I can sit for hours with her head against my cheek. We also hope to say good by to Evangeline and David [Bruce]. It is awful how all our friends are leaving us little by little."

On January 28 she wrote David in Vietnam: "Far's days in Ireland were not too illuminating anyway, even though he had a nice talk with a Catholic cardinal who was the only one who seemed to make any sense in that lunatic country. I am on their side in this. Like Lord Lucan who was so used to fighting the French that when they eventually were allied in the Crimean war, he kept forgetting it was the Russians he was fighting and shouting slogans against the dirty Frenchmen. But the world is so mad and so ugly and so unthinking these days no wonder one cant remember whom one is for and whom one is against. Far wrote a column saying how strange it was that the two best planned and best executed military operations of years the occupations of Czechoslovakia and the bombing of Beyruth airport, were both so disastrous diplomatically and politically, and he has been getting abusive letters by the bushel from angry American Jews. Not Israelis mind you but Jews who sit on their fat behinds in America and write insulting letters. Oh well."

On February 11, just before we took off for Cairo and Asia, Marina wrote David to say how much we looked forward to seeing him and added:

"One night we dined at the [Sargent] Shrivers* whom we like more and more, and it was an odd dinner. Mr. and Mrs. Michel Debré†who have as much charm as a tax collector. He said to Far *'Monsieur, vous n'aimez pas beaucoup notre politique.'* This to Far who is always accused of being a Gaullist was a bit much. I had Miss Julie Christie at my table who is lovely but less so than in the movies. Mr. Warren Beatty was there too and he much better than as Clyde. Also Peter Ustinov who kept us all in stiches, but alas I missed half because I was stuck in a corner with Mr. Duhamel whom I usually find irresistible but whom I would gladly have missed that night. One odd thing in the Embassy under the Shriver regime, not a single chair in the big living room and we all stood all night. Then three days ago we gave a dinner for the Shrivers and Mr. and Mrs. Edgar Faure‡ and it went very well thank god. We had From here to Eternity James Jones and his wife too, and they lent youth and wit to the evening. Mr. Faure is as bright as a monkey."

At the end of February we flew to Cairo, accompanied for that lap by the sweet and efficient Susan Sevray, my secretary, and then on to Pakistan. Marina wrote from Lahore to Marinette on March 4:

"We got to Cairo comfortably and to Shephard's hotel which although new is still with some nostalgia for me. Far saw Nasser the next day as forseen and it went very well but he had to write a news story as well as his column so he never lifted his head from the typewriter almost the whole five days we were there. Luckily he had Susan with him who was thrilled as you can imagine.

"The one time Far did manage a few hours off we went to see a solar boat of the Pharoah which is not yet open to the public but Far's friend, Mohamed Heikal, arranged to have it opened for us and we went. It is right next to the great Cheops Pyramid and alas the governement is building the most repulsive sort of cute boat shaped museum to put it in. Smack by the side of the Pyramid whose whole beauty lies in the stark landscape around

---

* U.S. ambassador to France.
† De Gaulle's first prime minister.
‡ Ex-prime minister.

it. Sheer folly. However we saw it in its temporary lodgings and it is exquisite. Forty three meters long exactly like a gondola with a kind of cabin on top. It was found by chance like so many things.

"Fancy, they knew there must be solar boats around the pyramids and had dug unsuccessfully on three sides and given up. Then King Saud of Arabia was coming on a visit and as he was a cripple they got an order from the governement to clear the whole hill behind the great pyramid to make a road. One of the workmen came to the archaiologists and said I have found something which looks like a great slab of stone. They said dont bother us, but he came back and said there is another slab and another. And they found thirty of them beautiful and hermetically closed. So eventually they opened a hole and they found the ship but brocken into two thousand eight hundred bits. We met the most enchanting old gentleman who put it together again. It has taken about fifteen years one way or another. First they had to photograph and catologue each piece before taking it out of its trench.

"He told us that as a little boy he used to break his sister's dolls for the pleasure of putting them together again. Then he became an artisan until a German archaiologist discovered this strange gift of his with his fingers and he has been playing jig saw puzzles with history ever since. He showed us vases and neclaces and a beaded belt he had already finished and it was spell binding. And he was so modest and nice. The proffessor was also marvell-ous. He scribbled hieroglyphics for us as if it were French, and he also told us that they are still confused and searching because the solar boat is forty three meters long and nine high (exquisite) and the trench it was in was only thirty. So they think this must be some strange unknown cult which ordered the smashing up of Pharaonic boats after death or something. He said that in hieroglyphics the word for putting together a boat is 'to sew a boat' which has puzzled them until they found this one and it is in fact held together only with ropes exactly as if it were a garment sewn together."

From the diary:

March 6, New Delhi: "Long drive from Lahore in Pakistan to New Delhi in India. Dull, flat country. Dust. Saw lots of carrots, one elephant, a lot of dead dogs and one dead child. No one was going near it until police came.

Sometimes they do that even if the victim is still alive."

March 10, New Delhi: "Cy saw Mrs. Gandhi. Found her pleasant."

March 19, New Delhi: "Bought some saphyres. They are beautiful. Zoo. Saw exquisite white tigers with blue eyes. Went to dance recital by Miss Krishnamurti. Fabulous. Wish I could, aside from saphyres, buy a new pair of hands like hers.

"Poor old Pakistan. The usual twenty-year after doldrums. It is so much easier to create a nation than to run it. *Sans compter* the really insurmountable problem of running a country cut up into two bits as far apart and as different as Greece and Sweden lets say. Not that India is much better, but at least they are all in one huge geographic bit. I have come to the not so original conclusion that revolutions are like love-making. One is supposed to do it in order to have children, but in fact one does it out of sheer pleasure and the children (or the results of revolutions) are an after effect and one never knows what they will turn into.

"I must say it is rather disconcerting to us poor technocrats when we hear the sweet voice of the air hostess saying 'In a few minutes *Insh Allah* we may be landing in such and such.' But only a few days in these places serve to proove that this is no idle theological curtesy, but a genuine hope for the best. Everything from the time of day to how many hours breakfast will take, to how far one point is from another or how many ruppees to a dollar, is in the hands not of one but of several non-coordinated divinities.

"But Delhi is really most pleasant. Our hotel is most luxurious and full of disastrous shops which haunt one at every step. The shopping is to die over. One is not accustomed in real life to even window shopping for emeralds saphires, saris, silks and gold, silver and amethysts. Yet here every step one takes is yet another argument with one's poorer self. Where and when else will I ever find this or that for only so and so. It is a losing battle and I HAVE bought myself a few strings of tiny saphires to wind around my pearls and they look so beautiful I wish to wear them even in bed.

"I am afraid by the time I hit Hong Kong I shall have just enough money left to buy a begging bowl. But dont worry I do do a bit of sight seing too and the museum is quite lovely although I dont much like many armed godesses and curly twisting limbs. But the Moghul things are beautiful. We went to a *Son et Lumière* at the Red Fort, and listened to dulcima's playing while a pale silver light flickers on the Pearl Palace and it is all very romantic. We had three not so succesful days when poor Papa wanted to go off somewhere to get cool and rest. Seventeen different people told us seventy different bits of advice as to where to go so in desperation he chose the one everybody told us not to go to and off we started for 'the Hills' as they are Kiplingeskly called.

"We had the worst driver in a population of 530 million bad drivers and the two hundred miles took us seven of the most agonising hours of our lives. People say one gets used to it eventually but I dont believe it. The whole thing is a perpetual game of chicken. Everybody drives in the middle of the narrow road and it is to see who will swerve into the ditch first. When it is the gigantic truks or busses loaded with eight times too many humans or bricks or cow dung or sugar cane, it was we who went in. When it was the vast assortement of other things pedestrians dogs water buffaloes widows and children, it was naturally they.

"We drove with eyes closed and fists clenched for seven and a half hours and when we got there *ça ne valait pas le détour*. 'There' being a hill station called Nainital. A tiny town clinging to the face of the hill (when I say hill we are already up several thousand feet but is only hill compared to the utterly astonishing and fabulous mass of the real Himalayas above us). In most places one gazes straight at mountains. Here one strains one's head upwards to see them. This is really something to see. One morning we took poneys up to the highest of our peaks believe it or not through a forrest of red rhododendrons in bloom, and when we got to the top there as far as our eyes could see row upon row upon row of snow covered blue mountains far up into the sky. One side China the other Nepal.

"One thinks one is dreaming all the more so as, even as we watched they vanished slowly before our very eyes and there was nothing there but sky. It is extraordinary these tricks of visibility. But that was the only nice thing we did. The first moment when we arrived and we saw the only intellectually pictureske little town, but in fact filthy and smelling of that so typical oriental combination of dust *pipi* and cardamon, four-floor houses of tin and wood holding together as by miracle. And one after another these same edifices named the Waldorf Hotel or the Pavillion or the Bristol, we got gloomier and gloomier. Luckily ours the Swiss hotel, which would make any Swiss turn in his grave, was *quand même* better and we cheered up slightly.

"Alas English the so useful lingua franca established during the British you know what, is vanishing more and more, and communication of any sort was out of the question. And not even a cool beer. Tiny dark damp room and to add insult to injury freesing cold at night and no lamps to read by. AND the prospect of the homeward drive. Still Far had left his typewriter behind so that alone was a psychological help. We went for long walks (Yes I) and picked flowers and read a lot and luckily the third day a dreadful family of rather ex colonial English with several loud children moved in next to us, so Far decided to come home a day earlier. I was not un pleased. Delhi seemed like home after that."

From Marina's diary:

March 22, Bangkok: "So hot and wet decided to forgo sight seing and do nothing. Had supper in room. Six mangoes each."

March 23, Saigon: "DAVID. He met us at airport looking adorable. Even had a haircut. Airport looks much less war-torn than three years ago. David's house charming. He gave us a dinner party. Excellent food. Generally marvellous."

March 25, Saigon: "Cy saw President Thieu. Went out to Cholon for Chinese dinner with 16 of David's best friends. All adorable, none more than 26. Smoked pot for first time. Cant tell if music, mangoes, people all looked specially nice to me because of that, or just because they *were*.

March 30, Saigon: "Three rockets struck but fell in the river bank. No damage."

Marina reported in a letter of March 31 to Marinette:

"We have been in Saigon a whole week, and somehow I have not managed to write to you yet. It is partly stupefaction from the heat, because I don't really have much to do. For the passers-by who are not journalists Saigon is deadly dull. Because lack of communications both physical and linguistic one depends entirely on some kind soul taking one about, but most kind souls here work all day including brother Polar who incidentally looks marvellous. Brown and somehow sturdier if not fatter and Far finds him perfect just to catch up with the times he considered him hopeless. They jabber away for hours.

"As for me I find myself plunged into his *parea* [group] and feel more and more like Dodo when she protests that I cant drag her around to 'everything' with my friends. Only more so because between fifty and twenty it is the whole world. I feel more nervous and coquettish going off to meet them, than if it were Don Juan. According to David they not only like me but find me Groovy. His *parea* is enchanting I must say and so different from each other one could study anthropology.

"Kevin his house-mate is a dream. His Chinese girl friend Gracie is ugly which is surprising as she is probably the only ugly one in town. But David says her quality is enthusiasm tottally lacking I gather in the local ladies who consider it plain buisiness. Her enthusiasm and the gentle way that all oriental women have of looking after their men. David says she jumps out of bed in the morning to get him orange juice and coffee. Then there is John who also shares the house who is a diplomatic type and most exasperatingly always looks cool and fresh in tie and jacket when the rest of us ordinary mortals look as if we had been dumped in a tub. You cant imagine how hot it is.

"John is serious and nice and the complete but rather useful restraint on his other friend Tim [Page] who is a hippy and smokes grass and pot and whatever. Not overwhelmingly exciting if it is just that. Tim has a girl friend too called Linda who is English (so is Tim) and she has been hitch hicking across the world for the last five years. Then there is a boy called Rob Straus who is a GI but sneeks away and comes as often as he can. This is the hard core but there are lots of others. A million dollar brain fellow from a think tank and one or two Vietnamese girls and a German Canadian who has the same name as the Red Baron. We dine out also every night together while Far works.

"Yesterday he was flying around near Laos for seven hours with his chum general Stilwell and had a marvellous time while I was green with envy. Helicopter at tree level and over unimaginably beautiful country. Alas discretion forbids him to ask to take me too. So I am quite *désoeuvrée* most of the day. I did find my old friends the Viet ladies of three years ago and went to hospitals and orphanages and things but they are much better organised now and one cant just walk in and help as one did then. Saigon in general looks much cleaner and less war like somehow in spite of the rockets. One fell last night about three blocks from here, but it was not as loud as I had expected. There is much less garbage on the streets and hardly any rats. It is astonishingly relaxed.

"On the whole except for the delight of seing David, I am rather counting the days until Thursday when we leave for Hong Kong all three of us. It will be so wonderful travelling with David. But I did have one marvellous day yesterday. Seven of us bundled into a car sort of 'borrowed' by John from his establishment (David having lost the keys to his which anyway only holds two and two squashed ones) and we drove down into the Delta and over the river (the mighty Mekong) to an island which has been given by a kind of gentleman's agreement between Saigon and the Viet Cong to a monk called the coconut monk and his disciples who are now about two thousand. He was an engineer studied at the Ecole des Mines etc but about twenty years ago formed his own sect (they grow here like political parties do in France) and kept a vow of silence for ten years but then started to talk again. He is a pacifist and a vegetarian and believes in goodness and peace and particularly that he will bring the end of the war to Vietnam. So he and his followers live on this island in a village built on stilts in the water (the jungly bit is full of Viet Cong so we were not allowed to wonder about) which is clean and sort of medieval looking with one tiny narrow street winding through it to the main *place* where there is the temple looking just like a fun fair.

"You cannot believe the odd combination of exquisite beauty and total vulgarity. The temple is a kind of bright green *papier mâché* cave with lotuses grown over it and then there is a big round *place*, surrounded by pink and blue and yellow dragons. In the middle of this lies the conference table. This is a table built by the Dao [monk] himself of six different symbolic woods and around this some day soon the South, Hanoi, the NLF, the Viet Cong the Americans the Russians and the Chinese will meet and fast and pray and be inspired and the war will end and peace and love will come to the whole world. The Dao himself is the last Stylite. Behind the temple there are two large columns joined by a tiny ladder and at the top of one is heaven and the other paradise and the ladder is the rainbow that joins them. He lives up there one in day and one at night and very rarely comes down.

"He has not eaten anything but coco nuts in twenty years and never lies down to sleep. He is four foot something and alas looks exactly like Alfred E. Newman in 'Mad.' But his disciples are fabulous. They pray to both Jesus and Budha six times a day and use both the sign of the cross and the bowing to the ground of the Muslims. We arrived just in time for noon prayer. The most beautiful boy I have ever seen was tolling the huge bell in a bright yellow bell tower and from everywhere the faithful came to the central *place*. They wear robes of simple cotton and trousers but they are deep deep egg plant colour or chocolate brown and have faded variously to every shade down to pale pink and light mauve. They dont cut their hair and wear sort of turbans each one tied somehow differently and they have the most beautiful faces I have ever seen.

"Everyone like a prince out of a Chinese fairy tale and a kind of imobility and spiritual quality which made us all feel like brash city folk. And their movements are exactly like the Khmer statues. One has the fealing of a story book or an ancient frozen temple suddenly come alive. They gave us sugar cane juice and coco nut milk and bananas and we sat and watched the praying and listening to the great bells and it was fantastic. So much so that on our way back when we met the first tanks guns etc we all jumped. We had quite forgotten there *was* a war going on."

David had managed to store up seventeen days of leave, so he joined us in Hong Kong and we went on from there *en famille* to Japan and South Korea, where Bill Porter, by now U.S. ambassador in Seoul, put us all up in a nice guest house. Marina's diary summed up this special holiday:

April 5, Hong Kong: "David arrived. Went wandering around the city. Everything is so beguiling, so tempting."

April 6, Macao: "Dream day. To Macao. We went sight seing, antiquing and to the Casino. Macao is so pretty. Looked across at China. Returned on ferry with strip-tease show. Quite an improper day for Easter. But such fun."

April 9, Hong Kong: "Went to the New Territories. Shopped at tiny village and picked our own fish and crabs and shrimps off the fishing boats and took them to a restaurant to cook. It was lovely."

April 19, Seoul: "Took off for Kanghwa island in a buss of the Royal Asiatic Society. Charming boy called Michael Gore was our Gruppen Führer. Crossed by ferry. Spent the night in old Korean inn. Eiderdowns of many coloured silk on indol floor, which means beaten earth heated from below. Oddly comfortable."

April 23, Seoul: "David left this morning. So sad but what a lovely month it has been. I must light a dozen candles."

She wrote Marinette on April 26: "Polar left on Wednesday and it killed me to see him go. He really was marvellous. The best of travelling companions gay and eager and curious and just as happy shopping as sight seing which will make some future wife happy it is so rare in a man. We went scrounging about Seoul for Celadon and he has become very learned about porcelaine and looks so impressive that in most places they asked him if he was a collector or a dealer. In his way he is a collector. He has ten huge plates and bowls of Vietnam pottery which are seventeenth century and perfectly lovely.

"How David will get back to ordinary mortal living I dont know, what with ambassadorial treatment here, suites in Hong Kong double rooms in Japan and just a slice of smoked salmon and strawberries for a snack in the orchid room when Far was working. David I may say responded to this kind of life as if he has never known any other and the flourish with which he signs bills in hotels made me chuckle. Korea was rather fun. The Porters, our hosts are the dearest people and kind.

"Eventually we managed to attach ourselves to a Royal Asiatic society excursion and went off for a two day trip to an Island. The first day was lovely and we pic nicked by a pretty temple in a pine forrest with sheets of wild pink azelea and also climbed to the top of a mountain with a superb view and remnant of a minimum great wall. That night we slept in a wonderful old Korean Inn so evocative of Kublai Khan type movies that had a group of wild Mongolian horsemen with pointed helmets and shields and bows and arrows shared our rooms we would not have been at all surprised. There was a large interior courtyard and lots of little ones and all the rooms had sliding doors a little like living in a chest of drawers but lovely.

"They have earthenware floors heated from underneith and it is most delicious to sleep on the floor on soft silk matresses covered with silk eiderdowns and have the heat come up under you like an electric blancket *à l'envers*. We were given a fantastic Korean dinner for which the only rule was if you can't recognise what you are eating just better dont ask what it is. Some of it was quite nice and some ghastly. But we were plied with rice wine and David had to keep up with the men and then they went on into the village and drank some more, so poor old David was sick all the rest of the night which was quite difficult seing that we were sleeping four or five in a room and he had to step over four cadavers on his way in and back. The next morning he had the largest hangover he has ever known and when at breakfast we were presented all over again with the unmentionable soup and sugar coated deep fried sea weed David turned sea weed colour all over and was only saved by a thimble full of hot tea left over in our thermos from the pic nic.

"My trouble is that when people say island to me, I naturally expect some land surrounded by deep blue water. Alas. The great Han river which starts god knows where in China, flows out around here and this island is surrounded by several miles of deep *mousse au chocolat* type mudd. So it was not very pretty sea-wards but the hills were lovely and full of wild flowers and pheasant and wild geese. A nice Korean Marine major had promised to take us to the place which is only one mile away from North Korea to look down into it and listen to their beastly radio screaming out insult and invective to us all, and although it was raining cats and dogs by the time we got to head quaters we could not refuse. We were then bundled into two open army trucks as our dear Royal Society buss could not drive up on the tiny cause-way between miles of rice paddies. The front truck with all the ladies in it broke down several times in three miles and it took us all told three hours to get there look at nothing as the fog was too thick and get back again and by then even my girdle was squeezable, and our shoes like PT boats. But everyone was in good spirits and good sports and we laughed a lot. But that was our only adventure and the rest alas was rather dull.

"The prime minister gave a Kaesang party for the men. This is a sort of super Geisha party where pretty ladies cut up your food in bits and pop it into your mouth and everyone sings little ditties and dances. Far's lady was called Hopeful angel and she made Far tango much to David's delight. He found it all 'so innocent' while all the older men felt such roués and gay blades. But Mr. Porter said that if one stays after the noodle soup then things got better. They all claim they left before the noodle soup. The prime minister sent me a present and I was so hoping it would be a bit of porcelaine or some brocade which in Korea is fabulous but when the packet four foot square arrived it was the most ghastly laquer and mother of pearl vase you have ever seen and the only way I could have taken it with me even had I wished to would have been to travel in it. So I bequeathed it to the Embassy guest house much to our hosts sorrow.

"David left on Wednesday direct for Saigon and we the next day for Tokyo. On arrival we found a cable from him asking me to go to the hospital here and try and find his friend Tim whom I wrote to you about from Saigon (the one who gave me the pot cigarette) who had been very badly wounded a few days ago. I was luckily able to find him and imagine, he had a piece of shrapnel right through his brain and god knows how many other wounds. But by a miracle he had neither lost his faculties nor even his sight. He is paralysed both leg and arm on one side but it is such a miracle that he is not only not dead but not a blithering idiot, that the doctors have every hope he may recover completely. But oh darling the things I saw. I did not sleep all night at the thought of the agony some of those boys in that ward were going through. The one in the next bed had no legs no arms and one eye missing. A nightmare. God help us."

We were in Honolulu for Marina's birthday. She wrote in her diary:

May 1, Honolulu: "Birthday. Cables from Marinette, David. Cards from Monica, Isabella. We had dinner downstairs and Cy sweetly gave me a cake, candles, asparagus, strawberries. All the things that make it a birthday. Also a lovely fat check as well as the rug from Hong Kong."

May 2, Honolulu: "We went deep sea fishing. I was seasick for nine solid hours. Cy caught 13 fish."

She wrote Marinette: "I have arrived at the conclusion that anyone over thirty eight who appears in a bathing suit should'nt. You cannot imagine the multitude of horrors in this hotel. All old (like me) and worse all bound to be rich else they would not be here, all frizzy haired pot bellied dressed in psychedelic coloured mumus and the men in long shorts and bright shirts all with loud New York voices and it makes one want to run and hide. Still poor old Far was looking forward to it so much and then of course the very day we arrived (luckily we had two Mondays this month so he was ill only one of them) he got a really bad attack of gout.

"Thank god at least it happened here where we are in Byzantine luxury and a view on the pool with my three old friends the dolphins gamboling around in the water and there IS a moon and a lagoon even though it is not yet June and the frangipani smells like a dream.

"I think your father has a built in 'keeper-going' when he has work to do and collapses the moment he can afford to workwise. However today he is better and has gone out to sit in the sun. Tomorrow we are going fishing."

Later Marina confided to her diary:

May 22, New York: "Fascinating evening with Commander Bucher of the Pueblo [a U.S. naval vessel surrendered to North Korea]. Such a sad thin weary face. I wanted to stroke his hair and hold his poor hands. So nice. So tragic when a modest quiet man is pitchforked into history."

I had just written a book that became a best seller and the publishers sent me on a nationwide tour to tout it. Marina wrote Marinette from New York:

"I have been reading it over again to find last minute mistakes in order to correct them for the second edition. It is marvellous really. What is so astounding is that our own history, the last twenty years, which should be as clear as one's own life, suddenly sound like history. Léon Blum and Herriot one reads about like Cromwell and François 1er. And when you read what people said and did. The same people in five year intervals. And you see the British fifteen years ago violently anti-Israel and the Russians their champions, and in no time at all the complete reversal. And it happens right under one's very nose and one is taken by surprise *quand même*. I can hardly put the book down."

She wrote to David at the same time: "Far saw the president [Nixon] but dont tell people and he was extremely nice and gave Far a photograph signed with admiration and deep respect from his friend. Also [Henry] Kissinger who suddenly realised that Far was your Far and said oh but of course his thessis was so good and he did not fall into any of the clichés so prevelent these days. Nice." [Kissinger had graded David's thesis on Vietnam.]

On June 17, from Paris, she sent him another letter betraying an extraordinary intuition: "For the first time I found the US had a sense of doom about it. Vietnam is out as a subject unless you want a fist fight. The other subject is the 'young' and there too it is either such clichés that one wants to scream, or then the ones who try so much to be with it, that you also find yourself arguing. And the race question or the war or poverty all seem to me to be used as alibis and simple explanations of the *malaise* but not really the deep down cause of it all. Perhaps it is that America is dying of *gigantisme*.

"She has the same problems as everyone else only everything is magnified by the very size of it, even the good things, like goodness or ideology or charity or self knowledge, end up by becoming man eating qualities and these are so much harder to fight, as they are good; evil is so much simpler to struggle against.

"Far went off on his book promoting tour and came back like a raped debutante. He has led after all a sheltered life far from the horrors of television and the 'hard sell' or even the soft one, and was amazed at the cheapness and shallowness and vulgarity of most of it. Also he had the fealing that the sell has become such a perfect science, that the thing sold has passed to quite a secondary plane, which is not too bad when it is soap or detergent but dangerous when it is political ideas, books, art etc. He came back exhausted and also the doctor saw his hand and told him it is the same thing that Uncle Arthur had, and will have to be operated on some day.

"Weekend at the Haywards was delightful. I argued with Mathias [a Hungarian-French friend] but not violent. He was full of questions about you and we played bridge together and won every rubber. But he made a booboo as he kept saying I *know* I have something to do tonight but cant think what, oh well *tant pis*, until at about six thirty a call came and an icy voice asked for him and it was Jacky [Kennedy-Onassis] who had asked him to the last gala performance of Sleeping Beauty with Margot Fonteyn and Nureev. So she was furious that he was still in the country and said you bloody well get on a train and come even if you are three hours late. The ballet lasts four. So sheepishly he had to leave but called us the next morning to describe the evening which he said was extraordinary because they had a souper at the Trees later sit down four course dinner at two in the morning and that Onassis and Nureev took to each other like two peasants of genius which they both are, and that it was fire works with the most brilliant chatter about everything from dancing to massacres and sex.

"After that went to Washington and stayed with the Alsops which was lovely socially by which I mean I went to a lovely party at the Bruces and met a dazzling black lady called the Princesse of Toro who is the number two model after Veroushka and deserves it, and Mr. Kissinger. The Bradens* also gave a nice dinner for me and I sat next to the Black commissioner for public safety of DC who looks like the twin of the fellow in I Spy. His wife also talked to me and how she knows she is black I dont understand as she was a blond compared to me. At one moment she looked around and said I have *had* equality. I can go to white dinners like this one seven nights a week if I want to and frankly I dont want to. What I want now is Money. Like all of *you*. So I said dont look at me, if you are wishfully thinking, set your sights much higher else you will be awfully dissapointed. I dont have one bean. To which she said, 'no matter, you feel and look rich.' Compliment? A strange woman.

"I read the Talese book on the NY Times called 'The Power and the Kingdom' and I have rarely read anything with such genius for the half truth. He manages to say about somebody he was beautiful upright noble wore exquisite clothes and had clean finger nails, and make it sound as if he is calling him a son of a bitch and a traitor. He too insists on saying I am related to the royal familly and Cy married me out of snobism. He also says Far had a lady of the aristocracy or if not that a very rich one in every port as it were and was interrested mainly in women and wine. Ho Hum."

On July 2, Marina wrote Avis Bohlen from Paris:

"The British Embassy party, the so called *deuxième affaire* Soames [the British ambassador] was really an enormous success. They had nine hundred people more than half from England and more than half not over twenty. I must say they looked adorable all of them and so gay and full of life. I sat in a corner and watched and thought how sad to be old and how nice to be old enough to enjoy sitting in a corner and watching. Somehow I think the English enjoy themselves more than the French and if this had been a completely French party it would not have been half as gay. There was a kind of informality about it in spite of Princesses Anne and Alexandra and ladies in waiting and curtseying and stuff. The house looking gay with

---

* Tom and Joan Braden, Washington friends.

pink tulle, curtains absolutely everywhere and tons of flowers and a most accomodating full moon somehow hung in exactly the right place in one gap in the trees. I have never seen so many beautiful women. Odette Pol Roger ravishing and Marie Rothschild in palest grey chiffon. And the English. But dazzling. Alas there were so many people that one hardly saw anyone for more than a glimpse and we found out next day about hundreds who were there and we never saw at all. I only danced twice. Once with a twenty year old boy whom I knew when he was four, and took me out for a shake kind of thing, and then to the other extreme with [former British ambassador, Lord] Gladwyn who walzed me around like some huge unleashed bear."

Marina flew to Greece with Benjamin Beagle for a summer holiday while I took off on a special French Boeing for the Apollo 11 moon shot. Greece worked its usual magic. She wrote David of a trip to visit Paddy and Joan Leigh Fermor in Mani, the rugged tip of the Peloponnesos:

"The place is a dream. Just like a nineteenth century drawing of Greece. Monumental mountains in the back ground, going in wave after wave of bluer to blue to pale, and in front dark acropolis-like hills with sheer drops and cypress trees in clusters. One could almost see the *evzone* [Greek soldier with skirt-like uniform] with a musket in the back-ground and the wicked turk lying at his feet. This is the heart of wild Mani and all over one sees abandoned towers and baby forterreses and churches.

"And Paddy has managed to make his house, which is not really finished yet, look like a combination of all three and as if it had been there five hundred years. Monastic in some parts of it, with arches and collonades, it opens up into a huge living room with Turkish style wooden window and sofas all round, stone floors, and courtyards everywhere done in pebbles like ours but only with geometric designs like the ancient Greek mosaics and he has put here and there a row of brownish red together with the green pebbles and the white and it looks too beautiful. They have no electricity but little church *kandilis* [oil lamps] everywhere and it is fantastic; not that we needed even the *kandilis* as it was full moon when I arrived and we could almost read by the moon alone. The sea is at their feet on one side, down a sheer staircase built in the rock, and on the other a bit further away through their olive grove lemons cypress and then kitchen garden with tomatoes and *melintzanes* [eggplants] and peppers and everything that smells sweet like *vassiliko* [basil] and thyme and marjoram.

"I had the most enchanting day and they really are two of the most civilised people alive. A pro pos of their wedding we got to the Credo and thence to the *Filioque* [a cause of schism between Orthodox and Roman churches] and down came the reference books and from the *Filioque* to Julian the Apostate and more books and more quotes and in the middle Paddy jumping up and saying 'I do think we need a fountain here, or another tree there,' and back to some other totally disconnected but equally fascinating subject, all day and more than half the night. I had to leave on Saturday morning, to my sorrow as both Seferis [Nobel Prize poet] and Ghika the painter were arriving for the week and the combination of minds and learnings of those three would have been utterly beguiling."

That August she wrote Michael Edwards from Spetsais: "You just cant imagine how glorious everything is. Blue sky and sea and rock and golden moon and sun and stars and from every corner a pleasing smile and gentle cry of welcome, 'Marinaki Mou' [my little Marina] friend and family and tree and thorn all loving all familiar all open armed and warm and oh so beautiful. I brought my family here to the island and got them all settled and going. I find the role of *Gruppen Führer* a bit alien to my caracter which would much rather be lead, than leading, but no one else can do it here on account of language and other barriers. So I market and get the boats and decide where we are going and when and how but I must say my *troupeau* is very meek and apreciative and there is never any argument and they all seem to like my plans so all is well. My only problem is calculating properly how many tons of fruit and vegetables and bread and cheese seventeen people are able to consume. It is fabulous.

"Having got the household going I then vanished for a week on a private holiday of my own back to Athens where I really had a dream time. I went to the theatre nearly every night and to several concerts to hear my friends perform and then go back stage and discuss matters. The lovely thing about belonging to a small country like this is that sooner or later your own generation does everything so that now all the people I was at school with are become ministers and painters actors musicians and producers poets and failures, and each one in his way IS the life of the country. Then after dinner or play or concert I meet one or the other and listen for hours to stories of their lives loves etc.

"What a relief to be once again with flaming people who consider it a duty and essential to their atavism and respect of their ancestors to invest their slightest cardiac flutter, their mildest emotions, with Sophoclean adjectives and Homeric exageration. They burn they quiver they have never felt anything like it. It is eternal it is unique it is all absorbing. And by sheer force of exageration and the magic of words these mild sensations do end up by being unique and eternal even when they last one glorious moon lit night. It seems to me this is the only way to live and stay young and alive. I have listened to more tales of love and misery (delicious) in the last ten days than in the years of Paris London or New York. Blessed be the exagerators for they shall inherit the kingdom of this earth."

As the lovely summer ended, Marina recorded in her diary:

September 8, Spetses: "David sent a cable: Have frangipani will travel."

September 9, Spetses: "David arrived at last. Skinny, long hair, but divine. Funny, covered with gifts. Talkative."

September 12, Spetses: "Absolute deluge. Now the first cyclamen will appear. We all dined at Spetsopoula [island belonging to Stavros Niarchos].

All lights out in Spetses from storm so the ladies had half their eye makeup. Arrived as bright young things. Returned more like *la retraite de Russie*. Soaked."

September 18, Spetses: "Stavros, Bob [Joyce], Peter [Payne] played poker here. Bob lost to Cy, Peter to Stavros. Too bad. Stavros should have lost to all."

I flew off to the Arab world and Marina (with Benjamin Beagle) to Paris. On October 9 she wrote David, back in Vietnam from his brief leave:

"Back in slavery. Shoes hurt. A desk piled high with bills, invitations, letters, telephone calls. And right back into this modern world where one can listen to the astronautes chatting from the moon, but cant get local telephones to answer. Or a man to fix the door bell which is brocken or the cleaner to give one back a badly needed coat in less than three weeks. I am sure I shall get back to the train of Paris life and enjoy it too, in no time at all, but for the moment I am on the fringe.

"Last night I was invited by the Embassy to a gala at the Palais de Chaillot for the astronautes and I must say it was very thrilling to hear three thousand people shout and applaude and call *'Vive l'Amérique.'* *Ça nous change un peu.* The three astronautes themselves were so nice and modest and genuine."

From Marina's diary:

October 21, Paris: "Sat between Ionescu and Chagal at dinner. Rare honor and privilege and Ionescu was dull as hell. How sad. Chagal more relaxed, chatty. Talked a bit of Russia, his youth, etc. He said he had never been poor as at once he found a *'maecinas'* who gave him 150 francs a month in Paris."

On November 22 she wrote David:

"Far appeared with the twelve volumes of his book and we have to correct it and cut it, as quickly as possible. You cant think what time this takes. I *know* I have seen this refference to the Hapsburg lip somewhere before but where, *et pan, on se tappe le livre* all over again. But it is fascinating and I am most encouraged. I mean by that, it is different enough from the last one.

"Here the conversations are much longer and on specific things and of course so near (and yet so far) to us all, that one is always delighted to read one's own history. I say so far, because you cant imagine how war-of-the-roses-ish things like Cyprus, or the re-armement of Germany or the Northern Tier alliance, sound. As for Vietnam . . . Ah me how terrible all this business of Pinkville and the rest. America is really a bran new pheanomenon it seems to me and we are just barely begining to know this. Think what would have happened in any other wars if every time one side shot someone on the other, there were questions asked in Parliament. Not that this does'nt alas sound extra so to speak. It is heartbreaking.

"We gave a very fancy dinner here. We had the Couves [de Murville]*

---

* Maurice Couve de Murville, French foreign minister and prime minister.

and Malraux and Louise [de Vilmorin] and the Van der Kemps and the Embiricos and the Bentincks and the Clermont Tonnerres and Chip and Avis arrived unexpectedly so gave the party a real *raison d'être*. I was petrified as the last time I sat next to Couve in his own Foreign Office he did not even say pass me the salt. But defeat suits him better than glory apparently because he was most chatty and for him even merry and so all went well. Malraux was marvellous. Every story he told we had heard already but this did not detract from its magic one bit. Like listening over and over to one's favourite Beethoven or Beatle record. The food was good except that the madly expensive turbot I got, Far thought was haddock. Really! They all stayed very late even Malraux who is seventy and lives in lovely sin with Louise in the country."

On December 10, Marina wrote David: "I have not been going out much as I have been working so hard on Far's book which is fascinating but hard work. I get more and more discouraged by politics and politicians as I read the utter nonsense they have said *à travers les années*. A talk of Far's with Mr. Pineau in fifty seven when he says the only trustworthy ally of the French in the Middle East are the Israelis. A talk with de Gaulle saying *les Arabes c'est de la poussière*. Talks with Dulles that make your hair curl. A conversation with Cocteau ten years ago in which he says in ten years all the youth of the communist countries will want to be capitalists and all the young capitalists will want to be communists. At least he was right, but then he was not a politician."

As the year was ending, she sent David another letter: "On Xmas eve we went to an extraordinary midnight mass at the Sainte Chapelle. There had not been one there since before the Revolution and the last King to be present was Louis XIV. Then Ambassador Shriver asked the Minister of Culture if he could borrow it for a joint Franco-American service. *Il fallait y penser*. The Minister was delighted and then the Shrivers brought over a fantastic *cantatrice* Anna Moffo, to sing and *le père* Bruckberger (you know the one who tossed his robes off and became a major in the war, who lived in America a lot and wrote controversial books and you met him once I think at Diana Cooper's) to officiate. The vestements were designed by Matisse, and the American priest recited parts of Murder in the Cathedral, while later medieval musicians trumpeted the announcement of the holy birth. The whole thing was fantastic and the Sainte Chapelle illuminated was almost more beautiful than by sunlight.

"And yet . . . I dont know quite how to explain it, especially I who if I ever do anything intelligent or witty or nice I long for the whole world to know about it. But somehow the publicity seeking side of it, the whole appearance of all the children as acolytes, the photographers on the alter, even the singing which was beautiful but oh so temporal (she sang Holy night and *Gloria in excelsis Deo* as if it were Mozart or Wagner) gave me a tiny uncomfortable feeling of phoniness. I may be wrong, but anyway it was a glorious spectacle if not a moment's religious cardiac flutter. Then afterwards we went back to the Embassy for *souper* and had onion soup and caviar which was a delicious if unwise way to prepare for the morrow and a great Turkey lunch. Which I cooked myself by the way.

"Tomorrow I have to go to a funeral alas. The husband of Far's old old friend Grace ex-Radziwill, now Dudley. He died on Saturday and so did poor Louise de Vilmorin who had had dinner here only about two weeks ago. She died after a few days of flue which is rather marvellous. And at the peek of a great new love affair with Malraux at the age of 67. *Pas mal.* So much better for a woman like her, or anyone for that matter, to die at the top sort of. Of course better not to die at all for a while but then . . ."

And somewhat ruefully in her little diary:

December 31, Paris: "For me the sixties have changed the world more than any others in the life of people."

XII

January 1970 - December 1971

The new decade of the seventies began happily for Marina because we found a modern, cheery apartment to replace our dilapidated old house which had grown too large for our childrenless family and too difficult for our aged servants to take care of. We signed our lease and then rushed off to take a health cure in Austria.

From Marina's diary:

January 2, Paris: "Got an apartment!!! Cy saw it this morning and liked it."

January 5, Schruns, Austria: "Arrived at Bludenz. Took taxi to Schrunz. Unpacked. Saw doctor. He prescribed baths, massage. Goodbye marrons glacés, spaghetti, bread. Started on our dreary diet."

On January 18, 1970, she wrote David, who was about to wind up his trip in Vietnam. First she cautioned him about a motor tour he was planning with a girl friend:

"After two years in Vietnam I am sure you know better than I do what is good for you and what is'nt so go with our blessing but for god's sake be careful. I dont see her changing a tyre. Of all travelling companions I would say she is the least useful and *débrouillarde* but obviously has other qualities far better than those of a scout mistress. My precious I count the days for you.

"Our stay in Schrunz far less unpleasant than I expected. It was just like the story of the Russian student in Rilke. I went armed with fifty good books tapistery even double crostics and above all a thousand unrequited Xmas cards to reply to and somehow never got down to doing anything. Between sleeping late and Far hurrying me off to a quick brisk in the slippery snow and then the SS taking over and giving us massage and exercise and mud baths and things, I managed three detective stories and one book on Charles of Orleans just to keep it a tiny bit of mind improving."

On February 6 she again wrote David: "I spent the most agreable weekend imaginable in England looking for furniture. Far was going to Italy anyway, and Michael Edwards happened to be going by car to Lincolnshire and Yorkshire that weekend, and said one could pick up all kinds of bits and pieces in the country cheaper than anywhere else.

"I did manage to get a nice Regency table, a side board and a little desk for two hundred pounds. We visited Lincoln cathedral which is beautiful and then drove on to spend the night with some charming friends of Michael's called Fletcher with a son who is a proffesor of medieval history at the University of York and a daughter who lectures at the Victoria and Albert on eighteenth century furniture and architecture. It was enchanting and bright and intelligent and gay.

"Then Saturday morning we went off to York which is only half an hour away, and visited the cathedral there too which is fabulous except that it is sinking in to the marshes. Funny thing is that as it sinks the foundations appear and turn out to be remains of the Roman barracks and covered with grafiti of Roman barrack-room humor which changes not a whit from present day toilet wall scribblings. So funny to think of so much worship built on scatological and other blue jokes.

"Later we went to have lunch at Nostell Priory and it really was kind of black humor funny to go from buying a regency table with trembling heart, to a house where even the toilet seats were made by Chippendale. Rowland [St. Oswald] was saying that he found on the inventory 'eight pairs of fire tongs' and thought how silly who in the world put these on the inventory together with the Poussins (7) the Holbein and the Breughel, until he discovered that even these were designed by Chippendale to match the legs of the chairs and the moldings of the Angelica Kauffmann cealings. Ah me."

On February 18, from Paris, she told David: "The nicest thing happened. One morning Far opened his mail and the fattest enveloppe was from the White House, an invitation to the dinner for Mr. Pompidou. I think the President does not know we live in Paris because this is the second invitation this year. So we looked at each other, and grinned and decided that one simply cant regret two invitations by the President in a row so we are off on Saturday to dine at the White House. Naturally my first question was What shall I wear, and Far threw a pillow at me. But what would HE wear was even more urgent, and we got out his tail coat and to his great pride it still fits him and with a new colar and tie from Lanvin and his waistcoat freshly starched he will do quite nicely.

"Liliane de Rothschild has lent me a splendid dark green silk coat all the way to the ground which has already been to the coronation of the Shah of Persia lent to Princesse de Metternich, and to the Elysée lent to someone else and now to the White House on me. Not bad for one coat.

"But the sad thing is that an hour after we had accepted, Marinette called up and she is having a Ceasarian on the 26th. So instead of taking advantage of this little trip to see a few friends, I shall have to take the plane the very next morning at dawn in order to get to London in time to greet my grandson the next day. I told Marinette to take a double room, because I shall probably need a hospital bed as much as she.

"Alas alas I have started packing your things from your room and it hardly seems possible that you were playing with dinky toys when we first lived here. I am afraid I have to give away your electric train. I struggled with myself but thought that we really live in a world where it is sadly impossible for children to inherit their father's trains. By the time you know where you will be living and get married and have children, it would have cost its weight in gold to transport that train from place to place. But it saddened me. *I have put all your Greek* things and *letters* and other treasures knife collection stamps etc. *in a safe iron trunk* so you will have some souvenirs *quand même*."

The hectic end of February was confided by Marina to her diary:

February 24, Washington: "Staying with Bohlens. Dinner at the White House for Pompidou. Touching, provincial."

Less succinctly, she wrote David from Paris on March 2: "The Bohlens were as dear and warm and adorable as ever, and Tuesday was naturally spent in seing as many friends in so little a time as possible. Alsops Harrimans Mrs Guest who asked lovingly after you.

"Getting the ladies dressed was as nothing compared to the men who are admitedly two of the worst dressed men on two continents but *quand même*. First crisis that Francisco had ironed Far's stiff shirt with such a hot iron that all the stiffness had melted away so he could not fix a stiff colar to a soggy shirt and there was a good inch of neck between it and the said shirt like the clowns in circuses who wear only the front you know. I left our room in a hurry as Far's temper was at over forty degrees, and took refuge with Avis but things were just as bad there because Mr. Bohlen's shirts were TOO stiff and he could not get the buttons in and in his agonies he had crumpled the whole thing as if a bear had walked all over his front.

"Well eventually we got them all fairly presentable and drove off with Mrs. B driving. Imagine our horror and giggles when we got into the hand shaking line, to suddenly see our men's backs, both covered from head to toe with long white hair. Mrs. Bohlen had forgotten to clean the car, and they had spent the week end shooting in Georgia and had at one point several large white labradors in the car. Hence the hair. We were laughing so hard we almost shamed ourselves face to face with two Presidents.

"But to go back. The arrival is marvellous with all the Marines dressed like in the movies of the Wild West, and making one feel at once like so many Scarlett O'Haras. And then one stands about for a while greeting friends and acquaintances and then four trumpeters appear and the whole thing takes on a Sheakespearian fealing when the loud speaker announces 'The President of the United States and Mrs. Nixon, the President of the Republic of France etc.' By that time one is in such a state of emotion and receptivity one sort of expects Henry the 8th to appear, so that when these four rather mediocre people arrive in the door way, its almost like a gag, visualy speaking. However one must not be undemocratic and this IS after all the age of the common man. Anyway then we all filed by and shook hands, and then went in to dinner which was alas as bad as all huge official dinners can ever be.

"I was fairly lucky as I had a French journalist on one side and a Cherokee Indian chief (in white tie alas not feathers) on the other. I would have preffered Mr. Kissinger but he was not *bout de table* as I was. It lasted for ever, and then there were speaches and nobody mercifully brought up Lafayette but almost. I kept wondering what would ever happen if instead of the 'lyrical and sonorous reafirmation of the obviously untrue' someone sometime made a speach saying exactly what they thought. *Ça fait rêver* . . . Anyway we had all the *Liens traditionels entre nos deux pays* etc and then it was over and we all filed out.

"And just as I was taking a cup of coffee what do I see, but dear old Papa standing grining between the two Presidents and chatting away. He told me later that as he was walking out a hand came out and grabbed him and a voice said 'Come over here Cy you know these people.' It was Mr. N. and 'these people' were the Pompidous. Then the President said to Pompidou, 'You know Cy has been a good friend to me for many years, and always good to me even when I was nothing which proves not only that he is a good man but also a good reporter.' To which Pompidou answered 'I can confirm this as he has been MY friend too when I was nothing.' Nice no? Well Far was delighted and all set for a nice talk when Alas we were ushered into yet another room and sat on little gold chairs for the 'entertainment.'

"You know I am usualy *très bon public*. I would sit happily even if Beagle were singing. But this was passed even my endurance. A miss Peggy Lee, older than I and a bad singer of sirca 1935 songs. WHY? Either have a string quartet or if you want to play up to the misguided idea of the Pompidous being with it, then give them some real stuff. And to top it all she sang nine songs. Too shaming. And of course by the time she finished her yapping it was all over, and we went home. Still it was exciting being there and I am thrilled to have been asked. Then the next day I almost missed my plane to London because of the traffic. But got it and even got three seats alone again which allowed me twenty winks before the ghastly orange juice was flung at me at what was three in the morning for me and nine in London. I took a cab straight to the house where I was met by Adrian with a grin from ear to ear who said. 'Your grandson has just arrived.'

"We flew to the hospital and Marinette was only just opening one eye, and Jonathan was probably the most beautiful twenty minute old man in the world. He looks just like Marinette and like Far. That is, he is entirely made up of a mouth and a nose and nothing else. But a dream. An actress was having illegitimate twins in the next room but ours was better.

"Far is still in the US but coming back on Thursday. Publishers very happy with second volume and like it even better than the first."

Two days later she wrote Avis Bohlen: "As you know I have been engaged in the all absorbing process of becoming a grand mother. To a BOY. You know I never thought she would make it. So much has gone so well for all of us for so long (touch wood) that I thought perhaps this one tiny dissapointement was due. Well no. Even in this the gods have been good to us and he is a bonny boy consisting in all of two large pink feet, a mouth from ear to ear, and an unmistakable Sulz-Lada nose. Nothing else. He was six pounds something ounces, which is not very big but as all Ceasarian babies, all pink and fresh looking and so adorable it was hard not to pick him up and squeeze him to bits. We took Jessica to see him on Saturday and she was intreagued and seemed pleased, but not half as much as with the rabbits in the zoo, which followed our outing.

"And now I am in that most unenviable state of moving. I thought I had done a bit of throwing away before leaving, and yesterday I went into the *foutoir* and found Oh god, box after box of tangled fishing tackle sleeping bags with holes in them boy scout equipment, a box full of sneakers, dressing up stuff including two father Xmas beards, on and on until I really feel that posessions are the root of all evil."

Marina wrote Christine Claudel (in French) on April 27: "The older I get the more I believe that nothing in the world equals friendship. That marvelous assurance that everything will always be true and good between two beings and that this state is unchangeable."

From the diary:

May 17, Royaumont: "Staying with Liliane and Elie de Rothschild. The *muguet* [lily of the valley] is fantastic. Walked long and far with Beagle. Picked biggest possible bunch of *muguet*."

May 24, Launay: "With Jean and Gilberte de Montulé [née Léauté]. Cy fished non-stop. Thirteen fish. I stole a most enormous bunch of lilacs. The theft worth all the weekend."

On May 29 she told Catherine Negroponte: "Cy leaves for Moscow on Monday and I go to London to see the grand children. Jonathan looks so much like Cy Marinette says it is a miracle he was not born with a typewriter in his hand. Then even though I cant quite believe it, David is coming home to Paris on the 8th or 9th. After two and a half years of anxiety and so so far away, can hardly wait. And if he gets here on time I will take him with me to Athens for ten days to see my mother who is so sad as none of us are going to Spetses this summer."

The next day Marina wrote Susan Mary Alsop: "We were cought between laughter and despair the other day; Cy has been having endless discussions with the Macmillan lawyers about every line in the book, for libel and the last straw came when they telephoned transatlantically to find out anxiously what '*crise de foie*' ment and was it disparaging in any way. Probably they thought it was deniying one's religion or something. Blissful Americans who dont know where the *foie* [liver] is.

"We went to see M.A.S.H. this afternoon which is a sick sick comedie about a medical unit in Korea with jokes over people's dead and wounded bodies, and I felt very very sad suddenly at the fealing that I have lived too long. I feel a stranger and lost in so much going on around me these days. We have just had two more mini-riot nights at the Quartier Latin, over the dissolution of the Gauche Prolétaire."

I flew to Moscow at the start of June and then traveled extensively in the Caucasus. While I was gone, there was tremendous good news. I quote from Marina's diary:

June 8, Paris [with a flower drawn at the top of the page]: "David's return. He looks thin, brown, well. Oh I cant believe he is home."

June 9, Paris: "David accepted at Harvard Business School. Now that he is in he is not sure he wants to go. I feel him kind of lost."

I gave Marina a trip to Greece as a birthday present. She wrote me in Moscow:

"Sweet little Prune. I am so sorry you are coming back to an empty house. I did not leave with any great delight this time, for the first time in my life. And I am sure that once I get there everything will seem lovely. But I find these short trips take it out of one. Too many people to see, too little time to do it in. However Dodo would have been so dissapointed, I could not do this to her. Polar went off to London to go to Marinette's for dinner and the election party and also discovered that Hector [Vasconcelos] and another room mate of Harvard are in England and his friend Bingo Gowry and Oliver [Hoare], so maybe a few days with all his old *parea* will do him good. He will call you on Saturday night and say he will be back almost immediately. I rather like the thought of you two men *en tête à tête* for a few days."

On August 2, Marina wrote to Marinette from Aspen, Colorado: "Here we are being Daniel Boons again. I think I told you that hippies had burned down the old cabin. Well now we are living in the one you and David had but it has a stove and an ice box and a fire place and except for the fact that the WC is even further now than it was from the old cabin and that the stingy nettles seem to be twice as tall, it really is quite cosy. From this cabin as you may remember one has to go over that damn, where we picked the dandylions, to get to the river and as I have already encountered four snakes, I go less and less. But on the other hand it is rather nice to be on our own.

"Poor old Far is out of his mind with pleasure. Alas alas he came down with gout again last night. In his fishing wrist at that. Sick and head achy and in pain. I could cry. Here of all places where he hates to waste three minutes away from the river. At least lets hope it is a small one. As he does not drink a thing and eats almost nothing as well, he may get over it soon. I am trying desperately not to eat. Grape fruit and hard boiled eggs. It is sad because as I have little to do here as you know, cooking became a sort of enjoyable pass time. *Que faire* . . ."

Both our typewriters were out of order so Marina had a spell of muteness. When one was repaired, she wrote Marinette:

"Susan Mary came for a week and I think she enjoyed it even though she hates mountains and this is hardly her home *spirituel*. The first night we gave her trout cought by Cy and beautiful beautiful mushrooms picked by me and wild strawberries so the log cabin atmosphere was perfect. A lady friend of Nancy's had taken me up a high mountain and our jeep broke down almost at once, but we were given lifts by all kinds of nice people and we spent the entire day looking for mushrooms which was a dream. At first we kept any old thing and then as we found more and more of the good ones *morilles* and *chanterelles*, we became snobish and threw the others out. It was a specially good day she said, and she had never seen so many in her life. Then people gave us a lift down also which was good as in this altitude I huff and puff at every step. Poor Susan Mary has bad luck. She had never been West in her life nor seen the Rockies, and she had only a week to spare, and out of it it poured non stop for three whole days, so I was never able to take her to float down the river.

"The other day, this same friend who took us up the mountain, took us to some caves not too far from here. They are the meeting place of all the hippies and they all live there in tents or just out doors in sleeping bags. The extraordinary thing is that more than half of them were stark naked and that a few minutes after the first surprise one hardly even noticed it. The background is so beautiful with strong smooth round rocks, and the water falls splashing everywhere and then a great tall narrow cut in the rock with a sheer fall of about fifty feet and here they all swallow dive into the water below. I almost died the first time I saw one do it, as one thinks he is going right into the rock opposite. But they seem to turn and twist in the very air, and plunge sideways into the roaring waters below.

"It is breath taking and I think they are all stoned when they do it but even so. I went over and pleaded with one not to try and he was sweet and pleasant and said if I did not want he would'nt and then he asked where I came from etc and took a cigarette, and you cannot imagine what an odd sensation it is, looking back on it, to be sitting side by side on a rock with a totally naked young man talking about Paris or other simple normal chit chat. I must say most of them were dazzling looking, long long legs and slender torsoes, and of course tanned almost black. The pink ones looked much more naked. Fewer girls had nothing on, and some were nursing babies. It is all too extraordinary and yet they are nice as can be. And so polite. Rather to our sorrow they addressed us all as Mam, and we in our blue jeans and tea shirts hoping we might perhaps look just a tiny bit hippy also."

Her last Aspen letter was addressed to Michael Edwards on September 1:

"Perhaps because of the rarity of water in Greece, I am so eternally bewitched by streams and rivers. The sheer glorious extravagance of rich pure bubbling sparkling water, flowing endlessly by our cabin fills me with delight. As if I had diamonds or saphires floating by. I can spend hours walking in the stream stumbling or jumping from rock to rock and when it is not too cold, taking off all my clothes (there is not a soul in twenty miles) and slipping into the pools and letting myself be carried downstream until a providential rock stops me from being taken off for ever into whatever Ocean is on the other side.

"Cy luckily established himself as a hermit and an excentric long ago and oddly enough almost everyone I meet, says Your husband is the only sane man among us doing ONLY what he wants to do, one month every three years. They could too of course, but most people really only admire solitude in others. However Cy is blissful and fishes all day every day with the same passion and enormous success. I have cought three little ones and one splendid one, all summer. I catch trees rocks the net and my own trousers much more frequently."

After a Washington visit Marina flew to Paris and I to Cairo, where Nasser had died and been replaced by Sadat. She wrote to Marietta Tree on October 12:

"Cy is in Egypt. I must say it was a bit of luck having bits of his book published in *le Monde*, at the same time as the General's [de Gaulle] memoirs are sweeping the country. It makes people read Cy with greater curiosity because the bits *le Monde* has chosen are mostly on the General."

From her diary:

October 25, Paris: "Far arrived from Cairo. He looks so well. Brown and fit."

October 27, Paris: "Orly for David, back from Asia. He looks marvellous. Pleasantest birthday present for Cy imaginable. I gave him a tape recorder with bedtime stories. Marinette a portrait of Jessica. David a Swat coat 58 years old [Swat is a small principality in the Himalayas]."

Marina's birthday present was indeed adorable. I had become an incurable insomniac, and she used to try and help by reading to me at night. She had dictated a whole series of stories onto cassettes so I could travel with her soothing voice or listen to it as I tossed at home. With the tape recorder was this note: "Happy birthday sweet Pee. It is not the box that is the important present but the two hours worth of stories at bed-time just in case I am not there to read you to sleep myself. All love Mumble."

From Marina's diary:

November 4, Paris: "Strange dinner at Nelly's [de Vogüé]. Sat between rector of the Sorbonne and his arch enemy M. Loste, de Gaulle's *chef de cabinet* for education. The duel at table was like stilettos in its elegance and deadliness. Can only be done in French."

November 5, Paris: "George and Mrs. Ratiani came to dinner. He is an editor of Pravda and they are both old friends of Cy's. Most nice. Easy to talk to, relaxed, excellent French and English. Say there is a generation gap there too. The young are fed up with *la guerre de papa* and being told they are not heros. Ah me. *Plus ça change . . .*"

November 10, Paris: "General de Gaulle died last night. We only learned this morning as Madame de Gaulle wanted the night alone with her grief. What a splendid way to die."

November 12, Paris [the page headed "De Gaulle funeral"]: "Watched funeral on tv. In the evening walked up Champs Elysées to the Arc de Triomphe in sheets of rain. Quarter of a million people, all silent. Extraordinary."

On November 13, Marina wrote to Susan Mary Alsop: "Well as you can imagine we have had a pretty *mouvementé* three days. Cy was on his way to Rome when the news of the General's death was announced. He would have really been sick if he had been away. Its funny how some people who enter history even before they are dead, do end up by seeming immortal, so that the surprise of their eventual abdication becomes total. But gosh what luck. For a man as proud as he to be spared even the minimum indignity of one trip in an ambulance, one moment of dependance on other hands other minds but his. Bed pans and thermometres, drops and pills and *analyses d'urine*.

"None of that. I have decided, even though alas I dont believe in an after life, that god in his mercy, MUST allow some people a kind of *sursis*, before they melt into nothing. I cant bare to think that he was not aware that his ultimate coquetry of asking for 'a very simple funeral' was realised to such perfection. Eleven kings, Ben Gurion and the Arabs side by side. Black Africa and South Africa, *contestataire* students and fascist beasts all together all mourning the man who had caused them as much trouble as good. David and I got up at dawn to go to Notre Dame, but Dawn was not early enough, and we did not get through. But we did go at six to the Rond Point and walked to the Etoile. A quarter of a million people all in total silence. And at six *tappant*, the rain came. It came in sheets, in buckets, in torrents, and not one person budged. It took us almost two hours to drop our little flower at the Arc de Triomphe and when we got home our shoes had melted."

Next day she added (to Avis Bohlen): "The French are really pass-masters of *Brule ce que tu a adoré, adore ce que tu a brulé*. Even Nelly de Vogüé who used to froth at the mouth at the very mention of his name, is now playing the widow. On television the other day one man was seriously talking of canonisation. If St. Louis why not St. Charles.

"I am afraid this was one of those typical precipitate gestures one regrets almost as soon as one has made. Like giving a friend your favourite scarf on the spur of a sentimental moment, or those deep confidences at three in the morning which one bites one's tongue off about, later. But in the first flurry of grief after the general's death I would not have been surprised had Paris been named Gaulia, or *Colombey les cinquante Eglises* or something.

"I dont believe in a sort of active *anthropomorphique* after life but I do hope God allowed the general in particular, a forty eight hour, suspended sentence as it were, for him to be able to look down and see all of his people whom he disliked so deeply, crying their eyes out for him.

"Last night we went to Ferrière to dine with Malraux and it was like a Dürrenmatt play. The poor fellow was really completely gone, swaying back and forth alone in the middle of the room making a kind of half moan half growl noise, and all of us not quite knowing whether to fly to his succor or tactfully pretend none of this was happening.

"The night before we were asked to the opening of the Théatre Nationale Populaire, and the play was about Queen Victoria who has Siamese twin sons. Albert and Disraeli plot together to kill the Queen but she falls in love with Florence Nightingale who is the fiancé of one of the two Siamese, and then Florence turns into the Scottish gardener and poisons Disraeli and the consort before they have time to do their plot. One of the twins dies and the other goes around with his brother's skeleton still hung around his neck. Gladstone comes to power as a communist leader and tortures a few people but then the Queen and her remaining child make a succesful treason and kill everybody. Scene two everyone is in a canibal paradise where everyone eats everyone else but legs and arms and heads grow back and no one feels any pain so they die happily ever after. I am afraid that I have lived too long. Molière for me."

From the diary:

November 29, Paris: "Amalia [Karamanlis]* called to say Costa [her husband] was leaving her. She came to supper and she is marvellous. Not a word of reproach or self pity."

December 5, London: "Took train for London. Italian countess next door escaping from kidnaping threats with her little daughter. Two policemen on either side. Rather exciting."

December 21, Paris: "Dinner Prince Paul, Olga. They told us amazing story of King Peter's death [of Jugoslavia]. Bishop Ireni and mistress Mitsi Low abducting body to burry in Liberty, Illinois. Fake will. False death certificate. Fantastic. Also reminisced about Russia, Hitler, etc. Charming evening."

December 31, Paris: "Supper at home tête à tête. Played two handed bridge. Cy sweet. It's been an awful year for the world at large but for us good. David got back from Vietnam. He got into Business School. He took a fabulous trip. Marinette had a son. We had a nice Colorado summer. Cy's 'Giants' published and successful. What more can one ask. That I get some dining room chairs."

The year 1971, began with a trip to North and South America. Just before going, she wrote Prince Paul of Jugoslavia, who had sent her a book for the journey:

"Darling Monseigneur. Some people grow older and more selfish or crotchety as the years go by and the better one knows the small or great

---

* Wife of Prime Minister Karamanlis of Greece, then in voluntary Paris exile.

faillings one discovers in them. You are the exact opposite. With each meeting one gets to see ever growing kindness, greater wisdom charm warmth, and above all a seemingly endless thoughtfulness for others, not only the privileged friends, but for humanity as a whole. And one leaves your presence each time more devoted, each time more indepted and more enslaved. I shall read my book with double pleasure as it comes from you."

From the diary:

February 28, Boston: "Very pleasant flight to Boston. Sunshine when we arrived. Polar waiting. Hair down to his waist. Went to the Ritz. Talked a great deal. He hates business school but will stick to it. Says he asked a professor a question and got the answer, 'Mr. Sulzberger, have you never had a meaningful cognitive, inter-personal relationship?' "

March 3, New York: "Dinner with George and Mrs. Ball [former Undersecretary of State]. Very interesting for Cy. He showed him documents of extraordinary interest and top secret. Most people do. It's flattering."

Our first stop was Bogota, from where Marina wrote Marinette on March 18:

"Our American bit of the trip was nice but both too short and too long. Much too short to see all friends, and not short enough if one decides not to call anyone and slip by unnoticed. We got a whole lot of awful news on arrival. Poor Mr. [Leland] Hayward is dying; he got a stroke and did not die of it but his brain has been damaged. Pam has not left his side for a moment in two months and is heroic. I saw her once only and him not at all. Then I went to see poor Mrs. [George] Backer who is also dying. And George Thayer you know who spent one Xmas with us, Avis' nephew, aged thirty, has had his leg cut off at the hip.

"We stayed the first three days in Boston with David and he is very well but hates the business school with passion. He says he does not understand half what they are talking about, and the half he does understand he wishes he did'nt. However thank god he is determined to see it through. The life saver is his house. A tiny eighteenth century wooden house in Hilliard

Place, one step from the university. He and his friend David Warsh share it; they have a large bedroom and bath each upstairs and a large living room sort of L-shaped downstairs with a kitchinette a garden trees and a huge wisteria all over the house.

"It is too good to be true. And they have done miracles. They have hung the boucharas sort of like a tent in one corner, with all their pictures and Viet treasures. David explained it is because they work eighteen hours a day and dont have time to be untidy. And so broke that they dont even go into Boston. The first night we went to the Union Oyster bar for old times sake, and the next day I went and cooked a gigantic moussaka and he had twenty of his friends to supper to meet us.

"Then we went to Washington to stay with the Bohlens who are wonderful as usual. And Pa got his great scoop. He went to see the President as usual very discreetly and not telling even me, and after they had talked for an hour and a half Pa sighed and said oh how I wish I could write some of this, and the President said go right ahead and write it all. When Far came to from his astonishement they had their photo taken together and Far could not believe his ears.

"And now begins a tale of such abject beastliness that it is hard to believe. Imagine; there he was struggling with his notes, his story for the paper and his column all without a secretary and in storms Abe Rosenthal [the managing editor] frothing at the mouth and yelling Who do you think you work for yourself or the Times. Why did you not tell me you were seing the President, and using really foul language. When Far tried to explain he had not known he was going to get a story and had not even told me Abe screached God damn your wife. I mean jealousy of such pro-portions that he really would rather have not had the scoop at all than have Far get it. And believe it or not the story appeared next day in mighty small letters and Far had been completely cut out of the picture leaving the President sort of lop-sided and funny.

"But in a way this was the best thing that could have happened to us; you and a very few others know that this kind of harrassement has been going on for years, but it was hard to really put it into words or make people believe such infantilism. And there it was right in the open for everyone to see.

"The night of the interview we were all dining together Stew [Alsop] and

Tish and the Bradens and the Bohlens and they all saw the pictures which were sent over by the White House so the next day they could all see what had happened. Its too gruesome. Far got congratulations from all kinds of people, TV chains, Averell Harriman, all sorts except from the Times people not one of whom even mentioned it *en passant*. Its really dreadful to think that the most powerful paper in the world is run by a bunch of sneaky hysterics, who put their own petty little jealousies ahead of the paper. It makes one want to cry.

"To console Far I only kept saying thank god thank god we dont really need them. Think if we were a young striving couple of poor reporters with a lot of children to feed. However on top of everything else this has been marvellous coming as it did on the eve of a long trip because every other president en route is now eager to see Far. *Au moins ça.*

"Well then we left yesterday for here and it is so high that our heads are splitting our hearts pounding and not a wink of sleep all night, except for a few moments in which I dreamed that I was sharing a very small bed with Mrs. Golda Meyer, so I woke at once. Not a shred of old Spanish charm. That Hilton type hotel, and hideous appartement buildings. And nothing works. Lovely bathrooms with no taps and no plugs. A lady called eleven times in a row asking for 'Gustavo por favor.' Hard to be furious in a tongue one does not master too well. However Far saw the President this morning and is deep in his typewriter so I know nothing of it as yet. I walked around a bit but there were hundreds of the local CRS [security police] out with helmets and shields so I figured I better not stray too far. They have a habit of killing and kidnapping around here."

The same day she wrote Avis Bohlen: "Thank god you dear ones, for perfect hospitality and perfect friendship. God knows we need it these days. In a way much as I hated Cy being so hurt, I am almost glad they did it so openly this time. Not you, but I think some of our friends were rather inclined to think that we exaggerated when ever we dropped discretion and talked of the really despicable way the paper had treated Cy. And with reason, because I do see that it is hard to remember how cheap and petty some grown-ups can be. I was amused to see just before we left the photograph of that lady reporter who saw the President spread a foot high across the entire page. And do you know, when Cy got back and went to lunch at the paper, not one single man on that miserable floor, even mentioned the story. Oh well the less we think about them the better."

On March 29 she wrote Marinette from Buenos Aires, after several days in Allende's Chile:

"The Korrys [U.S. ambassador to Chile] very sweetly asked us to stay, but Far was afraid it might embarrass them if he wrote anything they did not agree with, and him if he were staying in the very strong hold of international imperialist conspiracy so we stayed at the hotel but I spent all my days with them relaxing by the pool and catching up on six years of separation. It was lovely specially as there is nothing to see or do in Santiago at all. The Spaniards only came there, as a kind of backwater, without gold or treasures, so they never really built anything, and there is only one rather brocken down church and one delicious colonial house, a little out of town just exactly what one would wish to live in. Long woodden galleries and balconies, beautiful red stone floors, arched windows, tiny carved doors, and a garden to dream about, all roses and jasmin and lavander and avocado trees forty fifty feet high. Heavenly.

"Just being in Chile one would never know that there is anything changed at all. The municipal elections are in five days, and there were posters up and electoral lists, and speeches on the radio, etc., all *signes exterieurs* of democracy. But little by little one meets more and more people whose lands have been expropriated, proffessors who have been fired, journalists who cant get jobs, etc etc etc. Human capacity for not learning from experience seems alas endless. Here is a perfect set-up for a Marxist regime to do exactly the right thing. They have been voted in most correctly and democratically; on top of that, they are small which always makes things easier, they have as much land as they need for everybody, and they are rich. So the first thing they do is collectivise land, which is the one irrefutable error recognised as such everywhere from Moscow to Belgrade."

On April 5 she wrote Marinette from Rio de Janeiro: "The only time we went out of the city was to go yesterday for a drink with our correspondent who lives only about half an hour from the center, up on a steep hill, and even in so short a time we were in thick rain forrest, with tropical flowers, lianas, and ginger blooms everywhere smelling like a strong cross between gardenias and jasmin. I rushed off to pick some and got entangled in the strongest spider webb I have ever encountered. Like a tennis net. However even that could not keep me from picking, and I came back with an arm-ful and our room now smells like one imagines all those marvellous Maugham stories of the tropics do."

She noted in her diary: "Rio is enchanted. Five miles from the center jungle with ginger growing wild, scented like gardenias. Too lovely."

We flew nonstop to South Africa, not Marina's favorite country, and she noted:

April 6, Johannesburg: "Arrived Johannesburg like pretzels. And a bit dopy with five hour time difference. One can hardly believe the newspapers. Lead story whether whites can play cricket with non-whites. And use same washrooms. They are a vile group of people, really."

April 9, Lesotho: "Flew to Lesotho. The people are Basuto, the language Sesuto. Met Chief Jonathan. Very much like a hippopotamous but nice. Met marvelous man [South African] called Van Graan, chief of planning. So exciting to make a new country from scratch. Instead of yelling down with the consumer society, planning for milk and vegetables to be consumed, they have nothing but independance."

From Cape Town she wrote Marinette on April 13:

"Here it is really another world in another century. We open the papers day in day out, and not a word about Vietnam (thank god) or the Middle East, or anything except one after another sordid tales of some lady complaining because a Chinese girl was allowed to play tennis with the other children at school, or the Springbok team which is the main news all the time. And endless sorrowful stories of people separated from their children as they have been classified as non-whites. One can hardly believe it. In the little things above all, like tennis or cricket or even a play with one African voice in it. A passion play on Holy Friday at that, and hundreds of people complained.

"But what is upside down, is that in the U.S. for instance the gouvernement tries to impose some more good sense and the people dont follow, whereas here more than half the people are good and against all this, and it is the governement which tries to enforce wickedness. And stupidity. Because when you think what the ordinary every day problems of running any large country are, and then multiply them by three, then you get an idea of how this place works; or does'nt work.

"Far got me a fabulous bracelet for my birthday in Rio but wont let me even look at it yet. Daphne [Petrow] took me to a glorious place the other day where they cut and polish semi precious stones. One buys them by the pound like rice or beans. I got one delicious bit of amethyst for Pam who likes mauve. They are such fun to hold and play with and have romantic names like Aventurine or Cornelia, Amozonite, Jasper and Blue Lace.

"We came to Cape Town yesterday and I already feel better just being by the sea. But not swimmable. It is full of the strangest kind of thick dark brown sea weed as thick as my fist, and sort of tentacle-ish. And the waves are gigantic, not to mention that a poor German tourist was eaten by two sharks together, in full view of people on the beach, two days ago. Tomorrow we are going to visit a little town called Stellenbosch which dates from the Dutch East India company days so it might be romantic. Nothing else is."

From a long, summing-up letter to Susan Mary Alsop, I am quoting little bits: "Some places are better unvisited. Bogota for instance has ever since my school geography lessons, been confused with Shangri La in my mind. Alas. Dreary, modern of the worst 1930 type, rain rain rain, and even the terrorists are invisible to the naked eye. Just as well that. Diplomats HAVE to keep their car doors locked but that is as near to excitement as one gets. The only lovely thing, the pre Columbian gold museum, which is beautiful. Even arrows and hair pins, spoons, and fish hooks made of gold: its all they had poor things. Gold and God (ours) were their undoing. . . .

"In Santiago there are, as usual, no *signes extérieurs de tristesse*, except for row upon row of For sale signs on almost every elegant looking house; and innumerable Auction Sale announcements in the papers. The rich leaving the sinking ship presumably. . . .

"Then Rio. Which is always fun, in its deliciously absurd perpetual holiday life. Any city built almost IN the sea is bound to be gay and carefree. Imagine if Joe could put on his bathing suit, patter bare-foot down to Dumbarton Avenue and dive in. No one can concentrate on serious things with so much pleasure at their front door. And ten minutes away on the other side, mountains and rain forrest, orchids and ginger flowers, filling the air with a gardenia smell, to make even a brick wall feel romantic. . . .

"And now for the passed two weeks in this benighted country. To be wicked and unfair and prejudiced, when it is convenient and proffitable, is bad enough, but to be so when it means one's eventual destruction seems too stupid to believe. Yet we have met some most charming and exceptional people. However I shall be more than glad when this part of the trip is over. From now on, all is new and all fun. Mauritius on Thursday, and then Madagascar where our Ambassador, Tony Marshall, is Brooke Astor's son, and then above all the Comores where Cy does NOT have to write a column for a few days and we can swimm and sit in the sun and I can collect shells and even perhaps spear a decent fish, and look at the coral reef and all kinds of unknown flowers and fruit and plants."

From Marina's diary:

April 25, Mauritius: "We have a ghekko lizzard on the porch. He goes tick tack. Took a boat out. Tried goggles. Sea urchins a foot wide. Not very nice. Some pretty fish. No where near as lovely as Fiji. Long walk Cy. Dined with foreign minister who is an ass. Runs the black power party (everyone is almost black here) and wants rapprochement with South Africa. Mad!"

On April 28 she wrote Marinette from Tananarive: "Mauritius is where Robinson Crusoe should have been shipwrecked, instead of that dismal rock Juan Fernandez where he really was, and which has been enjoying a spurius reputation ever since. This is real real tropics, with bananas and bread fruit, vines and creepers, rivers and best of all, in the middle of the vast plane suddenly mountains like illustrations of some science fiction story. They are the result of some monumental explosion once upon a time, and really look like petrified bubbles or sprays of water.

"We drove all over the island between tunnels of emerald green sugar cane, and passed Indian villages and African ones, lovely Victorian houses of the *Grand Blancs*, and brocken down shanties of the 'humbles.' I cant think how they stand up to tornadoes, which are weekly things they tell us. We had a lovely room almost in the sea, on a mile long empty beach with bougainvillia and myrtle frangipani and ginger growing all around us.

"But as usual *le revers de la médaille*, the sea was so full of you know whats of the sea, and glucky looking sea weed, and some other furry creatures three feet long and wiggly, that for the life of me I would not have put my foot in. But we took a boat out to the reef one day and that was nice. Urchins here are like foot balls, and very creepy. Odd how familiar things when they change size become frightening. Some lovely fish and glorious blue orange and green coral. I found lots of tiny shells, and kept them for Jessica and Jonathan, as budding collectors. I hope to get better and bigger ones in the Comores. I did find one beauty striped mauve yellow and white.

"We stayed three days, which was about enough, because of the rain, and arrived last night in Tananarive. It was too dark to see anything, but this morning we woke up in a most enchanting and unexpected city. Built on innumerable hills, four thousand feet high, it looks like nothing we have ever seen before. Bits are like Austrian villages, with cobbled streets and Victorian gothic houses, next moment one is in an African market. Further down delicate pale pink brick, French and delightful, and by its side a concrete COOP [cooperative shop] and a MONOPRIX [French Woolworth's].

"And on Place de l'Indépendance, which looks almost the Midi, with arched streets on both sides, and in the middle a thousand large flappy white ombrellas, under which the market ladies sell the most beautiful fruit vegetables flowers hats baskets you have ever seen, and on both sides of the ornemental steps going down to the *place*, little stalls selling amethysts, rock crystal topaz agate etc, like you might sell pea nuts or chesnuts. Alas one franc here is worth two french ones, so that a bottle of Perrier becomes a luxury. We leave on Saturday for the Comores which is the high point of the trip and I shall write again from there."

The Comores were a disappointment: hot, uncomfortable, limited swimming, poor fishing, nothing else to do, only one plane out each week — and disaster at the end of the flight.

From Marina's diary:

Grande Comore, Comores Islands: "A little disappointing. The entire countryside is lava beds, great pointed black lumps. No flowers. Bananas, palms, ylang-ylang and gigantic fruit bats."

May 4, Grande Comore: "Took boat out for deep-sea fishing. Left from

Le trou du Prophète, a pirate nest. Caught two huge wahoos each. 21, 17, 16 and 14 pounds and one baracuda. But oh for five minutes of action, 9 hours uncomfortable in the sizzling sun. Not good enough."

May 6, Grande Comore: "Found small boy to row to the reef in a pirogue. Fabulous. More like a tropical garden with birds than an underwater scape. Coral like fields of thyme and heather. Yellow, blue, speckled fish. Found one marvelous shell, which bit me. Too surprised."

Rested but a bit bored after a week, we flew back to Madagascar where we were supposed to catch a plane to Kenya, our next stop. To our surprise, a delegation from the Embassy, including Jack Haney (to whom Marina had read in a Middle East hospital when he was temporarily blinded during the war), met us at the Tananarive airport. Jack beckoned me aside, showing me a cable that had been sent urgently from our Embassy in London. There was a message from Marinette: Jonathan, still a small baby, was desperately ill in hospital; the doctors feared he was dying. Could we come?

In that distant corner of the world there aren't many flights in any direction, and our Air France plane was booked solid. We had two seats as far as Nairobi, but there was nothing from there on. However, thanks to Haney and to Ambassador Tony Marshall's efforts, we were able to arrange one seat all the way through to Paris for Marina. Naturally we grabbed it. It was a glum flight to Nairobi; Marina was unable to keep tears from rolling down her cheeks as she gripped my hand tightly.

At Nairobi our ambassadorial couple, Bob and Alice McIlvaine, were waiting at the airport. They had received a copy of the London cable. There was little talk. We all hugged Marina and she promised to send a message as soon as there was news. Then wearily, lonely, sobbing, she climbed back aboard the plane. She wrote in her diary (May 8): "Longest flight on earth for me, imagining every horror possible."

Next day, finally in London, she jotted down again:

May 9, London: "Black Sunday. Arrived in Paris at 6:30. Had to wait till 8 to get plane to London. Went to hospital. Jonathan with septicemia. Just off the danger list today. Since Wednesday he has been dying. Marinette ash-white but fantastic. Quiet, brave, gentle and so strong. My heart aches for her."

Thank heavens McIlvaine got a cable next day saying that Jonathan had turned the corner and, although still under intensive care, was no longer on the critical list. I stayed in Nairobi, finished my job, and then took off for Cairo, where I had a rendezvous with President Sadat. Marina wrote in her diary:

May 14: "Cy called from Athens on his way to Cairo. So wonderful to be able to give him good news. Jonathan is definitely better. Talking and moving."

On June 6 she told Jane Joyce the story: "It is a real miracle that poor little Jonathan is completely cured, without a trace left. The worst part of all really was when they told us his life was saved but that we had to wait three weeks to find out if there was any permanant damage done. The main fear was the brain, and would he be a vegetable, or blind, or deaf or . . . I shudder even as I write this. Sitting there hour after hour, and watching Marinette's face as she passed her hand time after time in front of his eyes for a sign of sight and nothing, was really unbearable. And then not in three weeks but in ten days, one day he turned his head, and the next he wiggled his hands, and then finally one glorious day the nurse opened the door and he heard it.

"I must say having been sort of brave and dry eyed until then, when this happened we all disolved into floods, and the nurses came and gave us large cups of tea and muttered there deary and it was glorious. Who ever invented the idea that the British are cold and undemonstrative, must have been blind and deaf himself. You have never seen such sweetness and gentleness and real caring. There were six doctors and innumerable nurses around him all the time, each one nicer than the other, and saved him. And another detail, is that all this, seven weeks in hospital and the best care in the world, did not cost one penny. All on national health. Anywhere else, they would have been bond slaves for years.

"Well now it is over and he is home a dreadful thing has happened to me, at my age. It is real *amour* passion for the little fellow. I cant bare to have him out of my sight, and one smile of his throws me into delirium of joy, and holding him in my arms, soft and warm and velvety seems the best pleasure in the world. How I will ever leave here I dont know.

"Cy finally got home from his travels and came over here right away and spent a week end with us, but men are not very good around sick beds.

They get nervous and restless and unhappy, so we had to hold his hand as well as Jonathan's."

From Paris five days later she wrote Kitty Solomos (in French): "Well, Jonathan is now so well that he eats enough for four and crawls around on all fours so fast that we can hardly keep up with him. And he is on the verge of talking. So long as his first words aren't 'blood transfusion' or 'oxygen mask' everything will be okay. The advantage of being so small is that he probably won't remember anything of the entire affair. And I think I am its final victim because I have suddenly been overwhelmed by such a love for those two children that I can hardly bear being away from them. Jonathan fits exactly between my knees and my chin and he is so sweet and warm that my arms seem empty and sad without him."

That June, Marina went off to Greece and a well-earned holiday. She wrote me:

"Beagle has lost ten years, and swimms laughs talks eats better than ever. The boatman the other day could not believe his eyes; because Beagle was swimming to the boat and the boatman gestured with his hands that the ladder was on the other side. So Beagle came to the other side and climbed the stairs all by himself and went to the towel picked it up in his mouth and dried himself. A genius."

On July 15 she wrote Avis Bohlen: "Sometimes I marvel at the capacity of the human soul, to take in so many different aspects of life. A month ago we were holding our breath in a grey brick edifice of sorrow and hope, and praying for Jonathan, and today I am in Spetses with no other problem, but whether to have stuffed tomatoes for lunch or baked fish. Jonathan is completely, completely well and Marinette is coming next week with her sister in law and Isabelle de Waldner, for ten days, all of them in order to sleep and swimm and for a minute not to think of babies or husbands, stoves or supermarkets. . . . I am here with Nancy Smith and a friend of hers, and I think they are enjoying it. I was so delighted to be able for once to look after Nancy, instead of ever having her look after us and give us such endless hospitality."

She wrote me on July 26: "Last night I took Nancy Smith, Bill and Harriet Berry to Epidaurus and although the play was not very good, they loved it. Our taxi driver took us to a taverna after the show and insisted on paying, which was so dear and so Greek of him. He asked me if I could go and live with him and his wife for a few months and teach him English and he would even pay me something. Was sad when I said I live in France in the winter. He is a passionate hunter and said he would take you out for hare, in September if you wish."

On July 28, Marina again wrote me: "Last week I was whisked off by John Loudon* in his boat, and only got back on Tuesday. Bill Harcourt was on the boat, and a nice American couple. We went to Seriphos and Syfnos and Kythnos, which are not the prettiest of the islands, but the glory of a private boat is that it goes into all tiny coves and unknown places and the sea and the sun and the rocks were beyond words beautiful. I fished urchins for them and converted them all to addicts specially Bill who could not wait for more. It was lovely but in fact four days on someone else's boat, is just about enough, even though they were all so charming. I dont like being trapped somehow.

"We got into Passa Limani on Saturday evening and went to a very gay *taverna* with good food and even the Jonkheer [John] himself got up and danced a *sirtaki*, and then we went on to another place and listened to a famous *bouzouki* lady, and got home at three, which apparently is unheard of for John who likes to go to bed at ten. Then I took them to the airport on Sunday morning, and felt rather blushy, when the porters asked what line we were looking for and I had to say a private plane and they cant find their pilot. They took off for Holland and England, and I went to Kitty's. . . .

"We spent a nice day in the country at the Serpieris who were giving a rather fancy Sunday lunch, but suddenly a storm came up such as I have never seen, and we were fishing plates and glasses out of puddles. Then all the lights went out all over Attica. Later Kitty and I decided to try our luck at the theatre where the Munich philharmonic was giving the Bach *Grande Messe*, and we had no tickets nor any assurance that the lights would go on, but we tried anyway and the lights did come back at eight twenty and naturally so many people had given up all hope, that we not only got seats, but with no one in front or behind, so for once and once only we could

---

* Jonkheer Loudon, Dutch friend.

stretch our legs AND lean our backs against the wall. The performance was sheer magic and with the moon almost full, going from arch to arch behind the singers it was a memorable, memorable evening.

"Yesterday, I do think David had the loveliest birthday ever. He arranged it all. He really is in his funny little way a leader and an organiser without being bossy, which is so nice. He got Ghika and another boat and all the Woods and us went to Fokiano and had a lovely pic nic and swimm and discovered that the bit of land we want belongs to Nikolo's [a cab driver in Spetsais] maternal uncle so we will go back to the village one of these days and talk facts. The day was lovely and it only took two hours to get there, and then in the evening we had a fantastic combined birthday party, as it happened to be Leigh Bruce's birthday too, as well as Clem and Jessy's [Wood] anniversary and also Max and another girl guest's birthday. So we had fireworks and presents and kissing and four birthday cakes and all the children danced with us old ones and it really was a marvel. Full moon too."

From Marina's diary:

July 31, Spetsais: "Left for Epidaurus to see Medea. My patriotism stops there. I find Medea an inexcusable myth. Unless of course she was real."

To Avis Bohlen on September 5: "There is nothing like doing nothing for making one do even less. I have been meaning to write since July, and here we are September and I have only just managed to sit at my desk. Possibly because writing to Stew [Alsop] and Tommy [Thompson] was such agony, that it took up all one's reserves of energy [both had fatal illnesses]. Jane [Joyce] gave me your last letter to read, and it really is ghastly, how many many big and little tragedies there are around us. Every time we go swimming and come back whole, every time we have one of Eleni's huge delicious meals, every walk every smell of jasmine and thyme, makes me feel all over again how deeply grateful one must be, and how fragile it all is. I am almost ashamed and self conscious to tell you what a delicious summer it has been.

"Cy arrived ten days ago riddled with gout, but thank god is better now, and quite cheerful. And then the gift of gifts David arrived three days ago with three friends from both Vietnam and Harvard. So the house is alive again, and Eleni thrilled at the mountains of food the young can consume at one sitting."

On September 21 she wrote Michael Edwards: "Went to Leonidion which is a perfect little town with Frankish towers and houses and decided it was too sad to leave, so called up our respective houses and spent the night there. Some aspects of progress like the telephone, have their uses. Then we had a fabulous drinking eating dancing singing party that night, with the crew of our boat the mayor and several village people, which lasted till three A.M. and at six with the sun, we got up and climbed to two incredible monasteries which can only have been built by arch angels. No one else could carry bricks and stones and bells and iconostase, to such precarious hights. They are stuck in the cliff overhanging thousands of feet of precipice. Fantastic.

"In the woman's monastery David's morale was boosted, because everyone had been screaming at him for his long hair, and here the Higoumeni [abbess] took one look at him, and we all trembled at the thought of the scolding which was coming, instead of which she said, 'he looks just like St. John Prodrome. He must be a good boy.' Her opinion almost changed soon thereafter, when she opened a silver box and pushed it under my nose saying smell how sweet it perfumes, and kiss it, and to my distress it turned out to be the scull of saint Zachari, and David was taken with such histerical gigles, we had to rush out of the chapel and hide."

We learned on September 24 that Averell Harriman and Pam Hayward were getting married. We were very fond of both of them and their late spouses, and there seemed something especially apt and dear about their marriage. On that day Marina wrote Averell:

"How happy I am for both you and Pam. I know that you are going to be so very happy and this brings you every best wish and congratulations. Is'nt it lovely to think that when we come back to the U.S. next time, and stay with you, we will have two of our dearest friends together. I cant think of a happier combination of people than you two.

"Since the first of September Cy has been here, resting and swimming, shooting walking reading and sleeping, which is the greatest luxury for him, who never stops moving about, eleven months of the year. Luckily too he only got one small attack of gout. Alas all this is coming to an end soon. Autumn has arrived earlier than usual, and the wind has been blowing for days, so perhaps this will make it easier for us to go without the wrench it usually is. Although how I shall ever get back to wearing shoes and a watch, and living in a city I dont know."

And she added in a letter to "Pam Darling": "I am so glad for you my pet and I am sure you will make Averell the happiest of men. How clever of him to snatch you up, as I imagine the competition must have been tremendous."

To Avis Bohlen on October 21 on learning of young Charlie Bohlen's engagement:

"Congratulations. Ouf what a relief. These days when one can barely hope that one's child wont live in sin with a bearded woman's lib lady, or a ban-the-bomb passionara, not to mention pot ice, snow etc, to have one's son choose a sweet nice pretty girl, whose family one knows to boot, is almost to good to believe. I am so happy. I know the child from Marinette's Washington days and she seemed adorable. Oh darling I am so happy for you all. So glad too to have you in my generation of mother-in-laws soon.

"I just got back to Paris last night, and the very thought of shoes, stockings, a watch and traffic jams, gives me the shivers, after nearly four months of freedom from city life. I have been looking for another bit of land to buy, to keep for the bad new days, when inevitably Spetses will become a motel haven, or taverna infested tourist trap. It shows no signs of this yet, thank heavens, but sooner or later this must happen to an island so close to Athens, and Cy mainly wants the fealing of having another corner to move to.

"A friend of ours was lent a splendid yacht this summer and she took us all sailing down the coast of the Peloponissos, where we saw this magic place, which has no road not even a path leading to it, which is all to the good. It is a perfect semi circle of beach, with rocks on one side, the mountain behind, the sea in front, and covered with olive trees, figs oleanders (which means water) and at one end, miraculously one tiny church painted three different shades of blue, and one cypress tree. So I went off by land this time to do some detective work to see who it belongs to and if they will sell. Well it is the same old story; it belongs to ten different people, all saying they dont want to sell. But also letting it be *sous entendu* that they might. So I have left it in the hands of a young lawyer friend passing himself off as a nephew, and will just keep fingers crossed; and pray that something might happen. I spent ten days in Athens which was rather fun too, as I saw lots of old friends, cought up with family, school chums etc, and on the whole had a delicious time."

From her diary:

November 1, Paris: "Lunch — Malraux, Régis Debray, Clem and Jessie Wood. Absolutely fascinating. Old romantic revolutionary face to face with young doctrinaire ideologist. Hard to understand Malraux who talks like a radio with static. But what he says always makes sense, even when he rambles. Régis so young, so intransigent. Big blue eyes, moustache. Venezuelan wife like a man-eating mouse. Malraux comment, *'Ils ont beaucoup à apprendre.'*"

To Susan Mary Alsop on November 19: "One day we had an absolutely fascinating lunch here at home for young Régis Debray who had expressed a desire to Cy to meet Malraux about whose works he is writing a rather polemic book. We thought lunch, because by dinner time poor Malraux does not make too much sense these days. I must say it was really extraordinary to see the *face à face*, of the old romantic dreamer revolutionary, and the young doctrinaire unimaginative ideologist. Like a *dialogue de sourd*, in which both could hear part of what the other was saying. Malraux all generalities and abstractions, Debray almost like a computer. Debray full of regrets about Bolivia (a total faillure). Malraux full of lunatic fringe dreams about Bangla Desh with a hardly veilled desire to get himself killed there.

"It was really rather tragic and nice. One thing amused me and also saddened me. Because I get my own facts mixed up, I recognise it all too poignantly in others. Before getting into politics, we were talking about Greece (odd) and got to Lepanto, and Malraux gave us the most beautiful lyrical description of Cervantes's capture by the Turks and his subsequent escape, which was utterly marvellous to hear, except that Cervantes was captured four years later, and not by the Turks but by Algerian pirates. Ah me. If only one could pick one's time for dying."

To Avis Bohlen on December 7, just before Charlie's wedding: "All our thoughts are with you and I can imagine the excitement, the rush, the decisions taken and untaken, the whole delicious agony of Christmas plus wedding. Oh if only we could be with you.

"Cy has been having a hard time; off to Norway for five days, to Brussels for three, and now to Egypt tomorrow. And last night he was stricken again, with a real beast of a gout attack, and is in agony, but has to leave anyway. My heart aches for him specially as we were so hopeful, his having been free of the damned thing since September."

And Marina's summation in her diary:

December 31, Paris: "On the whole a year to be thankful for. Very much so. Jonathan did not die. Alexis did not go under. Cy finished book. Summer was lovely. Dodo well. Marinette got a new house. David came for Christmas. Took a fantastic trip. Alas, lost no weight. For the world, not such a good year but it squeezed through which is something. Thank God."

XIII

January 1972 - March 1973

The year 1972 started inauspiciously. Marina wrote her Greek friend, Dolly Voureka, on January 4:

"Poor old Cy had the worst attack of gout he has had in months. And you know what it is like to have a sick man in the house. *Tout s'arrête.* And on top of that Xmas. I must say I am very grateful that the Almightly god did not have two or three sons, to celebrate their birthdays. Apart from indigestion, exhaustion etc, we would all be in jail for dept.

"Our Xmas was rather miserable, with Cy in bed unable to even get up let alone think of plum pudding *foie gras* etc. But one great joy was David's presence for ten days. To our surprise short hair, grey gentlemanly costume, narrow neck-tie. *On n'en croyait pas nos yeux.* From the moment he set foot in the house, the door bell and the telephone never stopped ringing. God how I hate to think, that as of June when he graduates he will have to earn his living and we will only have him for two weeks a year, for fifty years. It is a grusome thought.

"This very morning Cy announced to me casually that on the 26th we are off to about twenty countries including India Pakistan Bangla Desh Vietnam and god knows what else. I think of silly things like having left all my sandals and bathing suits in Spetses, like what dresses do I have that dont take up space that dont crumple and that can be worn night and day hot or cold peace or war, snow or sun. None naturally. And unless we are shot by the Mukti Bahini, captured by the Viet Kong imprisoned by Bhutto, expelled by Indira Gandhi, or something, we will be back in Paris in April. And god willing another long delicious Greek summer."

To Avis Bohlen on January 15: "Feel like a lump of lead today. We have just had typhus tetanus cholera small pox and yellow fever shots in one day, and apart from looking like a sieve, I feel rather awful. So forgive this letter if it sounds lumpish too. We are off at the end of the month on one of these endless trips, and for the moment I am not even excited except at the thought, that all roads do seem to lead to Washington eventually and the hope of seing you. We are going to Israel first, then Persia, then Pakistan and then India, but god knows via what. Even that silly frontier, which one had to walk across, last year, is now closed naturally, so we may either have to go back to Teheran or more likely on to Kabul. Then Delhi Calcutta, Bangla-Desh if they will let us in, then Viet Nam, which will be sad without David glad as I am at his not being there. Then Hong Kong and Tokyo and then home (USA), and hopefully a few delicious days with you in April. I know myself and once we are on the way, I shall enjoy it. But for the moment, it seems to me, I have hardly started my Paris life, and hate to leave it.

"Our poor friend Gilberte de Montulé, died five days ago, leaving a ten year old little girl quite alone as her husband died three years ago. She was burried in Burgundy miles away from here, and then a mass the next day in St. Jacques and all of Monday I was at the hospital and Tuesday her old mother asked me to stay in the house, so that the body would not be alone so I feel that I have been at a funeral for a whole week. Poor little thing."

After Marina's own death I found among her papers a note I had written for our thirtieth wedding anniversary and I was pleased she had kept it:

"January 21, 1972. Sweet Dopeymou: Just think, 30 years ago you were a shy little girl of 22 and I had black hair and we were starting a dream together in a world that still knew how to dream. And it all went so fast, including the dreams. And nobody ever knows where it went; all one sees is tired fragments. Well, Mumbo, they haven't been the easiest years for you but maybe, since we 'clamb the hill togither' we'll be able to slide down it gently too, comforting each other on the sad road.

"I know this is the *pearl* anniversary so instead of giving you a present from Paris I give you a check ($10 for each year plus one to grow on) to spend on pearls of great price in Hong Kong or Tokyo. With all my love."

February 1 she wrote to Dodo from Israel:

"This country is like a mixture of the Bible, Philemon et Baucis and the *Paramthi horis onoma* [a popular Greek fairy tale, "Story Without a Name"]. After thirty years I can hardly recognize some places. There is an Inter Continental hotel on the Mount of Olives. Yet in others time seems to have stood still, and thank god rosemary and *pikrodaphni* [rose laurel] still grow in the garden of Joseph of Arimathea. As excavations take place everywhere all the time, new theories pop up, at the same speed.

"There is an idea, hotly denied by the Orthodox and the Holy Sepulchre of course, that this garden is in fact the place where Jesus was crucified, just outside the city wall, and was brought to Joseph's garden to be burried. I must say personally I would rather it were here. It is a real *jardin de cure,* with moss and cypress trees and the first almonds in bloom and a simple cave where the tomb is supposed to have been. Nicer than the gaudy competitiveness of the Holy Sepulchre. I am amused at the number of things one forgets one loves so. I mean I can live quite happily in Paris, unaware of the fact that there is no thyme around, no olive trees or cypress, no yellow light nor yellowish red rock no unexpected smells, no stray dogs or unhurried people.

"And then suddenly I find all these things again, and get a kind of violent retroactive nostalgia for them. Just to wake up in the morning in a room full of sun light, rather than electric one, fills me with pleasure. We have had a lovely five days. Cy saw Mrs. [Golda] Meir as well as [Moshe] Dayan and we had tea with Mayor Kollek who is an extraordinary man. Lives in a tiny humble sort of Harilaou Trikoupi Street flat, which is so filled with his treasures as he is an archeaologist, *dans ses moments perdus,* which are not many, that one can hardly sit down. Being Vienese in origin we of course were given coffee and cakes, and little by little as it was the Sabath people started dropping in. They retire all their generals at about the age of thirty eight, and they all become archeaologists or proffessors so there we were surrounded by about a dozen young men, every one a hero, now a humble or not so humble teacher. It is really a most moving country.

"I was given a car and a driver by the foreign office, so while Cy worked, I went sight seing frenziedly and managed to go everywhere. The weather was fabulous. I walked about the old city, lit candles to all of us, and enjoyed myself. Then we drove to Tel Aviv where we are staying with the American Ambassador in a charming house by the sea. Yesterday we went to Ceasaria, which is lovely, driving through all the part that used to be Jordan before the six day war. Almond blossoms everywhere and bright red anemonies and orange groves and olives. One can hardly believe that this was all battle field so short a time ago. We leave today for Teheran and lunch with the Prime Minister tomorrow. This is written both in a hurry and on a brocken typewriter. But hopefully I can get it fixed, as well as have more time in Persia to write again."

From Marina's diary:

February 2, Teheran, Iran: "Lunch with the prime minister [Hoveyda]. Pale beige caviar. Very attractive, intelligent man. Shrewd."

She wrote Marinette on February 5:

"In Israel where everyone knows the old testament like the back of their hands it was bad enough, but here it is quite hopeless. When the guide book opens with a phrase such as this 'La première construction fut sous les Deylamites et plus tard les Likhani les Agh Ghoyounlous et les Al Mozaffars . . .' you know you are in trouble. Not to mention that there are two Cyruses two Darius two Artaxerxes etc several hundred years apart. But I must say even without knowledge it was marvellous and for once Far managed to finish work in time to do it all with me.

"Iranian hospitality has no bounds and I found orchids in the room from the Information minister and then everything set for us to fly to Persepolis at five in the morning on Thursday. There we were met by a sweet lady guide who took us off from Shiraz to Persepolis. Via a desert rather gloomy beige road. But once there, it is most extraordinary. The *bas reliefs* are beautiful. The rest isn't, but very interresting. Shiraz itself is a bit of a dump. We saw the tent city put up for the famous celebrations [2,500 years after Cyrus the Great] and I must say they are almost as astonishing as Darius's palace itself. Jansen at his best, in the middle of nowhere. Crystal chandeliers and Nobilis chintz. Quite quite amazing. The tents themselves really look like a Cecil B. de Mille *décor* for a super film.

"The next day we flew to Isfahan which is also a dump but has the most beautiful moske in the world. I would not say *ça vaut le détour* if the detour is too great a one. But from Teheran it is only a half hour flight. We had an idiot guide who knew less than we did but still it was interresting and luckily sunny and blue. But oh so cold. My tropical *guarderobe* was not at all ment for 6 below zero which we found in Isfahan, and we nearly froze. Luckily the Ambassadress with whom we had dined in Teheran had lent me a pair of boots so at least my feet stayed on.

"We got back late last night, exhausted but happy and today we 'did' the museum, and the crown jewels which are beyond description. The smallest emerald is like an egg. Bowls full of diamonds gold tea pots enamel, pearls unbelievable. Forgive the wretched typewriter. This is the second time the hotel has sworn it was O.K. and charged us for its repair. I must pack and go to bed as once again we get up at five tomorrow to leave for Pakistan. But unless I can manage a quick trip to Taxila, which is fairly near Rawalpindi, to see the Greco Hindu excavations, there wont be a thing to do there so I may write again on a decent typewriter."

From Marina's diary:

February 7, Islamabad, Pakistan: "A Mrs. Garufi took me to a school for retarded children. So sad. Tears. Gave them 50 dollars. Mrs. G. had a big lunch for me with Pakistani ladies. All lovely intelligent and so bitter, discouraged and despairing about the fate of their country. All want reforms. All hard working. But how?"

February 9, New Delhi, India: "Staying at the embassy with Ambassador [Kenneth] Keating who at 71 looks like a naughty schoolboy."

February 10, New Delhi: "Shopped again for miniatures and rubies — the very words are a joy. Went to Ravi Shankar concert. It is alien to my ear. Lakshmi Shankar sang. A bit like bouzoukia [Greek music]."

February 13, New Delhi-Calcutta: "Cy's only day of rest. Went for a long walk in the zoo. Saw white tigers and the Lesser Panda. I want one!!"

Again to Dodo on February 17 from Saigon:

"It does make one very discouraged as to human nature and the implacable patern of greatness and stupidity alternating which comes over and over again just like night follows day. Specially disheartening when one is in a week-old new nation like Bangla-Desh and sees the enthusiasm and the euphoria, the heroism, the unselfishness, the fresh green hopes and determination, and KNOWS that sooner rather than later, politics ambitions, personal hatreds revenge poverty and above all disorganisation, will take their place. However, lets not denigrate the joyes while they last; and even though we only stayed twenty four hours it was heart warming and lovely, to see people so full of self-satisfaction so full of hope and promise.

"Specially after about ten months of unspeakable horrors. The stories of what the Pakistanis did, in the hope of destroying the very fiber of these people, so that even if they won their independence, they would not be able to rise again, for sheer lack of people, is something to make your hair stand on end. People talk of over two hundred thousand women raped, who are now pregnant and a problem. These are the survivors. Others had their hearts cut out, others their eyes limbs skins etc. The young Times man in Dacca who had probably led a sheltered American life up to now, is so shattered by his experience during the few weeks war, that there is not one vestige of objectivity left in him bless his heart.

"Cy saw Sheik Mujib for an hour and he is certainly a leader with all the qualities it takes to lead. How he will guide and administer a hopeless little nation god alone and perhaps the Indians and the Russians can tell. But oh what a nice change to be at the begining of everything. Dacca was much less of a hell hole than I expected, with grass and lovely mango and Banyan trees. The whole country is flat and has more rivers than roads. America is the arch enemy nowadays which did not prevent the crowds from pouring onto the tarmac for the arrival of Teddy Kennedy and greeting him like a messiah. He was there at the same time as we, on a private visit. But nothing is private when you are a Kennedy.

"But I must go back a little. The post from this part of the world is so awful you may not have had my letter from Teheran (almost surely) and one from Delhi. We had a most delicious lazy time there (I did I mean) shopping and sight seing and sitting by the swimming pool, and the Ambassador was absolutely charming. Gave a huge dinner in our honor Saturday night when I sat next to general Manekshaw, the hero of the war, who is charming and bright and looks almost like a carricature of a British brigadier, moustache and monocle and all. They are all very polite, but now and then one gets a real waspish anti American blast. All the good one does is taken for granted and all the bad remembered for ever. Ah me.

"We flew to Calcutta first, which is a really tragic awful place, and then to Dacca with three hours to wait, going and five on the way back. If I put end to end the hours I have sat on hard benches in airports I would have a second life to spend. But in Dacca I sat next to a sweet little Dutch refugee worker, who was carrying a little Bengali girl home with her. Imagine she had found her, by sheer miracle among a whole mass of dead bodies, about to be thrown onto a truck, and taken her out, and adopted her, and was taking her home to Holland. Apparently for the first three months she never spoke never smiled, never moved. And there she was, now runing around from one to the other of us, taking a stuffy old English man's hat, and pulling it over her eyes, nestling against me and playing with my ring, smiling talking and completely confident in humans. Needless to say I was in tears watching this little black crippled ugly adorable little thing knowing what a tiny tiny thread of luck her destiny had depended upon.

"Calcutta is terrible. Even without refugees. With them, one wonders that humans can survive on so little.

"Imagine, Japan Air Lines have lost all our luggage except one small bag. I was the lucky one as it held all the very light dresses. But I wont be when we get to Tokyo and New York with nothing but a cotton dress or two. And ALL my delicious shopping in Delhi, is gone. Saris miniatures dresses for friends for Jessica and Jonathan. All gone. And poor Cy has *nothing*. Just a thick tweed jacket he was travelling in, and a pair of grey flannels. Not a tooth brush not a razor and above all not a paper a book and all his notes are gone.* Its awful and yet strange that this should be the first time it has ever happened to us. The air port at Dacca is total chaos with people smoking on take off, or on the tarmac, with no one really knowing what

---

* Strangely enough, the missing baggage eventually turned up in Saigon.

they are doing. Well we arrived in Saigon yesterday evening and relieved as I was not to have David here, I missed his little face beyond the customs barrier. But the air port is covered with bright bougainvilia, which is a nice change from the mortar smoke it was covered in, when I first got here six years ago. We are staying with friends of Cy's in a nice air conditioned house, which I admit is nicer than the Caravelle hotel. Also there is greater hope of your getting this via them than any of the other letters up to now."

She wrote about Vietnam to Denise Boisot from Hong Kong on February 26: "One still hears thud thud thump in the background while sipping iced bloody maries in romantic gardens. I still dont know where and what and who is thumping at whom. But I did have one trip outside Saigon at long last. I felt rather sheepish about it, as I mentioned how sad I was never to have gone up in an army helecopter or seen anything outside the city, and then a delicious colonel arranged this trip for me to Long Bhin base, which I did not deserve as you can believe and it made me feel like a child who had wanted a ride on a fire engine, and that any moment someone would say dont you know there is a war on.

"However once it happened I was thrilled. Specially to see, in that grim beige treeless, air less ghastly place, young soldiers just like our own used to be. Proud and humble, old fashioned patriots, disciplined clean, quite unlike the grim picture of hopheaded fragging brutes that the press has lead us to imagine the entire Viet Nam army is like. The Major who took me up in his helicopter was a dream. Sort of like Paddy [Leigh Fermor] or Xan [Fielding] or Bill McClean [all three British paratroop officers in World War II] might have been. The helicopter is wide open on all sides, and I was afraid I might get *vertige* and make a *bruta figura,* but it was marvellous *au contraire* and I adored it. We flew over a few fire bases, that is small combat units hidden in the country side, as protection for the base. Alas also miles of defoliated forrest, like some kind of Dante-esk landscape of grey dead trees.

"Cy got an interview with General Abrams, which was terrific and also President Thieu, so his record is unbrocken. But what a struggle it all is. I am afraid that relations between authorities and the press are irreperably awful and neither trust the other, if they say the sky is blue. Which it is'nt here very often. I am also afraid that in this case the press is wrong. They all assume, that they know better than anyone else, that whoever is talking to them is hiding something, but worse than that only bad news is real. They all went around saying this was such a tense moment. The Tet offensive would be upon us any minute now, etc. etc and nothing happened at all.

"Perhaps this was even more nerve wracking than if it had happened. I cant tell. But everything seemed better to me. Bycicles have been replaced by Hondas, which is not such an improvement I admit, and the traffic death rate is gigantic, but at least denotes mounting prosperity. Almost no barbed wire, and hardly any sand bags. No American soldiers anywhere in sight. And no black market tooth paste and chewing gum, at every street corner. The Vietnamese on their own are doing much better. But then I sat next to a diplomat and a business man at dinner one night and they boasted of five and four sons respectively and when I asked, where they all were, three were in London, four in Paris, some in Canada. Not a single one in the army.

"We got to Hong Kong last night and it is like another world. We have been in places all this time, where there is both illiteracy and *exces de zele;* so they take half an hour to find the page on your passeport and another half to read it, and a whole one to find the right stamp for it, while one stands either freezing or boiling, in an agony of irritability. Here, we were through in three minutes flat. So curteous, so quick so bright. And ever since I have been saying a small silent prayer of thanks and for the preservation of that grand old friend the expence account. Our room in the loveliest hotel in the world. It is almost cold. I miscalculated there. Except for Bangkok air port, we have been near cold or very cold, and even Saigon was just right, which is amazing. February is the coolest month, breeding lilac out of the Tet land ha ha. I have not started on my shopping orgy yet, and only wish my little enveloppe of travellers checks were five times as fat. But even a little I hope will go a long way."

On February 29, Marina wrote Michael Edwards: "Arriving in Hong Kong after three weeks in the so aptly named sub-continent, was like coming to another world. We were escorted by a smiling employe, to a real Rolls Royce which was there for us. We drove to the hotel sitting up stiff like vice roys, and the hotel is a dream. Linen sheets, yellow spray orchids MANGOES, the deepest bath tub, bath salt, and the most beautiful view in the world. How I shall get back to everyday life I dont know. The harbour is so beautiful, except that progress has here too, supplied the junks with out board motors so alas those lovely dark brown sails are becoming more and more rare.

"Everyone here like elsewhere I suppose talk of nothing but the Nixon visit, and old China watchers feel that soon there may be no room for them in this generation. We are off tomorrow to Tokyo and I hope we may be able to take a tiny trip somewhere outside the city. Cy is seeing the Emperor the day after tomorrow and perhaps after that we can go. Then Hawaii for a few days mainly for Cy to collect his wits and his notes, and sleep a night or so before we plunge into a new continent."

On March 5 she wrote from Tokyo to Dodo: "Another country. The seventh in six weeks, and it is a bit dizzy making. I went into a shop the other day, and picked up a little blue and white cup and asked the price which was about three hundred yen. Three hundred anything seems fairly much to me and I was about to put it down when I discovered that this was one dollar. Its all rather confusing but oh so delightful. If only I had lots and lots of money just for this sort of time, and above all a private airoplane what fun it would be for everybody. I already have pearls for you Fanny Kitty and Eleni. But oh how I would like to also have kimonos and silks and coral and other silly things like stuffed birds and whiker chairs and five hundred year old chests, and above all, lots and lots of Imari china. I got David eight dear little cups for his new establishement wherever that may be.

"Here too we are staying at the Embassy, with old friends from Afganistan and Lebanon days and they are specially nice to put us up as they are going back to the US in about ten days and are out of their minds with fair well parties and with packing. Tokyo is hideous, and nothing to see except the museum and lots of little museums which show different things every month, such a good idea. But alas more than a lot to look at in the shops. More than eight million people live in Tokyo and the polution is such, that one hardly ever sees Fujiyama any more and the sky is beige. I wonder if a day will come when we will talk about the sky once having been blue, the way we talk about the earth once having been liquid and then flame and then ice? Think of the whole of the Greek population in one city. I hardly ever go for a walk alone as it is impossible to find one's way back. The streets have no names, the houses no numbers and even if they did I would never be able to say it in Japanese. Luckily the nice ambassadress gives me her car, so I can wander about with the chauffeur behind me.

"Tomorrow I have been invited to a Japanese lady's house for lunch which is a rare honor as they hardly ever ask one to their houses. Mostly out of inferiority complexes as they all live rather modestly. She is an old and very aristocratic lady and went to Cambridge about fifty years ago which shows they must have been very *évolué* even then. She is charming. We have already been to a couple of Geisha parties, and I worry so much about our friend Fred Warner coming here as British Ambassador next month. Do you remember him from Athens. He is almost seven feet tall and will never be able to squeeze his legs under a geisha table. One eats tiny delicate little things for hours on end and I do see that they take more pains with appearance than substance. Everything comes decorated like an etching, with a leaf or a petal or sprig of ginger and looks divine. But sweet raw fish I dont like, and sea weed which should be delicious is'nt.

"Cy has seen the emperor but everyone is in such a flap after President Nixon's visit to China and a potential raprochement, and Taiwan returning to China, that they talk of nothing else."

To Marinette on March 7 from Tokyo: "On Sunday poor old Far took his second half day off, since Persepolis, and we went to the museum and then a long walk in the Imperial park and had lunch believe it or not at a German beer hall. Typical. The little Japanese girls dressed in dirndles and frilly shirts hardly managed to look Bavarian but were very sweet. The women dont wear kimonos in the streets any longer, more is the pity, but when they do, as for special occasions they really look like a flower bed."

To Dodo from Honolulu on March 12: "We have been here for a few days now, and it is both lovely and ghastly. The hotel is too beautiful, with orchids everywhere and pools and water falls and my friends the dolphins. That is the good part. The bad is that we are back in the so-called civilisations, which means that all *courtoisie* vanishes. The Japanese with 8 million people living on top of each other manage to be as polite and ettiquettish as they were under the shoguns. Here one asks for a drink and they say Go get it yourself.

"On the plus side, is also the sea the climate which at this moment is paradisiac, the flowers etc. On the minus, the hundreds and hundreds of middle aged plump awful tourrists in flower or bird or geometric design ridiculous costumes of every imaginable shape and colour and it is awful when I remember that I too am middle aged and fat and wear some bright colours. It makes me want to put on black and a handkerchief round my head like the old Greek peasants.

"But we have found several friends on the island who have been kind and hospitable and taken me to lovely beaches away from the hotel area. One awful blow. I tried surf ridding and cant even paddle the board out any more, let alone *stand* on it. Ah me. Fifteen years does make a difference alas. So today I am not only stiff and achy in every limb but in spirit also. The children of this friend of ours took me out, and it was so sad making a *bruta figura,* but their mother called to tell me they had all said on coming back that I was 'neat' the highest compliment the young can express, and a good sport. Praise from the young is praise indeed. But little comfort for growing old. Cy poor fellow has had a lot of work here too, so did not get the well deserved rest he expected."

On March 14 to Denise Boisot from Honolulu: "A friend gave me the most beautiful little two-foot high Thai spirit house, and I cannot find in the whole damned place someone to crate it for me, so to Cy's immense releif I have to leave it behind. On arrival I almost died. The people in front of us at customs had every single thing looked at, even Kotex and tooth paste tubes, by a fiend of a woman and I had visions of myself (Cy was pretending not to know me by then) washing dishes to the end of my days in order to pay customs, but thank god, when my turn came she asked if I had anything not bought in the US so I said yes everything as I dont live in the States, at which she just waved me by and I almost fainted with relief."

She wrote Dodo on March 23 from New York:

"How lucky we are *mama mou glykia* above all with health and so many loving people round us. We arrived here on Thursday and then went off at once to the country to see my friend Pamela who just married Averell Harriman aged eighty and a widower of one year. They were going off to London for Easter so this was our only chance to see them. I had gone out Friday night with another old friend whose mother is terribly ill and who needed comforting, and when I got back who did I find sitting on Cy's bed busily talking but David on his way back from Texas where he had been to discuss jobs. He looks wonderful, shortish hair, and seems just one tiny bit heavier and absolutely eatable. He has several offers of jobs but says it is too difficult to concentrate on his thessis and exams and also think of jobs so he will try and forget about them until June. Everyone was always commiserating with me while he was in Viet Nam, but I find I am more worried and to be pitied now. To suddenly have a man for a son, is almost worse than have a soldier. A man with probably two weeks off a year now until the end of my life. We have been so spoiled for the last twenty six years, that I cant bear the thought of his being a grown up and living all alone. He came with us to the country and it was so lovely to see him and Cy heads together, all day long talking away, walking discussions and getting on like brothers.

"We are going to Cambridge on Friday to stay with him for three days and then on to Washington. Almost luckily most of our friends are away for Easter, so I dont have that problem of trying to fit them all in which with the best will in the world is not possible in ten days. But Christine Claudel *is* here and she is always a joy and I also saw Koutsi Ebon* yesterday and Deppy Messinesi who is really a friend from *dans la nuit des temps.*

"New York must have something poissonous in the air. Even people whom we knew abroad good friends nice simple hard working journalists, we meet them again here and they have been infected by the rat race of power and scrambling for survival. A card from Jessica which turned my heart over. See you soon grand ma and grand pa, on it in huge letters. I miss those children so it is a physical thing like a cold in the head.

"Here we have found a perfect epidemic of middle to old aged divorces. One friend of sixty five who is a millionaire and was sitting on his Florida terrace one day when he saw a strange sight in his pool. It was a dolphin who had somehow got lost from its Marine research centre several hundred miles away so he put it into his station wagon and took it back and its trainer turned out to be a lovely young woman also married with four children. The dolphin was called Tinkabelle and the next thing anyone knew he had left his wife of thirty years standing and run off with the dolphin lady. Oh well, the young have been rebbeling for the last six years. Its our turn now. I am sure the young will be horrified."

From Marina's diary:

March 24, Boston: "Polar waiting for us. Dinner at Guido Goldman's. Bingo [Gowrie] was there lovelier than ever and sad looking although Guido and Henry Kissinger are sick with love for her. Also a girl called

---

* Koutsi Baltazzi Ebon, a girlhood friend of Marina's.

Doris [Kearns] who is an assistant professor of social science and writing a book on presidential power. The young get cleverer every year."

The same day Marina wrote Marinette: "The most delicious surprise as Far may have told you was the sudden appearance of Polar on our doorstep Friday night. Looking very well and shoes on. He was so funny about them too. They are the best Made in England can offer, and he bought them last time for the only purpose of going to see people about a job. But he got them on sale and one had been in the window at least twenty years he says, so it is pale beige while its brother is dark brown. He is so funny about them and they hurt like hell.

"We all went up to Haywire house [Pam's home] for the week end. Averell had a cold. Sunday we all went over to Mrs. [Brooke] Astor's for lunch, the prettiest house, the best food and such flowers as one only sees at the Chelsea flower show. I was sitting next to a charming man, and saying how everyone commiserated with me when David was in Viet Nam, but that I was more worried now, at the thought of his suddenly being a real grown up and in search of a job, and how almost by accident he had gotten so interrested in oil and natural gas, via his trip to Algeria, and he said oh may I talk to him and turned out to be the President of Mobiloil. Nothing like a right word at the right time, except that David is a bit leary of working for such a gigantic organisation where one gets lost in the thousands of employees."

From Marina's diary:

March 29, Washington: "Lunch at [David] Bruces for Lucet farewell [French ambassador Charles Lucet was departing]. Charles made a speech all about Cy and de Gaulle. He must be punch drunk with farewells. Most embarrassing."

Back in New York, Marina sadly wrote *Mama mou glykia* (April 6):

"I must say it is grim to be getting to the deadable age. So many of our friends were either dead or dying, or ill, or divorced, it was a hecatombe. However it was lovely to see the survivors amongst whom thank god the Bohlens in spite of Chip having had three bad operations and about to have a fourth one. But at least not cancer. The worst tragedy is our beloved Stew Alsop* who has exactly the same thing as Gilberte and it is really heartbreaking to see a large handsome seemingly indestructible man, who knows that he is dying. I spent a week end with them and had a lump in my throat the whole time.

"The nice thing is that David can come down this week end and spend it with us and it will be a hard fairwell. I cant tell you how I hate the thought of his being a grown up and looking for a job. *Teleiossan ta psemata* [Let's face reality]. If only he can get a good one which will interrest him, I wont mind so much. And if god were to continue as kind to us as he has always been and get him a job starting in September or even August which would allow him a month of rest and sleep and Spetses then that would be the ideal."

Back in Paris, she wrote the Bohlens (April 18), after Chip had had another operation:

"Hoping that by now, it is all over, and all well. Ouf. I know you will have a million people to inform of the glad news, but if you can make it a million and one and send a post card we would be grateful. Of all the people I know Chip is the one who deserves most never never to have anything worse than a small hang-over. Because there should be a reward on this earth, for enjoying things and people and life and golf and other goodies as much as he does.

"If this letter is typed even worse than usual it is because the walls, floors and cealing seem to be coming up and down at me, with land sickeness, after five days on a demented Atlantic Ocean. The [liner] France looks like a super de lux tenement building. Gone the shiny brass, gone the mahogany and deep leather arm chairs of our childhood. Prison grey is the main colour, and masses of plastic, vynil, chrome, psychedelic tappisteries, and ALL chairs have spindly little steal legs like a second class *caffe de la gare.* However it is very comfortable and rides the waves like a dignified dowager so we were not too *secoué.*

"The poor little pale green Lucets could not avoid the purser's coctails

---

* Who wrote before his death the moving book *Stay of Execution.*

or the captain's gala and poor Charles must be in a trance of after dinner speaches, as I saw him scribbling notes on the back of his menu and he wanted the English word for 'houle' to quote some Baudelaire at us, but no one asked him or made a toast or anything and I felt him almost dissapointed. They were delirious about their presents incidentally and Charles saying *'Même la bibliothèque nationale n'a pas un livre comme le mien.'*

"The only other celebrities aboard were the [Salvador] Dalis, walking their two ocelots every morning on the promenade deck, and making all the poodles pommeranians dachshunds etc of the less adventurous animal lovers on board, look sheepish. He is sweet and crazy but friendly and chatty. Gala is waspish. But is eighty and looks sixty which seems to me wildely unfair, for a nasty person. Five days went quite fast, and I must say the French are the only civilised emigration authorities. We disembarked like royalty, and went through customs with one polite *'Rien à déclarer? Merci.'* And straight on to the train. France too was doing her best to welcome us home and the whole of Normandy was in bloom. Green fields and apple blossom and primeroses by the millions which made me think of you and our secret place.

"The house too was full of white rose bushes, sent thoughtfully by Bob and Jane [Joyce] so the return of the native was most agreable. Beagle barked for half an hour. And now a day later I am still trying to unpack *completely* for the first time in three months and answer the telephone, and read my mail and even though I swore I would not get into anything that moves, ever again, I cant resist going over to see my babies and the new house and all, so I shall go next week.

"Cy poor chap has to go to Rome as he was offered a thousand dollars for a face-to-face [on] television with Arthur Schlesinger and Eric Sevareid about the Pentagon papers and with the dollar at below zero these days, and hamburger at four dollars a pound, he thinks he had better. But he will join me in London direct from Rome."

In a letter to Pam Harriman on May 16:

"I was sort of half heartedly roaming around the house, when Cy called and said he felt fluffy too, and would I come and pick him up and we would go for a walk. This at two in the afternoon. We got back at four, found the back door torn from its hinges and the house like Stalingrad after a direct hit. Matresses torn from the beds, linen, under-wear, clothes books all on the floor, closets in a shambles, drawers up-turned and emptied and Beagle blisfully asleep on the sofa. All three of Cy's guns, out of their cases and one in each room (presumably in case we got back unexpectedly). And every bit of jewelry we own gone, as well as all the presents, all the things in our unpacked bags.

"Still we were lucky in a way. They did not take the Dali or any silver or my fur coat, or even the guns, which are worth more than my modest jewels. What breaks my heart is that figuring we wont be going back to the Far East every day, as we get older, I had spent every penny of my pocket money to buy pearl necklaces for all my family all the way down to our beloved cook. Twelve beautiful presents each in its little brocade bag, and I was so looking forward to the pleasure of giving them. ALL gone. And to add insult to injury, the beasts had even taken the time to eat our dinner and spit bits and pieces on the floor.

"And the police, when we went to report it, did not even lift their heads. *'Que voulez-vous messieurs-dames, vous êtes le huitième cambriolage de cette après-midi dans le quartier!'* And I shudder to think of what might have happened if we had indeed come back a half hour earlier and caught them in the act. Only yesterday a poor Mr. de Courcel (not Geoffroy) was killed in his office by robbers. I dont care that much about the jewels. Only humans are indispensable, but it does give one a creepy fealing, of being at the mercy of anybody these days. It took us days to get the house back in order, and that added to my lack of time or concentration for writing to you. And then a few days later I left for London as I was longing to see the babies, and it was better to go at once even before plunging into Paris life once again.

"They are just too dreamy for words and I adored having them both in my bed in the morning. And also managed to see lots of sweet friends, as one only can in London, where they rally round so fast and warmly. Went to two dances. One of the French Embassy, and one of Fred Warner's to celebrate *à la fois,* his birthday, his son's birth and his departure for Tokyo in no time at all. A thousand friends, in a strange studio full of plastic psychedelic rather anatomical looking sculpture which kept changing colour, all this somewhere by the docks. Alas the orchestra was so unbelievably loud, that our heads seemed to be coming off, and although there were so many people I longed to talk to, Evangeline [Bruce] and I sat huddled in a corner speaking in desparing sign-language."

From Marina's diary:

May 25, Paris: "Taxi driver offered me his jacket as it was raining so hard. Carried the flowers for me. So I, touched, bought him a bunch of flowers. Florist so touched she would not accept money for them. Ah me. If more of the world were like that."

To Avis Bohlen on June 14: "All well here. Cy's gout gone for the present (touch wood) but he is lunching with the Queen of Holland today, and if she pours Bols gin down his willing throat, he may come back with another attack. He called this morning to say hullo and the hotel operator gave me FIVE wrong gentlemen, before getting to Cy. The world is really becoming more and more inefficient in direct proportion to the rise of technocracy. I went to Morgan's on Friday to deposit thirteen hundred dollars and they gave me a receipt for fifteen hundred. I cashed a check for 2000 francs and they gave me three thousand. Alas my old fashioned up-bringing made me take it back. Your own dear letter to me took 14 days to get here."

From Marina's diary:

June 17, Paris: "Went to Grammont wedding at Vallière. The couple went off in a balloon. The Duchesse looks like a cook. The young were wildly dressed and all wore pants."

Marina went to Greece early that summer since her mother was unwell. As always she adored every moment.

From her diary:

July 5, Athens: "Catastrophic session at hairdresser's. I look like an aging leftwing liberal lesbian."

Magnum Opus by a gentleman orthodox priest philosopher and scholar named Georgius Florovski, whom I am ashamed to say I had never heard of, is a devastatingly beautiful Lithuanian called Vadim something, his Russian wife Masha, and an American with a beard looking more Russian than either of them. Apart from being good looking, intelligent and nice, Vadim sings like a nightingale and the other night Jane produced a guitar, and off we were from *Ochi Tchornia* to old Georgian ballads, reducing us to goo, what with the full moon and the jasmin and all. So yesterday I took all of us to Xylokeriza. It was possibly the prettiest day in weeks (I neglected to tell you the shocking news that it has been raining and cold for days) and the water was like melted emeralds. Vadim had his guitar and Rob his flute and I a bottle of ouzo, and Nata and I went out and got two hundred sea urchins, which we opened and spread along the rocks, and it was a Roman fiesta *la tête à l'ombre les pieds dans l'eau* and the singing so sweet, we forgot everything and got back for lunch at ten passed four."

She wrote Avis September 15:

"Heard with horror from Jane that Chip has had yet another operation, and that you could not go to Wyoming. I could cry and kick. Why why should such beastly things happen to people, any people, but above all to those who deserve it the least? I am shattered, for you all and for all your friends who love you so.

"There is a small possibility that we might come for the elections which are not far off, after all, and then we will see you and hug you and talk. All well here. David left yesterday and the house feels empty and a little sad but at the same time we are thrilled to have him go off to be a man. And he did have the most glorious summer, anyone can pray for. A really superb fairwell to irresponsible adolescance. And it was really so delicious to have four generations under the same roof, all so gay and dear and funny. Cy managed to come at the end of August so he had a few days, with grand children crawling all over his face and tummy and chest, like octapuses, and although he pretended to groan and moan, he loved it all. Adrian came too but only for three days.

"And now, *'hier c'était l'été, c'est aujourd'hui l'automne.'* Some rain, the first cyclamen, and practically no one left on the island, which is what Cy likes best. Miracle of miracles, he has only had a few twinges of gout, but no serious attack. I think it is the first pain-free summer he has had since we bought the house."

From the diary:

September 24, Spetsais: "I polished furniture, fixed flowers for party, etc. Claudette Colbert at 67 looks like she did in her first movies when I was a child. Fantastic. She came with Slim.* Rained through dinner. Claudette ate in Cy's raincoat and Chinese hat. Very gay."

September 30, Spetsais: "Went on pic nic to Agia Paraskevi. Picked a giant bunch of cyclamen. Cy walked. Saw a dear. Luckily did not shoot it."

October 9, Paris: "Fany drove me to airport. All smooth and easy except carrying three dozen tuberoses. Sat next to nice Frenchwoman two mettres tall. Almost crashed on landing, right off the field. At least my body would have been flower-strewn!"

Right after returning to Paris, Marina wrote Dodo (October 14):

"Each year I think, it cant be as lovely as it was last year, and each year it is better. This one was perhaps the best, with two new members in the family and Cy so well and David so happy and Marinaki [Marinette] enjoying herself like a little girl again. And you, observing it all, sort of from a warm and friendly distance, and as close as possible when necessary. And all our friends of all ages adoring you and envying me, because of you. Oh god we are lucky."

To Dodo again on October 30: "Well the birthday week-end went off like a dream. We managed to keep David's arrival a secret and on Friday morning, the door bell rang, and Cy said I wonder who it can be so early, and I said Oh probably another present, and in walked David. It really was the nicest present in the world. Poor old David. He rather hates his job, which has not turned out as interesting as it was supposed to be. He has a nice flat however and as soon as he gets a day off to go to Cambridge and

---

* Lady Keith, a friend.

get his belongings it will be quite nice.

"It really was amazing luck, how everything coincided. Cy's birthday, the British Embassy ball, to which all his friends from Spetses were also invited, and two more old old friends from London, who turned up unexpectedly and asked for me, only to find that David was here too.

"It was nice to look at one's children dancing and being so good looking. Marinette had a black dress on and her turquoise necklace and was irresistible. This in tremendous competition because I must say the young English were dazzling. We have never seen so many pretty girls all together. Even Cy enjoyed watching. Friday Cy David and I lunched together and talked a lot, and then David and Beagle and I walked home through the Tuilleries and the weather was gold-cold and sparckling, so it was lovely. Then in the evening we had the dance and Saturday lunch nineteen friends of David's arrived. Thank god I had made two large *moussakas* the night before (before going to the ball) and had some roast *pintades* and lots of cheeses and salads, and five raspberry tarts. There was not a crumb left."

From the diary:

November 29, Paris: "Karamanlis lunch. Sat next to Raymond Cartier who thinks the French revolution was the beginning of all evil and the end of civilisation. Funny."

December 3, Paris: "Beagle [Benjamin] worse. Shots every two hours. I feel he wont last long. Stayed home to look after him all day."

To Dodo on December 12: "Well, it was inevitable at fifteen for poor little Beagly to die, sooner or later, but later always seems so much sooner somehow. He was ill for only a week though. We got back from London, and found him looking very thin. I took him to the doctor who said at once that he had uremia so very advanced that he did not think there was much hope at his age. But we tried nonetheless every possible remedy for a week. But he was getting thinner and thinner and hardly ate anything and so weak he tried to wag his tail and could'nt.

"It was really heartbreaking. I have not seen Cy cry not even when his mother died. I cant tell you how empty and sad the house feels. No longer that enthusiastic welcome, behind the door, each time we came into the house, were it from three months in India or the grocer round the corner. No longer his head in our laps, no longer the walks, when we knew every tree, every lamp post every motor car tyre. We keep changing our minds and one minute think we should get a new puppy this instant, and another that we must never never again have another dog."

Marina wrote Dodo again on December 20: "Cy says we will probably take off for the US on the 15th more or less, which leaves really no time at all. However, with David in New York it makes the trip doubly pleasurable. I get calls all the time from various friends of his, giving us his news and all is well. Emma Soames is going to spend Xmas with him and he is taking her to Washington chez Alsop for Xmas day which will be very nice.

"We have just seen our last guests to the door, after a most succesful lunch party of tremendous grandeur. We had the new British ambassador and his wife, old friends, and with them one Rothschild, Prince Paul and Princesse Olga, Malraux who has given up drink and now talks so that one can understand all he says which is a great deal and all of it fascinating, and Mr. and Mme [Maurice] Schumann who I must say are marvellous company if not the best of Foreign ministers. And such errudition.

"The conversation was scintillating, and such a relief and change from endless 'are you going away for the holidays' type social chit chat. They were talking about Mazarin and Cromwell and the relative merits of princes of the church as heads of state, and it was delicious to listen to. Malraux is a genius. Prince Paul gave me the loveliest clock for Xmas, I was so surprised as usually it is a magnum of champagne, but as Cy has gout and they knew it they brought this little parcel mumbling 'this is not bad for gout' and I almost fainted when I saw it. Last year's Rothschild contribution to our wine cellar did very well and in spite of a *conseil de ministres* everyone stayed quite late. I was so glad for Cy who seemed to enjoy himmself, a rare occurence at one's own parties."

Right after we flew to New York at the end of January we went down to Washington.

From Marina's diary:

January 28, Washington: "Lovely evening with Henry Kissinger and his girl Nancy [Maginnes].* Spine chilling talk of corruption in the Pentagon, dishonesty of press, Russia and China, etc. I believe the last person I ever listened to. Hard to make out the other side's point of view. Hope there are some patriots left."

February 8, Washington: "Had a sandwidge nap and then off to War College for Cy's speech on Western European leadership. Speech good. Questions difficult. In time to pop in on the Harrimans for a nightcap."

To Dodo on February 4: "By sheer chance I spent practically every meal of the week end sitting next to Mr. Kissinger whom I found quite irresistible. Someone asked me if I would have found him as delicious as all that had he been an antiquaire, or a plain school teacher and of course *post facto* I cannot answer. There is undoubtedly something about power and notoriety that makes one look twice. *Ça fait gagner quinze jours* as Sagan says. And in this case *quinze minutes* is enough. Naturally he was talking about the negotiations and alas I cant remember what he said was confidential and what not, so I hardly dare repeat anything except what was told in front of ten other people. One fascinating thing he said to illustrate the total suspiciousness of the Vietnamese was that the night the protocole was finally finished accepted done with, initialled and sealed (at their demand with every single page having a hole and a ribbon through it) even then, they insisted that they keep the English copy and the Americans have the Vietnamese one, so as not to perhaps open it at night and add something.

"He said also that the one and only thing that you can never never do is put even one small card on the table, because their minds work in such a devious way that they would misconstrue it in a hundred different directions. One time he said, he was so bored fed up angry tired and despairing, that in a fit of devilry he said one or two outrageous things like linking together two clauses that had nothing to do with each other, or demanding some totally unwanted and unacceptable thing, in a sort of *exercise de style,* and he got more concessions out of these demands than out of any of his

---

* Now Mrs. Kissinger.

other logical possible hopeful ones. But the thing that I liked best in him, was how modest and curious about other people he is. He talked a lot about David whom he likes enormously, asked me all kinds of things and any time he made even the least disparaging remark about anyone, he almost always added some little justifying qualifications: 'Oh well you know he is an old man,' or 'well you know he is sad to be out of power,' or 'he is too young' or something.

"The only ones he was deeply bitter about was the press on the whole saying that after they have all been screaming for four years for almost unconditional end to the war, he had hoped and expected at least one day of generosity one day of rejoicing or granting credit where it was due, and he did not even get that. The most repeated comment was 'well we could have gotten all this four years ago anyway.' Which is just not true. But alas the biggest victim of this war has been truth and logic and I must say being less calm and disciplined than the good Dr. Kissinger I have a hard time keeping my temper with those who seem to take a special pleasure in attributing every ill of this world from war to flat feet, to the United States."

To Dodo from New York on February 15: "In Washington more than anywhere else, where life turns uniquely around politics, the devaluation of words strikes one as even worse than in our beloved country. You hear people talking of Nazi America. A book comes out, and half our friends denounce it as garbage, trash a pack of lies etc, and the other half greet it as the best book in all time, the most informed, the most objective etc. So one ends up by believing nobody.

"The one lovely touching heart warming thing is the gradual return of the prisoners, but even there poor old USA suffers from its own gigantism. Every tear, every embrace on Television. The nation as a whole has determined that they will be greeted with all the love and care possible. So hospitals are evacuated for them doctors mobilised psychiatrists alerted, so that one almost has the impression that they are letting the side down, but looking on the whole strong, thin but healthy and not at all destroyed freaks, as most of the bleeding heart peace-lovers would have them be. However it does bring the old tear to the eye, to see them fall into their mother's or wives arms, and greet little girls and boys aged seven nine ten, who they left as babies and whom they have to get to know now.

"We got back as I said a short while ago, and we have tomorrow and Saturday to unpack and repack and see David every minute we can, as we leave on Sunday morning for Mexico. You are so sweet to worry and admonish me to be careful, but you know we are not going to darkest jungles just yet. Mexico first, where we shall be staying with the Ambassador in great luxury, I am sure, and all the trappings which make short visits so much more agreeable. I mean cars and friends who take one to the right places, museums markets churches etc without wasting time. One of David's old Harvard friends lives there and he wants to look after me too. I do enjoy my children's friends and am so touched when they like me. We are even going to Acapulco for one day, which is a pleasure place and not on the usual journalistic circuit, but luckily the plane for Australia leaves from there, so we will see it. Fiji of course is the place I look forward to most, and if I get some exceptional shell it will be lovely. I feel I must get as much out of this trip as possible, as I am sure it will be the last one to the Far East."

To Marinette on February 17: "I must say I am totally discouraged by this our noble country. Nothing, but nothing seems to be pure or objective any longer here from politics to the church to newspapers to advertising. There is always 'an angle' somewhere and also another horrid fealing I have, that the selling buisiness has over-powered the thing sold, be it laxative or ideology, which both become incidental, and subservient to the chalange of selling it. And the credibility gap at zero, not only in the politicians but in authors journalists merchants schools. Washington was really confusing.

"I had made a great booboo too, as Pam and Averell had asked if they could give a party for us and I breesily said yes the 8th would be lovely and of course it was the night of the War College, the only thing we could not possibly change or chuck. But luckily we finished quite early and managed to go in after dinner and apologise in person. Pam looking ravishing and a lot of agreable people including chief Justice Warren who remembered me from Spetses fifteen years ago which flattered me no end. He had come on Kay Graham's mother's yacht one summer.

"Then the next night Joe and Susan Mary had a lovely party for us, and I sat between Stew Alsop and Mr. Hubert Humpfrey and had a splendid time. HH was at his best; funny, gay; serious lucid and nice. Alas perhaps too nice to ever have been a good president. On the other side was the notorious senator Eagleton. Poor Joe, when the cigars came around he took one, sniffed it, broke it in two pronounced it dry cut it in two threw it on the floor, crushed it with his shoe, took another, same thing, took a third, dipped it into his brandy glass, in the hopes of making it less dry, did not work tossed it off and took a fourth while Joe sort of pursed up all over 'like the oyster who has just received the drop of lemon.'

"Only Stewart Alsop it seems to me remains calm objective and sensible, without being pompous. Luckily he seems all right with two transfusions a week. We went to Mrs. Longworth's 89th birthday and she is phenomenal. Just up from weeks of flue, transparent but head high, quick repartee, and delicious smile wicked as ever. Celebrities coming in and out in droves. From there we went to dinner with Loraine and John Cooper, and Loraine was extraordinarily funny telling Henry Jamesian stories of her debut in Rome *dans la nuit des temps.* As most of our close friends were away shooting fishing golfing or lying in the sun in their *résidences secondaires,* we also had time to call on sadder older arthritic ones like the Gruenthers, and other dispossessed democrats or retired diplomats, or widows and Washington is a specially sad place for the 'outs.'

"Chip gave me a heavenly quote from Halévy which suits all the bleeding hearts so well, 'an excess of virtue is far more dangerous than an excess of vice, as it is not subject to the dictates of conscience.' Dinner at Marietta's the night before last, and chez Nin* yesterday for Berlins but Isaiah had flue, and Far ate a bad oyster, so the women were very much more numerous. Nin has been angelic to me. Susan Mary was in New York for a day, also on her way to Barbadoes and we went to the Metropolitan to see the downgraded Rembrandts and Velasquez and damned if suggestion is not so strong, that they actually did look less good to both of us. We leave tomorrow for Mexico and I shall be rather glad to leave 6 below zero behind me. It has been bitter bitter and your Far with only a tiny tropical rain coat. He IS a nut."

She wrote Marinette on February 28 from Fiji:

"Our stay in Mexico was fun and David's friend Hector [Vasconcelos] took me out to lunch and to see an old philosopher poet collector friend of

---

* Mrs. John Barry Ryan.

442

his, which was fascinating. The only other house like his I have ever been to is Teddy Kollek's in Jerusalem. Every inch of floor, chairs sofas book shelves tables, covered cealing high with figurines, masks, pottery gold objects, funeral bowls, all from five thousand to eight hundred years old. I almost sat on a five thousand year old plaque with lettering on it, and never dared put my cigarette out in anything, for fear it might be a Mayan treasure.

"Actually he considers the Mayans sort of *parvenue,* and it is the Lomecs who are his great passion. Very shyly he showed us one or two erotic statuettes, blushing and casting his eyes down, but all in the name of art and history. What would the poor man say if he knew I had seen 'Deep throat?'

"We stayed at the Embassy in a suite as big as all the flat in Paris together, and so many closets we almost went mad. One day we went to Cuernavaca and another to a lovely Colonial monastery in Tepotzopotlan (It took me three days to memorise that) and of course to the new museum which is the most astonishing building I have seen in a long time.

"The whole of Mexico city gives one a sense of enormous space and sort of nineteen thirty-ish *nouveau-richism.* What other big city these days has mile after mile of private houses three times the size of yours, and with vast gardens, in the middle of town. And then slums of course, but less than some. Nine million people live in Mexico City alone. One night our hosts took us to dinner *chez* friends of theirs to see their new house and we could hardly believe it. Bigger than a foot ball stadium with an Olympic sized swimming pool in the center, all in white or black or pink marble; then a trophy room with three hundred lion tiger elephant and rhino heads in it. Then a gothic room, followed by a *Louis treize* and by a modern one etc etc. You should have seen Far's face sunk in such dour disaproval that I almost laughed. Luckily he copped out after drinks, because we then went on to dinner at 11.30 which is sort of normal for Mexico and home at two."

To Dodo on February 28: "We arrived in Fiji on Monday evening having skipped Sunday completely, by going over the international date line; so yesterday we were suffering from such space-lag, that we did nothing but swimm and sleep. The reef is lovely and full of exciting things, but the hotel not as pretty as the one we had been to fourteen years ago. Alas progress mucks things up everywhere and we are now in modern bungalows with orange and green moquette on the floor and wall brakets, instead of bamboo and straw in the old days. However the air conditioning is to be thankful for as it is really hotter and damper than a turkish bath. It is the rainy season, and every half hour or so unexpectedly the skies open and it comes down like a bucket on your head and as quickly stops, and then the steaming begins. But today it is dreamy and clear and we are going up a river in a boat. Hardly any flowers oddly enough except the ubiquitus hybiscus.

"I wrote to you from Acapulco and believe it or not, the hotel had no stamps and the letter got so crumpled and dirty in my bag on the thirteen hour flight to here, that I threw it away and begin again. Acapulco is the anti-Spetses of all time. The very name seems common to me. A kind of cheap vulgar Miami Beach with endless hotels in every shape imaginable to man except the shape HOUSE, with swimming pools and ombrellas and tourrists in all forms of dress and colour and hats and high healed sandals. We only went there, as Qantas leaves from there for Australia, and as we were there any way decided to spend one day and look at the place and one day was enough. We drove from Mexico City just to see a bit of the country, but it was not a very exciting drive. Dry and cactusy *comme il se doit* but less romantic than it sounds. When we arrived at the hotel we were met with a lot of ceremony by a handsome Englishman public relations fellow and whisked off to a 'boufey' lunch by the pool and told we had the best cabana in the place with a private pool (bath size) and in the course of chit chat he asked Cy how long he had been publisher of the Times. When we told him we were mere employees we were dropped in six minutes, mercifully as we wanted to be alone, and anyway it was too late to do anything about our room, so we enjoyed undeserved priviledges with malicious pleasure.

"The vulgarity of the place was unbearable. Pink triple size bed, pink jeeps to take one up and down, pink drinks with flowers floating in them, pink clad bell-boys and as the various cabanas are scattered all over a hill built as a sort of phony castle it takes half an hour for the jeeps to bring up a glass of water or a ham sandwidge. Ah me; more and more I realise the absolute god sent privilidges of a place like Greece on the whole and Spetses in particular. The places other people have to struggle to for a bit of sun are beyond belief. We left on Saturday night and our plane was four hours late, in which we sat surrounded by a 'tour' of French Canadians going home and it really is the ugliest language I have ever heard. Thank god they were not going in the same direction as we. Luckily when the plane did arrive, it was not quite full so we each had three seats to ourselves and managed to sleep quite nicely on the first eight hours to Tahiti, and then the next five to Fiji passed quite quickly what with meals and detective stories. Distances in this part of the world really make little Europe seem divinely small. We have one more day here, of rest and *far niente,* all most welcome to poor old Cy, because from now on it will be work work work."

She wrote Dodo again on March 5, from Sydney: "Just two words to say how glad I was of your letter and how perfect I thought your description of Cy as a cactus bush with delicate flowers, is. He has been more cactus than flower recently, but it is often that way on trips, with all his problems and preoccupations. He is off seeing the Prime Minister at this very moment.

"Yesterday however, Sunday, he was flowerlike and we spent all morning looking at the Koala bears who are quite quite irresistible and I could have stayed all day, watching, as totally paralysed by their charm as they are by their laziness. The penguins too are a delight. It is late summer here, and a sort of gold warm weather, with a tiny cool breeze which is a nice change from Fiji.

"Holiday weather somehow and Sydney feels much like a holiday city, like all cities by the sea should. We went to a wonderful restaurant, taverna type, on the beach one night and it was almost exactly like Passa Limani and the food marvellous. Shrimps octapus lots of garlic. The new (not so much any more) immigration laws which allowed Italians Greeks Poles Hungarians etc in the country, have really given it a new zest and pep. Melbourne apparently is the largest Greek city outside Greece."

From Marina's diary:

March 6, Canberra, Australia: "Flew to Canberra. An urbanist's dream come true, and psychiatrists work over-time. If God made man in his own image, it was a big mistake."

XIV

March-October 1973

Marina adored the poetry of Edna St. Vincent Millay, and every time we zigzagged past, into, around, and along the frontiers of a China still forbidden to American journalists, she quoted that lovely tetrameter sonnet:

> "No further from me than my hand
> Is China that I loved so well;
> Love does not help to understand
> The logic of the bursting shell."

Along the Hindu Kush mountains of Afghanistan, in the snow-girt principality of Swat, peering at the top Himalayan layer from Nainital, when Everest burst from the clouds of Nepal, in dank Vietnam, in Taiwan, and flying in and out of Hong Kong, again and again, with its Greek-like mountain bays, Marina inevitably recalled these favorite lines to me as she peered across to the forbidden mystery of China.

When we flew from Australia back to Asia for yet another tour of that fascinating cradle of so much human civilization, we had no inkling in early 1973 that twice in the same year we would girdle the Far East and that the second time we would tour famous, ancient China itself, thereby satisfying an old dream. The initial Asian visit began in Bali.

Marina wrote Marietta Tree on March 10:

"Now we are in Bali, which is exactly as one would wish it to be in spite of this gracious Inter-Continental hotel in which we are housed. It is mercifully hidden from view by trees and things, so one has the best of both worlds, and in spite of a theoretical *nostalgie de la boue* and J. J. Rousseau etc., at our age, lets face it, a good bath and air conditioning and good coffee in the morning, are most welcomed. As for the country side, it is sheer magic. Douanier Rousseau jungle; great palm trees like fantastic fruit-bearing wind-mills, bread fruit trees with leaves like eagle wings, leachy and mango trees, the fruit in their brown wrappings hanging like neat little birthday presents from their branches. And bamboo groves of unbelievable beauty, dark mysterious and utterly romantic.

"All this interrupted by field after field, and steep exquisite terraces of rice, the green of which is surely the most pleasing green in the world. Deep crevasses with rocks and great fern hanging from the cliffs and in the muddy water dozens of young people splashing around like Indian miniatures. And everywhere the background of a deep blue sea, and here and there, a child-like pure triangle of a volcano. Not so child-like when it errupted in 1963 and killed hundreds of villages. Not only the volcanos kill. It is strange to think of these delicate tiny beautifully finished smiling people, with flowers in their hair, running amok (a Malay word incidentally) and hacking thousands of each other to pieces as they did not so long ago.

"There is something particularly pleasing to me, too about the infinitely multi-useful trees and fruit. One can eat them, drink them, wear them, build houses and boats with them, irrigation pipes and temple decorations, baskets, hats, almost every human need is met by the cosy coconut, the bamboo and the rice. Must make the aristocratic orange or peach tree very sheepish. The tide goes out for miles every evening, but my enthusiasm was quickly dampened, when I almost stepped right on to a seathing mass of something worm-like, on my very first venture. Strange how a thing so exquisite, when under-water, can suddenly become a creepy, cruel cross between Dante and Disney, when out of its natural habitat. This part of the island is inhabited on every inch, and the villages look very romantic, behind beautiful walls with heavenly scented paper-white clusters of frangipani, growing everywhere and lovely temple doors and tiny shrines everywhere."

We arrived in Jakarta on March 12, and she wrote Denise Boisot: "It has changed enormously since the last time I was here, twelve years ago. Large hotels, department stores, wide avenues, but something unreal about it, like a child pretending to be a grown up. Cy is already off to see the president and I am writing letters. . . . Will go off to the museum in a minute."

From Marina's diary:

March 13, Jakarta, Indonesia: "Dinner at the embassy. Martha and Frank Galbraith [the ambassador] are exceptionally nice and bright. It was a lovely evening. The Indonesian ladies *so* much nicer, easier, brighter than Japanese or Indians. Everyone in our embassy speaks Indonesian. *Chapeau!*"

March 14, Jakarta: "Lunch with Durdins and Mr. Brison of Ford Foundation. Very interesting on planned parenthood in West Irian. No anthropologist can find out what they do, what the plant they use is, or how they use it. But it works and on their own. Only ones in this part of the world."

March 15, Tokyo: "Left for Tokyo but at the reasonable hour of ten. Asiatic airports are like ant heeps. For every passenger there are fifteen relatives saying goodbye."

On March 21 she wrote Dodo from Tokyo:

"Our beloved friend Fred Warner who is British Ambassador here was away for the week end, but they came back yesterday so we went to a huge diplomatic dinner there last night with thirty people and mercifully just lunch alone with them today and gossip and window shopping which was fun. I must say that a lot of Japanese ladies all shuffling in to a room together in their incredibly beautiful kimonos, look like a swarm of butterflies or an orchard in flower.

"But *malgré tout,* I get a feeling that somehow relationships are false and that one is gropping around in the dark, like perpetual code-breaking. For instance they never say No. You say, shall we go to the movies tomorrow and they answer which movie and what time shall we meet, which you must understand means No. If it were yes, they would not ask the time or the movie but wait for you to tell them. Even people who have lived here twenty years, get confused. Window shopping only as in the last year Tokyo has become the most expensive city in the world."

And to Dodo from Hong Kong on March 25: "We lunched today with Yehudi and Diana Menuhin, who have been giving a festival here, and we met a marvellous missionary doctor lady who is taking me tomorrow to see one of the famous operations with only accupuncture aneasthesia. It will be most interresting. But what is even more remarkable is that they noticed that each time they did this to anyone brought in for an accident or an appendix or something, who also happened to be a drug addict, they suddenly left the hospital cured. They have only been testing this for five months but it has apparently worked a hundred per cent. This would really be a miracle. So many of the other methods are long and painful and can be addictive in their turn like methodon which cures you of heroine addiction but makes you methodon addicted.

"The lady doctor was telling me that they have had cases of abject withdrawal symptoms, all the vomiting and pain and shivers and quakes, and with three sessions, the victims have gone home, like new. So I cant wait until tomorrow to see this. On the whole this has been the most enjoyable of all the places up to now. But oh the fools. Right in front of our windows where we used to look out on the loveliest bay in the world with the delicious *va et viens* of boats ships junks, and the blue and green mountains in the distance, there now rises a fifty storey office building with a thousand round windows, of an ugliness beyond compare and known locally as the Hong Kong Stilton. They are so busy destroying even what little is left of a once enchanted island, that soon they wont even have room to stand up in. The money madness is upon them, like the plague."

From Hong Kong we flew to Manila. Marina wrote Marinette on April 1:

"Two of the most astonishing days of our lives in Manila. We got off our plane unsuspectingly and as usual rather bedraggled carrying hats and

David's old duffle bag and what do we see but ten TV cameras, three generals a pride of ministers, the President's daughter, and one or two fabulous looking ladies. All this for us, but standing at the first class exit so we almost missed them. Well after lights flashed into our bewildered faces, and our necks were hung with leis of a thousand *foulis* and our arms filled with orchids, we were introduced uselessly to a lot of faces and then took off in a motorcade of about twelve cars and motor bikes and felt exactly as if we had landed with the bad guys in a 'Mission Impossible.'

"So we arrived at a kind of story book palace, old colonial with terraces and pergolas and balconies in delicious iron-work and a jungly garden, and walked up a giant red-carpetted stair case, with endless generals and things all around and at the top of the stairs were met by Mrs. Marcos who is probably the prettiest woman I have ever seen. And so learned that we were to be guests in the Palace. After the greetings she took us in to the President who is small but impressive right away and he and Far started chatting right off like old friends. Then we were taken to our rooms, as large as Yankee stadium and in the bed room a bed like a foot ball field the very same given to Mr. Nixon and again such flowers as I could not believe and baskets of mangoes and other exotica and maids and servants and a *masseuse* and a *coiffeuse* and all just dizzy-making.

"My principles about democracy were 'ganging agley' at a most unseemly speed. Well that night we dined alone on a six course meal, and went to bed as they had to entertain Mr. Kishi [former Japanese premier] who had come to consecrate a shrine to the Japanese war dead. Which shows great magnanimity on the part of the President who is the war's greatest guerrila hero and was tortured and beaten and whose father was hanged by the Japanese. They asked him to surrender or else they would kill his father, and at the same time the father smuggled an urgent message to him not to do so, else the guerrila movement would expire.

"Well the next day I was taken in hand by several ladies in waiting who took me around and then we went to a department store with cottage industries and of course I admired everything and then discovered that every oh and ah was immediately given to me in dozens. I have dresses for me for you for Jessica shirts for Jonathan for six years, for Far for David, and shells to die over, and baskets and rings and even a giant Moslem chest inlayed with mother of pearl and I almost had the giggles at the sight of Far's face when these little things would start arriving in our rooms, but mercifully they are being sent courtesy of the Palace to the Philippine Embassy in Paris. We would have had to charter a plane otherwise.

"I have never been so overwhelmed in my life. And Far had warned me not to accept any presents. But how. He too was given gold and pearl cuff links books manuscripts photo albums the works. And then that night we were given a state banquet of three hundred people in the Palace halls which are gigantic and alas I had to have my hour of glory on the arm of the President walking through the reception line, with the national anthems playing, looking my worst as I had been ill fitted for a Philippino Barong Tagalog the national dress and looked like hell. Another gigly moment when the Star Spangled banner, not a great tune at best, was played on a bamboo orchestra by school children.

"The President I must say a most charming table companion easy and fascinating. The story of his life is like six adventure movies roled into one. Then there was dancing which is absolutely lovely. Much more alive and real than the beautiful but completely stilted Thai or Indian or Balinese. The Spanish and Moslem influence very apparent and oh such costumes and colours. All together a memorable evening.

"Then the next day more sight seing and a fashion show, and lunch with a lot of Jesuit priests and pretty ladies and more shopping including a green Tang (5th century) vase which will look lovely in your dining room and then a dinner party at one of the lady's in waiting house which was a dream. Somehow with super-Spetses atmosphere. A garden full of tropical trees and flowers and butterflies made of corn husks fluttering in the trees, and *foulia* scenting the air and lamps and caviar and champagne and everyone so cosy and intimate and joking and teasing the president about his having taken all their worldly goods away from them (which he sort of has) and saying if you tax us so hard the least you can do is sing for us (not what one imagines a dictator to be doing) and even oh shame ending up with me teaching them the *sirtaki* [a Greek folk dance]. Can you believe it? And we stayed long past curfew time with more jokes about his coming to get us out of jail etc etc. Too extraordinary.

"Got to bed at three and up at five to leave for Saigon and imagine our dismay and admiration when both our hosts were up to take us to the airport. WHAT hospitality. In the end only Mrs. Marcos came, and then there was engine trouble so out we came again and she was still there and whisked us off to breakfast with a dozen generals air force commodores ministers etc; a breakfast of fish and chicken and fried rice and mangoes and god knows what all, which one wanted like a hole in the head at five of a hang-overish morning. But you see the kind of welcome I mean.

"Living in the embassy in Saigon which would have seemed heaven to us compared with the old Caravelle hotel, now seems almost humble to us. The Ambassador [Ellsworth Bunker] alas had to leave almost as we arrived, to take President Thieu to San Clemente. I am sick at heart because a nice gentleman arranged a seat for me on a plane to go to Hué and Danang but Far called Frank Wisner who is coming down specially to see us, so says I cant leave."

Marina wrote Dodo the same day from Saigon: "We have just arrived here, and it is hotter than hell and sticky and outwardly at least, not much different from war time. No one really believes it is over, as the North is not even pretending, not to be pouring stuff into the demilitarized zone. Ah me. All these years, all these deaths; all this agony, just a postponement. Who knows, there may be a miracle yet, but it wont be because the North has stopped trying."

To Avis Bohlen she said on April 2: "The ceasefire violations are daily and poor Mr. Gauvin the Canadian [cease-fire chairman] pulling out his hair. Apparently at one time when there was quite a serious incident, he desperately tried to get the Poles and Hungarians to go and look and the excuse they found was that 'they had a social engagement' and could not go."

From Marina's diary:

April 4, New Delhi: "Lunch with Mr. and Mrs. Pat Moynihan [then U.S. ambassador] at Roosevelt House. They seem very nice. Not ambassadorial. Cy saw Madame Gandhi this morning."

April 7, Srinagar, Kashmir: "Exquisite Lake Dal. Took a shikara [boat] and floated on the canals. Visited the houseboats. The hotel is an old maharajah's summer palace. But oh so cold. Four blankets and hot water bottle. The town enchanting."

April 9, Srinagar: "The Moguls really knew how to live. Such flowers and trees and streams and open verandas. 'Paradise is here, is here, is here.' "

April 14, Teheran: "Cy off to the Shah. I bought a lovely Persian picture on glass. Drinks with Ramsbothams [British ambassador] in historic British embassy. Saw photos of Teheran meeting. Churchill, Stalin, Roosevelt, etc. Averell looking so beautiful at fifty."

Marina wrote Susan Mary: "Kashmir is even lovelier than expected. Even from the air Srinagar looks like one of its own famous carpets. Stripes of green and the incredible yellow of the mustard fields, speckled with a million blue and red flowers and the whole thing seen through a mist of pink and white peach and cherry and plum and almond blossoms. The whole vale is an orchard and all around way up into the sky the mountains of the magic names like Hindu Kush and Karakorams with visions of the caravans carrying their silks over the passes to the world of Henry the VIIIth and François Ier and Venice and the Borgias. You have to tilt back your head to see the peaks and suddenly what you thought was a cloud, turns into solid snow embroidered rock, and what you thought was rock turns into cloud and floats away still higher into the sun. Its quite amazing.

"And everywhere the lake like pale grey velvet, with thousands of vegetable boats and flower boats and tinker and tailor and post office boats and fishermen and gardeners tending their artificial floating gardens with long poles. And such a silence as one can hardly remember in our own over-developped lives. Even the heart-shaped oars dont seem to make a sound dipping into the waters. But oh such poverty. Even in the winter with ten feet of snow, the people go bare-footed. We went into the hills one day and fished in rushing crystal streams and Cy cought four trout, and I picked arms full of little pointed pink and white stripped tulips, exactly like the flowers in Persian or Mogul miniatures. It was enchanting. And very cold which was almost a joy after the sweltering places we had just been in."

We were back in Paris in the beginning of May. Marina wrote Dodo about a new maid we had obtained (with the help of my secretary) to replace a couple who had quit us just as soon as we departed on our last trip. Marina recounted:

"The next day I met Leontina for the first time. Quite nice looking in fact, oldish small trim and I can easily see how she could fool Cy's secretary into thinking that she was a pearl. Well she was'nt. Nothing can describe the disasters. Not least among them that the lovely silver tray which you gave me, my *prika* [dowry] in fact, has vanished, but of course I cant possibly proove that she took it. But oh little by little what I discover. Eight out of twelve plates gone, hardly a brandy glass left, forks in the linen closet and linen in the place where Cy's shirts should be. Well I sort of manage and in the evening she cooks an uneatable chicken which she brings to the table staggering, catches the pocket of her skirt in my chair and comes crashing down all over Cy, who leaves the table in a storm.

"I wait a second trying to find the right words to fire her, and those seconds are enough for me to hear another gigantic crash from the kitchen. I run and find on the one side of the table a chair brocken in two, several more plates, and glasses, some food and on the OTHER side Leontina flat on the *plakakia* [tile floor] but not sort of fainted, on the contrary in a kind of Mme Récamier position her head on her arm. And the following dialogue takes place. *'Que faites-vous là par terre?' 'Très bien merci madame.' 'Je ne vous demande pas comment vous êtes mais pourquoi vous êtes par terre?' 'Eh bien madame vous ne savez combien de fois je me le demande moi aussi.'* By this time I can hardly keep from laughing out loud. However I manage to say that she must leave and at once.

"Leave? *'Mais pas du tout. Je me trouve si bien chez vous et l'appartement me convient si bien. Non Non Non certes je ne part pas.'* Well somehow I managed to get her to her room where she fell into a sweet sound sleep, while I stayed awake fuming all night. And this little adventure in house-destroying has cost me two hundred and fifty dollars for her salary, another fifty for firing her, and another hundred and fifty which she managed to spend *sois disant* on her food for three weeks and other little matters. I must say it was catastrophic.

"Well then the next day I said all right pull yourself together, you have had four months of *dolce far niente,* now show what you can do. So with fear and trepidation I put all the dirty linen in the washing machine and carefully read the instructions in the little book. Put soap in compartement on left. I do so. Shut lid. I do. Turn the blue button to A and the red to 100. I do so. Push button X. Again I do so and in a noise as of Appollo 13, huge grinding buzzing starts and soap bubbles fill the entire room everywhere but in the clothes. Discouraged I stop that at once and turn to the vacuum cleaner. I see a little white paper on the blue rug, push button A again and pass the hoover over it. Not only has it not disappeared as supposed but in its place are three bits of white paper plus a lot of new dust and a hair pin. It was like a gag. And of course I could not find a thing as I had naturally forgotten where in a fit of *noikokyria* [housekeeping] I had put away the fish collection, the little boxes, etc etc. It really was a nightmare funny few days, and this with the telephone going non stop and people dropping in and Cy calling every half an hour to tell me that on Sunday we are giving a dinner party for the new American Ambassador, with twenty other guests including the foreign minister, Mr. Couve de Murville a few bank directors and two generals. Ah me."

Our very old friend Hamilton Fish Armstrong died that spring, and Marina wrote Christa, his wife, on May 12:

"I have thought of you so much all these months, and worried about you and wondered, long before we learned the news of darling Ham's death, on our return here a few days ago. It must have been so ghastly for you that probably now, the simple clean uncluttered pain of loneliness and loss may be almost more bearable than the months gone by. My heart aches for you and I wish I were nearer and could talk, or just stay silent near you, a touch of the hand, a look, a smile can say a thousand times more clearly what is in one's heart, than words, second hand words, used over and over, regardless of the gravity of the occasion."

After Marina had finally got our drunken Spanish maid out of the house, she told Bob Joyce on May 18:

"We even got organised enough to give a fancy dinner for U.S. Ambassador Jack Irwin with the usual dear old galaxy of Couve de Murville, Hervé Alphand, Maurice Schumann, [General] Billotte, etc, and also went to a gigantic Chase Bank party in Versailles for David Rockefeller, which was oddly enough rather fun. Enough Bank presidents around and business men to float a nation and we very much the out out outsiders but perhaps that is why I had a good time. John Loudon was there, with the Jonkhereen who looks older than he but nice. Gianni Agnelli too, and many 'international personalities.' Watergate is dinner party conversation but more on the lines of what a lot of fuss about a little corruption than moral indignation. As the Canard says 'Nous on a été Watergatés depuis des siècles.' "

To Dodo on June 12: "We gave a large fancy party last Wednesday for Susan Mary Alsop who is staying with us, and had Costa and Lia Karamanlis and lots of friends of Susan Mary's and at the last minute Mr. Kissinger invited himself which gave a fantastic *coup de fouet* to the party, which has become the talk of the town. Incredible what notoriety will do. Imagine that the very next day Peter [Payne] called me to tell me that Kissinger had been to see Karamanlis, and they had had a 'very significant' talk. *Comment s'écrit l'histoire.* They did chat at the dinner, but not very significant I imagine.*

She wrote Bill Burden,† who was wondering if his children should take a Greek holiday, on June 15: "As to your questions about Greece, would that I could answer them. I would be Prime Minister if I could. Would too that I could even know what to wish for. The end of Royalty in itself is not an unbearable blow. We do this to our kings at least once a generation. I am only sad, as it further complicates relations with the outside world, and does away with the last semblance of legality.

"Colonel Papadopoulo's speech sounded insane to me. On the other hand, the country as a whole has not moved a finger. That is where I dont know what to wish for. Having been turned into zombies in such a short historical time, seems such a tragedy. On the other hand, how could anyone move, without plunging the country into even more reprisals and repressions, and for what and above all for whom? If only we had a Joan of Arc tucked away somewhere, or (not wanting to ask that much) even one plausible, possible leader, around whom the nation could rally and become enthusiastic, things might be different. But alas I am old enough to know that people do not risk their lives for the almost abstract idea of parlementarism, or for a limited number of people in jail without trial, above all when the memory of bloody, ghastly, unbearable civil war, is still so clear in

---

* As a matter of fact, I did put the two Mr. K.s together alone for a pretty good private postprandial chat.
† Friend and former U.S. ambassador to Belgium.

our minds. So as far as your daughter-in-law and grandson go, I am sadly certain that they can go without hesitation, even though I would hate to feel responsible if anything were to happen. The chances are one in a thousand I am afraid. I say afraid because if there were any possible way of getting rid of the colonels without too much sorrow and fighting, I would be delighted."

Elise Bordeaux-Groult was desperately ill. Marina saw her almost daily and Susan Mary Alsop had flown over to be with her girlhood friend.

From Marina's diary:

June 16, Paris: "Lunch here. Malraux, Sophie de Vilmorin, André de Staercke, Manes Sperber, Susan Mary. Very interesting. Farytale party at La Grange for Gérard de Waldner's wedding. A tropical jungle under a green tent. Le Tout Paris. Gay and incredibly romantic in full moon. Spent the night at Billottes."

June 19, Paris: "Lunch at Prince Paul's. Poor Olga. The Colonels may take her passport away. Very stoical if sad at King's dispossession. It is the fourth time we lose all, she says."

June 27, Paris: "Elise died this morning. I was out all day and did not hear until late. Daphne [her daughter] away, does not know. Spent till dawn with Pierre and children in crypt of American Hospital. Elise looked really beautiful. Not literature. Truly. Oh, sad."

July 2, Paris: "Dinner rue du Bac [home of the Bordeaux-Groults]. Talk of stiff upper lip. All the family dressed for dinner. Made small talk. One by one they broke down. Susan Mary a rock. She is fabulous. But all of us undone."

July 13, Roquebrune [where Marina was staying with Sybil Billotte]: "Slept late and oh so well. One leaves pre-occupations at the gate in other people's houses."

July 18, Roquebrune: "Great mistral blowing so no swim. But the colours of sea, sky and flowers enhanced by the wind. Lovely. Scrabble. I feel uncomfortable. I've won over 150 dollars which for Sybil is peanuts and for me a fortune, and its me that feels bad about it."

We flew to Colorado.

To Susan Mary Alsop on August 8: "The first ten days at the seminar were hell for Cy who is suffering acutely from People-itis, but pleasant for me although during the sessions I felt a thousand years old and jaded and cynical, while everyone was being so high-minded and unrealistic and spending hours 'not recognising the obvious and trying to elucidate the obscure.' Bill Moyers our moderator is a preacher's son and it appeared with every phase. He rambled from Dürrenmatt through Thucydides to Machiavelli and ended with a Mr. Irving Kristol who I am told is a think man of the Nixon administration.

"We spent hours trying to define freedom and the only time I opened my mouth in exhasperation was then, just to say that we were all wasting our time as in my mind there were only two complete ones and one almost unconditional one, that is to love, to dream and to take one's own life.

"Watergate loomed largely, of course, but it was nice for me to spend ten days with a part of America which I hardly knew, the so called middle one, and I found them all dear and kind and generous in spirit and of course I was a curiosity to them and considered a genius for speaking some languages and having 'lived,' which is always good for the ego, if not taken too seriously. So all in all I enjoyed it. And then a few days ago mercifully for Cy it ended and we came up to the cabin which gets a bit shabbier and more spare every time we come. But Cy is in heaven so all is well. He fishes all day and goes to bed at nine and I must admit that the nights seem endless to me. The Coleman lamps are too dark to write by and anyway the typewriter would disturb him, so I read and read and read, and listen to the mice-in-residence who scurry around our flour, and wish I were married for the summers at least, to a gregarious millionaire with a yacht and a preference for night clubs.

"Chip and Avis arrived on Sunday. I got a message from Nancy [Smith] to go down to her house and there was an urgent message from Nicolas Nabokov* and my heart stopped, thinking it might be bad news, but mercifully it was only to say they had arrived and would we dine. Chip seems in constant pain and I dont know how he sits through the seminars in those modern horrible bidet-like chairs. They came up yesterday for

---

*Chip Bohlen had been invited to the seminar of the Aspen Institute, and although very ill, he and Avis had come along. Nicolas Nabokov, a writer and musician, was a guest of the Institute for several months.

supper in the cabin and for a while Chip sounded like his old self, but very soon he became grey-ish and silent. My heart aches for them. Avis is a marvel. When he takes his nap in the afternoons, I want to take her out picking flowers and walking by the river. Nancy is playing golf with her today and I hope she is getting a bit of a rest. We go to the gym together and girate horribly on the floor, but hopefully it will take a few pounds off me and firm up these aging muscles."

Marina tried to comfort Susan Mary about the death of Elise. She wrote: "I am so glad you are a little more calm. But please please my baby, get it out of your mind that you could have done anything more than you did. She had closed down the shutters of her life and loves, and would not let anyone in, not even Pierre not even you. So please do not brood. Weep, sigh, regret, miss, remember, but do not torment yourself with vain wonderings and questions, to which there is no answer."

In her diary:

August 14, Aspen: "Home to go fishing with Cy. Shortened pants. Made flapjacks."

Marina met a Frenchman at the seminar, where she still dropped in as an auditor after my ten days of participation had ended, and wrote Marinette:

"Yesterday I took a dear charming gentleman on a pic nic who is the director of the Musée d'Art Moderne called M. Laymarie and he told me he was a shephard boy in the Dordogne, and during the war the Louvre sent its most valuable pictures and treasures there, to hide in various chateaux and he became one of the guards, and when the war ended he loved them so, that he was taken to Paris as a special kind of guard and ended up where he is, and is about to be named Director of the Ecole du Louvre. Lovely story no?

"I just looked up from my letter and saw the biggest wood-chuck of them all, sitting up with his two tiny hands eating something. He is like a perfect toy. Gone."

Then, on August 21, when Marinette and her family had joined Dodo in Spetsais, she wrote her mother and her daughter jointly:

"Sometimes I sit and think what-it would be like to have Dodo and Eleni and the babies and all of you sitting on the porch here, watching the ducklings and the old Beaver and Woodchuck family and walking in the river and picking mushrooms and berries and dandelions. I think if you were all here with me, it might be quite lovely. I went mushroom picking yesterday up Ajax mountain with my mentor a lady called Priscilla and five years older, rushing up that steep mountain side like a goat while I huffed and puffed behind. Twelve thousand feet up I think justifies huffing if one is a sea-level person. Anyway we had no luck at all. But at the very end and almost when we were back at the car I found three Lacteria Deliciosas (see how learned I am getting) and one Boleta, and they were so large they were enough for six of us to have a nice *mezedaki* (hors d'oeuvre). Six because we had a dinner party. Far had cought twelve gigantic trout so we made a *bella figura* with hand picked food.

"The Bohlens left yesterday and I was sad to see them go. But we shall see them in Washington quite soon, although Chip goes back to hospital on the 9th. If they find more cancer it will be the end. Its too horrible and they are both so brave and gay and galant."

She wrote Dodo on August 28: "David arrived on Saturday, with short hair and neat shirt blue jeans and it is sheer joy to have him with us and he seems very pleased to be here. Cy and he have gone fishing *en tête à tête* all day today which is good for them both. He looks about fifteen and I can hardly keep my hands off him. We went splashing in the river yesterday which was icy and so beautiful, and then had a pic nic under the pines and it was so quiet and little chip monks came and nibbled at our bread and it really was bliss.

"To my surprise David who does not like fish ate two trout and said it was mother's cooking that made them so good. Ha. We have one more week here, and I must say, as always at the end of a summer, the thought of shoes and stockings, hair dressers and all that stuff, makes one very sad to leave."

Since 1956, when I had been granted a visa for China but Uncle Arthur had vetoed the trip, Henry Kissinger, David Bruce, and my old friend Etienne Manac'h, the French ambassador there, had all badgered the Peking government on my behalf. All of a sudden, I was promised visas for myself and Marina, and we were told to pick them up in Washington in

September and proceed immediately thereafter to China. Imagine my horror, therefore, when (as Marina recounted in her diary):

August 29, Aspen: "Just heard our China trip cancelled. Cy desperate. David, Cy came back from fishing frozen stiff. David cought a good trout."

We rushed back to New York so I could get to work by telephone trying to reverse the reversal. Marina wrote to Dodo on September 21:

"I have not written in a while, because we have been living on tenterhooks for weeks. The Chinese had granted us a visa after seventeen long years that Cy has been waiting, and then for some unknown reason took it back, and only on Monday after a lot of urging and pushing by *des personages haut placés,* did we get it. Actually get it, touched it saw it with our own eyes, and only then would Cy allow me to even talk about it to anybody. So every day I sat down to write to you and then thought what is the point if I cant tell her *the* most important thing of all, and every day Cy would say 'Tomorrow we will know,' and then we did'nt.

"Well now it is done and we leave in a few hours. Cy is like a small boy with a xmas tree. I have not seen him so excited in years. This rounds up his world-hopping carreer in a perfect way and after this trip he will feel that he had done his job to the full. Plus the fact that it IS a mysterious unknown provocative and apparently unparelled beautiful place. The few friends who have already been admitted, all came up with advice as to what to read, what to wear what climate etc so I hope I am well prepared. Actually it is supposed to be very much like New York weather so this must be the best time to go. I have a coat, sensible shoes sweaters and absolutely nothing fancy or *clinquant* so as not to look dirty capitalist. We leave for Hawai in an hour or so non stop and then to Hong Kong for two days and from there we are escorted to the frontier, which I believe we cross on foot, and then I hope by train to Canton. But the moment we cross into China we are in their hands and they tell us where and what and how.

"Except that we shall be staying with David Bruce our old and dear friend and our ambassador in Peking since May. It is so exciting I can hardly wait to get on the way, except that having waited seventeen years, they could have given us another seven days to go up and see David's little place in New Hampshire. He has been calling us constantly and sounds so well and relaxed and serious, he is a different human being. I dont tell you anything about the book [he was planning to write] as I dont know any thing to tell you. Well trained by his father, he does not talk about it. All I know is that it has something to do with a semi imaginary Mexican. He has given himself ten months to do it in, and if he fails he will do something else. He seems very sure that he can manage, and has made enough money to keep himself for a year, by selling his Far Eastern goodies, bouchara rugs, etc.

"All friends have been charming as usual and I have been lunching and dining constantly but alas no time to get to Washington to say good by to the Bohlens and I particularly wanted to as I have a horrid fealing we may not see Chip again. He has cancer all over and is in great pain. It breaks our hearts."

To Dodo from Hong Kong on September 25: "We spent the weekend in Hawai which was necessary so that we could shut ourselves up and read and read. Oh dear it is difficult and as for dates and names of revolutions and counter revolutions and party leaders, it is hopeless, above all when one cant pronounce the names. Also I have a fealing of reading science fiction.

"Apparently, if one throws away a pair of stockings with runs in them the maid gives them back to you, and one man was followed by a pair of holed socks mailed to him from one end of China to the other. If a worker makes a tiny bit more money than he needs for absolute subsistence, he gives the extra to the commune. Well *on verra*. From Hawaii we flew to Hong Kong and that is a long long flight. Seven and a half hours to Guam and then another five to here, plus going over the international date line so that we lost Tuesday completely."

Marina's diary:

September 29, Peking: "Beautiful sunny day. Mrs. Wu [our interpreter], Mr. Ma [assigned to look after me by the press department], Yen and Ching took us to the Great Wall and the Ming Tombs. One can only really feel the beauty and enormousness when one is *there*. Returned in time to dine with director Peng Ha, information chief. No English. Our friends Wu, Ma, Yen, Ching translated. Very free, easy conversation about Russia mainly and about the need for continuing revolution to keep a 'new class' from forming."

September 30, Peking: "Went to a commune near Peking. Saw pigs, force-fed ducks, rice, wheat, sorghum for making mao-tai [a powerful drink] and were given a lot of statistics and growth figures. Saw a commune house for family of five. Three quite nice rooms. All five sleep on top of a sort of flat oven, heated from below. Straw mats, eiderdowns, no mattress. No chairs. Posters on wall. One chest. But nice little garden, two private pigs, three chickens. Children at day school. Eight hour days but harvest time more."

To Dodo on October 4: "Even writing Peking at the head of this letter, seems like pretending. Often as we sit in David Bruce's living room talking of other matters, I suddenly come to and think My god we are in CHINA. I simply dont know where to start. The train from Hong Kong to the frontier, and a gloriously movie-like passing from one side to the other with our first glimpse of Red soldiers all looking most unmartial in their baggy green trousers, ill fitting jackets and defiant red star. Only difference between men and officers we discovered is that officers have four pockets and men only two. No difference between a major and a general. Rather nice that.

"Then we encounter the first step in the famed Chinese hospitality. Met by the man from 'Friendship travels' our Mr. Wu, who speaks impecable English and oddly enough there is not the slightest fealing of tension and artificial cosiness that we had in Russia or other Eastern countries. We plunge into conversation while lots of little people cope with our passeports tickets permits etc. Hours. Then taken into a gigantic dinning room (everything of the People is gigantic) and given an incredibly delicious meal and then onto the train. Odd how in this austerity ridden land, where the little red scarf on school children is the only frivolous note of dress, everything else is smothered in lace. Train seats covered in it, waiting rooms, motor cars have lace curtains and antimaccassers, lace even in the lifts.

"The train takes off and is most comfortable. We go through pleasant tropical country side much like pictures of itself on screens and scrolls. We are in the south. Pointed hats, buffalo rice fields banana trees. Two hours later, we are in Canton, but we dont see much of it as we have to catch a plane for Peking almost at once. Mr. Wu sees us safely on to the plane armed with Mao thoughts in the little red book, and three and a half hours later we land in Peking where David Bruce and a superb Chinese linguist from the American liaison office get our bags and bring us home. America is not yet quite recognised so we dont have an embassy here and David goes by the euphemistic title of head of the U.S. Liaison Mission to China. Up to now all is well and I can describe and tell it uncluttered by the total confusion that assails the foreign traveller the day after arrival. Nothing fits.

"The first almost unbelievable thing is to understand how 800 million people can be turned into self-denying altruistic impecably honnest saints in less than twenty five years? If you dont know how much something costs (which you dont of course) you open your bag and ask them to take what they want. You leave money jewels anything, anything, lying about in the street even and no one will touch.

"One night, the night of their National day celebrations we were asked to a banquet in the Hall of the People and Premier Chou was there, and two thousand guests and we drove through crowds and crowds of on lookers (and you can imagine what 'crowd' means in a country as populated as this) and nowhere in sight was there a single policeman, no cordons, no nothing, and not one person pushing or shoving. What makes them all so totally disciplined and honorable? Mao thought? The banquet itself was a bore like all banquets but the very idea of being there was astonishing. Then the next day our interpreter and Mr. Ma the press gentleman and Mr. Yu and Mr. Ching, all in charge of us, took us to the Great Wall and once again I was struck by how impossible it really is to 'feel' what things are really like from pictures films books etc. Of course, the Great Wall looked like we thought it would, yet I could never imagine the enormousness of it *par rapport* to one's self and how incredibly steep it is. One imagines that the top of a wall would be sort of straight. *Pas du tout.* In places this one has a forty five degree incline and one slips backwards going up and often comes down on one's behind in the decline. But fabulous. The great mountains all around would seem to be enough discouragement to any invading Mongol but apparently not. The wall of course is number one on any tourrist's ittinerary and rightly so, for Peking, and then we drove some more to the Ming tombs which are not so fascinating except for the great road leading up to them which is lined on either side with monumental marble elephants camels lions then generals and ministers, for miles. It is an amazing sight.

"Next day I went to the Forbiden city, which is like saying I went to another country. It really is a city. Mile after mile after mile, of gates bridges halls, pavillions, gardens, courtyards etc. All with the gold glazed tiles which only the Emperors could use, all with brilliant red walls, blue green yellow and gold roofs and cealings and dazzling dazzling. One bridge has pomegranate trees growing in giant tubs on both sides. The halls and pavillions have names to make one dream. Gates of heavenly peace, of persevering peace, of punctual Autumn of the Forgotten Favourites, of Earthly tranquility etc. Needless to say we try and try to say them in Chinese and it is out of the question. Our interpreter only laughes and we are probably saying mud-puddle when meaning apple blossom. We hardly ever do anything alone, but probably not for the same reasons as in Russia but from fear of our getting irrevocably lost and No way of asking our way home. It is most frustrating. Most impressed by the entire staff of this office, all speaking excellent Chinese except David.

"October 1st is the National day, but there was no parade this year, nor in the passed two years. Instead all the Parks were *en fête* and we went from one to the other, and it was a real sight. All the parks decorated with most un-flag coloured flags, pink and turquoise yellow and orange, and garland after garland of crepe paper and lanterns four and six and ten foot high, and enormous baskets dripping with paper flowers and real bushes covered with paper hybiscus to compensate for the flowerless season. And in these parks a million (litteraly) people, parents with little children held tight by tiny hands; or pigyback; young school girls all a-twitter with excitement rouged cheeks and red ribbons on top of their heads, ready to 'dance for the People' or sing or something, and endless stands with games like 'Pin the tail on the donkey' or Feed the Panda and magic fishing, and Shoot the elephant so like a million times multiplied the Gymkhana we loved so at the tennis club when we were children, that I almost had a tear in the eye. Also like when we were children and were allowed to go to the Oasis and have an ice and see the 'numera' [acts].

"Stand after stand with important theatrical performers, either from the Peking Opera, or acrobats or ladies reciting Mao's poems. In other places folk dances from the various 'minorities' Thibetans Mongolians Koreans, in national dress a nice note of colour in the sea of blue or grey of the entire nation. Cy says its what he likes best. You would too. We spent hours wandering around and there was an extraordinary fealing of inno-cence and purity and simplicity, compared to what the jaded, over-amused west needs for its pleasures. Every minute of our days is taken up and organised and planed, hence the impossibility of writing before. And the evenings when not at a banquet or a Peking duck dinner by a minister, we sit and chat with David and adorable Mary [Lady John] Manners who is also his guest, and then fall into our beds like dead, after eight or nine hours of walking and sight seing. Also so so much to read, even if one wants to keep three dynasties clear in one's mind. Very hard.

"David's servants all go home at five, so he makes his own supper. Another incredible thing. His house is quite open, no guards no doors locked, anyone can walk in and out at will. Hideous house, no furniture, and he who has lived submerged in beautiful things and precious belongings all his life is pleased as punch and sort of liberated. Evangeline alas had to go to Washington so he is rather pleased to have us and Mary Manners for company. The food here is beyond doubt the best thing I have ever tasted and we are fed so much and so often we feel like the force fed ducks we met, on our visit to a commune two days ago. Pigs and ducks and rice and wheat and endless statistics of growth progress etc. Cy has not seen any of the very big people yet, but keeps hoping. Apparently one is never told until half an hour before."

From Marina's diary:

October 5, Peking: "Deadly visit to a factory of building material and an air raid shelter: what a waste of everyone's time. Banquet by Information office. Lots of questions and answers but if you come down to it its all baby talk. Very tedious. I wonder if they know we know so much of it *is* twaddle or if they believe its true."

October 6, Yenan: "Hills all around. Quite pretty. One Tang pagoda rebuilt last year. The rest is shrine to Chairman Mao. Where he lived, his blanket, his ink-pot. The first central committee meeting. He lived here after the long march for about 13 years. Here is where he said 'If we lose Yenan, we win Yenan: If we keep Yenan, we lose Yenan!!!' "

October 9, Sian: "Drove early to tomb of Princess Yung Tai and the empress Wu. Very interesting but not compared to what Greeks, Egyptians, Romans, etc. had already done. In the evening we saw a dear acrobatic show: magicians, jugglers, etc. Classic form of entertainment here. Banquet by Mr. Liu. Very nice man."

October 10, Shanghai: "Left late for Shanghai. Planes so old they dont fly in the rain. Talked to David Bruce's group which we overlapped one night here. They told us war has broken out between Egypt, Syria and Israel on Saturday and Agnew resigned as U.S. vice president. We never knew any of this. Its too terrible."

October 11, Shanghai: "Cy off to see an English banker. Only two foreign residents in Shanghai, he is going crazy."

October 12, Shanghai: "Boat trip on the Whangpoo river to where it meets the Yangtse. Yangtse 6,000 kilometers long. Fifteen wide. Lovely junks. The sails are dipped in pig's blood to make them solid. Hence the colour and leathery look. Pig's blood coagulates slowly, so easy to handle."

October 14, Hangchow: "Hangchow is all that Marco Polo claims. The lake is pale green, turquoise and gold at sunset. Green thickly overgrown curly hills and woods. The hotel excellent. Took a boat on the lake. Went to the island of the three towers reflecting the moon. Then to Hua Kwang park. A dream of crooked bridges, pavilions, flowers, lotus plants. Wall in the middle of nowhere, with carved windows and round moon gates. In the afternoon went to Jade Fountain and Yellow Dragon spring and a nasty 20th century temple called Yin Liu. The landscape lovely. The inevitable banquet but this revolutionary chairman most charming. Straight. Talked of generation gap. He said there is one but not between him and his children but between him and his 80-year-old mother who believes in spirits."

October 15, Hangchow: "Went to another spring. The water so heavy with minerals that you can float pennies on it, or fill the cup half an inch over the edge and it wont overflow. Took plane to inner Mongolia at six. Comfortable but long. Arrived at Huhohaote at 11:30. Committee waiting for us. Nice hotel but cold."

October 16, Huhohaote, Inner Mongolia: "Visited city. A carpet factory. Alas dictatorial regimes are more interested in progress than history. But not much history around here. Mongolians look different. Also more relaxed. Obviously very pampered by central government as all minorities are. All convinced that the Russians have a million troops on the frontier and are about to attack. It keeps them on their toes. Instead of bread and circuses, Chairman Mao gives them bread and danger. Mr. Dergal, a Mongolian official, gave us best Mongolian feast. They eat meat, milk, butter here, unlike the Chinese. Most delicious and virile food."

October 18, Tatung: "Visit to two temples. Confirmed in my views that Chinese art can go just so far and no more. Pretty steps, pretty blue tiled roof. In the afternoon visited famous caves of 10,000 Buddhas. Frankly awful. In the evening usual banquet with vice chairman of revolutionary committee. Only one unidentifiable food. But quite good."

October 19, Tatung: "Visited a grim set of collective tombs in the coal mines. Killed by the Japanese. Then usual endless chatter and propaganda about dirty capitalists and how glorious everything is now."

October 21, Peking: "Went to Forbidden City with David, Mary. Dowager's apartments one can go to ten, fifty times and still discover new places, courtyards, long avenues. Tiny gardens. Dragon screens."

October 23, Peking: "Summer Palace with Cy. Its divine in all its vulgarity. Marble boat too funny."

October 24, Peking: "Up at 7. Two hour drive to an army division headquarters. More Mao thought. PLA [People's Liberation Army] makes its own soya sauce and curds. Big deal. Huge lunch. More Mao thought. No ranks in PLA. Met our host division commander. What endless contradictions."

Marina wrote Dodo on October 25 from Peking:

"We have just been whisked off on a forteen day trip around the country which was totally exhausting, especially for Cy who had to keep producing the damned column but fascinating. First we flew in a tiny world war one airoplane to a place called Yenan which is the birth place so to speack of the Revolution. After the famous long March, Chairman Mao came here with his ten thousand men and established a kind of first Chinese Soviet. So that today it is a cross between Mecca and Jerusalem. In actual fact it is a tiny very central Asian looking town. The plane lands almost in the middle of town on a sort of crazy pavement landing strip (rather disconcerting) with vegetables growing right up to the edge of the strip and high mountains in a ring all round. Not very pretty.

"As usual the vice chairman of the Provincial people's Revolutionary party, met us, and there was a lot of welcome and thank you and all that, which by now we are masters at, and we were taken to our hotel. Our bed room had five gigantic arm chairs in maroon velvet covered with lace and with prettily striped towels in pale blue pink and yellow. I cant tell you how odd it seems to have the revolutionary committee sitting on pastels stripes. I suppose it is that dry cleaning does not exist. As always we were given green tea and then whisked off to see the very humble mud house in which the great man lived, wrote thought and directed operations as well as ideology. And that night the usual 'banquet' given by the Committee at which we eat like force fed geese and carried on a laborious conversation through the interpreter. It is quite fascinating to hear the exact same phrases, down to the last semi-colon, repeated from one end of China to the next.

"We spent two rather dreary days there and then on through thick fog and our hearts rather in our mouths because of the age of the plane to another place called Sian, which was also a revolutionary capital as well as an ancient Sung or Han or something capital. We walk about with a little printed paper which tells one the Dynasties but try as one might it is impossible to keep them straight. Also they all last from two to five centuries so if you are told that this or that was built in the Chin (not to be confused with Cing or Shin) dynasty you dont know if it is sixteenth seventeenth or eighteenth century. And one's concepts change so that we found ourselves thinking of the Mings (14th) as almost *parvenue*. In Sian we saw a lovely museum with extraordinary bronzes two thousand years old, and pavillions and gardens and a pagoda and went through the same rigmarole of banquet and tossing down Mao Tai which is as strong as fuel oil, and then left for Shanghai.

"Rather dissapointing. All 'People's Republics' are far more interested in the present and future than the passed, so that we have a great struggle to see gardens and palaces and bureaucratic-capitalist landowner-oppressor things in spite of Chairman Mao saying 'put the passed to the service of the future.' We must have been told this seven thousand times. So we were whisked off to industrial fairs and Children's palaces; and ship yards and workers living quarters etc etc. Did see one delicious Ming garden. Garden here means an endless, but endless, series of pavillions inner courtyards bridges, rivulets cannals more pavillions with such names as Pavillion of the Azure Clouds, or the ten thousand flowers or the sweet awakening of the three hundred nightingales etc. Most enchanting.

"The workers housing I must say was most interresting. A very old man received us. Seventy three so he had been born under the beastly Empress dowager and seen wars and revolutions, starvation and colonial brutality enough for ten lives. The old workers decided to keep as an educational exhibit the places where they were born. And they took us there. A swamp with a line of triangular huts made of bits of wood a part of old *gazodeneke* [jerrican], some paper just high enough to crawl in, and nothing on the floor at all, and I am sure these are real. This is how they lived under British, French, German colonial administration and eat what they found in the garbage dumps. This I must say one has to keep in mind all the time, in order to just barely understand how one man in twenty five years can have undertaken the Promythean task of modifying the very core of human nature. As we were told that everyone is so honest, I deliberately left behind in our rooms everywhere some slight thing, like a hair pin and each time they followed us practically to the airfield to bring them to us. It is quite impossible to get rid of a half eaten apple. We had a pot of nescafe with us, and even there, they would not even wash the cups out for us in case we wanted the dregs. It is unbelievable.

"Well from the first horrible huts, the old man took us to another set of rather larger mud houses, but with floors and windows and mats on the ground and said that these were the houses they built for themselves 'after liberation' which is like saying A.D. Then he said 'when we lived in these we thought we had reached the epitomy of luxury and comfort. Never in our wildest dreams did we think we would ever live the way we live now. Come and see.' And with that we were taken to these gigantic housing projects, you know institutional grey cement mile after mile. One narrow smelly corridor off which each family according to size, have one or maximum two rooms, share a WC and a kitchin and own their own furniture. It was utterly heartbreaking. Any *contestataire* French worker or British Labour Union member would have spat on the flour if offered this. And these people were quite sincerely and profoundly greateful and happy.

"One day we took a trip on the river all the way to where it meets the Yangtse and alas it was pouring rain and grey and nasty but still interresting and I saw a lot of Greek ships. In every place we went we were taken to the theater at night. Acrobats are the great thing. And quite unbelievable. We saw one man stand on another man's head, stand a giant bamboo pole on his shoulder, have a girl climb to the top of that, whisk her whole body upside down and balance with one hand on this second man's head while swirling rings and hoops round her up turned toes. And the ballet which presumably infiltrated here via the Russian friends in the days of their idyl, which is so funny one hardly dare's look at a friend's eye for fear of unseemly laughter.

"I saw several. One called Steel flowers. A lot of lady welders *sur pointes* brandishing blow torches on steel girders. Then a splendid foreman comes and tells them they simply have to build an ocean going ship in no time at all. So great *pas de deux* and *entre-chats* with the blow torches flashing flames and sure enough in no time at all the ship is sailing away and everyone waves and then the foreman leaps back on stage with an ombrella twirling and gives it to the first lady welder and I in my bureaucrat-bourgeois insensibility think ah has he fallen in love with her and I whisper to the interpreter 'Are they going to get married?' In shocked surprise she whispers back 'Oh no, he has offered her the privilege of building a second ship for the masses.' And yet you know, as soon as the flippant laughter rises to one's lips, so one suddenly stops short because IT IS the way things are done. The Great Hall of the People, the station and the military museum which form the great Ten An Man square equivalent to Moscow's Red Square, were suddenly decided upon to celebrate the 10th Party congress and were built in ten months by 'voluntary' workers. They form the largest building in the world.

"The little children in the 'Children's Palace' were eatable and indoctrination starts at age two. They are tought unselfishness, helping others etc. I asked *à propos* of this splendid school how many orphanages there were in Shanghai and was answered in seemingly total sincerity 'Oh but there are no orphans since Liberation.' But I think this must have something to do with language difficulties. Even they cant think that I would believe no parents died 'since Liberation.' Probably orphan means 'abandoned with-no-place-to-go-to-child' or something. Again a banquet with the most unbelievable food including a pumpkin carved in the shape of a dragon and filled with crab shrimps and a lotus flower made of egg whites of unsurpassed beauty.

"The further one gets from Peking the more relaxed and natural our mentors become which is not to say that one can sit down and have a cosy chat. The questions they avoid, or refuse to answer are almost as interresting as the ones they do. Directives being as elastic and ever changing as they are, no one volunteers any information more precise than yes we have three harvests of rice 'since Liberation' and yes the rate of productivity has risen seventy three point eight and so on and so forth.

"From Hangchow believe it or not, we came back to Peking for one night and the very next morning at six they had us flying off to Inner Mongolia. This is more fascinating in thought than in reallity. The very word Mongolia somehow conjures up endless childhood books and mixed up pictures from Taras Bulba to Michel Strogoff let alone Kublai Khan, Genghis Khan, etc. and the fact that the place we went to is called Hu Ho Hao Te, all made us feel very excited. But in actual fact it was a flat endless plane covered with the century old dust from the Gobi desert and nothing but nothing to see. Except some nice horses and horsemen shooting bull's eyes in a gallop and standing in the saddle which is traditionally a Mongol thing. We also went to the inevitable theatre and were longing to see some real folk dancing but instead guess what. The Steel flowers again and bits of 'Red Detachement of Women.' Only one or two beautiful Mongolian traditional shephard songs which dont sound like anything we have ever heard before. Haunting and strange and weather freezing cold but sunny which was nice after the endless rain of Shanghai.

"From there to another place called Tatung also quite ugly. A flat beige mining town where we were taken at eight in the morning to see two giant collective tombs of dead bodies killed by the Japanese during the war. In between we sipped the inevitable green tea, and were told of the horrors of Class war. When I shyly said but this was not a class war it was a national war, they all explained that it was a class war because it was only the Militarist bureaucrat landowner Japanese who were wicked not the others, one cant win."

From Marina's diary:

October 26, Peking: "Suddenly the phone rang. All jumped. False alarm. Cy utterly dejected. Then the phone rang again. This time it *was* the invitation. People's Palace at 8:30. The big man himself [Chou En-lai] met us at the door. Looks frail and old. Talked for three and a half hours. Mainly about how bad the Russians are. Quoted Cy to himself. Full of charisma. Got home at one."

October 27, Paris: "Left at 6 A.M. Endless flight. Eight hours to Karachi and another nine to Paris. Cy worked *all* the way. Luckily had three seats each. Ouf. It's good to be home, to be able to read street names, to understand people without an interpreter. Gosh we are tired."

October 28, Paris: "Celebrated Cy's birthday one day late. He liked his Mao alarm clock and his basket dog."

After our return to Paris, Marina wrote to Bob* and Jackie McBride about China:

"It is in the theatre that one gets one's best understanding of their incredibly oversimplified life. A kind of *Image d'Epinal* [primitive] view of life where good is good and bad is bad and everything is educational. The latest popular song which we heard everywhere is entitled 'the glow of the declarations of the 10th party congress shines in the heart of the masses like ten thousand stars.' Can you imagine our young whisteling in their showers 'The latest findings on Watergate disturb the hearts of the people like ten thousand stingy nettles.' I was taken to one ballet which was hard to believe.

"A young couple *sur pointes,* dance around the stage greeting the new day in the form of a lovely yellow *papier-mâché* sun rising in the background. Then the boy stoops and picks up the chamber pot from under the bed and trips across the stage with it. His wife runs after him and wants to know where he thinks he is going. To put the contents on our turnips he says. Oh Ah you cant do that, what about the masses. There follows a stormy argumentative dance with her showing him the little red book where the good Chairman says that one must at all times think of the masses first, and finally he admits the error of his ways, is forgiven and together in a triumphant *pas de deux* they go off to give the potty to the people.

"And yet you know, just as the cynical chuckle rises to one's lips, so does the sobering thought occur that this may all seem childish to us, yet it is in this way that they have managed three crops a year, and done away with starvation, floods, illiteracy and epidemics."

Marina drafted an article for *Vogue*, from which I have taken excerpts:

---

*Retired U.S. ambassador with whom we stayed in Congo and Mexico.

"It is like living for a month or so in a vast boy scout camp. And their thoughts, their words, are over-simplified to such a degree, that I was balanced all the time between cynical disbelief, great admiration and a strange nostalgia for my own jaded loss of innocence. As in most of their ballet for example.

"There is one about a wounded PLA [People's Liberation Army] man who is found dying in a field by a gentle peasant mother. Quick as a bird she modestly retires behind a bush and fills a cup with her own milk, and just a sip of this restores the poor young man to perfect health, at which he thanks her gratefully and goes his way riffle on shoulder again, to serve the people.

"All the babies have slits in their little trousers, to make going to the bath room a bit easier, and it is a great surprise to see so many tiny bare bottoms everywhere. Another thing which Chinese people seem to need to do more often than we Westerners is spit, and it is quite astonishing the number of spittoons one faces both indoors and out. Unfortunately there are so many places which are closed that it is almost better not to look at guide books, even Nagel's because it only whets one's appetite and one is dissapointed. Like the historical museum, closed some of last year, no one knows why. But one can see the objects from the various recent excavations, in the Forbidden city itself and they are magic. When there was still ancestor worship no one would touch a tomb of course. But now that all that 'superstition' has been swept away there is no end to all the treasures still lying under that gigantic land waiting only for time and money to see the light of day . . . .

"From Sian one morning we were driven to the Tomb of little Princess Yung Tai who came to a sad end at the hands of her grandmother the Empress Wu. It is filled with the most beautiful newly excavated statuettes and a little further off the Empresse's tomb which has not yet been excavated. One looks at the tall hill and dreams of untold treasures which it has burried benieth that time browned earth. The avenue leading to the hill is lined on either side with monumental animals in stone of extraordinary charm, and at the very entrance there stands a sculptured group of foreign dignitaries, envoys from vassal lands, all standing stiff and grave, in their national costumes as if they had all been turned to stone, while paying their last respects to the great Empress. And in between the animals and statues grow gay percimon trees ladden with shiny orange fruit, almost imaginary, or like those made of jade or amethyst or gold, which decorate the rooms of yet another wicked Empress, the old dowager, in the Forbidden city. The view from the top of the hill is so breath-taking, and so vast one feels that one is looking down upon the whole of China . . . .

"On the Shanghai water front, like disposessed decrepit angry duchesses, the erstewhile Banks and places of amusement and buisiness of the Foreign devils look gloomily down on the muddy waters and ponder on their bygone wickedness. One of them is now turned into the 'Friendship shop' where foreign friends can pay with their own currency for silks and jade and porcelaine, none older than eighty or ninety years but, alas, costing six times what they would in London or New York. The only things one can afford are miserably untransportable. Beautiful earthern flower pots and baskets of extraordinary shapes and size, and animals made up of lackered straw which are quite wonderful. Chickens and ducks and marvellous green frogs and cats and dogs, but dear oh dear, how to pack them; specially from a place where every pound of excess baggage costs one eye."

XV

November 1973 - October 1975

Marina was unrelievedly glad to be back in her familiar Parisian world. She wrote Avis and Chip Bohlen on November 15:

"I must say that admiration is one thing and liking is another. In spite of strikes and grumblings and the principle of *rouspetance permanante* that governs this lovely land, the sheer joy of being back in an undisciplined country is boundless. I thought at times that if one more tiny tot put me in my place when I asked what he or she would like to be when they grew up, by looking at me sternly and answering 'what will be most useful to the masses,' I would hit it. Clare Hollingworth that dear old battle ax of a journalist says that everybody is so busy serving, that there is no one to serve.

"I have never seen people sleep so much or in such unexpected places and postures. Hanging from the buss door, clinging to the scaffolding of a new building, a stone under their heads, in David's bed, or right in the middle of the Park of Celestial Peace. In Hu Ho Hao Te (yes I am not making it up it is the capital of Inner Mongolia) the pillows are not filled with cotton or goose feathers as one might expect, but with rice husks which is astonishing but less uncomfortable than it sounds. Like bean-bags sort of."

We went to London to see the children and to purchase a three-month-old beagle puppy who was intimately related to Benjamin. He was promptly named Christopher after an obscure Greek Orthodox saint with the head of a dog. On November 28, Marina told her diary: "Beagelaki adorable, so damp and sweet."

In the wake of the Yom Kippur war and amid the Arab oil boycott, she wrote Dodo on November 29:

"If the Rennaissance was the century of great painting and the 16th of great litterature etc, this decade will certainly go down in history as the apogee of black-mail and mutual betrayal of everyone by everyone. Qadaffi was in Paris for three days and it was too sick making to see the governement fauning on him. He arrived very well dressed in suit and tie, and then just *pour marquer le point* I suppose, went to dinner at the Elysée in grey flannels and a turtle neck sweater. The only thing one can say is that at least the Arabs have some excuse in gloating, having been treated by the West as dirty Wogs and exploited for the last hundred and fifty years. One can hardly blame them for lapping up their superiority now. But when one thinks of the cheap self-seaking short sighted behaviour of France and other European countries it makes one quite sick. I lunched with John Loudon today, the Dutch head of Shell, and he said there were dozens of things which could have been done if only the Common Market members had held together. But they all fell apart in a panic betraying each other *à qui mieux mieux*. Oh Lord."

But she consoled herself with a few words about Christopher: "I cant tell you how adorable he is. It is a terrible gamble because no one can ever be like our very own Benjamin. But this little one is quite irresistible and the day he arrived he put his hand in mine and cocked his head to one side and I was done for."

Christopher was Marina's Christmas present and, like Benjamin before him, whom we still missed, he was presented under the tree with a little poem hung around his neck:

"Dear Mumbo
My name is Christopher Beagle
I'll try to do my part,
Amusing you and soothing you
To ease your aching heart."

He did.

Three days after Christmas, David flew over from the U.S.A. for a brief visit.

Marina headed the page for December 28 in her diary "POLAR!" and noted:

"Polar arrived in time for lunch, looking well and so sweet. I adore him." She wrote Dodo the next day: "He always fills the house with pleasure and with people. He looks very well and apparently is very well on his way to forming his little company for buying and selling art."

The year 1974 began tragically.

From Marina's diary:

January 1, Paris: "Chip died. What else can one write for today. Sorrow. Sorrow."

January 2, Paris: "Wrote to Avis and Marylin Holmes whose mother died. There has already been one air crash, one huge fire in a school and Mr. Sieff [Edward Sieff] shot in the head by Palestinians. Nice way to start the year."

January 4, Paris: "Evangeline [Bruce] came for early supper. Looked exquisite. Says a cold wind is blowing in China against everyone except the U.S. for the moment. Mrs. Wu [our guide of the previous year] has vanished. Mr. Ma [who looked after us for the press department] in a 7 May school [disciplinary institution] again. How confusing."

On January 15, before going to London, Marina wrote Dodo:

"We are giving an enormous party tomorrow night for twenty two writers. But it will be buffet and *makaronada* [spaghetti] sort of as everything is so unbelievably expensive and hopefully fun. Prince Michael of

Greece and Marina are coming, as writers not princes. And M. Maurice Schumann too not as an ex minister of foreign affairs but as a novelist. We have been killing ourselves the last week trying to read the works of all our guests. One is M. Larteguy you know the one who wrote *Les Centurions* which I gave you, about Algeria and the French army."

We went to The Hague and then on to Bonn to stay with Nicko (British ambassador) and Mary Henderson. Marina sent a postcard of the Villa Hügel at Essen to Avis Bohlen. The Villa Hügel was the astoundingly hideous home of the Krupp von Bohlen family, proprietors of Krupp, arms barons, and distant relatives of Chip (of which he hated to be reminded).

"Look what you would have lived in," she wrote on February 18, "if you had married into the other side of the Bohlen family. The interior is not to be believed. Solid pseudo gothic oak, gloomy as a tomb and of an ugliness beyond imagination. Only the park and gardens fabulous, even on a cold foggy Ruhr day."

She wrote Avis from Paris on February 24: "We went to a huge dinner at our Embassy a few days ago in honor of M. Jobert [the French foreign minister], the most talked about man in Europe after dear Henry [Kissinger], and I felt as if we were dinning at Princesse Mathilde's, it was all so nineteenth century. *Foie gras,* two duchesses a papal nuncio and Chopin after dinner in the Blue living room. All of us perched on little gold chairs. Even the underlying political tension over independence and nationalism, seemed of another epoch. Speaches with the pudding (your dear cook had out-done himself and the crystallised roses were fabulous). M. Jobert had the *grippe* and only came as this would have been the third time the dinner had been postponed (once he dashed off to Saudi Arabia, once Jack Irwin [U.S. ambassador] had been called to Washington and his flue would have been taken for a diplomatic illness). He did look green I must say and with his pitch black hair that looks like a wig, his personage fitted well with his reputation. He has apparently an American wife who is ill. That and Pompidou never having got over his Chicago experience [where he was spat upon]. This of course is gossip, but if true, ah me, what little things govern the destinies of humanity. Creepy.

"Virginia [Chambers] took me to the fancy *abonnement* evening at the opera ten days ago, when everybody who is anybody is there, all dolled up, and it was the opening of 'Swan Lake' and I kept thinking of you both and could almost not bare to sit through it. Chip saying he could dance every step of every caracter in the damned thing, and you giving us a demonstration of the Polovtsi dance over the living room sofa at Spasso. And how we laughed.

> " 'How mad and bad and glad we were
> But oh how it was sweet.' "

To Dodo on March 22: "A few days ago we had Jacky and [Aristotle] Onnassis to lunch and it was like a commedy really. Kitty [Solomos] and I were discussing the menu and Kitty said lets give them something different. *Angynares a la polita* [artichoke dish]. So off we went and got about twenty artichokes and spent all of the previous evening cleaning them polishing them with lemon rushing around to find herbs, etc and very proud we set them on the windows to cool. The next day oh horrors they tasted delicious but looked utterly revolting, all black and with a finger of oil floating over them. Catastrophe. Oh well we said, never mind we will buy some more and make them with Hollandaise. Off we rushed to the market, buy another twenty, leap into a taxi and get cought in a street demonstration of the striking bank clerks this time. Tic tic tic eleven, half passed, twenty to twelve, motionless. Obviously no time to boil artichokes. So we tell the taxi to be patient in case the *embouteillage* started to disolve. Flew off again and bought *caravides* [crayfish] which only need ten minutes to cook, and eventually got home about six minutes before the guests. I could have ordered *foie gras* and lobsters chez Maxim's for the price of three different sets of stuff as a first course."

From Marina's diary:

March 28, Paris: "Dinner at the home of Froment-Meurice [of the Quai d'Orsay]. Among those present were Maurice Schumann and Ambassador Seydoux. When the French are bright it's a joy to listen. But they can construct a most marvellous architectural syllogism, of infinite clarity and logic, on a totally false premise. In this case, that Nixon's name had not been mentioned once in the Kissinger Brezhnev communiqué."

To Dodo from Paris on April 6: "We have been sitting watching poor M. Pompidou's funeral on television. I must say humanity makes me more and more unhappy. All these months people have been going around talking about him as if being ill were a sin and not resigning a crime. They have called him power-crazy and obscessed with ambition and so on, and now they are all calling him a hero a captain who died at the helm of his ship a great patriot etc. *Trop tard.* And my god he must have been one.

"The trip to Russia alone, and that fifty kilometre drive over bumpy Caucasian roads, must have been enough to kill him. And it did in fact. Anyway it was nice that so many heads of State came and the service was very simple and moving. And now hardly underground and the death-dance of succession has already started with a show of dissaray in the majority which is too depressing and it is really quite possible that M. Mitterrand may be elected. With [Harold] Wilson in England and Mitterrand here *oti gelassame, gelassame* [we've done all the laughing we can]. However we so deserve all we get, we humans at large and so called conservatives in particular, that we must take what we get and not grumble.

"We gave a dinner party last Sunday for Mr. Heikal the ex editor of *Al Ahram* and best friend of Nasser's who has just been thrown out by Sadat, I suspect for being pro Russian and very against any *raprochement* with the U.S. But Cy believes above all in being nice to people who are out, and he is probably the only one. Last year when he had just written a book on Nasser and was at the hight of his power he and his wife were wined and dined everywhere. This year they had no engagements what so ever, except ours. Ah me."

On April 18, Marina wrote Dodo: "On Saturday we went to Cécile de Rothschild's who has the loveliest garden in the world and her cousin Victor was there [an English Rothschild] who is a brilliant scientist so David and Cy enjoyed him and we had fabulous wine and food and enjoyed every bite in view of the fact that if Mitterrand wins the elections (which is by no means impossible) it may be the last drop of capitalist luxuries we get in quite a while. She has some tulips in her garden which are green and white and the loveliest I have ever seen. I was given a large bunch to bring home so the house still looks festive even though David left last night and Cy for Cairo in a flurry this morning."

While I was away, Marina wrote me: "Jack's [Irwin] dinner was really deadly. Forty people of whom most were rich type Republicans *de passage*. I was lucky as I had M. Denis Baudouin [of the Elysée] next to me who was full of political gossip and naturally talked a great deal about Servan-Schreiber and his folly, and about Jobert who is a friend of his, but who, he says, lost his sense of proportion when he was bitten by politics and ambition and that he will really destroy himself with this idea of his own political party. M. Baudouin said you were the only journalist Pompidou ever saw with any sort of pleasure and that he told Baudouin *Lui toujours. C'est un ami.*"

To Avis Bohlen in April 1974: "I have stolen three days from every day life, to come to Ibiza and help Denise [Boisot] prepare her house for tenants. Cy is in Egypt so I have not abandonned anyone and I must say it is lovely being here. The fields are just like the Greek ones, covered in tiny dark pink gladiola and baby orchids and wild asparagus which it takes two hours to pick enough for one bite each, which is probably what makes one *think* they taste so good. Alas it is bitter cold and we only jumped into the sea once and that for our good and not our pleasure. Oh if only you could see what they have done to it. I remember so well coming for a few days from Mallorca on that 'our' summer, and it was then still a lovely village island with women in long black skirts and white painted straw hats. Now it is a sort of *sous-côte-d'Azur*, with giant blocks of flats and hotels all along the sea front, which seems to be a contradiction in terms. The mountain bits however are still lovely and Denise's house is enchanting."

May 1, Marina wrote Dodo: "If I had one present to choose for fifty five years of life, it would certainly be what you say, that I have not caused you a moment's sorrow. Often one does so inadvertantly by falling ill, or dying or being miserable, but we really have been lucky touch wood. I got back from Ibiza yesterday after five delightful days although it rained four out of the five. And so cold. One never suffers more from cold than in so called hot climates.

"Cy got back an hour after I did from Damascus, tired and grumpy. This evening the Claudels are coming to supper so it will be a nice birthday. I just burned the duck I was cooking for them. Damn. It is recuperable though thank heavens as everything is shut and I would have had to give them baked beans out of a can. We have asparagus and strawberries as warranted by tradition. How well I remember some birthdays in the big house when we picked our own first strawberries for the party."

To Dodo on May 13: "Cy has been thinking for quite a while that with things as they are in the *patrida* [fatherland], it might be good to have another little *apokoumbi* [fall-back position] in France, so this week end we went to Normandy. There is an old count who like many old French counts has lots of land and no money who had proposed to give us an old mill of his within the property of his chateau for nothing provided we fixed it and could then live in it for twenty years. It sounded like a good idea. Not owners, so less taxes less responsibility etc and a nice place for Cy to fish in. So off we went and met the old boy, who looked so exactly like Samuel Whiskers that I almost burst out laughing and *en plus* he was drunk as an owl at three in the afternoon.

"He took us to see the *moulin* 'un petit bijou' as he kept saying on the way there, and the *bijou* turned out to be four walls (thirteenth century) and that was all plus a rotting millstone and a lot of rats. The French are really incredible. We gathered later that he is not as poor as all that, being the owner of seven hundred hectars of rich wine land in the Loire. He makes all that lovely Pouilly fumé wine. Yet he cant have spent one drachma on his *moulin* since the thirteenth century. Then he said we might like to do the same for the Chateau and off we went to a real magic place half a mile away. A thirteenth century cubic house really, and a fourteenth century chapel, a *dongeon* and a *manoir* with Mansard roof and miles of stables *dépendances* etc, all in a wild state of decay over-run by lilac gone wild and white with falling apple blossom and grass so high we kept losing Beagle. And of course a stream. A kind of Grand Meaulnes place to dream about.

"Alas, it would take more than a hundred thousand dollars to fix even three rooms in the whole place and ten years to do it, and anyway even if he gave it to us we could never afford to furnish it or heat it or anything. Oh well I am not desolate about it because Normandy is all very well when the fields are green and the apple trees in blossom but in the winter . . . .

"We have a very *mouvementé* six weeks ahead of us. Cy goes to America on the 10th of June as it is his 40th annyversary from Harvard and he has been invited to make a speech. So he will take advantage of that to also go and receive the Overseas press club award for his last book which is a gold watch. Also see his Publishers."

To Catherine Negroponte on June 1: "From the few friends I have spocken to since yesterday [after Giscard d'Estaing won the French elections], I get the impression that they are all still too surprised about their new government to have made up their minds as to whether they wish to be furious or delighted, scornful or worried. But they all seem to agree that all this *sois disant* simplicity, the walk, the driving himself to the Elysée etc, are just a wee bit phony. *On verra.* No one can be a magician these days, above all for a highly critical, highly irreverent people like the French.

"The Prime Minister is reffered to by one and all as Chateau Chirac a refference to the famous juggling that went on a few years ago when he bought a chateau and three months later had it made a *'Monument historique'* presumably not to pay taxes. Oh tiny tiny shade of Watergate. I found Cy and Beagle both well."

From the diary:

June 7, Paris: "Cy sold the Dali. I shall miss it so." (This was in order to get money for a new apartment.)

To Vane Ivanović, our Jugoslav émigré friend whom she had visited in Mallorca, she wrote on July 9 from Paris: "I remembered the name of Merimée's imaginary Serbian poems. They are called 'La Guzla,' after a Serbian musical instrument and he ascribed them to a fictitious author to whom he gave the lovely name of Hyacinthe Maglanović. After the enormous success of Ossian apparently the vogue for exotic folk songs in Europe became very great and everyone was passionately interrested in all folk songs and legends above all a man named Claude Fauriel who was made a proffessor of foreign litterature at the Sorbonne for the 1st time in its history.

"One day it appears that Mérimée went to call on him and the proffessor handed him two large volumes of Serbian poetry with the blunt injunction 'Learn Serbian.' Easier said than done and Merimée never did, but his interrest in Illyria had been awakened and he began to wonder how he could manage to travel to that lovely land. He had practically no money however at that time, so he decided to compensate for his disappointment by composing his own collection of Illyrian balads and if he managed to sell them he would be able to fulfill his wish and go see for himself. So while on a holiday in 1827 he tossed off a balad a day until he had enough for a respectable anthology. No one suspected that it was anything but genuine and it was very well received by critics and readers alike and translated into German and English almost at once.

"Everyone admired Hyacinthe Maglanović greatly as he was supposed to be a romantic mysterious caracter half poet half out-law. Even Mary Shelley was so impressed that she translated three of the balads herself. Voilà. I am off tomorrow at dawn and I have not even packed yet. How I shall get on to the plane with enough hand luggage for a mule, plus Cy's shot gun and Beagle god only knows. Mercifully if one looks helpless enough; someone always turns up to lend a hand."

I was in Saudi Arabia when Marina wrote to me from Spetsais on July 19, 1974, just after the Greek colonels' regime sought to murder Cypriot Archbishop Makarios and only succeeded in provoking a Turkish assault on the island and their own political suicide. She said:

"The news of the Archbishop's murder had just been whispered and at the same time half of Attica was on fire. From Koropi to Tatoi down to Pikermi Bojiati etc up to Pendeli and Melissa and all the way down again to Vouliagmeni, the whole land was blazing. Athens was litterally surrounded by fire, the sky was black and red the heavy wind brought flakes of black and white ash on to everything and every scrap of Byzantine atavism and superstition in me cried out They have killed a man of god and this is the punishment. Our leaders here all talk like *Malbrouc* [the Duke of Marlborough]. Ah me. I hope you dont return at the head of an invading army. Po po po po."

To Susan Mary Alsop she continued her account on August 3: "We have just lived through two weeks which feel like two years and gone through every conceivable human emotion with such speed, that our heads and hearts were litterally swimming. Like malaria; one moment burning with patriotic fervor and righteous indignation the next frozen by a sick fealing that it was all our fault and that we were deep in the worst crisis of our crisis ridden existence with no one at the head and never have we had such a frustrating feeling of being taken for and treated as utter imbeciles by our own governement.

"During the worst first days our radios spoke of Ethiopia and Portugal and the export of morella cherries to Germany. The very first day, actually when the first whispers about Makarios having been assassinated by the national guard started moving around Athens was the worst. By a nasty coincidence, half of Attika was destroyed by forrest fires such as we have never seen before and to my own surprise strange nameless fears came forth from unsuspected depths and Shakesperean phrases about the death of kings, and an apocalyptic sense pervaded all of us.

"No one knew anything, but only one thing became certain in no time at all. The colonels would have to go. But how, and replaced by whom? There followed several days of suspence and worry and speculation and endless rumours and quarrels. I just managed to get through to Marinette to tell her not to come with the children and five minutes later general mobilisation was announced all communication with the outside world came to an end. And then the news of Turkish landings and bombings of open villages. One can always trust the Turks to do the wrong thing.

"While undouptedly the first foolish fault was ours, which is a horrid fealing, they then went all out and killed and cut off heads and did their time honored horrors and broke the truce so many times that there was no way of remaining objective and keeping a balanced judgement. The radio was blaring martial music from 1940 and the young men began leaving the island a carnation behind their ear and patriotic fervor in their hearts. There is something to be said for old fashioned under-developpement. Rather that, than the flag used for underpants like in Viet Nam. It is a strange and dreadful truth that war or even the possibility of it brings out the best in most people. In no time at all the whole of Greece seemed to become as one, united in two common hopes. Save Cyprus and overthrow the governement. Which incidentally managed to vanish completely and we neither saw nor heard the Colonels once during the entire crisis.

"Mercifully the internal telephones never came to a stop and we all talked to everyone every two minutes. And what endless false news flew over the wires. The 3rd army corps was advancing from Salonica. The president had been fired. The colonels were in jail, not at all they were jailling all rebel officers etc etc. Then one day the destroyer Velos which had led a fool-hardy coup last year and taken refuge in Italy, sailled back to Pyreus and the officers put themselves at the disposal of the nation. One night Kitty Monica and I were sitting on the terrace and the new moon appeared in a tiny gold sliver in the sky and we all three made our seven bows and seven times our wish and then looked at each other and said 'Karamanlis?' We nodded and never in my life has a wish been granted so fast so unexpectedly and so completely.

"Two hours later once again our telephone rang and we were told he was on the way and that Giscard [d'Estaing] had taken him personally to Orly and lent him his own airoplane. We could not stand to be away from it all and thank heavens Kitty had her car across the bay so we took a boat over and drove like lunatics arriving at two in the morning, which was just about the time he landed. Delirium. The whole of Athens was in the streets with flags and rose petals and beaming faces. Even the departure of the Germans had not been as wonderful, or so it seemed. It must have been such a thrill for him after eleven years of bitterness dissapointment and exile albeit self imposed."

She continued her tale to Michael Edwards on August 25: "Malaria is nothing in comparison with the pitch of fever and the icy anxieties we have been through in such rapid succession that our heads and hearts were whirling and as for our minds, at a complete stand still. Try as we might, nothing made any sense and we were submerged in such wild rumours, that in the end like Alice we were capable of believing six impossible things before breakfast. We were glued to the radio and when not listening to news we were arguing and quarrelling amongst ourselves.

"All ships and cars commandeered to carry the men to their bases. Yet the mobilisation itself was total confusion and so were our own thoughts and emotions. One bit of brain telling us that all this was madness, and the other that madness or not this was our country threatened, and sudden bursts of blind patriotism bubbled forth to the point of us trying to get the red cross (no wounded yet of course) but one thing became clear right away and was unequivocably welcomed and that was that the colonels having gooffed beyond the wildest dreams of goofingdom, they would have to go.

"At one moment tanks were seen crossing Constitution square and there was a brief moment of anxiety but it was too late to worry. People were kissing and embracing in the streets, and shouting He is coming, and walking arm in arm in long straight lines to greet him. Karamanlis eventually got here at three in the morning amidst a pandemonium of warm enthusiastic welcome. And of course everyone like in fairy tales began to think 'and we lived happily ever after,' but not being in a fairy tale the real problems have only just begun. Starting with such passionate anti Americanism that even some of my oldest friends wont speak to me. It is heart breaking and infuriating but my dear compatriots have never been too strong on objective thinking and there is no doupt alas that dear Henry [Kissinger] waffled this one. And in the mean time the cease fire violated eighty seven times in Cyprus and the island destroyed and god knows how we shall ever extricate ourselves from all this mess.

"Cy arrived *sur ça* and one of the papers published excerpts from his book about the original Greek affair which brought us celebrity as well as invective. Most of our old friends have become ministers but I dont envy them their tasks. *Tout est à refaire* and ghastly Andreas Papandreou has returned as well as Melina [Mercouri] with one thought in mind, to put as many spanners in the works as possible. Luckily she talks such arrant nonsense that she is being demythified most rapidly. But he is dangerous and bad.

"Yet in all this, the house has been a joy, the jasmine sweeter than ever, the sky blue as blue eyes, the sea like liquid velvet, urchins by the baskets full and Kitty and Monika and various other friends a source of infinite pleasure and at least this *parea* in complete agreement about everything. Cy went to Turkey for a week and got stuck but finally arrived two days ago."

She wrote Avis Bohlen from Spetsais on September 19: "Karamanlis has so many problems to face that he will need superhuman powers to achieve anything, and alas alas he has an all too human raw material to do it with. The newspapers, muzzled for seven years, have suddenly gone barking mad and the least esteemed or considered element in the Greek press today is a fact. The more pro Junta the paper, the more violently anti American it is now. One reads such things as that the American military attaché in Cyprus led the Turkish invasion of the island personally. That the whole thing was plotted by the CIA and Kissinger and Israel together. For whose benefit and why, no one bothers to explain. Even I have had one of my oldest friends turn her back on me and call me a liar a traitor and question my right to spend the summer on Spetses, just because I was married to an American. You can imagine what a thing like that can do to a tiny island like this one."

And on September 20 to Roxane Panas,* in Johannesburg: "Nationally sad, and family delightful. Marinette came in spite of her mother-in-law's worry about her 'taking the children into the jaws of death' and we had four generations in the house. The children are just at the age when everything is an adventure and you cant think what joy it is for me to relive my own childhood through them; watching them do and love exactly the same things as Alexi and I did fifty years ago. The same fig tree the same light house the very same *amaxi* [coach] and coachman. It is the highest priviledge in this maddening world, to own a little corner of the earth where nothing changes."

Back in Paris, Marina wrote Dodo on October 16:

"Cy was supposed to arrive at nine this morning but apparently the plane ran into a flock of birds which got entangled in the engines and they had to go back to Tel Aviv and begin again and it is now four in the afternoon and he is still not here . . . . Just arrived, white and exhausted having left Jerusalem at two A.M. Oh me air travel. He has gone straight to have a hot bath."

Again to Dodo on October 29: "This week we had both children as it was Cy's sixty-second birthday. We had the British Ambassador and his wife who are old friends and Bill Deakin even older and that nice Thérèse Larteguy who was in Spetses and Marinette and I cooked a splendid lunch and it was nice although Cy very depressed and feeling a hundred."

There was a long French mail strike which interfered with Marina's correspondence. In her diary she wrote:

---

* South African friend.

November 6, Paris: "General Stehlin in big trouble after story on Mirages broken by Cy. Demotion called for. Poor chap. His son just lost an eye."

November 10, Pont Ste. Maxence [at the Billottes]: "Cy angelic mood. Drove to Billottes. Walked in the forest with Beagle. Lovely blue sky for half an hour. Pierre told us all about the Markovic scandal. Photos of Pompidou as a transvestite. Operation Véronique, the peddling of drugs to the U.S. to get money for France's intelligence. Makes Watergate look like a boy scout meeting."

November 21, Paris: "Dinner at Diane's [de Mouchy] with President Giscard d'Estaing [at his request]. Giscard started by asking *why* this was the age of mediocrity [title of my last book]. Margeries and Pierre Brossolettes the other guests. Interesting but one is not at one's best when so formal and deferential."

Marina wrote Dodo that evening:

"I am going to London for ten days to do nothing but play with the babies. We were supposed to go this week but then we were invited to dine with President Giscard d'Estaing, just six of us, so we could not refuse and I put it off until after the dinner. Dont tell this to anyone as he preffers we dont say we saw him."

To Dodo on December 8 from Paris: "At last the mail men are back at work and we feel as if a siege has been lifted. Today I got your letter of November 4th. Well I have just returned from ten days in London where the main attraction was the little ones of course, who are dreams. I cant tell you what joy they are to me. Marinette gave two dinner parties for me bless her heart and she is fantastic the ease with which she cooks for ten and one hardly sees her lift a finger. One week end we went to Oving [home of Adrian's father, Lord Hartwell] and the second to Hackwood [Lord Camrose's house]. It is really pre 1914 luxury. Beds warmed and cosy with huge eiderdowns and flowered cretonne and chaises longues and baths 'drawn' and warm towels drapped over the chair. Huge amounts of very good food, and suit cases unpacked (so one has a hard time finding anything) and re-packed so beautifully with so much tissue-paper that one is loath to unpack it, ever. David [now living in London] came too and at one point Marinette skidded and we landed in a ditch. Nothing happened to either the car or us, but we had a silly time composing telegrams to poor Cy telling him his whole family had been done for. It was a pleasant week end but the English are odd people. Mostly small talk about people and movies and things, and suddenly one realises that Joan* has just finished a book on the Bogomils and another one on the Hanseatic League.

"Cy has finally decided *une fois pour toute* that Normandy is out. I cant tell if he is doing this purely for my sake or if he too saw that it would be difficult to live in the wilderness at our age and with life and money getting shorter by the minute. So we are looking for a flat."

To Dodo on January 6: "We went to Royaumont to Nelly de Rothschild's wedding to Axel Münthe's grandson Adam and that was lovely. The Chateau is beautiful and had little lights on the steps and only a little lighting on the balconies and windows and looks so romantic in the very black night. So we had a lovely time and Beagle was invited too and he was delirious because he does not have much fun in Paris.

"Cy left for Rome much to my regret because his flue was the real thing, and indeed he called this morning to say he is back in bed with fever in his hotel in Rome. But he is so stubborn nothing I say will do any good."

Mary Henderson always drew her own talented and amusing Christmas cards, and on January 7, Marina wrote to her and Nicko in Bonn:

"If only I had kept all your Christmas cards through the years I could make a fortune, with a retrospective 'Henderson' at the Grand Palais. I have not written in ages, but not out of lack of love. Mainly lack of time and geography . . . .

"I was in despair in the middle of Piccadilly one night after a play with Aline Berlin and twenty taxis went by without stopping and finally one did because of the red light and I put my head in his window and said I suppose you too dont have enough petrol to go to Kensington and he grinned and said 'For two quid I 'ave luv.' Most Unbritish. Paris I am afraid is still the Marie Chantal of Western Europe, and apparently the polls say there has never been so much money spent on *foie gras boudin* chesnuts etc as this year. *Après moi le deluge,* sort of thing."

---

* Princess Joan Aly Khan, friend of Lord Camrose.

Marina wrote Dodo on January 15: "Your sweet letter and the giant bag of pistaches arrived almost at the same time. I must say it is wonderful after fifty five years of acquaintance (intimate) that you should still think I am a perfect daughter. It is only because you are a perfect mother, but still I like to hear it. The other day I was sitting at a table with five people I did not know (at a dinner party) and ALL five admitted sadly that their children hated them, and that they themselves did not feel any tremendous devotion for their progenie. Too sad. How lucky that I should have had it both ways."

And again on January 25: "Ever since you wrote to me about Anika and now Vassilaki and also poor Frank Wisner's young wife Geneviève dead at twenty eight I keep thinking of those beautiful angry lines of Edna St. Vincent Millay's.

" 'I am not resigned to the shutting away of loving hearts in the hard
     ground.
So it is, and so it will be, for so it has been, time out of mind . . .

" 'Gently they go, the beautiful, the tender, the kind.
Quietly they go, the intelligent, the witty, the brave.
I know. But I do not approve. And I am not resigned.'

"And yet resigned, resigned; there it is mama mou and I am so sad for them and for you. One by one our friends go. I wish I were there to hug you and hold your hand and comfort you. January is almost over and from February on I always feel that winter is almost over and we can begin counting the days until July."

To Avis Bohlen on January 27: "Call from Polly [Wisner] to say she had just married Clayton [Fritchey]* and they are coming to stay four days with us, which delights me. I am so very glad for both of them. Tried to get a party going for them but NOBODY is free for dinner in the next week so they will have to content themselves with us.

"This morning Giscard [d'Estaing] abolished titles all over again. I dont

---

* U.S. newspaper columnist.

suppose any of our friends will change their visiting cards, but it will please the workers. Ah me, how transparent politics have become. Or is it that I am getting old and so much is déjà vu. Everything he does is all right *sur papier,* like walking or driving alone in the streets late at night, or wearing a tea shirt and inviting himself to dinner with his *encadreur,* and yet somehow a tiny bit silly. Still silly on the right side, so at least that."

On February 5 she wrote to an American friend, Liz Fondaras: "The sun has been out for two whole days in a row and all Parisians are out trying to dry their damp spirits after the weather which you know. We went to the Senate the other day to a reception for Maurice Schumann's entry into the Académie. Apparently the Duke de Castries who made the welcoming speech said two words about Schumann and the rest of the two hours talked viciously against Gaullism. Scandal and how the French enjoy a good scandale. But oh how beautiful the Senate is, inside."

I flew to the Middle East. Marina wrote to me on February 24:

"It is so comforting to read your columns and know that you are alive and not eaten up by a revolutionary or high-jacked to some place even hotter than Khartoum."

Marina wrote Rosie Cartier that month. Raymond, her husband, a distinguished French author and journalist and our friend, had died. Marina said:

"Alas we have been away, but our thoughts our minds our hearts were with you every second since we heard of your tragedy and your immeasurable loss. Strange how the heart is slow to learn what the swift mind perceives at every turn; even though we knew it was inevitable even though we feared it was but a question of time, when it did in fact happen, we were as shocked and horrified as if Raymond had gone in a motor car accident. Oh darling Rosie how my heart aches for you. Eyes closed, hands folded on so much goodness and courage so much intelligence and kindness and love. My every fiber rebels against such sorrow.

"There is so little love in the world alas, so many people who do not understand or care that when a couple, a real couple like you exists, one wishes it could go on forever, not only for its own sake, but also as an example to others, like a ray of sun-shine in a darkening world. So it is my dearest, why I cannot find it in me to tell you to be brave and strong and patiant in your deep belief and faith, partly because I know you are all these things, and partly I fear, because in moments of sheer almost physical grief and pain, courage and strength, are useful in one's behaviour to the outside world, but do not really help the abyss of internal loneliness and misery."

On March 29 she wrote to Mary Manners, who had invited us for a fishing weekend in England:

"Cy got back two days ago and imagine my delight when he said he would do everything in his power to write a few columns ahead of time etc, so that we could come for the week end of the 6th June. I can hardly wait. We shall be free and dancing for joy to come and see you."

To Pam Harriman on April 1: "My god the world is in a mess only France seems to be floating in a kind of euphoria on the surface. Except that it is more like Xmas than Easter. After all the daffodils and primroses came out in January, it suddenly turned to snow and rain and the Easter holy day was spent in ski pants. We did not go anywhere and I must say Paris when all the Parisians are gone is bliss. The busses were galloping down the Champs Elysées enjoying an almost unique traffic-less vista; taxi drivers stopped to ask if one needed a lift, and the only language not heard in the streets was French."

On April 14 she sent a nice, gossipy letter to Avis Bohlen: "We found a flat in the Boulevard Montparnasse which was built by Mansard for Mme de Maintenon. It is tiny but with a lot of caracter and good floors good windows good proportions. There is a pretty little entrance and then a corridor (not Mansard's alas) and on one side of it is a study for Cy a nice living room a small bedroom and a rather nice size dressing room which can also be my *foutoir* [den], desk, television etc. And a very ugly bath room. On the other side is a tiny guest room, with its own bath, a kitchen and another fairly good size room. My dream is to move the kitchen to this other room plus all closets washing machine etc and make the present kitchen into a minute dining room. Everyone says one needs no dining room these days, but the less servants one has the more one needs one I think. Just to close the door and leave everything for later.

"Two nights ago there was a wonderful TV program with Solzhenytsin and a lot of French journalists including Jean Daniel who said he was so dissapointed in him (said it to his face) because he was not doing anything to help the down trodden people of Europe. Implying that while S. was in his Goulag, Western Europe also had its own goulag and American Imperialism was as bad as anything in Russia. I could have brocken the set I was so angry. But Solzhenytsin was fabulous and so quiet and gentle and one felt at every word the boundless wisdom of a man who has suffered everything and seen everything and lost all illusions all hope, except love of men *malgré tout*. And not an ounce of bitterness, not even towards imbeciles and show offs like Jean Daniel. But there are so many like Daniel alas in the world.

"Philippe de Rothschild lunched here yesterday and HE claims to be ruined. And it is true that the wine people have had a terrible time. And this weather wont help. Eighty per cent of all the fruit has been destroyed. As I look out of the window at this very moment, there is a bright ray of sun and snow flakes dancing in it. Its too crazy."

On April 29 she wrote to Mary Henderson, still stationed in Bonn: "The best news we have heard in years is that you are coming here. Too good to be true. Who would have thought when we were young, so young, in Athens that you and Mary Averoff and Frosso Zarifi would one day all find each other again in Paris [Mary Henderson was also Greek-born]. When are you coming?

"Cy has to have a little operation in the intestine next week but god willing it will only be that and he actually rather looks forward to it, so as to stay in bed for a while and rest. He has been travelling like a lunatic in the last few months. Middle East first and then Greece and Turkey but Turkey not for politics but to take part in a Bilderberg meeting. He was the only poor man there. All the other hundred or so members came in their own planes. But it was interresting. He saw a lot of Shan and Rox while in Athens who were adorable and most hospitable and mercifully did not get into political discussions because Roxani considers even the one hour change to daylight saving as a sort of leftist plot.

"Imagine what an amusing and absurd thing happened a few weeks ago. I was at home when the phone rang from Teheran and a voice said to me *'Marina ici Hoveyda le premier ministre d'Iran.'* My first thought was that it was my cousin Peter who often pulls that sort of joke on me and I almost made some silly crack back when the voice added *'et je suis en train de manger du caviar avec votre mari qui veut vous parler.'* Apparently he asked out of sheer *politesse* about me and when Cy said I was in Paris and he had been unable to telephone me from the hotel, he had got some minion to call my number and had handed the receiver to Cy with a grin saying *'Voilà cher ami, vous voyez il y a certains avantages à être ministre.'* I spoke to Cy for a while, and then he said Hold on there is another friend of yours here who wants to talk to you. And an American voice said to me 'Hullo Marina do you remember me this is Lou.' I almost could not believe it. Do you remember Lou, the teacher from Athens college whom I was engaged to for one brief spring just before the war. Six foot seven and eyes like the Aegean and came from Sioux City Iowa which made mummy so distressed because she thought I would spend the rest of my days taking part in pie baking competitions with a kind of Covered Wagon mother-in-law. The chances, after thirty odd years of his and Cy's having dinner *en tête à tête* with the Iranian Prime minister, you must admit are pretty extraordinary. I was so taken aback I hardly know what I said to him but I did understand that he is no longer a school teacher but a banker. In petroleum no doupt. And probably madly rich. But be that as it may I got a very funny telegram from Cy the next day saying 'I may be grumpy selfish difficult to live with etc but I am still the best thing that ever happened to you because your Lou although still six foot seven is as bald as an egg and about as bright.' "

And the same day to Dodo: "Marinette is coming for my birthday and I am just having the Paynes and Boisots like the old days and we will play some bridge. It is awful how unold I feel. The only place I feel my age is in my total disbelief in human beings alas. There is not one evil in this generation, on this earth, which could not have been avoided, were it not for basic human weeknesses and bloody mindedness and self preoccupation with no thought for anyone else. What a pity. No more mama mou. This is not a real letter. Just a *pour mémoire* of my devotion."

The day after we went to spend a weekend with old friends.

From Marina's diary:

May 2, Varaville, Normandy: "Chez van Zuylens. Cy's first weekend off since September. Gaby met us with David Bruce [no longer assigned to

Peking]. Vangie [Evangeline Bruce] lovelier than ever. We took a long walk. Beagle crazy about Pandora [the van Zuylens' enormous, fat black Labrador bitch]. The countryside is a dream but few flowers."

To Dodo on May 10: "Cy was in the hospital; nothing serious. He was in from Monday to Thursday and was fine really except that he is so obsessively secretive about his own health that I could not tell anyone and it complicated my life no end being at the hospital all day and thinking up things to say I was doing. He came home on Thursday and almost at once got a most awful tooth infection; spent an hour and a half at the dentist and woke up this morning with a cheek like a pumpkin and very miserable. He keeps quoting De Gaulle 'La vieillesse est un naufrage.'

"Cy will be going to Germany soon and then to Brussels for the summit meeting and directly from there to London for the referendum. I will join him there for a week end of fishing at a friend's Elizabethan castle. I am so glad for Cy and also to see the famous castle before it is turned into a recreation place for Labour leaders or something. I am absolutely convinced that Europe cant last for more than a maximum of ten years the way it is now."

To Mary Manners on June 17: "How ever to thank you for such a wonderful weekend? Cy has been in an angelic mood ever since, because he did catch a few fish and enjoyed himself more than he has in years. He is off in Belfast at the moment dodging bullets, while I got back to a most unexpectedly fancy three days here.

"On Saturday the Princesse de Faucigny Lucinge married the Prince Brandolini and it was THE event of the season. I went to the church in the morning sort of like a concierge to have a good look and it was well worth it. I found Evangeline [Bruce] and Nin Ryan sitting together also with eyes round their heads and I have never seen so many well dressed women together. One could tell the various nationalities as the *Tout Paris, Tout Rome, Tout Londres* etc came prancing in, by their clothes. The Italians all looked as though they had walked straight out of a Visconti movie. Large hats and veils and exquisite *glissé* dresses. The flowers in church were breath-taking and the music lovely which made up for the rather endless admonitions of the priest to the young couple to keep to the ways of god, something they are most unlikely to heed.

"Then later in the afternoon there was a giant reception in the gardens of the Cercle Inter-Allié for two thousand people and it was all so pretty and the weather was so warm and friendly that we all had a marvellous time and stayed till deep into the night, much to the distress I am sure of our hosts who had been at it since dawn. It was almost as if everyone there sensed that this was probably the last party of its kind in a coming world of *'Bleu de travail'* almost as if we knew that the very day after the communists would sweep the land of all those elegant Italian *principessas* and industrialists.

"And as if this were not enough pomp for a time, yesterday I was invited to the opening of the new rooms at Versailles, at night with candles and flowers everywhere. I have never seen so many beautiful things in my life. In the King's *petit appartement* a pair of hand-painted *chinoiseries* pink curtains to sell one's soul for. It is to disgust one of poverty for ever. The Queen's bed re-done up to the last ostrich plumes at the top of a gold and silver *baldaquin* to dream under. Entirely embroidered with her peacock feathers lilac panzies and roses. Exactly what would look right at Hadden. Ah me. I must say Gerald Van der Kamp who has done it all almost single-handed, ought to be decorated from head to toe.

"The embroidery in the King's bed chamber took ten years to do. How they found craftsmen to do it all, is too incredible. And what research and hard work. Gerald has such charm that he can get money out of Shylock Scrooge and almost every rich American he smiles at, but also (which is hardest of all) out of other museums and the Louvre, albeit reluctantly, has been shamed bullied beguiled and coerced into giving back almost everything IT had which came from Versailles. With the result that it now looks not like a museum but like a palace about to give a party. It was wonderful."

She wrote Dodo on June 17 to tell her about David's new business setup with his old school friend Oliver Hoare. Oliver had headed the oriental art division of Christie's and was both an expert and a linguist, including Persian among his tongues. Together they conceived an idea that selling Islamic art to newly rich Islamic oil sheikhs, thus recycling the petrodollar, had a sound economic future. This proved to be eminently sensible. Marina told her mother:

"David's new office is beautiful. They have a very large window full of huge cushions and he and the two pretty secretaries and Oliver often sit there and have sandwidges and coffee which makes people pop in thinking it is a tea house or a restaurant. The buisiness is going well and Oliver is off with the Sheik of Kuwait in a private airoplane looking for objects for the Sheik's collection.

"David left for Rome on the same day I came back here, and was hoping to stay with Nelly de Rothschild. She lives in a very romantic brocken down castle outside Rome. WHAT about the Italian elections? They make our aristocratic fancy week end of fishing knee deep in Dukes seem even more retrograde and delightful.

"I was so delighted for Cy. We went to Diana Cooper's nephew who lives in a Norman castle in Derbyshire and the weather was like August in Spetses. Our co-guests were two dukes. The house is the most romantic thing in the world. Norman walls covered in roses and the most heavenly tiered gardens all the way down a hill to the river dark and shadowy with great trees. And filled with trout. One day we went to call on yet another Duke, Devonshire, at Chatsworth which is quite unbelievably beautiful and a mile of hot houses built by Paxton in glass and white wood. I have never seen such flowers."

Marina wanted me out of the way while she finished the tedious job of moving to our new apartment, so I had been traveling constantly and, when I got back in August, the following letter was waiting for me written before she left for Spetsais:

"Sweet Pea,

"WELCOME to your new house. It is still a terrible mess but I did my best. And you cant think how hard that best was, with almost everybody off on holiday, everybody promising things they could not do etc. The only really nice ones were the painters and the carpenters and a sweet pitch black Camerounian I found who helped carry really heavy stuff and wash the floors. And Jovita [our maid] has been really marvellous. Hard work from day to night and never a complaint and always willing and smiling. As for Linda [Lamarche, my secretary], she was a really moral as well as physical support of the most marvellous sort. There were moments when we all almost burst into tears and thought we would never move two thousand books off one end of the floor to another and then back. We were covered in dust and dirt from top to toe. However you now have a bed room a dressing room (I hope you find all your belongings in their place) and a bath room, which in spite of its size is really rather cosy. I wonder how far you will be able to stretch your legs. However for reading it is comfortable.

"A big kiss and thank you for getting us such a nice home.

"Yours very truly with much love

"landlady Smou"

After a splendid Greek summer holiday, we returned to Paris and preparations for another very long journalistic trip — the very last, alas, we would ever enjoy together.

To Marinette and David, from Washington on October 27:

"Far's birthday and the last place in the world that he would wish to be in to celebrate. Even New York he likes better. I must admit that this is an incestuous city with everybody scratching everybody else's back but also eyes out. Depending on the time of day.

"Polly [Fritchey] was giving a large Sunday night supper kind of party and Kissinger was there as well as twenty two other people. The good doctor took me by the hand after dinner and said 'Any Greek who says hullo to me I want to talk to,' and so we sat on a sofa *en tête à tête* half the evening. Both he and Mrs. K sent their special love to David and he said that any party he goes to at which David is present Nancy scolds him if he does not spend all evening with him. She looked exhausted having come straight from Williamsburg where they had been taking the Sadats sight seing.

"Every time we come here I must admit I am scared for the world. The capital of the most powerful country in the Western world, run by a bunch of self satisfied smug self important provincials. First and foremost the press, who has bamboozled everybody into thinking it almighty, and from there on say anything that comes into their minds and take it for gospel. It is very scary.

"We go back to New York on Wednesday and then start the big trip on Sunday begining with Panama and then Ecuador which is the only new country on this trip and I hope beautiful. Then Peru, then Chile Argentina Brazil and then across to South Africa and after that *on verra.* We heard from Jovita that Beagly who was really desperate the day we left (he cried all night and unpacked my entire suit case twice) is better now but simply wont ever go into our room. What a dog!"

To Dodo on October 30, from New York: "The nicest thing about Washington was our hostess Polly with her new husband. They are so happy and gay so funny together that it is contageous and the house is full of laughter and singing in the bath tub. But out of the goodness of her heart she has taken a whole family of Vietnamese refugees as servants and it is Tovaritch all over. I wonder if the Russian archdukes were as bad servants as these are. The man was director general of some big company and the wife a proffessor (Chinese) and the three sons students. They do EVERY-THING all together. They all five shop together sweep clean cook together, drive the car together so that there is hardly room for Polly if she wants to be driven anywhere, and they answer the telephone together, which means that no one can get through to her at all. This of course frustrated Cy who was expecting a call from the White House or some senator all the time."

XVI

November 1975 - August 1976

It is sad for me to recall that Marina's last long trip was on a route she knew well — Latin America and southern Africa. Oddly enough, the beginning of our travels spanned those same continents. In 1942, we took off via Sudan, Chad, and Nigeria to Brazil, Trinidad, and Puerto Rico on our start in married life. Then, of course, it was all lovely, new, and most exciting, with the United States our final goal, the traditional "America" of Renaissance poets. But at the end of 1975 there were fewer dreams.

We started in Panama and Ecuador. Marina wrote Dodo as soon as we got to Quito:

"We left New York on Sunday and arrived in Panama which is quite a dreary place. But there is so much to be said for being Greek. Imagine. We arrived on a three day national holiday with everything from museums and churches to bars and barbers closed like coffins. But we did go out to lunch with the Ambassador and his wife turns out to be Greek American from Kardamili. So we have a lovely heart to heart and she tells me that the President of Panama *gia onoma tou theou* [in God's name] is Greek. His family comes from Kranidi [near Spetsais]. His parents emigrated to

Pitsburgh but during the wars of 12 and 22 the father could not stand being away from the *patrida* and came dashing back to fight thus forfieting his U.S. citizenship.

"Later they came to Panama where Dimitri started as nothing and ended up president of the country. Is'nt it unbelievable. So the next day the Ambassador was at the Presidencia with all the other diplomatic corps notables etc and he said to him 'You know Sulzberger of the N.Y. Times is here and his wife is Greek' at which the president said 'Why are they not here. Send a car for them at once.' This was eight o'clock in the morning as the Fiesta starts at 5.30 A.M. with fire works and a serenade and goes on till night-fall. So we were called and rushed into our clothes and a mile long presidential car was waiting for us. At one moment we got into an *embouteillage* because naturally the whole of Panama was in the streets so very calmly the driver jumped the little flower bed in the middle of the Avenida and drove merrily on the wrong side of the street syrens blowing and on-coming cars scatering like mice.

"The Presidencia is a pretty colonial house white with balconies and patios and white egretts by a fountain and there we stood and watched the parade. I said all of Panama was in the streets but it must have been only half of it for at least the other half was parading. The parade lasts six hours. Schools, guides, airmen, nurses, all of them with drums until one feels really in a jungle voodoo ceremony and all of them walking rather like the chorus of a rhumba ballet than a militarist nation. It was too endearing and now and then one saw the face of a by-stander light up as it cought sight of its own child proudly walking by.

"Then we were taken upstairs to meet the President who is, mama mou, about six feet tall and must weigh at least three Katsimbalis [a very fat Greek intellectual] together. A jaw like a monster and a hand like a ham and speaking broad Texas American with every other word shit or F——— or something. Vulgarity personified and yet . . . GREEK. *Vre ti kanis patriotaki vre stin Spetsais menis, akou thee mou* [Well how are you little compatriot? You live in Spetsais? Can you believe it?]. Mrs. President a tiny pretty little thing and a ghastly spoilled brat daughter called, *parole d'honneur,* Zaharoula [a very sugary name]. I could not believe any of it. A lot of the entourage was Greek; a charming beautiful Matina, a dear old lady in black and no teeth. The whole thing. Needless to tell you it made our stay.

"And today we left for Quito where we have been invited to stay at the

Embassy which is the prettiest I have ever been in. Built on a hill we look right down through a gap in two mountains to a long thin green green valey covered with clouds that come and go. We are two thousand mettres up and I feel very fluffy."

From Lima, Peru, she wrote to Koutsi Ebon: "Once more I am confirmed in my belief that it is essential to be Greek. The President of Panama is Dimitrios Lakos!"

On November 12 she wrote Slim Keith from Lima: "Spent three days going to Cuzco and Machu Picchu which is absolutely incredible. However much one may have read about the place nothing prepares one for the delight of an old Spanish medieval town, twelve thousand feet up in the air built on the ruins of the Inca city. The entire town is pale pink tiles and patios and convents and the Cathedral which make one expect Pizarro himself to come out at any moment.

"And as for Machu Picchu, it is mind boggling. And I so love jungly things. And the roaring white foamy river. At one moment I escaped the awful guide and wandered alone amid this vast dead city and picked a giant bunch of deep white gladiola and pink or red begonias two orchids and a handkerchief full of the more familiar wild strawberries. This in sheets of rain but so much fun I did not even notice I was wet to the skin. My only worry later was my borrowed Dior coat which looked a bit Inca itself after three hours in a deluge."

She informed the children that on arriving in Cuzco: "We were lucky to be chosen by one of the fifty taxi drivers who fling themselves at one as one walks off the plane, and who turned out to be a dream, Leonardo Flores, who took us everywhere and was an excellent guide as well. We saw the Inca ruins and tried to pat a llama in a field but he showed ugly camel-like teeth so we didn't."

From Santiago, Chile, she summed it up for Dodo on November 16:

"[In Cuzco we had] our first sight of llamas and alpacas which look like a cross between a camel and a lamb. Then one starts down through desert exactly like those common pictures of 'sunset in Mexico' or something and gradually into more fertile country where the little stream we had been following turns into the Urubamba river, rushing and frothing and cascading down, white water over great grey brown smooth rocks that look like fossilised turtles. Poor Cy longing to stop and fish. And suddenly real jungle, trees and lianas and berries and such flowers that it was all I could do not to jump off the train to investigate.

"Machu Picchu — the most dramatic site in the world. A kind of Mycenean world right in the sky. Incredible building capacities when one thinks that the Incas had no writing and no wheel. It is not beautiful in itself but just so staggering this complete dead city which no one knows much about. Straight down at our feet in sheer drop the valley and the river and all around us still higher mountains some white with snow some blue some deep dark green with jungle. Unfortunately three hundred fellow tourrists mostly German took away some of the majesty of the place so I slipped away on my own.

"Now we are in Chile which you with your political ideas would love. Cy was whisked off in a tiny airoplane to Antofagasta to see the president and I dont envy him poor fellow as it takes four hours and the weather is foul. (He just called to say he was glad I was not with him as I would have been sick as a dog.) So I am alone for a moment or two."

We went on to Buenos Aires and Rio de Janeiro. Marina wrote Dodo from the latter on November 26:

"Buenos Aires only three days and completely submerged in kindness and hospitality by the Sossides (he is Greek ambassador there). I am once again staggered by the difference between reading about a place or a situation, and living it. Buenos Aires outwardly looks as peaceful and even gay as if there were no problems at all. Streets full of busy people shops bursting with things. Inflation is such that one is totally confused when one person talks in hundreds one in thousands and another yet in millions. But for foreign exchange things are so cheap that people come from all over South America just to do their Xmas shopping. The Common market shut down on their imports from Argentina, and that plus the oil costs has brought ruin. One can buy a whole cow for seven dollars and dogs are fed on filet mignon. As for leather goods they are for practically nothing.

"It is tragic in a way, how impervious nature and every day life is to the sufferings of the few. Because invisibly, one knows that every day someone is killed or kidnapped or destroyed. Mrs. Peron must be out of her mind to wish to remain president. But like in so many countries everyone is furious angry and unhappy but dont have anyone else. From B.A. we came to Rio and then went straight off to Brasilia which is hell. I had imagined that the eight years since we were here last would have brought some little improvement in this soul-less city but if anything it is worse, because tattiness and bad maintenance have been added to the inhuman quality of the place. We stayed only two days mercifully and were glad to get back to Rio. I met an old friend here and she asked us to her house which is the most romantic thing in the world.

"Apparently it belonged to Lord Cochrane who after helping to liberate Brazil became governor or something and was such a pest that they finally got rid of him, whereupon he came to help liberate Greece. He is the [battle of] Navarino* chap. So his property remained dormant for over a hundred years, and when my friend's father bought it it was completely overrun by roses. Mama mou. Tall giant palm trees, a lake, an island, their own sugar-loaf, green slopes, mango trees as big as the house, magnolias jacarandas flamboyant and bougainvilia all mixed together and the ever present scent of ginger and frangipani. And black servants with bandanas and long skirts. Another world specially after Brasilia.

"I am going with them to another of their houses by the sea tomorrow for a day or two but Cy has to work. He preffers me out of the way as he has to finish with South America before we face the entirely new but even uglier problems of Africa. We leave for Johannesburg on Monday and will write again from there. Hopefully we will have some mail. I feel as if I were on another planet."

Just before flying off to Africa, Marina wrote David from Rio (December 1): "Brasilia is sheer hell. Palladio, Bramante, Gernier and co, must be turning in their graves each time they look down on this insult to their art and trade. *En plus* nothing works and the faithful in the famous cathedral pray under their open ombrellas as it rains as much inside as out. As the

---

* Where British, Russian, and French ships destroyed a Turkish fleet, helping the Greeks to achieve independence.

rainy season lasts five months *c'est beaucoup*. Back in Rio I stand at the window and look down at the main avenue of the Copacabana and this looks like an entire nation on holiday. One sees more bikinis than suits. And the waves I could look at forever. Big giant ones, curley ones, tricky ones. Beautiful all of them."

Africa was a disappointment. Marina never really liked it much — no part of it — and I had hoped to go to Angola, where the civil war was still on, and also to Mozambique, where I had a tentative interview scheduled with President Machel of the newly liberated government. But the South Africans (who had intervened in Angola) welshed at the very last moment when they canceled their promise to fly me in by military plane to Lobito, the Angolan city where their own and anti-government rebel forces had their forward base. And then Machel suddenly left for a consultation with other African leaders in Tanzania. So I had a rather fruitless journey. Marina, however, was cheered up by one basic fact — we would just manage to get back to Paris in time for Christmas!

Marina wrote Dodo from Johannesburg on December 13:

"All our plans are up side down as the Independant black nations catch their feet in their own beards and bureaucracy is so rampant one never gets a straight answer to a straight question. Last night a Pan American plane took off from here and as it was approaching Zambia [a hitherto friendly country] it was refused permission to overfly and had to come back. Our own Mozambique permission gets given and taken away once every other day. In the mean time we went for two days to South West Africa which is on the boarders of the Kalahari desert. Nothing. A kind of wild West frontier town. This kind of trip is only nice if you have a land rover and can move about; see the desert the animals etc. Sitting in a hotel room in a tiny Germanic city is no fun at all. And hot as hell. This was part of the German empire lost after the 1st world war. The day we arrived hotels and restaurants had been opened to blacks. Can you believe it?

"Then we went on to Cape town which is lovely. We found two friends and went swimming on Saturday. *Façon de parler* swimming as the Atlantic here comes direct from the South Pole and is painfully frozen. And an undertoe and giant waves. And sharks. The new film called Jaws has just been showing here and it has made people very scared. Its all about sharks eating people. We visited two absolutely beautiful Cape Dutch houses which are now museums but were the oldest wine growing estates in the cape in late seventeen hundreds. Too beautiful and such trees and flowers a cross between mediterranean and jungle.

"We got back yesterday and had to go off straight from the airport to lunch in the country, come back and drive to Pretoria which is an hour away and dine with Chief Buthelezi the Zulu chief. I keep thinking of the *Didima* [*Twins,* a children's book] and the *Diaplassi ton paidon* [Children's Encyclopedia]. How long ago."

On the same day a letter to Marinette: "Poor Far had to go off again this morning to see some general. Our Mozambique trip seems less and less likely. And from all we hear I am not distressed. Bureaucracy rampant in a never never land of drunken soldiers and policemen drunk both on liquor and independance who arrest you because they dont like your nose or your dress. Twice our permission to go has been granted and taken away on the same day. If we dont go we only have one more country and then mercifully home."

From the diary:

Lusaka, Zambia: "Lusaka is really pretty driary, poor thing. No longer native, not yet modern. Worse of both worlds. Dinner at embassy. Ambassador [Miss] Wilkowski charming."

On the day after Christmas, Marina sat down and wrote a summary of her impressions to Susan Mary Alsop:

"After ten weeks away from Paris, the very sound of French voices was like music after the Afro-English we had been listening to for days, as well as the Africaans English of South Africa. Odd how one can rant and grumble against the French for all their varied short-comings but one is always so delighted to return to them.

"This trip on the whole was not much fun. Latin America and Africa are fun only if one is sight seing or hunting or fishing or travelling in the wilds, down the Amazon or in the bush or the veld. The cities are just like cities everywhere else only less pleasant and alas the Intercontinentals have inherited the earth.

"And work work work for Cy in difficult conditions and the endless suspence of pending *rendezvous,* cancelled at the last minute and the vision of that long empty [column] space on Sunday or Wednesday. But what struck me once again is the invisibility of sorrow or danger or dictatorial methods, to the man-in-the-street traveller. Chile looked, felt, smelled no different than all the other times. Except for a soldier here and there in front of a public building with a machine gun over his shoulder one might as well be in a Jeffersonian democracy, at first glance.

"As for Buenos Aires, where my Heiskell cousins, Marian and her husband, had gone with private body guards, it was the gayest most alive place we went to on all the trip. Streets full of elegant people all looking like polo players, shops full of goodies and restaurants cinemas etc doing brisk business. Only the poor U.S. Embassy people are under orders not to go anywhere except other Embassies.

"But with all its faults South America is at least colourful. Whereas South Africa is really pretty deadly if one does not go bird watching or diamond-searching. Luckily I have two old Greek friends there who took charge of me, while Cy was struggling unsuccessfully against bureaucracy and bone headedness. Three times we started off for Lourenço Marques and three times Mr. Samora Machel changed his mind. Probably with reason poor chap as he had a palace revolution on his hands but still very frustrating.

"And the South Africans also promised to fly him in to a bit of Angola and also let him down. Just as well I suspect because it is easier to sneek in than out. What a *panier de crabes* that is.

"Then we went to Zambia and I must admit that being *à cheval* between the middle ages and the twentyeth-and-a-bit centuries is the worst of both worlds. Its all right if one knows one will live in a hut, travel on foot and communicate through witch-doctor and tribal chief. One knows where one is. But going to see the president [Kenneth Kaunda] seven hundred kilometers away in the north, in the rainy season, in a storm worthy of Noah, in a first world war piper cub piloted by a man retired seven years before from BOAC for old age, is something rather nerve-wracking. The president's village has no gasoline pump (indeed no airport and one lands in a field) so the plane went somewhere else to get gas, and never came back.

Mercifully Mrs. Kaunda lent Cy her Mercedes and he drove all night in the rain counting forty two over-turned busses trucks etc. on the *parcours* and just made it back to Lusaka in time to catch our Paris plane so as to be back for Xmas. Ouf.

"And they are queer folk. All protestations of good will and liking for the U.S. but having voted ninety two times with the Russians in the U.N. in the last few years.

"We got back to the new flat as I say Xmas eve rather dejected thinking we might have to go to a bistro for Xmas lunch, but darling David had taken charge and we found Xmas tree flowers, holly, presents, turkeys, plum pudding and he even remembered the hard sauce and cranberries."

Marinette came over at New Year's to help fix up our new home. That evening Marina wrote Roxane Panas:

"No fairy with a magic wand appeared in the time we were away to fix the washing machine, put down carpets, hang curtains take the books off the floor etc. And we are so broke, we probably wont be able to do it either. I spend my days fiddling and achieving nothing. Marinette is a great help moraly if not physically. We sit and groan together and wish we had the fortune we deserve and could go off and buy two Louis XV commodes, a few Rembrandts for the walls, sixty yards of taffeta for the curtains and a couple of Aubussons for the floors. All we have bought for the moment is two hooks to hang Cy's pajamas on in the bath room, and three coat hangers. Oh well. By some miracle the PLUMBER has just appeared. The only man not on holiday til February, in the whole of France."

We took a brief trip to the Benelux countries, and Marina wrote Dodo on January 24:

"We went because the U.S. Ambassador invited us to dine with princesse Beatrix and her German husband and as she is heir to the throne Cy felt it would be useful business-wise. It is so near that we could afford the time. Actually it was not madly interesting but I sat next to the Prince who is German but very nice and lovely to look at and as he was brought up in Africa we had a lot to talk about in view of our recent travels.

"The last day my hostess said I am sorry but we have to go to a ladies' lunch at a frau Van den Graaf and I dont know who or what she is and dont dare ask, as she has asked me dozens of times and I could never go, so if you dont mind we will go together. Well mama mou, Madame turned out to be a Kyria [Mrs.] Toula from Kalamata fat bossy vulgar incredible with long black curley hair *à la Louis XIV* who somehow, god knows how, had married this Dutch diplomat. Well the other guests about fifty in a small sort of Othos Patission [modest bourgeois] appartement, were Pakistanies and Indians, Koreans and Japanese, Dutch Rumanian Yougoslav Poles and a Turk, no one really speaking much of anyone else's tongue and I chatted merrily away with the Chek in German and then of all things after the *pastizio bourekakia lahabodolmades* etc. [Greek food], she put on the gramophone and dragged us through a *kalamatiano* [a Greek dance] at two P.M. in a tiny flat in the Hage . . . *gia onôma tou theou* [in God's name]. Life is so full of non sequitors it is almost worth living. Then we went on to Brussels to say good by to the poor Bruces who are retiring this week [as U.S. envoy to NATO]."

She wrote her thanks and goodbyes to Evangeline Bruce on January 27:

"I discovered that half the cealing in the bran new kitchen is about to fall on our heads. The architect says it is the plumber's fault, the plumber that it is the boiler-maker, he that it is the weather, and the weather does'nt care. And no one wants to do anything about it. I do think that Karl Marx was right about property, and at this moment I would gladly settle for an igloo in the Tuilleries.

"To cheer me up Cecile de R. took me to hear Rosencavalier last night, which was beautiful beyond compare as far as the voices went, but the décor and costumes were awful. I just dont understand this extraordinary tendency to change things around and the terror of being bourgeois about things, by doing them as they were meant to be. This urge to set Rosencavalier in a Clock-work orange *décor,* or Mozart in a super-market and Vivaldi in the said supermarket but the Beatles at Royaumont. I feel very old and *dépassée par les évènements.*

"It was rather fun however, after all these months in darkest Africa, to find myself once more surrounded by floor length mink coats, ostrich feathers, diamonds, and all those faces which so impressed me when we first came to Paris. The world may well be galloping on its way to Goulags but at least Le Tout Paris will go down in style."

From Marina's diary:

January 26, Paris: "Books and flowers for Cy who insisted on going to hospital on his own [for an operation].

January 28, Paris [the page headed by the word "operation"]: "Cy operated today. Thank God all well. He slept almost all day."

She added in a letter to Dodo on February 11: "Cy is a lunatic. He got home from hospital last Friday stayed in bed the weekend, and left for Madrid on Wednesday."

March 8, Paris (the page headed "Pauline [Baroness Philippe de Rothschild] died yesterday"): "Denise *has* cancer. It's so shocking I can't take it in. Went to see her. She looks incredibly well. Cheerful. Will have cobalt. Rage. Rage." (Denise Boisot was Marina's closest friend in Paris.)

Four days later she wrote Dodo: "Cy has definitely decided that we wont go to Aspen this summer. Marinette has invited god knows how many people for August but she will have to disinvite some and then in September I have sworn to Cy we shall be alone as he really deserves quiet and rest after an almost non stop travel year. Denise has returned from the hospital and looks and sounds fantastically well and brave. But she has to have forty cobalt treatements and that is rather helish. One feels tired and sick and dizzy apparently."

On March 28, Marina again wrote her mother: "I wish I had some of that magic water. Not to cure me of illness, as thank goodness I am exceptionally well, but of a kind of zombie-like state in which I am falling, in which people, nice people talk to me about politics or theatre art or themselves, and a glassy look comes over my eyes, as my mind has wandered to the eternal problem of the plumber electrician etc. Imagine that last week I put the water in Jovita's room; that I called up and told him not to bother as I had found another company to do it. Well in less than half an hour he was there (which means he could have done it any time he had wanted to) but that is not the end of the story. He made a last hole in the wall, left three pipes on the floor and next day he did not turn up nor the next, so I telephoned and was told, *'Monsieur est parti aux sports d'hiver pour dix jours.'* And these people vote communist. We have had a train strike for a week or more, called on the very day that seven hundred thousand (repeat thousand) people, mothers with children dogs cats luggage etc. were leaving for the spring school holidays. You have never seen such a shambles as the railway stations. On the other hand I do have an angelic black market Italian carpenter who is making closets and at long last the book cases for Cy's study, so *siga, siga* [slowly, slowly] things will get organised."

On April 25 she told "Nursey mou": "Far who is an angel disguised as a cactus-bush has been pretending for weeks that he really does not care that much about going to Aspen any more, because the old cabin burned down. So he decided we would go to Greece anyway this summer. I am sure he is doing this because he knows Dodo feels this to be if not her last, at any rate one of her last summers alive and wanted to give her pleasure. When I rang up to tell her she was speachless with joy. Poor lamb she really hated the thought of another year before seing me. I was going to go for Easter, but we cant afford two trips so I will only go for the summer. Not a bad exchange.

"Far has been travelling like a lunatic all these months but is getting back on Friday to stay a while I hope. We have been asked to fish in Normandy in end of May and June and if anything can keep him here, that will. But his morale good. His Chinese post script book has come out in French and so is the abridged version of the memoirs so maybe we will be able to buy curtains after all. Some day."

The day after her last birthday, Marina wrote to Susan Mary Alsop:

"In a world that gets more and more unfamiliar, and cold, the fealing of permanance and invulnarability of being with you seems doubly, nay a thousand times more precious each time. Years go by or days or hours, lots of letters or none, meeting every day or not at all, and then together one hears the marvellous 'and so?' as if we were continuing a conversation left off yesterday. It is life giving pleasure giving, and totally satisfying and absorbing to be with you, whether we talk about ourselves or politics children or clothes lovers or litterary critics. Damn the Atlantic ocean. I would so love to talk to you every day.

"May 1st and Sunday AND Monday everything was closed. I was fascinated to watch the streets. No garbage collecting because of the holiday and in three days Paris looks like Bombay at its worst. Amazing what a fragile equilibrium we all live in. No wars or earthquakes or revolutions needed any longer to destroy us all. No garbagge collectors and in no time a great city is reduced to tears."

A few days after her last birthday, in a strange mood, Marina put the following entry in her diary:

May 13, Paris:

"I wish I loved the human race,
I wish I loved its funny face.
I wish I liked the way it walks.
I wish I liked the way it talks."

She told Dodo on June 15: "As I wrote you we had the Norstads [former NATO commander] for three days and the party went off superbly. *Tifla na ehoun oi traiteurs* [The caterers might as well be blind]. I spent fortunes for *petits fours* etc. and the thing every one threw themselves at was the *kolkythakia tiganita* [fried zucchini]. A touch of Spetsais chez Louis XIV. Then on Friday we abandoned them as they were leaving at dawn Saturday anyway and went off to friends near Dieppe to fish. Cy has not taken three days off since last May and it was heaven except practically no fish. The drought is getting so serious that it is declared national disaster which means we had the most glorious weather all the time hotter than Spetsais and clear blue skies but the rivers low as can be and the fish not bitting. But delicious companions and Cy at his best, sociable and talkative and our hosts adorable and Normandy a dream. Every fifty mettres a Norman church, a manoir, a chateau, and we went to visit some famous gardens which made me drool with envy.

"Jessica's news is both good and bad. Good in the sence that it is not osteolimielitis or anything horrid, but she does have to have an operation.

And the only time the doctor can do it is in the middle of August which bitched up their summer. However the doctor may say that a month at the sea would do her good in which case I will bring her with me in July and see to it that she swims but does not walk or get tired.

"Marinette did something very clever. Borrowed Monica's crutches for her to use them and get familiar with now while she is still well, and apparently Jessica was thrilled and went off triumphantly with them to school showing off and very proud. Thank heavens for an enthusiastic nature.

"Cy went off to Spain on Friday and like a good wife I drove him to Orly at seven in the morning and when we got there he discovered he had left his brief case behind. Impossible to leave without it and impossible not to leave as he was meeting the Foreign Minister at twelve. So he went in to hold the plane if possible and I drove like Fangio himself back to the house and believe it or not there on the public bench outside our front door was his brief case large as life and NO ONE had taken it. I flew back and leaving the car to the care of an astounded policeman raced upstairs and managed to get the briefcase delivered to Cy in the plane.

"Two hours later I got a telex message straight from the ministry of foreign affairs saying 'You are a genius and I adore you.' I have stuck it on to the mirror where he shaves every day, to serve as reminder for the less adoring days. He got back this morning and went straight to the office. I gather he had a lovely time because the Interior Minister took him fishing, very quietly and secretely as it was in full Basque country where all the irredentists want his head. So I am relieved that Cy is back all in one piece."

She wrote Avis Bohlen that June: "The flat is nice and there is a *tilleul* [linden tree] outside our windows which smells like real country so we are happy. Cy has been travelling like a maniac because aside from his column he is trying to write a book about the Romanoffs, the Hapsburgs and the Hohenzolerns all in one and wants to go and see various remnants of those noble hopeless families. But he is well and coming to the U.S. for the conventions. I wont because my mother has something wrong with her eyes and the sooner I get to Greece the better.

"Paris as usual in a frenzy of June-*mondanités,* in spite of everything, and we who dont go out much, have had a few too, including a delicious *fête du village* at Anet with fire works and the little school girls acting out Diane de Poitiers and Henry II. Also a beautiful party at Loulou de Waldner's for her daughter Diane's wedding to David's partner Oliver [Hoare]. You have never in your life seen such flowers. I counted thirty eight bunches in the *small* sitting room, and she had so many left over that the bath tub in the guest room, was one mass of roses head to head like a victorian carpet.

"I shall be going to Greece on the 11th of July. If by any chance the doctors say what you need after the operation is rest and sun and sea, I hope you remember where to find it. Open arms any time— so just call and say I am on my way. Would that you could."

From the diary:

June 17, Paris: "Lunch Prince Paul, Olga. Cy wanted to talk about Romanovs for book. Fascinating. And they are so sweet."

This small item marked a pause in her diary; and she wrote only one more letter, a tiny pen-and-ink note to Avis Bohlen saying, "What idiotic times we pick for ailments. Not only my summer plans all destroyed, but so many friends, children, grandchildren etc. In a big hurry as I have not packed yet for hospital." The only further personal record among her papers was an ominous entry in her carelessly scribbled personal journal:

June 24, Paris: "Hospital."

As I look back, it seems difficult now to realize that this was so tragic a date. Marina's doctor had examined her several times that spring and had finally decided she should probably have a hysterectomy but wished to have final tests made first and therefore committed her to the American Hospital, whither, on that bright June day, I drove her through the leafy avenues of Neuilly. Christopher Beagle was perhaps more perceptive than I. As Marina stoically, even cheerfully, packed her little bag, taking along only a minimum of things, he whined, drooped his tail, sought to get in the way, tried to make himself so attractive that we would have to take him along.

After a very brief time in hospital, the doctor deferred tests. He allowed

Marina to go home for several days and to lead a normal life while resting up.

He did not, of course, realize what "normal life" meant for such an irrepressible, inordinately gay and active woman. She did try to be good and to take it easy but was only relatively successful. Apart from a few close friends in on the secret, nobody realized that the Marina circulating happily in Paris late that June and early July was any less energetic or bubbling with health than ever before. On June 29 she had a particularly good time at her last party — to celebrate the wedding of young Frank Wisner and Christine de Ganay, attended by dozens of French and American friends.

We told Dodo simply that Marina had to have an operation but it was not worrisome and she still hoped to get to Spetsais fairly soon. Marinette went on to Greece to be with the children and her grandmother; David was in London.

Marina had been very excited about that summer. Our new apartment in Paris had slowly been taking shape, and she was filled with particular zest, enthusiasm, brimming with confidence and a desire to tell Dodo every last detail. Moreover, little eight-year-old Jessica was coming along with Marina to have at least a week or ten days alone with her, and Marinette and Jonathan (whose school finished later than his sister's) were bringing up the rear. Then all these precious dreams were dashed when she was told she required routine surgery.

In late June, Marina underwent the slight operation (a curettage) to see if she had cancer. She seemed scarcely to worry about this but regarded it as a nuisance that might delay her vacation.

On July 15, she had her operation. She was in pain for almost three days, but she recovered her spirits and strength rapidly thereafter.

Denise Boisot, Mary Henderson, and Mary Averoff were there as much as they could be: available, but only when Marina was up to seeing them. Philippe de Rothschild, who had just lost his Pauline, came with a splendid bottle of claret. Prince Paul and Princess Olga sent her an icon of a saint reputed "to make the most miraculous cures."

Friday I arrived outside her room. The door was open, but as I started to go in a nurse emerged, stopped me, explained that *"Madame a eu un malaise,"* and asked me to wait outside. Perplexed, worried, I stood there when her wheeled bed was rolled rapidly by me attended by a cluster of doctors and nurses.

Where could I go, I asked a nurse, to find out what was the matter? I was sent to the Intensive Care room one floor up. The door was shut, but there was a bell to ring for inquiries. I rang and in a fairly short time a nurse emerged, told me kindly that a doctor would come out and talk to me when it was possible, but my wife was very ill and that was the first problem.

After an interminable wait, the door again opened and out came the young anesthetist who had handled her first operation. *"Je regrette,"* he said. *"J'ai une mauvaise nouvelle."* It was all over. Noon.

The children were wonderful. Marinette got a helicopter to pick her up in Spetsais and help her catch an Olympic flight to Paris. David flew from London. And Mary and Nicko Henderson,* dear old friends, were magnificent. Mary wanted to kidnap me and take me for the night to the British Embassy. I refused, although she sent their car and chauffeur. I said I had to get used to things pronto. But they did put up Marinette and Adrian (who also flew from London). David stayed with me. They kept a kind of open house for us at all meals. Mary brought Aristide Pilavachi, the Greek ambassador, over to my office and he helped immensely on a lot of dreary bureaucratic details.

On Wednesday, July 28, a funeral service was held for Marina in the Greek Orthodox Church on rue Georges Bizet. It was conducted by Archbishop Metropolitan Meletios, who flew from Athens for the purpose. He is a sweet man, and he had officiated at the marriage of Marinette and Adrian in the same church. Marinette, Mary Henderson, and other close friends had done a wonderful job of arranging the masses of flowers sent, including all Marina's favorites — lilies, *muguets* (where from I cannot imagine), rose petals, cut flowers. The bier was entirely covered, and the whole space behind it.

At 10:30 A.M. the golden doors before the altar, behind the bier, swung very slowly open and there was the Archbishop, in glorious Byzantine robes and black cylinder hat, bearing a gold crook, his white beard and hair bursting around his face and glowing eyes, standing stone-still looking up at the choir as it sang its medieval paeans. Two priests helped Meletios, and they chanted magnificent trios, with the choir coming in afterward. It was tremendous indeed, impressing even me, an atheist who detests all funer-

---

*British ambassador to France.

als, and I noticed that such a cool, reserved Protestant as Maurice Couve de Murville had tears streaming down his face when the hundreds of people present were summoned, according to Greek custom, to file past the bier and extend their sympathy to the children and me. Almost everyone in the church wept.

At the end the children and I left dearest Marina's coffin still covered with flowers.

The last act occurred in Spetsais on August 6. On the previous day David and I flew from Paris with Marina's ashes. We arrived on the evening of August 5, and on August 6 we scattered her ashes in the Aegean Sea, with the full approval of Dodo, her mother. Only those present knew.

Peter Payne, Marina's cousin, took us out in his motor yacht that dismal Friday evening. It was clear, but suddenly the moon vanished behind thick black clouds and it rained. Aboard were Peter, his sailor, Françoise Payne, Monica, Clem and Jessie Wood, the children, Christopher, me. Clem read aloud some excerpts from my book, *My Brother Death:*

Here the impassive, diurnal contrast between light and dark, life and death, is cozily expressed. Here one is pushed by simplicity toward truth.

When one lies upon a mountaintop in Greece, one's mind drawn up into the Eastern Mediterranean sky, one knows why so many gods were cradled in these seas, among these stones. For here, when one regards the subject vertically, one grasps the infinity of distance and the eternity of time. And death is the brother of eternity; religion the search to flee it....

The way home is long. The grass bends with pity, the cypress tree bends with grief. And there is a strange sound, the sound of autumn that comes before a bleak and devastating winter. That stark naked fellow my soul stretches forth asking protection and boon. And now you know not, you know not, for there is not so dark a thing as light....

I am weary, infinitely weary. And spring is but a word and not a feeling; a beautiful woman is become a phrase. Corrosion withers my soul and eats my bowels. I shrink from its touch. And the future in which I lived, the scene of my hopes, is gone; and there is only past.

Now, come my Brother Death; now, old, old, old, with hair like thistledown, I sink with fatigue into the soft Aegean waters that bear me northward and backward into time.

That was the only interment service. Then David scattered the ashes. Afterwards, first Marinette flung after them a bouquet of everything from our garden — all kinds of flowers, tuberoses, foulia, lemons, jasmine, together with a basket of seashells Marina had collected in Spetsais — then Jessie cast her bouquet, largely made up of blossoms she had snitched along the way, just as Marina loved to do. Christopher trembled; he knew something terrible had happened.

Marina herself would have loved her end: the beautiful ceremony, the people, the flowers. (Marinette whispered to me in church, "Oh, if Mummy could only peek out of the coffin for two minutes and see it all.")

And finally the pagan ash-and-flower-scattering ceremony in the wild August sea with the moon darting in and out of storm clouds.... Now there is nothing but a hollow that will never be filled.

Postscript:

Marina of the Rocks

In this world of confused theology and credo, where Christian, Jew, and Moslem, sect and sect, have always killed each other in the name of the God they all agree exists, Marina's lovely, generous life-filled paganism, derived from the old Greek sense of beauty — land, sea, and sky, plus humanity and flowers — made existence a joy while she lived and a leaden sadness when she died.

Marina was a great personality, a maker of music. She was an astonishingly vivid woman with an eye for beauty, an ear for rich sonorities, a face endowed both with liveliness and also with what Constantine Cavafy called "a dreamy appealing beauty." She had exquisite taste in painting, a vast knowledge of music, and was exceptionally well read.

Like most Greeks, Marina had a passionate interest in and little understanding of politics. She was more fascinated by the action, the movement, than the goal. Also, like most Greeks, she was exceedingly vital, generous, gay, courageous, patriotic, and, in the sense of human equality, immensely democratic. Everyone, from the meagerest fisherman or peasant, called her Marina or, at most, Mrs. Marina. All people, rich and poor, black and white, were the same to her, if she liked them. Her only prejudice was her personal choice, not abstract generality. She cherished the huge majority of people she encountered.

Also, like most Greeks since the days of Homer and all the bards who preceded him, Marina adored hearing and also telling a story. That her versions of the same tale often varied considerably according to her audience or according to her own mood bothered her not in the least. "I am," she confessed with a delicious smile, "unshackled by the fetters of fact."

Apart from her family and her dogs, Marina most loved picking wild flowers and plucking sea urchins from the bright Aegean. Benjamin Beagle, our eccentric companion, could swim like a seal for ten kilometers without touching shore even at the venerable age of fourteen, shortly before he died; but Marina swam like a dolphin or a mermaid.

Summer was her season and the Aegean was her earthly paradise: that bright sea filled with friends like timid red mullets and gleaming, large-eyed minnows who swam beside her face, rock pigeons and gulls wheeling overhead as she dove and dove again to explore the gleaming depths.

I have put this memorial together not as a writer or editor but as a sculptor. A sculptor can always see the perfect shape encased within the flawless marble, and I have tried to discern and preserve all the most tender and most vital beauty contained in Marina's mixed and informal writings, discarding only the immaterial dross in order to emphasize the inner loveliness.

I hope I have managed thereby to enhance and preserve the picture of Marina, above all for those who had the good fortune to know her. You cannot re-create the past and you cannot escape the future, but I hope I have allowed readers to see in this compilation how Marina always welcomed the present, no matter where, or what it brought.

No man can know life except at the side of a dear, loyal, warm woman. I basked in this privilege and never for a single moment of all the time we were together did it occur to me she might die first, she who was seven years younger and came from durable stock (her grandparents died in their nineties). Were I as wonderful and sweet as she, I would be glad for her sake that her death preceded mine, but I am not, alas. The world is a lonely place without her.

On August 24, 1962, when I was flying to America after my mother's death, I wrote Marina: "All I want to say in this brief note, which I am writing on the plane after saying goodbye to you, is that I am a goddamn coward and will do everything possible to insure that I die before you. I just couldn't bear to be alive without you. Thank heavens yours is a long-lived family.

"You are so sweet, so nice, so attractive, so good, so amusing, so sympathetic (none of which I ever say when I'm with you) that I can't even imagine the world for other people when you die, much less for selfish me.

"How hard it is to reconcile with death. Hard, my foot, impossible. I intend to leave the problem with you. Because when I go, you will still have hundreds of people who love you and that will be a comfort of a sort."

One death is a tragedy; mass death is not. A hecatomb overwhelms but appalls rather than requiring consolation. Yet Marina's death left as much sadness as if she had been thousands of people embodied in one soul alone, for she had so many adoring friends. That they share my sadness is, however, no consolation. Each carries in his or her heart a separate burden that cannot be shared. And the fact of this burden does not alleviate the desperate loneliness bequeathed by Marina's love.

Marinette wrote me on July 28, 1976, when she had to fly back to Spetsais after Marina's funeral, saying: "It occurred to me last night, as I was going to sleep, that although we said 'good-bye' to little Mummy under her mountain of flowers in that beautiful ceremony, it was only the actual small shape of her which left us. Already it seems to me that her warmth and tenderness and fondness of people seems to be coming out of you — and it is an enormous strength to us."

David Bruce wrote in the London *Daily Telegraph:*

> Her blithe spirit was infectious. In conversation she was a delight, her store of picturesque anecdotes inexhaustible. As a letter-writer she had an unusual gift for combining wit with a keen power of observation, description and erudition. Her intense joy in life never diminished. Her affection for her family and friends was unstinted. Gregarious by nature, she animated people of all ages. To those who knew her well it is almost indescribably sad that one so intensely charged with vitality, charm and kindness will no longer be of their company.

At the end of August 1977 a few friends and the family gathered at our house in Spetsais. The local stonemason raised a simple plaque above the door, on which Nata Constantinidis had engraved in Greek and English these lines from "Marina of the Rocks," by Odysseus Elytis, a poet popular when Marina herself was young:

"Deep in the gold of summer
And the perfume of hyacinths — But where did you wander
Descending toward the shores, the pebbled bays?"

MARINA

S'agapo apo edo os ton ourano.

Acknowledgments

Marina wrote such vivid letters that many, many of her friends kept them for years. This trove provided the material for this book when I sent out widespread requests for help. Among the letters used in this volume are those kindly sent on to me by the following: Susan Mary Alsop, Christa Armstrong, Marinette Berry, Avis Bohlen, Denise Boisot, David Bruce, Vangie Bruce, Peggy and Bill Burden, Rosie Cartier, Virginia Chambers, Aglaia Choremi, Christine Claudel, Tatiana Colonna, Monica Curtis, Pussy Deakin, Cleo Dunford, Koutsie Ebon, Michael Edwards, Liz Fondaras, Fred Fresco, Polly Fritchey, Averell and Pam Harriman, Marian Heiskell, Mary Henderson, Vane Ivanović, Jane and Bob Joyce, Beatrice Kahn (estate), Slim Keith, Rev. Pacificus Kennedy, Eve Labouisse, Dora Lada, Alexis Ladas, Linda Lamarche, Kakia Livanos, Jackie and Bob McBride, Mary Manners, Laurie Marchetti, Catherine Negroponte, Isabelle Norstad, Princess Olga, Jane Page, John and Roxie Panas, Eleni Panayatopoulou, Françoise and Peter Payne, Chris and Daphne Petrow, Beatrix Payne, Avi von Ripper (estate), Nin Ryan, Liliane de Rothschild, Pauline de Rothschild (estate), Nancy Smith, Kitty Solomos, Maria Sotiriadis (estate), A. C. Sedgwick, Emily Stanbury, Arthur Hays Sulzberger (estate), Iphigene Sulzberger, David Sulzberger, Marietta Tree,

ACKNOWLEDGMENTS

François Valéry, Dolly Voureka, Fred Warner, Louie Woods.

Some of Marina's letters had to be condensed or even deleted from a manuscript that simply became far too long. But I should like to thank everyone who contributed.

I would like to express my enormous gratitude to Eda Pallier and Linda Lamarche, who patiently, tactfully, and sympathetically helped in typing, preparing, and editing the text.

Finally, I am deeply appreciative of the sympathetic patience and skill with which David and Marinette helped me.

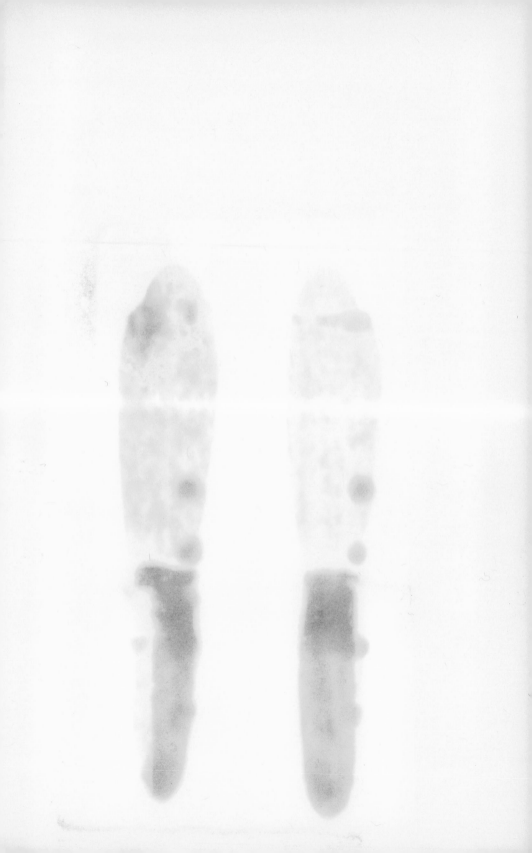

DATE DUE

GAYLORD   PRINTED IN U.S.A.